Oh, My Horses!

ELGAR
AND THE GREAT WAR

Also in this series

The Best of Me - A Gerontius Centenary Companion
ed Geoffrey Hodgkins

Also published by Elgar Editions

In the Bavarian Highlands by Peter Greaves
Half-Century: The Elgar Society 1951-2001 ed Michael Trott

Also by Lewis Foreman: books and theses on music

Havergal Brian: a collection of essays (1969)
The British Musical Renaissance (1972)
Discographies: a bibliography (1973)
Archive Sound Collections (1974)
Systematic Discography (1974)
Factors Affecting the Preservation and Dissemination of Archive Sound Recordings (1975)
British Music Now (1975)
Havergal Brian and the Performance of his Orchestral Music (1976)
Edmund Rubbra: composer (1977)
Dermot O'Byrne: poems by Arnold Bax (1979)
Arthur Bliss: catalogue of the complete works (1980)
The Percy Grainger Companion (1981)
Bax: a composer and his times (1983; 2nd ed 1988; 3rd ed in preparation)
Oskar Fried: Delius and the late romantic school (1984)
From Parry to Britten: British music in letters (1987, 1988)
Farewell, My Youth and other writings by Sir Arnold Bax (1992)
Lost and Only Sometimes Found: a seminar on music publishing and archives (1992)
British Music 1885-1920 (1994)
Koanga: the 1935 production of Frederick Delius's opera in the context of its performance history (1995)
Vaughan Williams in Perspective (1998)
Elgar & Gerontius: the early performances (1998)
British Choral Music (2001)

for Leslie Head
unsung Elgarian
and a pioneer of the Elgar revival

*Concerning the war I say nothing -
the only thing that wrings my heart & soul
is the thought of the horses -
oh! my beloved animals - the men -
and women can go to hell - but my horses; -
I walk round & round this room cursing God
for allowing dumb brutes to be tortured -
let Him kill his human beings but how CAN HE?*
Oh, my horses.

*letter from
Elgar to Frank Schuster
25 August 1914*

UNE VOIX DANS LE DÉSERT

Poem by Emile Cammaerts

Music by EDWARD ELGAR

Alfred Craven

LONDON:
ELKIN & Cº LTD
8 & 10, BEAK ST. REGENT ST.
NEW YORK: G. RICORDI & CO.

The Music of Elgar - vol 2

Oh, My Horses!

ELGAR
AND THE GREAT WAR

edited by

Lewis Foreman

with a compact disc of historical recordings

 Elgar Editions

Published in Great Britain by

Elgar Editions

the publishing imprint of

Elgar Enterprises
20 High Street, Rickmansworth, Herts WD3 1ER
(e-mail : editions@elgar.org)

First Published : November 2001

British Library Cataloguing in Publication Data
A Catalogue record for this book
is available from the British Library

ISBN 0 9537082 3 3 (Elgar Editions)

Printed and bound in Great Britain by Antony Rowe Ltd,
Bumper's Farm, Chippenham, Wiltshire

FRONTISPIECE : *Cover of the published voice and piano score of*
Une Voix dans le Désert *(Elkin, 1916)*

CONTENTS

LIST OF ILLUSTRATIONS

Those illustrations not attributed are from the editor's collection

MUSICAL EXAMPLES

INTRODUCTION AND ACKNOWLEDGEMENTS

The First World War was such a major fracture-line in European life, such a divide in both life and art, it is strange that its impact on music has not been studied in greater detail. My purpose in proposing this symposium in response to Elgar Editions' invitation to contribute a volume to their series 'The Music of Elgar' is to document Sir Edward Elgar's life and music during 1914-18 in some detail and set it against the changing music of England at the time. In this respect our sub-title should, perhaps, be 'Elgar, *music in England*, and the Great War'. Also on this occasion we have the luxury of a CD recording of historical recordings of some of the music discussed as an integral part of the book. This will be found on the inside backboard. References to the tracks on this CD are made by on-page footnotes throughout the text.

Inevitably when nine authors are discussing at length various aspects of the same short period there will be some duplication as they shine their individual searchlights across similar material. In the interest of a multi-faceted discussion I have allowed some repetition to remain, though extended quotations of poems, Elgar and Lady Elgar's diaries or others documents are keyed from chapter to chapter to avoid unnecessary repetition.

We have assembled a varied selection of illustrations which I hope will give the reader a more vivid appreciation of the period. Many of these come from the editor's collection. These have been supplemented by superb photographs of Elgar and his family from the collection of Raymond Monk, and from the Elgar Birthplace Museum at Broadheath. I also have to thank David Michell, Stephen Lloyd, Andrew Byrne, Malcolm Macdonald, Joseph Herter and Charles Hooey for their invaluable provision of various items.

Some of the material assembled here has appeared in print before, though all has been revised for its present purpose. Andrew Neill's studies of Elgar in the First World War have variously appeared, notably in the *Journal of the Elgar Society,* which also published earlier versions of the chapters by Charles Hooey and Joseph Herter. Stephen Lloyd's chapter has been developed from his book *Sir Dan Godfrey: champion of British composers* with acknowledgements to Thames Publishing. Professor Porter's chapter first appeared in the *Journal of Imperial and Commonwealth History* and is reproduced by courtesy of Frank Cass, London. The editor's chapters draw on some material that first appeared in his *From Parry to Britten* (1987) and *Music in England 1885-1920* (1994), with acknowledgement to B T Batsford and Thames Publishing, though they are now integrated into a new and much more wide-ranging discussion. The editor's account of the Ruhleben prison camp in chapter 3 is taken from a script first written for BBC Radio 3 and broadcast at Christmas 1995.

Musical examples have been set by the editor using Sibelius software, with thanks to Rodney Newton for assistance with bit-map formatting. We are most grateful to Novello and Co for the generous use of extracts from works of Elgar published by Novello and by Enoch and Co.

For the recordings, in addition to the editor's collection we are greatly indebted to Ruth Edge of the EMI Archives, to David Michell, to Stephen Lloyd and to the conductor Leslie Head. Dubbing was by Michael J Dutton and David Michell, and digital processing by Michael J Dutton.

As ever, general library requirements were met by the Central Music Library collection at Westminster Music Library, the Barbican Music Library and the London Library and I have to thank them and their librarians, without whom no music research in London would easily be possible. Thanks also to the FCO library and especially John Sweeney for his research in Hansard. All my fellow contributors have made significant contributions to the final volume and I am grateful to them for their enthusiasm. Garry Humphreys read the second proofs and found a shoal of inconsistencies and typographic issues with his customary gimlet eye - for those problems that remain the editor accepts responsibility. My wife Susan compiled the index using Macrex software and I am most grateful to her for her speedy preparation of a substantial and invaluable tool. John Norris has designed and generated the printed text using Quark Express software and all contributors are grateful to him for his patience a\nd good humour in evolving the final layouts.

Although each contributor makes their individual acknowledgements below for copyright material quoted, the publishers and editor wish to thank the following for the use of copyright material which appears throughout this book. The over-riding source has been Lady Elgar's unpublished diaries at the Elgar Birthplace which have been used by permission of the Elgar Foundation. The discussion of Elgar and Laurance Binyon has required extensive quotation of Binyon's poetry and we thank the Society of Authors as the literary representative of the Estate of Lawrance Binyon for various quotations from Binyon's poetry. To A P Watt Ltd, on behalf of the National

Trust for Places of Historical Interest or Natural Bueaty, for quotations from Kipling's poems 'Submarines' and 'My Boy Jack'. To William Heinemann and the Estate of Robert Graves for 3 lines from 'Recalling War'. To the Estate of John Masefield for a stanza from his poem 'August'. To the Estate of Alfred Noyes for a quotation from 'Song of Victory' and two stanzas from *A Pageant of Empire*. To the Literary Estate of A P Herbert for an extract from his new words for *Pomp and Circumstance No 4*. To Thames Publishing and the estate of the late Christopher Palmer for quotations from his book *Herbert Howells a centenary celebration*. For the inevitable quotations from the giants of the literature of Elgar: Wulstan Atkins, Jerrold Northrop Moore, Michael Kennedy, Robert Anderson, Diana McVeagh and Dr Percy Young as acknowledged throughout the text and are © Wulstan Atkins; © Jerrold Northrop Moore; © Michael Kennedy; © Robert Anderson, © Diana McVeagh; © Dr Percy Young. We thank them for their pioneering research and acknowledge the use of quotations from their copyright books with thanks. For the quotations from Rosa Burley as published in *Edward Elgar the record of a friendship* we acknowledge Mrs I M Fresson and Barrie & Jenkins Ltd.

The authors of individual chapters have also contributed their own detailed acknowledgements as follows:

Andrew Neill: Where possible I have acknowledged the sources I have quoted. The study of Lady Elgar's diaries has, of course, been fundamental to an understanding of this period. I first saw the diaries at the home of Mrs Sybil Wohfeld, the former companion of Carice Elgar Blake, nearly thirty years ago and have since examined them when this unique record was deposited at The Elgar Birthplace Museum. I would like to express my gratitude to the curators of the museum over the years for the assistance they have given me in undertaking research, namely the late Jack Mackenzie and Jim Bennett. More recently I have been helped by Melanie Weatherly, Catherine Sloan and Chris Bennett. I was assisted greatly in this study by Elgar's biographer, Dr Jerrold Northrop Moore, who allowed me to examine his transcription of the diaries that cover this period. I am also grateful to David Ward, the grandson of William Rothenstein for information on the life of Charles Conder, and to Sara and Jonny Shaw for their help when I stayed in their home in Rosshire over Easter 2000.

Lewis Foreman: I am particularly grateful to the Elgar Birthplace Museum, and especially Chris Bennett, Melanie Weatherly and Catherine Sloan for ready access to Elgar's Cuttings book for 1914-1919. David Michell provided a variety of documentary material and made available recordings from his superb collection. David Mason shared with me his enormous knowledge of the popular recordings made during the First World War, and contributed materially to that section in my first chapter. Stephen Lloyd provided assistance on specific points from his wide knowledge of Elgar and his period as well as loaning his copy of the original printing of Carillon. I have to thank the Hon Lora Ponsonby for her hospitality at Shulebrede Priory and for providing access to the Parry diaries and supplying the printed music of Parry's setting of *A Hymn for Aviators*. I am most grateful to Stuart Robinson, Archivist of the Hallé Orchestra, who kindly identified members of the Hallé Orchestra in 1908.

Bernard Porter: I am grateful for help and advice given by Chris Bennett (especially) and Melanie Weatherley at the Elgar Birthplace Museum; Andrew Neill, Tim Barringer, Eric Cross, Barry Collett, Finlay Murray, Kajsa Ohrlander (for playing some unrecorded pieces to me on the piano),and fellow historians and musicians to whom preliminary versions were presented at Yale University, Stanford University and the University of Texas at Austin early in 2000.

John Norris: In addition to established Elgarian biographers, notably Michael Kennedy and Jerrold Northrop Moore, I am particularly indebted to Charles Hooey for his research into early performances of *The Spirit of England*, published in the Elgar Society Journal for November 1996.

Charles Hooey: Thanks to everyone who helped over much time put to put together my tribute to Mott, notably Dame Norma Major for direction to British government information services. The Commonwealth War Graves Commission, John Davies, Dennis Foreman, Ewen Langford, Lawrence Holdridge, Jim McPherson, Graham Oakes, photographer Tom Tulloch-Marshall, Wayne Turner and John Ward. Also to Geoffrey Hodgkins and Michael Messenger for their later contributions. I am most grateful to Alan Kelly who compiled the exhaustive Mott discography which follows my article.

Brian Trowell: I am grateful to Mrs Avis of the Worcester County Council Record Office for kindly checking that Elgar did in fact write 'fifty years ago' in the letter quoted on page 353 and to Mr Edmund Gray for permission to print the two poems by his grandfather, Laurence Binyon, on page 359.

LEWIS FOREMAN
Rickmansworth
October 2001

Prologue

CHAPTER 1

ELGAR'S WAR
From the diaries of Lady Elgar, 1914–1918

Andrew Neill

When Great Britain declared war on Germany in August 1914, Elgar was 57 years old and therefore considerably beyond fighting age. He was also too old to be involved in such activities as Red Cross work in France, unlike younger friends such as Laurence Binyon (1869-1943) and Algernon Blackwood (1869-1951), both important figures in this narrative. Elgar faced a challenge which, if not dangerous, was nonetheless a demanding one. He had to provide what was required and expected of a major artistic figure during a catastrophe unprecedented in his lifetime and that of his fellow countrymen. Elgar's response is clear from the diary excerpts given below[1], and is perhaps greater and more substantial than has been appreciated by some in the past.

There is nothing new in suggesting that the period 1914-1918 imposed a psychological as well as physical strain on Elgar. The period was a new and eventually horrifying and depressing experience for all those caught up in the substantial changes to their lives and their country 'which had hitherto been shielded by their navy, [and] that war could threaten with death the manhood of a whole nation.'[2] For most of the war, Elgar composed little music that was not either in response to a commission or at the suggestion of others, and it was not until he left hospital and moved to Sussex in the summer of 1918 that he began composing again from within, 'his insidest inside'. These works, three chamber pieces and his cello concerto, were in a form that was more economic than his more recent pre-war compositions such as the E flat symphony of 1911.

Artistic change was already in the air as war began, for in 1912 the first British performance of Five Pieces for Orchestra by Schoenberg and the performances of the Ballets Russes had challenged existing musical perceptions. Other composers were already turning against existing forms, and 1912 also saw the composition of Marcel Dupré's

FACING PAGE: *Alice Elgar by E O Hoppé, 1916*
(Raymond Monk collection)

Prelude and Fugue in G minor with its terrifying reworking of Bach's model. Elgar's *Falstaff* in 1913 had pointed towards a change in style, with its leaner scoring, snatches of melody and occasional tonal uncertainty. Although, during the war, he rarely initiated or responded directly to the patriotic needs of his countrymen, Elgar responded enthusiastically to ideas that would make a valuable contribution in this area. It is significant, all the same, that his most substantial 'war' work, *The Spirit of England,* is in a sense a requiem. It is no call to arms, and in keeping with the mood of the time he also felt unable to compose a celebration of victory in 1918.

For Elgar, the war was particularly challenging as he struggled with exceptional periods of ill health and an apparent sluggish creative response in his country's hour of need. Questions spring to mind, to which there are no obvious answers: was there any direct relationship between the conduct of the war and Elgar's compositional difficulties, and was his return to good health and composition in 1918 a direct response to the road to victory? Why did he compose relatively little during this time and why did he produce no really 'big' work for the war, beyond *The Spirit of England?* Elgar's largest wartime score, *The Starlight Express,* could have been written in peacetime.

As a source for deducing possible answers to these questions, the diaries of Lady (Alice) Elgar (1848–1920), and occasionally those of Elgar himself are invaluable, for not only do they tell us a great deal about the life of the Elgar family during this period, but also how they both reacted to the events of the war. Shortly after a significant event occurred, Alice Elgar – who lived in London for most of the war – would often comment on the routine of her life, such as her Sunday morning visits to Mass at St. James's Spanish Place. At the time the Elgars were living at Severn House in Hampstead.

It soon became apparent that it was not possible to answer these questions fully by isolating the diaries as a source of information. Furthermore, these questions and others I asked subsequently, and the corresponding answers, are more complex than I first presumed. Nevertheless, the diaries enable a researcher to paint a portrait of the lives of the Elgars during the four years their country was at war and compare these to the events of the war and the wider world with the purpose of seeing how these may have influenced Elgar and his music.

If Edward Elgar is the hero of this narrative then Alice Elgar is the heroine, as she sought servants capable of sustaining a big London home (and working in a country cottage), entertained constantly and nurtured, bullied, worried over and cared for her husband. Her diaries show how she loved the social life of London, visiting and receiving guests at Severn House. As *Lady* Elgar, she was well aware of her social standing and the correct way of conducting herself socially, but her diaries also show her happy to involve herself in charity work and to be immensely practical, using all means of transport and taking a great interest in the development of the war and much that was new.

The devotion of Alice in supporting her husband from the moment they married through the remainder of her life has been scrutinised at length by others, some suggesting that their relationship was based more on convenience than affection. These wartime diaries do nothing to assist those who wish to read something else into their relationship, other that that of a devoted couple. Despite the nine-year age gap between Alice and Edward, the diaries reinforce the view of mutual devotion, with Elgar telephoning or telegraphing nearly every day they were apart. She encourages the company of other women and supports (admittedly uncritically) everything Elgar did or wrote. She also takes a quiet pride in the work of their daughter, Carice.

For those unfamiliar with her writing, Alice's use of baby language when referring to her husband can be disconcerting. However, the diaries were written as a personal document with no view to subsequent publication, and display a restraint that is an example to us today. Indeed the diaries help us to gain another impression of Alice and discover someone of energy and humour that is often obscured by her rigid adherence to Victorian standards. Despite her enjoyment of London life, Alice knew that a retreat from the city was necessary for the well being of her Edward and, in Brinkwells, a cottage buried deep in the Sussex countryside, she found the Elgarian ideal. In doing this, she sacrificed her socialising and the comforts of home.

To say that Elgar was happy at Brinkwells is an understatement, but his contentment was not just because he could cut himself off from London, for Alice encouraged friends to stay locally as another part of the diversions she organised for him. Brinkwells did not even divorce them from reality for they bought newspapers almost daily, and the sound of southern guns was a reminder of the war across the Channel. It seems that Brinkwells satisfied something deep in Elgar's soul; a return to the land and his roots or some deeper atavistic craving. He may well have been happier there than anywhere else he lived.

Quietly supportive in the background is Carice Elgar (1890-1970), the only child of the Elgar's marriage, who engaged in translation work in the Government Censorship Department from early in the war. Her mother's diary references show how she remained constantly at hand, particularly during the crisis in Elgar's health in 1918.

The diaries reveal more, particularly in demonstrating the Elgars' constant activity during this period. From the outbreak of war until the end of 1917 Elgar is constantly on the move, trying to find the right task for himself in a new and alien environment. His attempt to find a rôle as a special constable or a 'volunteer' may seem naïve with the benefit of hindsight, but we can see how he must have felt as he adjusted to the fact that he could contribute little physically. Although this distracted him from composition, it was clearly something he had to do, and 'get out of his system'. Many others felt the same at the time.

Throughout the war Elgar worked hard. At times he drove himself non-stop. He conducted a great deal, travelling substantial distances in the process, participating in countless performances of *Carillon*[3] and *The Spirit of England* across the nation. He produced music to deadlines, such as *The Fringes of the Fleet* and *The Starlight Express* as well as performing as a music hall artist at the Coliseum in 1915 (with *Carillon*) and on tour with *The Fringes of the Fleet* in 1917. He went to fund raising events, recorded his music and survived bombing raids and generally coped well with the depressing atmosphere which beset the country as 1915 wore on. The end of the run of *The Fringes of the Fleet* in 1917 signalled a change of direction. Elgar then seemed to retreat into himself, allowing the medical profession, the healing atmosphere of Brinkwells and the involvement in country pursuits to create a sense of well being and peace to prevail during the summer of 1918.

It is easy to assume that the mounting losses on the Western Front, and a war that dragged on and on, added to Elgar's worries and contributed to his poor health at the time. Clearly he was deeply concerned, and his own few diary notes show this. Nevertheless, although he made some initial attempts at composition whilst recuperating in London after his March 1918 operation, it was not until the initiative passed to the Allies in the August that Elgar arranged for a piano to be delivered to Brinkwells and he turned to composition with an obvious sense of purpose.

Certainly the war news was better in the summer after the German spring offensive, but after four years there were few who would have

Carice Elgar, early in the war
(Raymond Monk collection)

forecast the German retreat and the eventual collapse of the German forces within three months. Much has been written about the 'artist' being able to sense changes and that these are reflected in their art. Suggestions have been made that Elgar's E flat symphony, from 1911 anticipated the end of the Edwardian era and foresaw the conflict ahead. We can never really know, and as the truth of the symphony may well lie in another direction such a claim may be tenuous: 'It is a farewell to a vision that had been glimpsed but never held, to an illusion, stubbornly maintained in the face of overwhelming evidence, that the dignity of 19th century society was real, its values true, its structure stable.'[4] All the same, the perception of the artist should not be dismissed lightly. Did Elgar then sense the end of the conflict, and feel content to devote himself to composing once again when it was clear that an Allied victory was likely. He could now turn his back on the past and look to a future that was to give him nearly two years of creative happiness. What is also clear is that Elgar could return to his roots in the country in an atmosphere detached from twentieth century technology at its worst. It is the equilibrium thus achieved which allowed creativity to flourish.

Alice Elgar's diary shows how the war came close to home, with air raids, the loss of friends, the German attack in March 1918 and the impact of the sinking of the *Lusitania*. Alice, sympathetic to German culture and its language, soon became disillusioned about her enemy as the German army marched ruthlessly through Belgium. 'The Germans were obsessively concerned about violations of international law. They succeeded in overlooking the violation created by their presence in Belgium in favour of the violation committed, as they saw it, by Belgians resisting their presence.'[5] This chapter is neither a history of the war, nor does it consider the causes of the conflict that Lloyd George felt the European Nations had 'slithered into'. All the same, it is important to put the Elgars' diaries in context as Europe 'slithered' inexorably towards conflict.

Despite the deterioration in Anglo-German relationships prior to the summer of 1914, there is little to support the view that the British public or the Government were anticipating having to go to war that August. Nor was it appreciated by any but a few, that Britain would become committed to a war that would involve the army in a long campaign on the near continent. Indeed this is supported by Alice Elgar's diary entries, in that no mention is made of the European situation until 1 August, three days before war was declared. The European crisis, which began with the assassination of the heir to the

throne of Austro-Hungary, Archduke Franz Ferdinand and his
consort the Grand Duchess in Sarajevo on 28 June, developed away
from London, primarily managed in Vienna and Berlin at first, only
moving to Russia, France and Great Britain during the last few days of
July. For most of that month the British Government had been
preoccupied with the Home Rule issue in Ireland, and the British
court ordered a week of official mourning. It was not until 23 July,
with the Austrian ultimatum to Serbia, and the appeal of the Serbs to
the Russian Tsar the next day that Sir Edward Grey, the Foreign
Secretary in London, proposed four-power mediation (Great Britain,
Germany, France and Italy), which Germany felt inclined to accept.
Events began to spiral out of control as Russia mobilised forces on the
Austro-Hungarian border on 25 July, the day Serbia mobilised.

Under the London conference of 1831 both Britain and Germany
guaranteed the neutrality of Belgium. Nevertheless, the German
Government faced the dilemma of how to implement the Schlieffen
Plan. This required Belgium to acquiesce to the German army,
allowing it to march through it on its way to attack France. 'Britain,
which had awoken to the real danger of the crisis only on Saturday 25
July, still hoped on Thursday 30 July that the Russians would tolerate
an Austrian punishment of Serbia but were determined not to leave
France in the lurch.'[6]

The immutable Austrians declared war on Serbia on 28 July,
having refused mediation proposals. Although the German
Government was conciliatory it threw any responsibility for war on
Russia. It was the following day that Britain warned Germany that she
could not stand aside if Germany went to war with Russia, but
Germany ordered general mobilisation on 30 July, the Russians
following later in the day. As late as 26 July the Prime Minister, Henry
Asquith, declared that Britain had made no pledge to Belgium. 'In the
end, Asquith permitted events on the Continent to outpace and
influence decisions of the British Government. The German ultimatum
demanding submission by Belgium within twelve hours forced Britain
to choose. Asquith's achievement was that, when the choice was made,
Government, Party and Country were united behind him'.[7]

On Friday 31 July, Austria mobilised fully and Germany declared
an 'imminent-danger-of-war situation' and demanded to know if
France would remain neutral. Belgium decreed mobilisation and Sir
Edward Grey worked, as best he could, to offer mediation between
Austria and Serbia whilst seeking assurances that Germany would
respect Belgian neutrality. Saturday 1 August saw France and

Germany mobilise with German troops invading Luxembourg and Poland the following morning. That day the Belgians received the notorious note from Germany stating that she must be allowed to violate Belgian soil in order to 'anticipate' a French attack. On 3 August the Belgians rejected the German demand and appealed to Britain to intervene, and later that day Germany declared war on France, with Britain ordering mobilisation immediately.

It was Sir Edward Grey who was responsible for conveying to his Liberal party and Government, the Unionist opposition and his fellow countrymen the issues involved in a speech to the House of Commons on the afternoon of Monday 3 August. 'This momentous speech ... which decided the fate of Europe ... converted [a] very large number of Englishmen to the horrid necessity of war'.[8] It is Grey's words which echoed those of Alice's diary when he ended by saying: 'If in a crisis like this we ran away from those obligations of honour and interest as regards the Belgian Treaty, I doubt whether whatever material force we might have at the end of the war would be of very much value in the face of the respect that we might have lost.'

The next morning the German army crossed the Belgian border before declaring war later in the day. Britain had already begun to mobilise, and the Government issued an ultimatum to Germany to withdraw her troops by midnight, German time. Lord Beauchamp, brother of Lady Mary Lygon,[9] was Lord President of the Council and was present at Buckingham Palace for the meeting of the Privy Council convened by the King to declare war on Germany, which took effect at 11 pm (midnight in Berlin). The fateful 4 August began with Britain protesting to Berlin against German violation of Belgian territory, but it was too late. At 11 pm, Britain and Germany were at war.

As a perspective on the war Alice Elgar's diaries are of greatest interest in the first few months of 1914 and from the spring of 1918 until the Armistice. It was then that there is great movement leading to uncertainty and fear and eventually confidence in the outcome. For much of the time, for those fighting, the war consisted of a mixture of 'boredom, stark horror and fear', as the poet Siegfried Sassoon eloquently put it. Alice Elgar shows us that for those at home boredom was replaced by activity, and fear by constant worry. Her diaries are an important historical document and make fascinating and at times amusing reading.

∽   ∽   ∽

The text that follows is supported by a brief war commentary that amplifies, where relevant, the Elgar diaries as well as highlighting important developments in the course of the war to which no direct reference is made in the text.

1914

The Sarajevo assassinations occurred on 28 June. For the next five weeks, Alice Elgar does not refer to the events that were beginning to engulf Europe, and in mid July she was organising a family holiday.

> July 16. A. & C. [Carice] to Harrods. Bought waterproofs for Scotland.[10]
> July 19. Had to await [sic] until 11 before embarking in train. Most comfortable. E. Slept well.[†]

They travelled to Glasgow by train and took the ferry from Gairloch through the Crinan Canal to stay at the Station Hotel, Oban, which placed them well to explore the Inner Hebridean islands of Mull, Staffa and Iona.

> July 20. Lovely view across the bay but Oban a dull little place & dull hotel.
> July 21. Managed to miss the crowd & wandered by our souses very lovely. Cathedral [Iona] in imposing position but looks so plain & distressingly Protestant.

The Elgars moved on to Inverness, through the Caledonian Canal and then to Dingwall and Achnasheen. Carice recalled the driver being slightly drunk and singing nonsense songs in the back of the taxi with her father.

> July 25. Found taxi for us. Had tea & started, A. outside. Wonderful drive but terrifying. The taxi raced...frightful road, taxi leapt and plunged and tore through huge puddles...arrived safely D.G. Nice Hotel and fire very reviving.

June 23-25. Kiel Canal re-opened (after deepening) by German Kaiser. Visited by British fleet under the command of Sir George Warrender; the Kaiser, as Admiral of the Fleet in the Royal Navy, inspects HMS *King George V*.

June 28. Assassination of Archduke Franz Ferdinand (heir to throne of Austro-Hungary) and Grand Duchess Sophie in Sarajevo.

July 23. Austrian ultimatum to Serbia.

July 27. Russia Tsar states Russia cannot be indifferent to the fate of Serbia.

July 28. Austria declares war on Serbia.

---

† - All quotations are an accurate transcription of the original, retaining as far as is practicable the punctuation, capitalisation and spelling of the original.

Edward Elgar by E O Hoppé, c 1915
(Raymond Monk collection)

July 29. Russia mobilises.
July 31. Germany demands to know if France will remain neutral.
August 1. France mobilises.
August 2. German troops invade Luxembourg, Poland & East Prussia.
    German note to Belgium saying she must violate Belgian soil.
August 3. Germany declares war on France & Belgium.
August 4. Britain declares war on Germany.
August 10. Liège occupied by German forces.
August 12. Great Britain declares war on Austria-Hungary

There followed days of fishing and walking in typical Scottish summer weather: squally showers followed by bright sunshine and blue skies. At last Alice records details of the events that would engulf all their lives.

August 1. Rainy, wired for news of Novello – most anxious – Feared Government would not take action and feared betrayal of Belgium and treaty &c.
August 5. Frightfully anxious for news. Had a telegram saying Germany declared war against us.[11]
August 6. Very anxious for news. E. very worried about everything. ... Very stormy still managed to be out a great deal. Very thrilling & touching seeing the Lovat Scouts start. ... Stood out and waved.

The Elgars were desperate to get home, but were delayed as most local vehicles had been commandeered by the military.

August 10. Very stormy. E. A & C. started about 10 in the Charabanc. Wonderful drive – Rain and wind. Found ourselves wet through and changed to the skin in Achnasheen. Lunched there & lovely journey to Inverness Loch Luichart so beautiful & sad. Slept at Inverness.
August 11. Inverness full of dear Kaki [sic] soldiers – It is a sweet place. Left at 10 & spent 3 or 4 hours at Perth.... Walked to see the Bridge and to Fair Maid of Perth's house.

Meanwhile the first soldiers of the British Expeditionary Force were beginning the journey for France. On 12 August the 1st Battalion of the Irish Guards embarked from Southampton on the SS *Navara,* and '... as dusk fell, she passed HMS *Formidable* off Ryde and exchanged signals with her. The battleship's last message to the Battalion was to hope that they would "get plenty of fighting".' [12] Alice and Carice arrived back at Severn House on 13 August whilst Elgar travelled home via Leeds where he was to conduct. The following day Marie Joshua, a German-born widow and patron of music, wrote to Alice. 'My sympathies are entirely with England and France. The despotic

German ruler & his horrid influence arouse my greatest indignation, & I am glad my dear Mother's family were all French, and I love this great England which has sheltered me so long & which has a conscience even in Politics.' [13]

Back in London, Elgar's music was inevitably being used for patriotic purposes.

> August 15. A. & C. to Queen's Hall in evg. 'Sospiri' [14] lovely like a breath of peace on a perturbed world. Wonderful effect of Land of Hope and Glory. Enormous audience rose   Shouts.

As the destruction of Belgium became the main news in every newspaper Elgar undertook his first act for the war effort.

> August 17. E. went up to the Hampstead P Court and was sworn in as a Special Constable. When one of the police saw the O.M. he said. 'there are not many of them going about.' C. to work for Navy League & first aid.

Alice noted the desecration of Louvain in her diary. British forces had now been in action for the first time but she was unaware of the retreat, as the military authorities began their effective control of news. 'Mons ... it was not understood that eighty thousand British troops with three hundred guns ... were meeting twice that number of Germans on their front, plus sixty thousand Germans with two hundred and thirty guns trying to turn their left flank, while a quarter of a million Germans, with close on a thousand guns, were driving in the French armies on the British right ... .' [15] However, they could not disguise the reality of the German advance, so close to home, and the potential consequences of a successful encirclement of Paris.   Alice

---

August 17. Sir John French, commander of the BEF, sets up HQ at Le Cateau.

August 19. German Kaiser's order to destroy General French's 'contemptible little army' allegedly given.

August 20. Brussels occupied by German forces.

August 23. Japan declares war on Germany. Battle of Mons begins; German advance checked by British forces

August 25. Retreat from Mons begins.

August 26. Battle of Le Cateau, British 2nd Corps delay German advance, but retreat continues.

August 29. Battle of Heligoland Bight, three German cruisers sunk.

September 2. BEF withdraws to Chantilly-Nanteuil.

September 3. German forces cross the River Marne.

September 6. The Battle of the Marne begins. By 12 September   German forces have fallen back to the line of the Aisne.

and the rest of her fellow countrymen and women became transfixed
with the daily developments.

> August 29. Heard of Navy success in the North Sea. So thankful – Wonderful
> pluck and skill. Thank God not many Eng. killed. ... Heard serious
> accounts of German advance in N. France & how our Army had suffered.
> ... Lovely hot days & harvest moon, looking down on what a death
> harvest through one nation's depravity.

The original Schlieffen Plan which asserted the German right wing to
march, not only through Belgium but Holland, had already been
compromised by General von Moltke.[16] He had refused to violate
Dutch neutrality and had reduced the number of men involved by
1,500,000. The plan required the force to touch Rouen, encircle Paris
and meet up with the German left wing which should have entered
France through the Saarland. The eventual failure of the plan
occurred when the German right wing under General von Kluck[17]
swung left after Amiens across the front of Paris, eventually opening
a gap in the German front line.

Meanwhile the German army had enlisted reservists in a
desperate attempt to sustain the momentum of their advance on
Paris, and Alice, in her diary, no doubt reflected the anxious state of
mind of all back home.

> August 30. To see Special Constables Parade – E. looked very distinguished
> and was photographed in front of the body. ... Afterwards a 'Times' with
> harrowing account of destruction of so much of our glorious Army –
> September 1. ... Still no very good news very anxious.
> September 2. E. to Police Station. Mr Broadhurst to see him about a song – A.
> firing into shops about recruiting &c – Very anxious days – still German
> advance goes on –
> September 3. Still little news. Advance on Paris. Very anxious. Our splendid
> Army seems to have such fearful numbers against it. E. feeling unwell –
> Very hot – Lovely day. Very choky to think of our lovely Country in these
> misty evenings & sunny days –
> September 4. Lovely day – Long walk. Much harrowed thinking of English
> killed and prisoners.
> September 5. Frightfully anxious about War & beloved army & ships.
> Abominable mine destroyed 'Pathfinder' E. busy – & may have to go out
> in the night, any night –
> September 8. Lovely day. Very hot. E. to his Station 10-12. Beginning of
> another great battle. Pray Heaven English win & French.

Elgar composed *The Roll Call – A Soldier's Song* over the next few
days, which was sung by Clara Butt at the Albert Hall in October.
Later he withdrew it. His mood at the time is clear from a letter he

wrote to Frank Schuster[18] on 25 August:

> My Dear Frank,
>   I don't know where you are so I send this home. I hope you are well
> & getting some clean & clear air. Here we are very hot but atmosphere
> quite bearable – London looks normal; it seems incredible that things shd.
> go on so well. Alice is well but worried. Carice spends her whole time in
> practical ways – learning nursing &c &c. I am a s[pecial] constable and am
> a 'Staff Inspector' – I am sure others cd do the work better, but none with
> a better will. I was equipping (serving out 'weapons') & taking receipts &
> registering my men for hours last night: this morning at six I inspected the
> whole district – so one does what one can – its a pity I am too old to be a
> soldier[:] I am so active.
>   Everything is at a standstill & we have nothing left in the world –
> absolute financial ruin – but we are cheerful & I will die a man if not a
> musician.
>   This is all about us[:] & how about you? do write.
>   Concerning the war I say nothing – the only thing that wrings my
> heart and soul is the thought of the horses – oh! my beloved animals – the
> men – and women can go to hell – but my horses; – I walk round and
> round this room cursing God for allowing dumb brutes to be tortured – let
> Him kill his human beings but – how CAN HE? Oh, my horses.

Despite this, Elgar had already written to A C (Arthur) Benson[19] to
create some topical words for *Land of Hope and Glory*, which were
now being sung across the nation. Daily exchanges between Elgar in

---

September 14. Battle of the Aisne (until 28) begins, as Germans halt north of
    Rheims. This battle marked the end of the war of movement as the
    armies began to take up positions in trenches.
September 20. Bombardment of Rheims Cathedral.
September 22. HMS's *Aboukir, Hogue* & *Cressy* sunk by submarine.
October 9. Surrender of Antwerp (the seat of the Belgian Government since
    17 August).
October 13. Ypres occupied by Allied forces.
October 15. Ostend & Zeebrugge occupied by German forces.
October 16. Battle of Yser begins with German attack on Dixmude.
October 17. HMS *Undaunted* & destroyers sink four German destroyers.
October 18. British monitors under Admiral Hood bombard German forces
    on the Yser.
October 19. First Battle of Ypres begins (to November 17).
October 28. Lord Fisher becomes First Sea Lord in succession to Prince Louis
    of Battenberg.
October 31. On the Yser the French recover Ramscapelle, crisis of the Battle
    of Ypres, British line broken but the position is recovered by the 2nd
    Battalion of the Worcestershire Regiment.

Hampstead and Benson in Sussex thrashed out a new version that satisfied them both by early September.[20]

> September 19. Still terrible fighting. Longing for news of British Victory-

Although The Battle of the Marne frustrated the German plan to take Paris, heavy Allied losses began to become apparent, as did the poor communication between the French and British forces that was to undermine so much of the allied effort in the first half the war. The news made Elgar restless and on 22 September he went to Stoke Prior (The Elms) to stay with his sister Pollie but returned to London three days later.

> September 21. Heard of destruction of Rheims Cathedral – Much upset.
> September 22. Lovely day – E. to the Elms after visit to his station. Travelled with wounded Soldiers (Mons) & gave them tea – he said, 'wonderful men.' Heard of loss of the 3 Cruisers in North Sea. Dreadfully grieved –
> September 25. E. returned – Too opprest with the war to stay away – Frightful battle still going on – Lovely weather like summer –
> October 5. A. to Emergency Corps to ask if cd teach Soldiers French – Was asked if she wd take a class that minute almost!
> October 6. A. Chelsea Barracks. Pupils very nice especially 2 of them, & very interested.
> October 7. A. to Chelsea Barracks later to tea at American Embassy. ...

The Belgian army now fell back to the coast, and in an attempt to stop the German army from reaching it first the BEF moved into position, basing itself on Ypres.

> October 10. Much distressed at fall of Antwerp. E. to Albert Hall. First part of concert trying. Then E's splendid Roll Call & at end The Kingsway & Land of Hope & Glory. Audience began to applaud as soon as that began & all stood at 2. verse & many joined in singing. Wonderful thrill. C. Butt sang the KingsWay[sic] splendidly.
> October 11. Terribly anxious regarding War News – & Germans trying to advance to Ostend.
> October 14. Still very anxious Germans near coast.
> October 17. E. to The Hut – Lovely day – Cheered by more & hopeful news –
> October 18. E. at The Hut. A. to Spanish Place P. & Circumstance splendid as outgoing Voluntary. Much cheered with good naval news –
> October 21. Anxious as to great fight on Coast, but thankful news seems encouraging.
> October 22. Anxious about the great fight on the coast – Monitors seemed splendid.
> October 23. Nice day – Frightful battle still going on. Longing for good & great decisive news. E. to his station.
> November 3. Mr R. Hichens to tea & long talk Mr Streatfeild came too – Very nice time –

Good news was grasped, even if far away. Alice noted that Japanese (with some British) forces seized Germany's only possession in China, the fort at Tsingtao.[21]   This event would have overshadowed the disaster at Cape Coronel.

> November 7. Tsing-tan[sic] surrendered Great Russian success.

By the end of November the German advance was halted, but at great cost. The exhausted armies now sank into the trenches that would stretch in a line from the Channel to the Swiss border, remaining virtually unchanged for four years. It was now that Elgar began to take stock, artistically, of what had occurred during the first terrible, fast-moving months of the campaign.

> November 9. E. thinking of Carillon Music –

The following day Elgar telephoned Tita Brand Cammaerts[22] who, as the wife of the Belgian poet Emile Cammaerts, had translated his poem *Carillon* into English.   Elgar had been commissioned to contribute to the Belgian Fund by publishing a work in the commemorative *King Albert's Book*. The destruction of Belgium's many bell towers was remembered in the poem, as is the destruction of Belgium itself. He took the advice of an old friend, Rosa Burley,[23] and provided an illustrative prelude and entr'actes as background music for a recitation of the poem.

> December 6. to Queen's Hall – Delightful rehearsal of Carillon – wonderful sounds and orchestration.
> December 7. To concert & am [sic] gorgeous performance & immense enthusiasm.   E. wd not take the applause & always came on with Cammaerts but at last <u>had</u> to come by his ducksie souse – A wonderful scene and ovation. <u>large</u> audience.

The next day, Cammaerts wrote to Elgar. 'I cannot let this day pass without thanking you again for your glorious work. I have met a

---

November 1. Battle of Coronel (off coast of Chile). Admiral Graf von Spee defeats lightly armoured British.
November 5. Great Britain declares war on Turkey and annexes Cyprus.
December 8. Admiral von Spee's squadron defeated off The Falkland Islands, by a fleet under command of Admiral Sturdee.
December 16. Hartlepool, Scarborough and Whitby bombarded from sea.
December 25. No action was reported on the Western Front, although British naval airmen bombed German warships off Cuxhaven.

good many Belgians to-day and they all wonder how you managed to share so completely our pain and our hopes.' [24]   *The Times* commented, somewhat sourly but perceptively. 'If this is all that the tragedy of Belgium can bring from a musician it seems a small tribute'.[25] However, the popularity of *Carillon* continued throughout the war and *The Times* was able to comment in May 1915:[26] 'those which secure large audiences listen to Elgar's *Carillon*, and those which secure small ones for other music'. A cut version of *Carillon* was recorded with the distinguished actor, Henry Ainley, during Elgar's visit to the recording studio on 29 January 1915, and was to become, in its own terms, a 'best seller'.[27]

> December 17. Raid by German Cruisers on Scarborough & Hartlepool – Low barbaristic to shell a defenceless watering place – …E. conducted most splendidly & the Carillon sounded greater than ever. Most beautifully played & aroused enormous enthusiasm – recalled & recalled & shouts of 'bis, bis'.
> December 20. A. not out. Very cold. M. A. de Greef[28] & Kalisch[29] to tea – Mr de Greef, very interesting. Immense gratitude to England –

For those at Severn House, the first Christmas of the war was uneventful, but on Christmas Eve Alice noted something she was to record with great interest throughout the remainder of the war.

> December 24. German aeroplane threw bomb at Dover, went into garden & did no harm.

At the same time the British dropped bombs on German air sheds near Brussels.

> December 25. No news at all, all day. Seemed a strange blank – Longing to hear – Nice letters & little things. E. & C. well thankful to say. Miss Burley here – Alice S. W. came to tea, brought flowers & E's lovely lavender water.
> December 31. Year ends in great anxieties but with invaluable consciousness that England has a great, holy cause – May God keep her –

1915

Following the success of *Carillon*, 1915 began well for Elgar, although Alice had to deal with servant problems.

> January 7. Florence Drake returned but did not wish to stay then but to be home for some days – A. sd. she must stay or leave – She left. Sarah & Beatrice so good carrying on house –
>
> January 11. New cook, Alice Bee came. Seemed nice.
>
> January 14. Anxious about news. The French having had to lose a little ground. German paper punished as it stated B. Hollweg[30] said the situation was precarious & Germany cd Hold out till Oct.
>
> January 15. Anxious for news, the French had a slight setback – Good news aftn. British charged & gained a hill at La Barrée & nearly a kilometre of ground – Trust small losses –
>
> January 17. E. to Albert Hall, Rehearsal of Concerto. Quite delighted with A. Sammons playing.

The concert took place that night. Meanwhile the war came closer to home, and the demands on Elgar's time as a policeman were never far away.

> January 19. Seemingly tranquil but at night a German air raid on Yarmouth & that part of East Coast. They damaged houses & caused some loss of life, engulfing themselves more deeply in crime than ever. Brutes – E. called out about 10.40 – Roamed around till a telegram released the Specials. E. in about 1 a.m.
>
> January 23. Very cold. Alice came up to tea – Much talk of Germans in London & traitors &c. Why not turn them out –

The Dogger Bank action delighted the British public, although it achieved little strategically.

> January 24. All morning Naval Battle in N. Sea & great success for the wonderful Navy.
>
> January 25. Joy hearing of Naval success. Such a relief –
> E. to dentist, vesy peased with his gold toof! – Then to Brit. Museum & saw L. Binyon & lunched with Mr Streatfeild –

Laurence Binyon, poet and keeper of Oriental Manuscripts at the Museum had been an assistant to Sir Sidney Colvin[31] who had

---

January 19. Zeppelin drops bombs on Yarmouth and King's Lynn.
January 24. The Battle of the Dogger bank in the North Sea. The German cruiser *Blücher* was sunk.

suggested to Elgar 'Why don't you do a wonderful requiem for the slain – something in the spirit of Binyon's *For the Fallen*?'

The first 'war poem' by Henry Newbolt appeared in *The Times* on 5 August, and from then onwards poems were published almost daily for a year. Poets included Bridges (the Poet Laureate), Kipling, Hewlett and Gosse. Elgar took a close interest and on 26 October he wrote to Ivor Atkins 'Have you read Masefield's poem [*August*] in the *English Review*? That is the best thing written yet...'.[32] The publishing of poems was not confined to Britain for in Germany 'several million war poems appeared in newspapers or popular anthologies [during the war].[33] Laurence Binyon's *The Fourth of August* appeared within a week of the declaration of war, and his *For the Fallen,* written after the retreat from Mons, was published on 21 September. All twelve of his poems were published as *The Winnowing-Fan* in December 1914.[34]

Binyon was deeply attached to the Flanders countryside and one of his best friends, who had become a Benedictine monk, had entered a monastery in Louvain, where he was killed in the German attack. The volume contains an impassioned eulogy on the destruction of the University City, including its 'incomparable Library, founded in 1426 when Berlin was a clump of wooden huts'.[35] The distinguished journalist, Richard Harding Davis was but one American who witnessed the desecration, and his headline in the *New York Tribune*: 'Germans Sack Louvain; Women and Clergy Shot' sent the German propaganda machine into full speed as it tried to convince an unbelieving world that 'the entire responsibility for these events rests with the Belgian Government'. Binyon, in one of his poems, wrote an imaginary appeal to Goethe:

> If still those clear, Olympian eyes
> Through smoke and rage
> Your ancient Europe scrutinize
> What think you, Sage?[36]

The destruction of Louvain, which began on 25 August was a turning point in the war, in that neutral world opinion began to form against Germany from that time, and in some ways did not recover for fifty years or more. 'The gesture intended by the Germans to frighten the world – to induce submission – instead convinced large numbers of people that here was an enemy with whom there could be no settlement and no compromise'.[37]

Later in the war, Binyon was to serve in France as a Red Cross volunteer. As Jerrold Northrop Moore has pointed out, his poems 'were an early attempt to reckon up the psychological cost of the war'.[38] It is *For the Fallen* that made the biggest impact at the time, and there are few who do not know its most famous verse today.

> They shall grow not old, as we that are left grow old:
> Age shall not weary them, nor the years condemn.
> At the going down of the sun and in the morning
> We will remember them.

Rudyard Kipling was sent the lines, shortly after his son was reported missing in 1915, and he later told Binyon that he had thought the lines 'were old, – something classic, – and then I realised they were just it'. Even Siegfried Sassoon wrote to Binyon that ' "For the Fallen" remains as the finest expression of a certain aspect of the war'.[39]

> January 31. A. & C. to Albert Hall for Variations. Beautiful performance…L. Ronald[40] conducted them wonderful E's real spirit in them.

On 7 February, a Sunday, Binyon joined other guests at Severn House. A few days later, Alice supported an old friend, the violinist W H (Billy) Reed.

> February 12. E. to Bradford…for rehearsal.
> A. & Doris Whitehorn to Leighton House. Mr Reed's quartet played Debussy and Fauré – Debussy very charming like all birds & insects & creatures all pweaking at once in the country – …Nice telegram from E. there all safes –

At the beginning of March the Elgars began an exhausting conducting tour of Scotland and the north of England. Before leaving home he resigned from the Special Constabulary. Late night calls, the cold weather and his age contributed to the decision, as no doubt did the realisation that the war would not be easily won. The initial fun of joining in a new adventure had also gone, and he needed time to think over Binyon's poems. Edward and Alice went to Birmingham

---

February 11. Formation of the Battalion of Welsh Guards.
February 18. Heavy fighting near Arras.
February 19. Naval bombardmant of Dardanelles begins.
March 10. Battle of Neuve Chapelle begins, to March 12.
March 14. Battle of St Eloi (south of Ypres) begins. German cruiser *Dresden* sunk by British warships off the coast of Chile.

together and Elgar travelled on to Manchester, Sheffield, Glasgow, Edinburgh Newcastle and Leeds.

> March 10. E. returned from Leeds all well, very slight cold. So thankful to see him safes. Vesy hapsy evening – Much to hear –
>
> March 12. E. raser cold –
>
> March 13. E. raser cold – Bed to breakfast. A. with E. to park & then to Albert Hall Ballad Concert. J. Coates sang 'Speak Music' <u>most</u> wonderfully and it is a wonderful song. Outrageous to have a horrible Music Hall song just before it. A. came away very directly.

Alice was happier the following week.

> March 18. Concert quite wonderful. Carillon was played as never before, most splendid & Ainley very fine. Impossible to describe the Symphony. E. conducted splendidly & most vehemently. The 2nd movement is the greatest thing in all music, indeed so is all the Symphony. Much enthusiasm. Carillon was repeated. Deo Gratias for such a beautiful evening.

Whilst Elgar stayed at Stoke, Alice and Carice went to an exhibition.

> March 25. A. & C. to see Lindsay & his pixtures [sic]. Glorious glowing red wheat fields & Cotswolds in distance. One feels the summer glow & the spirit of Masefield's August.

Elgar was planning to set two additional poems from the Binyon collection, in addition to *For the Fallen* that would provide the third movement and be the climax of the work. The opening line of the first poem, *The Fourth of August* gave the work its overall title, *The Spirit of England*. The third poem was entitled *To Women*. Already, by early March, he had been able to show and play his sketches to his friends; but towards the end of the month it became clear that Novello, the music publisher, had agreed to publish a setting of *For the Fallen* by another composer, Cyril Rootham, a pupil of Stanford. Novello advised that they could not contemplate publishing two versions of the same piece. Elgar met with Rootham and then wrote to Binyon on 24 March.

> I have battled with the feeling for nearly a week, but the sight of the other man comes between me and my music. I know you will be disappointed, but your disappointment is not as great as mine for I love your poem & love & honour you for having conceived it.
>
> I am going to the country & will see if I can make the other settings acceptable, without the great climax.[41]

Binyon replied to Elgar the following day:

> Your words about my poem touch me deeply. My disappointment matters nothing, keen as it is: but think of England, of the English speaking

peoples in whom the common blood stirs now as it never did before; think
of the awful casualty lists that are coming, and the losses in more & more
homes; think of the thousands who will be craving to have their grief
glorified and lifted up and transformed by an art like yours – and though
I have little understanding of music as you know, I understand that
craving when words alone seem all too insufficient and inexpressive –
think of what you are withholding from your countrymen and women.
Surely it would be wrong to let them lose this help and consolation.[42]

On 26 March Henry Clayton of Novello wrote to Elgar stating the
following:

Many thanks for your letter. It is very good of you to stand on one side
for the benefit of Dr. Rootham, & I am very sorry indeed that our
commercial views of the matter should be the cause of interfering with the
plans of an artist like yourself.[43]

That day Alice recorded her feelings in her diary:

March 26. Heard from E. that he had written to give up 'For the Fallen'
'Wrotham's[sic] disappointed face comes between me & my work.' Vesy
vesy beautiful of E. – sad loss to the world.

Elgar, after considering his response to Binyon, wrote to the poet on
31 March.

Very many thanks for your most kind and sympathetic letter: I quite feel
all you say and would give anything that the publication might proceed;
but under all the circumstances this is not conceivable.
        There is only one publisher for choral music in England: Mr Rootham
was in touch with Novello first – my proposal made his MS wastepaper &
I could not go on.[44]

March 31. A. to lunch with Mrs Joshua – Percy Pitt there – he bought a
photograph of himself for Mrs J & by the side he had written some bars of
the Slow Movement of E's 2nd Symphony – Very nice thought –

At last Novello agreed to publish both settings of *For the Fallen*, but
Elgar's heart had gone out of the project. He was to continue with his
composition of the two other poems, *The Fourth of August* and *To
Women.* However, others were not so easily dissuaded. Richard
Streatfeild, a colleague and close friend of Laurence Binyon at the
British Museum and music critic of the *Daily Graphic*, took it upon
himself to further Binyon's cause and therefore Elgar's too. He also
found Elgar still sympathetic to the idea of some form of 'war service'.

April 5. Mr Streatfeild to tea – induced E. to join Hampstead Volunteer
Reserve – Mr S. so distressed that E. had given up Binyon's poems –
because he had so generously retired in favour of Wrotham but quite

<u>angry</u> too – (quite right.)

April 7. E. to his first drill – with Mr Streatfeild who returned with E. & stayed for dinner & played Spelka.

Servant difficulties also intervened again.

April 9. … Bee, the cook, returned with haemmorage from dentist at 10 P.M. A. telephoned to Drs. & chemist, at last got a Dr. to come – who stopped it just before 2. Pleasant night! So glad nothing worse.

April 11. Spanish Place. Very nice morning – London is so quiet at that hour – Sir Sidney Colvin to tea – Sidney overwhelming in his <u>attack</u> on E. to go on with L Binyon's poems – E. a little moved I thought.

April 12. E. to tea with the Colvins – Hope more influence for the great music –

April 13. Młynarski[45] came to see E. Longed for him to write something for Poland as he did for Belgium.

The same day Sir Sidney Colvin wrote to Elgar pursuing him to make a decision on 'For the Fallen'.

I heard with great distress last night that my wife's utmost petition to you on behalf of us all seemed to be in vain and that you persist, now that the original occasion for such misfortune has passed away, in abandoning the scheme on which we had built such hopes. Well it is cruelly hard on that fine poet & fine fellow, my friend Binyon, to whom the association with you would have brought just the lift in fame & status which was lacking to him and which, since the war began, he has so splendidly deserved.

… You put it on the indifference of our race & public to art; but what has the poor British public done now which it had not a month ago, when you were full of the project and raised all our hearts with the anticipation of a great & worthy expression & commemoration of the emotions of the hour, such as you alone are capable of giving them?

… I cannot bring myself to believe – nor to crush the hopes of the poet by having to tell him – that in the end you will not consent. –
Ever affectionately yours
Sidney Colvin

PS The above is not to be answered except by deeds. SC[46]

So, despite Elgar learning to drill and hold a rifle as a new member of the Reserve, Alice was able to record a day later:

April 14. E. turned to his beautiful music again, loved it himself. So there is hope. A. to see Frances Colvin who was longing to hear if her & Sidney's entreaties had had any effect on E. to persuade to write for L. Binyon's Poems again –

April 14. Australian Government commits its men to the war.

The second battle of Ypres now began and by the end of the battle, Ypres had ceased to exist, the mediæval buildings and famous cloth hall gone for ever.

> April 25. M & Made Cammaerts in aftn & Mary Trefusis[47] & Mrs Hewitt. Then Mr Streatfeild and Lawrence[sic] Binyon & Mrs B. – E. turned to his music again and played it to them, Streatfeild knelt beside him – enraptured. All so pleased … Then Cammaerts read us his mystic Drama …

The following morning Alice and Edward travelled to Stratford, where over five days they saw six plays. Whilst there Elgar ordered his reserve uniform.

> April 28. Warm & lovely – E. & A. to lunch with Mrs Leggett – Lovely house & garden. E. to Study Rifle with Sergeant – Mary de Navarro motored over [from Broadway] – Very dear & nice – Embraced E. at front door!
> April 30. After lunch had a car & motored near Rifle Range – E. stayed there to practise, –   E. much excited about shooting – Hit target at 600 yards, wonderfully good as he never tried a rifle before.

Back at Severn House Elgar continued with his Binyon settings.

> May 2. E. turning to his music – played his music to Landon Ronald who was entranced with it.
> May 3. E. busy with his Binyon music. J Coates came over & sang through it – most impressed & thought it wd be one of his greatest things.
> May 7. …horror struck one – Sinking of the Lusitania – truly German deed –

As the battles in the Dardanelles and at Ypres continued, Elgar worked on *Polonia* the work that had developed from his meeting with Młynarski. But his military duties also continued to divert him.

> May 20. E. to Meeting Volunteers –
> May 21. E. to drill in evening.
> May 22. E. out in aftn. Severe drill &c.
> May 23. E. out for March &c – Came in very hot … M. de Groote to tea & E. played his *Polonia* to him & then the Binyon Poem Music with wh. he was enthralled. Italy declared war.

On 31 May the first Zeppelin raid on London killed six people. Alice noted the event in her diary. The next day Elgar finished *Polonia* and Alice took the score to the publishers, Elkin. They hired a taxi on 3 June to look at the house wrecked by the bomb. This was the first of many excursions, which took place whenever a bomb fell in the vicinity, until Elgar's health gave out.

> June 12. Lovely day rather hot & tiring. E. very busy with his parts, score & rest of parts arrived too of Polonia. … Better war news D.G.

June 15. E. finished his parts & he took them on omnibus to Mr Elkin.[48]

June 16. E. working at the Binyon music all the morning
wis him to Euston – The train nearly left wisout him as he was telling A. what Orch. to set –

Elgar stayed at Stoke Prior until 19 June, whilst back in London Alice stayed loyal to his music.

June 17. In evening to Albert Hall – Carillon gorgeous & then the great 2nd Symphony No words cd. Describe it – the music is beyond Earth. The greatest music ever written.

June 20. Very nice afternoon – The Landon Ronalds – ...Landon so nice & went through Polonia with E. & loved the Binyon music, said there had been nothing like it since the 2nd Symphony –

June 22. E. & A. to Bert [Albert Hall]. Variation most beautifully played – Landon is wonderful & a poet/interpreter for E

Elgar travelled to Bournemouth to conduct *Carillon* and returned the following day, a Saturday, to find Severn House empty as Alice and Carice were at the Albert Hall with Mrs Joshua and others listening to yet another performance of *Carillon*. As ever the war was not far away and intruded in other ways:

June 25. E. to Bournemouth in afternoon – Travelled with Made Vanderwelde[sic] – She had to report herself at Police Station. E. escorted her there in the dim evg.[49]

June 27. ... A. S.W. took E. for drive rather rainy – Loebs[50] called. Mrs.L. much distressed by her father's (Richter) attitude towards England.

On 5 July the first rehearsal of *Polonia* took place in the Queens' Hall, and the next evening the Elgars were joined by Alice Stuart Wortley[51] for the concert.

July 5. E. to Rehearsal, the first, of Polonia, at 10 at Queen's Hall – A. wis him – Landon & Streatfeild & Alice S. W. there – Very very fine & thrilling.

April 22. Second Battle of Ypres begins. Germans use poison gas for first time against French.

April 25. Allied forces land on the Straits of the Dardanelles.

May 7. *Lusitania* torpedoed off southern coast of Ireland. 1198 were drowned (including 124 US citizens).

May 14. Internment of enemy aliens begins in Britain.

May 23. Italy declares war on Austria.

May 25. Coalition Government formed in Britain. Asquith Prime Minister, Lloyd George – Munitions, Grey – Foreign Secretary, Kitchener – War.

July 6. 2nd Rehearsal of Polonia at 10. E. much peased – The Orch. beautiful & the music sounded wonderful – Such a wonderful <u>sound</u>, as dear Rody[52] used to say, <u>his</u> sound, drums like guns – To Concert in evening. Small audience – Badly advertised & managed – … The first notes of Polonia seemed to open out a new world – A splendid performance in the work magnificent & enormous enthusiasm, the real <u>roar</u> there is for E. his own roar I always calls it & recalled again & <u>again</u> – D.G. for such a beautiful evening & for E's success –

July 11. E. vesy busy – Alice S. W. & Frances Colvin came first. E. played all his Binyon music to them, Frances quite white with excitement – Much impressed.

Meanwhile Cammaerts had persuaded Elgar to begin work on another recitation, this time incorporating a song for mezzo-soprano.

July 17. E. took his darling score of The Voix dans le Désert to be copied – Goodwin & Tabb – A new arr. of Pomp & Circumstance there. E. looked at it, the assist. Pointed it out. E. sd he did not know it. 'Not know it?' indignant surprise. 'But there is Land of Hope & Glory' – pointing out where it came. Still E. saying he did not know it, more indignation till E. said 'I wrote it but do not know this arrangement.' Horror and surprise of the poor man –

July 20. Very anxious about Coal Strike, trust it is settled. Also grieved that Russians have to retire.

July 28. E. into town, saw Mr Elkin & then to the Grand Guignol Plays – Very Frightening. …Trusting Russians may hold the horrid enemy –

July 30. E. writing much – …M de Greef to dine … – Very nice evening. E. played his lovely Voix dans le Desert & De Greef sang the song –

During the first two weeks of August Elgar conducted *Carillon* twice a day at the Coliseum. He also tried a run through of *Une Voix dans le Désert* with Agnes Nicholls and Carlo Liten, the Belgian actor.

August 9. To Coliseum – E. & A. at 11 – Orch. Played through 'Une Voix dans le Désert' wonderful & lovely – Liten declaimed & Mrs Landon Ronald [sic, ie Mrs Hamilton Harty] sang –

After the Coliseum run, Alice and Edward took a holiday at Liphook in Hampshire. They walked and drove about in glorious weather, receiving guests including the Streatfeilds. They returned to Severn House at the end of the month. The war was now never far away and in early September the Zeppelin raids began to increase. Alice witnessed one of the first large raids on London which killed 27 people.

September 4. E. & A. for long omnibus drive to Leyton & saw the damaged houses where the brutal Zeppelin dropped bombs & the sweet old Almhouses damaged. E. took A. to find booful boots –

July 9. Germany surrenders S W Africa.

~ ~ ~

September: Further allied advances at Loos. British victory at Kut el-Amara in Mesopotamia.
September 8. Zeppelin raid on London kills 20.
September 13. 59 killed in Zeppelin raid.
September 21. Battle of Verdun begins.
September 25. Allied offensive begins at Loos and Champagne - To 16 October.
September 26. French & British gain ground in the Loos offensive.

> September 8. Evening – all in bed except A. Suddenly Boom Boom, wonderful deep sound. A. ran to the window and then fled out to look through other windows. The sky was lit by flying searchlights – part of Zeppelin visible like a gilt box, and star-like shells bursting more or less near it, and the boom of guns sounding!

Alice was very upset and reluctant to leave London at the time, but joined Elgar in the Lake District on 10 September, where he had been for four days. They met the Stuart Wortleys and the Beresfords[53] and explored the area thoroughly. Elgar went on to Hereford and Alice returned to Severn House on 23 September.

> September 28. Good news of English French advance & of Russia D.G.

The losses in France were now becoming appalling. At the beginning of October two performances of *Polonia*, before large and appreciative audiences, did nothing for Elgar's mood, which was not helped by 'inadequate' performances of *Carillon* by Lalla Vandervelde at the Coliseum.

> October 13. E. restless and wanting to be away. Late Guns about 12.30. Atrocious Zeppelin raid again, but farther off.

Alice stayed at home whilst Elgar went with Carice to Stratford, Broadway and Stoke. They returned on 21 October.

> October 22. E. very bad cold, hard, tiresome cough. At last said A. might go with him to Bournemouth. Started by 6.15 train.

Alice Stuart Wortley should have been at the concert but was unable to get there. On 24 October Elgar wrote to her:

> The concert went off very well – Rain – Sammons played very beautifully and you were desired – missed but scarcely expected – it seemed too difficult. The train journey was horrid – crowded and very hot train down

which made me ill. Today I have been nursing and cannot go out tomorrow unless the weather is quite fine and warmer, which seems impossible. I feel dreary and not well but my cough is better – I had to take so many jujubes etc etc that my head aches from the sheer force of numbers and remedies. We returned home in the rain and the dark last night and I am desolate.

Elgar returned home to the Binyon settings – his requiem for a lost generation. The contrast with the memories, which must have been stirred by his luncheon with William Meath Baker ('WMB', the fourth of the *Enigma Variations*, a work of great optimism) would have been clear. But he stuck to his music, with an obvious sense of duty, leaving the issues of the constant changing domestic staff to Alice.

> October 24. M. Cammaerts came to talk about "Voix dans le Désert" – E. played it to him & wept a little. Cammaerts profoundly moved –
> October 27. … E. & A. went to lunch with W. & Sybil Baker at Claridges – very pleasant time – Willie most cheerful and laughed his old delightful laugh at E's sayings. Then back & Robert Hichens came – E. played to him & he wept at 'The Fallen' & thought the music overwhelming – & prayed E. to finish it – Then Mr Streatfeild came & he and E. had a great talk in the Library on Literature. Harrowing accounts from Serbia.
> October 29. E's cold still very badsley Asked Sir Maurice [Abbott Anderson] to come. He was very nice & kind and said E. would be muss better very soon.

October ended with the news that steel helmets were being introduced into the British Army. After a trip to Leeds, November began in a way that would lead Elgar to two months of feverish activity, banishing ill health and introspection. On 9 November he received a letter from the critic, Robin Legge proposing that he write the music for a Christmas play that was being adapted from Algernon Blackwood's novel, *A Prisoner in Fairyland*, which had been published in 1913. The adaptation, to be called *The Starlight Express* would be produced at the Kingsway Theatre by the actress Lena Ashwell. Elgar moved quickly.

> November 10. E. raser tired. Lena Ashwell came up & showed E. the play – she longs for his music to go with it. E. drove into town with her.

Alice and Edward were invited to see the current production at the Kingsway Theatre, 'Iris Intervenes', which they enjoyed, finding Lena Ashwell 'wonderfully clever in it.'

> November 13. Lena Ashwell came and E. settled to do or adapt his music for her play – she was moved to tears by E's music from The Fountain.
> November 15. Lena Ashwell and Algernon Blackwood came up and E. played to them, they wept. Had a delightful talk &c A. Blackwood seemed charming. Told E. about rearing a horse to run in the Derby on dried milk –

> October 27. Serbian Army in retreat on several fronts.
> December 6. First meeting of Allied War Council in Paris.

> E. drove into town with them and returned at 3.30 and settled adapting Wand of Youth.

Blackwood and the Elgars became firm friends, and within a month Elgar had completed 300 pages of score containing over an hour's music. His enthusiasm was uninhibited and Alice's diary shows how *The Starlight Express* became the most important thing in their lives. Diversions did occur however, particularly when another 'Variation', a reminder of another time, reappeared.

> November 21. Stuart Powell to tea & T. Beecham came earlier & had long talk with E. in library & came into tea & ate cakes and drank water.

Alice and Edward dined with the Stuart Wortleys at their Cheyne Walk home on 23 November where, Lord Montagu, a cousin of Charles Stuart Wortley, was also a guest.

> November 24. E. vesy hard at work – E. to Kingsway Theatre – E. peased with the Theatre rehearsal.
> November 25. Mr Blackwood here very early to go through Play with E.
> December 3. E. to rehearsal at Albert Hall – Kept waiting for Tita Brand so took up a violin and played in Orch. – much delight at this incident.
> December 4. Very wet – E. to rehearsal at Coliseum. Kept waiting – Lunched at Athaneum [sic] & then to Albert Hall – Enjoyed the Creation. Party in Box ... till the Carillon wh. Was splendid with fine Orch. Do not like Tita Brand's Reciting.

From *The Starlight Express* another friendship was begun, one that was to be tragically short-lived.

> December 6. E. very rushed – Mr Mott at 9.30. Very good & nice.

Later that day Elgar met Clytie Hine, the soprano, who with Charles Mott were the two soloists in the play. Alice noted '<u>very</u> delightful singing'.

> December 7. E. not out all day – absorbed in his 'Starlight'. Mr Blackwood to dine – very pleasant & interesting. E. told him many stories. Blackwood entranced with E's music. Glorious Orion & Pleiades at night-
> December 8. Ballet Mistress. E. came much absorbed in his work.
> December 9. E. very very busy – Music most fascinating and lovely – E. to try and find an [barrel] organ – went to all sorts of wonderful places in London – no success. Miss Ashwell to dinner, & to go over points of the play –

All was not well however, and about this time Elgar received a letter from Blackwood which ended with the following:

> I hear that Mr Wilson,[54] the artist, has designed the Sprites in the spirit of Greek Fantasy – Lamplighter a quasi-Mercury, Gardener as priapus or someone else and Sweep as Pluto. It is a false and ghastly idea. There is nothing pagan in our little childhood play. It is an alien symbolism altogether. It robs our dear Sprites of all their significance as homely childhood figures. Don't you think so too? If our play means anything at all, it means God — not the gods. But Mr Wilson is obsessed with Greece, dear thing.

Although many of Wilson's ideas were discarded, differences between Lena Ashwell and Blackwood did nothing to produce cohesion in the crucial days before the opening.

> December 11. Mr Mott early and sang some of the music delightfully. Mr Elkin came later to discuss publishing 'Starlight'. Novello gave it all up[55]
> December 13. Breathless time with 'Starlight Express'.

Breathless it was, for Alice's next entry was not until 27 December. Elgar finished the score on 15 December, just fourteen days before the first night. On the same day Sir John French resigned and was succeeded by Sir Douglas Haig as Commander in Chief. Militarily the year had seen neither breakthrough nor any sign that there was a way out of the stagnation on the Western Front.

Elgar now virtually lived at the Kingsway Theatre, and no doubt the faithful Alice would have accompanied him most days. Despite his great disappointment with the sets and costumes he worked up to the night of the first performance. The darkened streets of London were perilous, particularly for elderly ladies.

> December 27. Accident to A. – brought back from Chelsea by kind ladies – A. remembers nothing about it – but is told she spoke most politely & behaved with much dignity.

Suddenly the last days of 1915, which had begun with so much promise, turned sour with the news of the death of Elgar's nephew, William Henry, from pulmonary tuberculosis on 21 December, and the nightmare of the *Starlight* production reached an anti-climax.

> December 29. First performance of the Starlight Express – E. wd. not conduct as the mise en scene was so repulsive – & was not even present – Music wonderful –

To compound his distress over Alice's accident, which kept her in bed for ten days, and the failures of the *Starlight* production, news

December 15. Sir John French resigns.
December 28. British cabinet decides for compulsory service.
December 30. SS *Persia* torpedoed off Crete. 333 lives lost.

reached Elgar on 31 December of the loss of the P&O liner *Persia*, with Lord Montagu on board. On 2 January 1916 he wrote to Alice Stuart Wortley:

> What an awful year: I had hoped and now the crowning horror of the P&O All else seems nothing – our invalid is going on all well but more fidgety at which we are not surprised – the tedium must be very great.
>   I am very sad and nothing goes right. we have had people here – but I was not here – I am somewhere else and am not happy.

Happily Lord Montagu was rescued, and Elgar forgot the poor quality of the *Starlight Express* production by absorbing himself in his music.

1916

> January 1. May this year bring hope & Victory – & blessed Peace. Starlight Express every day. E. there very often –

The Starlight Express could not survive, as most critics perceived. That from *The Observer* summed up the problem. 'Where it would be just humbly telling the audience a story, it is preachy and pretentious. It pretends to be meant for children, but it is canvassing all the while for grown-up sentiment.' But *The Times* could not forget the music. 'Apart from the charming tunes and the glorious orchestral colour which carries away in mind, a great deal which one does not carry away – which one hardly distinguishes – plays its part very subtly and yet very simply. Whosoever is "wumbled", let him listen to Sir Edward Elgar'.

> January 29. Starlight Express – ceased with a beautiful ending for the present – E. A. & C. to the Shaftesbury Theatre where E. conducted 'Une Voix dans le Désert for the first time – <u>Most</u> beautiful & impressive & had an <u>immense</u> reception – Then on to Kingsway Theatre   large audience & much enthusiasm. *Lovely* play & music <u>enchanting</u> killed by bad setting &c.
> January 30. E. felt the ceasing of The Starlight very much –   so did Mr Blackwood indeed all the nice people concerned.

All was not lost, however, even though Elkin felt unable to publish the music. On 25 January, The Gramophone Company had suggested to Elgar that he sign a new contract, and as an enticement proposed recording four songs sung by Charles Mott, from *The Starlight Express*. But Elgar wanted eight sides, a large undertaking in 1916, and on 14 February the Company met his demands. Although he was working flat out on his Binyon settings, he found the time to modify the *Starlight Express* music for recording purposes, and the records were duly made at Hayes on 18 February.

Alice was now out and about again:

> February 11. Agnes Nicholls to sing Laugher music – Sang perfectly beautifully. Mr Elkin to lunch – to talk over Star music for Gramophone –

On February 21 the Germans began their assault on Verdun, which would continue for the next eighteen months.

> February 26. Anxious about Verdun & the glorious heroic French – ... E. wrote all day, finishing his orchestration of his wonderful Binyon music.
> February 29. Very busy finishing my work for E's wonderful Score – Took it to Novello & Starlight parts to Elkin.

During the first part of March Elgar took the London Symphony Orchestra on a successful tour of the North of England and Scotland.

> March 13. Mr Blackwood came to stay – Starlight Express records came – very exciting hearing them. <u>Very</u> good –
> March 27. Nice evening. Just A. Blackwood & souses Mr Streatfeild came. So kind like a champion wanting to write to that wretched Wrootham [sic] – so indignant for E.

Streatfeild indeed wrote a long letter[56] to Rootham, making clear that Elgar had withdrawn in his favour and that it was Elgar's friends who had persuaded Novello to publish both works. Sadly Rootham could not accept the position, with the consequence that 'a shadow was thus cast for Elgar over his greatest piece of war music'.[57]

The consequence of this emotional stress was not long in coming.

February 21. Battle of Verdun begins.
March 1. 'Unlimited' submarine campaign begins.
March 9. Germany declares war on Portugal.
March 17-24. Constant fighting near Verdun, Dutch, French & British vessels sunk.
April 20. Sir Roger Casement lands in Ireland and is arrested.
April 24. Rebellion in Ireland, Dublin Post Office seized.

April 8. E. ready to start for Stoke. Said he felt giddy and was not sure he wd go. A. in bed and afraid of the cold house, no coke, for him so did not persuade him to give it up – hoping change wd do good. A. dismayed to hear by telephone from Cap. Dillon that E. was ill in the train and Capt. D. took him out at Oxford & motored him to Acland Nursing Home – A. told Sir Maurice who gave directions. A. telephoned C. and she went off to Oxford & sent comforting account. A. so mis.

April 11. E. & C. arrived all safely about 6 – E. a good deal better. A. so thankful to see him safes – Very disappointing to have this touch of former illness but hope & trust it was only caused by influenza & wd pass.

April 14. E a little better … Very cold wind & showers, hail, snowy &c. – Nice Capn. A. Bliss – stayed nearly 2 hours, heard gramophone &c. He said 'this sort of thing bucks one up tremendously.' To leave next day. May he return all safe & well. I pray –

April 15. E. raser better – out a little while but very cold in the wind – not a genial Spring. Nice Mr Streatfeild in evening. Then Gerald Grafton[58] came & seemed to enjoy himself very much – & so glad to be in present history.

Elgar's health did not improve, and it is now that it becomes increasingly a background consideration to most of his activities for the next two years. For the remainder of April there are no diary entries, but it is clear that here had been little improvement as his responsibilities to Embleton[59] and Leeds intruded. But this was an important event, and one that Elgar would not have wanted to miss.

May 3. E. far from well. It seemed quite cruel for him to travel, so unfit for exertion – … E. got a little better & found the train did not upset him. Mr Embleton so pleased to see us – Rehearsal in evening. Very wonderful to hear the new works for the 1st time.

May 4. The Concert was magnificent. Enormous audience & orch. Very good & chorus perfect. E. conducted superbly –

So, at last Elgar conducted part of *The Spirit of England*, the music of the war that he had been destined to write. The public could hear his reaction to a changed world. His response is both angry and sad for the waste, horror and carnage that would destroy the life he knew. Although for 'England', these pieces are for any country and its dead, but in particular for the countries of the Empire which fell in behind the mother country in 1914 and 1915.

The title covering all three settings in *The Spirit of England* has an implied chauvinism that has inevitably restricted the appeal of the work. For now Elgar satisfied his audience as he did later in the month in London for a week of performances, to which Alice and he returned on 6 May after a night in Bradford.

May 7. (Sunday) E. to rehearsal at Queen's Hall at 10 – ...Most deeply impressive, especially 'To the Fallen' [sic] E. not too tired –

May 8. E. keeping fairly better. Enormous crowds at Queen's Hall, people not able to get seats – Performance wonderful. ... New works made most profound impression. A. Nicholls' 'We will remember them' never to be forgotten. The semi-chorus perfect in Gerontius, the opening Kyrie breathed out PP in perfect time.

May 10. This afternoon was even more beautiful – & performance still more perfect – Enormous audience. King & Queen present. King seemed fidgety and un-King like in demeanour – They had to catch a train at 4.45 – & I cd <u>feel</u> E. hurrying and feeling the constraint of their want of interest. The King <u>was </u>said to be much affected by 'For the Fallen' but Gerontius was evidently too long for him. They seemed to have no music &c. So different from King Edward.[60]

May 13. The last day of this memorable week & a most perfect performance. Each time seemed more beautiful than the last. It is probably unprecedented that for a whole week, one composer's work shd. be repeated every day. D.G. that that has happened for E. Enormous audiences each time & it seemed as if there wd be just as great crowds if the works were repeated for another wk.

The week was a triumph for Elgar, a reminder that he was still in touch with his public and that the combination of 'For the Fallen' and *The Dream of Gerontius* could satisfy a craving and speak to an audience, perhaps uniquely, in his time. £2,700 was presented to the Red Cross from the proceeds of the series of concerts which had been organised by Clara Butt.[61]

Elgar was exhausted by the end of the week and with Alice he was drawn to Sussex, staying in Eastbourne, which Alice disliked. She compensated for this by organising trips to Wertham, Pevensey and Hurstmonceux. Even so, the war continued to intrude.

May 20. Terrible Verdun fighting all this time, May the great French stand be continually victorious.

Elgar experienced days of headaches when back in London and on 26 May visited his physician, Sir Maurice Abbott Anderson. May gave way to the terrible months of June and July. On the night of 31 May the German High Seas Fleet clashed with the Grand Fleet off Jutland. This inconclusive battle demonstrated the superiority of German armour and gunnery, but that the greater numbers of the Royal Navy would win any engagement. Admiral Jellicoe[62] fought a cautious action – he was no Nelson – but then he was, in the words of Churchill, 'The only man who could have lost the war in an afternoon'. Alice, staying at Broadway, whilst Elgar was at Stoke,

> May 31. Battle of Jutland to the following day.
> June 2. Third Battle of Ypres begins.
> June 5. HMS *Hampshire* sunk by mine with Lord Kitchener on board.
> June 8. Compulsion replaces voluntary enlistment.
> July 1. Somme offensive begins.
> July 6. Lloyd George becomes Secretary of State for War.

reacted perceptively to the news of the battle.

> June 3. ... Terrible shock hearing of naval battle & loss of English ships – but it
> seemed as if nos. of Germans had been sunk and they had fled – but still –
> June 4.   ... As news came, it seemed we had a great Naval Victory –   so
> thankful and might have been spared the first horrid shock.
> June 5. ... Hampshire with K. of K. & his staff sunk off Orkneys about 8 PM
> June 6. In evening the dreadful shock of hearing Kitchener[63] and his staff were
> lost in the Hampshire. Expect some horrid treason and German murder.
> Stormy sea so fear few rescued. D.G. that the great man had finished his
> work – & that his great army was made.

The battle for Verdun continued, the Canadians retook lost positions at Ypres and the Government introduced daylight saving. As July began, the French and British launched their great offensive along twnty-five miles of the River Somme. On the first day British casualties amounted to 60,000.

Elgar returned to London at the end of June and then moved first to Ridgehurst before spending a few days at The Hut (Frank Schuster's home at Bray, Berkshire) in early July. The Somme offensive was barely noted by Alice, she being concerned with Elgar's health. Eventually he got away again to Stoke whilst Alice took to her bed with a chill. However she was well enough to entertain again, receiving Arthur Bliss[64] and Richard Streatfeild for tea on 21 and 27 June. From Stoke Elgar sought accommodation for Alice and himself.

> August 1. A. to Bridgnorth & met E. at Arley – both had real excited joy in
> meeting. He had a garland of clematis and threw it over A's head.
> Looked better & very keen about the holday. Intensely hot.

From Arley they travelled to the Lake District for a few days where they were joined by Lalla Vandervelde and the Speyers. They were overjoyed to be back in a region they both loved, and Alice recorded a touching scene whilst caught in a rain squall on Ullswater.

> August 16. E. & A. sat at end of bench on boat very close together & vesy
> hapsy under one umbrella, & a man who had been standing by talking to

another suddenly said, putting his face close to theirs, 'You are luvers still like me & my wife.' A. rather speechless with surprise, E. said in a sweet way 'I hope so.'

August 20. E. feeling throat. A, very anxious for him to be home to see Dr. feeling sure his throat needed treatment.

August 21. E. still not very well – E. & A. started at 10 & drove to Windermere … E. hated coming to town but was not well to go out without seeing Drs &c.

August 25. Sir Maurice found throat wanted doctoring – ordered painting etc.

August 29. To Sir Maurice. Found throat better but needed electric cautery. E. bore it so splendidly.

Elgar went to stay at Ridgehurst until 4 September, and in London Alice was able to observe, with enthusiasm, the destruction of a Zeppelin in the night sky as autumn approached.

September 2. …A. …watched & suddenly a great flare lit up everything shining on the mist curiously it came a 2nd time & there was joyous shouting Hip hip hurrahs & great clapping so A. hoped she had seen the Zeppelin's death flare. This was confirmed in morning paper – D.G. nothing here hurt.

On 8 September both Alice and Edward went to stay with the Berkeleys at Spetchley; 'Warmest welcome to the stately dignified delightful house.' This was a wonderful break for them both, Alice enjoying a Roman Catholic environment and Elgar pursuing country activities; chasing weasels and catching seventy fish. On 14 September Alice returned to London and Elgar went on to Stoke Prior, before returning to London on 18 September. There, the war was never far away.

September 23. … E. & A. to London Bridge on omnibus, … Very touching seeing the wounded being driven from Charing Cross Station great crowds there – Raid at night & 2 Zepps brought down – great rejoicing.

September 27. E. in bed all day – chill, headache, &c. … Very good news, Combles & Thiepval ours – great stores & prisoners –

October 1. … Zepp raid late at night. A. heard shouting, but guns were too far away. Joy at another brute being brought down at Potters Bar. Crew taken prisoners by a single Special –

October 6. … E. & A. early to … see Zepp remains – Great crowd –

October 8. … Mr & Mrs Elkin to tea & Mr. Blackwood who met E. coming up from Finchley Road with a toad in his pocket. E. had bought it of[f] some boys for 2d. He did not think it was happy with them – He put it in the garden and calls it Algernon as he met A.B. at the time – He puts his head out of the window & says 'Do you think he will come out if I make a noise like a worm?' Algernon invisible.

September 2 – 3. 13 airships raid Eastern Counties of England.

September 15. Tanks used for the first time north of Pozières.

September 23. Numerous airships raid Eastern England.

September 26. British capture Thiepval & Combles & storm Gueudecourt.

October 3 – 7. Rumanian advance turned into retreat.

November 7. President Wilson re-elected in USA.

November 21. Austrian Emperor, Franz-Joseph dies aged 86, succeeded by Archduke Carl.

November 27. Two Zeppelins brought down after raid on N.E. Coast of England.

November 29. Admiral Jellicoe becomes First Sea Lord and Admiral Beatty C in C of Grand Fleet.

The local press was unable to resist the story under the headline 'Toad und Verklärung'.

October 9. An account of the Toad incident & reproduction of Phillip B. Jones' pixture [sic] of E. in *Daily Mirror* today. Dr. MacNaught came to see E. Wants him to write a Bugle call symphony very appealing to all the Army – J Littleton said about the Toad incident Toad & Verklarung Sym – ! –

October 25. All this time harrowed & depressed over Rumania – trust for better news.

October 26. E. to Book Sale & A. S. W. came to tea & played the lovely phrase of Piano Concerto.

October 27. E. lunched at Athaneum with S. Colvin then to see Safonoff who wants him to go to Russia to conduct in Dec.

October 29. A. to Queen's hall to hear the Introduction & Allegro – Thought H Wood conducted it better than anything else of E's A. had heard. A. back with C. & A. S. Wortley. Percy Anderson had arrived & was playing billiards. Then Muriel & Ludo came & Safonoff & A. Alexander & Barclay Squire. Very pleasant time – The C. Butt & her mother – C. Butt sang some of the 1st No. of the Spirit of England – It sounded gorgeous.

On 31 October Alice met with Safonoff to explain that it was too dangerous for her Edward to go to Russia and Elgar saw Laurence Binyon again as his ideas for completing *The Spirit of England* developed in his mind. By the second week of November he was feeling ill again, but on 20 November he was well enough to rehearse Agnes Nicholls in 'For the Fallen' at the Queen's Hall and to hear Albert Sammons perform the Violin Concerto the same evening, in a concert conducted by Safonoff. Elgar then conducted *The Dream of Gerontius* in Manchester returning in time to rehearse 'For the Fallen' in the Albert Hall on 24 November. Three days later he conducted his E flat Symphony at the Queen's Hall.

November 27. A detestable audience not worthy of hearing the great music. Raid over east & N East coast Zepps – but scarcely any damage.

Elgar now turned his attention to cutting his violin concerto for recording on four sides of gramophone records. As December began a political crisis developed over the conduct of the war.

> December 3. … Very trying news. Enemy's advance in Roumania & troubles in Greece wh. Seem so avoidable – Cabinet crisis.
> December 4. We are longing for Asquith to go
> December 10. Laurence Binyon … talking about a new poem –
> December 12. A. in bed with a bad cold – All this time immensely excited over new Government. D.G. Asquith gone and Lloyd George Prime Minister.
> December 15. Marie Hall & discreet companion in afternoon to rehearse concerto for Gramophone.
> December 16. Frightful fog & cold. Gramophone sent car E. & A. started soon after 9am. Very horrid, E. did not like it. A cart ran into us & road was up continually. Nice Gramophone men so kind and cheerful. Marie Hall very late, delayed by train. Lovely to hear concerto – beautiful. Then E. changed & started home very late, nearly smashed by Red Cross car coming wrong side, E. very tired & headache.

Winter descended on London with bitter cold, dense fog and snow. Elgar took to his bed but was up again for a quiet Christmas. Charles Stuart Wortley was ennobled in the New Year's honours list, which was published earlier then. On 20 December Elgar wrote to the new peer's wife.

> I am out of bed for the first time since Saturday & I use the first minute to send you love and congratulation on the event, – I gave you a coronet long ago – the best I had, but you may have forgotten it – now you will have real one, bless you!' The letter ended: 'Everything pleasant and promising in my life is dead – I have the happiness of my friends to console me as I had fifty years ago. I feel that life has gone back so far when I was alone & there was no one to stand between me and disaster – health or finance – now that has come back & I more alone & the prey of circumstances than ever before.[65]

On Boxing Day Alice and Edward lunched with the Stuart Wortleys at Cheyne Walk before going to the theatre, and on 28 December, he was well enough to receive Jaeger's widow and children on Boxing Day. They now called themselves Hunter.

> December 26. E. & A. to lunch with Alice S. W. Went by train. Then she motored us to S. James's Theatre for 'Charley's Aunt' – very poor & silly – coming out *dense* fog & darkness – Eventually we drove to S. Kenn. Station & Alice drove home. We had to wait quite fifteen minutes for train in the fog & cold – of course it gave E. bad cold.

December 1. Lloyd George declared himself unable to remain in the Government.

December 5. Asquith resigned as Prime Minister

December 6. Bucharest falls. Continued unrest in Athens.

December 7. Lloyd George becomes Prime Minister

December 15. General Nivelle launches great attack on Verdun, having succeeded Joffre as C in C.

1917

The prospects for 1917 seemed little better as Elgar's poor health occupied his and Alice's minds, no matter what diversion she organised for him. News of Richter's[66] death on 5 December came through and Elgar wrote to Richter's son in law, Sydney Loeb, referring 'to my dear old friend'.[67] This news was a reminder of how much he owed to the many Germans or those of German stock who had befriended him, such as the Speyers, Marie Joshua, Lalla Vandervelde, Frank Schuster and August Jaeger.[68] Sir Thomas Beecham, in answer to the question 'Where have all Elgar's friends gone?' answered unkindly 'they are all interned'.

Although militarily there was stalemate, the success of the U-Boat campaign against merchant shipping was reaching crisis point. In April 545,200 tons of shipping would be lost from an annual total of 3,373,000. Britain would starve unless this rate of loss could be halted.

> January 3. A. to lunch with Mrs Joshua – Most kind and pleasant, mourning really mourning for Richter, Drove A. back & insisted on sending fruit and chocolate to E –
>
> January 5. E. to see Sir Maurice. A. wis him. Throat again burnt with electric cautery – poor ducksie –

Elgar's treatment continued for a number of days, but he was able to attend the memorial service for Sir George Warrender.[69]

> January 12. E. & A. to the Church of the Annunciation – Very touching. Bluejackets standing by the coffin. First the Angel's farewell, most beautifully played –
>
> January 23. ... Mr Embleton came to tea & had talk over May projected week of performances & urged E. to have 3rd part of Apostles ready for him for March year & 4th part of Spirit of England for this March – wish he might

The intense cold did not inhibit movement around London and general socialising, but Elgar was lost.

> January 26. ... E met A. at M. de Navarro's Savoy Hotel – Nice time She was <u>most</u> affectionate & dear – E. played some Bach music to her & his lovely fragment of piano concerto over & over again.
> January 29. Very cold hard frost less wind – Gulls flying round – Read of Cruiser Laurentic being sunk – sad –
> February 1. ... Diabolical Germans threatening to sink Hospital Ships –
> February 2. Diplomatic relations between America & Germany broken off <u>at last</u>.
> February 3. E. busy with arrangements for Gramophone – out to lunch – Cold raw day –
> February 7. E. in his bed & his room all day but raser better – just came down in fur coat to see I Lowther ... [who] came to lay the Chelsea Ballet idea before E.

Instantly Elgar's imagination was kindled as the ideas for *The Sanguine Fan* took root:

> February 8. E. better and in the music room in afternoon – Mr Elkin to talk over the Chelsea Ballet idea –

There was news of the death of another 'variation', a link with a happier past severed.

> February 9. Shocked to read in paper Dr. Sinclair died suddenly – so glad E. has his new music to occupy his thoughts. Ina Lowther here to talk over Ballet.
> February 12. Thinking much of our friend George Sinclair. The funeral this day – E. keeps G's last letter in front of him on writing table & thinks much about him.
> February 16. E. writing <u>lovely</u> Fan music –
> February 17. E. busy with Fan Music. Alice S. of W. came & had a walk with E. Immensely excited over E's new music.

On 19 February Elgar began to orchestrate *The Sanguine Fan* Ballet.

> February 23. Ivor Atkins came – delighted with Fan music – ... Ina Lowther & Gerald du Maurier came re the Fan scene – L. George's great speech – Economy &c

Elgar was still occupied with *The Sanguine Fan* orchestration when he heard of the death of his uncle Henry on 24 February. His next preoccupation was with the setting of four poems by Rudyard Kipling, which had been published under the title *The Fringes of the Fleet*. Potentially the combination of Elgar and Kipling was a heady one, but matters did not run as they might have done a few years earlier. The poet's son had been reported 'missing' in 1915, the truth about his death had still to be discovered and Kipling was not happy with the projected settings by Elgar. His world had changed even more than Elgar's:

> My Son was killed laughing at some jest. I would I knew
> What it was, and it might serve me in a time when jests are few.

and

> If any question why we died
> Tell them, because our fathers lied.

> February 24. E. & A. to Kilburn by train & walked some way. A. not liking it <u>at all</u> Dutch Ships sunk by horrid submarines –
> March 5. Mr Broadhurst came re R. Kipling Songs – Much telephoning. Mr Elkin had score of Fan. Started for Leeds from King's Cross – ...Mr Embleton waiting for us in Hotel. Dined with him & ... Dr. Coward –
> March 7. ... in car to Rehearsal – Orch. Arrived late – Some of them new to the works. E. raser worried & annoyed with them. A. Nicholls sang 'To the Women' [sic] without having tried it most beautifully.

Alice and Edward returned to London on 8 March and, although he caught another cold he worked on *The Sanguine Fan*. By 12 March Sir Maurice Abbott Anderson thought him well enough to travel to Worcester, and that day Elgar attended the first rehearsal of the ballet. Even though he felt unwell on the morning of 14 March they travelled anyway, dining with Ivor Atkins[70] that evening.

In the Cathedral the following day, Elgar conducted 'For the Fallen'. As they travelled home, momentous news greeted them for, on opening a newspaper at the station, they read of revolution in Russia and that the Czar had been deposed. Alice then added, somewhat surprisingly: 'May it have all success.'

January 25. Southwold shelled by enemy vessel & HMS *Laurentic* sunk by mine off Ireland.

January 31. Germany declared to all neutral countries 'unrestricted naval warfare' within the war zone.

February 3. President Wilson, in a speech to Congress, invites all neutrals to join USA in breaking diplomatic relations with Germany.

February 22. Seven neutral (Dutch) ships sailing from Falmouth were attacked by a German U Boat which sank four vessels.

February 24. German withdrawal on the Ancre begins in face of successful British attack.

March 12. Russian Tsar suspends Duma & Council of the Empire. Provisional Government formed.

March 15. Tsar Nicholas abdicates.

Back in London *The Sanguine Fan* now dominated their lives. Alice attended a rehearsal:

> March 17. First rehearsal of Conder Ballet – Supposed to begin at 3? Kept E. waiting nearly an hour, doing stupid vulgar things – Then a <u>very</u> poor unworthy orchestra – Made A. start from her seat at some of the noises theymade – Everyth. very confused – G. Du Maurier & Thesiger delightful of course –
> March 18. dress rehearsal. Watteau dresses lovely. Shepherd's <u>very</u> trying! Ballet promised to be lovely.
> March 19. To rehearsal at Wyndham's Theatre – Orch. More bearable – Ballet lovely, other scenes vulgar, in bad taste & wretched –

The following day the ballet, based upon Ina Lowther's scenario from a picture painted in sanguine on a lady's fan by Charles Conder, was given its only intended performance as part of the revue 'Chelsea on Tiptoe'.

> March 20. Stupid music first & some stupid things. Ballet perfectly beautiful, music exquisite & enchanting & actors delightful. Ina Lowther <u>very</u> good just filling the part with gaiety & spontaneity. Much applause. Then E. & A. had tea & dined with Lalla Claude & Robert Ross to dinner.
> March 22. … violent snow showers, just managed to go to Mesopotamia Office to offer to help…
> March 23. … E. orchestrating – & playing with the Shepherd's Dance to be added to Conder Ballet.
> March 24. … Ina Lowther came & discussed Conder ballet affairs, the mistakes, & muddles &c – & talked of a new one –
> March 25. E. busy orchestrating R. Kipling Songs – A. 'set' an Orch. In afternoon for E. but might only put words without notes – rather damping.
> March 27. E. (& A.) to Queen's Hall in evening & Carice. Tessie Thomas played <u>wonderfully</u> – E. very pleased. Concerto <u>most</u> beautiful. Rapturous meeting of T Thomas & her father in Artist room – What a wonderful happy evening for her. Mr Reed conducted Wand of Youth splendidly.

As spring became a reality, British air superiority on the Western Front was unable to contribute to the hoped for breakthrough. The disastrous offensive by the French under General Nivelle resulted in a large scale mutiny in the French army. At one stage there were

> April 6. USA declares war on Germany.
> Apil 9. Battle of Arras begins, Canadians take Vimy Ridge.
> April 28. US Congress decides for conscription.

barely any combat troops in the front line. General Ludendorff, now responsible for German strategy in the west, only heard of his opportunity after General Pétain had replaced Nivelle and restored order.

On 2 April President Wilson asked Congress to declare 'a state of war' with Germany, and four days later the declaration was made. Conscription was introduced immediately, and America went to war with that enthusiasm with which it embraces anything new. At home the U-boat campaign had imposed further restrictions on food. Elgar could now see his enemy clearly.

March 30. E. turning towards Spirit of England –

Elgar had found the missing key to his completion of *The Spirit of England* in the demon's chorus from *The Dream of Gerontius* and he was able to complete 'The Fourth of August', as the words had their music at last:

> She fights the fraud that feed desire on
> Lies, in a lust to enslave or kill,
> The barren creed of blood and iron,
> Vampire of Europe's wasted will . . .

The final Cammaerts setting, *Le Drapeau Belge,* was rehearsed at the Queen's Hall on 13 April in advance of its first public performance.

April 14. E. lunched with Maud Warrender & came with her to Queen's Hall. A. & C. there & Frances Colvin. Orch. played the Voix beautifully, it is an exquisite poignant picture – Liten not dramatic enough, O[lga] Lynn very good. Then the Drapeau Belge was splendid & Liten did it very well. Much enthusiasm & E. was stopped just leaving platform & the president Dr. Philippe presented him with a wreath & read him a really beautiful address.

April 19. Much good news of both fronts. D.G.

April 20. E. not very well, postponed going to Stoke. After lunch went on omnibus to Westminster, most reviving to see flags flying, numbers of American, & cheerful looking crowds out in the bright sunshine. Saw the strange sight of American flag waving from Victoria Tower –

April 23. E. not vesy well but thought he wd like to start for Stoke. A. with him to Paddington 1.40 train he just went into Station but felt he cd not go on so we returned – Poor Ducksie so disappointed. ... Fresh advance in France – ...Lalla to tea – said admiration for England in France was unbounded.

April 25. Proofs of the beautiful Spirit of England came so E. put off starting till 1.40 train –

Importantly, Kipling had given his reluctant approval to the setting of his poems from his 1915 publication, *The Fringes of the Fleet*, and Elgar now turned to their orchestration. Also, Alice had found in their beloved Sussex the home she had been seeking for some time:

> May 2. A. & C. to Fittleworth to see a cottage – a 2 seater met them but after arriving at Inn preferred to walk – <u>Lovely</u> place, sat in lovely wood & heard a nightingale, turtoo [sic] doves, & many other dicksies & saw lizards and heard Tuckoo [sic] first time. Lovely <u>hot hot</u> day. A. much perplexed as cottage is so very cottagy but large studio & <u>lovely</u> view & woods. dear place – finally took it for June – Lovely walk thro' woods & by primroses to Station …
>
> May 4. So dreful peased to have E. home & looking muss better & burnt by out of door air & sun – He had played through his Spirit of England proofs with Ivor Atkins – May 9. E. to Novello – Found his 4 Augt. Spirit of England had stirred the House – It was thought so wonderful. E. to see Mr Stoll who liked the idea of the Kipling Songs at Coliseum – Then to Enoch to consult them about it.
>
> May 11. E. orchestrating & vesy busy – Finished orchestrating Spirit of England.
>
> May 14. E. to Fan Ballet rehearsal. Back to lunch – A. to Novello with precious parcel score of 4th Augt. Gave it into Dr. McNaught's hands – lunched out & bought hat &c – Long walks, no omnibuses – Shameful to strike at this time – & shame on engineer strikes in North –

Strikes around the country had affected, amongst other services, the omnibuses of London.

> May 18. E. with car to Palace Theatre, Orch. rehearsal. A. wis him. Very nice Orch – & very keen to do their best. E. quite happy with them – Music enchanting. Mr Elkin found taxi for E. with some difficulty. C. to rehearsal also – Still cold –

Preparations for the stay in Sussex were now being made.

> May 19. E. very busy arranging schemes, & tidying his workshop &c &c – A. busy preparing. …

But *The Sanguine Fan* revival was to happen first.

> May 21. E. to rehearsal at Palace Theatre. A. wis him – Lovely music & so beautifully played.
>
> May 22. E. & A. to Palace Theatre for Conder Ballet – Most things dull a <u>very</u>

May 3. Mutinies in French Army.
May 15. General Pétain appointed to command N & NE French Armies.
June 7. Battle of Messines begins.

heavy dull audience – Why shd. Philanthropy make ladies so oppressively stupid? The Ballet a perfectly lovely gem – The music entrancing & <u>beautifully</u> played – Actors charming – lighting not quite right – The Italian Masque senselessly dull – lovely costumes. ... E. rather depressed, such a dull house to hear that perfect work – Mott came & sang the Fleet Songs, perfectly & <u>splendidly</u>. They sounded gorgeous.

The Fringes of the Fleet cycle was signed up for a run of performances at the Coliseum as part of a wartime variety. Charles Mott again agreed to sing for Elgar and to take the lead in the production. The songs were to be sung outside a pub in an imaginary fishing village 'in', as Elgar wrote, 'a broad salt-water style'.

At Brinkwells the weather was glorious and Elgar took to it immediately. With Alice they spent the time gardening, sightseeing and walking. Carice joined them on 26 May. Their tranquillity was only spoilt by the possibility of Charles Mott's imminent call up preventing him from performing at the Coliseum.

> May 23. A. very busy preparing & settling all in house & collecting things to take [to Brinkwells] – E. to Enochs & rehearsed Songs for Fleet with Mott – A. very busy paying & settling.
>
> May 24. E. & A. left Severn House for 10.20 train – ... Pulborough ... A cart came for luggage & E. & A. walked. ... E badsley headache in aftn. but thought it 'too lovely for words' & satisfied with house much to A's relief. A. very busy making it look a little nice –
>
> May 25. E. & A. enjoying their souses very muss – Wandered around woods &c & to Stopham after tea to post letters – Heard Mott was called up & cd. not sing the Fleet Songs after all – a <u>real</u> disappointment.
>
> May 31. E. heard from Maud [Warrender], who had everything ready for his Sailor Songs – & from Enoch saying Mott cd sing for 3 days & suggesting some one for the rest.
>
> June 4. E. & A. left Brinkwells, hoping to return – [Carice would stay until June 18] ...Found all well & house very delightful warm & sunny – E. pleased with prospects of Songs –
>
> June 5. Rehearsing at Enoch's Maud Warrender there & carried E. off to the Admiralty & settled about going to Harwich.
>
> June 6. Rehearsing at Enoch's – Crowd in street, begins to hum and whistle the tunes.
>
> June 7. E. away all day, going to Harwich for <u>Kit</u> from Ships – .

Rehearsals for *The Fringes of the Fleet* continued daily until the first performances on Monday 11 June. The previous day Alice had entertained members of the cast to lunch. The next two weeks would be very demanding with matinees and evening performances daily. Alice basked in the first night atmosphere:

> June 11. Rehearsal at Coliseum had car & took down E's luggage. A. with E. to
> 1ˢᵗ performance. <u>Very</u> good & very enthusiastic receptn. Back to Severn
> House & E. rested & then again in Car, & A. to evening performance. <u>Very</u>
> good & most exciting & much enthusiasm. Maud & many Admirals there –
> June 12. E. quite peased & enjoying the Songs – Everyone happy & all made
> pleasant. A. with E. again in evening.
> June 13. Raid in morning. Heard guns but cd see nothing. Sad sad list of
> casualties – E. & A. into town, …

The performances continued, sometimes without Mott, but with
another number, *Inside the Bar*, to words by Sir Gilbert Parker set by
Elgar as a part song, added to the performance on 27 June. A few days
earlier, on 15 June, Elgar had invited the Coliseum orchestra (composed
largely of women) to lunch at Gatti's restaurant.

> June 27. … E. getting on well with Coliseum & peased with new part Song,
> his men singing it –
> July 3. E. had a tremendous ovation at Coliseum at night. Applause wd not
> stop, he & the others had left after many appearances but they had to
> return and stand on Boucher's the next turn's stage – E. very peased.

The *Fringes* were a phenomenal success, and the performances were
extended into the summer, some days of which were 'intensely hot'.
Elgar clearly enjoyed the popularity of the songs despite the unlikely
figure he cut as a music hall artist. On 4 July the Elgars travelled to
Hayes where four gramophone records were made under Elgar's
direction. Later, on 27 July the four singers travelled to Hayes alone
to record the additional part-song setting of *Inside the Bar*. The test
records were produced very quickly:†

> July 14. Tried the new Fringes' records – Quite <u>wonderful</u> Sweepers so
> splendid –
> July 22. Spanish Place – In aftn. The 4 Singers came & Mr Geisberg[sic], the
> new records here – … Also L Binyon came & Mr & Mrs Reed & Mrs
> Henry. … The Records were delightful & the 4 Singers sang the Pt. Song
> beautifully – There was a warning of a Raid about 9 p.m.

George Parker replaced Charles Mott for a provincial tour, but before
it commenced Alice recorded a touching ceremony on the stage of the
Coliseum, following a tea party given by Alice Stuart Wortley.

June 13. Daylight raid on London kills 162.
June 25. First 'fighting' American troops arrive in France.
July 31. Third Battle of Ypres (Passchendaele) begins.
August 15. British attack at Lens.

---

† - For the four songs, see the accompanying CD, tracks 2-5

July 27. E. & A. walked around after tea party & found a little silver ship for E.
to give Mott – at 5.40, tea party to E. on Stage – Very nicely arranged, Ladies
Orch. gave it & a silver inkstand to E. – (A had been told of it as a secret) Mr
Croxton made a witty & delightful speech & E. a charming one & a head
lady spoke charmingly, All was so simple & sweet – pure hero-worship the
lady sd. 'if Lady Elgar does not mind my saying so we all love him' –

July 28. ... Last evening for the present for Mott – his voice better than ever. ...

July 31. Great new movement at the Front began – Pray all go well –

The third battle of Ypres continued through the following months
until November, the climax of which was the taking of Passchendaele
Ridge by the Canadians on the 6 November. If the soldiers were not
shot they risked drowning in the sea of mud and water which
Passchendaele became. Five miles of territory were gained at the
expense of 250,000 lives. The gains would be lost in the spring of 1918.

During the early part of August Elgar spent some time in
Manchester and Leicester 'on tour' with *The Fringes of the Fleet*,
whilst Alice had gone back to her roots, staying in Herefordshire and
Worcestershire, in particular at Hasfield Court, the home of the
Bakers ('WMB' of the *Enigma Variations*). It was now clear that
Kipling wanted to stop further performances of *The Fringes*, which
Alice felt was 'mean spirited'.

The Elgars had Algernon Blackwood to lunch on 27 August, but
despite stormy weather travelled to Brinkwells two days later, where
they quickly met up with the Colvins who were staying nearby. They
were able to keep up with the war news through the Post Office in
Fittleworth and by visiting the Swan Inn at Fittleworth where most of
their guests stayed.

August 29. E. & A. started 10.20 train. Walked up & found nice fire & all ready
– Garden too dreadfully wild – 5 kittens frolicking about <u>not</u> wanted by A.
– E. enjoying it at once –

September 7. Lalla (Vandervelde)[71] telegraphed she would come. E. in pony
carriage to meet her – after tea E&A. & Lalla walked to Bognor Common and
then by the Pine walk round by Bedham & the sinister trees – Most lovely.

The next day they were home for a week of *Fringes* performances at
the Chiswick Empire theatre, and to worries over Kipling's attitude to
continuous performances. The demands of touring began to impose
on Elgar as the year drew to a close and the war news grew worse. At
the end of September they travelled to Chatham.

September 13. E. not at all well – E. & Lan[don Ronald and Alice] ...all on to
Enochs – Enoch & E. & Lan discussed Kipling situation. Lan much
perturbed & sorry –

> September 14. E. still not vesy well – C. with him to Gunnersbury in evening
> – Last time but one at Chiswick – All most successful there & very nice
> understanding & very enthusiastic audience – Expecting every day
> answer from R Kipling. none coming.
> September 15. Still no answer from R. Kipling.
> September 24. Wretched station, E. walked, A. drove with luggage. E.
> rehearsed, then lunch. … Then E. to theatre almost immediately lights
> went out, & a raid – A. sat in Hall & watched for E. feared he wd be quite
> exhausted & at last was able to send him some sandwiches – he returned
> & we dined – <u>no</u> performance cd take place, Raid over, E. returned.
> Fearful noise more or less all night –

There was a raid the next night, but the next day all was quiet for two
performances.

> September 28. … got through one performance of 'The Fringes' & then
> another Raid & no second cd. be done – Very tremendous guns &c – D.G.
> not hurt –

They returned to London and another air raid on 30 September. Elgar
escaped to Stoke for a few days, returning on 7 October, where he
would have found the following letter awaiting him from a serving
officer in Flanders.

> Although unknown to you, I feel I must write to you tonight. We possess
> a fairly good gramophone in our mess, and I have bought your record
> "Starlight Express": 'Hearts must be soft-shiny dressed', being played for
> the twelfth time over. The Gramophone was anathema to me before this
> war, because it was abused so much. But all is changed now, and it is the
> only means of bringing back to us the days that are gone, and helping on
> through the Ivory Gate that leads to Fairyland, or Heaven whatever one
> likes to call it . . . Music is all that we have to help us carry on.[72]

Further performance of *The Fringe of the Fleets* followed at the
Coliseum until 13 October before Elgar spent a few days at The Hut,
where Alice joined him on 20 October. There was 'anxious' news
from the Italian front and air raids on London continued almost

---

September 20. Battle of Menin Road Bridge.
September 24. Aeroplane raid on London & SE Coast.
September 25. Raid on SE London.
September 26. Battle of Polygon Wood.
September 28. Raid on SE Coast (and for following 2 nights).
November 6. Passchendaele captured by Canadians.
November 8. Coup d'Etat in Petrograd.
November 20. British advance at Cambrai.

nightly. Alice and Edward travelled north on 29 October to hear *The Spirit of England* with 'The Fourth of August' for the first time, as part of a concert in Leeds on 31 October. Agnes Nicholls and Gervase Elwes were the soloists. As usual the Elgars were welcomed and entertained by Henry Embleton and his committee.

> October 31. ... G. Elwes could not sing – Telegraphed for tenors – Useless – Orch. quite good – Then in Evening to Concert Elwes did what he cd. hardly audible sometimes – ... A. Nicholls splendid 4th Augt. Gorgeous & the other 2 numbers most beautiful & heart moving. E. conducted splendidly.

The first complete performance of *The Spirit of England* had already taken place on 4 October in Birmingham with soprano Rosina Buckman as soloist under the direction of Appleby Matthews.[73] The Elgars travelled to Huddersfield for a further performance on 2 November before returning to London the following evening against the background of increasingly worrying war news, which caused them both concern. However, they entertained Algernon Blackwood, the wife of the landscape painter Rex Vicat Cole and their son before Elgar travelled to Stoke again.[74]

> November 6. ... E. looked tired & dreadfully worried over the war news.

On 8 November the Bolsheviks, under Lenin deposed Kerensky in Petrograd and sued for 'an immediate democratic peace' with the Germans, who would now be able to concentrate the bulk of their resources on the Western Front.

> November 16. Better news from Italy from Russia wildly confused & conflicting statements.

Alice, receiving daily messages from Elgar, watched a military parade across Waterloo Bridge from the balcony of Somerset House and heard Louis Godowsky play his piano arrangement of Elgar's Violin Concerto on 14 November.

Elgar's health now began to deteriorate markedly, and he needed immediate medical attention when he returned to London on 18 November. He was not well when he attended a concert at the Albert Hall later in the month. Agnes Nicholls was again the soloist for 'The Fourth of August' and 'For the Fallen' and Gervase Elwes for 'To Women'.[75]

> November 23. E. raser better. To rehearsal at Albert Hall – Had to wait while Stanford did his common Songs & a dreadful new one.[76] Then the great music began – E. looked like the High Priest of Art – 'The Spirit of

England' is great, wonderful music –

November 24. E. raser better To Albert Hall at 3. Wonderful music & most
impressive performance. Large audience who seemed held – A. Nicholls
gave a beautiful rendering of 'For the Fallen' All 3 parts are great, great
music. ... In the box were Lady Horridge, the Colvins, Lady Martin, & Mrs
Thesiger & Carice & Miss Evans, A. S. of W. & Binyons next box –

Three days later Elgar wrote to Alice Stuart Wortley: 'I am not well
alas. It was lovely seeing you on Sunday. Are you coming to the
"Fringes"? The funeral this week is so sad'. Kipling had withdrawn
his consent for *The Fringes of the Fleet* and their 'funeral' was to be
held at the Coliseum for one last week. Elgar went there feeling more
and more wretched as the week progressed. Algernon Blackwood
came to stay once again.

November 26. E. to Coliseum for rehearsal. ... A Blackwood arrived dined
together & had pleasant talk.
November 27. Algernon much perturbed about his friends' troubles. E. & A.
to Coliseum, A. returned & went down to fetch E. at night just as Algernon
came in – E. not at all well.
November 28. ... E. vesy unwell.
November 30. E. still not at all well. To Coliseum in aft. in car – ... Sir Gilbert
Parker came & had tea after the performance – Delighted with it & to hear
the Pt. Song.
December 1 (Saturday). E. & A. to Coliseum in car. E. still very unwell – short
walk – last of these long evenings till nearly 10.30 but E. got through D.G.

And so *The Fringes of the Fleet* disappeared from view, their memory
preserved on disc; a distant view of an entertainment of, and for, its
time. For the month of December, Alice records Elgar's ill-health
virtually every day, with their doctor, Sir Maurice Abbott Anderson,
visiting frequently. Her diary noted diversions such as the explosion
of an ammunition ship in Halifax, Nova Scotia and a Gotha bomber
raid on Hampstead, but she did not note the successful advance at
Cambrai during late November and early December. From the 12 to
21 December there are no diary entries, and when Alice took up her
pen again it was no different.

December 28. E. muss the same. All the disagreeable feels. Expecting
specialist next day – stayed upstairs all day. Lalla came in aftn. E. enjoyed
a talk – & evidently wants more society & some pleasant excitement.

December 9. Surrender of Jerusalem, General Allenby enters city 2 days later.
December 22. 3 British destroyers sunk off Dutch coast.
December 26. Admiral Wemyss appointed First Sea Lord.

Where is it to come from in these times?

December 29. Sir Maurice brought Dr Hale White to see E. ... They decided, such a merciful relief, that there was <u>no</u> organic trouble. Urged smoking, golf, change &c &c – Gave a new Meddi – D.G. that there was no serious malady – ... Read of loss of 3 Destroyers.

That day Elgar added a postscript to a letter his Alice wrote to Alice Stuart Wortley:

'The doctors say nothing the matter: but I am not well'.

Militarily, 1917 had achieved little, whilst at sea a reluctant Admiralty introduced the convoy system at the insistence of Lloyd George, and increasingly more and more eyes were being turned on the United States and the effect its resources would have on the outcome of the war.

December 31. Maud Warrender came for nice long visit. E. much the same. Deep thankfulness for much of this year. Still spared to one another. Success of Fringes – Can only pray E. be better soon – & that a Victorious Peace may come.

1918

1918, as General Ludendorff[77] realised, would be crucial for achieving a German victory in the west, by diverting troops from the east, now that Russia was out of the war. It was essential to achieve a quick victory, before the fresh American troops were deployed effectively. Ludendorff's strategy was to drive a wedge between the British and French armies. In 1914 the strategy had been partly that of destroying France before Russia could mobilise effectively, now it was vital to defeat the 'French and British before the Americans arrived in force.' [78]

For Alice and Edward January was no better, with Alice going alone to a performance of the A flat Symphony on 6 January conducted by Landon Ronald. At the end of the month Elgar was fitted with a belt for a dropped stomach diagnosed earlier in the month. In February Alice attempted the stimulus of theatre trips and visits by musicians and other friends, with little effect.

February 15. E. & C. to Sir Maurice, later E. with Lalla to lunch with the Bernard Shaws, Granville Barker there – Much interesting conversation. ... A to Eresby House, to hear Ld. Edmund Talbot & others speak on responsibility of women with their voting power. Very interesting speeches & very large audience –

February 16. … Raid in Evening. Only 1 Gotha got through but it dropped bomb on house by Chelsea Hospital & buried the poor people in it – horrible –

February 17. Lalla & Mr Boult[79] to tea. Quite a nice quiet man. E. went through 'In the South' with him – He seemed to really understand. Raid in evening – Lasted rather a long time.

February 18. E. & A. to Queen's Hall at 10.30 – to hear Mr Boult rehearse 'In the South'. Too few strings but reading of it really good – Feared audience wd be almost none on account of raids, & so it was, fortunately & mercifully not one Gotha got through – D.G. …

February 24. Spanish Place – Lalla to lunch – Last unrationed day! Mr Gaisberg to tea – Pleasant long visit. E. for a walk in morning – Still unwell –

March 3. E. still feeling ill, not out. Spanish Place. … News all depressing Russia a helpless prey –

March 4. E. a little better – Arranged to see Mr Tilley.

March 6. E. & A. to Mr Tilley, met Sir Maurice just arriving. A. waited in much anxiety. Sir Maurice said tonsil was not right, … tonsils wd have to be taken out – horrid idea –

Through this litany of gloom, occasional flashes of Elgarian humour appeared:

March 7. E. to Caledonian Market with Lalla – Saw an officer & E. gave him his arm to Devonshire Place – He wrote a very grateful letter & fell nearly flat! when E. told him who he was – … All gone to bed, when whistles and maroons began – Heavy guns & one tremendous report, windows vibrating &c probably the bomb wh. fell in Lyndhurst Gardens making a great hole & smashing windows – …

March 8. E. feeling … – alas – very unwell – …Russian & Scandinavian prospects very terrible.

On 10 March W H Reed and fellow members of a quartet came to Severn House to play. Guests included Percy Anderson, Frank Schuster, Robert Nicholls, Lalla Vandervelde, Mr & Mrs Ernest Thesiger, Hew Steuart-Powell and the Stuart Wortleys.

March 11. Sir Maurice urged removal of tonsils – pray God it may cure him. Horrid to think of E. being touched – E. telephoned to Sir Maurice that he wd go through with operation –

March 14. E. feeling so ill, glad to go and try something – A. wis him in car about 5.30 – The Home (Dorset Square Nursing Home) & a cheerful room …

The operation was not until 3 p.m. so Alice spent an anxious day awaiting the result.

March 15. (E.) Nursing Home Operation on Throat Tilley surgeon

March 15. … A. spent an anxious horrible 40 mins. Then Sir Maurice & Tilley came & told her all was well. Sir M. showed her the worst tonsil all over

February 7. Peace treaty signed between Germany & Finland.
February 10. Trotsky declares that Russia is now out of the War.
February 17. 21 killed in air raid on London.
February 25. Meat, butter & margarine rationing came into force in London
      & Home counties.
March 21. 2nd Battle of Somme begins with 50 mile wide German offensive.
March 24. British Fifth army all but destroyed.

abscess matter & a black stone, pea size in it. E. in great pain not knowing
how to bear it.
March 16. Drs. satisfied – Dreadful pain.
March 19. E. a little easier. A. S. of W. to see him – E. very depressed and
annihilating things –

The German attack on the British lines began on 21 March at 4.40 am.
Within three days, the British Fifth Army was in disarray,
communications with the French severed. Despite her personal
anxiety, Alice could not ignore what was obviously a crucial moment
in the conflict.

March 22. Preparing to leave Dorset Sqre. Mr Tilley very pleased with the
throat – A. & C. lunched at Canuto's & C. helped arrange all. Car was late
& E. was very worried waiting – the Home had upset his nerves & all he
had suffered – He was <u>so</u> peased to be home & loved everything – Very
anxious time. Battle impending.
March 23. E. so peased at being home. Throat feeling better & his colour muss
better … Very hot & lovely, E. in garden, cleared out fountain…
March 24. Frightfully anxious for our dear Army – wonderful day – hot as
summer – E's throat muss better.

As the German Army smashed into the British right flank south of
Arras, Elgar relaxed at home and, for the first time since he completed
The Fringes of the Fleet the previous June, wrote some music.

He was in a great deal of pain for several days; [there] were not anything
like the sedatives etc. that we have now, but nevertheless he woke one
morning and asked for pencil and paper and wrote down the opening
theme of the 'Cello Concerto …'.[80] This bold 9/8 statement would indeed
form the main theme of the first movement of the Cello Concerto, which
would not, however, be completed until August 1919. Two days later, on
25 March, Elgar began writing a subject for a String Quartet, the first
intimation of the three chamber works which would herald Elgar's last
great creative period.

March 25. E. began a delightful Quartett. A remote lovely 1st subject. May he
soon finish it – Wrote all day –

This sudden sense of well being was carried through into a witty letter Elgar wrote on the same day to his friend, W G McNaught of *The Musical Times*:

> I wish somebody would write an account of people to whom music has been dedicated, (I could have written 'dedicatees', but I scorn to be pedantic) – there are so many names which don't seem to exist apart from some quartet or other small composition; and then I should like to know all about the Grosshandler TOST to whom Haydn dedicated a whole string of IVtets [—] nearly a dozen! I expect it is all in Pohl but I haven't got P. Do ENCOURAGE, say, Selfridge, as a useful Grosshändler, to order some quartets from me.[81]

Elgar's recovery was not easy, nor was it helped by the war news:

> March 27. E. feeling so unwell – …
> March 29. …E. much the same – …Most anxious for news – Terrible fighting & having to give ground – Was there ever a Good Friday so much in harmony with Sacrifice & Suffering? …

By 5 April the German forces on the Western Front under Ludendorff had achieved an advance of forty miles, the greatest since November 1914. However he had extended his supply lines to breaking point, which gave the hardened British Third Army time to regroup. Ludendorff broke off the attack and moved north to Flanders where he launched the Lys offensive that lasted until the end of April. Haig with no reserves issued his famous order: 'There must be no retirement. With our back to the wall and believing in the justice of our cause each one must fight on to the end.' The German advance was halted after ten miles, with substantial losses on both sides, but in particular to the cream of the German Army.

For Elgar the good days began to outnumber the bad. As his health improved, a stay at The Hut was recommended provided the authorities, now that rationing had been introduced, would allow it.

March 26. Allied unity of command at last agreed. Foch becomes C in C.
March 27. German advance continues.
April 5. Formal end to 2nd Battle of the Somme.
April 9. Lys offensive begins
April 16. Attacks near Bailleul repulsed, but Germans force British withdrawal from Passchendaele.
April 22. Raid on Zeebrugge & Ostend successful.
  Fighting very heavy in Somme region. 102 German divisions employed against British alone.
April 29. Formal end to Battle of Lys.

April 11. E. slightly better. A. busy with preparations. To Petrol Control
everybody very polite & had full permission for Sir Maurice to drive E. –
April 12. Lovely day – warm & sunny – Sir Maurice sent his car for E. early &
they had a nice drive & E. showed Sir M The Hut & the garden wh. pleased
him very much – A. by 2.20, slow oh! slow train – but country so lovely
White blossoms, fresh green, lambs &c – Met E. who came to look for A.
near Hut – Strolled & strolled in lovely evening thought spring had come –

Elgar began an occasional diary, where his factual notes contrast with
the more elaborate entries of Alice:

April 12.(E.) Beautiful day – Sir Maurice motored me to the Hut. Alice arrived
by train.

Elgar stayed at The Hut until 25 April, where among the other guests
were Lalla Vandervelde, the poet Robert Nichols and from the world
of music, Adrian Boult. Whilst there he was not immune from war
news, as he records in his diary.

April 17.(E.) River very high. Bad news Bailleal[sic] etc. Cheque 42L from
Gramophone.

There was very heavy fighting on the Bailleul-Wulverghem line,
where continued German attacks put the British and the new
American front line under intense pressure.

April 18. Rather better account of himself from E. very depressed by the War
News. ...

The Allies responded to Ludendorff's success by appointing General
Foch C in C Allied forces in France: the need for effective co-
ordination had never been more vital. Although the social life
continued as usual for Alice, the prospect of taking her Edward and
away at last became a reality as she prepared to spend the summer at
Brinkwells. Carice recalled the time vividly:

Mother was meanwhile arranging for the move to Brinkwells for
recuperation. She had to think what would be wanted in the country, as
there was a scarcity of furniture and comforts there, and also the business
of shutting up Severn House safely. Father's only contribution to all this
was choosing tools which he would need for the woodwork he did and
the repairs and small improvements he made.[82]

Elgar's diary entries record the move to Sussex:

May 1.(E) Brought map of Brinkwells – prepared for journey tomorrow.
May 2.(E) to Brinkwells. A.S.W. angelically met E. at Vic: lunch there. Alice came
by car. Carice from office – left comfortably at 1.36. Alice drove from Fworth
sta. to Cottage. Carice & I walked. Navy boots great joy for wet woods

> May 3.(E) Better day – warmer. C. & I for walk in a.m. Killed snake 2 ft 2 C.
> back to town 5. 1. Mr Aylwin drove A. & C. to F'worth much unpacking
> Got Beer & Cider from Swan Great thunderstorm began abt 9 o'c.

They were there for most of the remainder of the war, where a southerly wind brought the sound of guns from the Western Front. Within a few days Elgar was feeling better: better than he had felt in a long time. He took to the rustic life with a passion, happily gardening, exploring, walking and making a variety of things from wood. Through June and into the late summer they watched first the hay and then the wheat and barley being harvested. Occasionally he helped. There was another reason for a sense of well-being, for at last there was a realistic chance that the war would end, as the allied forces on the Western Front began to push back the German army after its successful spring offensive; and above all Elgar wanted to compose.

Occasional visits to London and a visit to The Hut were the exception, as Brinkwells became the cradle for the last great creative spell of Elgar's life. It was to see the composition of the three chamber works and his final work for the war, *Big Steamers*, a setting of a poem by Kipling. 'Anything for the cause' was his reply when Alice commented on his generosity of spirit in setting Kipling again.

Alice records her worries over a letter published in *The Times* on 7 May by Major General Maurice accusing Ministers of mis-stating the military situation:

> May 9. Anxious for good result for Ll. George – Such a moment for a General,
> of all people, & other wretches to raise a quarrel –

A motion by Asquith, during the debate in the House of Commons on Maurice's letter was defeated, substantially.

> May 10. Overjoyed to hear of smashing majority for Ll. George. Saw the news
> in Pullboro'[sic] so anxious for it. … Nice lunch at Swan Inn, & explored
> & did some wonderful shopping. The Village has three Shopping Centres
> – Decided to return over fields & had lovely walk back. … tired after quite
> 7 miles. …

Elgar was more interested in the practical issues of life. He also recorded the shopping trip, the arrival of boots and overalls from *The Fringes of the Fleet* and that Mark shot a pigeon and a rabbit which he sold for 6d and 1 shilling respectively. He spent more and more time outside, putting up with minor irritations such as the occasional shortage of tobacco as the weather became warmer.

May 18. Daylight raid by British Air Force on Cologne.
May 19. Heavy fighting around Beaumont Hamel.
May 26. Increased artillery activity north and south of the Avre.
May 27. 3rd Battle of Aisne begins with new German thrust on Paris.
May 29. Allied retreat continues, Germans take Soissons.
May 31. Germans advance on Chateau Thierry.

> May 17. Lovely day – Hotter – Air vibrating with Song of birds –
> May 17 (E). Warm evening sat out till eleven. Nightingales seen – owls &c.
> Moon.

In Ireland 150 Sinn Fein leaders were arrested for 'plotting with Germany', and on 19 May twenty Gotha bombers raided London killing forty-nine, but five of the Gothas were shot down.

> May 20. Very hot lovely day. Heard of Irish arrests, so glad, & raid on London
> much wanting details. 4 [sic] raiders down seemed successful – Guns
> sounding –

The war now entered its final phase with increasingly heavy fighting on the Western Front and the new German thrust on Paris beginning on 27 May. The battle began with a German barrage at 1 am that was 'of a violence and accuracy that in the opinion of the most seasoned soldiers far outdid any other barrage they were under.' [83] At 3.40 am, the German advance began, storming the Chemin des Dames ridge, and over the next few days swept all before it advancing at a rate not seen since the armies sank into trenches 3½ years before. By the time the action finished on 3 June, the Germans were once again on the Marne only 56 miles from Paris. 'The most spectacular, and the most equivocal, victory of the War had been won.' [84] But, by mid July, at the second Battle of the Marne, Ludendorff had to admit defeat as allied aircraft and artillery destroyed his supply lines.

Elgar recorded in his diary:

> May 30 (E). Bad war news this & succeeding days Incessant gun fire (distant
> cannon)

This was the most anxious time Britain since the first Battle of the Marne in September 1914.

> June 1. Very anxious for news – Nothing good yet – E. & A. for lovely stroll in
> woods, late – Saw 3 Cockchafers all at once burying themselves in the
> ground about 9 P.M.
> June 2. Longing for good news but hardly expect to hear anything till next

day. Lovely, exquisite day – E's dearest birfday – No letters & no pesents[sic] had come for him except some asparagus from Rosa. ... Only praying for good news.

During June, through July and into August, the allied forces began to reverse the German successes, with the American forces at last having an effect militarily at Belleau Wood which was captured on 25 August. The British at Soissons and Meteren and the French near Rheims demonstrated the passing of the initiative westwards at last.

> June 13. News slightly better at some points. ... Then walked to Colvins. Great joy at seeing us. Very nice visit. Sidney read a Clough poem & A. found her favourite, & all exclaimed, <u>the </u>thing to set now.

An old interest caught Elgar's imagination as Lalla Vandervelde arrived to stay:

> June 15. E. & Lalla to Little Bognor for E. to try fishing. Much peased, caught 2 trout – ... news better D G.

That evening Elgar records: 'started worm tub'.

> June 22 (E). Fishing with A. (Tackle & landing net arrd. from stores) ... Caught one good fish – weather became too bright. E. walked to Henwoods Green to examine river. Saw <u>wild cat</u>

During July at Brinkwells, varied summer weather interfered little with the activity there. Algernon Blackwood (Alice called him 'Starlight' in her diary) came to stay, as did Alice Stuart Wortley on 3 August.

> July 19 (E). Blackwood left (Mr Aylwyn) at 9 o'c. He jumped wonderfully with a pole.[85] Found wasps nest. Began orchestrating 9/8 Very wet, warm & dull day
>
> July 22. A. to P.O. & to Miss Steel's after lunch – then heavy rain. After tea clearer & E. & A. to Bognor Pond – No fish. Much better news D.G. Horrid threat of strike. Czar Nicholas shot on 16th – a cruel murder.
>
> August 4. The memorable date – Finer morning & sunny later – E. & A. of W. for a walk.
>
> August 4 (E). <u>Soissons.</u>
>
> August 5 (E). Walk to Bognor Pond A. to Fittleworth before tea Good news <u>Albert</u>

Elgar noted the French re-taking of Soissons on 2 August and the German retreat from Hamel north of Albert. On 8 August the second and decisive Battle of Amiens began, with the British Fourth Army, under General Sir Henry Rawlinson, going over the top on the Somme, this time achieving the surprise in attack that eluded Haig in

1916. Ludendorff was to call this 'the black day of the German Army in the history of the war', as his losses totalled 27,000. Three days later the German Kaiser noted 'We have nearly reached the limit of our powers of resistance. The war must be ended.' The British Official History recorded 'the collapse of Germany began not in the Navy, not in the Homeland, not in any of the sideshows, but on the Western Front in consequence of defeat in the field.'

It was now that the British Army (of which the Australians under the brilliant General Monash, New Zealanders and Canadians were such a formidable part) and Field Marshal Haig came into their own. Haig was convinced that the Germans could be beaten in 1918, and with the Third Army entering the front line on 21 August the advance eastwards began in earnest. The Commander in Chief, Marshal Foch listed no less than nine separate actions of the British forces during this advance, stating that 'Never at any time in history has the British Army achieved greater results in attack than in this unbroken offensive lasting 116 days, from 18 July to 11 November.' It was at a terrible cost, for the Germans were by no means beaten and between 8 August and 26 September, when the Hindenburg Line was stormed, 190,000 men were lost in the British Army alone.

For the British in their war weariness, this triumph was largely ignored at home. The previous year the reserved status of farm workers had been lifted, so no doubt Elgar's assistance in the field would have been as welcome as much as he enjoyed the opportunity to work. The last days of rural England could be appreciated by someone who understood the countryside and his roots, even if there were those who had anticipated the resolute destruction to come. 'The whole face of England is being rapidly altered, and this is perhaps more noticeable in the country, even in the most remote districts, than in the towns, where we look for change…'.[86]

June 3. German forces 'on the Marne'. Formal end of the 3rd Battle of the Aisne.
June 25. American capture of Belleau Wood.
July 4. Australians 'peaceful penetration' at Le Hamel.
July 18. 'High-water mark of the war: Great Allied counter attack begins on 27 mile front.
July 20. Germans pushed back across Marne river.
August 2. French retake Soissons.
August 4. Fourth anniversary of the declaration of war.

> August 9. Great Cavalry charge – Good news Western Front. Such a mercy – Lovely day – Wheat field being cut. … In wheatfield after tea & E. worked hard 'Stooking' A. helped too with a good many but found the sheaves heavy.
>
> August 11. Glorious sunny day – Splendid for harvest. D.G. Mark mowed lawn! To our surprise – Such good news still – Germans <u>must</u> begin to know something.

At last Elgar's mind was turning to composition again.

> August 19 (E). <u>piano</u> arrived & blind from A. S. W. for garden room very busy all day with piano and blind. Mr Aylwyn's waggon brot. up piano.
>
> August 20. Wrote some music.

It was another glorious day, and the Elgars had been joined by Sir Sidney and Frances Colvin. Elgar's curt diary entry records the beginning of the Violin Sonata which even the sensitive Alice failed to note in her diary. Four days later though, she wrote:

> August 24. E. writing wonderful new music, different from anything else of his. A. calls it wood magic. So elusive and delicate.
>
> August 24 (E). Lovely day. … Squirrels ravaging nut tree. E. busy with music A. & C. to rectory to tea. Ham came & MS. paper from Novello

So the Violin Sonata progressed, aided by visits from the conductor Sir Landon Ronald and violinist W H (Billy) Reed:

> August 29. Busy expecting Mr Reed – E. happy over his booful new music – … Soon tried the new music & was delighted. … Much time over the Sonata, so lovely to hear it –

Elgar had to travel to London for a few days on 31 August where he visited Lalla Vandervelde and travelled on to lunch with the Speyers at their home, Ridgehurst in Hertfordshire. He returned to Brinkwells on 3 September where he picked up his music again. He continued writing every day.

> September 6. E. worked all the early morning … & really all day. The Sonata was vibrating through his very being – He wrote and offered dedication to Mrs Joshua –

It was not all work, for there were diversions.

> September 13(E). 'Bowls from E.V. Lucas came. … Rector called & to tea Mem: left bowls on lawn: they were taken to be black pigeons by the farm boy & two men with guns got out ready to shoot them.'

The next day both Alice and Edward record the shock of the news that Marie Joshua had died suddenly. Elgar paid tribute to her in his music, by recalling the second subject of the slow movement at the end of the Sonata.

> September 14. ... E. writing end of last movement of Sonata, ended it with a
> wonderful soft lament ...   This was after hearing with great shock &
> sorrow of sudden death of one of our dear & very kindest of friends Marie
> Joshua –

Marie Joshua had, in fact, intended to write and say she felt unable to
accept the dedication of the sonata, but that she was overwhelmed by
the honour. When the Sonata was published, Elgar was able to record
their friendship, publicly by inscribing her initials above the title: 'M
J – 1918'. With that dedication to a part-German by birth Elgar was,
perhaps, subconsciously declaring his feelings on the four years of
carnage and destruction that had achieved nothing. Marie Joshua
had befriended the Elgars after Hans Richter had introduced her to
them. Elgar had written to her earlier in June. 'I think over all the
great days with Richter while I am working with the hoe or plane and
little of the actual manual labour, and I regret that such hours can
never come again; your letters tell me that you live on the past
glorious art life sometimes;   but happily for you, you have so many
interests in the present.'
     There was no break between work on the Sonata and that on the
Piano Quintet.

> September 15. E. writing, 3rd movement of Sonata growing most beautiful –
> Wrote part of Quintet wonderful weird beginning same atmosphere as
> 'Owls' – evidently reminiscence of Sinister trees and impression of
> Flexham Park –

Billy Reed visited Brinkwells three days later and with Elgar they
played through the Sonata and the sketches of the Quintet. Elgar
negotiated the purchase of woodland near to Brinkwells and
proceeded to clear and cut it back almost everyday, as he finished the
Sonata.   This pattern continued into October, Alice recording
frequently 'wood & music' as the Quintet took shape. Elgar was now
writing against the background of continuously better war news and
the arrival of autumnal weather, although for some days he was not

---

August 11. Ludendorff offers resignation – it is not accepted.
August 14. German retreat gathers momentum.
Early September: Allied advance continues.
September 12. The Americans under General Pershing victorious at Saint-
     Mihiel.

well. As the end of the war became inevitable, he interrupted the
Quintet to turn back to the Quartet he had begun in the spring. The
Sonata was sent to Novello on 1 October, and by the second week of
the month Elgar was 'possessed with his wonderful music' as he
developed the Quartet.

> September 27. E. writing wonderful new music real wood sounds & another
> lament wh. shd. be in a War Symphony.

They celebrated Alice's seventieth birthday on 9 October and travelled
back to London. The war's end was now inevitable and Elgar was
forced to confront, again, his position as composer laureate. However,
his heart was not in this enforced rôle as is clear in a letter of 5
November to Laurence Binyon who had sent him a 'Peace Ode'. 'I
think your poem beautiful exceedingly – but – I do not feel drawn to
peace music somehow.'

On 11 October Alice and Edward returned to London and then
Elgar spent several days with Frank Schuster at The Hut, from where
he travelled to the Palace Theatre for rehearsals and a revival
performance of *The Fringes of the Fleet*. Alice's diary then falls silent
for three weeks, possibly over concern for the operation she
underwent on 29 October to remove a wen from her forehead. Elgar
also spent a few days with the Speyers at Ridgehurst, returning to
London for the final tense days of the war. Tense it was, with the
retreating German forces resisting to the end. October alone cost the
British Army 5,438 officers and 115,608 other ranks. However,
through constant rain the British advance never faltered.

> 'An Armistice was declared at 11 a.m. this morning, November 11' at last.
> Men took the news according to their natures. Indurated pessimists, after
> proving that it was a lie, said it would be but an interlude. Others retired
> into themselves as though they had been shot, or went stiffly off about the
> meticulous execution of some trumpery detail of kit-cleaning. Some
> turned round and fell asleep then and there; and a few lost all holds for a
> while. It was the appalling new silence of things that soothed and
> unsettled them in turn. ... For the first time since August 14 the monthly
> returns showed no officer or man killed, wounded or missing.[87]

Alice and Edward were at Severn House for the morning of Armistice
Day but, despite the excitement, Elgar could not wait to return to the
country where the essentials of life continued, as his diary records:

> November 11 (E). Armistice – ran up Flag. Car to Victoria. A. & E. to
> Fittleworth 1.36. Flags. ... Threshing barley at Brinkwells

---

September 18. Substantial advance of British forces north of St Quentin.

September 26. British Army storms Hindenburg Line.

September 28. Anglo-Belgian attack in Flanders.

October 4. Germany & Austria address pleas for Armistice to President Wilson.

October 5. Allied forces break through the Hindenburg line.

October 9. British take Cambrai.

October 10. British take Le Cateau.

October 19. Bruges recaptured.

October 26. Ludendorff resigns.

October 29. German naval mutiny begins. Austria signs Armistice.

November 8. Marshall Foch meets German delegation and lays down terms of Armistice.

November 9. German Kaiser abdicates.

November 11. Canadian Division of British Fifth Army capture Mons before dawn. Armistice signed at 5 am. Hostilities cease on all fronts at 11 am.

Alice was more expansive.

> November 11. E. & A. heard Armistice was signed. E. put up our Flag, it looked gorgeous – Crowds out & all rejoicing. D G for preservation & Victory E. & A. to Brinkwells – Lalla came to train at Victoria – C. tried too but just missed & went to Coliseum where 'Land of Hope & Glory' was sung twice the 2nd time the words of refrain were thrown on the screen & people stood & joined in – Very exciting & moving –
>
> November 12. Very bright & cold – E. beginning to work – A. unpacking &c. Very exciting paper. New republics[88] – Gn. rejoicing in London, much Hope & Glory being sung –
>
> November 12 (E). Tidying up, unpacking at Brinkwells. Lovely day – Threshing machine ploughed up lawn. Put up Flag.

Life began to take on its former pattern again and Elgar was in the mood for continuing the composition of his Quartet.

> November 13 (E). Wrote music & tried to recover the threads broken. Worked in wood Threshing at Springs – walked up – A. to PO in afternoon before tea. Lovely bright day Flag flying

Thus Alice and Edward merged back into a happy normality as they spent as much time as possible over the next year at Brinkwells, that 'very cottagy cottage' which had become the inspiration and crucible for the last great creative period of Elgar's life.

NOTES and SOURCES

1. For more extended detail of the chronology of this period of Elgar's life, see Martin Bird's chronology in the Reference Section, pp389-456.
2. Keegan, John: *The Face of Battle* (Barrie & Jenkins, 2nd edn, 1988) p 248
3. On one occasion *Carillon* was performed in five different halls in London on the same day. See Lindley, Jeanne: *Seeking and Finding, The Life of Emile Cammaerts* (SPCK, 1962) p 103
4. Pirie, Peter J: 'World's End', *Music Review* (1957) p 89. Quoted by Kennedy, Michael: 'Elgar the Edwardian' from Monk, Raymond: *Elgar Studies* (Scolar Press, 1990) p 114
5. Tuchman, Barbara: *August 1914 (The Guns of August)* (Constable & Co, 1962 (Papermac edition 1991)) p 309
6. Keegan, John: *The First World War* (Hutchinson, 1998) p 74
7. Massie, Robert: *'Dreadnought' Britain, Germany, and the Coming of the Great War* (Random House, 1991 (Canadian Edition)) p 900
8. Colles, H C: *Walford Davies* (Oxford, 1942) p 104
9. The subject of the Variation 13 from Elgar's *Enigma Variations*.
10. All the diary entries are by Alice Elgar, except where noted. For the sake of clarity I refer to Alice and Carice Elgar by their Christian names, and only do so for Elgar for the same reason.
11. This was of course the reverse of the case.
12. Kipling, Rudyard: *The Irish Guards in the Great War,* vol I (first pub 1923) (Spellmount Limited, 1997) pp 29-30
13. Moore, Jerrold Northrop: *Letters of a Lifetime* (Oxford, 1990) p 285
14. Sir Henry Wood conducted the premier of *Sospiri* the previous evening.
15. Kipling: *op cit*, p 31
16. General Helmuth von Moltke (1848-1916), Chief of the German General Staff at the outbreak of War. To avoid compromising Dutch neutrality, he fatally undermined one of the basic concepts of the Schlieffen Plan.
17. General Alexandrer von Kluck (1846-1934)
18. Leo Francis (Frank) Schuster, a patron of the arts, with homes in London and in particular 'The Hut' at Bray on the River Thames in Berkshire.
19. Arthur C Benson, son of Edward Benson, Archbishop of Canterbury (1883-1896). He wrote the words for Elgar's *Coronation Ode*, Op 44, thus helping to immortalise 'Land of Hope and Glory'.
20. Moore: *op cit*, pp 277-283
21. Britain, fearing Japanese expansionism, lent a token force of 1,500 to aid the 23,000 Japanese under General. Kamio. It was not until the Washington Conference of 1922 that the Japanese agreed to leave.
22. Tita Brand Cammaerts, daughter of Marie Brema, the first Angel in *The Dream of Gerontius*, 1900.
23. Rosa Burley (1866-1951), formerly Headmistress of The Mount School, Malvern where she befriended the Elgars. She worked with Carice Elgar in the Government Censorship Department during the war. Her book, *Edward Elgar, the Record of a Friendship*, written with Frank C Carruthers (Barrie & Jenkins Ltd, 1972), is an important document of Elgar at home in Malvern and Hereford.

24. Moore: *Letters of a Lifetime*, pp 277-283
25. *The Times*, December 8, 1914
26. *The Times*, December 15 1915
27. Moore, Jerrold Northrop: *Elgar on Record* (Oxford, 1974) gives details of all Elgar's recordings and recording sessions.
28. Arthur De Greef, pianist & friend of Grieg.
29. Alfred Kalisch (1843-1923), Jewish music critic, based in London.
30. Theobald von Bethmann-Hollweg (1856-1921), German Chancellor from the outbreak of war until 1917.
31. Sir Sidney Colvin (1845-1927), former director of the Fitzwilliam Museum, Slade Professor of Art & Keeper of Prints and Drawings at the British Museum. His wife, Frances (1839-1924), had been close to R L Stevenson.
32. Moore: *Letters of a Lifetime*, p 284
33. Chickering, Robert: *Imperial Germany and the Great War, 1914-1918* (Cambridge University Press, 1998) p 17
34. Binyon, Laurence: *The Winnowing-Fan* (Elkin Matthews, 1914)
35. Tuchman: *op cit*, p 311
36. 'To Goethe' from Binyon's *The Winnowing-Fan* collection
37. Tuchman: *op cit*, p 314
38. Moore: *Edward Elgar: A Creative Life* (Oxford, 1984) p 674
39. Hatcher, John: *Laurence Binyon Poet, Scholar of East and West* (Oxford, Clarendon Press, 1995) p 198
40. Sir Landon Ronald (1873-1938), composer, conductor and later record probducer, champion of Elgar's music.
41. Moore: *op cit*, p 674
42. *ibid*, pp 674-675
43. Moore, Jerrold Northrop: *Elgar and his Publishers, Letters of a Creative Life* vol 2, (Oxford, 1987) p 788
44. Moore: *Edward Elgar: A Creative Life*, p 675
45. See Herter, Joseph A: 'Solidarity and Poland', chapter 11 in this volume
46. Moore: *A Creative Life*, pp 675-676
47. Formerly Lady Mary Lygon, (1869-1927), sister of Lord Beauchamp and the inspiration for Variation XIII of the *Enigma Variations*. On marriage in 1905 to Major the Hon H W Hepburn-Stuart-Forbes-Trefusis and moving to Cornwall, she became closely associated with the Folk Song Society.
48. William W A Elkin (1863-1937), music publisher and founder of the eponymous publishing house.
49. Lalla Vandervelde, daughter of Edward Speyer and wife of the Belgian Socialist leader, Emile Vandervelde living in exile in London.
50. Sydney Loeb (1876-1964), half German Jewish son-in-law of Richter.
51. Alice Stuart Wortley, daughter of the painter Millais and wife of Charles (later) Lord Stuart of Wortley. She was the inspiration for many of the themes of Elgar's violin concerto and became an intimate of both Alice and Edward.
52. Alfred E Rodewald, an understanding business friend and supporter of Elgar in Liverpool. He died suddenly in 1903 aged 43.
53. Admiral Lord Charles Beresford (1846-1919), Commander of the Mediterranean Fleet (1905). Beresford and his wife invited Elgar and Frank Schuster to sail

with them. Beresford commanded the Channel Fleet (1907) but disagreed with Lord Fisher over his proposals for reform of the Navy.

54. Henry Wilson, the President of the Arts and Crafts Society.
55. Novello allowed Elkin the publishing rights. The score was never published.
56. Moore: *Elgar and His Publishers,* vol 2, pp 789-790
57. *ibid,* p 790
58. Gerald Grafton (1886-1950), nephew of Elgar, only son of Pollie [Elgar] & William Grafton of Stoke Prior.
59. Henry Embleton (1854-1930), businessman & secretary of the Leeds Choral Union.
60. It was about this time that King George V began to take the steps that would remove the German titles from the Royal Family. The Royal House still bore those of Hanover, Saxe-Coburg, Gotha and Wettin. The King accepted the suggestion of Lord Stamfordham, his private secretary, and the Royal House became The House of Windsor.
61. Hooey, Charles A: 'Spirit Insights', *Elgar Society Journal,* vol 9 no 6 (November 1996) p 297
62. Admiral of the Fleet Earl John Jellicoe (1859-1935), Commander of the British Grand Fleet 1914-1916.
63. Field Marshal Horatio Herbert Kitchener, First Earl of Khartoum (1850-1916), the hero of Omdurman, he was Secretary of State for War in Asquith's Government, where he presided over the creation of Britain's 'New Armies'. He was a popular public figure, and his death caused a great outpouring of national grief. He was the 'only outstanding military figure on either side who came to a violent end'.
64. Sir Arthur Bliss (1891-1975), composer and soldier during the war, later Master of the Queen's Musick.
65. Moore, Jerrold Northrop: *Edward Elgar: The Windflower Letters* (Clarendon Press, Oxford, 1989) p 172
66. Hans Richter (1843-1916), conductor of Elgar's music including the first performances of the *Enigma Variations, The Dream of Gerontius* and the A flat Symphony.
67. Fifield, Christopher: *True Artist and True Friend: A biography of Hans Richter* (Oxford, Clarendon Press, 1993) p 456
68. August Johannes Jaeger (1860-1909), German-born editor of Elgar's music at Novello. 'Nimrod' of the *Enigma Variations.*
69. In 1907, Sir George Warrender had been on the cruise to the Mediterranean with Elgar, under the command of Lord Charles Beresford. His wife, Lady Maud (sister of the Earl of Shaftesbury) was close to Alice Elgar.
70. Sir Ivor Atkins (1869-1950), composer and organist of Worcester Cathedral (1897-1950), close friend of Elgar and champion of his music.
71. see note 49
72. Moore: *Elgar on Record,* p 18
73. Hooey: *op cit;* Geoffrey Hodgkins, the Editor of *The Elgar Society Journal,* makes the point in the same edition, that Elgar was staying only a few miles away at Stoke at the time of this performance. No mention is made that he attended the concert.

74. Brinkwells had been rented from the landscape painter Reginald (Rex) Vicat Cole (1870-1940). Biographer of Byam Shaw in 1933, Cole also published *The Artists Anatomy of Trees* in 1916. He was the son of the better known George Vicat Cole (1833-1893).

75. Hooey: *op cit*

76. The songs of Stanford were *Songs of the Fleet* and *A Carol of Bells*. Parry's *The Chivalry of the Sea* and Frederick Bridge's *The Inchcape Rock* were also performed.

77. General Erich von Ludendorff (1865-1937). Appointed quartermaster-general of the German Army in August 1916, Ludendorff masterminded the military strategy in the west, strengthening his forces after the collapse of Russia.

78. Terraine: *op cit*, p 160

79. Sir Adrian C Boult (1889-1983), distinguished conductor of Elgar's music. Boult was the first conductor of the BBC Symphony Orchestra and the second Director of Music of the BBC from 1930 to 1942.

80. Young, Percy – see also *op cit*, pp 179-180

81. Moore *Elgar and his Publishers*, vol 2, pp 798-799

82. Young, Percy: *Alice Elgar* (Dobson Books, 1978) pp 179-180, from a MS by Carice Elgar Blake

83. Terraine: *op cit*, p 169, quoting Rogerson, Sidney: *The Last Ebb* (Arthur Barker, 1937)

84. Terraine: *op cit*, p 169

85. Blackwood frequently carried a long pole on walks which he would use to vault fences, hedges and gates. Alice Elgar was very taken with his ideas, so much so that they frequently became 'fact'. It is likely that Blackwood contributed substantially to the rumours associated with the trees in Flexham Park which in turn influenced Elgar's ideas for his Piano Quintet. (From a conversation with E. Wulstan Atkins, May 2001).

86. Pulbrook, Ernest C: *The English Countryside* (B T Batsford Ltd, 1915) p v

87. Kipling: *op cit*, p 290

88. As the Central Powers collapsed, a Yugoslavian Government was announced, Bavaria declared itself a republic and on 14 November the Republic of German-Austria was proclaimed in Vienna. Over the next few days, the National Assembly of the Czecho-Slovak State held its first meeting and the Hungarian Republic was declared in Budapest.

Part One

~ ~ ~

Life & Times

Elgar and Music in England 1914-1918

CHAPTER 2

The DEATH of a CULTURE
Germany and British Music Before 1914

Jeremy Dibble

> I have my own confession to make. For I have been a quarter of a century
> and more a pro-Teuton. I owed too much to their music and their
> philosophers and authors of former times to believe it possible that the
> nation at large could be imbued with the teaching of a few advocates of
> mere brutal violence and material aggression; with the extravagance of
> those who talked about super-morality; with the ruthless implications of
> their insistence that the State is power, and nothing but power, and has no
> concern with honour, right, justice, or fair play.[1]

It was during an address to the students of the Royal College of Music
in September 1914 that Parry made this personal admission. 'We
cannot help recalling the splendid hexameter in our English version of
Isaiah, 'How art thou fallen from Heaven, O Lucifer, son of the
morning! . . .' This is the German nation which in former times was
glorified by producing some of the noblest minds that shone in the
world of art. Heinrich Schütz, Johann Sebastian Bach, Handel, Gluck,
Beethoven, Schumann, Brahms – the nation which has produced
great poets, great philosophers, great scientists, great scholars, great
inventors of things which have benefited humanity to the utmost.'[2]
Parry was one of many who had grown up to believe in the
supremacy of German music and culture. His adherence to German
aesthetic ideals emanated from his profound belief in evolutionism as
the engine of history, and in the Darwinist notion of polygenesis, the
product of which was a racial hierarchy in which northern European
composers were seen as superior to their southern counterparts.

A reverence for German culture can be traced back to the accession
of the Hanoverian monarchy in the early eighteenth century and to
the dominance of Handel, particularly as the epitome of Protestant
choral music. A similar reverence for Haydn was shown at the turn of
the century, but it was Mendelssohn who ultimately succeeded
Handel as Britain's musical icon in the nineteenth century. *Elijah* and

FACING PAGE: *Hans Richter*

Messiah between them provided the pillars of British choral festivals at Birmingham, York, and the Three Choirs, with *The Creation* and Spohr's *Last Judgement* as secondary alternatives. Mendelssohn's particular breed of romanticism, informed heavily by classical and baroque formal paradigms, was *sine qua non* for most British composers (particularly between 1840 and 1870) in every genre from song, symphony, oratorio, and light opera, and it was aesthetic *Weltanschauung* enthusiastically endorsed by the Prince Consort, an advocate and the instrument of British assimilation of German scientific and artistic ideals. After the foundation of the Leipzig Conservatorium in 1843, Mendelssohn's position as a pedagogical idol was also cemented, as was the reputation of the city with its famous Gewandhaus Orchestra as the Mecca for all those in the German- and English-speaking world who considered music the stuff of a career. Leipzig maintained its reputation for the rest of the nineteenth century, though by the end of the 1870s, Reinecke's conservative regime caused many young aspirants to look elsewhere, to Berlin (where Friedrich Kiel and Heinrich Urban had a major following), to Frankfurt, Stuttgart, Cologne, and Munich. The list of British students is considerable. Sullivan, Dannreuther, Rosa, Algernon Ashton, Swinnerton Heap, Cowen, Stanford, Luard Selby, Harwood, Delius, and Smyth are among the many names to study in Leipzig; Parry spent a short but profitable time with Henry Hugo Pierson (the English composer who voluntarily exiled himself to Germany in the 1840s, writing under the *nom de plume* Edgar Mannsfeldt); Mackenzie was educated at the Realschule in Sondershausen between 1857 and 1862, studying theory with K W Ulrich and violin with Eduard Stein; Stanford, Somervell, Cowen, and George Bennett (organist of Lincoln Cathedral) worked under Kiel in Berlin; Grainger, O'Neill, Quilter, Scott, and Gardiner all studied with Iwan Knorr in Frankfurt; Philip Heseltine worked in Cologne; in 1897, Vaughan Williams studied with the elderly Max Bruch in Berlin, and the young Scottish composer, Cecil Frederick Gottfried Coles, won a scholarship to the Stuttgart Conservatorium where, after four years of study, he was chorus-master to the Royal Opera and assistant conductor to Max von Schillings.

Although a musical career in Germany was a serious temptation – Henry Hugo Pierson was one who happily yielded to complete Germanisation in the respelling of his name to Piersen – few Britons put down permanent roots in the German-speaking countries of the continent. Even Sterndale Bennett, admired by both Mendelssohn and Schumann, turned down the offer of the conductorship of the

Gewandhaus Orchestra in 1853 (for reasons no-one has yet been able to discover) which would have been a serious accolade for an Englishman. Conversely many Germans and Austrians (including those from nations in the Austrian Empire), such as the Cramer family, Moscheles, and Julius Benedict, saw Britain as a major economic opportunity or as a place of political refuge. This was certainly the case for Wagner during his year as conductor of the Philharmonic Society in 1855. His legacy of near-bankruptcy was one the Society wished to forget, but Wagner's meeting with Karl Klindworth, who had settled in London in 1854, planted some of the earliest seeds of Wagner appreciation in Britain. Klindworth appeared at intervals in London as a pianist and conductor of orchestral concerts. One of Klindworth's principal achievements during the 1850s and 60s was the arrangement in vocal score of

Wagner's *Ring* cycle, a task sanctioned by the composer while he was in London. Klindworth's enthusiasm for Wagner found a broad sympathy in the young Alsatian-born American pianist (as he was at that time), Edward Dannreuther, who had arrived in London fresh from Leipzig in 1863, under the protective wing of Henry Chorley.

The friendship of Klindworth, Dannreuther, Walter Bache (a Liszt pupil), and the Dane, Frits Hartvigson, gave rise to the informal 'Working Men's Society' which began to meet on a weekly basis in 1867. Its main brief was to explore Wagner's music, act by act, though other contemporary works were discussed and played. After Klindworth left for Moscow, Dannreuther kept alive the Wagnerian flame and his own unquenchable ardour for

Dannreuther and Richter

Wagner's music was nourished by his acquaintance with Wagner and
Hans von Bülow. The laying of the foundation stone at Bayreuth in
1872, and Wagner's performance of Beethoven's Ninth Symphony,
were deeply formative in Dannreuther's development and from that
time his promulgation of Wagner's artistic mission became a more
public enterprise with the establishment of the London Wagner
Society.

During the 1870s Dannreuther was regarded as one of London's
most radical musicians. Besides promoting Wagner in concerts,
articles, and books – his book *Wagner and the Reform of Opera* was
one of the first significant monographs on Wagner's theories of opera
and drama – he was a major catalyst in the introduction of piano
concertos by Tchaikovsky, Grieg, Liszt, and Scharwenka to English
audiences. Though a dyed-in-the-wool Wagner disciple, he
nevertheless refused to serve Wagner to the exclusion of other music,
and was equally keen to promulgate the work of Schumann, Brahms,
Dvořák. It was through the intellectual atmosphere of his semi-private
chamber concerts at 12 Orme Square, that Dannreuther's German
outlook found its natural expression. In particular it was Dannreuther's wide interests in literature and philosophy that informed his
understanding of music, and articles such as 'Beethoven and his
Works: A Study' for *Macmillan's Magazine* betray that wider
perspective of German *Kultur*.[3] Dannreuther's cerebral outlook was to
touch the lives of many British musicians of the period, including Fuller
Maitland, Stanford, Walford Davies, Hurlstone, and most of all Parry.

If Dannreuther was Parry's mentor, then Joachim may be fairly
cited as Stanford's. It was Joachim who was responsible for directing
the young Irishman towards Friedrich Kiel in Berlin. Soon after, with
Joachim's help, Brahms's First Symphony was heard for the first time
in England at Cambridge, an event which sealed the friendship
between the two men, and which established an unbroken tradition
of annual visits by the violinist to Cambridge until the early years of
the twentieth century. Joachim was indeed a British 'institution'. His
regular visits to London, since 1865, made him a fixture in the concert
calendar, but he was also a visitor to many other cities in Britain,
namely Birmingham, Manchester, Leeds, Oxford, Edinburgh,
Glasgow, and Dublin; universities conferred degrees on him and the
RCM (as part of their propaganda) advertised his rôle as examiner.
Joachim provided a spiritual link between Bach, Mendelssohn, whom
he met as a boy, and Brahms whose music he promoted among British
concert societies. He was also the embodiment of classicism and was

Joachim performing at the Guildhall, Cambridge after his installation as a D Mus in March 1877. In the audience, extreme right, we might identify Sir Julius Benedict.

largely responsible for the inculcation of those Brahmsian tenets of 'absolute music' for which the RCM, through the proselytes of Grove, Parry, and Stanford, was an apologist.

Joachim and Dannreuther did much to encourage the British composer and performer. One must also add the name of August Manns whose German values informed the content of the Crystal Palace concerts and chimed happily with Grove's unabashed preference for the Teutonic triumvirate of Beethoven, Schubert, and Mendelssohn. Manns' pioneering work was superseded in 1879 by the advent of Hans Richter. Richter personified the cult of the great Austro-German *Dirigent*. He was already renowned as conductor of the first *Ring* cycle at Bayreuth and was known to London audiences through his appearances during the London Wagner Festival in 1877 (when Wagner came to the British capital as a guest of Dannreuther), but he was a positive revelation to orchestras, audiences, and native composers in terms of his interpretative abilities, his sense of authority, and his powers of orchestral cohesion. Richter was ultimately responsible for the birth of a new orchestral standard in Britain. He, more than any other conductor, broke the monopoly of Italian opera in London with his performances of *Fidelio*, *Der Freischütz*, *Euryanthe*, and all of Wagner's operas in their original language, and it fell to another German, Carl Rosa, the Hamburg-born violinist, to promote both opera in English and opera by British composers.

Richter's promulgation of Wagner did much to nourish a sense of Wagner-worship in the late 1880s and 1890s. Bayreuth became a Mecca for many British composers: Stanford visited often, especially to hear

G R Sinclair, Richter and Elgar

Die Meistersinger and *Parsifal*; Elgar made his pilgrimage in 1892, and Vaughan Williams followed in 1896; furthermore, Richter established the German canon of Beethoven, Weber, Brahms, and Wagner at his concert series at St James's Hall which created a benchmark for all conductors who followed him. Other German conductors – Bruch (in Liverpool), Bülow, Mottl, and even the young Mahler (who came to London in 1892 to conduct Wagner) had a following, but Richter's presence in England, like that of Joachim, was deeply formative not only in London but in Birmingham where he conducted the festival from 1885 until 1909, in Manchester where he directed the Hallé Orchestra from 1897 until his retirement in 1911, and the London Symphony Orchestra from its foundation in 1904. Like Dannreuther, Richter also did much to promote British composers, notably those who adhered to the Teutonic creed. He was quintessential to the promotion of the British symphonic tradition, conducting works by Cowen, Parry, and Stanford, and was 'true artist and true friend' to Elgar, whose *Enigma* Variations and First Symphony owed their energy and confidence to Richter's encouragement and stature.

Dannreuther, Joachim, Manns, and Richter, as four icons of German culture in Britain, established yardsticks by which most Britons judged the progress of native musical culture, and excellence was seen to preside in all things German, whether in publishing (many German publishing companies had set up branches in London), orchestral playing, municipal support for national opera, chamber music, or even the fledgling discipline of municipality which had been led not only by Dannreuther but also by others such as Carl Engel and Francis Hueffer (critic of *The Times*). Engel in particular did much to raise the consciousness of the British Library (the Museum) to cultivate a national collection of music, and his seminal essay 'A Music Library' (in his volume *Musical Myths and Facts* of 1876) in which he questioned the absence of a musical lexicon in English, appeared a timely juncture as the first volume of Grove's *Dictionary of Music and Musicians* was being prepared.[4]

In Scotland's capital, music was enhanced by Mackenzie's German acquaintances. He persuaded the Düsseldorf violinist and theorist, Friedrich Niecks to settle in Edinburgh in 1868. Niecks soon established himself as a viola player in Mackenzie's Edinburgh quartet (with Adolf Kuchler and Hugo Daubert) and a regular contributor to the *Monthly Musical Record*. With publications such as the *Concise Dictionary of Musical Terms* (1884) and Frederick Chopin as *Man and Musician* (1888), and numerous articles in *The Musical Times* (after

The Hallé Orchestra in 1908. This is almost the personnel that gave the first performance of the First Symphony that year. In the large ovals are Hallé and Richter. Others shown are : 1. Dr A Brodsky, Director, Royal Manchester College of Music; 2. Carl Fuchs, principal cello; 3. F Paersch, first horn; 4. Otto Schieder, first bassoon; 5. A Wichtl, second bassoon; 6. Simon Speelman, principal viola; 7. M M G Speelman, viola; 8. W Klippé, first violins; 9. A Hamer, second violins.

1879). Niecks' reputation as a musicologist and lecturer on music led to his appointment as Reid Professor of Music at Edinburgh University in 1890.

German musicians such as Ludwig Straus led the Philharmonic Orchestra; Otto Goldschmidt founded and conducted the London Bach Choir; Charles Hallé founded his eponymous orchestra in Manchester which was inherited by other Germans, Richter, and Michael Balling; and there were many instrumental performers and teachers who made their home in England, among them Ernst Pauer (who was a piano professor at the RCM until his retirement), Paul David (son of the great German violinist Ferdinand David and music master at Uppingham School), Joseph Ludwig (violinist at the RAM), Robert Hausmann (a cello professor at the Berlin Hochschule and a close friend of Joachim and Stanford), and Ernst Franke, the prime mover in the establishment of Richter's 'Festival Orchestral Concerts' in London in 1879. Franke was one of many pupils of Joachim, who, through their teacher, had their eyes turned towards Britain as a land of economic opportunity. Richard Gompertz was employed as a violin teacher by the Cambridge University Musical Society, helped promote the Wednesday Popular Concerts, and was a Professor of Violin at the RCM, and Johann Kruse, his natural successor after Gompertz left London for Dresden in 1899, did much to promote British and German chamber music through the Broadwood concerts and his own orchestral festivals in London.

To this close society of performers we should add the names of other German immigrants, who, in their different ways, also brought their influence to bear on British music before the war. Edward Speyer, the son of a wealthy Frankfurt merchant, settled in London in 1859 where he was a magnet for the likes of Joachim, Clara Schumann, and their musical circle. Like Dannreuther, he became a British subject, and devoted his time and money to the future of the nation's music. At his Hertfordshire home, 'Ridgehurst', he entertained Joachim, Elgar, Strauss and others of the younger generation and underwrote the visit of the Meiningen Orchestra to London in 1902. Speyer's second wife was Antonia Kufferath, daughter of the German pianist and conductor, Hubert Kufferath. She retired from a career as a singer when she married in 1885.

One of the most retiring yet influential personalities among the German community was August Johannes Jaeger, born in Düsseldorf but settled in London in 1878, becoming an employee of Novello in 1890. Jaeger's fame rests principally on his rôle as musical mentor

A J Jaeger, photographed by E T Holding

to Elgar, but it should also be noted that he was a close adviser to Parry, Walford Davies, and Coleridge-Taylor. Jaeger's rôle is often taken for granted, but as a facilitator for British music in Germany he was essential in attracting the attention of German conductors such as Julius Buths, Fritz Steinbach, Walter Josephson, Felix Weingartner and Richard Strauss.

Since the very edifice of British music was predicated on German values and measured against German standards, it was also an essential part of the equation that ultimate success for a British composer was to gain recognition abroad, but chiefly *in* Germany from his German peers. This was key to the success of Cowen's music and particularly for his *Scandinavian Symphony* (No 3) which was performed in Vienna, Prague, Berlin, and other German cities. It was clearly important to Stanford who, in the earliest stages of his career in the late 1870s, considered the performances of his operas, symphonies, chamber music, and choral works to be a vital criterion of Britain's musical renaissance. To some extent Stanford relied on his network of Austro-German friends – Frank in Hanover, Richter in Vienna, Bülow and Joachim in Berlin, Hiller in Cologne, Bruch and

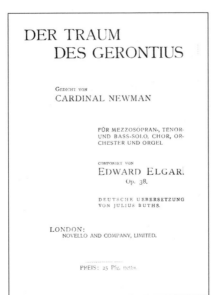

Promoting German editions of Elgar's choral works was a major preoccupation of his publishers in the early 1900s. Ultimately, however, few copies were sold outside those needed for performance.

Loewe in Breslau – but he was also facilitator for others such as Mackenzie and Parry in organising concerts at the Berlin Singakademie and in Brussels (where Kufferath presided) during the 1890s. Parry, a naturally less ambitious man, could only be persuaded to visit Germany the once when *Blest Pair of Sirens* was given at the Duisburg Festival in 1903 in a translation by Josephson. 'It is an exceptional occasion,' Jaeger wrote to Parry insistently, 'and surely for once you may be allowed to take exceptional liberties with your work. The Committee are inviting *all* the conductors of big societies in Rhineland and Westphalia (Steinbach, Buths, Schwickerath, Heubner, Haym, Reuter, Müller, etc, etc, etc. They can do much for your music and English music generally. So once more – Do go!'[5]

It was Jaeger who, in inviting Julius Buths to hear *The Dream of Gerontius* at Birmingham in 1900, helped to secure performances of the oratorio at the Lower Rhine Festivals in 1901 and 1902, the first time an English work had enjoyed such an honour. Buths' successful performance of *Gerontius* (and Strauss's endorsement of Elgar as the leader of the English progressivists) was the catalyst towards the oratorio's recognition in Britain, and other performances of the work throughout Germany were vital in elevating his status at home. A third Lower Rhine appearance with *The Apostles* in 1904 at Cologne under Fritz Steinbach placed Elgar in a different league from his older contemporaries, and with the First Symphony, which Richter, as its dedicatee, tirelessly promoted, Elgar's continental reputation had reached its apogee. Only Delius, who enjoyed support from Haym (at Elberfeld), Buths (at Düsseldorf), Cassirer (Berlin), and Witte (Essen) in works such as the Piano Concerto, *Appalachia, Paris, Das Lebenstanz, Koanga, Im Meerestrieben (Sea Drift)*, and *Romeo und Juliet auf dem Dorfe (A Village Romeo and Juliet)*, seriously rivalled Elgar's popularity, though the circumstances surrounding Delius's recognition was quite different, he being better known in Germany before his work was exported to England. It was only Delius who would be taken up again after the war, when *Fennimore and Gerda*, which had been promised for Cologne in 1914, was produced at Frankfurt am Main. It would not be heard in England for over forty years.

Elgar, as had so many other ambitious young musicians of his generation, aspired to study in Germany. All that kept him away was lack of money: he could not afford it. In fact, he first went to Germany in 1883, visiting Leipzig for a fortnight while Helen Weaver, the first of the girls to which he was engaged, was there to study German. All over Germany there were English-speaking expatriate communities, notably students attending language and finishing schools. In his autobiography the composer Arnold Bax remembered Dresden in 1906 which he found 'infested by finishing schools for Anglo-Saxon misses'.[6] When Elgar went again it was nine years later, in 1892; he was now married, and with Alice he went to Bayreuth where they saw *Meistersinger*, *Tristan* and *Parsifal*. Afterwards they went to Garmisch and experienced the Schuhplatt'l dances which would soon engender Elgar's *From the Bavarian Highlands*.

The following year the Elgars and Rosa Burley went to the Wagner Fest at Munich, hearing a variety of Wagner operas including *Meistersinger*, *Tristan* and *The Ring*. They found their experience of German life and culture so congenial they returned in 1894, again in 1895 and in 1897. In her account of the 1893 visit Rosa Burley underlined how at one with Germany she found Alice Elgar to be: 'German culture was one with which she was clearly in deep sympathy and I suspect she felt more at home in Munich than she would have done in many parts of England . . . she spoke in excellent German'.[7] Burley underlined the European nature of Alice Elgar's culture remarking on Hermann Sudermann's then recently published novel *Frau Sorge* which she was reading in German.[8] It is interesting in view of later history that this is a novel set in Prussia.

The pro-Teutonic mindset of the British musical establishment continued unabated until the First World War. Brahms, Wagner, and (to a lesser extent) Humperdinck were displaced by Richard Strauss whose visits to London after 1903 were the main annual attractions. To some of the older generation, led by Stanford, the influence of Strauss and the philosophy of Nietzsche was seen as unhealthy and was associated with a new breed of German nationalism. With the emergence of Germany as a major industrial power to rival Britain's won predominance, a cultural as well as political nationalism also began to assert itself in the last years of the nineteenth century, fed by an antagonism towards Germany's pro-Boer stance after the Jameson Raid and during the Boer War itself. The upshot of this rivalry was to question the pre-eminence of German cultural values. At first those pro-Teutons who owed much to their German mentors were reluctant to join the discourse, but the appointment of Richter, first to Birmingham (in 1885) and later to the Hallé (in preference to Cowen), provoked public protest from Sullivan who believed the posts should have gone to Englishman. This sentiment may have had few subscribers in the 1890s, but in the years before the outbreak of war it

The audience at Bayreuth as the Elgars would have experienced it in 1892, here congregating during the shorter interval.

grew into a chauvinistic juggernaut epitomised in Cecil Forsyth's attack on the immigrant musician. 'How long will it be,' Forsyth demanded, 'before we realise the fact that where the foreign musician is there is the enemy? He may come to this island in shoals, but he comes for one purpose only – the money he can take back across the water, and he well knows that the surest way to make his position firm here is to denationalise our music.' [9] By this time Joachim, Dannreuther, Goldschmidt, Manns, and Jaeger were all dead, and Richter had retired to Bayreuth.

When war broke out in August 1914, hostility to Germans and German music was a predictable if regrettable reaction, and it was not helped by Richter's and Bruch's repudiation of their honorary doctorates. (Bruch's was from Cambridge, Richter's from Oxford.) Politically liberal, Parry genuinely believed that Germany and Britain would not go to war, a sentiment he expressed with some fervour and irony in his incidental music to Aristophanes' comedy *The Acharnians* in February 1914.[10] He considered the arguments of his son-in-law Arthur Ponsonby, a prominent apologist for the Union of Democratic Control which advocated neutrality, but, losing patience with the German press and the military fixation of the Prussian mind, he supported the war effort. His association with the propaganda machine of Francis Younghusband's 'Fight for Right', which produced 'Jerusalem', was brief, and he robustly repudiated any suggestion of retribution after hostilities had ceased, though as we know, Parry did not live to see this come about. Stanford was probably the most vocal of his generation during the war, and was vituperative in the extreme in his rejoinder to Bruch's reaction of his Cambridge degree. He nevertheless fiercely condemned the notion that German music of the 'older' generations should be boycotted. Instead he blamed the decadence of Prussian nationalism on Strauss and Reger and lamented the demise of a great nation into musical anarchy. In acknowledging that the massive depletion of Germany's financial resources would seriously impede the progress of her orchestras and opera houses, Stanford saw the war as a cultural watershed and urged all branches of the musical profession in Britain to re-examine their artistic and commercial ideals:

> Much has been written about patriotism in business, and its utilisation to give stimulus to the nation's inventions and manufactures. Little has been said about its influence in the arts, and especially in music, the wholesomest aid to patriotism in the field and outside it. To stimulate artistic patriotism is the need of the moment; we must cultivate a trust in

British ideals and British effort at least as great as other nations have long shown in their own. If this patriotism has been long dormant, it is not too late to wake it. If it is restricted in amount, it can be extended. But the need of the moment is a lead, and a strong lead, not in the direction of exclusion of the best from without, but of the encouragement of all that is good within; and, given conditions of equal ability, a preference to the men and the productions of our own country.[11]

Stanford was correct in predicting a new patriotic fervour in the arts after the war; 'Englishness' became a watchword of the new generation and the expression of English nationalism in music, particularly in the works of Vaughan Williams, Holst, and Howells, was *de rigueur*. But what Stanford witnessed, and which left him culturally isolated, was the rejection of German aesthetic values in an English musical milieu where German musicians, publishers, professors, and conductors no longer existed as a cultural coefficient. Moreover, Stanford, the father of this new generation of British composers, looked on despondently as his pupils and the public at large rejected the values of their Victorian and Edwardian forbears.

NOTES and SOURCES

1. Parry, C H H: *College Addresses* (London, 1920) p 222
2. *ibid*, p 220
3. For further details on Dannreuther's Orme Square concerts, see Dibble, J: 'Edward Dannreuther and the Orme Square Phenomenon' in Bashford, C and Langley, L (eds): *Music and British Culture 1785-1914* (Oxford, 2000) p 275-98
4. See Dibble, J: 'Grove's Musical Dictionary: A National Document' in White, H & Murphy, M (eds): *Musical Constructions of Nationalism: Essay on the History and Ideology of European Musical Culture 1800-1945*, pp 33-50
5. Letter from Jaeger to Parry, 13 May 1903, Shulbrede Priory; see Dibble, J: *C. Hubert H. Parry: His Life and Music* (Oxford, 1992) p 390
6. Bax, [Sir] Arnold, ed Foreman, Lewis: *Farewell My Youth and other writings.* (Aldershot, Scolar Press, 1992) p 27
7. Burley, Rosa and Carruthers, Frank C: *Edward Elgar: the record of a friendship* (Barrie & Jenkins, 1972) p 65
8. *op cit*, p 62
9. Forsyth, C: *Music and Nationalism* (London, 1911) p 260
10. See Dibble: *op cit*, p 467-8
11. Stanford, C V: 'Music and the War', *Quarterly Review* (1915) p 408; also in *Interludes, Records and Reflections* (London, 1922) pp 123-4

PRO PATRIA

1914–1918

ARTHUR ARMSTRONG-DASH
RUPERT BOROWSKI
GILBERT HEARN BREACH
ERIC BROWN
GEORGE BURCHELL
GEO. SAINTON KAYE BUTTERWORTH
PHILIP EVERSHED CHAPMAN
DONALD JOHN STUART CHAPMAN
ROHAN CLENSY
ERNEST COSTER
CHARLES DIXON
ROGER MACDONNELL EVANSON
WILFRID RUPERT BUCKNALL EYRE
ERNEST BRISTOW FARRAR
SEYMOUR THOMAS GOODWIN
ADOLPHE GOOSSENS
WILFRID JOHN HARE
JOHN HATCHMAN
ARTHUR CLEMENTS HEBERDEN
HERBERT NOEL HOSKING
ELI HUDSON
JOSEPH KNOWLES IRELAND
HARRY DUKINFIELD JONES
CLAUD PERCY MACKNESS
EDWARD MASON
ALBERT MIDGLEY
ALFRED GEORGE MILLARD
RALPH WINDSOR PARKER
HAROLD WILLIAM PICKETT
HENRY PYCOCK
HARRY RETFORD
ERIC WALTER ROPER
LEONARD SADGROVE
KENNETH BRUCE STUART
WILLIAM HIBBERT WANKLYN
FRANCIS PURCELL WARREN
ARTHUR BENJAMIN WILKINSON
CECIL KEITH FOYLE WRIGHT

CHAPTER 3

The WINNOWING-FAN
British Music in Wartime

Lewis Foreman

The First World War broke out during an August Bank Holiday and
the unexpected ending of normal life in a matter of a couple of days
was unprecedented. Indeed, for the music profession it must have
seemed like the end of the world – certainly of the world as it had
been known. For overnight, disaster struck: with the cessation of
normal musical activity, which had been at a frenetic level throughout
'that sinister carnival time',[1] the London summer of 1914, not only
was music suddenly silent but for many professional musicians the
majority of their income seemed to have gone too. The necessity of
making a living was, of course, most musicians' immediate concern,
in view of the apparent disaster that faced most of them in August
1914: nothing less than the total collapse of British musical life for the
duration. The five major choral festivals due that autumn were
cancelled, as were the main competitive festivals; music teachers were
suddenly not required; sales of pianos fell dramatically. One wonders
how many joined up in August 1914 merely for the meagre army pay.

The outbreak of war was initially received in many quarters with
enthusiasm, excitement and a euphoric outburst of jingoistic feeling.
Very quickly music returned to a more normal pattern; even so, many
leading players and composers joined up and were not available for
musical engagements. The war certainly signalled a new culture
characterised by the rise of popular songs later indissolubly linked
with the period.[2] Typical was the establishment of 'Tipperary' as a
song associated with the war effort. In December 1914 *The Musical
Times* told the story of what by then was the army's pre-eminent
marching song, including a facsimile of the manuscript and a music
type version of the tune, noting that 'sales have now passed the
second million'.[3] It was probably the music publishing coup of all
time, and indeed may be said to have saved the record industry, or at
least HMV, with its biggest hit since the invention of disc recording.

FACING PAGE: *The Royal College of Music war memorial.*

There were many recorded versions, though possibly John McCormack's has proved most enduring (Victor 64476, variously reissued on LP and CD).

In a profession in which continental attitudes had previously had so long-standing a sway, many individuals found themselves the unwitting victims of the new reality. In the summer of 1914, music was probably the most cosmopolitan activity in daily life, with foreign and particularly German musicians revered for their assumed innate musicality and connection with the musical world. The War was especially traumatic for the musical profession, for in almost no other aspect of British life were German practice and German practitioners so fully integrated into the day-to-day round. Immediately many British musicians who had previously found it politic to adopt continental names found the opposite was true. Others who were of continental extraction changed; thus the conductor Basil Hindenberg found it expedient to become Basil Cameron, the name he used for the rest of his life. Cheltenham born and bred, Gustav von Holst, known to his great friend Ralph Vaughan Williams as 'v', and of Baltic extraction several generations before, found himself harassed by the police and eventually changed his name by deed poll, dropping the von. The pianist Mark Hambourg had to sue for libel when reported German in the press, the court finding showing him to be of Russian parentage on both sides.[4]

Anyone with a German name was likely to become the butt of super-patriots, and strangely Stanford, one of the most integrated of British musicians into German life and practice, and a bilingual German speaker, initiated an action against the music publishers Augener. Parry noted in his diary on 13 October 'Stanford's case against Augener collapsed ignominiously. The Board of Trade deciding that they were not 'Alien Enemies', but technically a British Firm.'[5] A similar attack on the publisher Bosworth was answered by the reprinting of an earlier article on Arthur E Bosworth's status as an English music publisher in the November issue of *The Musical Times* with the caption 'the above serves as further answer to a contemptible attack on Bosworth & Co'.[6]

There was what in retrospect now appears to be excessive anti-German sentiment extending to such matters as the use of British rather than 'German' fingering on the piano! The much publicised renouncing of his English honorary degrees by Hans Richter elicited the response 'it would be impossible for him to resign the degree, though he can cease to use the title of Doctor of Music of this University which was conferred upon him'. After his death in 1916 *The Music Student* published a letter from him [7] to an English friend which seems perhaps somewhat nearer the truth of a great musician's sadness at the turn of events:

A World-Famous Conductor

No one would deny Hans Richter a place among the greatest of conductors . . . One of . . . Richter's last letters was to a London friend and arrived on December 5th [1916], the very day of this great conductor's death. It ran: 'Give my love to my friends, and all the artists who worked with me, when you meet them. They are with me in my waking hours and in my dreams, and my thoughts of them are always good and pleasurable. With thankfulness I think of the hours I spent with them. They were the happiest of my artistic life.' These are not the words of a man who hated England!

The war also gave the British piano industry an unprecedented opportunity to develop in the absence of German competition, and leading musicians were favourite targets if they performed on German instruments. Unfortunately, without German competition 'prices rose almost as rapidly as quality deteriorated'. [8]

Many German-born musicians whose careers had centred on the United Kingdom either left the country or were expelled. An example was Maria Janotha, the pianist, who it was reported was suddenly deported on Sunday, 8 August 1915. Janotha had been the court pianist to the Kaiser and as one press report surmised: 'it must be assumed that she has betrayed her German sympathies too openly. She was born at Czestochova, near Warsaw, and has generally been regarded as a German Pole. She was given a Jubilee medal by Queen Victoria.' [9]

Yet, surprisingly quickly, stability was achieved. The Promenade Concerts carried on – much against

MISS JANOTHA.
COURT PIANISTE TO H.I.M. THE GERMAN EMPEROR

expectations and, noted *The Musical Times* in its September 1914 issue, 'the success that has so far attended the Queen's Hall Promenade Concerts is one of the most encouraging signs of the times'. *The Musical Times* reported the first concert:

> The opening of the season on Saturday, August 15, presented a scene of great enthusiasm. The principals of the Orchestra were welcomed one by one, and lastly Sir Henry Wood received a great ovation. The National Anthem, 'La Marseillaise' and 'God Bless the Prince of Wales' were sung, and a typical 'popular' programme succeeded. Mackenzie's 'Britannia' Overture, Sibelius's 'Valse Triste', and Percy Grainger's orchestral adaptations of the Londonderry Air and 'Shepherd's Hey' were enthusiastically received, the last being encored . . . and songs . . . in patriotic vein [sung] by Herbert Heyner.[10]

Later Wood's orchestrations of the Belgian national song, Campenhout's *La Nouvelle Brabançonne*, was introduced on August 29 and the Russian national anthem on 1 September.[11]

Initially anti-German feeling resulted in attempts to suppress the German music of the previous fifty years, and the first night of the Proms saw Tchaikovsky's *Italian Caprice* substituted for Strauss's *Don Juan,* and a Franco-Russian programme for a Wagner night. But this phase soon passed and, by the time of the first Queen's Hall Symphony Concert on 17 October, a traditional 'safe' programme of Beethoven, Brahms and Tchaikovsky was offered, though 'patriotic' programmes were also being given everywhere.

Wood was criticised for playing German music, an invective that continued into 1915 and beyond, but was not reflected by the wider public who supported him. The following year's Proms saw a renewal of the objection to the performance of German music. Sir Arthur Markham, MP, during an adjournment debate before the Autumn recess in 1915 remarked:

. . . the House does not appreciate the fact that we are at war. Take, for instance, the case of Sir Edgar Speyer,

Sir Henry J Wood

MUSIC AND THE WAR.

PATRIOTISM AT THE FIRST PROMENADE CONCERT.

Sir Henry Wood was received on Saturday night at the first concert of his twentieth year of the Promenades with something more than the usual enthusiasm. Every seat in the Queen's Hall seemed to be occupied, and there was no possibility of walking about down below.

This large audience had gathered together partly for old sake's sake, partly to show their appreciation of the decision to keep the concerts going just as usual, and partly, no doubt, to avail themselves of the opportunity of singing the National Anthem and the Marseillaise in conjunction. This was done with a quiet conviction which was far removed from any jingo spirit. Other opportunities will be given, and with a little better acquaintance with the words of the former and the tune of the latter, so musical an audience might produce a wonderful effect. " God bless the Prince of Wales " was then played, but nobody knew the words. The Russian and Belgian national anthems are to follow as soon as possible.

Some alterations have been made in the early programmes. These are days in which neither Strauss nor Don Juan can mean very much to us ; and for the traditional Monday evening there was substituted last night a Franco-Russian programme. This was done not from any narrow conception of patriotism, but out of respect for the natural feelings of the audience. It would be a pity, however, if those feelings were allowed to descend to the level of prejudice, and if the conductor thought it necessary to hamper himself unduly in his choice of music.

The Press were generally sympathetic to the performance of the German masters.
This cutting is from The Daily Telegraph.

who, as everyone knows, is the proprietor of the Queen's Hall. I suppose it is because he is of German origin that we in this country are to be treated during the next few weeks by Sir Henry Wood to a series of concerts entirely composed of German music. I have the whole of the programmes here, from which it will be seen that some of the concerts are to be devoted entirely to Wagner's music. What would France or Russia do under conditions of this kind? The people are not recognising the seriousness of the position. I cannot understand how people can go to listen to German music, when every people in the world, except ourselves, would not tolerate during a time of war that they should be entertained by German music. But as the Queen's Hall belongs to him, I suppose we in this country are to be instilled with German virtues.[12]

But wiser counsels prevailed. 'Should Teutonic music of any period whatever be performed in this country at the present juncture?' asked *The Musical Times* and referring to Sir Arthur Markham's remarks noted that he had 'wrongly attributed the programme to the supposed influence of Sir Edgar Speyer, who has now nothing to do with Queen's Hall or its newly organised orchestra'.

Speyer had previously headed the Queen's Hall syndicate and had been responsible for bringing Richard Strauss to London. As a significant financial player in London music he was therefore resented by those who may have felt he kept British music from the platform. In fact Speyer had asked Elgar for the Second Symphony in 1911.[13] Speyer's eventual emigration to the USA was in the longer term a significant loss to music in England.

The composer Hubert Bath vehemently supported the attempt to boycott. However, Sir Henry Wood produced programmes, which, while they excluded the music of living Teutonic composers, drew freely from the classics, including Brahms and Wagner. *The Musical Times* applauded this solution: 'We think the compromise is a perfectly rational one. The music of these composers has been our mother's milk, and we cannot banish it from our memory even if we would, because it is part of our mental equipment. Bach, Haydn, Mozart, Beethoven, Mendelssohn had nothing to do with 20th century mad German megalomania. Both England and Prussia were on the side of the angels in Beethoven's time.'

According to one annual review of the time 'nearly all the concerts and recitals arranged for the autumn were cancelled'[14] but it is clear that while the usual visiting virtuosi, particularly those from Germany and the Austrian Empire, did not come, now technically being enemy aliens, and the opera season did not take place, there was a fairly active scene, though activity varied in different parts of the country.

The young pianist Arthur Alexander, friend of Arnold Bax and a recent graduate from the Royal Academy of Music, had returned to his family home in New Zealand before war broke out and his friend Tim Braithwaite's letter of 5 December vividly evokes the London scene after three months of war.

Now for the news. I will begin with the war and work back to myself. Just what is happening you will know as well as I do, but I can perhaps tell you a little bit about London: – Soldiers everywhere, drilling, marching, eating, drinking, riding in trains, trams & 'buses, you can't escape them, and there is no need to, as they are a fine, wholesome looking lot of men, and mostly well behaved & pleasant to meet. The male civil population is rather small, but millions of women have come to the front (I wish they had gone) so that London is about as full as ever. After sunset most of the lights are either lowered or out, so that it is almost dark. Search lights at Hyde Park Corner, the Admiralty, and at other points, search for Zeppelins, and I believe other games much favoured by darkness go on in and around the Squares of Leicester & Soho – but of this I have no personal knowledge, and I only have the support of rumours. The Theatres are mostly open and 'business as usual' is the generally accepted motto. We travel in trains with the blinds down (here again you'll see possibilities) and on foot under the protection of bomb-proof umbrellas, or so *Truth* had it a fortnight or so ago. Mr Shaw has written a long pamphlet entitled 'Common sense about the war' which seems to have upset a lot of sober minded people, though I believe that when the air has cleared and we can see by the cold light of day we shall find in it a lot more truth than malice; in fact, most of it reads, for me, as very clear, cool-headed common sense, though some of it I can't swallow. A number of Irish newspapers have been writing rather nasty things, or so I believe, but on the whole we are more or less unanimous, and all most hopeful & cheery. Now as to how the war has affected music. The Promenade Concerts were held as usual, & the Symphony & Philharmonic are on again. A few British compositions have figured in the programmes, including Arnold's [Bax] Fatherland, a new piece by Delius, & some less interesting things; but Bach, Beethoven, & Brahms still hold the field. Patriotic concerts are being given in most parts of England, & a host of vulgarities bearing Union-Jack covers come for review in *The Music Student*, and get very small shrift from me. Mackenzie is giving an all British orchestral concert this term, when one can absorb the subtle beauties of Cowen, Edward German, Eric Grant, Parry, & F Corder;[15] the latter having unearthed an Operatic Aria of the mid-Victorian era, containing a martial strain accompanied (in short chords) by the whole band! I believe that German & Austrian musicians have been banished from our large orchestras, & that all the Blue Hungarian bands have become Pink Belgian, without undergoing any other change, which matters not at all, as the players are, & were, all English! César Franck's Symphony is to be done in January, Beecham conducting, Psyche I heard at the Promenades, and Eolides was done one

OUR MUSICIANS AND THE WAR PAGE

MAJOR A. CORBETT-SMITH

Now invalided home, Major Corbett-Smith has spent some useful hours in writing *The Retreat from Mons*—a thrilling book. He is Secretary General of the Naval and Military Musical Union, and a gifted singer, pianist, lecturer and composer. It may be interesting news to some of our readers if we let out a little secret. Aston Tyrrold, the popular song composer, and Major Corbett-Smith are on very intimate terms; it is rumoured that they even share the same boots.

LIEUTENANT EDWARD MASON

"He was a brave man, Sir—a pattern for officers and men." So said Edward Mason's Sergeant, after his death. He was only in his thirty-seventh year when he was killed in a hail of machine-gun bullets near Fromelles. As 'cellist and 'cello teacher at Eton College, as quartet player, and as choral and orchestral conductor, Mason will be greatly missed. The Edward Mason Choir had become one of the outstanding features of London musical life.

LIEUTENANT ROBERT MADDER

With sadness we record the death, in action, of our former secretary of the *Music Student* "Three Years' Fund," Robert Madder (born 1887). He was first flautist and hon. treasurer of the London Shipping Orchestral Society, a member of the Sutton Circle, and later, of the Central London Circle of the Home Music Study Union. He was attached to the Machine Gun Section of the 1/5th Gloucesters, and was killed instantaneously when leaving a captured trench.

BENJAMIN JAMES DALE

On holiday in Germany when war broke out, B. J. Dale has been at Ruhleben ever since. He was born in 1885, became an R.A.M. student in 1900, and was awarded the Costa Scholarship for Composition in 1901. Later he became a professor of the R.A.M. His compositions include the piano piece affectionately known as "the Dale Sonata," *Night Fancies* for piano, and a Suite for viola and piano. At Ruhleben Mr. Dale is active in musical work.

A typical feature from the wartime pages of The Music Student

Sunday in October. Dale is a prisoner now in Berlin; he went a Germanying for his summer holidays & was captured at Munich when war broke out. Kastner, Beringer & Wesseley are still with us; Cole & Bell have gone to fight; there is no change otherwise at the Institution. I dare say, we shall feel the pinch next term, but we are all busy so far.[16]

The major choral festivals announced for the autumn, including Norwich, the Three Choirs and that at Birmingham were cancelled, but one continued, that at Brighton which was successfully given in November and received an up-beat report in *The Musical Times*[17] not only for the British and other new music performed but also for Sir Henry Wood conducting the last act of *Lohengrin* and extracts from *Parsifal* and *Die Walküre*.

Seven concerts were to be given [in the Dome] . . . beginning with Elijah [and] ending . . . with Messiah, and including . . . orchestral music ranging from Debussy and Stravinsky to the modest efforts of two young lady composers.

It was a sign of the times that in a concert of new music conducted by Beecham including Debussy's *Printemps*, Rimsky-Korsakov's *Antar*, Stravinsky's suite from *The Firebird* and Delius's *First Dance Rhapsody,* one Miss Doris Woodall sang *Abide With Me*. The beefy patriotic aspect of British choral music was represented by Sir Frederick Bridge's settings of Kipling's *The Ballad of the Campherdown*, while Edith Swepstone's *Two Scenes from Morte d'Arthur* heralded what would be a growing wartime trend of playing music evoking British military and naval exploits of the past, not least the legends of heroes such as King Arthur and Sir Francis Drake[18] sleeping until they heard the call.

The festival commission for Brighton was Sir Hubert Parry's tone poem *From Death to Life*. Doubtless it had been first asked for before war had become a reality, but it was only completed in October. At Brighton its two linked movements were subtitled 'Lament' and 'Consolation', but by the time it was heard again at Queen's Hall these had become 'Via Mortis' and 'Via Vitae'. The writer of the programme notes for those early performances summarised it as 'Death, arm-in-arm with fate, walks ever in our midst, while life unceasingly protests, deplores, defies, despairs and finally triumphs spiritually'.[19] Despite its many attractive features it lacked the brilliance of Elgar and although at the end the march theme of the second part rises to an affirmative peroration, one could well imagine its message was one some might have preferred to avoid in the early months of the War.

> Its importance rests upon the lofty beauty of the first slow movement and
> the fact that its thought has been directly suggested by the War. The
> second part recalls the quick-step march with which a regimental band
> leaves the soldier's grave.[20]

Parry was not happy with it, uncertain that he had struck the right
note. After its second performance at Queen's Hall the following
March he noted in his diary 'Death to Life went capitally but I could
feel it was not a success'.[21] Others seem to have agreed with him and
it remained unplayed for 76 years until revived for two recordings
made almost simultaneously in 1991.[22]

Many young composers enlisted, although a small number of now
famous names - including Bax, Ireland and Heseltine - did not, the
first two having failed medicals. Lists were quickly published of those
who had joined the forces, as well as photographs of musicians, both
well-known and unknown, in uniform.

It is interesting to contrast the opposing views at the time, as
stated by Arthur Bliss and Philip Heseltine. Only three years
separated Arthur Bliss from the younger Philip Heseltine (later
known as Peter Warlock). Bliss wrote:[23]

> The crash of a European War on our very beaches sucked me into its
> undertow without my ever probing the consequences. My action was
> purely automatic, sparked off by a feeling of outrage at the cause of the
> war, of a debt owed, and added to this was the spirit of adventure and the
> heady excitement which the actions of my own contemporaries
> engendered. Since then, the ever-deepening horrors of wars have made
> the very word the more hideous in our language, but at that time its vague
> unknown possibilities made it remote from realistic definition.

Heseltine expressed his thoughts at about the time war broke out in
1914, in a letter to his mentor Frederick Delius:[24]

> I have never been able to understand the sentiment of patriotism, the love
> of empire: it has always seemed to me so empty and intangible an idea, so
> impersonal and so supremely unimportant as regards the things which
> really matter – which are all the common heritage of humanity, without
> distinction of race or nationality . . .

Possibly Sir Hubert Parry best expressed the position occupied by
many fair-minded artistic people when he confessed[25] that he had
been for a quarter century or more a pro-Teuton.

At the Royal College of Music, Parry felt it all deeply, particularly
concerned that irreplaceable talent was being put at risk. When
Vaughan Williams decided to join up, Parry argued:[26]

You have already served your country in very notable and exceptional
ways and are likely to do so again: and such folks should be shielded from
risk rather than be exposed to it.

Vaughan Williams's war experiences as a private in the 2/4th Field
Ambulance were clearly arduous and have been explored by Stephen
Connock[27] and others. RVW enlisted in the RAMC Territorial Force
on New Year's Eve 1914 at first remaining near home at Chelsea
Barracks. Early in March his unit found itself at Watford, when,
incidentally, Delius was living there as a refugee from his home in
France. RVW's unit was first posted north of Arras, which saw fierce
fighting in 1915, and later they moved to Ecoivres and the Somme;
from June to November 1916 his unit was near Vimy Ridge. Later
they were posted to Salonika before RVW underwent officer training
and subsequently found himself in France during the German
advance of March 1918. These must have been experiences that were
common to many, but we now know in Vaughan Williams' case they
engendered his *Pastoral Symphony*. Although initially not recognised
for what it was, Vaughan Williams's symphony uniquely
encapsulates the sorrow and the pity of war in a major work of art
which will last.

∽   ∽   ∽

Summer had been the time to visit Germany, as Elgar himself had
done in the 1890s. Thus on the outbreak of war, as mentioned in Tim
Braithwaite's letter quoted above, a sizeable number of Brits found
themselves trapped in Germany, at first scarcely able to take in the
fact that war had been declared. Among these was a goodly number
of musicians, who had been visiting Bayreuth and other summer
festivals, had been students, or had been residents occupying
positions as teachers, conductors and players, all essential experience
before 1914 for a good job on returning home.

Initially the German Defence of the Realm Act required all foreigners
to register and report to the police every day. But the internment of
German civilians in Britain sparked the Germans into reprisal, and
they chose the Ruhleben racecourse near Berlin, one of the largest
trotting courses in Germany, to improvise a prison camp for civilians.
There were 14 stone stables, and each was used to house 250 men.

British women had been repatriated during October, and on 5th
November British male civilians began to be sent from all over

Germany to Ruhleben and some 4,000 arrived during the first few weeks. This included nearly 1,000 businessmen and almost as many from the professions and academia.

A M D Hughes who was repatriated after only a short internment wrote about the pre-war British community in Germany:

> One saw with surprise how many of the British of all classes earn their living in this country - jockeys and trainers, golf and tennis professionals, foremen and workers from factories, seamen and ship's stewards . . . merchants and business men, some in a big way; artists and musicians from the schools and centres of art, and the first fruits of the holiday traffic from England, which had just arrived on 4 August, and in which the most conspicuous elements were undergrads, public school masters and invalids for the Spas.[28]

Musicians held at Ruhleben included composers Edgar Bainton, Benjamin J Dale and Ernest Macmillan from Canada; Carl Fuchs the first cello of the Hallé Orchestra and cellist of the Brodsky Quartet; the Welsh composer Bryceson Treharne recently returned from Adelaide; Leigh Henry self-style avant-gardiste; Percy Hull of Hereford Cathedral; Frederick Keel singer and writer of ballads, and Roland Boquet, songwriter, friend of Bax and a long-time resident in Dresden. Other musicians interned, who were more or less celebrated in their day, included conductor Charles F Adler; the Scottish violinist and conductor J Peebles-Conn, who for five years had been leader and sub-conductor of the Bielefeld-Municipal Orchestra; William Lindsay; Quentin Morvaren; Waldemar Pauer; Arthur Speed; Charles Weber conductor of the Lübeck Opera House, and Arthur Williams. By the summer of 1915 the forty or so professional instrumentalists became so organised they had formed a camp Society of Professional Musicians which 'took charge of the concerts and gave all qualified conductors their chance with the orchestra'.[29]

After an initial period of privation and disorganisation, Ruhleben became unique among prison camps in Germany for the self-governing structure that emerged and for the extensive educational and artistic pursuits that were organised including many concerts which the *Lageroffizier*, Baron von Taube, viewed benignly and would himself attend. The report of the first concert season in the printed camp magazine extends to three and a half pages and is remarkable for the central place given to German music including a 'red letter programme comprising works by Schillings and Strauss'.[30]

∽   ∽   ∽

SCENES FROM RUHLEBEN

ABOVE: *The musicians in Ruhleben;*

LEFT: *three prisoners of war at Ruhleben (note their dress), 27 March 1915, drawing by W O'Sullivan Malone;*

BELOW: *a concert at Ruhleben, illustration from* The Ruhleben Camp Magazine *No 5, Christmas 1916, showing the original 1916 caption.*

LEBEN MUSICAL SOCIETY.   FULL ORCHESTRA.

And thus the war continued. During 1915 there was an enormous range of musical activity. At the end of May, Sir Henry Wood indicated he had conducted 112 concerts in the previous 9 months. Although the great choral festivals were in abeyance, choral music was performed throughout the year. In Manchester on 7 January, Thomas Beecham, a recurring name synonymous with quality and enterprise, conducted the Hallé Orchestra and choirs in Berlioz's *Te Deum* as well as *Fatherland*, Arnold Bax's short choral setting of words that later became the Finnish national anthem, but in fact was intended by Bax as a hymn to Ireland. He must have been nonplussed to find it sung as an expression of patriotic fervour. Also in Beecham's concert came Delius's *Paris* and the last scene from Stravinsky's *Petroushka*.

On 21 January Beecham deputised for Bantock at three days' notice to conduct a complete performance of Bantock's epic setting of Fitzgerald's *Omar Khayyám*, a work which runs for about three hours and makes enormous choral and orchestral demands. Clearly a large constituency of talented performers was still available as was their audience. Continuing this vein of exploratory programming, Beecham's later novelties included Ethel Smyth's short but difficult choral works *Hey Nonny No* and *Sleepless Dreams* on 4 November.

The Ladies Night of the Bristol Madrigal Society on 14 January celebrated the fiftieth concert conducted by Mr Daniel W Rootham, Stanford (*Ode on Time*) and Parry (*La Belle Dame Sans Merci*) producing new works in a desperate attempt to maintain normality. Provincial choral societies also continued, *Messiah* being most popular, though *Gerontius*, which was becoming a work of consolation for many, also enjoyed many performances. This was perhaps brought into closest focus by Clara Butt's week of *Gerontius* at Queen's Hall from 8-12 May, 1916, preceded by performances in Leeds and Bradford. The *Yorkshire Observer*[31] reported:

> Quite a brilliant start was given to Mme Clara Butt's remarkable venture last night, when the Leeds Town Hall held a crowded audience gathered to listen to 'The Dream of Gerontius' under the composer's direction, the performance of that now famous work being preceded by the production of two new choral pieces from his pen, illustrating phases of the nation's present ordeal. The orchestra was as well filled as the body of the hall – tenanted by the ranks of the Leeds choral Union and the Hallé Orchestra, neither of which seemed to have suffered material diminution though Derby drafts or others, while the picturesque costume of some nurses at the top lent a touch of colour and a hint of significance to a concert closely associated with the war.

Clara Butt's remarks on the significance of the occasion were widely quoted. Her aim was 'not to provide a series of concerts calculated to attract the public in the ordinary manner, but to challenge London at the present time with something definitely spiritual and mystic.' [32]

The central part of Butt's thesis appears in the extract reproduced overleaf from an unidentified cutting, after which Butt concluded 'there is a new attitude to death . . . many people that had no faith before the war are now hungering to believe that beyond the grave there is life.' [33]

As an example of local enterprise the Central Croydon Choral Society gave Bantock's early cantata *The Fire-Worshippers* on February 13, 1915. On 10 April that year, Worcester Cathedral hosted 725 voices from across Worcestershire for Bach's *Christmas Oratorio* in Ivor Atkins' 75-minute version excluding all but one aria, and presumably sung in English.

Yet musical activity varied from place to place. In Birmingham, for example, the December 1914 issue of *The Musical Times* reported[34] that after the cancellation of the Festival 'musical matters are assuming their normal aspect to a certain extent' and the Birmingham Festival Choral Society mounted a performance of Mendelssohn's *Elijah* on October 21. Yet the following spring season was the poorest anyone could remember and the Festival Choral Society and Theatre Royal Promenade concerts were abandoned. Although there was only one concert anywhere during September 1914, a full range of activities were later promoted, including Sullivan's *The Golden Legend* on October 16. Big names could still attract a crowd, but only allied artists and artists who were technically refugees were available. This not only enabled a new generation of British artists to emerge but also guaranteed support for those performers on the circuit.

Thus when Clara Butt returned from her world tour and chose to make her début in Birmingham Town Hall on 1 February 1915 hundreds were turned away. Butt's appearance in London on 27 February marked her earliest full assumption of the rôle of the angel in Elgar's *Gerontius*. Elgar himself first appeared in Birmingham with the London Symphony Orchestra in a programme which included Dvorak's *New World Symphony*, the eminent Belgian pianist Arthur de Greef in Saint-Saëns' G minor Piano Concerto and de Greef's own *Fantasia on Old Flemish Folksongs*, as well as Elgar's *Carillon* recited by Constance Collier. Sir Edward and the LSO were in Liverpool on 2 March and Glasgow on 5 March.

a widely felt desire on the part of the public in these trying times.

Madame Clara Butt expressed her views in a conversation with Mr. Harold Begbie, when she asked :—" Don't you think that people will be glad to hear something which is definitely spiritual? Isn't it time, I mean, that art in England should try to express the new attitude of the English mind towards the life after death? I feel so strongly that one performance a year in London of a work like ' Gerontius ' is utterly ridiculous, especially when it is done in a hall four times too large for it. I want the people to get it into their bones, and to really love it, and I am sure they will, given the proper chance. I cannot tell you how I feel the need for something in the nature of a protest or a challenge. We are a nation in mourning. Life as it existed two years ago has ceased. And in the midst of this tremendous upheaval, when youth is dying for us, I want the people to come to the Queen's Hall, and, with the help of Cardinal Newman's wonderful poem and Elgar's music, to realize some spiritual truths, and to give them a week of beautiful thoughts. I am the last person in the world to deride comedy and amusement," she said, " but my point is this : the greater things in life should never be neglected by art; but to neglect them now, in a time like this—in a time of such sorrow and pain—to limit art only to amusement—this is bad. And I am not afraid to go much further. I am sure that no nation can be great which is not religious. I am perfectly certain that nearly all our tragic blunders—perhaps all of them—can be traced to our materialism, for materialism breeds apathy and self-satisfaction."

Madame Clara Butt believes that there is a new attitude towards death. She holds that many peo[...]

ABOVE: *Clara Butt's remarks on the spiritual life at the time of the series of performances of* The Dream of Gerontius *were widely reported in the press*

RIGHT:
Clara Butt, a 1914 portrait by Swaine

There were notable Delius performances; Beecham repeated *Paris* in London at a Royal Philharmonic Society concert on 26 January, and accompanied young Benno Moiseiwitsch in Delius's Piano Concerto at the LSO's Queen's Hall concert on 8 February.

On 12 January, the violinist Albert Sammons, having been discovered by Beecham as a restaurant violinist before the War and led Beecham's orchestra since 1910, made his solo début in Beethoven's Concerto in Glasgow, a performance well received and repeated at Queen's Hall on 12 April, while in Liverpool Ysaÿe appeared for the first time in public since his adventurous and well-reported escape from Belgium, where he had lost all except his Strad, on which he played Viotti's Violin Concerto No 22. At Liverpool, Sir Henry Wood included Brahms's Third Symphony, and the great German composers, including Wagner, which continued to be supported by the public. Typical was the Bach-Beethoven-Brahms Festival at Queen's Hall in April. Recent Teutonic works were embargoed, but Strauss's *Tod und Verklärung* was heard in Belfast on 26 March, though Strauss's royalties were frozen for the duration.

Many organisations were active: the Committee of Music in War-time; the persistent efforts of Isidore de Lara, especially for British composers; Broadwood's Camp Concerts, and many others, were widely supported and reported. Longstanding series, such as Thomas Dunhill's Chamber Concerts and the Royal Philharmonic Society, contrived to keep going, a typically interesting programme being the second Dunhill Concert of works by women, which included Katherine Eggar's Piano Quintet. De Lara's concert on 25 March heard John Ireland's new Trio for Piano, Clarinet and Cello, much later rewritten as his Third Piano Trio, while that on 10 June featured the early Piano Quartet in A minor by Arthur Bliss which despite being printed, Bliss later withdrew.

THE PROMOTER OF "ALL BRITISH" CONCERTS

ISIDORE DE LARA

Isidore de Lara from the pages of The Music Student

The pre-war craze for child prodigies, usually from Europe was reflected in young British instrumentalists brought forward at an early age, notably at the Edgbaston Botanical Gardens on June 5 when Grieg's Sonata Op 8 was given by Master Paul Beard. Previously 'Master Solomon' had appeared at the Promenade Concert in Grieg's Piano Concerto.[35] Generally concerts ended much earlier than hitherto, and the Royal Choral Society pioneered Saturday afternoon performances.

At the colleges of music, young artists continued to emerge, a typical example being the Australian Arthur Benjamin, who had made a considerable splash as a pianist with Herbert Howell's romantic big-boned Piano Concerto[36] in a Royal College of Music concert at Queen's Hall, conducted by Stanford, on 10 July 1914. He subsequently appeared in the César Franck *Symphonic Variations* also conducted by Stanford on 16 February 1915 at the Royal College of Music. Soon after this Benjamin joined up, later transferred to the Royal Flying Corps and was shot down and taken prisoner for the remainder of the war.

New music by the allies – notably French and Russian – included the works of Debussy, Stravinsky and Ravel. March 17 saw the first English performance of Ravel's *Trois Poèmes de Stéphane Mallarmé* given by Jane Barthori-Engel with Beecham conducting. The Societé des Concerts Français at the Aeolian Hall on 18 June presented the Italian pianist-composer Alfredo Casella in the first performance of Ravel's new piano trio which seems to have been well received. The Music Club at the Grafton Galleries on 25 January included Carrie Tubb in Stravinsky's *Three Japanese Songs* with small orchestra and Albert Sammons introduced Delius's *Légende* with three of Delius's songs newly orchestrated.

The closure of Covent Garden Opera House ended an era. But after a brief period when opera was not staged in London, opera in English flourished, notably under the influence of Sir Thomas Beecham. During the Spring of 1915, London's Shaftesbury Theatre had a remarkable success with a ten-week run including *The Tales of Hoffmann*, *Madame Butterfly*, *La Bohème* and *Rigoletto* under the batons of Hubert Bath and Hamish MacCunn. A second season at the Shaftesbury Theatre started with Gounod's *Roméo et Juliette* on October 2. The season was long-running, four other conductors taking over from Beecham.

But the opera public does not seem to have been automatic, for in

May, Vladimir Rosing's season of French and Russian repertoire at the London Opera House in Kingsway failed for want of public support, though artistically it may have been the better venture, including Tchaikovsky's *Pique Dame* and the first UK performance of Rachmaninov's opera *Aleko,* along with *Madame Butterfly* and Delibes' *Lakmé,* the latter two with a Japanese Mimi and a Hindu singer respectively. Benefit concerts were held on 15 and 17 July to relieve the financial distress of the performers.

The London season also saw the Carl Rosa Company at the Marlborough Theatre, Moody-Manners at Croydon, and D'Oyly Carte at Hammersmith. Out of London, Moody-Manners (who premièred Colin McAlpin's prize-winning one-acter *The Vow*) were in Nottingham in May; Carl Rosa and the O'Mara Opera Company at Manchester's Gaiety Theatre. The newly-formed Harrison-Frewin Opera Company appeared at Birmingham's Alexandra Theatre with popular operas, plus Halévy's *La Juive* and Alfred Bruneau's powerful anti-war drama from the Franco-Prussian War *The Attack on the Mill,* but its biggest success was Balfe's *The Bohemian Girl.* Later came Moody-Manners with a week at the Bordesley Palace Theatre, where Balfe's *Puritan's Daughter* was revived and was followed by Saint-Säens's *Samson and Delilah,* plus *The Lily of Killarney, The Bohemian Girl, Carmen, Rigoletto* and *The Daughter of the Regiment* conducted by Aylmer Buesst, later in the 1930s to have a career in the BBC Music Department.

In Liverpool, Adrian C Boult, soon to be called up and at one time to be responsible for the supply of boots to the army, promoted his popular orchestral concerts aimed at the growing working audience, in the Sun Hall, but they were not well attended, receipts being less than half the costs, causing Boult to have to make a full call on the guarantee fund established to underwrite them. Later a series of six fortnightly orchestral concerts was announced by Boult from 6 October at the David Club Theatre.

In London the 1915 Promenade concerts cemented their success of the previous summer, despite the anti-German remarks in Parliament already quoted. The first programme drew an immense audience, and the novelties included the Alsace composer Loeffler's *The Death of Tintagiles* (17 August); Debussy's 'Fragments Symphoniques' from *Le Martyre de St. Sébastien,* and Haydn Wood's Piano Concerto played by Miss Auriol Jones (26 August). Of the special 'Allies programmes', the Russian night on 12 September had an overwhelming audience for Tchaikovsky but also Stravinsky's *Fireworks* and Sibelius's *Finlandia*. A Wagner night on 6 September is reported as drawing a large audience. Moiseiwitsch played the Delius Concerto, and a substituted programme on 15 September was mainly Italian but included Frank Bridge's heartfelt *Lament*, the latter Bridge's personal memorial to 'Catherine aged nine' who was drowned with her family when the *Lusitania* was torpedoed on 24 June 1915. The critic Edwin Evans recalled the reception it received after the war when he wrote 'The audience was too spell-bound for a noisy demonstration of favour, but the eloquence of the music had achieved what a more ambitious or studied composition could not have effected.'[37]

What can the musicians who had faced the nightmare of the trenches and returned have thought when they encountered the vigour of British musical life at the mid-point of the war, and a vigour not too different to the climate that had preceded it. Arthur Bliss was one who was not inclined to keep his outrage to himself, writing to *The Musical Times* in a celebrated letter:

> Sir, As one of those musicians who have fought German aggression in France, I should like to express my thanks to Edwin Evans and 'Musicus' for their championship of English music and their fight against the predominating influence of Germany at home.
>
> It seems to me unseemly that a fine institution like the London Symphony Orchestra should have to put its financial security in front of its national feelings – if all had followed suit we should never have declared war. Moreover, by its choice of works it has missed a signal opportunity of showing its appreciation and gratitude to those of the profession who are fighting to maintain all the cherished institutions this country.
>
> The names of two such occur instantly to my mind. One is Dr. R. Vaughan Williams, who for eighteen months had been through the drudgery of a private's work in the R.A.M.C.; the other is Lieutenant G.S.K. Butterworth, M.C., who was killed in action. The works of either would add to the prestige of the English orchestra that included them in its programme; nor do I think that a performance of Vaughan Williams's Symphony in London would be altogether unfitting at this time. I am delighted to think that Dr. Allen is doing the 'Sea Symphony', together with works by Stanford and Parry later in the season to commemorate those of the Senior Service who have died. All honour and success to him!
>
> I do not know whether as a class musicians have been less affected (except financially) than other professions, but when straight from being wounded on the Somme I went into a London concert hall and heard a public vociferously applauding a German soloist, it gives me furiously to think.

This was written less than a fortnight after his brother Kennard – cellist and Bliss always said the more talented brother – had been killed at Thiepval. In fact Bliss's attitude was permanently coloured by the view he took then, a very positive influence in his activity after the War as a champion of the new in the development of a highly personal style which took little if anything from German models. In 1921 he lectured to the Society of Women Musicians on 'What Modern Composition

Captain Arthur Bliss

is Aiming At', and in celebrating the music of Stravinsky, Bartók, de Falla and the younger British composers declared 'I take my hat off to him [Stravinsky] and the others . . . not only for what they have created, but also for what they have killed', and among a varied selection of the pre-war musical world celebrates the demise of 'the symphonic poem à la Strauss', the 'pseudo-intellectuality of the Brahms camp followers' and 'frothing Wotans and stupid King Marks'.[38]

သ   သ   သ

All too soon the roll-call of those who fell included promising young musicians who had started to make their name before the outbreak of war. One of the first was Lieutenant Edward Mason, cellist and conductor of the choir that bore his name, who was killed on active service on 9 May 1915 in his 37th year. Soon he was followed by William Denis Browne, who was killed at the Dardanelles on 7 June.

William Charles Denis Browne (1888-1915) was a friend and student of Dent at Cambridge and is remembered for two songs, *Diaphenia* and *To Gratiana Dancing and Singing,* out of some 10 songs, a ballet and a few short choral pieces that survive. He was present when Rupert Brooke died on Skyros, his letter of 25 March to Edward Marsh describing the occasion being reprinted in the *Collected Poems*. The following account is from a letter by his composer-friend the brilliant Australian pianist F S Kelly:[39]

> The events of to-day made a deep impression on me. Rupert Brooke died on board the French hospital ship at 4.45 pm, and in view of the ship's orders to sail at 5 am the following morning, arrangements were at once made to bury him on the island he loved so well . . It was about a mile from the shore to the grove, over very difficult stony ground, and the petty officers who bore the coffin had to go very slowly. We reached the grove at 10.45 pm, where, in the light of a clouded half-moon, the burial service was read . . . It was a most moving experience. The wild sage gave a strong classical tone, which was so in harmony with the poet we were burying that to some of us the Christian ceremony seemed out of keeping. When all the others had gone back to the boats, Lieut-Commander Freyberg, Ock Asquith, Charles Lister, Denis Browne, and I covered the grave with stones and as many pieces of marble as we could . . . . The body lies looking down the valley towards the harbour, and, from behind, an olive-tree bends itself over the grave as though sheltering it from the sun and rain. No more fitting resting-place for a poet could be found than this small grove, and it seems as though the gods had jealously snatched him away to enrich this scented island. For the whole day I was oppressed with the sense of loss, but when the officers and men had gone, and when at last the five of us, his friends, had covered his grave with stones, and took a last look in silence - then the sense of tragedy gave place to a sense of passionless beauty, engendered both by the poet and the place.

Kelly survived Gallipoli long enough to produce an affecting *Elegy for Rupert Brooke* for harp and strings, in which he evokes the rustling of the olive tree over the grave; but Kelly himself was killed on the Western Front, leading an advance in the last battle of the Somme at Beaucourt-sur-Aube on 13 November 1916.[40] 1916 was the year which also saw the death of George Butterworth, perhaps the best-remembered of the British composers who died in the war.

Yet curiously Butterworth wrote no overtly war works, and it has only been the association of his music with the poetry of A E Housman that gives it so powerful a feeling for us, redolent of impending war. Specifically we think of the orchestral rhapsody *A Shropshire Lad*.

W Denis Browne   *George Butterworth*
Ernest Farrar   *F S Kelly*

'We understand, as we listen to it' wrote Sir Thomas Armstrong 'why Butterworth's death on the Somme in 1916 seemed to be a disaster for English music: and we wonder, as his friends did at the time, what his final achievement might have been if he had lived'.[41]   This is a work which underlines the potential lost when George Butterworth was shot through the head near Thiepval on 5 August 1916.

Butterworth's death gives an added piquancy to his two sets of Housman songs – *A Shropshire Lad* and *Bredon Hill* - and in the latter the song 'On the idle hill of summer' seems to gain enormous significance from our knowledge of Butterworth's fate, as it also does in Ivor Gurney's even more haunting setting. The dreamer enjoys his reverie on the sunlit hillside and while feeling war to be all foolishness lightly joins the soldiers who pass by. Both Butterworth and Gurney draw great effect from a subtle presentation of 'the steady drummer drumming like a noise in dreams'.

Butterworth's closeness to Vaughan Williams, his whole-hearted commitment to folk-dancing – he was a virtuoso and athletic participant – and a wide experience as a folk-song collector made him a central figure in the construction of tradition that focused on Cecil Sharp in the immediate pre-war years. Sir Thomas Armstrong, in a celebrated anecdote, tells how, on seeing the young Butterworth and R O Morris in Oxford, Sir Hugh Allen remarked 'there goes more red revolution than in the whole of Russia',[42] presumably in that statement aligning Butterworth with Elgar in his rejection of the then musical establishment. However one wonders whether Butterworth's dissatisfaction with the musical establishment of his day would have resulted in anything more than perhaps him eventually becoming the Director of the English Folk Dance and Song Society? There are no clues, for he had not resolved the problem of reconciling composition with earning a living when he closed not only a chapter but the book, on 31 August 1914, when he enlisted.

The potentially most significant British composers to be killed included (in order of their passing) W Denis Browne, and F S Kelly,[43] Butterworth, and, the teacher of Gerald Finzi, Ernest Farrar (1885-1918) (in 1997 the subject of an eye-opening Chandos orchestral CD[41]). Farrar was lost in the closing weeks of the war when, only two days after his arrival at the front, he was killed on 18 September at the battle of Epéhy Ronssoy.

If Denis Browne, Kelly and Farrar had almost passed from view before the present exploration of the music of these composers, it is reasonable to assume that there are doubtless others worthy of our attention. Recently the conductor Martyn Brabbins has championed the music of the Scottish composer Cecil Coles (1888-1918), some of which was actually written in the trenches. Coles, friend of Holst, and one of those commemorated by Holst's *Ode to Death,* lived and studied in Stuttgart for several years, where he worked under von Schillings. Coles's *Behind the Lines* was intended as a four movement suite from which the 'Cortège' is dated 'in the field Feb 4, 1918' (and has been completed in full score by Martyn Brabbins); two months later Coles was dead.

Others, such as E J Moeran and Ivor Gurney, were damaged when wounded or gassed. Yet would it be reasonable to suggest that despite a number of lamentable deaths, the future creativity of British music was probably not massively diverted by losses during the First World War?

Surprisingly no major vocal work of a memorial nature appeared during the war apart from Elgar's *The Spirit of England* and Delius's *The Requiem,* and the latter was not performed until after the war, and when it did was far removed from the mood of the time and was not well received. However, several substantial works were written, of which M U Arkwright's *Requiem Mass* for soprano and baritone soli, chorus and orchestra was published in 1914.[45] This was by Marion Arkwright (1863-1922), whose idiom suggests to us both Brahms and Stanford. Her intention is made absolutely clear by the opening funeral march and the superscription:

> No matter where or when
> Or how we die, the while you say to us –
> "O, nobly died! O glorious Englishmen!"

It was little if ever performed.

During the war *The Last Post,* Stanford's Boer War choral setting of words by W E Henley, was heard again, particularly by local choral societies. The vivid, even corny setting is characterised by the well-known bugle-call. Also 'Farewell' from *Songs of the Fleet* was, not surprisingly, often heard. But after the war Stanford's celebratory mass-setting, *Via Victrix 1914-1918,* was completely ignored. This was a large-scale mass in six movements with an exultant 'Gloria in Excelsis' which is also available separately. Dated December 1919 it was published in vocal score in 1920, but was barely noticed. It must have been a crushing blow for Stanford.

It is the *Short Requiem* – running around 18 minutes – that Henry

Walford Davies wrote for all too practical purposes in 1915 that stood out. In nine movements this sequence is one of those works which turns what is almost cliché into something timeless, it seems familiar yet is new. The printed copies are written without organ accompaniment, which doubles when required. In an introduction the composer counsels using the organ sparingly if at all. 'It would seem best to restrict it to a few pedal notes to play over the Chants and the Hymns' and to the use of its full tone for the Gloria. With its solos in the first, fifth, sixth and ninth movements, natural chant, the hymn 'No more to sigh', and ending with John Lydgate's emotive text with the words 'Tarry no longer', its impact must have been devastating when used during the war.

෯   ෯   ෯

Nevertheless the war had enormous practical implications. If music printing and engraving was heavily dependent on German practitioners, German-trained craftsmen and the German printing industry particularly around Leipzig, the record industry was even more truly international from the first. The Gramophone Company had been developed in the first fifteen years of its existence as a Europe-wide enterprise, though with its eyes also on the Empire, especially India and the Far East, and the company's factory in Hanover housed all HMV's metal masters (from which records could be re-pressed when required). They actually supplied ostensibly 'British' HMV records as well as local HMV labels to the whole of Europe. When the German and Russian governments seized their local branches, this major loss of assets and manufacturing capability coupled with a brief but almost total absence of disposable income by the public at large almost destroyed HMV. They saved themselves by halving staff wages, by taking on munitions work at their new factory at Hayes, and by developing a wartime craze for popular recordings, at home and in the trenches, started by the biggest best-seller then experienced – 'Tipperary'.[46] From the first both HMV and Columbia emphasised such patriotic titles and recorded new ones, though the craze for overly nationalistic music was only a phase at the outset of the war.

Similarly with the Columbia catalogue, which on Columbia and their more popular Regal label, at first issued a wide variety of such titles. They 'raked up all the patriotic records they could find . . .' and 'rushed them out as war records' and within ten days they were

NEW
Patriotic Records

Mr. STEWART GARDNER
10-inch Records, 3s. 6d.

4-2493	One United Front	*Bradwell*
4-2498	Sons of Old Britannia	*Forster*
4-2492	Little Mother	*Buchanan*
4-2497	Sons of the Motherland	*Monckton*
4-2496	The Soldiers of the King	*Stuart*
4-2495	Private Tommy Atkins	*Potter*

12-inch Record, 5s. 6d.

02548 England! Thy Name! *Lewis Barnes*
(*Composer of The King's Command March
coupled with Trot of the Cavalry, by Coldstream Guards Band, No. B222, 10-inch, 3,6).

DESCRIPTIVE RECORD
10-inch Record, 3s. 6d.

9473 British Troops passing through Boulogne

12-inch Record, 5s. 6d.

C 377 { **A Drill Sergeant**
Words of Command
A Signalling Sergeant-Instructor
Morse Code—Alphabet and Message

METROPOLITAN MILITARY BAND
12-inch Records, 5s. 6d.

C 378 { " Allies in Arms." Selection I.*
" Allies in Arms." Selection II.†

*Selection I. contains Opening, " Hearts of
Oak (England), " La Brabanconne " (Belgium),
" St. Patrick " (Ireland), " Russian Hymn "
(Russia), " Rule Britannia " (England), " See
the Conquering Hero " (England). Finale.
†Selection II. contains " La Marseillaise "
(France), " The Garb of Old Gaul " (Scotland),
" The Maple Leaf " (Canada), " Marcia Reale "
(Italy), " Men of Harlech " (Wales), " God
Save the King " (England).

C 379 { Salut à Liège (dedicated to the Brave
Belgians) *Entwistle*
United Forces March

C 380 { " Our Sailor King," Patriotic March *Gay*
" Fighting for Liberty," Patriotic March *Kaye*

BUGLERS OF H.M.
COLDSTREAM GUARDS
10-inch Record. 3s. 6d.

B 261 { Regimental Calls. No. 1
" " " 2

B 262 { Camp Calls. No. 1
" " " 2

From the HMV catalogue for October 1914

issued. . . . Soon records everywhere were expressing the warlike sentiments of the nation. Often these records promised to pay a royalty to war charities. In the event 1915 proved to be Columbia's best year ever, a growth that continued, with Louis Sterling reporting in 1918 that 'our sales during 1917 showed a gain of 25 per cent over 1916 making this year the best in our history'.[47]

Among patriotic songs 'We don't want to fight, but by Jingo if we do' had been a musical hall song dating from 1878, associated with the music hall artist G H Macdermott. It is said it gave the word 'jingoist' to the language, and its wartime revival not only added to the cannon of popular patriotic songs but also, as did others, became a catch-phrase of the time.

Records also proved to be a useful medium for the dissemination of recruiting songs which were a significant feature of ballad concerts and music hall in the early days of the war. A typical example would be 'Your King and Country Want You', also known as 'We Don't Want to Lose You'. A cylinder recording of this sung by Helen Clarke has been reissued on CD.[48] Another example, by the lady tenor, Ruby Helder, was issued by HMV. The London newspapers promoted their own recruiting songs, and the HMV recording of the *Daily Telegraph* Recruiting Song, 'Courage' by Vanden Heuvel (presumably a Dutch or Belgian composer), was sung with 'palpitating feeling'.

Typical wartime picture postcard

Such material came from a variety of less dominant labels, notably Pathé. The *Daily Sketch* song 'The Flag That Never Comes Down' sung by 'Mr Lionel Rothery' with orchestra was on Pathé's cheap label Diamond (0.130). Other recruiting songs included 'Call Us and We'll Soon Be There' by 'Wheeler and Weston' which was sung by 'Mr Robert Howe with orchestra' on Pathé 5680. Finally, of interest because the piano accompaniment was played by the composer Hubert Bath, one of those in the forefront of the campaign to keep German music out, 'We Are All Plain Civilians' ('England Wants You'), words by Foden Williams, music by Ernest Hastings, was on Pathé 5688. This was also of note as the singer was Thorpe Bates, a rising concert singer of the day, who also recorded 'The Deathless Army' for HMV (02312).

These songs were also issued by big name concert artists; Edna Thornton, for example, recorded 'Your King and Country Wants You' (HMV 03390). Columbia, too, brought its serious artists to the fore in its wartime patriotic recordings, examples being Maggie Teyte yet again in 'Your King and Country Want You'[†], coupling it with 'The Homes they Leave Behind' (Columbia 2467). They ensured their dissemination by making them the first recordings to be issued by top-line artists at a non-premium price.

Possibly it was Clara Butt who achieved the widest such audience, transferring her activities to Columbia from HMV in 1915 and for her new company not only recording a widely disseminated tub-thumping version of 'Land of Hope and Glory' (Columbia 7156) but also Parry's *A Hymn for Aviators*[‡] - in retrospect a less than successful patriotic piece - and the first ever recording of vocal extracts from *The Dream of Gerontius* to coincide with Butt's week of *Gerontius* at Queen's Hall in May 1916 and her other charity performances in the rôle of the angel at the time.

Butt's recording of the melancholy ballad 'Have You News of My Boy Jack?' which Edward German wrote for her, setting words of Kipling written after the loss of his own son, very much reflected the concerns of so many at the time (Columbia 7145). With orchestral accompaniment directed by Beecham, Butt is perhaps better replaced for the historian by Kirkby Lunn's competing version which is directed by its composer.[§] It is significant that there should be competing versions of such an item, surely signalling an industry which had regained its health and manufacturing output.

Haydn Wood was the composer of various popular ballads that were recorded. His song 'O Flower Divine', sung by the lyric tenor

---

† - see track 10 on the accompanying CD; ‡ - see track 9 on the accompanying CD
§ - see track 7 on the accompanying CD

Hubert Eisdell, was a feature of HMV's March 1915 list. But his 'hit' and another song indissolubly associated with the war was 'Roses of Picardy' recorded for HMV by Ernest Pike (793). It was also recorded by John McCormack (Victor 64825). It was said that Haydn Wood's income from this one song was such that it financed his musical career after the war.

Another substantial strand in the rapidly developing wartime record catalogue was songs from the shows. After the first shock of the outbreak of war, these became a major feature of musical life and increasingly the leading numbers were recorded. The first of these was *On Duty* which opened at the Holborn Empire on 24 August and set a patriotic tone soon emulated by *England Expects* at the Stoll on 17 September, but these appear not to have produced any songs that were recorded.

It was Louis Sterling at Columbia who 'realised that the soldiers, who flocked to London to see these shows in London whilst on leave, would want to take back to the trenches records of the songs and music performed by the original casts'.[49] *Business as Usual*, a revue full of topical and patriotic numbers which opened at the Hippodrome on 16 November was probably the first show to produce such recordings, including a sketch 'Fortifying the Home Front' featuring Harry Tate and Violet Loraine (Columbia 504), 'When We've Wound Up the Watch on the Rhine' (Columbia 2484) and 'Three Cheers for Little Belgium' (Columbia 2488). Peter Martland, in his history of EMI, prints a fascinating session photograph of Harry Tate, Violet Loraine and Morris Harvey recording these numbers.[50]

Immediately after Christmas 1914, Martin Shaw's children's play *The Cockyolly Bird,* with words by Mrs Percy Dearmer - she called it 'a musical adventure' - appeared at the Little Theatre, though the 'Bubble Song' was not recorded until the early 1920s when Frank Titterton sang it for Vocalion (X-9118). It was variously revived in the 1920s, and the overture played at the Proms.[51] We need to note it, however, as an important precursor of Elgar's music for *The Starlight Express* which would open on 29 December 1915.

It was 1915 before the songs from the shows began to appear on records in any significant way. Possibly the first was Herman Finck's review *The Passing Show of 1915* which opened at the Palace Theatre on 9 March. One may survey what was on offer from a selection of the numbers recorded by HMV on 23 April and issued almost immediately (HMV C 405). Finck himself conducted the Palace Theatre Orchestra in two orchestral numbers 'Le Revue de l'Amour'

(HMV B 288) and the Palace Girl's Dance 'Cheero' (HMV B296). Soon afterwards *Rosy Rapture, the Pride of the Chorus* opened at the Duke of York's and was recorded by Columbia, the records being in the shops within ten days of the show's opening.[52]

Reputedly *The Bing Boys are Here* was the most popular show in London during the First World War, with its hit number 'If you were the only Girl in the World' sung by George Robey. This opened on 19 April at the Alhambra, but although George Robey and Violet Loraine made the cast recording of the song (as 'If you were the only boy in the world') neither of the two main record companies had the exclusive use of the music, and HMV issued two selections of 'vocal gems'.

Most of these shows are not remembered today, though one or two songs have survived. It would be the end of August 1916 before such celebrated scores as *Chu Chin Chow* arrived at His Majesty's and on 10 February 1917 the *Maid of the Mountains* at Daly's, both extensively recorded, and long remembered.

The arrival of the fox-trot, followed by American popular numbers was a notable feature of the recorded repertoires of the war. Brian Rust identifies Elsie Janis as introducing the foxtrot to London with Basil Hallam. This was in *The Passing Show of 1915* where she

From the HMV catalogue for May 1915

instructs her partner in the dance in the number 'Balling the Jack' (HMV 2-4251). Rust goes on: 'the first instrumental record of the fox-trot must be the one released in December 1915 by the Van Eps Trio'.[53] Fred van Eps was an American banjo player, but initially American music seems to have been shunned in response to American neutrality. Only after America entered the war did American artists and shows begin to assume a widespread popularity.

The cessation of normal operatic activity and the development of opera in English with English artists was turned to advantage by HMV who started their series of 'Opera in English' launched in 1915. They included a few English operas including all the main numbers from Ethel Smyth's *The Boatswain's Mate* (at first on single sided discs later on D 445-8) and a complete *Mikado* in the summer of 1918 'eleven double-sided records contained in a beautifully decorated album price £3/11/6d complete'.[54] However the main thrust of this movement was to record established operas in English, even making a high point of Kirkby Lunn singing 'O Righteous God' ('Gerechter Gott') from Wagner's *Rienzi* (HMV 02440)!

Elgar in the recording studio at Hayes, 1915

Elgar came to be associated with the gramophone in a quite unprecedented way, and he is usually considered the first significant composer personally to record most of his serious work. He made his first recording (*Carissima*) on 21 January 1914, a performance which actually constitutes the music's first performance as it did not have its first public hearing until 15 February that year. In June 1914 Elgar conducted *Pomp and Circumstance* marches Nos 1 and 4, *Salut d'Amour* and *Bavarian Dances* Nos 2 and 3 at the Gramophone Company studios. These were cut to fit single sides, *Pomp and Circumstance No 1* almost immediately launching into the trio tune. It was Elgar's first wartime issue, and HMV's catalogue sought to promote 'Land of Hope and Glory', subtitling it 'introducing Land of Hope and Glory', as a great cultural symbol, writing:

> At a time when patriotism is welling up in the breast of every British-born citizen, Elgar's super-patriotic suite [sic] is doubly welcome, especially a performance conducted by the great composer himself. In 'Pomp and Circumstance' Elgar reaches great heights of national feeling. The patriotism of the artist shows itself as vividly in this work as in his acceptance, despite his age, of an active part in protective work during the war: Sir Edward has become a Special Constable in Hampstead. That thrillingly broad march-melody now known to every British ear, 'Land of Hope and Glory', is played with unspeakable breadth of tone and majesty by these fine players directed by Elgar. No one can listen without experiencing feelings of noble patriotism, such is the nature of its immediate appeal. Every Britisher should possess this unique record.[55]

Yet when the third dance from *Three Bavarian Dances* was issued in May 1915 its overtly Germanic subject matter appears not to have caused anyone difficulty, the music being presented as picturesque: 'the joyousness of the music is easily descriptive of the rustic scene with its background of heavily-gabled booths and towering green and grey peaks searching the hearts of the cloud-lands'.

Elgar's wartime recording sessions were really comparatively few, centred on three dramatic or semi-dramatic presentations which had a significant following at the time. These were first *Carillon*, the recitation with orchestra of words by the Belgian playwright and poet Emile Cammaerts, secondly the songs from Elgar's children's play with music, *The Starlight Express*, and later his song cycle *Fringes of the Fleet* which was a hit when presented by four singers in costume. Between these came a truncated version of the Violin Concerto played by Marie Hall, and drastically abridged versions of *Cockaigne* and the 'Prelude and Angel's Farewell' from *Gerontius*. *Bavarian*

Dance No 1 and two movements from *The Wand of Youth* complete Elgar's wartime recorded repertoire. *Polonia*, his other significant wartime orchestral work, was not recorded until May 1919, and even then only in a truncated version, while extracts from the ballet music for *The Sanguine Fan* had to wait until 1920. *Carillon* and *Fringes of the Fleet* are discussed elsewhere in this book, but entries in Lady Elgar's diary for May 1918 suggest that Elgar may have attempted a recording of *Polonia* then but not been satisfied with the results.

ဢ   ဢ   ဢ

Various initiatives were launched to promote British music, perhaps the most interesting being Beecham and Młynarski's Festival of British Music at Queen's Hall, a series of three concerts on 11, 13 and 15 May 1915. It was given by the London Symphony Orchestra and London Choral Society, with Młynarski, Beecham, Elgar and the choral conductor Arthur Fagge on the podium. The first programme included music by O'Neill, Delius, Bantock, Holbrooke, Ethel Smyth, Percy Grainger and Stanford. Elgar himself only appeared in the second concert when he conducted his Violin Concerto played by its

---

QUEEN'S HALL, LANGHAM PLACE, W.

Lessees   Messrs. Chappell & Co., Ltd.

FESTIVAL
OF
BRITISH MUSIC

DIRECTORS :
EMIL MLYNARSKI
THOMAS BEECHAM

TUESDAY,   MAY 11th, at 8.30 p.m.
THURSDAY, MAY 13th, at 8.30 p.m.
SATURDAY, MAY 15th, at 3 p.m.

(Under the management of L. G. Sharpe)

LONDON SYMPHONY ORCHESTRA

LONDON CHORAL SOCIETY

CONDUCTORS—

EMIL MLYNARSKI | Sir EDWARD ELGAR
THOMAS BEECHAM | ARTHUR FAGGE

Telephone No.: 5564 Gerrard.   L. G. SHARPE
Telegraphic Address : "Musaceous, London."   61, Regent Street, W.

PROGRAMME.

SATURDAY, MAY 15th, at 3 p.m.

1. Rhapsody   -   " Spring "   -   *Frederic Austin*

2. Songs   -   (a) " Chanson de Bilitis " -   ⎫
                      (b) " Mandoline "   ⎬ *Pitt*
                      (c) " Au Jardin de l'Infante " - ⎭
                      Madame KIRKBY LUNN.

3. Pianoforte Concerto -   -   -   -   *Scott*
                      (First Performance.)
                      CYRIL SCOTT.

4. Symphonic Impression —
        " In the Fen Country"   -   *Vaughan-Williams*

5. Introduction and Allegro for String Orchestra   - *Elgar*

6. Songs -   (a) " A Celtic Lullaby " -   *Bax*
                  (b) " The Wood's Aglow"   *McEwen*
                  (c) " Muse of the Golden Throne " *Bantock*
                  Madame KIRKBY LUNN.

7. Fantasy   " In the Faery Hills"   -   *Bax*

8. March - " Pomp and Circumstance " (No. 3) - *Elgar*

THE LONDON SYMPHONY ORCHESTRA.

Conductors—
EMIL MLYNARSKI
THOMAS BEECHAM

newly recognised champion Albert Sammons. The third concert on
Saturday afternoon with works by Frederic Austin, Cyril Scott,
Vaughan Williams and Bax included Emil Młynarski conducting
Elgar's *Introduction and Allegro*, not then a frequently heard score,
and the least well-known *Pomp and Circumstance* march – no 3,
which closed the series. The programme book remarked 'This March,
perhaps better than any other, might be used to celebrate our Russian
alliance'. After the series Beecham, in puckish mood, was heard to
remark 'Well I think we have successfully paved the way this
afternoon for another quarter of a century of German music!' [56]

During the War a variety of special concerts took place, notably to
raise money for war charities and usually under aristocratic or royal
patronage. Notable among these were a variety of Red Cross concerts,
a typical example of which was the Clara Butt Concerts Committee to
plan her season of performances of *The Dream of Gerontius* with the
premières of the two parts then completed of *For the Fallen*. These
were held under the aegis of the British Red Cross Society and the
Order of St John of Jerusalem in England. Another occasion was
when Elgar's *Carillon* was performed in a concert for the British
Society for Relief of Belgian Wounded Soldiers in October 1915.

THE BRITISH RED CROSS SOCIETY
AND THE
ORDER OF ST. JOHN OF JERUSALEM
IN ENGLAND

Invite you to join the " Clara Butt Concert Committee."

The first Meeting will be held on **Tuesday** the
21st March, at 4 p.m., at The Royal Automobile Club,
Pall Mall, London, S.W.

Speakers :—The Rt. Rev. Bishop Boyd Carpenter.
The Rev. Father Bernard Vaughan.
Sir Edward Elgar, O.M., Mus. Doc., LL.D.
Rt. Hon. G. W. E. Russell, and others.

Tea will be served after the Meeting.   R.S.V.P.
This Ticket will admit yourself *and friend.*   [P.T.O.

From the point of view of music by other British composers used to commemorate recent tragic events we might note examples of three concerts among many:

12 December 1916
A concert at Queen's Hall
to commemorate the loss of the *Invincible* at Jutland
Parry: *Chivalry of the Sea*
(specially commissioned, first performance)
Stanford: *Songs of the Fleet* (concluding with 'Farewell')
Vaughan Williams: *A Sea Symphony*

15 December 1917
The Mons Memorial Concert at the Royal Albert Hall
in the presence of King George V and Queen Mary
(Memorial to the Seven Divisions who fought at Mons and Ypres)
Elgar: *Cockaigne*
Vaughan Williams: *Toward the Unknown Region*
Howells: *Elegy*
Parry: *There is an Old Belief*
Somervell: *To the Vanguard 1914*
Stanford: *Farewell*

20 January 1918
Tribute to France conducted by Landon Ronald
Verdun, 1916 Concert
included Stanford: *Solemn March* and *Heroic Epilogue*
(orchestration of the of 2nd and 3rd movements of Organ Sonata no 2)
1st movement entitled 'Rheims', 3rd entitled 'Verdun' 1916.

ഗ   ഗ   ഗ

Of those who were injured or damaged by the war we shall only know of the later celebrated – the many 'might have beens' who were lost we can only glimpse – the Royal College of Music War memorial, for example, names 38, of which only two are now remembered as composers.

In brief, we have already noted the Australian Arthur Benjamin, later a successful pianist and composer, who was shot down and taken prisoner but who returned to an active career. Arthur Bliss, whose brother Kennard was killed and who was himself wounded and gassed, likewise developed a brilliant and outspoken career. The conductor and composer Eugene Goossens whose brother was killed (and is named on the RCM War memorial), and Ivor Gurney, poet and composer, whose pre-war waywardness was exacerbated by being gassed and who ultimately became insane, spending the last dozen years of his life in the City of London Mental Hospital in Dartford.

Of the others, the composer Gordon Jacob was taken prisoner in April 1917 and was long affected by the death of his brother, Anstey, on the Somme. The war cast a long shadow and many works paid conscious tribute, many more unconscious memorial to those who had not returned. In Jacob's case, he dedicated to his brother his First Symphony some ten years later.

After the war the thought was of memorials for the dead and the Cenotaph in Whitehall became its focus. It was at first intended to be a merely temporary structure for the peace celebrations in July 1919, but Sir Edwin Lutyens' design so caught the public imagination that the lath and plaster version erected for the march past in 1919 was replaced 'in all respects in permanent form'.[57]

Elgar's publisher, Novello, recognising what they took to be a commercial opportunity, asked Elgar for a much truncated version of his setting of 'For the Fallen', the third part of *The Spirit of England*. This was intended for use at the unveiling of the Cenotaph on 11 November 1920 but in the event the music on that occasion consisted only of hymn singing. For outdoor use Elgar had scored what was now called *With Proud Thanksgiving,* for military band. He now re-scored it – largely reverting to the original – for its first performance at the Royal Albert Hall on 7 May 1921. It was not a success and was little performed, choirs preferring to do the longer original version as 'the whole piece was reduced from 218 to 98 bars'.[58]

After the Cenotaph, the return of the Unknown Warrior for burial in Westminster Abbey provided a second focus for national remembrance. Both were unveiled on 11 November 1920. Stanford's short *At the Abbey Gate*, written immediately after the event, sets brief emotive words by Judge Darling which describe the arrival of the Unknown Warrior at the Abbey, the vocal exchange encompassed by a pent-up funeral march. It was not widely heard and at its first performance at the Royal Albert Hall on 5 May 1921 it was little more than a curtain raiser to *Gerontius*.

More poetic but also soon forgotten was *Out of the Mist* by Lilian Elkington (1901-1969). Elkington was a young student of Bantock, and her tone-poem was first heard at a student concert in Birmingham in 1921 and later played at both Harrogate and Bournemouth. The following is from the programme note which appears in the score:

This short[59] tone-poem is the outcome of a poignant memory connected
with the War. . . when the Unknown Warrior was brought home to his last
resting place there was a thick mist over the Channel, out of which the
warship slowly emerged as she drew near to Dover. This explanation of
the title will give some clue to the understanding of the music.   The
opening is quiet, with muted lower strings, as the ship feels her way
through the murk . . . After a pause mutes are removed, the air grows
brighter, and the deep gloom upon men's spirits is somewhat relieved . . .
Gradually the style enlarges and becomes more elevated as larger views of
the meaning of sacrifice calm the spirit . . . [in] the final section,
Largamente appassionata ff, as with a burst of sad exaltation the
representative of the nameless thousands who have died in the common
cause is brought out of the darkness to his own.[60]

Another curious reminiscence of the war is one not designated as such
by its composer. This is the *Storm* that Bliss composed as incidental
music for *The Tempest* in 1921. Scoring it for a barrage of percussion
as well as piano, trumpet and trombone it generates a prodigious
volume of sound, a remarkable tour de force of drumming which
surely relives Bliss's experiences of the barrage on the Western Front.

The Nash Ensemble conducted by Martyn Brabbins recording Bliss's Storm *at
London's Henry Wood Hall in February 1998, showing the barrage of
percussion required.*

At the time, possibly the most striking work to result from the war,
and one which briefly found a wide public following, was John
Foulds' *A World Requiem*, first performed in the Royal Albert Hall on
Armistice Night 1923. This took a whole evening to sing and seriously

challenged Elgar on his own ground in a work which would find no competitor in intention and scale until Benjamin Britten's *A War Requiem* almost forty years later. As Foulds' biographer Malcolm Macdonald has written[61] the intention of the British Legion in promoting the work was 'to replace "Armistice Jazz" which had celebrated the first few anniversaries of the war's end'. It was also given an active focus by the title 'Festival of Remembrance' coined apparently by Foulds' wife, Maud MacCarthy. The first performance on 11 November 1923 was given to a 'packed auditorium by a chorus and orchestra of over 1,250'. 'The audience was ecstatic, many of them in tears: the ovation . . . lasted ten minutes'.[62] Curiously it was not a success with the critics, and although there were three more performances, all enthusiastically received, after 1926 it was dropped and only a few excerpts have been heard since, in an isolated performance in 1983. It remains a significant tribute to those lost in war which will surely have its day again.

As time passed various works appeared which may have originated from the war. Arnold Bax's aggressive First Symphony in 1922, with its searing funereal slow movement was ascribed to the war by many in the 1920s, though it is far more likely to have actually recalled the events in Dublin at Easter 1916. Vaughan Williams' *Pastoral Symphony* has been widely discussed as an elegy for RVW's companions on the Western Front where he was an orderly with the field ambulance.

We should end with Sir Arthur Bliss again who after more than a decade returned to the war in his own 'war requiem' *Morning Heroes*, dedicated 'To the memory of my brother Francis Kennard Bliss and all other comrades killed in battle'. Here, by taking texts from the *Iliad*, from a Chinese poet of the seventh century, from Walt Whitman and from Wilfred Owen and Robert Nichols, an inspired anthology libretto, makes the work universal and timeless as well as personal and specific. It was first performed at the Norwich Festival – one of the choral festivals that did survive the war – on 22 October 1930. What particularly aligns it with Elgar's war music is the use of orator in the first and fifth movements. A peculiarly difficult medium before the days of microphone, the use of orator with orchestra when successful communicates like no other medium and here Bliss provides a flowing accompaniment for Hector's celebrated farewell to Andromache in the first movement and no accompaniment for Wilfred Owen's 'Spring Offensive' other than drums at the point of the bombardment.[†]

† - Basil Maine, the orator in the early performances, features on track 17 of the accompanying CD.

ROYAL ALBERT HALL
Manager   :   :   :   :   HILTON CARTER, M.V.O.

UNDER THE MOST GRACIOUS PATRONAGE OF

THEIR MAJESTIES THE KING AND QUEEN

AND IN THE PRESENCE OF

H.R.H. THE PRINCE OF WALES
(Patron : BRITISH LEGION)

FESTIVAL COMEMMORATION

FOR ALL WHO FELL IN THE GREAT WAR

ARMISTICE EVENING
———————1923, AT 8———————

A WORLD REQUIEM

By JOHN FOULDS.
(FIRST PERFORMANCE)

IN AID OF

BRITISH LEGION
(Registered Under the War Charities' Act, 1916)

FIELD - MARSHAL EARL HAIG'S APPEAL
FOR EX-SERVICE MEN OF ALL RANKS

SOLOISTS:

IDA COOPER   WILLIAM HESELTINE
OLGA HALEY   HERBERT HEYNER

Chorus and Orchestra of Twelve Hundred

Conductor: JOHN FOULDS

Leader of Orchestra: MAUD MacCARTHY.   At the Organ: C. H. KEMPLING

Programme: PRICE ONE SHILLING

So, soon they topped the hill, and raced together
Over an open stretch of herb and heather
Exposed. And instantly the whole sky burned
With fury against them; and soft sudden cups
Opened in thousands for their blood; and the green slopes
Chasmed and steepened sheer to infinite space.

Later Britten would write, in Wilfred Owen's words, of the anguish and the pity of war. Bliss does so too, though he had a more immediate devil to lay.

The War was the end of the old musical order. Afterwards a new generation of composers flourished and even Stanford and Parry were soon forgotten, while former leading figures such as Mackenzie and Cowen, both of whom lived until the mid-1930s now seemed like fish out of water. Elgar survived, but although he was still treated as an honoured name his following began to wane and, for example, the first performance of the Cello Concerto in October 1919, played to a disappointingly small audience. Yet new champions of Elgar would arise, and with them different works were promoted. Perhaps chief among these was Adrian Boult who became the architect of the later popularity of the Second Symphony, and Malcolm Sargent whose championship of *The Dream of Gerontius* underpinned its continuing success to the mid-century and beyond. As Arnold Bax later wrote:[63]

'The catastrophe of 1914 certainly threw a cloud upon the imaginations of men and bundled away dreams such as those in which I had hitherto indulged. Yet despite the restless and sombre mood of the world, or perhaps because of it, many creative artists managed to continue with their work and even gained in strength. The demon of the times seized us and forced us to his will.'

NOTES and SOURCES

1. Bax, [Sir] Arnold, ed Foreman, Lewis: *Farewell, My Youth and other writings* (Aldershot, Scholar Press, 1992)
2. For a selection of wartime recordings reissued on CD see *'Oh! It's a Lovely War' Songs & Sketches of the Great War 1914-18* Vol 1 CD41 - 001
3. 'It's A Long, Long Way to Tipperary – An Army Marching Song', *The Musical Times* (Dec 1914) pp 696-7
4. *The Musical Times* (Dec 1914) p 697
5. Sir Hubert Parry: Diary for 1914 at Shulbrede Priory
6. *The Musical Standard* (February 1917) facing p 200.
7. 'The House of Bosworth', *The Musical Times* (November 1914) p 642 (reprinted from the *London Musical Courier,* 1 November 1913).

8. Ehrlich, Cyril: *The Piano - A History* (Dent, 1976) p 159
9. *The Musical Times* (September 1915) p 533
10. *The Musical Times* (September 1914) p 589
11. *The Musical Times* (October 1914) p 625
12. *House of Commons Hansard*, session 1914-15, 28 July 1915 col 2326
13. Moore, J N: *Edward Elgar A Creative Life* (Oxford, Oxford University Press, 1984) pp 573-4
14. Foreman, Lewis (ed) : *Music in England 1885-1920 as recounted in Hazell's Annual* (Thames Publishing, 1994) p 96
15. Corder was the composition professor of both Alexander and Braithwaite at the Royal Academy of Music.
16. Foreman, Lewis: *From Parry to Britten - British Music in Letters 1900-1945* (Batsford, 1987) pp 67.
17. *The Musical Times* (December 1914) p 701
18. See also pp 194-5; the image of a sleeping King Arthur was found evocative after the death of Kitchener on 5 June 1916.
19. Programmes at Shulbrede Priory.
20. 'Brighton Musical Festival', *The Musical Times* (December 1914) p 701
21. Parry's diaries at Shulbrede Priory.
22. The two recordings are by the London Philharmonic conducted by Matthias Bamert (Chandos CHAN 8955, recorded 5-6 January 1991); and the English Symphony Orchestra conducted by William Boughton (Nimbus NI 5296)
23. Bliss, [Sir] Arthur: *As I Remember* (Faber, 1970) p 30
24. Smith, Barry (ed): *Frederick Delius and Peter Warlock - a friendship revealed* (Oxford, OUP, 2000) p 141
25. Graves, Charles L: *Hubert Parry - his life and works*, vol 2 (Macmillan, 1926) p 70
26. Vaughan Williams, Ursula: *R.V. W. - a biography of Ralph Vaughan Williams* (OUP, 1964) p 117, letter dated 19 January 1915. See p 223 for a more extended text.
27. 'VW and The First World War' issue of the *Journal of the RVW Society* No 16 (October 1999). This includes articles by Stephen Connock, Alan K Aldous, Roger Juneau and Henry T Steggles.
28. Hughes, A D M: 'Ruhleben', *Cornhill Magazine* (Nov 1915) p 666
29. Ketchum, J Davidson: *Ruhleben - a prison camp society.* (Toronto, University of Toronto Press, 1965) p 204
30. *In Ruhleben Camp* No 1 Sunday June 6th 1915 p 22
31. 'The Butt-Elgar Festival: Leeds Concert', *Yorkshire Observer,* 4 May 1916.
32. ' "Gerontius" Week. Mme Clara Butt's Remarkable Undertaking', *The Westminster Gazette,* 9 May 1916
33. Unidentified cutting, May 1916 in Elgar Press Cuttings books, Elgar Birthplace, Broadheath.
34. 'Birmingham', *The Musical Times* (December 1914) p 709
35. *The Musical Times* (October 1914) p 625. Solomon appeared on 3 September 1914.
36. Howells did not promote his concerto after the war and although the score lay in the library of the Royal College of Music for many years, the last page was lost and it was not performed again until the ending was reconstructed by John Rutter. It was recorded by Chandos in May 2000 (CHAN 9874) and

published in full score by Novello.
37. *The Musical Times* (January 1919) p 59
38. Roscow, Gregory, ed: *Bliss on Music - selected writings of Arthur Bliss 1920-1975* (Oxford, Oxford University Press, 1991) p18
39. Edinburgh, Reid Orchestral Concerts (programme), 19 February 1921, pp 14-15
40. Davies, Rhian: 'Brother Officers – F S Kelly and Rupert Brooke', Armistice Day Festival (programme) (London, November 1989) p 50
41. Armstrong, [Sir] Thomas: 'George Butterworth – Rhapsody: A Shropshire Lad' Foreword to the miniature score (Ernst Eulenburg, 1981)
42. Barlow, Michael: *Whom the Gods Love – The Life and Music of George Butterworth* (Toccata Press, 1997) p 31
43. Some of the issues were discussed in my review in *Tempo*, no 168, pp 46-8 of the revival of Kelly's *Elegy in Memoriam Rupert Brooke* at the St Martin's in the Fields' Armistice Festival on 11 November 1988. See also Rhian Davies' account of Kelly in 'Warlock Down Under', *The Peter Warlock Society Newsletter* No 69 (Autumn 2001) pp 7-8
44. CHAN 9586
45. Arkwright, M U: *Requiem Mass for soprano & baritone solo, eight part chorus & orchestra.* (vocal score) (Carey & Co, 1914). Presumably Marion Arkwright or her publisher felt that a requiem written at that time would be more likely to find success if it was not apparent that the composer was a woman, hence the rather stilted use of initials.
46. For an illustrated account of the war years see Martland, Peter: *Since Records began - EMI The First Hundred Year* (B T Batsford, 1997) pp 71-77.
47. Martland, *op cit*, p 110 quoting *Talking Machine World,* April 1918
48. 'Oh! It's a Lovely War' Songs & Sketches of the Great War, 1914-18, vol 1 (CD41-001) *op cit*
49. Martland, *op cit*, p 113
50. Martland, *op cit*, p 114
51. Shaw, Martin: *Up to Now* (Oxford, Oxford University Press, 1929) p108
52. Martland, *op cit*, p 114
53. Rust, Brian: *Gramophone Records of the First World War* (Newton Abbott, David & Charles, nd), p (11)
54. *His Master's Voice New Records* (July 1918) p15
55. *His Master's Voice Records* (October 1914) p 3
56. Bax ed Foreman, *op cit*, p 81
57. Foreman, Susan: *From Palace to Power – an illustrated history of Whitehall* (Brighton, The Alpha Press, 1995) pp 129-31
58. Notes by Garry Humphreys for the revival by the Broadheath Singers conducted by Robert Tucker at Eton on 24 September 1988.
59. When revived by the Windsor Sinfonia conducted by Robert Tucker at Eton on 24 September 1988 it ran for 6'45".
60. Quoted in the programme note by David Brown for the Windsor Sinfonia performance, *op cit.*
61. MacDonald, Malcolm: *John Foulds and his Music: an introduction* (White Plains, New York, Pro/AM Music Resources, 1989) pp 28-37
62. *ibid,* p 36
63. Bax ed Foreman, *op cit*, p 167

CHAPTER 4

ELGAR and EMPIRE
Music, Nationalism and the War

Bernard Porter

Elgar's 'imperialism' has dogged him for years. It still does. Among many non-musical Britons, and most foreigners, he has the reputation of being little more than a jingoistic tub-thumper, a manifestation of the worst aspects of late Victorian and Edwardian bombast. For some – hooligans at England football matches, for example, and yuppies at the Last Night of the Proms, belting out *Land of Hope and Glory* as if they still had any shred of either left – this may be no bad thing. It shows Elgar had the common touch. For others, however, it has been an embarrassment. It resembles the problem posed by Wagner's anti-semitism in this way, although of course to a much lesser degree. His jingo pieces diminished him. His fiercest contemporary critic, Cecil Gray, claimed they did much more. He pictured the tune of *Land of Hope and Glory* – the melody on its own, note, not the words – arousing 'such patriotic enthusiasm in the breast of a rubber planter in the tropics 'as to lead him 'to kick his negro servant slightly harder than he would have done if he had never heard it'. That is quite a load of responsibility for a mere tune to bear. He also believed that Elgar's imperialism 'contaminated' all the rest of his work, including even the beloved *Enigma Variations*, whose last section he characterized as 'undiluted jingoism'.[1] Elgar's reputation has never entirely recovered from this.

For non-hooligans who still love his music,[2] there are three main lines of defence against this. The first is to see his 'jingo' pieces as aberrations, not fully representative of the rest of his art. They could sometimes bring promising works down, like his 1898 oratorio *Caractacus*, whose Finale suddenly transplants us from ancient Rome to modern times, bidding Britons be 'alert' to the dangers surrounding them and their empire. Most music critics have found that anomalous, to say the least. They included many of Elgar's contemporaries and even friends.[3] Others thought the *Coronation*

FACING PAGE: *While the British public cheered their troops returning from South Africa, Elgar was composing in Worcestershire.*

Ode he wrote for Edward VII was spoiled by having *Pomp and Circumstance No.1* tacked on to the end of it, with A C Benson's new words.[4] (This, of course, was the first outing of 'Land of Hope'.) Other works had to be dismissed entire. Elgar's biographer Diana McVeagh thought the *Crown of India* Masque and Suite (1912) reached 'rock-bottom in his occasional music'.[5] His music for the 1924 Wembley Empire Exhibition – *A Pageant of Empire*, including an *Empire March* – was also widely attacked for its vulgarity. But you could dismiss these, and still be left with the bulk of Elgar's creation intact. The marches, the masques, *Caractacus*, and possibly one or two other bits of larger works, like that final Variation, could be disregarded, air-brushed out of the Elgar canon. You would still be left with the symphonies, the concerti, the oratorios, the part songs, the chamber music, the overtures, and 14/15ths of the *Enigma Variations*; which should be enough serious and uncontaminated music for anyone. They are evidence enough – save for the cloth-eared – that, if Elgar was a jingo, he was also much more than that, expressing a range of emotions and aspirations that goes far beyond what appears to be the cruder message of *Land of Hope*.

This, by and large, has been the approach of his main champions.[6] It is often supplemented by a second line of defence. This is that the aberrations were provoked by the ethos of his time. Imperialism was in the air all around him, infecting everyone. 'We should remember', writes one authority, 'that most of Elgar's life was spent in the reign of Victoria and that he witnessed the ascendancy of the Empire.'[7] So it would have been difficult for him to escape. One school of thought holds that it was impossible. The colonial ethos was just too dominant and ubiquitous in Western culture, and had been for years.[8] That of course could be taken as an excuse for Elgar, if one were needed. Unfortunately – as we shall see shortly – it may not square with the empirical facts.

The third common defence of him is quite unacceptable. This is that his supposedly 'jingo' pieces have been misinterpreted. That argument mainly rests on the words of *Land of Hope and Glory*, which we have seen were not Elgar's own, and which some of his champions claim he disliked.[9] That is almost certainly false. There is no evidence that Elgar disapproved of Benson's words, at least initially.[10] He accepted them, when he could have rejected them if he had wanted to: it was his call. There is, true, no direct testimony that he positively liked them either; but there is in the case of the earlier *Caractacus*, which was also criticized for its blatant nationalism, as we have seen. Elgar's response to that was robust. He might have blamed it on his librettist, the amateur (and clearly inadequate) Harry Acworth, but he did not. He boasted that it was his own idea to 'dabble in patriotism in the Finale'. Perhaps, he suggested, Acworth went in a little too deep: 'instead of merely paddling his feet [he] goes and gets naked and wallows in it.' But he stood by him. 'I knew you would laugh at my librettist's patriotism (and mine)', he wrote to his friend Jaeger in June 1898; ' – never mind: England for the English is all I say – hands off! There's nothing apologetic about me!'[11] There are other similar whoopings in his correspondence, especially early on. In one he even complained at the relative patriotic restraint of his countrymen, by comparison with him. 'It's no good trying any patriotic caper on in England', he wrote to Jaeger again; 'we applaud the "sentiment" in other nations but repress it sternly in ourselves: anything like "show" is repugnant to the real English.'[12] And this was in November 1899, at the beginning of the Boer War, which makes one wonder just how much popular jingoism it would have taken to satisfy him. But in any case this seems to knock on the head any idea that he has been fundamentally misjudged over *Land of Hope and Glory* and the like. If he was not a jingo, he had only himself to blame for appearing one.

The purpose of this chapter, therefore, will not be to try to exonerate Elgar from the charge of 'imperialism'. That would be absurd. Elgar himself would not have wanted it. But there are still difficulties with it. His was not a straightforward sort of imperialism, either in its nature or in its origin. If we examine it closely, it looks atypical, uneven, even ambivalent. In some ways it appears anomalous. Elgar, when we dig deeper, does not seem a 'natural' imperialist. Nor is it easy to explain where his imperialism came from; far less so than the 'cultural imperialists' assume. If it was in the general culture around him, in his early years in particular, it was in a highly elusive form. The question of Elgar's imperialism, therefore, is problematical. That will surprise those who have taken him to exemplify, almost to the point of caricature, the ubiquity of empire feeling in his time.[13] Analyzing these problems is obviously necessary in order to understand Elgar more fully. It may also fulfil a broader function. Elgar was a creature of his place and time, though he also transcended it, as all great artists do. By appreciating better his personal relationship to the empire, we should also be able to refine our view of the latter's impact on contemporary British society.

I

Studying British society through the life of Edward Elgar can be unexpectedly rewarding. The reason for this is that Elgar came from a class of English people which is less well known than certain others, but which due to his fame has been minutely researched in his case. That research has thrown up some surprises, though historians have been curiously blind to the clear implications of at least one of them. That is: how deafeningly *non*-imperialist Elgar's early background was. That, of course, is unexpected, for the composer of 'Britons, alert!' and 'Land of Hope'. It will also be puzzling for anyone brought up on the assumption that nineteenth-century Britain was deep-dyed in imperialism, from top to bottom and north to south. It suggests that at least some sections of society could escape it, of which the Elgar family's was one.

Even a cursory glance at his background makes this likely. He was a provincial; a tradesman (at the beginning); a Roman Catholic; and an artist. All these characteristics alienated him from the dominant British culture of the time, which was metropolitan, upper class, Church of England and philistine. They certainly did in his own mind. We have ample proof of this, including the testimony of his close friend Rosa Burley, who could scarcely credit the bitterness with which he spoke of these things to her, the keenness with which he felt the disgrace of his lowly origins, and resented the religious prejudice that had blighted his career.[14] Critics who assume a 'national' mood in Britain in the nineteenth century often forget how variegated and fissiparous the society of that time really was. There were several English nations, quite apart from the Scottish and Welsh. Each had its own ethos, focus, system of values; overlapping, certainly, but distinct. 'Empire' was associated with just some of those nations: the upper and upper-middle classes, mainly, including the military, which was tiny, and the Church of England. Others were largely excluded. This is not to say that they were necessarily *against* the Empire, only that it did not impact greatly on their daily lives. That was the situation of Elgar's set.

If the Empire had impacted on the young Elgar one would expect it to have left *some* visible marks. But in all we know of his childhood there is not the slightest reference to it, even indirect. He was born in the year of the Indian Mutiny: but that is a coincidence, not a connection. He had no close family ties with the colonies, so far as can be gathered: no soldier cousins, no uncles in Australia; not even a pen-pal. That was unusual, but by no means unique. Worcestershire, where he lived, was apparently a great place for the imperial gentry class to retire to, but he only ever met those in the unsympathetic and even humiliating rôle of a servant, accompanying his father on piano-tuning trips.[15] His childhood friendships were restricted to his class, and within that – though to a lesser extent – to his religion. He was educated at local 'Dame' and Roman Catholic schools, and by violin tutors, not usually at that time regarded as founts of imperialism. By all accounts he did not like joining in boys' games, preferring instead to wander by the river, imagine fairies, and write pretty tunes. There is a hint that he may have been attracted to ceremony.[16] The greatest influence on his early life was a beloved mother, whose own ideological world we know about in remarkable detail from the commonplace books – cuttings from popular journals – that are still preserved at the Elgar Birthplace, and none of which indicates the slightest interest at all, even indirectly, in things imperial.[17] (The nearest they come is the theme of 'chivalry', of which more anon.) Ann Elgar was not the least like the strict imperial matriarch – the builder of empire-builders – that was such the rage in other social circles, and later on. Even if she had been, it is clear that he would not have provided very malleable material. 'Nervous, sensitive and kind' was how she herself described him at seventeen; and (later) 'terribly shy and quiet'.[18] He was also sickly and moody, to put it mildly, throughout his life.

Even with the most sensitive antennae imaginable it is difficult to detect many imperial – or even potentially imperial – messages here. Nor can they be anticipated in what we can gather about his early political interests, which appear to have been minimal. We know that by 1885 (when he was 28) he was a Tory, but that is not necessarily saying much. In a letter of October that year he recounted joining in the electioneering in Birmingham, and helping to unseat the incumbent Radical; but the main focus of the letter is his dog Scap who, we are told, 'wore his colours like a man'.[19] The Conservative allegiance stuck, but there is never any sign – as there was in the case of Kipling – that any sophisticated thought went into it. He later grumbled that the 1906 Liberal landslide, for example, had 'installed the *waiters* in place of the gentlemen'.[20] That hardly indicates a refined political intelligence. But Elgar wrote very little about politics in any case; and nothing at all that has been preserved before 1885. If that year, when he 'came out' as a Tory, was also when he became one, it is possible that there were 'imperial' reasons for it, as we shall see. If he was Tory before 1885, however, it might mean anything. People voted Conservative for a variety of motives. Patriotism was certainly one, after Disraeli had appropriated the slogan for the party in the 1870s; but there were also others. They included literal conservatism – simply wanting to keep things as they were; fear of domestic radicalism or socialism; the Tory association with the countryside, so beloved by Elgar; admiration for one's 'betters', despite in Elgar's case his treatment at their hands; and purely local factors. There was certainly no reason why a Tory had to be an imperialist in any committed or even vaguely aware sense, before the events that may have turned Elgar in this direction in 1885.[21]

Indeed, looking objectively at both his background and his personality at this time, there was no reason for him to be aware of his imperial identity – even perhaps his national identity – at all. Imperialism was not an issue in Worcester in the 1860s and 1870s. It was coming to be so in intellectual circles, with – for example – the publication of Sir Charles Dilke's *Greater Britain* in 1868, and John Ruskin's extraordinary Oxford inaugural lecture as Slade Professor in 1870, when he seemed to be advocating imperialism as a means to spread art in the world;[22] but it begs an awful lot of questions to assume that Worcestershire folk, and especially of Elgar's class, had any idea at all of that. It hugely underestimates Britain's cultural unevenness; and the factors that will have cut Elgar off from this milieu: geography, class, education, religion. Even patriotism will not have been much in evidence. Worcester people did not fly Union Jacks. The army – a common focus of national loyalty in other countries – was generally hidden. We need to be aware of this peculiar *restraint* in the English when it came to expressions of patriotism in mid-Victorian times. Elgar often referred to it himself, as we have seen. He knew he was reacting *against* his environment when he affected jingoism eventually. Nothing in his early life contributed to it. Everything we know about his first 28 years, from his letters, reminiscences of friends and family, and his activities, suggests a young man whose horizons were rigidly bounded by his provincial – not his national – surroundings; by his music, which was the only thing that encouraged him to transcend those horizons, and then straight to Germany, the fount of great music; by the sights and sounds of nature; and by his introspective dreamings. This is not the soil in which imperial plants are grown.

And then, if any doubts remain: there is the music. The earliest extant Elgar composition – a slight one – dates from 1867.[23] From 1878 to 1885 he wrote a great deal, most of it now forgotten, except occasionally in recycled forms.[24] What is interesting about this corpus is the un-Elgarian feel of it – according to conventional notions of Elgar – almost entirely. Those of his compositions that involve words – songs, religious pieces, instrumental or orchestral works with illustrative titles – avoid the national, the grandiose, and the bombastic almost perversely. Many of them are dances, or religious pieces. Several involve jokes. The subjects of the rest are typically love, nature, the wind, babies (lullabies), friends and small dogs. Several writers have remarked on their 'femininity'.[25] In 1883 he wrote and had performed an orchestral *Intermezzo Moresque* which might possibly be considered 'orientalist', and therefore imperialist by association: if it were not for the fact that to most contemporaries it sounded less 'Moorish' than French or Slav. The commonest comparison was with Delibes.[26] He also wrote a *Peckham March*, a very slight piece;[27] and – perhaps more redolently – *A Soldier's Song*, for voice and piano, in 1884. That could be described as militaristic, but is not at all patriotic.[28] Nor is it easy to detect a patriotic or imperialistic tendency in any of his more abstract music: no pre-echo of the 'nobilmente' style, for example, before the middle 1880s. Elgar once famously declared that he plucked his music from the air around him.[29] In that case the air around Worcester in the 1870s and early 1880s – and probably in most other places in Britain – must have been singularly devoid of imperial themes.

II

Whatever it was that made Elgar into an imperialist, therefore, it was not his background. Before the mid-1880s he represented that other Britain, the non-imperialist one, which is usually forgotten in modern cultural historians' accounts. He became an imperialist quite late on in his life. The first of his compositions which are unambiguously imperialistic – that is, they mention the empire – date in fact from 1897, when he was 40 years old. (They are *The Banner of St George*, whose Epilogue celebrates the

> ... great race, whose empire of splendour
> Has dazzled a wondering world!

and his first proper march, which is called the *Imperial*.) But of course one should not be pedantic about this. Imperialism does not always call itself such. Its presence can be indicated by other tell-tale signs, references to other values – or even language – which are commonly associated with it. We must be careful here, because some of those values – what John MacKenzie terms his 'ideological cluster'[30] – can also be used for entirely different purposes. Some ludicrous errors have been made by cultural scholars who, glimpsing a flash of a dolphin's fin in the water, have assumed it belonged to an imperial shark. In this case, however, we can say that it probably does, because we get a closer view of the shark later on. At the very end of the 1880s the character of Elgar's music suddenly changes. It becomes more confident, celebratory and bold. The best-known example is his concert overture *Froissart*, completed in June 1890, whose brassy, leaping opening is unprecedented in Elgar's output. There are definite pre-echoes of *Land of Hope* here. So this is where it starts.

There are two possible reasons for that. A couple of things happened at around that time, which clearly affected Elgar. The first was in the public sphere. That was the surge of popular interest in imperialism that took place in the middle 1880s, surrounding three main events: the controversy over Irish home rule, which had an imperial dimension; the first Anglo-Boer war; and the death of General Charles Gordon in Khartoum in January 1885. We have no idea what Elgar thought of any of these things at the time they happened – there is no reference to them in any exactly contemporary documentary sources – but we do know that he felt deeply about the Gordon issue a little later on. In the 1890s he toyed with the idea of writing a symphony about it, though that came to nothing.[31] Nonetheless Gordon is an obvious tangible link between Elgar and the Empire. Whether it was the imperial aspect of the affair that attracted him, however, is another matter, to which we shall return.

The other event of this time that affected Elgar was more private. That was his marriage to Alice Roberts. That took place on 9 May 1889, two-and-a-half years after they met. Alice's importance to Edward in all kinds of ways is well known. She ruled his manuscript paper when they were too poor to buy it; wrote poems he could set

to music; apparently spotted the possibilities of the *Enigma* theme
before he did, while he was aimlessly extemporizing;[32] and bucked
him up, which often took some doing. She may also have made him
into an imperialist, in two ways. The first is very speculative, and may
be felt to be indelicate. One of the new qualities to be seen in *Froissart*
is its stirring, exhilarating, masculine tone. The same is true of many
of the more minor pieces he wrote at this same time – of his meeting
with Alice – often to words by Alice, and on patriotic and military
themes. There is a great deal of 'thrusting' in them (of 'flashing
swords').[33] The first time this kind of thing appears is in a song called
The Wind at Dawn of 1889, again to a poem by Alice, which is fairly
calm for three stanzas, but then bursts out exultantly with this:

> To his tawny mane and tangle of flush
> Leapt the wind with a blast and a rush;
> In his strength unseen, in triumph up-borne,
> Rode he out to meet with the morn!

Is it fanciful – or even prurient – to see in that, and also of course in
the motto Elgar attaches to *Froissart* – 'When Chivalry lifted its lance
on high' – a hint, at any rate, of Freudian undertones? The completion
of *Froissart* coincided with the birth of the Elgars' daughter, Carice.
They may have had the same genesis. Elgar was almost certainly – of
course this is unproveable, but it would certainly be expected of a
young man of his background – a virgin when he married Alice. She
therefore, as the phrase goes, 'made a man' of him. Masculinism and
imperialism are supposed to be related.[34] But these are murky waters
for a historian to venture into.

Besides, there is a far more direct and obvious 'Alice' link. She was
the one with the 'hard' opinions of the two. Everyone noticed this:
her 'violent political prejudices' against the lower orders, for
example;[35] and her vindictiveness towards the 'diabolical' Germans
during the Great War.[36] She was also an overt imperialist. There can
be no dispute about that. She came from an Indian army family –
father, brothers – and had even been born in the subcontinent.[37] She
was very definitely a part of that 'other' Britain, from which Elgar had
been rigidly excluded before then. In linking his life with hers, Elgar
was laying himself open *for the first time* to that Britain's cultural
influence. Alice helped it along with the patriotic verses that, initially,
came more naturally from her than from him. This is the most
obvious cause of his conversion to imperialism; though it may not be
the deepest, as we shall see.

III

'Conversion', however, may be too strong a word.   Converts are usually zealous for their new faiths. It is not at all clear that Elgar was. Outside his music – in his correspondence, for example, his writings and people's memories of him – there are almost no references to it. Though widely travelled for his time, in Europe and even the Americas, he never visited a single British colony, with the exception of a few days in Canada, which he found 'drearily cold'.[38]   He expressed no recorded opinions about the many burning imperial issues of his day, with two half exceptions: a pro-Unionist petition he signed in March 1914,[39] and a couple of glancing references in letters to tariff reform.[40] (Both these questions of course also had a domestic side.) The *most* burning imperial issue of his day seems to have left him cold, or at least distracted. In the year 1900, when everyone else was apparently getting in a frenzy over the war in South Africa, and one or two other composers were writing music for it (Sullivan, for example, a *Te Deum* to be ready for the victory), Elgar was immersed in very different worlds: those of the *Enigma Variations*, the *Chanson de Matin, Sea Pictures*, the *Serenade Lyrique, Three Characteristic Pieces*, some songs, and the *Dream of Gerontius*. No-one knows his view of the war itself. It should not be assumed that he automatically supported it. His friend Jaeger did not.[41] The Great War of 1914-18, which it is possible (though not convincing) to regard as an imperialist war, distressed Elgar – as we shall see – beyond measure. If it were not for his patriotic music, no-one would have particularly noticed him as an 'imperialist' at all.

So, how about the music? The first and most obvious point to be made about it is how little of it after the turn of the twentieth century – and the first flush of his marriage – can be characterized as imperialistic, or even patriotic, in any way. The *Banner of St George,* the *Imperial March* and *Caractacus* all date from the late 1890s. Afterwards came the *Pomp and Circumstance* Marches (two in 1901, followed by the others in 1904, 1907 and 1930); the *Coronation Ode* (1902, then revised for 1911); a *Coronation March* (also 1911); the *Crown of India* music (1912); *The Spirit of England* (1916); *Fringes of the Fleet* (1917); and the *Pageant of Empire* music of 1924. There are also some minor patriotic songs; and occasional pieces that are not patriotic but sound as though they ought to be. (Other composers –

Haydn and Bruckner, for example – wrote bold brassy *Te Deums*, but only Elgar (1897) could have seen it as a March Past, with God taking the salute.) Even including marginal pieces, however, this only represents a very small fraction of his total output. As well as this, some of it is very thin. His longest explicitly imperial pieces (the *Crown of India* and *Pageant of Empire*) are no more than occasional music; which is not to say that the former, at any rate, is not good in its way. He did not invest a great deal of his talent in it. He saved that for his more serious works.

Secondly: the sort of imperialism that is expressed even in these few pieces is highly selective. That of course was not uncommon. Much of the wide appeal of imperialism in the late nineteenth and early twentieth centuries derived from the fact that it could mean different things to different people, ranging from highly aggressive expansionism, associated with militarism and race pride, through to a beneficent idealism that could be said to be almost internationalist. (The best example of that is the scheme that George Bernard Shaw – one of Elgar's great supporters, as it happens – drew up in 1900 for a socialist Commonwealth.)[42] Elgar leaned to the latter of these two positions, if either. That finds its clearest expression in the late *Pageant of Empire* music, whose Finale, after a series of songs representing the different 'white' dominions, lauds the spirit that draws them together.

> 'Twas love that linked our realms in one
> And love in joy that crowned them!
> Then Freedom took her throne,
> And peace was breath'd on ev'ry sea
> And music swelled around them.
> No more the dreams of war shall sound
> When hearts and realms in one are bound:
> For love binds all our hearts in one.

The other major themes here, besides 'unity', are 'freedom' and 'peace'. 'Freedom' comes up repeatedly in Elgar's patriotic pieces. It is prominent, of course, in 'Land of Hope and Glory', whose second line lauds Britain as 'Mother of the free'. It also appears in the Finale of *Caractacus*. Of course it is possible to regard this cynically (has not every aggressive power claimed to be advancing some kind of 'freedom'?), but there are reasons we shall come on to later for thinking that it was genuine in Elgar's case. The pacifism may be more surprising, and will probably be more distrusted as a consequence. Disapproval of Elgar rests largely on his reputation as an *aggressive* patriot. No-one much minds gentle nationalist composers (*Finlandia, Ma Vlast, Sverige...*), but not a 'jingo'.[43] And one cannot be both a jingo and a pacifist.

Elgar would not have called himself a pacifist, and was certainly not one in his (comparative) youth. The evidence for that is the settings he made of Alice's swashbuckling poems in 1892, poor as they are:

> But sword in hand we'll board the foe
> And shouting loud old England's name
> We'll storm their deck with thrust and blow,
> Then welcome death or life the same...[44]

and the frankly expansionist sentiments of his early patriotic works. The best known of these is the second stanza of *Land of Hope and Glory*:

> Wider still and wider,
> Shall thy bounds be set...

but there are others.[45] It is difficult to conceive of any way Britain could have widened her bounds at that particular time in history without fighting. It follows – assuming Elgar approved the words he set (which is reasonable) – that he was an imperial expansionist, and therefore by implication a militarist, up to 1902.

Beyond that, however, the evidence for any kind of militarism in Elgar runs very thin indeed, and at some points directly counter to it. 1902 saw the composition of arguably the most grimly militaristic music he ever wrote: a section of the *Coronation Ode*, 'Britain, Ask of Thyself', for bass solo, male chorus, and orchestra dominated by trombones and drums; but it was the militarism of desperate resistance rather than aggression.

> Britain, ask of thyself, and see that thy sons be strong,
> Strong to arise and go, if ever the war-trump peal;
> See that thy navies speed, to the sound of the battle-song,
> Then, when the winds are up, and the shuddering bulwarks reel,
> Smite the mountainous wave, and scatter the flying foam,
> Big with the battle-thunder that echoeth loud and long;-
> See that thy squadrons haste, when loosed are the hounds of hell:-
> Then shall the eye flash fire, and the valorous heart grow light,
> Under the drifting smoke, and the scream of the flying shell,
> When the hillside hisses with death, – and never a foe in sight.
> So shalt thou rest in peace, enthroned in thine island home;-
> Britain, ask of thyself, and see that thy sons be strong!

The context for that was the enormous blow to Britain's pride that her military embarrassments in the Boer War had occasioned, and consequent fears about what was called 'national deterioration', which dominated public debate at this time.[46] Later in the same work comes a section pleading for 'Peace, Gentle Peace', for unaccompanied voices, which aptly complements it. So in a sense does the music of the trio of *Pomp and Circumstance No.1* which rounds off the whole *Ode*, if we ignore Benson's upbeat lyrics, which several contemporaries felt fitted the tune's descending cadences rather badly.[47] The genesis of that tune may in fact confirm this reading; several of its key phrases are first found, in Elgar's notes, in a setting he contemplated, but then abandoned, for Kipling's *Recessional*, which of course is a sombre warning against national triumphalism.[48] Against that it has to be said that the orchestration of the *Ode* version is not at all sombre; but that may have been simply to whistle up national courage in the dark.

Thereafter Elgar clearly lost his taste – if he had ever really had it – for war. That is shown in his subsequent works. The marches were not for fighting by, but for ceremony; hence the overall title of his most famous set. There is nothing intrinsically militaristic about them.[49] *Pomp and Circumstance* No 1 has been used as a Socialist signature tune (in Spain in the 1980s), a football song ('We hate Nottingham Forest ...'), and at American University Commencements (played very slowly on the organ). No 4 – the other one with a 'big tune' – has been fitted with at least three sets of words: the first, by Alice in 1910, celebrated a newly-built London street, *The King's Way*, ending with a stirring plea to 'England's sons across the sea' to 'fight to keep it free' (for what – traffic?); in 1928 that was replaced by Alfred Noyes's *Song of Victory*; which in turn gave way to A P Herbert's *Song of Liberty* in 1940. It works just as well as a democratic march as an imperial one.[50] Elgar always intended to make one of the set a 'Soldier's Funeral March', but never got round to it.[51] That he had regard for the terrible side of soldiering as well as its glories is evidenced by a fine part-song he published in 1907, *The Reveille*, which is full of doubts and omens. No one would want to march to that.[52] At this time, however, this kind of thing seems to have come more easily to him than the braggadocio that was more often expected of him. About the same time as *The Reveille*, he was asked for a 'Marching Song' by Novellos; he obliged eventually with *Follow the Colours* ('Roll the drums and blow the fifes, And make the bagpipes drone ...'), but it was only after a huge struggle: 'I am truly grieved about these marching verses but I really cannot *feel* any of them' he wrote back at one stage; and not to his satisfaction.[53] In 1909 he started writing a *Patriotic Song* but put it aside: Percy Young claims this was because it was too anti-German, but no words survive, and the musical sketches appear sad and wistful.[54] That takes us up to the real test of his 'militarism', which was the Great War.

IV

Elgar failed that with flying colours.[55] His failure was all the greater because of what was expected of him: He was pestered for new battle songs. 'This is not the moment when Elgar should be silent', wrote Hall Caine to him, pompously, when he turned down one such request in October 1914.[56] He tried his hand at one or two, not very successfully.   *The Chariots of the Lord*, premièred by Clara Butt, set some words of a hymn urging that 'the power of God be shown, To quell satanic might; To rescue those who strive alone, Despondent in the fight.' One of Elgar's biographers calls it 'frankly a pot-boiler', but it has its moments.[57]   *The Birthright* is an odd piece, scored for boys' voices with bugles and drums, and reading rather like a Boy Scout promise:

> Serve thy God, thy king, thy land;
> By thy comrade firmly stand;
> Grimly fight, if duty call,
> All for each, and each for all –
> Freedom's joy in life possessing,
> And in death, thy Country's blessing'[58]

The Roll Call (September 1914) seems to be lost. It too was sung by Clara Butt, but then withdrawn and probably suppressed by the composer. It cannot have been very good.[59]   *Fight for Right* (1916) is a stirring injunction to 'loosen thy sword in the scabbard and settle the helm on thine head, For men betrayed are mighty, and great are the wrongfully dead'. The words are taken from one of the Socialist William Morris's Old Norse pastiches.[60] Elgar's best war music of this rousing kind is probably the *Fringes of the Fleet* cycle he composed to words by Kipling in 1917 – their only collaboration – and conducted, with his singers kitted out in sou'westers, in various music halls all over the country, until Kipling stepped in and scuppered it. A contemporary review characterizes the piece well:

They were songs permeated with the breath of the sea, vibrating with the great pure life of the out-of-doors; and the joyous freedom of wind and waves. I loved these songs; there was a fine feeling of patriotism about them; they spoke to one of the throbbing, restless life of the sea, and the courage and the daring of the men who make it their home.[61]

All in all however these pieces must be reckoned failures as war weapons, which is what Elgar had been expected to provide. None of them was anything like as inspiring as *Land of Hope and Glory*, which consequently took on a new lease of life in 1914 as a popular patriotic tune. (In the meantime Elgar had altered the words to make them seem less aggressive.)[62] Alice Elgar's press cuttings books are full of accounts of spontaneous renditions at public meetings, and letters like this, from a private at the front in 1916 describing the excitement of his first moments under fire, and his emotions on seeing a picture of home: 'I knew that England depended on us; and the knowledge set me aglow with pride. I wanted to sing "Land of Hope and Glory" '.[63] But *Land of Hope and Glory* was an old joint, re-heated. It did not represent the Elgar of *now*.

The Elgar of now was the Elgar of *The Starlight Express*, a long children's piece written in 1915; of the recitations: *Carillon* (1914), *Une Voix dans le Désert* (1915) and *Le Drapeau Belge* (1916); and of the cantata *The Spirit of England* (also 1916). Of all these genres the escapist one would seem to be the least relevant to Britain's war needs at that time; but another letter from the front suggests otherwise:

> Though unknown, I feel I must write to you tonight. We possess a fairly good gramophone in our mess, and I have bought your record 'Starlight Express'... It is being played for the twelfth time over. The Gramophone was Anathema to me before this War because it was abused so much. But all is changed now, and it is the only way of bringing back to us the days that are gone, and helping one through the Ivory gate that leads to fairy land or Heaven, whatever one likes to call it ... Our lives are spent in drunken orgies and parachute descents to escape shelling or Bosch aeroplanes. In fact the whole thing is unreal, and music is all that we have to help us carry on.[64]

But it was the other pieces that Elgar considered his genuine 'war work'. All of them concentrate on the *pity* of war, the recitations in order to stir outrage against the inhumanity of the enemy. Emile Cammaerts' poetry touched his deepest feelings at that time, which were of confused, depressed anger at how his beloved Germany – the home of music and of so many of his closest friends – could now have turned so bad.[65] They are all about the violation of 'plucky little

Belgium', Cammaerts' homeland. *Carillon* begins with a dead march, then blazes defiance, salted with a melancholy description of children's graves 'neath scented poplar trees. *Une Voix* further develops the 'innocence defiled' imagery with a young girl's voice singing of spring from a ruined cottage in the middle of a dead, silent battlefield. It is far more subdued. The brief *Drapeau Belge* makes play with the colours of the Belgian flag, black denoting the 'blood of soldiers' and 'tears of mothers', and the red and yellow the triumph to come. It also contains a wistful little oboe theme that could have come straight from *The Starlight Express*.[66] These are affecting pieces, and were popular at the time. So was the better-known *Polonia*, a rousing orchestral *fantasia* on Polish national themes.[67] Poland, of course, was another innocent victim of the Hun. All these works embody patriotism, but generally it is the patriotism of other countries, or of Britain – by implication – in defence of freedom and the weak. It should go without saying that they are not 'imperialistic', or even British-nationalist, in any sense.

The Spirit of England, his major war work, sounds from its title as if it should be just that.[68] It also undoubtedly starts badly, for those who disapprove of this sort of thing.

> Now in thy splendour go before us,
> Spirit of England, ardent-eyed,
> Enkindle this dear earth that bore us,
> In the hour of peril purified.
>
> The cares we hugged drop out of vision.
> Our hearts with deeper thoughts dilate.
> We step from days of sour division
> Into the grandeur of our fate.

'Sour division' has a clear contemporary right-wing resonance, for those familiar with the political history of the pre-war years. (It refers to democracy.)[69] The mood gets stronger, with a description of Germany as Europe's 'vampire' – to a brief snatch of the Demons' music from *Gerontius* – which has been much criticized. The liberal Elgarian's defence of this rests on the fact – which is true – that he completed the first part last, a good 14 months after parts 2 and 3, and with great difficulty, *especially* the anti-German stanza, where he resorted to the *Gerontius* music only because he could not generate any decent new hatred in 1916. His heart was not in it. But it did quicken to the poetry (by Laurence Binyon) of the other two sections, which are about the sufferings of women in war, and death and mourning. In Part 3, 'For the Fallen', wrote Billy Reed later, 'he was able to resume once more his own noble, natural style'.[70] C W Orr described it as 'a work so poignant in expression that it seemed almost too painful to listen to during those times of agonized grief and suspense'.[71] Elgar himself regarded 'For the Fallen' as equal in merit to *Gerontius* and *The Kingdom*.[72] It may be thought to compensate for the bitterness (but not the jingoism, still) of the rest.

That bitterness was as much against the War itself as against the Germans. He made few explicit statements about it outside his music, or at any rate that have been recorded; but this famous one from very early in the War, already printed above as a motto, encapsulates his view.

> Concerning the war I say nothing – the only thing that wrings my heart & soul is the thought of the horses – oh! my beloved animals – the men – and women can go to hell – but my horses; – I walk round & round this room cursing God for allowing dumb brutes to be tortured – let Him kill his human beings but – how CAN HE? Oh, my horses.[73]

Someone who can be stirred to such depths of misanthropy as this is not a warrior. No wonder he found it so difficult to celebrate the War – or even its ending. In November 1918 Binyon asked him to set his new 'Peace Ode' to music, only to be rebuffed on the grounds that it seemed too comforting: 'I regret the appeal to the Heavenly Spirit which is cruelly obtuse to the individual sorrow & sacrifice – a cruelty I resent bitterly.'[74] In the end the lugubrious 'For the Fallen' became Elgar's peace anthem, re-named, abridged and arranged (for chorus and military band), to accompany the dedication of Lutyens' Cenotaph in Whitehall in 1920: although as things turned out it was not performed there.[75]

Many people at that time had their jingoism squeezed out of them by the experience of the Great War. In Elgar's case there was probably no need. Militarism was one of the Roberts family influences that never really rubbed off on him. He tried to take it on board, with that early doggerel she wrote for him; and even managed to persuade himself occasionally that he had 'some of the soldier instinct in me'.[76] At best, and early on, he could swashbuckle with the worst of them – flashing swords, whizzing bullets, 'up and at 'em boys!' – but rarely convincingly. He found writing explicit marching songs a terrible drudge. It was alien to his nature, or upbringing, or whatever else it was that gave him the gentleness and ultra-sensitivity he was always trying to hide. There is one reported remark of his that suggests an actual antipathy towards the military life he so purported to admire. It came when Alice complained that since her marriage to him she no longer had access to the Army & Navy Stores. 'No', Elgar replied, 'abruptly', according to Rosa Burley; – 'because I don't make it my business to kill my fellow men.'[77] That was either a result of mere petty irritation at not getting a store card; or a moment when the mask slipped.

V

That does not however entirely dispose of the matter. Elgar had one passion – almost an obsession – which can be seen as *quasi*-military. It is sometimes confused with militarism, or dismissed as a mere cynical cover for it. In Elgar's case, however, it was almost certainly not.   This is why it must be dealt with (in this paper) entirely separately from the question of his 'jingoism'. The passion was for 'chivalry', which infuses nearly all his patriotic and imperial music.[78]

Chivalry is a strong theme in his early (pre-1900) works in particular. He first learned about it, as we saw, at his mother's knee, and then direct from the pages of Holinshed. It appealed to him as an ethical code, 'demanding personal honour, generosity, loyalty and courage', as a recent definition has it.[79] It is mainly associated with pure-souled mediæval knights righting wrongs.   It was almost certainly this that first attracted him to the Gordon affair: not the expansionary or military aspects of it, but the pervasive contemporary myth of Gordon as Christian martyr-hero, which was heightened for Elgar when either his fiancée or his priest – we cannot be sure which – presented him with a copy of Cardinal Newman's *The Dream of Gerontius*, with marginalia transcribed from Gordon's own copy of the poem, which he had been studying in Khartoum when he died.[80] Some Catholics believed this indicated that Gordon was about to go over to Rome.[81] That would have given them a link with the British imperial enterprise they had sorely lacked before. So far as Elgar is concerned it is unlikely that he would have responded to the Sudan adventure as he did without that allusion to his religion and to chivalry. It must be significant, surely, that this is the only imperial event in his lifetime that directly inspired – albeit abortively – a serious musical work.

The *Gordon Symphony* came to nothing (unless it was

re-cycled);[82]   but the chivalry came up again repeatedly in other forms. The *Froissart* overture of course explicitly celebrates it; and his mediæval cantatas – *The Black Knight* (1892) and *Scenes from the Saga of King Olaf* (1896) – inevitably hint at it. Elgar's first major patriotic piece is even named after the patron saint of chivalry. *The Banner of St George* retells the familiar story of the brave knight rescuing a virgin princess from the clutches of a 'mighty dragon vast and dread', thus putting the city of Sylenë – which up to then has had to furnish the dragon with a regular diet of such delicacies – out of its misery.   It is at the end of this that Elgar places his first explicit imperial exhortation, with the help of a noble tune and some terrific percussion effects. The context of the poem, however (by Shapcott Wensley), makes it very clear that this imperialism is conditional on its being used in a chivalric way. St George is vital to it, just as his cross is 'central' (Wensley's word, though it is difficult to see the literal logic of it) to the Union flag. And St George only fights in noble causes.

> Where the strong the weak oppress,
> Where the suffering succour crave,
> Where the tyrant spreads distress,
> There the cross of George must wave!

Then, in case the message was missed the first time:

> O ne'er may the flag beloved
> Unfurl in a strife unblest,
> But ever give strength to the righteous arm,
> And hope to the hearts oppressed! [83]

It appears again in that notorious final chorus of *Caractacus* (1898), following on from the passage cited already ('Britons, alert!'):

> And where the flag of Britain
> In triple crosses rears,
> No slave shall be for subject,
> No trophy wet with tears,
> But folk shall bless the banner,
> And bless the crosses twin'd
> That bear the gift of freedom,
> On every blowing wind. [84]

St George is not mentioned by name. But he is still there, in spirit. The moral is plain. Elgar believes the British Empire to be a force for good in the world. But it is the good he is fundamentally interested in, not the force. This is salutary, not celebratory.

Of course there were many people in Britain who said this kind of thing at the time, and may not have meant it. Chivalry can be used as a tawdry excuse for aggression. At least one of Elgar's modern critics suspects that this was what he was up to.[85] But in his case there is no reason – no underlying militaristic spirit apart from this, as we have seen – to think so. He was probably naïve and idealistic enough to genuinely believe in the myth. Another reason for thinking this is that the theme disappears from his work for a while after the turn of the century. *Land of Hope and Glory* may be thought to imply chivalry, with the 'Mother of the free' a kind of female version of St George, and the 'nobilmente' markings – Elgar's neologism, of course – hinting at it. (Chivalry was an essentially aristocratic – 'noble' – virtue.) Ten years later it makes a brief appearance in the *Crown of India* masque: the 'Entrance of St George'.[86] Apart from this, however, the brave knight is scarcely visible again before 1914.[87] That may be because he seemed less convincing an image for the British army after the latter's well-publicised 'atrocities' against women and children (the 'concentration camps') during the Boer War. It was then that the 'chivalric' illusion of imperial warfare was pricked for many Britons.[88] We have no direct evidence for this; but Elgar may well have been one of them.

The Great War saw a temporary resuscitation, albeit in far less jaunty attire. The recitations clearly refer back to the St George legend, with Germany as the dragon and Belgium and Poland ideally cast as damsels in distress. What is lacking is any convincing appearance of the hero himself, in what are mainly angry and desolate pieces. Elgar's best contemporary stab at that came in his boys' marching song *The Birthright* (1914), mentioned already, which embraces the knightly creed,

> Simple, courteous be thy word,
> Straight and true as knightly sword.
> Be for woman's honour bold,
> Gentle to the weak and old ...

but to music, unfortunately, which is risible. On the assumption we have been broadly following in this chapter so far, that the worse his music is, the less committed he probably was to its subject,[89] it seems that he had little confidence in the saving power of chivalry any more. And when that was taken away, the imperialism became an empty husk.

VI

The two large-scale celebratory imperial works he wrote late in his career – the *Crown of India* (1912) and the *Pageant of Empire* (1924) – illustrate this perfectly. Both were pleasant but facile, and not highly regarded by Elgar. The first was commissioned to celebrate the Indian coronation of the new king-emperor, and for a very large fee. (Elgar often complained that the more trivial his music, the more he was paid for it.)[90] In its original form it was a long work, in twelve 'tableaux': the version on record today is a scaled-down *Suite*. Even so it was not considered long – or perhaps attractive – enough to fill a whole programme at the London Coliseum, where it was staged, and so shared its billing with – for example – an overture by Wagner (*Tannhäuser*) and a march by Fabiani (*Le Lion de St Marc*); the 'Five Cliftons, Gymnastic Equilibrists'; 'Billy Merson, The New London Eccentric Comedian'; 'Thora, a Ventriloquial Novelty'; 'Dimitri Andreef, The Famous Russian Solo Harpist'; some songs by 'Rudolfo Giglio, the Chanteur Neopolitain', a scene from J M Barrie's play *The Twelve-Pound Look*, starring Miss Irene Vanbrugh; a whole pantomime, called *Pierrot's Last Adventure* (that came straight after the Masque); and – to round things off – a view of some 'Topical and Interesting Events' through 'The Bioscope'.[91] This was the *context* of Elgar's piece. It was not intended seriously. Nor was it originally supposed to stand on its own, without the gorgeous settings that were expensively built for it:

SCENE: – A Temple typifying the legends and traditions of India. At the back is a view of the Taj Mahal at Agra. In front of it and occupying the entire scene is a semi-circular amphitheatre of white marble, its boundary defined by steps at the summit of which is a semi-circle of sculptured and fretted seats of marble, for the Twelve Great Cities of India...
At the rise of the Curtain, INDIA and her CITIES are discovered ... INDIA is raised aloft upon the central throne, the seats to right and left of her being vacant, but upon the right one is placed a cushion covered with cloth of gold, bearing a Chaplet of Lotus and a palm branch.
After a Musical prelude, the Curtain rises on darkness, upon which a faint steel blue light gradually dawns, warming by degrees to amethyst, which slowly changing to rose is finally succeeded by a golden glow which deepens and increases till all the scene is flooded with full light.
When the lights are up a NATIVE CROWD, or rather the indication of one, is seen to be gathered at either end of the semi-circular rostrum, some

characteristic FIGURES lying and squatting across the full width of the
Stage in front of it. At one end is A NATIVE MUSICIAN with a tom-tom,
at the other a couple of SNAKE CHARMERS with pipes ... As the light
begins to brighten there file up on to the stage from the two archways
right centre and left centre a double line of INDIAN NAUTCH GIRLS.
When there takes place

AN INDIAN DANCE ... [92]

It is easy to see why Elgar – the boy in him, perhaps – thrilled to
all this. The music he wrote for it was perfectly fitted for it: illustrative
and 'mood' music, rather in the nature of film scores today. Judged
by these standards (compared with William Walton's film
masterpieces, for example), it certainly does not deserve Diana
McVeagh's verdict on it ('rock bottom'). It achieved great popularity
at the time, raking in the money for Elgar, and retained it for some
years afterwards, with the BBC broadcasting it 102 times (including
extracts) between 1922 and 1934.[93] Some of the snootier contemporary
critics had some fun with it, especially with St George's 'electric light
halo', which apparently caused the singer (Mr Harry Dearth) much
discomfort; and everyone was a little disappointed that the composer
did not manage to come up with another *Land of Hope and Glory*,
which most of them seem to have gone there in anticipation of. St
George's song *The Rule of England* – obviously Elgar's stab at this –
was, they all agreed, not quite up to it. (It did not find its way into the
Suite.) Some of them had also expected more 'orientalism'. [94] But *The
Crown of India* succeeded in its general purpose, which was to
entertain. Elgar probably would not have objected if it had also
bolstered British imperial pride. That probably depended on whether
it was the 'March of the Mogul Emperors' and the 'Entrance of John
Company', two of the most spectacular tableaux; or the 'Ventriloquial
Novelty'; or possibly the winsome dancing Nautch Girls, that were
uppermost in the minds of his punters as they left the Coliseum.

Pageant of Empire comes from the same stable. It was written to
a commission, for music to mark the opening of a grand British
Empire exhibition that was being planned for Wembley stadium in
1924, as a desperate attempt by imperialists – this at least is one way
of looking at it – to revive a popular enthusiasm for the empire that
was flagging. It consists of an *Empire March* and a set of eight songs.
The March Elgar described only as 'a bright 4½ minutes'.[95] But it was
not used anyway, allegedly because of a shortage of rehearsal time,
and was replaced by the earlier *Imperial March*. Elgar conducted part

of the programme, which also revived 'It comes from the misty ages' from *The Banner of St George*. Conservative newspapers found the occasion imperially exhilarating: the *Morning Post* for example read 'the very spirit of that broad and tolerant Imperialism, to which the King had referred in his speech' into the Elgar march;[96] but Elgar himself, as it happens, hated it – 'all mechanicil [*sic*] & horrible – no soul & no romance & no imagination...' He was also irritated by the philistine King's forever demanding *Land of Hope and Glory* when he wanted to play him other tunes.[97] The songs are very tame. The contemporary critic Cecil Barber noted that 'on examination neither the lyrics nor their settings are aggressive'.[98] One imagines he felt he needed to say that because of Elgar's reputation. In fact one of them is distinctly gloomy: a lament to 'The Immortal Legions',[†] the soldiers who died to 'save England', which harks back to his Great War mood.[99] Another could be read as implicitly anti-imperialist. It is based on the idea of the endurance of great art, compared with the dust into which all earthly empires ultimately crumble. This is also hinted at in the earlier *The Music Makers* (1912), his personal artistic manifesto (and a strange hotch-potch of self-quotations), one stanza of which relates how:

> With wonderful deathless ditties
> We build up the world's great cities
> And out of a fabulous story
> We fashion an empire's glory:
> One man with a dream, at pleasure,
> Shall go forth and conquer a crown;
> And three with a new song's measure
> Can trample a kingdom down.

One critic, the ridiculous Cecil Gray, took that literally, to mean that the artist could inspire the conquest of 'real' empires, presumably by whipping folk up with stirring tunes – yet more evidence of Elgar's gross jingoism[100] – but in fact it simply describes (surely?) the power of the imagination to build fictitious wonders and knock them down. 'Shakespeare's Kingdom', the opening song of the new cycle, elaborates that, contrasting the endurance of Shakespeare's poetry when set against the transience of Britain's material glory when he arrived, penniless and unknown, in London.[101] That is really quite a subversive thought for the occasion it was written for. It may be little wonder, then, that the *Pageant* music, unlike the *Crown of India*, was not even successful as entertainment.[102]

† - see track 15 on the accompanying CD

So: where does this leave Elgar as an imperialist? A less
whole-hearted one, it seems – certainly a more complicated one –
than is usually assumed. He was – to recapitulate – not born or
brought up an imperialist, or even with any significant awareness of
the empire, until his thirties, at the earliest. He possessed none of the
attributes, personal or in his social environment, that were likely to
turn him to imperialism, until his marriage in 1889. That, together
with the special circumstances (for him) attaching to the Gordon
affair, effected a conversion at around that time. It was always
however a very partial conversion, with his appearing to take
virtually no practical interest in the empire itself at any point in his life
thereafter, and embracing only a very few of the 'cluster' of values
that are said to have essentially accreted themselves to the empire
then. We have discussed his lack of a convincing militaristic attitude,
despite the efforts of a bellicose wife and the demands of his public in
the Edwardian years. We have not yet mentioned – simply because
there is only negative evidence to suggest it – that he does not seem
to have been a racist (certainly not an anti-semite),[103] or an 'orientalist'
of the derogatory type.[104] He felt highly ambivalent about the
capitalism that has often been seen at the 'taproot' of British
imperialism, especially in his own time.[105] The only thing linking him
intimately with the empire was a pure myth – the trope of 'chivalry'
– which he found evaporating startlingly, however, after the turn of
the century, effectively casting him adrift from the empire, certainly
emotionally. Hence the deliberate superficiality of his later imperialist
works; and the paucity of them throughout his career, with the
possible exception of the late 1890s, by comparison with one or two of
his contemporaries: especially Sir Arthur Sullivan, who wrote a larger
number of explicitly imperial pieces, even if few of them were as good
as Elgar's.[106] Of course we can only be certain of those of his
compositions with words or titles. We have not discussed – because
the present writer is not equipped to do so – the question of whether
'imperial' traits can be inferred from his abstract works. (Is there such
a thing as a 'jingo' cadence or key?) Judged by his representational
pieces, however, Elgar comes over as a pretty toothless sort of
imperialist, as these things went; more dolphin, really, than shark.

VII

There remains one final puzzle. Elgar did not mind being *taken* for a jingo. He even encouraged it. His whole life after the age of thirty was a performance, choreographed to make him appear 'blimpish', ultra-patriotic, militaristic, stupid, even – for goodness sake! – a philistine. Hence the soldierly bearing, the moustache (to make his upper lip look stiffer), the country sports,[107] the outrageous political opinions, and the pretence that he did not understand the technicalities of musical composition when strangers tried to discuss them with him.[108] Everyone close to him knew that this was a huge bluff, a mask. It irritated many of them, and even seemed pathetic.[109] It is entirely contradicted by the great bulk of his music, and what we know of his underlying personality. His reputation since his time has been enormously damaged as a result of this. So why did he do it?

One obvious answer is that it was to conform to the dominant imperial ethos of the time. No matter how temperamentally un-imperial Elgar was, the argument goes, he could not hope to escape the spirit of his age, even if it was only to pretend to conform. Unfortunately that will not wash. Other artists, after all, did not give in. Only a very few composers went even as far as Elgar along the 'jingo' path. Most resisted.[110] Many of them were less 'English' than Elgar, of course (Stanford, Delius, McEwen, MacCunn), but that by no means disqualified them from sharing in the imperial enterprise at that time.[111] The main reason why they (and Parry, Cowen and Corder) abstained was that this was thought to be not a proper artistic concern. Art was above politics, and certainly above this crude, boisterous, tribal sort. This was not lost on the imperialists. Contemporaries noticed how little support the empire got from the cultured set.[112] Some of them would not have wanted it otherwise. Many instinctively distrusted art. This was a common reaction, in what may well have been one of the most philistine cultures (the British nineteenth-century middle classes) in recorded history. Foreigners tended to assume that this betrayed a lack of taste or sensibility or capacity, but it was very largely deliberate. Art was widely believed to be (a) useless, and (b) effeminate. Britain's greatness – first commercial, then imperial – was based on utilitarianism and manliness. Art threatened both. It is difficult to find texts to support this – philistines were too busy doing useful and manly things to want to write about it – but there are some,[113] and plenty of broader hints. Gilbert and Sullivan's operetta *Patience* (1881) expresses it satirically. The Oscar Wilde affair (1895) heightened contemporary suspicions about the connection between art and 'effeminacy'. So the stand-off was mutual. This was yet another of the conflicting currents that ran through British society at this time. Elgar himself felt it. In 1902 he wrote to Jaeger of 'the horrible musical atmosphere ... in this benighted country'; with which Jaeger (of course) agreed: 'England *ruins* all *artists.*'[114] So it would have been possible for him – even natural, in view of what he revealed of his deepest feelings in *The Music Makers* – to become part of this alternative discourse. He would have been in good contemporary company.

The reason he did not was, at bottom, social. It had nothing at all to do with the seductive power of imperialism *per se*. He was fairly immune to that. But he was not immune to the need for social acceptance. We have noticed already his almost pathological sense of social insecurity throughout his life, even suspecting people of referring to his lowly origins – 'his father keeps a shop' – behind his back.[115] Class was a far more powerful force in British life in the later nineteenth century than patriotism, which more often than not was an artificial device exploited by the upper classes to try to defuse its dangers, usually in vain. Elgar was obsessed by it. This was not all simple snobbery. His origins – coupled of course with his religion – *were* a terrible drag on his art. None of his colleagues (or rivals) had the social disadvantages he had. Or at least if they did we do not know about them, because they simply went under, their talent snuffed out, probably by the need to teach the piano in order to eat.[116] Edward German was the closest to Elgar in social origins, and he made ends meet only by pandering to the taste of the philistines.[117] That was one way to survive: collaboration with the enemy. (It was Sullivan's, too.) Elgar was too principled, and convinced of his higher potential, for that. A second way was to have an established social position and private means, like Parry. But Elgar was not as fortunate. A third was exile. That was Delius' way. In retrospect perhaps Elgar should have uprooted to Germany, where he felt that his serious music was more appreciated than in England: except that this would have taken him from the Malvern Hills he was so emotionally attached to, and dependent for inspiration on. So he was trapped.

This was where the 'Alice' factor really kicks in. Whether or not this was why he married her (he seems to have loved other women romantically more), her great value to him was her *class*. She rescued him from social ignominy, which gave him a chance to be an artist. But it was at a price to them both. Alice's relatives disapproved of her marriage, believing it dragged her 'down'. 'They said he was an unknown musician; his family was in trade; and anyway he looked too delicate to live any length of time.'[118] Elgar – sensitive soul that he always was – was painfully aware of this, and determined to prove them wrong. The obvious way to do this would have been to give up his work as a musician entirely, and take up farming or join the stock exchange like other respectable bread-winners. But that was out of the question. (Quite apart from the violence it would do to his muse, he simply did not have the capital.) So he tried as far as he could to reconcile *his* music with *her* class. His 'imperial' pose and 'patriotic' music can be explained almost entirely in terms of that.

'Imperialism' carried a number of specific advantages for this purpose. First, it gained him an entrée into the upper (imperial) classes, in a way that Alice's appalling family would be forced, surely, to accept in the end. *Pomp and Circumstance* linked him with the pompous and circumstantial, rising even as high as royalty when a new monarch needed music to process by. Both of them enjoyed that, but Alice especially. (Edward went off royalty when George V came to the throne. He had managed to persuade himself that Edward VII was something of a music-lover, unaware apparently that he had slept through his own Coronation Ode until woken up by 'Land of Hope and Glory' at the end.)[119] 'I am so glad for Mother's sake that Father has been knighted', Carice is reported to have said in 1904. 'You see – it puts her back where she was.'[120] There is a story, which may be apocryphal or exaggerated, that after Alice's death Elgar threw all his honours into her grave, saying that he had sought them only for her.[121] Only patriotic music could have achieved that for her, and so enabled her to support him.

More important than the patriotism, however, was the *usefulness* of it. That addressed one of the main problems which faced most British artists throughout the nineteenth century: which was that their work was seen as marginal to the central – essentially material and practical – mission of the British economy and state. This certainly exercised Elgar. In his early cantatas *Caractacus* and *King Olaf* he gives very practical rôles to bards or 'skalds', who are the wise men of their tribes, respected even by kings and chiefs. There was little chance of that kind of respect in nineteenth century Britain. So Elgar settled for something less. This was the idea of the musician as what he called a 'troubadour', who could 'step in front of an army and inspire the people with a song'.[122] Coronation odes and military marches were a move in that direction. They were needed. You could not crown your king in silence. You had to have a beat to keep your army in step. Both were *useful*, at a stretch. Critics who have taken the well-known 'troubadour' quotation as evidence of Elgar's nationalism miss the *utilitarianism* that is clearly implied in it too. That was meant to appease the philistines.

Lastly, imperial music could be presented as 'masculine'. Elgar himself, in his writings, made much of the 'healthy, out-door' thing, which he claimed was one of the distinguishing characteristics of English – as opposed, one assumes, to Continental – music.[123] Marches of course are explicitly healthy and out-door: not only the walking up and down stiffly, but also the hard blowing and thumping that are necessary in military bands. So are sea-songs, which were another popular English form.[124] We have seen how Elgar's contribution to this genre, *Fringes of the Fleet*, was specifically commended at the time for its bracing qualities. And then, of course, there were the noble, self-disciplined, manly values celebrated in his 'chivalric' pieces. Maybe Elgar needed to emphasize these characteristics for his own personal reasons, in view of the 'weak' and 'feminine' qualities which others certainly saw in his personality and his music, and which he may have been frightened by.[125] As well as this, however, it must have reassured the philistines. It was good for them to have an English composer who they were told was 'great', and so played to their patriotism in this way (someone at long last to put up against the Germans),[126] but without any of those 'arty' qualities that so often tainted this kind of enterprise. It made Elgar socially acceptable, even something of a trophy.

Elgar's 'imperial' music, therefore, was essentially part of his answer to the problem of artistic survival in a philistine land. The philistinism affected it far more than the imperialism, which he did not embrace wholeheartedly, and, insofar as he did embrace it, did so only as a means to that other end. As an answer it was successful on the whole, enabling him to compose much great music with no patriotic agenda, and some lighter but terrifically exhilarating music under patriotic colours (*Pomp and Circumstance*), as well as the relatively small amount of occasional 'whooping' that was necessary to keep up his reputation. Of course it created tensions. Art is not really useful, or (particularly) manly. It was a strain pretending it was. This may account for Elgar's many black moods, especially after 1911 (the Second Symphony), when he felt both out of sympathy with his times, and rejected.[127] The latter may have been strictly unwarranted: it has been shown that his popularity remained high right through the 1920s and '30s;[128] or it may really have expressed a sense of being *misunderstood*. (It was the deeper Elgar that was neglected.) But looking at his mental struggle against the climate of his age it is remarkable – even heroic – that he managed to achieve as much as he did that so transcended that age; and ironic, to put it mildly, that the means he chose to wage that struggle leaves him open to so much misunderstanding still.

For if Elgar was an imperialist – and that is not a thing that matters greatly, being more a question of semantics or, at most, degree than of fact – he was not 'natural' one; nor a very deep or fierce one; nor an 'inevitable' one because of the dominant imperial ethos of his time. He came to imperialism accidentally, through his marriage, and in order to find some sort of social space to compose in, in the stifling social and artistic environment of his day. His life and works tell us much more about these aspects of British life than they do about its imperialism.[129] The superficiality of his imperial beliefs may also tell us much: if they reflect, as I believe they do, the uneven spread of the imperial spirit in the country more generally. For a small minority of people in *fin-de-siècle* Britain – mostly upper-class – the Empire was their religion, dominating their whole lives and values and 'discourses'; they desperately wished the majority of their countrymen to share it with them, in order – apart from anything else – to ensure its preservation, and worked hard to persuade them: but with mixed success. The majority of Elgar's compatriots were affected by empire, often in ways they (and historians until fairly recently) were largely unaware of; but there is no reason to suppose that it took them over completely, any more than it took over him. They had other priorities, other interests, other – sometimes conflicting – value systems. Occasionally imperialism could be harnessed to one of these; a well known example is the way Labour MPs played on the imperialists' fears of national 'physical deterioration' to secure social reform.[130] Sometimes it might distract them from those priorities, temporarily. More often than not it was a façade, or abjectly misunderstood, or simply a source of entertainment, or of harmless pride. There are probably not many cases where it came with marriage, as a kind of dowry, and as a means of gaining social acceptance, to counter the stigma of being an artist in a philistine land; but the triviality of that explanation must have been repeated in a thousand other ways. Imperialism was a veneer. This chapter is no place to try to demonstrate this as a general proposition. But if it was true for Elgar, of all people, it is at least a possibility that it was true more commonly.

NOTES and SOURCES

1. Gray, Cecil: *A Survey of Contemporary Music* (OUP, 1924) pp 79-81. The last section of the *Variations* ('EDU') has always seemed to me something of a self parody.
2. Here I should declare a personal interest. I am a passionate admirer of the music of Edward Elgar (I won't diminish him by calling him 'Sir' in this article: a merely temporal title, unworthy of his rightful position among the gods). I have tried however not to let that affect my objectivity.
3. Like Ernest Newman, who called the final chorus 'a serious blot ... much conventional doggerel ... flatly nonsensical ... lamentably inept ... banal ... The cantata is thus made to end in a splutter of bathos and rant' (Newman, Ernest: *Elgar* (London, 1906) pp 43-44); and Rosa Burley, who thought it 'so wildly absurd as seriously to endanger the whole cantata' (Burley, Rosa and Carruthers, Frank: *Edward Elgar: The Record of a Friendship* (London, 1972), p 115).
4. Young, Percy (ed): *Letters to Nimrod* (London, 1965) pp 151-52 (for Jaeger); Newman, Ernest: *Elgar*, p 48
5. McVeagh, Diana: *Edward Elgar: His Life and Music* (London, 1955) pp 186-7
6. See, for example, Kennedy, Michael: *Portrait of Elgar* (London 1968) ch 9
7. Lace, Ian: 'Elgar and Empire', in *Elgar Society Journal*, vol 10, no 3 (Nov 1997), p 130
8. I am referring here, of course, to those who argue that any members of a society involved in imperialism – its victims too – are inescapably entrapped in its discourse, whether they know it or not. Edward Said comes close to this reductionist position in his essay 'Yeats and decolonisation' (Eagleton, T *et al: Nationalism, Colonialism and Literature* (Minneapolis, 1990) p 74), though he later stepped back from that. Granted that the influence of empire can be subversive, and is more widespread than appears on the surface, there is no philosophical or empirical reason to believe it was more ubiquitous in Elgar's time than certain other – and even opposing – discourses.
9. For example *The Guardian*, 'Corrections and clarifications', 25 June 1999: 'Sir Edward Elgar was not responsible for the "rather nationalistic" jingle of

Land of Hope and Glory, Pass Notes, page 3, June 23. He wrote the music. The words, which Elgar strongly disliked, were written by Arthur Benson'.

10. For later doubts, see below, p 148
11. Elgar to Jaeger, 21 June and July 1898, in Young, Percy (ed): *Letters to Nimrod* (London 1965) pp 13, 16
12. Redwood, Christopher (ed.): *An Elgar Companion* (London, 1982) p 144. Elgar often referred to this alleged restraint in the English. 'We are not a patriotic people', he told an interviewer in 1916. 'We think we are, of course, but in the sense in which one might call the French or Russians patriotic, we are not. Perhaps we are a little too much afraid of that awkward self-conscious feeling, that so readily attacks the Briton, to let ourselves go in the matter of patriotic expression.' (ibid, p 144).
13. For example, Morris, James: *Pax Britannica* (London, 1968) pp 341-42, though Morris is sensitive to Elgar's other sides.
14. Burley and Carruthers: *Record of a Friendship*, pp 25-26, 44-45
15. Moore, Jerrold Northrop: *Edward Elgar: A Creative Life* (Oxford 1984) p 25
16. This is the story of his once cutting school to watch a piece of local pageantry, in which the High Sheriff visited his locality in a carriage and four with twelve javelin men, four footmen and two trumpeters; but even that was suggested to him by another boy, and in the event they both somehow managed to miss it. If it were not for his later 'Pomp and Circumstance' style it might not appear significant (ibid, pp 39-40).
17. Elgar Birthplace, EB 1556
18. Moore: *A Creative Life*, pp 68, 131
19. Elgar to C W Buck, 29 November 1885, in Young, Percy M (ed): *Letters of Edward Elgar and Other Writings* (London, 1956) p 21
20. Elgar to Frank Schuster, 20 Jan 1906 (ibid, p 167)
21. Elgar was certainly constitutionally anti-democratic. Billy Reed claimed he loved ordinary village people, but clearly in a very patronising way (Reed, W H: *Elgar as I knew him* (London, 1936) p 43). There are traces of this in the music: for example the 'Slay the Briton' chorus in *Caractacus*, and the portrayal of Judas as a Lefty revolutionary in *The Apostles*.
22. Cook, E T and Wedderburn, Alexander (eds): *The Works of John Ruskin*, vol 20 (London: 1905) pp 41-43
23. *Humoreske*, mentioned in Anderson, Robert: *Elgar* (London, 1993) p 4, and listed in Christopher Kent's invaluable *Edward Elgar: A Guide to Research* (New York, 1993) p 3
24. Kent lists 131 separate pieces, including transcriptions and fragments (ibid, pp 16-94).
25. For example Moore: *A Creative Life*, pp 100, 127
26. See Anderson: *Elgar*, p 14; Young (ed): *Letters of Edward Elgar*, p 9
27. This was one of the pieces he wrote for his wind band in 1877.
28. After its first outing, at the Worcester Glee Club on 17 March 1884, the song had two further incarnations, in 1890 and (re-titled *War Song*) 1903. The words are by C Flavell Hayward, and describe the excitement of battle:

> Hear the whiz of the shot as it flies,
> Hear the rush of the shell in the skies...

The last stanza pictures the war dead. It also has a refrain:

> Ah! Glory or death, for true hearts and brave,
> Honour in life or rest in a grave.

See Anderson: *Elgar*, p 284: 'It starts as rumbustious Valkyrie music in the minor and 9/8. Unfortunately Elgar marches into the major at 'Glory or death'. Despite Valkyrie resumption and a touching slow-down for 'Now the warfare is o'er' the song remains a lost cause.' It has been recorded by Stephen Holloway (bass) on *The Unknown Elgar*, directed by Barry Collett, on Pearl SHECD 9635.

29.   Interview with Elgar in the *Strand Magazine*, May 1904, reprinted in Redwood: *An Elgar Companion*, p 112

30.   MacKenzie, John: *Propaganda and Empire: The Manipulation of British Opinion, 1880-1960* (Manchester, 1984) p 2

31.   The progress of the symphony, such as it was, is chronicled in Moore, Jerrold Northrop (ed): *Elgar and his Publishers* (London, 1987) vol 1, pp 93-4, 96, 108 111, 114, 123. One of the reasons he gave for abandoning it was his belief that the British did not take to this kind of thing, giving rise to the 'patriotic caper' remark quoted above, p 3.

32.   Moore: *A Creative Life*, p 247, fn 199, tries to trace back the source of this well-known story.

33.   For example the songs *A spear, a sword*, and *1588: Loose, loose the sails*, both of 1892. The text of the former appears to be lost, except in a scribbled parody version copied at the Elgar Birthplace (EB354), which suggests that the song was not a huge success:

> A sword, a spear, – a spear, a sword
> A spear a sword – a sword, a spear!
> The audience is slightly bored
> They rush to purchase pots of beer,
> And still drink it while I'm singing here,
> Here all alone!

34.   For example Sinha, Mrinalinj: *Colonial Masculinity: The 'manly Englishman' and the 'effeminate Bengali' in the late 19th century* (Manchester, 1995); Dawson, Graham: *Soldier Heroes: British Adventure, Empire, and the Imaging of Masculinities* (London, 1994); and Rutherford, John: *Forever England: Reflections on Masculinity and Empire* (London, 1997).

35.   This is 'Cumberland' quoted in Redwood: *Elgar Companion*, p 131.

36.   Young, Percy M: *Alice Elgar: Enigma of a Victorian Lady* (London, 1978) p 178. Apparently this is characteristic of stay-at-home women in wartime: see Bourke, Joanna: *An Intimate History of Killing* (London, 1999) p 161. Some commentators refer to an earlier radicalism in Alice, which she later stifled: for example, Young: *Alice Elgar*, p 61; but it is difficult to find any convincing evidence for this. Her diary for 1917 welcomes the Russian Revolution; but that must have been because she misunderstood what it was. See pp 43-44.

37.   See Young: *Alice Elgar, passim*

38.   Elgar to Alice Stuart Wortley, 18 April 1911, in Moore: *A Creative Life*, p 612

39. Young, Percy: *Elgar OM: A Study of a Musician* (London, 1955) p 169; Moore: *A Creative Life*, p 664

40. One is a letter to Troyte, 24 March 1909, in Young (ed): *Letters of Edward Elgar*, p 188. (I have misplaced the other.)

41. '. . . this glorious campaign for Goldmines,' as he called it in a letter to Elgar of 14 Nov 1899 (Moore: *Elgar and his Publishers*, vol 1, p 149). It is possible that some of this rubbed off on Elgar. Another reason for speculating (only) that Elgar may not have been entirely happy with this most imperialist of British wars is given below, p 152

42. Shaw, G B: *Fabianism and the Empire* (London, 1900)

43. The *Oxford English Dictionary* (2nd edn, Oxford, 1989) defines a 'jingo' as 'one who brags of his country's preparedness for fight, and generally advocates or favours a bellicose policy in dealing with foreign powers'. Cecil Gray believed that the distinction between nationalism and imperialism in music was crucial: the former could inspire great works, the latter could not. 'The reason for this is simply that national feeling has its roots in the very soil... Imperialism, on the other hand, has no such basis in reality.' (*A Survey of Contemporary Music*, p 80). See also Ould, Hermon: 'The Songs of Sir Edward Elgar', in *English Review*, vol 47 (1928), pp 358-9.

44. *1588: Loose, loose the sails*, printed in Young: *Elgar OM*, p 112

45. For example, from the Finale of *Caractacus*:

> And ever your dominion
> From age to age shall grow
> O'er peoples undiscover'd,
> In lands we cannot know . . .

46. See my 'The Edwardians and their Empire', in Read, Donald (ed): *Edwardian England* (London, 1982)

47. For example, Rosa Burley: 'no tune the principal phrase of which works steadily down the scale can possibly produce an effect of hope, whatever it may achieve in the way of glory.' Burley and Carruthers: *Record of a Friendship*, p 154.

48. This is documented in Moore: *A Creative Life*, pp 338-39. The correspondence about *Recessional* (with Sir Walter Parrott) took place in late November and early December 1900; the first sketch of what later became *Pomp and Circumstance* No 1 was made on New Year's Day 1901. At the time Elgar claimed that 'I've had that tune in my pocket-book for twenty years without using it!' but that – as with so many of his other autobiographical *dicta* – should probably be taken with a pinch of salt. (McVeagh: *Edward Elgar*, p 36). On the other hand, of course, if it is true, then it means that the 'tune' pre-dated his imperial conversion.

49. Dozens of other composers' marches must be easier to keep step to. Figaro's *Non più andrai* leaps to mind. By all accounts the tunes the British First World War Tommy preferred to march to were music hall songs, sometimes with deeply subversive anti-war words. Examples are *It's a long, long way to Tipperary; Pack up Your Troubles; I don't want to be a soldier;* and *Gassed last night (and gassed the night before)*.

50. Anderson: *Elgar*, p 293. Two of these versions are on record: Alice's sung by

Teresa Cahill on *The Unknown Elgar* (above), and A P Herbert's sung by
Dennis Noble with chorus and the Band of the Coldstream Guards, in a
vintage (1940) performance reissued on the Elgar Society's *Elgar's
Interpreters on Record*, vol 2: Dutton Laboratories, CDAX 8020. The latter's
trio section goes:

> All men must be free,
> March for liberty with me
> Brutes and braggarts may
> Have their little sway
> We shall never bow the knee . . .

51. Interview in *Strand Magazine*, May 1904, reprinted in Redwood (ed): *An
     Elgar Companion*, p 123
52. This features on the London Symphony Chorus disc of *Choral Songs of Sir
     Edward Elgar*, cond Vernon Handley: Hyperion CDA 67019.
53. Moore: *Elgar and his Publishers*, vol 2, pp 679-87 *passim*. It is performed by
     Stephen Holloway on *The Unknown Elgar*.
54. Young: *Elgar OM*, p 140. The sketch is in the British Library, BL Add MS
     63160, f55v, with a copy at the Elgar Birthplace.
55. On Elgar's war music see chapter 1 and part 2 of this book.
56. Moore: *A Creative Life*, p 671
57. Ibid, p 662. McVeagh calls it 'a nasty piece of pretentiousness' (*Edward
     Elgar*, p 137), but it is sung quite upliftingly by Stephen Holloway on *The
     Unknown Elgar*. The première came just before the outbreak of war – but
     when that catastrophe was widely anticipated – on 24 June 1914.
58. Words taken from printed music at the Elgar Birthplace. It too appears on
     The Unknown Elgar, sung by the Tudor Choir, director Barry Collett, with
     trumpets and side drum.
59. See Moore: *A Creative Life*, p 670; Anderson, *Elgar*, p 118. There is some
     mystery over this. An entry in Alice's diary for 6 September implies that
     Elgar withdrew it *before* it was performed. But then comes this report of a
     concert at the Royal Albert Hall on 10 October: '. . . Then E's *splendid* Roll
     Call . . . Sir F Bridge came and s[ai]d, is not that Roll Call of Elgar's splendid'
     (EB 942). Yet contemporary concert programmes and newspaper reviews in
     the Elgar Birthplace collection contain no mention of it. Could Alice have
     been confusing it with *The Birthright*?
60. Also performed by Stephen Holloway on *The Unknown Elgar*.
61. *The Voice*, Oct 1917 (copy at Elgar Birthplace, EB 1333). The original
     performances (and settings) are described in Moore: *A Creative Life*, pp
     708-9. Even McVeagh tolerates these songs, crediting them with 'a not
     unpleasant raciness' (*Edward Elgar*, p 138). It was that raciness, however,
     that led Kipling to cancel the whole enterprise in December, because it no
     longer chimed in with his mood after the death of his own son in the war.
     The cycle has been recorded by Paul Kenyon, Stephen Godward, Simon
     Theobald and Russell Watson (baritones) and the Rutland Sinfonia,
     conducted by Barry Collett, on the CD *Elgar: War Music*, Pearl SHECD 9602.
62. It was the 'Wider still and wider' part that was changed, sometime in August
     1914, on the grounds that it was 'liable to [be] misunderstood now':

presumably by those who needed to be reassured that Britain was fighting a defensive war, only, against Germany: Elgar to Benson, 24 August 1914, in Jerrold Northrop Moore, *Edward Elgar: Letters of Lifetime* (London, 1990), p 278. Elgar's own replacement words are to be found pencilled in the margin of the bound edition of the score (Boosey, 1902) at the Elgar Birthplace, EB 1392:

> Leap thou then to battle, bid thy troops increase
> Stand for faith and honour, smite for truth and peace!

By this time, incidentally, Benson's own imperial and militaristic enthusiasms had waned considerably. See Hyam, Ronald: 'The British Empire in the Victorian Era' in Brown, Judith and Louis, Wm Roger (eds): *The Oxford History of the British Empire*, vol 4 (Oxford, 1999), p 47; and Young, Percy M: 'Elgar and Cambridge', *Elgar Society Journal*, vol 11, no 5 (July 2000) pp 272-73.

63. Elgar Birthplace, EB 1333, vol 3b. No source or date is given for the letter.
64. J Lawrence Fry to Elgar, 5 Oct 1917, quoted in Moore: *A Creative Life*, pp 694-95
65. '[T]he horror of the fallen intellect – knowing what it once was & knowing what it has become – is beyond words frightful': Elgar to Ernest Newman, 17 June 1917, in Moore (ed): *Letters of a Lifetime*, p 307.
66. All three works are included on Collett's *Elgar War Music* CD, with Richard Pasco a terrific narrator, and Teresa Cahill the innocent young girl in *Une Voix*. For other recordings of *Carillon* and *Une Voix*, see accompanying CD.
67. See Herter, Joseph A: 'Elgar's Polonia, op 76' (chapter 11 of this book)
68. As Andrew Neill points out on p 35.
69. It was a constant theme among pre-war imperialists that 'party politics' were largely to blame for what they saw as Britain's alarming weakness at that time. Some advocated a centrist or one-party government as the solution. Lord Rosebery's 'Liberal Imperialist' group was intended as a focus for such a government. Strife on the industrial, women's and Irish fronts was also looked on as enervating and unpatriotic. Imperialists of this ilk were often found wishing for war as a means of national unity against an external threat, and then welcoming it for that reason when it came in 1914.
70. Reed: *Elgar as I Knew Him*, p 55
71. C W Orr: 'Elgar and the Public', in *Musical Times* (January 1931) reprinted in Redwood: *An Elgar Companion*, p 272. Andrew Neill (p 216) characterizes the mood of these pieces as one of 'heroic melancholy' (quoting W B Yeats). To my untutored ear they have much in common with Britten's *War Requiem*.
72. Elgar to Alice Stuart Wortley, 12 Sept 1923, in Young (ed): *Letters of Edward Elgar*, p 284. I agree.
73. Elgar to Frank Schuster, 25 Aug 1914, in Moore: *A Creative Life*, p 670. Cf Billy Reed's account of their returning from one musical engagement discussing 'how awful it was, and how we hoped that it would all be over quickly': *Elgar as I Knew Him*, p 55.
74. Elgar to Binyon, 5 Nov 1918, in Moore (ed): *Letters of a Lifetime*, p 320

75.   The new title was *With Proud Thanksgiving*. See Anderson: *Elgar*, pp 143, 150; Moore (ed): *Windflower Letters*, p 233

76.   Rudolf de Cordoba, 'Elgar at Craeg Lea ', in *Strand Magazine*, May 1904; reprinted in Redwood: *Elgar Companion*, p 123

77.   Burley and Carruthers: *Record of a Friendship*, p 60. Burley goes on: 'Despite his military fantasies, Edward had little of the soldier in him'. She thought his 'military bearing... – a total contradiction in the least military of men – was an unconscious offering for Alice'. (*Ibid*, pp 183, 197)

78.   This of course is not a new idea. The 'chivalry' theme was picked up in much early Elgar criticism: for example Newman: *Elgar*, pp 127-30 (vis-à-vis *Froissart*), and in *Sunday Times*, 25 Feb 1934, reprinted in Redwood (ed): *An Elgar Companion*, p 155; Barber, Cecil: 'Elgar – Englishman', *Progressive Review*, vol 91 (1928), pp 554, 557; Scott, Hugh Arthur: 'Elgar: the Man and his Music', *Contemporary Review*, vol 145 (1934), p 468; and Hogarth, Basil: 'Edward Elgar – The Noble Romantic', *English Review*, vol 58 (1934), pp 432-33. The ultra-critical Cecil Gray compared Elgar himself to 'a knight errant who rides out seeking for any adventure that may cross his path': *A Survey of Contemporary Music*, pp 88-89.

79.   Cannon, John (ed): *The Oxford Companion to British History* (Oxford, 1997) p 203

80.   There is some confusion over this in the literature. Elgar himself claimed he received this volume as a wedding present from his parish priest in 1889: interview in *Musical Times*, October 1900, reprinted in Redwood: *An Elgar Companion*, p 48. Michael Kennedy follows this in *Portrait of Elgar* (1968) pp 24-25. Anderson, however, has him already in possession of it by May 1887, when he passed it on to Alice (*Elgar*, p 18); and Northrop Moore refers to Alice's copy of it at the Elgar Birthplace, with the Gordon markings taken from Edward's copy, and 'clearly dated', in *A Creative Life*, 120, fn 141. The relevance of this to our concern is that it might have a bearing on the precise date of Elgar's 'conversion' (above, p 142) to imperialism.

81.   Moore: *A Creative Life*, p 120

82.   There has been speculation that some of it later appears in *Pomp and Circumstance No 1*, and the First Symphony (1908).

83.   Elgar, Edward: *The Banner of St George* (Novello, 1897) p 2

84.   Elgar: *Caractacus* (Novello, 1898) p xiv

85.   McVeagh, Diana: *Edward Elgar*, p 184

86.   This doesn't appear in the Suite.

87.   There is also of course the comic-sad version in *Falstaff* (1913).

88.   On this see Krebs, Paula M: *Gender, Race and the Writing of Empire* (Cambridge, 1999) chs 2-3

89.   Of course this involves subjective judgements. One way of avoiding these might be to note which of his own compositions Elgar did, and did not, assign opus numbers to. Presumably he attached less value to the latter. *The Birthright* is one of these.

90.   For example Kennedy: *Portrait of Elgar*, pp 39, 44, 50, 93-4; and Moore (ed): *Letters of a Lifetime*, p 244: 'When I write a big serious work eg Gerontius we have to starve'.

91.   Taken from the original programme at the Elgar Birthplace (EB 1129).

92.   This is from the original libretto, at the Elgar Birthplace (*loc cit*). It was published by Enoch and Sons, creating trouble with Elgar's usual publisher, Novello, who complained at his not offering the work to them. Elgar replied that he didn't think it was 'in your line at all', ie that it was not serious enough. Moore (ed): *Elgar and his Publishers*, vol 2, pp 761-63.

93.   Moore: *A Creative Life*, p 630; Taylor, Ronald: 'Music in the Air: Elgar and the BBC', in Monk, Raymond (ed): *Music and Literature* (1993) pp 336, 352.

94.   These reactions are taken from cuttings of reviews in *The Times*, *Daily Telegraph*, *Morning Post* and *Morning Leader*, 12 March 1912, and the *Observer*, 17 March 1912, in Elgar Birthplace EB 1332.

95.   Letter to Percy Hull, 19 Feb 1924, in Young: *Letters of Edward Elgar*, p 285. The *Empire March* is another work to which he did not bother assigning an Opus number. A very early recording of it, by the BBC Wireless Symphony Orchestra conducted by Percy Pitt in August 1924 appears on the Elgar Society's CD *Elgar's Interpreters on Record*, vol 2.

96.   All this according to an article in the *Morning Post* on 'Music and the Empire', 24 April 1924. Other items were the Trauermarsch from *Götterdämmerung*, which must have raised people's spirits; the *Meistersinger* overture; Walford Davies's *God be in my head;* Purcell's *Soul of the World;* Parry's *Jerusalem;* and – at the end – the predictable *Land of Hope and Glory* and *Rule Britannia*, and the now forgotten Graham's *The Champions*. I have been unable to find the last-named in any of the normal musical dictionaries. Elgar Birthplace, EB 1334.

97.   Elgar to Alice Stuart Wortley, 26 April 1924, in Young (ed): *Letters of Edward Elgar*, pp 286-87.

98.   Barber, Cecil: *Elgar – Englishman*, p 556.

99.   The near-contemporary part-song *Zut, zut, zut* (1923) has a similar theme. It is probably Elgar's only successful marching song, but only because it depicts a ghostly march of the dead, remembering 'How we worked and drilled together... Gloried in danger, our sinew tight'ning...', and fading into silence at the end. Elgar wrote the words himself over a pseudonym. It is recorded on the Hyperion disc of *Choral Songs*.

100.   Gray: *Survey of Contemporary Music*, pp 79-80. The words of *The Music Makers* were by Arthur O'Shaughnessy. Not all of them are as bad as this.

101.   The words are by Alfred Noyes. The music of the middle stanza alludes faintly to the trio section of *Pomp and Circumstance No 1*. Was this meant to emphasize the superior hope and glory of art? Elgar was, of course, fond of musical riddles. His most mischievous and enduring riddle – the theme that is supposed to lie beneath the 'Enigma' melody – need not be addressed here, except to say that many of the 'solutions' that have been offered to the problem – for example *God Save the Queen* and *Rule Britannia* – may have been only thought of because they were presumed to be the kinds of pieces that Elgar, the imperial troubadour, would use. If his underlying priorities were not patriotic or imperial, however, it suggests other options. I have long thought that I could hear a connection between the 'Nimrod' variation (though not the main theme) and Schubert's *An die Musik*; but I am not a musician, and every musician I have suggested this to has given it short shrift. On extraneous grounds, however, that would certainly fit. So would

another solution that has been offered recently: *Twinkle, twinkle, little star* (*Observer*, 14 Feb 1999), which would tie in with Elgar's lifelong childish concerns.   On the whole, however, Jerrold Northrop Moore's preferred solution in 'The Return of the Dove to the Ark', *Elgar Society Journal*, vol 11, p 3 (1999), which does not require there to be a specific musical theme, carries more conviction.

102.   Two of the cycle, 'Sailing Westward' and 'The Immortal Legions' (nos 5 and 7), appear on Barry Collett's *The Unknown Elgar* CD; another, 'Shakespeare's Kingdom' (no 1), is on a Hyperion CD with that title, CDA 66136, sung by Sarah Walker, while 'Immortal Legions' and 'Song of Union' appear on the CD accompanying this book. Excerpts from the cycle were given 23 broadcast airings by the BBC between 1924 and 1934, most of them probably of 'Shakespeare's Kingdom', which is the only one to have achieved any kind of popularity (Taylor, 'Music in the Air', p 354). Otherwise the enterprise appears to have been a commercial failure; fifty years later the publishers still had most of the sheet music on their hands: Moore (ed): *Elgar and his Publishers*, vol 2, p 838.

103.   No-one has ever suggested that he was anti-semitic; see his letter to Adela Schuster 17 March 1933, quoted in Young (ed): *Letters of Edward Elgar*, p 316. The diary of his Mediterranean cruise he kept in 1905 reveals some prejudices against lower-class foreigners, but whether because they were foreign or lower-class is unclear.   The following entry may indicate something: 'I had a berth with a young Greek. Bouillon & then to bed: did not attempt to undress' (ibid, p 48).

104.   See ibid, pp 151, 158, for his sympathetic appreciation of Eastern music, heard in the course of this same voyage. We have noticed already the entire absence of 'orientalism' in his own music, even the *Crown of India* masque. Whether this implies more or less contempt for it is an open question; since the publication of Edward Said's *Orientalism* (1978) artists have not been able to win on this.

105.   'Economic taproot' was J A Hobson's expression, in *Imperialism: A Study* (London 1902). Elgar's distaste for capitalism was not highly developed and is only to be inferred from his strictures on the British music market (above, p 153), and his distaste for America's money-grubbing 'vulgarity': 'They asked me what I wd. take to settle in the States & conduct one of the big orchestras – I said nothing in the world wd. induce me to spend six months here – not $10,000,000 – this they do not understand': letter to Alice Stuart Wortley, 26 April 1911, in Moore: *A Creative Life*, pp 613-4. In 1928 Bernard Shaw tried to explain capitalism to him, but by then it was probably too late: Shaw to Elgar, 30 May 1928, in Young (ed), *Letters of Edward Elgar*, p 326. This does not really bear on the question of his 'imperialism', however; it was quite possible at this time to be both an imperialist and an anti-capitalist.

106.   Until his death in 1900, Sullivan was the real imperial laureate. His explicitly imperial pieces include an *Ode for the Opening of the Colonial and Indian Exhibition* (1886); another *Ode for the Laying of the Foundation Stone for the Imperial Institute* (1887); an *Imperial March for the Opening of the Imperial Institute* (1893); *Victoria and Merrie England* (1897); a 'Grand National Ballet', which includes dances for 'Colonial Troops' and an

Imperial March; and the already-mentioned 'Boer War' *Te Deum* (1900). He was also responsible for the famous – and very stirring – tune of *Onward Christian Soldiers* (1871), which reappears in the *Te Deum*.

Sir Alexander Mackenzie runs him close, with a *Jubilee Ode* and a choral song *The Empire Flag* (both from 1887), a *Coronation March* (1902), an *Empire Song* (1908), and a *Canadian Rhapsody* (1905) and *Four Canadian Songs* (1907). For the Crystal Palace performance of the *Jubilee Ode* we are told that 'the conductor had electric buttons beside the score to detonate cannon in the grounds, though not all came in on cue': Brian Rees: *A Musical Peacemaker: The Life and Work of Sir Edward German* (London, 1986) p 207.

Edward German is Elgar's only other competitor in this field. None of his works is as explicitly imperialistic as Sullivan's, but his operettas contain some stirring patriotic songs: for example 'The Yeomen of England' in *Merrie England* (1902) and 'We Red Soldiers Serve the King' in *Tom Jones* (1907); he contributed his share of the coronation music that was expected of establishment composers at that time, especially in 1911; and he set far more Kipling than Elgar did.

107. See Elgar to Jaeger, 21 Feb 1899: 'I'm just off to the Beagles & shall be away all day – no music like the baying of hounds after all'. He took up golf in 1892. Anderson: *Elgar*, pp 26, 42.

108. Rosa Burley commented on his 'rather trying pose of not being interested in music' (Burley and Carruthers: *Record of a Friendship*, p 62; and cf Reed: *Elgar as I Knew Him*, pp 140, 150.

109. Burley is the main proponent of the 'mask' idea (Burley and Carruthers: *Record of a Friendship*, pp 43, 45, 60; but it is corroborated by Ernest Newman's and Arnold Bax's contemporary impressions of him as someone trying to hide his unhappy and tortured soul by a 'show' of bluff (quoted in Moore: *A Creative Life*, pp 354, 358), and accepted – as I think it must be – by nearly all of his later biographers. For example McVeagh:, *Edward Elgar*, pp 86, 90; Trowell, Brian: 'Elgar's Use of Literature', in Monk (ed): *Music and Literature*, p 277; and many others.

110. For the exceptions see above, fn 106. Of the remainder, Charles Villiers Stanford wrote a *Jubilee Ode* (1887) and a *Jubilee Te Deum* (1898); a choral *Last Post* (1900) which had reference to the Boer War; some fine sea songs (more convincing and durable than Elgar's), and of course some Irish Rhapsodies. Hubert Parry wrote some coronation music, notably *I was Glad when they Said Unto Me* (1902), and a song called *England* (1916) which Diana McVeagh claims is superior to any of Elgar's patriotic songs: *Edward Elgar*, p 138; but in which Bernard Benoliel can only see 'a tired backward-looking quality': *Parry Before Jerusalem* (London, 1997), p 134. Parry's *Jerusalem* has, of course, been hi-jacked by jingoists (with help from Elgar, who provided the most stirring orchestral version), but that cannot be blamed on him. Apparently he was better pleased when the Women's Institute asked to be allowed to use it as their anthem. His cantata *The Vision of Life* (1907) includes some explicitly anti-imperialistic lines. Frederick Cowen wrote *Jubilee* (1897) and *Coronation* (1902) *Odes*, and an *Indian Rhapsody* (1903). A search through Frederick Delius's corpus

produces nothing, except possible orientalisms. Hamish McCunn wrote a choral work on Livingstone (the missionary-explorer) in 1913. George Macfarren is credited with a *St George's Te Deum* (1884). That is all I can find.

111. See MacKenzie, John: 'Scotland and the Empire', *International History Review* (1993); Fitzpatrick, David: 'Ireland and the Empire' in Andrew Porter (ed), *The Oxford History of the British Empire*, vol 3 (Oxford, 1999); and the contributions to this genre by the Scot Alexander Mackenzie (above, fn 106).

112. For example Salmon, Edward and Longden, Major A A: *The Literature and Art of the Empire* (London, 1924)

113. See my ' 'Monstrous Vandalism': Capitalism and Philistinism in the Works of Samuel Laing (1780-1868)', *Albion*, vol 23, p 2 (1991)

114. Elgar to Jaeger, 3 Jan 1902, quoted in Kennedy: *Portrait of Elgar*, p 99; Jaeger to Elgar, 8 Jan 1905, quoted in Moore: *A Creative Life*, p 452. Mary Beatrice Alder recalled him complaining that in Britain 'Great musicians are things to be ashamed of' (ibid, p 172).

115. This is from Burley and Carruthers: *Record of a Friendship*, pp 25-26, 44-45, 147-8. Burley is the one who makes the 'social stigma' point most forcefully; but it is corroborated by Elgar's interview with 'Gerald Cumberland' (C E Kenyon) reprinted in Redwood: *Elgar Companion*, pp 125-36; and developed by Meirion Hughes in ''The Duc d'Elgar': Making a Composer Gentleman', in Christopher Norris (ed): *Music and the Politics of Culture* (London, 1969). The 'father keeps a shop' quotation comes from a letter from Elgar himself to the editor of *The Musical Times*, 19 Sept 1900, quoted in Moore: *A Creative Life*, p 326.

116. That of course was how Elgar earned his keep early on: teaching violin and piano accompaniment, with no great enthusiasm. He was apparently bad at it (Burley and Carruthers: *Record of a Friendship*, pp 24-25), and determined not to return to it.

117. They shared similar backgrounds (West Country; fathers in 'trade'); both had crude right-wing political opinions; and they admired each other's music (Rees: *A Musical Peacemaker*, pp 20, 138, 225ff). But German seems to have been perfectly happy writing only 'light' music. That is the difference.

118. Young: *Alice Elgar*, p 95

119. The Edward VII story is told in Moore: *A Creative Life*, p 409. For the Elgars' feelings towards his successor, see Alice's comment in 1916 when she caught him fidgeting during a performance of *The Dream of Gerontius*: 'how different . . . was it in the days of King Edward' (Young: *Elgar OM*, p 181); and a letter from Edward (Elgar) to Alice Stuart Wortley in 1924, when he really went for him: 'everything seems so hopelessly & irredeemably vulgar at Court..' (Young: *Letters of Edward Elgar*, p 286).

120. Burley and Carruthers, *Record of a Friendship*, p 174

121. *ibid*, p 202

122. Elgar's first Birmingham lecture of 1905, quoted in Moore: *A Creative Life*, p 459

123. Interview for *Strand Magazine*, May 1904, reprinted in Redwood: *An Elgar Companion*, p 123

124. For example, Stanford's *Songs of the Sea*, op 91 and *Songs of the Fleet* op 117
125. For example he hated Philip Burne-Jones's portrait because he thought it made him look effeminate. Moore: *A Creative Life*, pp 642-43. See also McVeagh: *Edward Elgar*, pp 5, 46 and Trowell in Monk (ed): *Music and Literature*, p 277: 'the weedy lad . . . evidently needed . . . to feel kinship with his nation's fighting men'.
126. See for example reviews of the First Symphony reproduced in Moore: *A Creative Life*, pp 546-47.
127. There were a number of surface reasons for this: illness, the death of his friend Jaeger, the new reign, the relatively apathetic reception of the Symphony, and possibly simple burn-out.
128. See Taylor, Ronald: 'Music in the Air'; and Gardiner, John: 'The Reception of Sir Edward Elgar 1918-c1934: A Reassessment', *Twentieth Century British History*, vol 9, p 3 (1998)
129. Of course the two things are not necessarily unrelated. Utility and manliness – the aspects of philistinism emphasised here – served an imperial agenda in the later nineteenth century. If they originated in imperialism, or served its agenda exclusively, then it might be argued that their effect on Elgar was an indirect result of a hegemonic 'imperial' discourse, albeit indirectly. But that would be a difficult case to sustain historically and empirically.
130. See Gilbert, Bentley B: *The Evolution of National Insurance in Britain* (1966)

A wartime group at Bournemouth, 22 May 1918, with (left to right):
Back row: Godfrey's sons Frank and Dan (in uniform) flanking his daughter Joyce;
Middle row: Rev G A Johnstone, Godfrey's daughter Phyllis, Mrs Henry Robson,
Mrs Johnstone, Mr Hamilton Law;
Front Row: Dan Godfrey, Mrs Godfrey, Alderman and Mrs Bishop (Mayor and
Mayoress of Bournemouth), Sir Charles Villiers Stanford.

CHAPTER 5

BOURNEMOUTH
A Microcosm of Musical England

Stephen Lloyd

The Easter 1914 holiday season at Bournemouth, bright and sunny, began with record-breaking crowds. As described by the *Bournemouth Guardian*: 'The crowds which descended on Bournemouth were phenomenal. The rush commenced on Thursday 9 April when thousands of people came from all over the country. Excursion trains were packed, and by Thursday night nearly all the accommodation in the town was taken. The sands and promenade were crowded, the paddle steamers had a busy time, and 30,617 people strolled along the Bournemouth Pier as against 20,501 the previous year. As far as Bournemouth was concerned the black clouds of war which were starting to appear over the Continent did not exist.'[1]

By the time of the August Bank Holiday, as the threat of war was fast becoming a reality, the crowds had dwindled. Excursion trains and long sea trips farther than to Weymouth had been cancelled. The Sunday and Monday were quiet: on Tuesday war was declared.

Bournemouth, which had gained municipal borough status in 1890, had long earned itself a name as a fashionable middle-class resort in no small measure because of its health-enhancing climate. The railway link inaugurated in 1888 from London's Waterloo Station put the town within easy reach for the day trippers. While the beaches and the surrounding countryside may have been the chief attractions for most visitors, for a smaller culturally-minded number (that included, of course, a core of its residents) there was another attraction, stronger even in the winter than in the summer. As the March 1914 *Musical Times* observed:

> The amount of serious music that is packed into each week of the winter season is indeed phenomenal: the big cities of the kingdom, with populations seven or eight times as large as Bournemouth, do not show a greater musical activity than this South Coast resort exerts. It is indeed a remarkable manifestation of civic enterprise, revealing a spirit which is

> alone emulated in the enlightened centres of artistic thought on the
> Continent. Only as regards opera, which lies outside the domain of the
> municipal authorities does stagnation prevail.

This had been achieved through the efforts of one man, Sir Dan Godfrey (1868-1939), who gave Bournemouth the reputation it enjoyed, more than any other town, as a regular home for music, especially for British composers. Since 1893, when he had answered a request (actually addressed to his then more famous father) to supply a small band for the re-opening of the Winter Gardens, Godfrey had made it his duty, in addition to fulfilling the general need for music in the bandstands, in the gardens and on the pier, to expand his band of 30 into a full-size municipal orchestra and instigate regular seasons of orchestral concerts. This he had achieved within a remarkably short time. In 1895 (coincidentally the year in which Robert Newman and a young Henry Wood inaugurated the Queen's Hall promenade concerts) Godfrey gave the first of 39 annual series of weekly Symphony Concerts lasting from October until April, often with a parallel series of Popular Concerts, and with a rather less prestigious series of Symphony Concerts in the summer season as well. His other dream was to promote British music, whenever possible by inviting the composer to conduct his own music. *His* music ? One of Godfrey's great achievements was to provide an opening for women composers, and in 1927 he gave a concert entirely devoted to British women composers, probably the first of its kind.

In May 1896 Dan Godfrey's Band became the Bournemouth Municipal Orchestra, about 40 in number, and Godfrey was appointed the Corporation's resident Musical Director and Entertainment Manager. Dan advanced his plans cautiously, only too aware of the danger of upsetting his public and especially the town council with whom relations were rarely cordial. Fortunately he had his supporters.

In 1897 Edward German conducted a programme largely of his own works (he was to remain among the most frequently played of British composers), and other composers soon followed suit. The facing table illustrates how British music gradually infiltrated the programmes, often with the composer conducting.

The name of Elgar first made its appearance in the Winter Gardens programmes in April 1898 when his *Three Bavarian Dances* were performed. Yet despite the ready charm of this work it was not heard again for seven years. It was to be some while, too, before Elgar was

WINTER SYMPHONY CONCERTS SERIES

SEASON	TOTAL NO. OF WORKS	BRITISH WORKS	NEW BRITISH WORKS	COMPOSERS CONDUCTING
1895-6	193	15	6	0
1896-7	207	27	11	0
1897-8	255	24	14	3
1898-9	268	30	21	7
1899-1900	258	45	15	6
1900-01	228	41	25	15
1901-02	249	77	44	20
1902-03	265	75	39	26
1903-04	269	70	37	23
1904-05	252	58	28	21

to appear in person. As his fame spread, so gradually his works entered the Bournemouth programmes: in 1900 the slight *Sevillana* in January, the *Meditation* from *Lux Christi* in April, the *Mazurka, Salut d'Amour* (instead of *Serenade Mauresque*) and *Contrasts* in October, and the *Serenade for Strings* in November. Even this last appealing work was not repeated until two years later. In 1901 were introduced *Chanson de Matin* and *Chanson de Nuit*, the Overture *Froissart*, and, in December, Elgar's first masterpiece, the *Enigma* Variations, conducted by Godfrey because, as he announced at the start of the season, Elgar 'is so busy that he cannot spare the time'. Elgar was to elude Dan Godfrey for a few years yet.

When in February 1902 the Orchestra notched up its 400th concert, *Pomp and Circumstance* March No 1 was heard at Bournemouth for the first time. For the occasion the band was enlarged to 60. The *Cockaigne* Overture, the most frequently performed at Bournemouth of all Elgar's substantial works, was introduced by Godfrey in January 1903. In April he conducted the *Coronation Ode*, first given at the Sheffield Festival the previous October. Towards the end of the year Godfrey gave the Prelude and 'Angel's Farewell' only from *The Dream of Gerontius*, a work he considered to be 'one of the few really inspired religious works we have had since Handel's *Messiah* and Mendelssohn's *Elijah*'.[2] Five years were to elapse before he was able to give the complete work.

In March 1905 came the first of many hearings of Elgar's expansive *In the South* overture, and in April 1908 Elgar's *Introduction and Allegro for Strings* was performed. This work, which had been generally slow to establish itself since its first performance in 1905, almost certainly because of the relative complexity of its string writing, must have taxed the smaller complement of Bournemouth strings (up to the war about 27) as much as any work at that time. Although Godfrey repeated it in May, he did not take it up again until 1925. (These three were the work's only Bournemouth performances during Dan Godfrey's time. Similarly, Vaughan Williams' *Fantasia on a theme by Thomas Tallis* received only two performances, in 1923.)

It was not until the 1908-9 season that Elgar made his first visit to Bournemouth, the first of eight.[3] In his end-of-season speech Godfrey spoke of 'unavoidable obstacles' having stood in the way of 'the only one of our leading English composers who had not favoured us with a visit'. In September Elgar wrote to Alfred Littleton, chairman of his publishers, Novello & Co: 'I have been asked for so many years by Godfrey to go to Bournemouth & he has asked me again now . . . & I think I ought to go there if possible. Godfrey has done so much English music &c.'[4] Although immersed in proofs and preparations for the première of his First Symphony, Elgar wrote to Worcester Cathedral organist and close friend Ivor Atkins: 'I have to conduct on S Coast watering places for needed bread . . .'[5] Consequently on 21 November, three days after he had conducted two concerts at Eastbourne with the Duke of Devonshire's Orchestra (an afternoon concert in which he shared the conducting with Pierre Tas, and an evening performance of *Gerontius*), Bournemouth was at long last able to welcome Elgar at the Winter Gardens for a special Saturday afternoon programme similar in content to the first of his Eastbourne concerts but with the addition of the *Enigma* Variations: the *Meditation* from *The Light of Life*, the new *Wand of Youth Suite No 2*, *Pomp and Circumstance* Marches Nos. 2 and 4, and *Sea Pictures* with Maud Santley.

In his autobiographical *Memories and Music*[6] Godfrey wrote of Elgar: 'My personal acquaintance with Sir Edward Elgar is slight, for he is not the kind of man with whom it is easy to get on terms of intimacy. He has always appeared to me to be very reluctant to acknowledge public applause, a habit which is apt to be misunderstood, and I am told that it is far easier to get him to talk about his pet hobby than music.'[7] But it is Eric Coates who tells the story of a hobby that Dan Godfrey unwittingly led Elgar into:

It was in Dan Godfrey's rooms at the Winter Gardens, Bournemouth, that the famous composer of *Gerontius* turned his attention to something far removed from the religious . . . Elgar was very mystified at the frequent and sudden entrances to and exits from the room of a small page-boy, who was continually handing Godfrey little slips of paper in exchange for sums of money, some small and some large. He was even more mystified when he heard 'two-thirties' and 'three o'clocks' and 'three-thirties' and such enigmatical expressions as 'both ways', 'ten to one' . . . and so on . . . What could Godfrey be playing at? Unable to check his curiosity any longer, he politely enquired of the musical director what it was all about. Horses![8]

At first horrified, Elgar was eventually persuaded by Dan to place a small bet, and when this proved a winner, another followed until by the end of the afternoon he was well and truly 'hooked'. The upshot was that some weeks later Godfrey received a telegram suggesting the name of a horse as a sure winner in a particular race – from Elgar!

Within a fortnight of Elgar's first appearance at the Winter Gardens came the première in Manchester of his first symphony under Hans Richter. Performances in London and the provinces followed in rapid succession, the Queen's Hall audiences witnessing two with Richter in December and three with Elgar in the new year. Quickest off the mark to take up the new symphony was Joseph Sainton on 16 January for his first Brighton Festival with the normally 40-strong Brighton Municipal Orchestra, pipping even Henry Wood to the post. George Halford gave it exactly a month later in Birmingham, four days before Richter conducted it at Eastbourne with the Duke of Devonshire's Orchestra augmented by 27 London Symphony Orchestra players, and at a 'special concert' on Saturday 27 February 1909 Godfrey introduced the work to Bournemouth. 'At great expense' ran the advanced publicity for this special concert, and members of the LSO were hired to swell the orchestra to 60. Ticket prices were raised to cover the additional cost, and a large audience braved bitter winds and snow to hear the new symphony. Godfrey repeated it at another special concert in April, this time with extra players from the Queen's Hall Orchestra, but Bournemouth had to wait until 1922 before Elgar came to conduct it himself.

Despite the work's popularity, it was only to achieve seven performances during Godfrey's time. Its comparatively infrequent scheduling had less to do with the demands of the score but instead rather more with a reason Dan Godfrey put forward in a 1923 *Musical Mirror* article:

> Elgar is our greatest man, but it is a pity that the performance of his works
> is so handicapped by big performing right fees as it is . . . Seven guineas for
> such works as *Falstaff*, etc., will place them on the shelf. At the same time
> the composers' and publishers' interests must be guarded, but I believe in
> the end it would pay them to allow permanent orchestras to purchase sets
> of these works for their own performance at a reasonable price.

Elgar was certainly the star of the 1908-9 season, and Godfrey followed the Symphony's two hearings with a performance on 4 May of *The Dream of Gerontius*, repeating it the following April, with Gervase Elwes in the name part on both occasions. Of the second performance *The Musical Times* commented that 'Madame Newling's choir sang the music with insight, but narrowly escaped disaster in the exacting Demon chorus. The playing of the Municipal Orchestra was magnificent.' That season also included the two *Wand of Youth* Suites, *Cockaigne* and *In the South*.

In July 1910 the Bournemouth Centenary was celebrated with a ten-day festival planned 'on a scale quite unprecedented in modern English life'.[9] In addition to military tournaments, balls held on the pier and masked balls in the covered skating-rink, athletics meetings, car rallies, motor-boat regattas and the first international aviation meeting (at which C S Rolls crashed and died shortly afterwards), there was music of all varieties. The chief focus was on the Winter Gardens concerts with such celebrated artists as Nellie Melba, Agnes Nicholls, Clara Butt, Wilhelm Backhaus, Mischa Elman and Vladimir de Pachmann. The highlight of these was an all-British composer-conducted programme. Godfrey began with Sullivan's *Macbeth* Overture, after which Parry conducted his *Symphonic Variations*, Mackenzie his *Burns Rhapsody*, Stanford his *Irish Rhapsody No 1*, Elgar his *Pomp and Circumstance* March No 1 and the second *Wand of Youth* Suite, and German his *Welsh Rhapsody*. Uncertain that British music alone would ensure a good audience, Godfrey saw to it that each half of the concert concluded with songs at the piano from a popular vocalist of the day, Margaret Cooper.

This historic occasion was suitably snapped for posterity: photographs were taken of the orchestra with its six conductors, and two of just the conductors.[†] What these photographs do not reveal is the tension that existed between two of the participants. Elgar and Stanford were not then on speaking terms, a situation that had arisen over nine years ago and was to last for nearly 20 years.[10] For the camera the two sat at extreme ends of their group. Alice Elgar recorded in her diary that Stanford 'fled when he saw E.' Another

† - see page 199

observer of this split was Parry who, unlike other visitors who had arrived either by car or train, had sailed all night from Littlehampton aboard his yacht *The Wanderer*, arriving at Bournemouth at 4.30 am. Only then did he get a 'little sleep & was quite tired out by the morning'. His diary entry confirms the hostility:

> Fine – had a bathe. Went ashore at 9.45 and up to Pavilion. Rehearsed Variations, the band playing with great spirit. Stanford, Mackenzie, Elgar, German came: Stanford refused to speak to either Elgar or Alfred Littleton [of Novello]. We were all photographed – I suggested photographing the band, which was done. Came off to the yacht for luncheon . . .

At the concert 'there was a large & very exuberant audience. Everything went well & the audience cordial. The programme was lightened by Miss Katie Cooper who was very charming. Got on board at 10.30. Bad night.' Parry set sail at 4.30 the following morning.

A special booklet published at the time of the Centenary included a complete list of works performed by the Municipal Orchestra since October 1895. This drew attention not only to the extraordinary breadth of Godfrey's repertoire but to his unflagging devotion to British music. This booklet and the Centenary concert probably provided the spur for some well-deserved recognition the following year. On 1 March 1911 Stanford wrote to German:

> I have had a talk with Mackenzie and Parry, and we all agreed that it would be a right and proper thing to give Dan Godfrey a dinner from the composers of England whom he has so nobly backed. (There are 114 of them!) It will probably be on May 15. Mac will take the chair. Wallace has undertaken to be the Secretary. We all felt that the circular to go out had best be signed by the five in the photo – Mac., Parry, Elgar, yourself and me. Will you agree to this?[11]

A circular was duly sent out, signed by the five composers with the addition of Cowen, and stating that 'It is proposed to entertain Mr Dan Godfrey, Conductor of the Bournemouth Municipal Orchestra, at a Dinner at the Criterion Restaurant [London] on Monday the fifteenth of May, at 7.30 pm, in order to give the Composers of this Country an opportunity of showing their appreciation of his persistent and practical championship of native art, and of his successful efforts to make the public familiar with the best music of all Schools'.

On the afternoon of 15 May 1911 the Municipal Orchestra, as part of a Festival of Empire, gave its first London concert at the Crystal Palace, the home for August Manns' enterprising concerts from 1855 until his orchestra was disbanded in 1901. All six signatories to the circular were represented in another similar all-British programme: Elgar's *Imperial March* and second *Wand of Youth* Suite, Sullivan's *Macbeth* Overture, Parry's *Symphonic Variations*, Stanford's song-cycle *Cushendall* with Plunket Greene, German's *Welsh Rhapsody*, Cowen's scherzo from the *Scandinavian* Symphony and *Yellow Jasmine* from *The Language of Flowers* Suite, and Mackenzie's air de ballet *La Savannah*.

The dinner that evening in Godfrey's honour received detailed coverage in the Press. There were speeches from Mackenzie (who took the chair), Parry and Stanford. Both Mackenzie and Stanford went as far as suggesting that Godfrey had assumed the much-respected mantle of Manns, with Mackenzie stating that Godfrey had achieved a record only equalled by that of the Crystal Palace under Manns, and Stanford calling him 'the greatest friend of the British composer since the days of the late dear Manns'.[12] It was a parallel that Godfrey was pleased to accept as a compliment both to Bournemouth and to his orchestra. Press reports do not mention Elgar, and although his name is included on a typed list of over 80 musicians who attended (with a few hand-written additions), only a week previously he had returned from a six weeks' tour of North America and was now busily preparing for the first performance of his Second Symphony in nine days' time, so quite likely he was not present. Perhaps, too, Stanford's involvement acted as a deterrent.

The greatest excitement of the 1910-11 Bournemouth season was generated by Elgar's new Violin Concerto, premièred at the Queen's Hall on 10 November 1910 with Elgar conducting and Fritz Kreisler as soloist. With remarkable alacrity Godfrey secured the first provincial performance, with Kreisler, at a special concert on Wednesday 23 November, a week before the work's original exponents were able to repeat their success in London. Bournemouth audiences were even treated to two further performances of the Concerto that season, at special Saturday concerts on 4 February again with Kreisler, and on 22 April with the 20-year-old May Harrison (who played the Mendelssohn concerto as well). The Elgar was heard yet again in the summer when the soloist on 22 August was the 27-year-old Marie Hall who, when only 11, had a lesson from Elgar and in 1916 was to record an abridged version of the Concerto with the composer. Godfrey conducted all four performances.

During the 1911-12 season the limelight was again stolen by an Elgar work, this time the Second Symphony, which had been premièred at Queen's Hall in May 1911. The new symphony was first heard at Bournemouth,[13] the composer conducting, on the afternoon of Saturday 9 March 1912 in a special 'Grand Orchestral Concert'. Members of the LSO augmented the orchestra to 60 and the programme, which was rehearsed by Godfrey, also included the new *Coronation March*, the *Meditation* from *Lux Christi* (*The Light of Life*) and the Overture *Cockaigne*. On 6 February a busy and unwell Elgar, involved with the first performance of his masque *The Crown of India* at the London Coliseum only two days after the Bournemouth concert, pleaded with Godfrey for a change of date:

> We have moved to the above address [Severn House, 42 Netherhall Gardens, Hampstead] & Lady Elgar wishes me to ask if the promised photograph was ever sent to you. I hope so but in the confusion of leaving Hereford it may have been forgotten – but it was in a special memo:
> I have heard from Messrs Novello about Concert: first is there any possibility of altering the date as the Coliseum people want me urgently very urgently on the 9th – a month later or even a fortnight wd. be a blessing to me.
> > Will you wire to me
>
> > Queen's Hotel
> > > Leeds
> > tomorrow Wednesday
>
> saying if this is at all possible ? I have only just discovered that I am urgently wanted on the 9th

Clearly Godfrey offered no alternative and on 18 February Elgar was again pleading with him:

> Dear Mr Godfrey
> I wish you could let me off March 9th. However, if you really cannot, how wd the following do ? and what about you conducting ?
>
> > ? Opening piece Coronation March ?
> > > Meditation Lux Christi [crossed out: or Sursum Corda]
> > Symphony II
> > Over. Cockaigne
>
> Do you want it all me ? or wd. you prefer an opening piece by some other 'person'. Please settle this and let me know.

However, the concert went ahead as announced, with the programme that Elgar had suggested. A second hearing of the symphony was given just over a month later, under Godfrey, but, in keeping with its generally poor reception in the country at large, it was nine years before it was heard again in the Symphony Concerts. It is interesting to note that the performances of the Elgar symphonies during Godfrey's tenure (1893-1934) just outnumbered those of Parry's, all of which except the first were heard at Bournemouth, usually under the composer's baton. But both were outnumbered by the performances of Stanford's symphonies of which the third, *The Irish*, proved the most popular, and the fifth's tally of performances equalled those of Elgar's First Symphony.

In the early months of 1914 the Bournemouth Municipal Orchestra's first gramophone recordings were released by HMV. They were recorded in London – after the war the Orchestra would use its home, the (old) Winter Gardens for recordings – and these four acoustic releases include Godfrey's only Elgar recording, of the third *Bavarian Dance*, issued on HMV C352.

The nineteenth series of concerts (1913-14), the last before a world war was to change everything beyond recognition, could hardly have opened with anything more optimistic than Elgar's First Symphony, but its composer's 'massive hope for the future' [14] that the work embodied was soon to be shattered. In sharp contrast, one of the toughest works that Bournemouth audiences had to contend with came a week before Christmas: Sibelius's Fourth Symphony, which the composer himself, through his friend Granville Bantock's influence, had introduced to Britain at the 1912 Birmingham Festival (a unique occasion when Delius, Bantock and Sibelius had sat together to hear Elgar conduct *The Music Makers*).

On Thursday 21 May 1914 the Orchestra 'came of age', a good enough cause for celebrations that were to be the last before war erupted across Europe. As at the Bournemouth Centenary celebrations in 1910, a clutch of notable composers was invited to conduct: Mackenzie with his *Song of Thanksgiving* from the *London Day by Day* Suite, German the *Valse Gracieuse* from the *Leeds* Suite, Vaughan Williams making his first conducting appearance with the première of his revised *Norfolk Rhapsody No 1*, and Parry (his last visit, this time driving down to Bournemouth) with the Overture and Minuet from *The Acharnians of Aristophanes*. The programme also included two Bantock songs, Brahms' *Academic Festival Overture*, Debussy's *L'Après-midi d'un faune*, and Stravinsky's *Fireworks*, which had been given nearly a month before at one of Godfrey's benefit concerts, the first note of Stravinsky to be heard in the Winter Gardens. Stanford and Elgar were not present on this occasion. Instead they sent congratulatory telegrams.

∽   ∽   ∽

The 1914 summer season, the last few months of peace, consisted as usual of frankly popular works but with an occasional novelty, such as the first performance of Edith Swepstone's tone-poem *Woods in April* (as already mentioned, Godfrey was ever a champion of women composers). War had broken out by the time of the first concert of the 1914-15 winter series which included two pieces written in France that in mood could not have been farther removed from the realities of the moment, Delius's *On hearing the first cuckoo in spring* and *Summer night on the river*. Also in that first programme of the season were Mackenzie's witty Overture *Britannia*, Parry's cheery and robust *English* Symphony, and Beethoven's *Emperor* Concerto with York Bowen as soloist.

1914-15 [15]

Symphony Concerts: *Enigma* Variations,
Froissart Overture, *Sospiri*

Popular Concerts: *Enigma* Variations,
Pomp & Circumstance Marches, *Grania and Diarmid*,
Crown of India March and Suite, 'Meditation' from *Lux Christi*

Special Concerts: *Carillon*

During those troubled war years serious music provided an air of stability and comfort, and these concerts' existence was not seriously challenged. When there was talk of the Bournemouth beach being strewn with anti-invasion barbed-wire entanglements, people wondered good-humouredly why the Germans should want to invade Bournemouth of all places. There was a ready reply: 'Because they are a musical nation and would like to hear Dan Godfrey!' [16] Outwardly the series of Symphony Concerts remained largely unaffected by the war, although the days when such ventures could turn in a profit were long past. The war years were to bring increasing financial loss. But fortunately in 1915 there was support from the Mayor, Alderman Robson, who quelled any fears by giving a public undertaking that, despite wartime economies with lighting and other restrictions, if the war continued the orchestra would still be left intact. Godfrey's policy continued unchanged, as the pianist Mark Hambourg recalled:

> At Bournemouth the flag was kept flying by my old friend Sir Dan Godfrey. How he kept his orchestra together through those difficult

times, how good it was under the circumstances, and how much Godfrey helped both then and always to give the works of young British composers a good hearing, was a marvel. When Bournemouth was crowded with families who left town because of the air raids, or to seek the winter sun for which the place is famed, because they were debarred from the Mediterranean, the weekly symphony and other concerts by Godfrey's orchestra were no mean part of the major attractions of the place.[17]

Bournemouth, in the words of the *Morning Post* critic, was a:

> musician's paradise . . . Here alone of all English towns one can hear 'everything' all the year round . . . Not even the Londoner, with his Queen's Hall, London Symphony, New Symphony, Beecham Symphony and other orchestral concerts, can boast such programmes of music . . . More wonderful, however, is Bournemouth's splendid detachment from war-panic, when one remembers how many of the great provincial festivals and concerts have been cancelled . . . Bournemouth has, quietly and without fuss, provided its quota of eligible fighting men in the nation's crisis. But that epic motto 'Business as usual' means to Bournemouth also music as well, and the work done in that direction since the war began is surely unparalleled in the United Kingdom.

Just as in 1900, at the time of the Boer War when the Municipal Orchestra held concerts to support the Mayor's appeal fund, so there were numerous concerts in aid of war charities. The National Anthems of the allies became a regular feature of popular concerts. The name of Richard Strauss was absent throughout the war period, but there was no purge on German music of past years. Each season saw almost the complete canon of Beethoven symphonies (with, when programmed, the Ninth without its choral finale and with the second and third movements interchanged as was Godfrey's fashion). While the war progressed, single programmes were allotted to Beethoven and Wagner as well as those given to Russian and Belgian composers and music of the Allies. The continued playing of Wagner's music clearly annoyed one concert-goer who, on a postcard signing herself 'a disgusted Englishwoman', challenged Dan Godfrey: 'What the devil do you mean by playing German music, you beastly pro-Germans?' (While Wagner's occasionally aired *Kaisermarsch* was understandably not heard again after 1913, his rarer overture *Rule Britannia* had a single hearing in the early months of the war.)

The orchestra's personnel changed as men were called up. Equally unfortunate was the effect that the 1914 Defence of the Realm Act had on one of the players and his family. All persons of German nationality were required by the Act to obtain a special permit from the police if they were to remain in the town. Most affected were those working in the hotel trade, but the principal viola, Wustenhagen, who had joined the band in 1894, was German. His wife was English, and his son, who played in the first violins, spoke no German and had never set foot outside England. But Wustenhagen's presence as a member of the orchestra was discussed at a Council meeting when there was some opposition to a German being employed. Ultimately, although he was granted a permit and even applied for naturalisation, he resigned his post and left Bournemouth.[18]

The first (1914-15) series of the war years had none of the leading composers present. But amongst those who did come were Richard Walthew, who conducted his incongruously named overture *Our friend Fritz* first heard at the 1914 Proms, and the Staffordshire composer (and great supporter of Elgar in his years before recognition) Havergal Brian, who conducted his *First English Suite* on 26 November. By then Brian had enlisted with the Honourable Artillery Company, so, to facilitate his release for the concert, the ever-resourceful Godfrey stipulated that he conduct in khaki. This public advertisement for the HAC regiment on the rostrum did the trick. Many years later Brian recalled the occasion:

> The performance of my work took place on the last day of my leave. Before it began I realised that unless I deleted several movements or quickened the tempo of all of them I should miss my train to Waterloo. I decided to quicken the tempi. When I came off the platform I found Godfrey killing himself with laughter. I said, "What are you laughing at?" He replied: "Splendid. I've never heard my trombones and basses play like they did in the 'Carnival' " [the last section]. I caught my train.[19]

The true reason for Brian's metronomic haste was not the infrequency of the rail service but instead gastronomic urges: he wanted to catch the last train with a buffet, and he apologised to the band for driving them so hard. 'That's all right,' they replied. 'Go and write us something else, even quicker!'

That season introduced the name of Ernest Farrar, whose Rhapsody No 2 *Lavengro*[20] was played on 22 April. Godfrey wrote of Farrar as 'the most modest of men and I shall never forget the difference between the shy and retiring youth I met at Harrogate and the stalwart soldier . . . I encountered some twelve months later'.[21] Farrar was destined to become one of the 'lost generation' of composers to die in action during the war.

A list of other British composers represented (some forgotten today, some perhaps not even known) gives a flavour of the period: Ernest Austin, Granville Bantock, Learmont Drysdale, Percy Fletcher,

Balfour Gardiner, John Greenwood, Arthur Hervey, Josef Holbrooke, Gustav Holst, Alexander Mackenzie, Charles Maclean, Hamish MacCunn, Geoffrey O'Connor-Morris, Hubert Parry, Percy Pitt, Alfred Pratt, Roger Quilter, Ethel Scarborough, Ethel Smyth, Arthur Somervell, Arthur Sullivan, Edith Swepstone, Frank Tapp, Samuel Coleridge-Taylor, Arnold Trowell, and Walter Twinning. But perhaps the season's most important event was the third performance anywhere of Vaughan Williams' *A London Symphony* on 11 February, important because of the endeavours that were necessary in order to achieve the performance. After its London première under Geoffrey Toye the previous March and a second with Julian Clifford conducting the Harrogate Municipal Orchestra on 12 August (just over a week after the outbreak of war), the manuscript full score had amazingly been sent to Germany either in the hope of a performance or for engraving – and was lost. Clifford was a friend of Godfrey's, occasionally visiting Bournemouth, and he would almost certainly have acquainted him with the work. A score was then reconstructed from the band parts by the composer and three friends, George Butterworth, Geoffrey Toye and Edward Dent. Godfrey's was the first performance of this reconstruction. Subsequently Vaughan Williams was to make three revisions of the symphony, generally tightening its structure by making cuts, and Godfrey was to become particularly associated with it.[22]

As the war continued, one of the early concerns was the plight of neutral Belgium, brought home forcibly to the people of Bournemouth by both the influx of refugees and the number of Belgian casualties hospitalised there. A Belgian Refugee Committee was kept very busy housing the many arrivals until, in November 1914, the town was designated a prohibited area for any further Belgian refugees. Over the next 12 months nearly 400 of that country's sick and wounded received treatment in hospitals and nursing homes in the Bournemouth area. This was the more poignant for the several Belgian musicians in the orchestra, such as the Gennin brothers, Jean and Pierre, both flautists, who in 1915 were joined for a while by another of their family, Julien, on double-bass. A number of gaps in the orchestra left vacant by those who enlisted were filled by Belgians unfit for war service: the oboist P Craen (followed in 1920 by Joseph Craen) and the trumpeter J Ardenois, who joined in 1916, clarinettist L Van Ingh, who came at the beginning of 1918, and Joseph Govaere, who joined the orchestra in 1914 and became deputy leader after the war until he died in a road accident. By 1918 at least 15 of the

Orchestra's 50 were Belgian. Jan Blockx' popular *Flemish Dances* would have struck a nostalgic chord in such players; similarly the *Fantasia on Flemish Folk Songs* for piano and orchestra by the Belgian composer and pianist Arthur de Greef heard in January 1916 (a work that was in Elgar's repertoire when touring with the London Symphony Orchestra in 1915 with the composer as soloist).

Elgar's dramatic recitation *Carillon* ('Sing, Belgians, sing!') of a text by Emile Cammaerts was an English musical response to the Belgian nightmare. It was performed up and down the country, producing a deep emotional response. Its first provincial performance was given in January 1915 at the Winter Gardens with Sir Alexander Mackenzie's daughter, Mary, as reciter. 'Hardly dramatic enough in her delivery of the impassioned lines', wrote *The Musical Times* critic. Elgar himself conducted it on 26 June at a Belgian Repatriation Fund concert shared with Godfrey when the words were declaimed by Madame Vandervelde, wife of the Belgian Minister of State and daughter of the wealthy banker Edward Speyer, whose support Elgar enjoyed. He repeated it the following season on 23 October with the Belgian actor Carlo Liten, also conducting the Violin Concerto with Albert Sammons, while Godfrey was in charge of the *Wand of Youth* Suite No 2 and the second and fourth *Pomp and Circumstance* Marches. 'The concert went off very well . . . Sammons played very beautifully . . . The journey was horrid – crowded & very hot train down which made me ill,' Elgar wrote to a friend.[23] Lady Elgar's diary for that day adds an extra dimension: 'Watched army horses being ridden into the water. One rolled over rider & all – not hurt. Then rehearsal. E. not liking music at all & saying it was all dead &c – E. rested & then conducted splendidly & evidently music had revived – Wand of Youth delightful to hear. At the Tame Bear A[lice] heard someone say, 'they do not allow it now'. So they understood the poor Bear – captive, made to dance.'[24] Debussy's *Berceuse Héroïque*, played that same year just before Christmas, was another timely work. Like Elgar's *Carillon*, it appeared in piano reduction in *King Albert's Book*, an anthology of prose, poetry and music inscribed to the King of the Belgians and his people, and sold in aid of the *Daily Telegraph* Belgian Fund.

Belgian music featured prominently in the Bournemouth programmes. On the German invasion of Belgium, the composer Joseph Jongen had evacuated to England for the duration of the war, and on at least five occasions he conducted his own works at Bournemouth, his *Fantasia on Two Walloon Carols*, *Tableaux pittoresques*, and his Cello Concerto, of which Maurice Dambois gave the British première on 17 February 1916. Principal flautist Jean Gennin was soloist in the first British performance of the Belgian Pierre Benoit's *Symphonic Poem for Flute and Orchestra* on 4 May 1916, and a little earlier, on 6 March, Paul Goossens, conductor of the Kursaal Royal Orchestra at Ostend[25], brought a specifically Belgian programme with César Franck, Blockx, Grétry, and Paul Gilson, his *Deux Humoresques* and his best-known work, the symphonic poem *La Mer*. At the end of the war, in recognition of his sympathies for Belgium, the Belgian members of the orchestra presented Godfrey, on behalf of themselves and a number of refugees, with a large silver inkstand and two cut-glass mounted inkwells.

1915-16

Symphony Concerts: *Cockaigne* Overture

Popular Concerts: *Froissart* Overture, *Enigma* Variations, *Carillon*, Violin Concerto (Sammons), *Wand of Youth* Suite No 2, 4 Military Marches, 2 *Sea Pictures* (Violet Oppenshaw)

Two works in the 1915-16 season that by chance seemed to match the mood of the hour were Walford Davies' *Solemn Melody* of 1908, first given in November and then each year up to 1919, and Arthur Somervell's Symphony *Thalassa* (1912) whose elegiac slow movement *Killed in action* is a heartfelt nine-minute threnody actually composed with the death of Captain Scott of the Antarctic in mind[26] and notable for its plaintive cor anglais solo. (Another member of that ill-fated Polar expedition, Captain Oates, was remembered in the second of Howard Carr's *Three Heroes* heard in 1918, the outer movements relating to O'Leary VC and Warneford VC.) Charles Hoby conducted his Elegy *On the Brave*. There was a strong national element in the Municipal Choir's November programme of Sir Frederick Bridge's *The Flag of England* (conducted by the composer) and Elgar's *The Banner of St George*, Godfrey repeating the whole programme the following month.

Elgar's visit in October to conduct *Carillon* in the all-Elgar concert already mentioned (at which Godfrey shared the conducting) was the last of his war-time appearances at Bournemouth. Other British composers who came to conduct their own works included Hubert Bath, Rutland Boughton, the local composer Arthur Burton, Adam

Carse (who had changed his name from von Ahn Carse), Hamilton
Harty (his *Irish* Symphony), Charles Maclean and O'Connor-Morris.
The William Sterndale Bennett Centenary was marked on 13 April
1916 with *The Wood Nymphs* Overture and the Fourth Piano
Concerto. His Symphony in G minor Op 43 was heard a week later.
(This work and several of his overtures that were quite frequently
given at these concerts were hardly heard at all after the war.) The
season also introduced works by the composer and pianist Dora
Bright, Learmont Drysdale, Ernest Farrar again (his *Variations on an
Old British Sea Song* for piano and orchestra), Amy Woodforde-
Finden's *Four Indian Love Lyrics*, the Manchester-born John Foulds'
once-popular *Keltic Suite*, and the name of Eric Coates appeared on
Bournemouth programmes for the first time.[27]   Coates was then
principal viola in Henry Wood's Queen's Hall Orchestra and he was
not to give up orchestral playing and devote himself full-time to
composition until 1919.   In his autobiographical *Suite in Four
Movements*[28] he remembers how as a young player he once asked
Godfrey if there was a vacancy for viola in his orchestra.   Dan had
replied that 'all his men were obliged to be double-handed on account
of having to play in the Military Band on the pier each morning' and
asked if Coates played another instrument.   Coates acquired a flute
and took weekly lessons, but progressed no further than becoming
'conversant with the woodwind side of the orchestra', knowledge that
was, however, to stand him in good stead as a composer.   After the
war he frequently conducted his own engaging pieces at
Bournemouth, with increasing popularity.   'You are the man who
writes tunes' he was once greeted by Ethel Smyth[29] who came herself
that season to conduct the Overture to *The Boatswain's Mate* and the
Prelude 'On the Cliffs of Cornwall' from *The Wreckers*.

   Rutland Boughton's visit introduced his three *Folk Dances* for
strings and the Love Duet from his opera *The Immortal Hour* which
had had its first full staging the previous year at the Winter Gardens.
Two years before that, with a failed marriage, Boughton's relationship
with the designer Christina Walshe had shaken the sensibilities of the
Glastonbury fraternity.   When backing for a proposed Festival
production there of his choral drama *The Birth of Arthur* crumbled,
he had turned for help to Dan Godfrey who not only provided much
needed moral support but effectively put the Municipal Orchestra at
his disposal.   In August 1913 Boughton rented a large house in
Bournemouth and, with Christina Walshe's assistance, ran a three-
week school which culminated in the public first performances at the

Winter Gardens of the Prelude and First Scene from Act 2 of *The Birth of Arthur* conducted by Edgar Bainton. His most famous work, *The Immortal Hour*, was by then completed, and with a foot in the Bournemouth door, he was able in January 1915 to realise its first presentation with full orchestra, in costume with a curtain back-cloth doing duty as scenery and only the simplest of stage fittings. With a single full-dress rehearsal, four performances were given in the Winter Gardens under the baton of Charles Kennedy Scott. (Boughton had much to thank Godfrey for because Bournemouth was the venue not only for further performances of *The Immortal Hour* and the Nativity drama *Bethlehem* in 1919 but a mini Boughton operatic festival was given in April 1925 as part of that year's Bournemouth Musical Festival.)

Godfrey's adventurous programming continued undimmed by war. Brief listings can only give a flavour of what both the knowledgeable and the untutored ears in Bournemouth audiences had to contend with, but works from abroad that season included Joachim Quantz's Flute Concerto and the first British performances of Lalo's Symphony in G minor, Glazunov's *March on a Russian Theme*, Pietro Nardini's Violin Concerto in E minor, and from Poland Witold Malischevski's Symphony No 1 and *Joyous Overture*. The strong representation of Russian music included, besides familiar works, the first British performances of Arensky's lyrical one-movement Violin Concerto, Alexander Goedicke's Concertstück, a Suite *In Modo Populari* by César Cui, second hearings of the Arensky and Balakirev Piano Concertos, and new works such as Rimsky-Korsakov's *Sinfonietta on Russian themes*, Nikolai Laduchin's musical tableau *Crépuscule* for strings, Nikolai Sokolov's *Serenade for Strings* and Venanzi's ominously titled tone-poem *Satan's Dream*.

In January 1916 compulsory military service for single men was introduced, with the age limit raised the following year. Dan Godfrey submitted himself for examination and was listed Class B, exempting him from active service. Twenty-seven of the Orchestra and Band joined the services, and their losses were fortunately few. Only two were killed in action. Meanwhile, life in war-time Bournemouth was thankfully free of air-raids and other major occurrences. Indeed, as Godfrey himself remembered, practically the only war incidents were the disruption to an afternoon concert when a mine, washed up on the beach, exploded, and a scare when the audience at an evening concert were about to be warned of an approaching airship *en route* for nearby Swanage when it was realised that the report had confused

that town with the more distant Swanick.   Air-raid alarms were
confined to practices, the signal for which was worthy of *Dad's Army*:
policemen cycling through the town, ringing a handbell and wearing
a placard which read 'All take cover'.

Because Bournemouth escaped any air bombardment, it retained
its popularity as a resort, although with restricted train services and
the higher rail fares there were no longer the great numbers of regular
day-trippers.   But the town also took on another rôle, as a garrison
town, billeting soldiers in their thousands during the winter period
after a summer under canvas.   Khaki soon became a familiar sight
everywhere.   There were other changes.   The Military Band was
suspended during the summer season for economic reasons, with the
full orchestra playing instead on the pier in the mornings and sections
in the afternoons, and with lighting regulations and the tram services
finishing earlier than usual, there were no evening concerts at the
Winter Gardens.   As the war progressed, there was a noticeable
falling-off in receipts from the piers and the Winter Gardens, with
annual losses often as much as £1,900.   However, the summer events
continued to turn in a profit which helped towards the financing of
the winter Symphony Concerts.

1916-17

Symphony Concerts: *In the South* Overture, *Cockaigne* Overture,
Pomp & Circumstance March No. 2

Popular Concerts: *Cockaigne* Overture, *Three Bavarian Dances*,
Pomp & Circumstance Marches Nos 1 & 4, *Serenade for Strings*,
Dream of Gerontius: Prelude and 'Angel's Farewell'

The 1916-17 series introduced another Belgian musician who was to
become a familiar name to Bournemouth audiences, the composer
Juliet Folville.   A professor at the Liège Conservatory from 1898, she
settled in Bournemouth at the beginning of the war, teaching, and in
October she was first seen as soloist in her own Piano Concerto.   She
was to display a wide range of talents at a special concert in February
1921 when she not only repeated the solo rôle in her own Piano
Concerto but conducted the *Fragments symphoniques* from her
abandoned opera *Jean de Chimay*, and then took up the bow as
soloist in Godard's Violin Concerto *Romantique*.   This multiplicity of
talent, quite common at Bournemouth, was in evidence again when

the New Zealand composer Arnold Trowell, as well as conducting the first performance of his tone-poem *The Waters of Peneios* (which was to have at least five Bournemouth performances), in the same concert was also the soloist in Haydn's D major Cello Concerto.

Other composers appearing that season as conductors were Howard Carr (better known as a theatre conductor), Giovanni Clerici and Montague Phillips. Stanford's visit in December brought the first British performance with Benno Moiseiwitsch of his romantic and lyrical Piano Concerto No 2 (the popular *Irish* Symphony and *Irish Rhapsody* No 1 were also heard that season) and in March Cyril Scott was the soloist in his own First Piano Concerto. Innocent enough to today's ears, Godfrey considered the work 'most complicated', and it was with 'heartfelt relief' that orchestra and pianist finished together.[30] In a letter to *The Times* at about this time, Godfrey complained of the absence from London programmes of such works as the Stanford Concerto and Bantock's impressive *Hebridean Symphony*,[31] pleading with Sir Thomas Beecham to include at least one important British work in each of the Philharmonic Society's concerts. While British music had not been neglected in those programmes, it had not enjoyed the prominence given to it at Bournemouth.

There were works new to Bournemouth by Algernon Ashton, Bantock, Coleridge-Taylor, Frederick Corder, Learmont Drysdale, Molyneux Palmer, Cyril Rootham, Masters van Someren-Godfery, and Vincent Thomas. From abroad there was Rimsky-Korsakov's Third Symphony and his Overture *La fiancée du Czar*, Goldmark's Overture *Prometheus*, Emile Wambach's Suite *Belgiana*, a Suite *L'Enfant Prodigue* by the French composer André Wormser, and Glazunov's *Paraphrase on National Hymns of the Allies*. The current fashion for Scriabin, who had died in April 1915, was met with performances of the first and second symphonies, the latter 'magnificently played', and the Piano Concerto. There was also a *Dance Scherzo* written by a former RCM student, the Australian composer and pianist Arthur Benjamin while on active service in France, 'in remembrance of happy nights spent at Drury Lane, Russian season, 1914' and first heard at a RCM concert. Far off the beaten track were some Maori songs arranged by the Australian composer Alfred Hill, and *A Maori slumber song* by Princess Te Rangi Pai (who had herself sung at the Winter Gardens back in 1903) sung by a Princess Iwa.

The first week of the summer season brought a tone-poem *The Passing of Arthur* by Cecile Ruthven Reeve, dedicated to Lord

Kitchener, the Secretary of State for War, who had been drowned the previous year when his ship had struck a mine off Orkney. The orchestra took its habitual week's holiday in July. As usual, most of the summer works were predictably popular ones, though with the inclusion of Raff's *Lenore,* Svendsen's Second, Somervell's *Thalassa* symphonies and Rheinberger's Piano Concerto.

1917-18

Symphony Concerts: *Froissart* Overture, *Serenade for Strings*

Popular Concerts: *Imperial March,* 4 Military Marches

The United States entered the war on 6 April 1917, and the first concert of the 1917-18 season opened with a *Triumphal March*[32] by Glazunov which, by a timely association, quoted the Civil War marching-tune *John Brown's Body.* Composer-conductors were again in short supply that season. Those who did appear on the rostrum were – possibly with one exception – forgotten figures today: Giovanni Clerici, Joseph Jongen, P Marinari, William Fenney, Percy Godfrey (no relation), Percy Elliott and the Bournemouth resident Dr H V Pearce (Godfrey did much to encourage local talent). In November Christian Carpenter appeared both as the piano soloist (in Paderewski's *Polish Fantasia*) and as the composer (a *Suite of Dances* for strings); in December the British-born Bluebell Klean made her one Bournemouth appearance as soloist in her own Piano Concerto; and in February Julian Clifford revived his own Piano Concerto, substituting it for the Saint-Saëns concerto he had originally planned 'owing to an injury to his hand', ran the curious programme insertion.

Godfrey gave the first performances of a *Concert Overture* by the organist and composer Harold Darke (to be more widely known for his setting of *In the bleak mid-winter* which rivalled Holst's for popularity, and for his long residency of St Michael's, Cornhill), and a tone-poem *Taj Mahal* written in 1916 while on active service by Bertrand Peek, who was still serving with the Hants Regiment in India. Other new but now forgotten works included an overture *Ellangowan* by the Edinburgh organist and choirmaster Charles O'Brien, *Three Elfin Dances* by the violist H Waldo Warner, and, all in the same programme, a *Minuet and Bourrée* for piano and strings by E M Oakeley who was a master at Clifton College, Bristol, an *Orchestral Prelude* by Charles A Rudall, and *Three Dale Dances* by the

Orchestra's former flautist turned London theatre music director, Arthur Wood.[33]   Bournemouth programmes can provide many examples of works slipping from popularity to obscurity: Frederic Cliffe's Symphony No 1 had its eighth and last Winter Gardens performance[34] that season.   From a new generation of rising British composers however was a *Miniature Phantasy for Strings* by Eugene Goossens, and John Ireland's atmospheric *The Forgotten Rite*, the work's second performance.   On 6 December there came a harsh reminder of war with the first of many Bournemouth performances of the Rhapsody *A Shropshire Lad* by 'the late Lieutenant Kaye-Butterworth, MC', who had been killed on the Somme in 1916. Premièred by Nikisch at the 1913 Leeds Festival, it had its third performance during the summer at the Proms. The 'immense promise' one critic remarked upon was tragically to remain unfulfilled.

The diversity and enterprise of Godfrey's programmes are further illustrated by a brief list of other works Bournemouth audiences heard that season: a Concertstück for Piano and Orchestra by Cécile Chaminade (whose ballet suite *Callirhoë* was heard the following season), de Swert's Cello Concerto, the Cello Concerto by the Glasgow-born pianist and composer Eugen d'Albert[35] having its fifth Bournemouth performance (with Felix Salmond who was to première the Elgar Concerto the following year in London), a *Concerto passione* for cello, the first part of an ambitious trilogy of concerted works by a certain Georges Dorlay, who was in fact a member of the Queen's Hall Orchestra,[36] Sinigaglia's Violin Concerto, and the British premières of Antonio Scontrino's *Sinfonia Marinaresca* and Goedicke's *Dramatic Overture*.   Ippolitov-Ivanov's *Scènes Caucasiennes*, first heard in Bournemouth in 1912, was joined this season by his Suite *Iveria* and the first British performance of the Symphony.   This, ventured the *Musical Times*, 'will probably also be its last here, not a single passage relieving its deadly monotony and uninspired staleness of phraseology'.   It was not repeated.   New also were two tone-poems, Lyadov's *Kikimora* and Svendsen's *Zorahayda*. A more serious note was struck when the *Prélude à l'après-midi d'un faune* was played 'In memoriam' on 11 April, Debussy having died the previous month.

The cessation of hostilities was still several months off when, on 22 May 1918, the orchestra's 25th anniversary was celebrated with afternoon and evening concerts.   Carrie Tubb was the vocalist at both concerts, but the tone was generally subdued, as befitted the times. Stanford conducted both his sturdy *Irish Rhapsody No 5*, 'dedicated to the Irish Guards' and first performed in June 1917 in Norfolk,

Connecticut, and the *Marcia Funèbre and Epilogue Verdun*, an orchestration of the last two movements of his Second Organ Sonata and first heard earlier that year at an Albert Hall Sunday concert under Landon Ronald. In place of Bantock who was detained by illness, Godfrey conducted *Pierrot of the Minute* and (possibly its première) a *Coronach* which commemorated the death in 1915 of Lieutenant John Kennedy, Vicar of St John's, Boscombe. The mood was lightened by the *Welsh Rhapsody* and two shorter pieces of Edward German, who also conducted. The evening programme opened with 'Two Military Marches' of Elgar (almost certainly *Pomp and Circumstance* Marches) conducted by Godfrey. Was Elgar's absence due to Stanford's involvement? Instead he was one of many sending congratulatory letters and telegrams. His message read: 'Congratulations and thanks for your twenty-five years' wonderful work for English music'. Stanford again spoke of Godfrey as a natural successor to Manns, and the Mayor handed Godfrey war bonds to the value of £400 in recognition of a quarter of a century's association with Bournemouth. The statistics revealed that 1,500 different compositions had been played in the 23 series, of which 685 were the works of 140 British composers, nearly one hundred of whom had conducted their works at various times. 'You say the Winter Gardens has lost £12,000 during 25 years?' Stanford challenged Godfrey's critics. 'But you are wrong,' he struck back, 'for you have not lost it, you have only paid £12,000 in educating the people to a knowledge of good music, and £12,000 in a quarter of a century is, I think, extraordinarily cheap. In Bournemouth you have a possession – a good thing. Stick to it.'

1918-19

Symphony Concerts: *Froissart* Overture,
In the South Overture, Violin Concerto

Popular Concerts: *Pomp and Circumstance* Marches Nos 1 & 2,
Crown of India Suite, *Wand of Youth* Suite No 2,
Dream of Gerontius: Prelude and 'Angel's Farewell'

The 24th (1918-19) series began while Europe was in the closing stages of war. Parry had died three days before the start of the new season, and his *Symphonic Variations* was played 'In memoriam' at the second Symphony Concert. Throughout the season a number of works again matched the mood of the nation: Harry Keyser's Elegy *In*

Memoriam for brass and drums was given at the first concert to follow the Armistice; in December there was a tone-poem *In Memoriam 1914-1918* by Throsby Hutchison; and the BMO's leader (since 1896) Frederick King-Hall, who by the start of the season had been succeeded by A Renges, directed the first performance of his Overture *To the Fallen* in April.

Russian music, as much a favourite of Godfrey's as it was of Henry Wood's, was as ever much in evidence, with new works by Vladimir Rebikov, Rimsky-Korsakov, and Sistek (*Two Serbian National Dances*). A *Suite of Russian Fairy Tales* by Bagrinoffsky was programmed twice, Godfrey feeling obliged first to warn his audience of the work's seeming grotesqueness. Scriabin's first two symphonies were heard again, and the season included three Glazunov symphonies of which Godfrey seemed especially fond.

A new name in February was that of the Gloucestershire-born Herbert Howells with his 1914 Suite *The 'B's*, each of its five movements being dedicated to a RCM friend (himself included) whose nickname bore the initial B. Many years later, in a broadcast conversation with Bliss (one of the dedicatees), Howells recalled the occasion:

> I remember the best performance I ever heard of [the scherzo movement 'Blissy'] was curiously enough down at Bournemouth. Do you remember the way we used to go down at Easter-time to dear old Dan Godfrey, who was one of our greatest friends, I mean of British music, and you were there I know and Eugene Goossens was there and . . . [Arthur] Benjamin [another dedicatee]. They were wonderful occasions, and I heard a magnificent performance . . .[37]

It is of some interest, to Elgarians at least, that the season's works also included a Violin Concerto (soloist Jessie Snow) by the London Symphony Orchestra's leader (until 1935) and close friend of Elgar, W H Reed, who eight years earlier had given the composer much help in the bowing and fingering of his own concerto. Reed's rôles as orchestral leader and also as Elgar's friend and biographer have totally obscured a third rôle: that of composer. His concerto was not heard again at Bournemouth but other works of his that also had single performances there in Godfrey's time are a Rhapsody in E minor for violin and orchestra (also played by Jessie Snow, in 1920); *The Lincoln Imp* (dedicated to Elgar, at the 1922 Bournemouth Musical Festival); *Will o' the Wisp* and *Italian Serenade* (1924 Musical Festival), the Suite *Aesop's Fables* (1925), and the Suite *Shockheaded Peter* (1933). Reed himself conducted all performances except that of his Violin Concerto. These works only represent part of his output. Considering the many demands on his time made by teaching and as an orchestral leader, he was a fairly prolific composer. It would surely be of considerable interest to revive at least a couple of them so that we might assess them.

The season ended in peacetime. Just before the start of the first post-war season, the Orchestra embarked on its first tour, setting a precedent for its successor, the Bournemouth Symphony Orchestra. Difficult times lay ahead for the orchestra but it was to maintain its association with British music. From Elgar in his post-war decline there was only to be a handful of new works to find their way into Godfrey's programmes. In January 1921 a young Giovanni Barbirolli was soloist in the Cello Concerto (he had been an orchestral cellist in the work's première under the composer only three months earlier) – 'not entirely equal to the demands of the solo music,' *The Musical Times* reported, 'but his playing unquestionably gave a considerable amount of pleasure.' (No-one was then to know that he would become one of the finest of Elgar interpreters, as conductor rather than as cellist.) That season saw both symphonies, both concertos and all three concert overtures programmed and it is worth noting that Sir Dan Godfrey's interpretations of the symphonies in particular were much admired: of the First in 1924 *The Morning Post* reported 'a great and powerful reading'. In Godfrey's remaining years the Bach and Handel arrangements were given on a few occasions, likewise the *Nursery Suite*, and he seemed particularly to relish the addition of the fifth *Pomp and Circumstance* March which he gave frequently in his so-named Popular Concerts.

Dan Godfrey and Elgar with four other composer-conductors at Bournemouth:

Back row: Edward German, Hubert Parry;

Front row: next to Godfrey, Sir Alexander Mackenzie, and at the right (keeping far away from Elgar) Sir Charles Villiers Stanford.

In the inter-war years Bournemouth's celebrated Easter Music Festivals were inaugurated, but in 1929 the Orchestra moved from the familiar if certainly not ideal home of the Winter Gardens to the new Pavilion, not itself an ideal concert venue but one which more readily met the new demands of a variety of entertainments against which the Orchestra had to compete. It was a time of change. Dan Godfrey's happiest days had passed.

WORKS BY ELGAR PERFORMED AT SYMPHONY, CLASSICAL AND MUSICAL FESTIVAL CONCERTS, BOURNEMOUTH

This is a list of the works by Elgar performed in the Symphony, Classical and Musical Festival Concerts at Bournemouth from 1895 to 1934 (the year of Godfrey's retirement), together with those found to have been given in the Popular Concerts and summer series from 1929 until 1934 for which no programmes seem to have survived. This should therefore not be taken as necessarily a complete list of all Elgar performances from that period.

fp = first performance; fpp = first provincial performance;
MF = music festival;
* = composer conducting
remainder, unless otherwise stated, conducted by Sir Dan Godfrey

Bach-Elgar : Fugue in C minor	Caractacus : Triumphal March	Chanson de Matin	Cockaigne Overture (cont)
20/4/22*	4/12/19	14/11/01	31/1/10
4/5/22		2/1/05	23/10/11
MF 4/4/23	*Carillon*		26/10/11
(and Fantasia)*	1/15(fpp)	*Chanson de Nuit*	9/3/12*
24/4/24	23/10/15*	14/11/01	14/11/12
	c 11/15	2/1/05	4/11/15
The Banner of St George : It comes from the misty ages	26/6/15*		15/3/17
	Cello Concerto	*Cockaigne Overture*	7/5/17
	27/1/21 (Barbirolli)	15/1/03	6/11/19
14/11/31 (cond Frank Idle)	1/3/23 (H Bliss)	23/11/03	7/10/20
	MF 10/4/26	22/12/04	1/3/23
	(B Harrison)*	17/12/06	13/3/24
	28/1/33 (Harrison)	14/12/08	MF 4-5/24
			MF 16/4/25

Cockaigne Overture (cont)

7/1/26
MF 10/4/26*
11/10/28
21/3/29
22/9/29
20/4/30
8/6/30
21/9/30
14/1/31
25/1/31
7/5/31
11/10/31
20/1/32
3/8/32
11/9/32
21/5/33
2/8/33
17/12/33
26/9/34
30/9/34 (Godfrey's last concert)

Coronation March

9/3/12*
8/5/20

Crown of India : Grand March and Suite

7/12/14
4/11/18
4/7/30 (March only)

Dream of Gerontius

4/5/09
26/4/10
21/3/31
25/1/34 (2 perfs, cond Idle)

Prelude and Angel's Farewell

3/11/04
12/4/06
16/4/08
13/4/11
4/4/12
12/1/14
5/4/17
14/4/19
19/4/20
8/11/23

Sanctus Fortis

MF 19/5/24 (William Boland)
14/4/32 (Steuart Wilson)

Dream Children

15/1/03

Falstaff

19/2/19 (Interludes)
1/3/23
4/4/23*

Froissart Overture

4/11/01
18/4/04
16/3/11
24/4/13
30/3/14
25/2/15
31/1/16
7/3/18
16/1/19
11/4/21
1/4/26
MF 21/4/27
19/1/28
1/8/29
11/8/29

Froissart Overture (cont)

29/5/30
27/7/30
23/9/31
6/7/32

Grania and Diarmid : (Introduction and Funeral March)

8/2/15
6/11/24
11/11/26 (F March)
MF 4/27 (F March)
28/2/34

Handel-Elgar: Overture in D mi

17/4/24

Imperial March

18/3/18

In the South Overture

30/3/05
19/10/05
29/4/09
24/11/10
14/11/12
17/2/13
29/1/14
19/10/16
20/3/19
24/2/21
26/10/22
3/4/24
7/5/25
MF 21/4/27

In the South (cont)

11/4/29
4/10/33

Introduction and Allegro for Strings

9/4/08
11/5/08
12/3/25

The Kingdom

9/4/33 (cond Idle)

Lux Christi: Meditation

23/4/00
12/4/06
21/11/08*
9/3/12*
22/12/13
21/12/14

Nursery Suite

7/10/31
6/2/32
22/11/33

Polonia

17/1/24
MF 23/4/24
24/1/29

Pomp & Circumstance Marches Nos 1,2,3,4

20/2/02
15/1/03
19/11/03
10/10/04
24/10/04
27/4/05
10/10/07
9/4/08

Pomp &
Circumstance
Marches
Nos 1,2,3,4 (cont)
21/11/08 [2&4]*
14/12/08
27/2/09
17/4/09
8/7/10 [1]*
10/2/13
14/4/13
12/10/14
26/4/15
23/10/15 [2 & 4]
1/5/16
28/12/16
12/3/17
15/10/17
22/5/18
28/4/19
1/3/20
MF 4-5/24

Pomp &
Circumstance
March No 5
17/5/31
13/7/31
1/9/31
10/10/31
11/10/31
24/11/31
28/1/33

Sea Pictures
11/4/04 (Maud Santley)
21/11/08 (Maud Santley)
25/10/15 (*In Haven*: Miss Oppenshaw)
MF 3-4/23 (C Butt)
25/3/32 (*Where Corals Lie*)
13/8/33 (*Where Corals Lie* : Brunskill)
29/8/33 (*In Haven*)

Serenade
for Strings
22/11/00
1/1/03
1/5/05
22/10/06
22/10/09
13/12/09
5/2/12
22/1/17
1/11/17
23/5/29
24/7/30
12/8/30
16/12/30
31/10/31
16/1/32
10/1/34
22/8/34

Sevillana
22/1/00
16/1/05
2/1/05
25/11/07

Sospiri
18/2/15

Symphony No 1
27/2/09
17/4/09
9/10/13
21/10/20

Symphony No 1
(cont)
20/4/22*
24/4/24
MF 10/4/26*

Symphony No 2
9/3/12*
18/4/12
10/2/21
28/4/21

Three Bavarian
Dances
25/4/98
27/11/05
1/11/09
15/12/13
26/3/17
MF 3-4/23
20/10/29
31/8/30
28/1/33

Three Pieces:
Mazurka,
Salut d'
Amour [sic],
Contrasts
25/10/00
17/10/04
28/1/33 (*Salut*
d'Amour only)

Variations on an
original theme
(*Enigma*)
5/12/01
15/1/03
13/10/04
28/2/07
21/11/08*
30/10/12

Variations on an
original theme
(*Enigma*) (cont)
12/11/14
15/3/15
3/4/16
13/11/19
8/4/20
1/3/23
8/8/23
1/5/24
8/9/25
17/12/25
24/10/29
17/11/29
24/2/32
29/3/33
11/4/34

Wand of Youth
Suite No 1
15/10/08
21/12/11
11/1/09

Wand of Youth
Suite No 2
21/11/08*
14/12/08
14/10/09
18/4/10
8/7/10*
23/10/15
28/4/19
1/3/20 MF
3-4/23
MF 22/4/24 (B
Robinson)
11/11/29
7/10/30
10/12/32

Violin Concerto

23/11/10 (Fritz Kreisler - fpp)	24/12/24 (1st. mvt.: Issay Schlaen)
4/2/11 (Kreisler)	21/1/26 (N Evans)
22/4/11 (May Harrison)	3/8/27 (Albert Voorsanger)
22/8/11 (Marie Hall)	2/1/30 (Melsa)
23/10/15 (Albert Sammons)*	8/4/31 (Melsa)
30/1/19 (Nanette Evans)	19/10/32 (Voorsanger)
7/4/21 (Tessie Thomas)	17/12/32 (Sammons)
MF 4/4/23 (Margaret Fairless)*	12/9/34 (Sammons)

WINTER SYMPHONY CONCERTS SERIES

	1914-15	1915-16	1916-17	1917-18
Number of concerts:	61	59	59	59
Number of works:	359	326	286	280
First time at these concerts:	33	53	37	35
Number of British works:	67	56	53	53
New British works:	20	21	18	18

NOTES and SOURCES

1. Quoted in Edginton, M A : *Bournemouth and the First World War: The Evergreen Valley 1914 to 1919* (Bournemouth Local Studies Publications, 1985) p 1
2. Godfrey, Sir Dan: *Memories and Music: Thirty-five years of conducting* (Hutchinson, 1924) p 137
3. Elgar's conducting visits were on the following occasions (with MF denoting a Bournemouth Easter Music Festival): 21/11/1908; 8/7/1910; 9/3/1912; 26/61915; 23/10/1915; MF 20/4/1922; MF 4/4/1923; MF 10/4/1926
4. 1 September 1908. (Moore, Jerrold Northrop: *Elgar and his Publishers: Letters of a Creative Life Vol II 1904-1934* (Oxford, 1987) pp 707-8)
5. Letter, 13 November 1908. (Atkins, E Wulstan: *The Elgar-Atkins Friendship* (David & Charles, 1984) p 185)
6. Godfrey, *op cit*
7. *ibid*, p 186
8. Coates, Eric: *Suite in Four Movements*, p 207. The incident almost certainly took place at the 1923 Bournemouth Easter Music Festival. This was the occasion when Elgar was staying at the same hotel as German who was suddenly seized with an attack of lumbago before conducting at an evening concert. Elgar suggested that they shared a table before the concert and surprised his fellow composer by saying, 'German, I am going to give you a

pint of the best champagne they have in the hotel.' Then, carrying the score in one hand, he took German with the other and walked him to the Winter Gardens. By the end of the concert the lumbago had vanished.

9.   *Musical Times* (August 1910) p 527
10. Michael Kennedy has admirably examined the Elgar-Stanford estrangement in his *Portrait of Elgar*, 2nd ed, pp 154-5, as have also Robert Stradling and Meirion Hughes in *English Musical Renaissance 1860-1940: Construction and Deconstruction*, pp 51-60, and Harry Plunket Greene in *Charles Villiers Stanford*, pp 149-159. As regards their posing for the camera at Bournemouth, Elgar and Stanford still occupy similar extreme positions in the photograph taken in 1922 on the occasion of the unveiling of the Parry memorial at Gloucester (reproduced in Brewer, A Herbert: *Memories of Choirs and Cloisters* (Bodley Head, 1931) p 200). It was then that the two were brought together by Bantock and what differences they may have had were forgotten.
11. Reprinted in W H Scott, *Edward German: An Intimate Biography* (Cecil Palmer, Chappell, 1932) p 161
12. *Bournemouth Echo* report, quoted in *Memories and Music*, pp 82-3
13. Julian Clifford gave the first provincial performance of Elgar's Second Symphony at Harrogate on 9 August 1911, before Manchester (composer, 23 November), Liverpool (composer, 2 December) and Birmingham (Beecham, 6 December).
14. 'There is no programme beyond a wide experience of human life with a great charity (love) and a *massive* hope in the future', Elgar had told Walford Davies.
15. These brief summaries of Elgar works performed concern the winter series only. Oddly enough, no programmes (possibly not printed) and no records were kept of works given during the summer season concerts which were anyway of a more popular nature. Details can only be gathered from local newspaper reviews.
16. Edginton: *op cit*, p 2
17. *From piano to forte: a thousand and one notes*, Cassell 1931, p 244
18. Edgington: *op cit*, p 3
19. *Musical Opinion*, January 1942, quoted in Eastaugh, Kenneth: *Havergal Brian: the making of a Composer* (Harrap, 1976) p 193
20. First performed with Farrar conducting the Harrogate Municipal Orchestra on 4 June 1913. It was also given at Hastings by Julian Clifford on 25 March 1920.
21. *Memories and Music*, p 154
22. Godfrey's next performance of *A London Symphony*, on 11 November 1920, was of the second (1920) revision and the first published edition. The third revision (1933) was the version used when Godfrey replaced an indisposed Vaughan Williams on 22 August 1934 in his last season. On that occasion the programme claimed that the symphony had 'been performed here more frequently than by any other orchestra'. That would seem to have been its 25th Bournemouth performance, not counting the 1924 Festival, when the first and third movements only were played. At about that time Godfrey recorded those two movements, very much abridged, for Columbia (L1507/8), not with his Municipal Orchestra but with the LSO. In March 1926 a complete recording of the work by the same forces was released, also by Columbia (L1717-1722). This recording includes sections that were omitted from the final

revision which is the version heard today. Despite their considerable interest, these recordings have not been reissued in any format.

23. To Alice Stuart Wortley, 24 October 1915. Moore, Jerrold Northrop: *Elgar: The Windflower Letters* (OUP, 1989) pp 155-6

24. Anderson, Robert: *Elgar in Manuscript* (British Library, 1990) p 133

25. Paul Goossens was a cousin of Eugene Goossens II.

26. In the score the second movement bears the heading 'Killed in Action. Near the South Pole. March 28th 1912.'

27. Although a frequent visitor to Bournemouth, chiefly at Festivals, rather surprisingly Eric Coates did not conduct any premières there as he did at Eastbourne, Folkestone, Harrogate and Torquay.

28. Coates: *op cit*, p 44

29. *ibid*, p 152

30. *Memories and Music*, p 192

31. Bantock's *Hebridean Symphony* was to enjoy seven performances at Bournemouth in Godfrey's time, the composer conducting on two occasions.

32. Commissioned for the 1893 Chicago Exhibition.

33. Yorkshire-born Arthur Wood (1875-1953) was flautist and solo pianist in the Municipal Orchestra from 1898 to 1902. After leaving Bournemouth he soon became known as a London theatre music director, although he occasionally returned to conduct his own works at popular concerts. His music, if not his name, reached a wider audience when in 1950 'Barwick Green', the last movement of his suite *My Native Heath* (heard at Bournemouth in 1931), was chosen as the signature tune for the long-running BBC Radio serial *The Archers*.

34. This work enjoyed a rare revival in December 2000 at West Norwood with Christopher Fifield conducting the Lambeth Orchestra.

35. d'Albert succeeded Joachim as director of the High School for Music in Berlin and was the dedicatee of Richard Strauss' *Burleske*. He was generally unpopular in the UK during the war for his proclaimed allegiance to Germany and residence abroad.

36. The *Concerto passione* was given by Sir Henry Wood with Warwick Evans as soloist at the Proms in September 1913, and heard again in 1914 and 1915. The second part, a Symphonic Fantasia *La Lutte et l'Espoir*, was given by Wood and Benno Moiseiwitsch at the Queen's Hall in June 1916 and at that year's Proms. The third part, *Les Flammes*, was awaiting production. Other works by Dorlay were heard at the 1906, 1907, 1909 and 1920 Proms. The November 1916 *Musical Times* Prom review suggests that 'Georges Dorlay' was a pseudonym. However, Sidonie Goossens, who knew Dorlay, confirms that it was his name and remembers him as 'a dapper little man'. He was no longer playing in the Queen's Hall Orchestra when she joined it in 1921. (Letter to the author, 3 February 1995.)

37. BBC 1977, in Palmer, Christopher: *Herbert Howells: A Centenary Celebration* (Thames Publishing, 1992) p 374. It is assumed that Howells is referring to that 1919 performance and not to the 1923 Festival when he himself conducted the 'Blissy' movement on its own. The work was first given at a RCM concert in June 1915; Godfrey's performance was its second.

CHAPTER 6

ELGAR'S CREATIVE CHALLENGE 1914–1918

Andrew Neill

> They are fallen, those famous ones
> Who made this kingdom glorious, they are fallen
> About their King, they have yielded up their strength
> And beauty and valour.

These lines by Laurence Binyon from his play *Arthur* of 1919 were written during Binyon's final artistic collaboration with Edward Elgar. This produced one of the few great pieces of music written in response to war, Elgar's setting of Binyon's poem *For the Fallen*. Beginning early in 1915 this relationship lasted until the performances of *Arthur* in 1923 with incidental music by Elgar. During the war, Binyon and his wife became part of the Elgar's circle visiting their Hampstead home, as well as faithfully following performances of *The Spirit of England* of which *For the Fallen* formed the third section.

In his poems of 1914 Binyon perceived that the war was likely to be longer and more horrific than any conflict before. Others, such as John Masefield (1878-1967) in his poem *August, 1914*, seem to guess this. Three verses from the poem show how he creates an atmosphere of peace that is almost tangible but which is about to be destroyed by the coming of war.

> So beautiful it is. I never saw
> So great a beauty on these English fields,
> Touched by the twilight's coming into awe,
> Ripe to the soul and rich with summer's yields.

> These homes, this valley spread below me here,
> The rooks, the tilted stacks, the beasts in pen,
> Have been the heartfelt things, past speaking dear
> To unknown generations of dead men.

> Who, century after century, held these farms,
> And, looking out to watch the changing sky,
> Heard, as we near, the rumours and alarms
> Of war at hand and danger pressing nigh.

FACING PAGE: *Elgar at Severn House, 1919 (Raymond Monk Collection)*

Binyon's was a rare insight for, as we have seen, the British only became aware of the possibility of war little more than a week before it began. Richard Strauss had conducted Mozart in London at the end of June and the conductor Sir Henry Wood 'earmarked a week to spend in Bayreuth in order to hear *Parsifal* on August 4, 1914'.[1] Wood did not travel to Germany, but others were less fortunate, such as the composer Edgar Bainton and the assistant organist of Hereford Cathedral, Percy Hull, both of whom were interned at Ruhleben for the duration of the war.[2]

Alice Elgar's diaries show how Elgar devoted himself to work for much of the war. His efforts display hard work, imagination and patriotism. It is true he had the occasional break and visited his sister and her family at Stoke Prior, but his constant activity in conducting and composition as well as police and military duties eventually took its toll. It was the breakdown in his health toward the end of 1917 that enabled Elgar to take up composition once again, aided by the knowledge that he was not suffering from a fatal disease and from the move to the Sussex countryside. Although we may feel disappointed that he did not compose more music during the war, there is little doubt that Elgar began determined to support the cause to the best of his ability.

It is easy to conclude that Elgar found composition difficult during the first three and half years of war. However, things are never that simple, and it is perhaps more accurate to suggest that it was the spark of inspiration that was elusive for, once he began a piece, Elgar does seem to have worked fluently and at times passionately. This is particularly true, for example, in parts one ('The Fourth of August') and three ('For the Fallen') of *The Spirit of England* once the way became clear for their completion. We cannot know the truth, but the environment in which Elgar worked was unique, not only to him, but his fellow countrymen.

In his first post Armistice diary entry of 12 November 1918, Elgar does not mention his work, but the next day he looked forward once again as he concentrated on his Quartet. 'Wrote music & tried to recover the threads . . .'. At last the war was history. It is easy to assume that Elgar's operation in 1918 performed a psychological as well as physical healing particularly as he began to compose again once he felt well, but his real work did not commence until the German forces were in retreat and there was some certainty of an allied victory.

The Spirit of England and the three Belgian recitations: *Carillon, Une Voix dans Le Désert* and *Le Drapeau Belge* counter Elgar's apparently undemonstrative approach to the fighting. To this wartime collection we should add *Polonia, The Fringes of the Fleet, The Sanguine Fan, The Starlight Express* and some songs. If we consider the chamber music as post-war music (only the sonata was completed before the Armistice), this does not add up to a great amount for a composer at the height of his powers. Little of this music is considered to be a significant part of the repertory today and, for reasons beyond Elgar's control, too much became beset by controversy. He did not so much write 'war music', more he wrote music of or for the war, such as the three recitations, *The Spirit of England* and *The Fringes of the Fleet*. Elgar's inability to see a way to complete 'The Fourth of August' until 1917 says much about his feelings.

The time Elgar took to complete 'For the Fallen' cannot just be lain at the feet of Cyril Rootham, although Elgar's sensitivity (and natural courtesy) meant that he was not able to brush aside the interest of Rootham, as Verdi was able to do in a similar situation.[3] Matters would have been further complicated if Ivor Gurney had completed his setting of the poem which he considered whilst serving at the front in 1916. On 5 July Gurney wrote to the musicologist Marion Scott.

> ... but have you heard Elgar's setting of 'To the Fallen'?[sic] Is it any way worthy of the poem? I *would* like to set that! One of the best things I know 'in memoriam'.

Two months later on 29 September he wrote asking her to send him a copy of Binyon's poem, but on 25 October he wrote again to Scott: 'The Binyon poem is too long, too big, I fear, for any setting I could give it, but perhaps, perhaps...'. There is no evidence Gurney ever set a word of Binyon's poem.[4]

Despite Elgar's affection for *The Fringes of the Fleet*, he may well have had some sympathy with Rudyard Kipling's reluctance to allow them to be paraded as part of a revue, for he would surely have known of Kipling's grief for his son reported 'wounded and missing' at the end of September 1915. To occupy himself, Kipling spent the autumn turning to poems and articles, which were published as the pocket book, *The Fringes of the Fleet*, in the December. He had spent some time in the September with the Dover Patrol and Harwich Flotilla. It is probably fair to assume that Elgar had no idea of 'the intense personal feelings' which Kipling associated with the writing of *The Fringes of the Fleet*, for it is unlikely he would have called Kiplng's attitude 'perfectly stupid' when Kipling tried to stop performances.[5] Possibly Elgar understood Kipling's grief, but it may be that he was unable to 'read between the lines' in the Kipling verses. As we have seen, the poems are set in what Elgar called 'a broad saltwater style'. This is a fair description except for *Submarines* which is as sinister as the poem and might well have been respected by Kipling had he been prepared to listen.

> The Ships destroy us above
> And ensnare us beneath,
> We arise, we lie down, and we move
> In the belly of Death.
>
> The ships have a thousand eyes
> To mark where we come . . .
> And the mirth of a seaport dies
> When our blow gets home.

The relationship between Elgar and Kipling is worth exploring further, for this disagreement between two artistic giants seems, on the surface, to be improbable. We need to understand the state of Kipling's mind and that of his wife Carrie once the fortunes of war turned against them in 1915. Kipling had persuaded Field Marshal Lord Roberts to find a place in the Second Battalion of the Irish Guards for the Kiplings' only son John. He was just seventeen when he received his commission in September 1914. Originally it had been assumed, from an early age, that he would join the Royal Navy, but his poor eyesight ruled this out early in the war. Short, naïve, inexperienced and young for his age John Kipling was mortally wounded during the battle of Loos on 27 September 1915. The report of the action tells of the charge, in which 'Second Lieutenant Kipling was wounded and missing'; it further implied that advancing German forces might have captured him. Rudyard Kipling, born in India, was brought 'home' to England and, at the age of five, his parents, on their return to India, left him behind in Southsea in the care of a Captain

Rudyard Kiplin

Holloway and his wife. This miserable experience was to stay with
Kipling for the remainder of his life. It is possible that Kipling, who
had 'pulled every string in his book' to find John Kipling a place in the
forces, suppressed his own guilt at abandoning his son. Thus he was
to spend months using every avenue available to him to establish the
truth before, finally, accepting the reality of John's death.

Therefore, any collaborator with Kipling had to tread a delicate
line between various and deep sensitivities. The mutual eminence of
Kipling and Elgar may have been a barrier to communication, for
Kipling felt able to respond to the approach of Edward German (1862-
1936) who achieved a level of understanding of Kipling and his state
of mind as he sought to establish the truth about his son. The
younger, perhaps less threatening composer was able to establish the
right level of sympathy with the poet. When German set Kipling's *My
boy Jack?,* German successfully perceived the poem's passion hidden
by a thin veneer of stoicism. Reflecting Kipling's work with the coastal
forces the poet asks after the fate of his son and concludes that if he
were lost then his death would have been honourable. German
understands and matches Kipling's mood. He never patronises the
sentiment but draws the listener into sharing the Kipling family grief
and hope that a miracle had occurred. The recording German made of
the song in 1917 with Louise Kirkby-Lunn[†] shows his identification
with his task as passionate advocate and conductor.

> Have you news of my boy Jack?
>> *Not this tide.*
> When d'you think that he'll come back?
>> *Not with this wind blowing, and this tide.*
>
> Has any one else had word of him?
>> *Not this tide.*
> *For what is sunk will hardly swim,*
>> *Not with this wind blowing, and this tide.*
>
> Oh, dear, what comfort can I find!
>> *None this tide,*
>> *Nor any tide,*
> *Except he did not shame his kind-*
>> *Not even with that wind blowing, and that tide.*
>
> *Then hold your head up all the more,*
>> *This tide,*
>> *And every tide;*
> *Because he was the son you bore,*
>> *And gave to that wind blowing and that tide!*

Missing the point? A contemporary advertisement underlining the importance of associating a song with a popular artist, here Clara Butt.

That he satisfied Kipling is clear, for German was invited to set his poem *The Irish Guards,* which was published by *The Times* on 11 March 1918. German even considered setting a version of *The Fringes of the Fleet,* but only set one of the poems that had also been used by Elgar, *Be well Assured.*[6] If Elgar and Kipling never became close, and Elgar would have found it difficult to accept Kipling's strong and continuous anti-German rhetoric: 'his hating condemnation of the enemy',[7] he was later happy to nominate Kipling for membership of The Beefsteak Club.

After the report that John Kipling was missing in action his grieving father allowed more and more of his personal affairs to pass under the control of his wife Carrie, whose loathing of all things German became as vehement as that of her husband. 'She would not let him [Kipling] write to any friend without knowing who the correspondent was.'[8] It is clear that Elgar did not have to deal with Rudyard Kipling alone as he fought to keep *The Fringes of the Fleet* performances afloat in 1917. A fellow Irish Guard's officer of John Kipling, Rupert Grayson, became a friend of the Kiplings and also a frequent visitor to their home, Bateman's in Sussex.

Grayson had visited Bateman's when the idea of making the verses [*The Irish Guards*] into a song was mooted and had suggested that Elgar be invited to compose the music. 'No,' he (Kipling) said abruptly, 'Edward German will set my verses to music.' Grayson commented, 'German's music was melodious and charming, but I was disappointed it was not Elgar – a great composer with a superb sense of pageantry. I said nothing because I had learned to keep my mouth shut whenever Carrie shot me one of her warning glances. I would dearly have liked to know what Elgar had done to offend Kipling ... If Kipling was the leading poet of that period, Elgar was surely the leading composer. [9]

Elgar, like Kipling, had to come to terms with the sudden abnormalities of war, which produced inevitable anti-German propaganda from the start when attempts were made to ban German music and musicians of German origin. As an artist he would have tried to put his creative gift above the conflict. Early on the writing was on the wall with the cancellation of Strauss's *Don Juan* that was to be part of a promenade concert on 15 August 1914. This situation did not last long, and the manager of the Queen's Hall published a notice toward the end of August, which ended:

The Directors ... take this opportunity of emphatically contra-dicting the statements that German music will be boycotted during the present season. The greatest examples of Music and Art are world possessions and unassailable even by the prejudices and passions of the hour. [10]

Edward German

Elgar may well have found ridiculous the efforts of the composer Joseph Holbrooke, who was at the forefront of the 'All-English Concerts' and the 'No-German Concerts' in the spring of 1915, and, although not of the writer's circle, Elgar was no doubt aware of the suppression of D H Lawrence's

The Rainbow. Officially, this was because of its denunciation of war, although ostensibly the action was brought on the grounds of obscenity.[11] The thinking of many at the time was demonstrated by writers such as J C Squire in the New Statesman, who suggested that Lawrence might be 'under the spell of German psychologists'. Lawrence's German wife hardly helped their case either.

During the war the issue of 'British art' was to raise its head from time to time, and *The Musical Herald*, a monthly journal, considered 'The effect of the War on British Music' in 1915. Gustav Holst (1874-1934), in a letter that September wrote:

> ... but the importance of the question of national art lies not in the finding of the solution, but rather in the attitude of mind which is brought to bear on it. It is useless to approach the question without an entire absence of prejudice and a delicate sense of artistic values.[12]

Elgar's recorded comments on the war and the course of the war are few but, after completing 'The Fourth of August' in 1917, he wrote to Ernest Newman explaining the use of music from the Demon's Chorus in *The Dream of Gerontius*.

> Two years ago I held over that section hoping that some trace of manly spirit would shew itself in the direction of German affairs: that hope is gone forever & the Hun is branded as less than a beast for very many generations: so I wd. not invent anything low & bestial enough to illustrate the one stanza; the Cardinal [Newman] invented (*invented* as far as I know) the particular hell in Gerontius where the great intellects gibber & snarl *knowing they have fallen*:
>
> This is exactly the case with the Germans now;-the music was to hand & I have sparingly used it. A lunatic asylum is, after the first shock, not entirely sad; so few of the patients are aware of the strangeness of their situation; most of them are placid & foolishly calm; but the horror of the fallen intellect – *knowing* what it once was & *knowing* what it has become – is beyond words frightful ... And this ends, as far as I can see, my contribution to war music.[13]

His letter to Frank Schuster of August 1914 is more obvious.[14] This is not a callous disregard for human life but a subtle cry for those caught up in an affair they cannot control, the waste of war and the uncomplaining support horses have given and would continue to give to all armies. No doubt Elgar would have seized on these sentiments, subtly expressed by Julian Grenfell in his poem *Into Battle (Flanders 1915)*. Grenfell, a courageous soldier who was to die of wounds during the Second Battle of Ypres in May 1915, took an objective view of war. He captures, in a few words, the essence of waiting for the dawn of battle:

> In dreary, doubtful waiting hours,
>> Before the brazen frenzy starts,
> The horses show him nobler powers;
>> `O patient eyes, courageous hearts!

Of course Elgar's letter is emotional, but Elgar was an emotional artist. In his lecture on 'The Nature of Genius', Ernest Jones draws attention to a pair of opposites… . 'For there is every reason to suppose that men of genius are characterised by possessing exceptionally strong emotions and usually a correspondingly strong capacity for containing them'. [15]

Elgar was not as successful as some in disguising his emotions. On the other hand he 'soldiered on' throughout most of the war in circumstances that he might have avoided in peacetime. He was a realist therefore. Although we know very little of his thoughts at the time there is little doubt that, if he had spoken out against his enemy as loudly and as often as Kipling we would know about it, for it would have affected his reputation. We are left only with few pointers as to Elgar's true feelings, and perhaps his only overtly 'anti-German' statements are the 'Gerontius' excerpt in 'The Fourth of August', and his letter to Ernest Newman quoted above.

One analogy might be that 'he had his enemy in his sights', but if he let loose a round it was one only, and before long Elgar's objectiveness, which shines out of Alice Elgar's wartime diaries, becomes apparent. Shortly after the end of the war Elgar extended the hand of friendship to Richard Strauss.[16] During the war, when he heard of the death of the conductor and dedicatee of his A Flat Symphony Hans Richter, he wrote to Marie Joshua.[17] Perhaps this is as it should be, the creative artist reaching out over conflict and political barriers. This stood him good stead. For once Elgar's state of mind seems to have prepared him for the future, and he could move forward, composing and attempting to find his place in the new world of 1919 and beyond. In contrast, poor Kipling, unable to accept the loss of his son 'became tormented with the idea that Germany was not going to be made to pay in full, and for ever, being "Evil Incarnate".' [18]

In some ways we can see that Elgar reflected the course of the war in his response to events and attitude to friends and outside stimuli. For the first few months he threw himself into every sort of activity, composing *Carillon*, corresponding with A C Benson, becoming a Special Constable, and embracing Binyon's poems early in 1915. Slowly it became obvious that the war would go on and on and become a debilitating and draining experience for the country and its people.   More and more difficulties arose for Elgar too, both of a practical and creative nature.   Thus he became detached or perhaps distant from events.   It is this attitude that allows us to perceive his operation in early 1918 as the catharsis that enabled his creative impulse to be stimulated anew on his return to good health and his retreat to Sussex.

Then, as throughout the war, Elgar does not seem to have seen himself as the vehicle for expressing overt patriotism at a time when several 'Land of Hope and Glorys' might have been expected.   The completed *The Spirit of England* could have taken centre stage, but it took too long to produce to have the long-term impact that Binyon's poems had made originally.   By the time the work was performed complete in late 1917 time was running out for its acceptance as a centrepiece for wartime concerts, even though audiences were, at times, ecstatic.   Demands for frequent performance, as with *Carillon,* were neither made nor could then be justified, even though Elgar's instinctive reaction to Binyon's poems was sound.   'For the Fallen' became the finest example of their mutual 'heroic melancholy' emphasised by Binyon's coincidental echo of a line from the great lament from *Caractacus,*[19] 'O my Warriors 'in a verse in 'For the Fallen'.

> And the god shall give you heeding
> And across the heav'nly plain . . .

and

> As the stars that shall be bright when we are dust
> Moving in marches upon the heavenly plain . . .[20]

Although the poem 'For the Fallen' (through its one oft quoted fourth verse) has remained in the mind of the public, Binyon's other poems and Elgar's wartime music faded slowly from view, as the war became a memory, until a rekindling of interest took place fifty or more years later.   During the war the audience for both changed, and the 'heroic melancholy' of Binyon and Elgar became out of place in the post war years in such works as *Arthur.*   The combination then only served to emphasise the unsympathetic climate of opinion.[21]   A fissure had opened between those who could not go to war and those who could. Neither Binyon nor Elgar was a combatant so could not express their feelings for the horror of the Western Front from first hand experience.   However, Binyon by his visits as a Red Cross volunteer came close to the fighting and on returning from France in early June

1917 he researched and wrote a volume, *For Dauntless France* which,

> despite its dry subtitle – *An Account of Britain's Aid to the French Wounded and Victims of the War, Compiled for the British Red Cross by Laurence Binyon* ... ranks with 'For the Fallen' and 'Fetching the Wounded' as Binyon's major contribution to the non-combatant literature of the Great War.[22]

In 1914 Binyon possessed the ability to perceive the heroism, self-sacrifice and loyalty of the individual fighting for his country in a way that was ahead of his time. He had to come to terms with an unprecedented change in warfare, the consequences of which were to be felt in every home in the country. How could he have represented the war after Loos, The Somme, and Passchendaele and how could Elgar set the same sentiments to music? Binyon's service in the Red Cross provided the inspiration for *Fetching the Wounded,* but because he was not 'fighting' his difficulty is only emphasised. 'The short sentences [of the final lines], clinging close to the action –

> The village sleeps; blank walls and windows barred.
> But lights are moving in the hushed courtyard
> As we glide to the open door. The Chief
> Gives every man his order, prompt and brief.
> We carry up our wounded, one by one.
> The first cock crows: the morrow is begun.

- hint at one direction in which his poetry might have developed had he been a younger man fighting at the front.'[23] He did get close, for he was sent to France a month before the Armistice as a lecturer to the advancing Allied forces, and ended the war close behind the advance. By then it was too late.

Shortly before he died in 1942, Binyon wrote his last poems, including *The Burning of the Leaves.* This has been described as

> one of the major lyrics of the home front, and it is remarkable, to say the least, that the poet who produced the most famous consolatory poem of the First World War should also have written during the Second World War what George Gilpin has identified as 'the poem that spoke most poignantly for the besieged and for the era'.[24]

> Now is the time for the burning of the leaves.
> They go to the fire; the nostril pricks with smoke
> Wandering slowly into a weeping mist.
> Brittle and blotched, ragged and rotten sheaves!
> A flame seizes the smouldering ruin and bites
> On stubborn stalks that crackle as they resist.

The last hollyhock's fallen tower is dust;
All the spices of June are a bitter reek,
All the extravagant riches spent and mean.
All burns! The reddest rose is a ghost;
Sparks whirl up, to expire in the mist: the wild
Fingers of fire are making corruption clean.

Now is the time for stripping the spirit bare,
Time for the burning of days ended and done,
Idle solace of things that have gone before:
Rootless hope and fruitless desire are there;
Let them go to the fire, with never a look behind.
The world that was ours is a world that is ours no more.

They will come again, the leaf and the flower, to arise
From squalor of rottenness into the old splendour,
And magical scents to a wondering memory bring;
The same glory, to shine upon different eyes.
Earth cares for her own ruins, naught for ours.
Nothing is certain, only the certain spring.

Gradually the nature of the problem was established, and many,
including the journalist Philip Gibb, summarised it clearly:

> If any man were to draw the picture of these things or to tell them more
> nakedly than I have told them . . . no man or woman would dare to speak
> again of war's 'glory', or of the 'splendour of war', or any of those old lying
> phrases which hide the dreadful truth.[25]

It took more than forty years for the voice of the Western Front to find
its comprehending partner in a work with a pacifist message, the *War
Requiem* of Benjamin Britten, first performed in 1962. However, this
was more a culmination than an original idea, for Arthur Bliss in his
Morning Heroes of 1930 not only used a poem by the then little known
Wilfred Owen, but also excerpts from *The Iliad,* the eighth century
Chinese poet Li Tai-Po's *Vigil* and Walt Whitman's *Drum Taps.* Bliss's
younger brother, Kennard, had been killed on the Somme in 1916.

> In 1928, ten years after the bloody events Bliss had lived through, he
> became a victim of nightmares in which he relived scenes he could not
> forget. The need to externalise them became imperative, and he returned
> to the battlefields to seek out the grave of his 23 year-old brother, whose
> loss he had never ceased to mourn. Out of that experience grew *Morning
> Heroes,* a symphony more on heroism than war.[26]

Morning Heroes was born through a personal need for healing and
reconciliation, and it is perhaps its intimacy that has left it
overshadowed by Britten's larger work. The *War Requiem* is, in many

ways, the concluding chapter of a book of which *The Spirit of England* was the first. Wilfred Owen's poetry was, by 1962, as well known as 'For the Fallen' became during the war, but nothing as public had been written since Elgar's settings. Britten, born in 1913, was nearly a generation younger than those who fought. He could at last see how to combine the words of a great war poet in a musical context, and lay to rest those which had by the 1960s become overshadowed by those who had fought between 1939 and 1945, and the climate of the cold war.[27]

Paradoxically, the *War Requiem* serves to show how great Elgar's achievement was in finding a voice in *The Spirit of England*. In a changing and rapidly darkening world Elgar's musical insight is all the more remarkable. It is clear that Britten recognised this when he wrote of 'For the Fallen' in the 1969 Aldeburgh Festival programme-book:

> [It] has always seemed to me to have in its opening bars a personal tenderness and grief, in the grotesque march, an agony of distortion, and in the final sequences a ring of genuine splendour.[28]

Ernest Newman's considered reaction at the time in the *Birmingham Post* of 9 May 1916 anticipated Britten.

> 'For the Fallen' is as moving a piece of music as Elgar has ever given us – a work of passionate sincerity and a beauty that is by turns touching, thrilling, and consoling. ... The emotional basis of the music of the music is proudly elegiac, with moments of soaring rapture. ... Technically [it is a work] of the rarest quality. It takes a lifetime of incessant practice to attain a touch at once so light and so sure as this.[29]

Before this, Newman had already nailed his colours to the mast:

> In the 'Carillon' Elgar gave expression to the best that is in us at this time of trial. It was not mere war-music; it was music that transcended the shouting and the trampling, the blood and murk of war. ... In no country, one almost dares say, can the emotion for the dead have quite the same thrill as ours; for the men who have died for England have for the most part given their lives as a voluntary sacrifice. As Mr Binyon sings:
>
> > They laughed, they sang their melodies of England.
> > They fell open-eyed and unafraid.
>
> It is love and gratitude and pride and sorrow for these children of England and their self-sacrifice, – a sacrifice of which Rupert Brooke, in the eyes of lovers of art, will be for ever the shining symbol, – that Elgar sings in such noble accents in the third of these new works of his.[30]

Rupert Brooke had been buried on Skyros on St George's Day 1915 and the heart of the volunteer army was about to die on the Somme.

Never again could these sentiments, both simple and pertinent be expressed so directly and honestly.

The *Fringes of the Fleet*, another work born and sustained in controversy, is patriotic in a quiet domestic way, reflecting the heroism of the ordinary man 'doing his bit' for the war. It is also worth considering Elgar's other compositions written before 1918, which throw into relief the achievement of 'For the Fallen'. Brilliantly orchestrated, *Polonia* was composed for a country on the Eastern Front, at a time when eyes at home were concentrated on the Front in France. *The Sanguine Fan* has little to do with the war beyond its composition for a war charity. Elgar's music 'for the cause' remains the three Belgian recitations, *Polonia, The Spirit of England* and *The Fringes of the Fleet*. This is hardly the result that might have been expected from the country's composer laureate in 1914. But it was in *The Starlight Express* that Elgar became most absorbed, but that failed for reasons beyond his control.

This was an enormous score, Elgar's largest since the E flat Symphony of 1911. It had nothing to do with the conflict; everything else was brushed aside to meet deadlines and the opening night. Even this music was touched by controversy, for the composer and singer Clive Carey had originally been asked to write the music.

During the war Elgar composed and completed most of his scores quickly and happily. He may have been happy working, but the initial idea for composition was rarely his. With inspiration from within frustrated, it is possible to see his moves to involve himself in the Special Constabulary and Hampstead Volunteer Reserve as an attempt to do something for the war other than compose. When the elusive muse did come it was when others showed him the way. He was not alone, as Samuel Hynes has shown. 'It is striking how few of the great Edwardians had found an adequate wartime voice, or the heart to use it.' Mr Hynes, who gives an American perspective, goes on to point out how Bridges (the Poet Laureate), Kipling, Galsworthy, Conrad, James, Masefield, Hardy 'lapsed into virtual silence particularly during the pivotal year of 1916'.[31] This echoes a letter of Virginia Woolf of 1922 when she wrote to Janet Case: 'But don't you agree with me that the Edwardians, from 1895 to 1914, made a pretty poor show. By the Edwardians, I mean Shaw, Wells, Galsworthy, the Webbs, Arnold Bennett.'[32] Inevitably these comments are not entirely fair, for Masefield like Vaughan Williams, volunteered as a medical orderly, and was sent to France in early 1915.

However, all those artists of Elgar's time and the generation following, had to come to terms with the way war had changed their lives and country and to face the impossibility of reflecting the sentiment and reality of a time without precedent.[33] Hynes refers to 'the voluble Shaw' in the same context, although Shaw's 'virtual silence' is more a creative than a literal one. Shaw, who was to become Elgar's friend, took advantage of his renown to put across his ideas.

From the beginning of hostilities, George Bernard Shaw spoke out against the war, condemning both sides for their failure to resolve their differences. In a letter to his German translator, he wrote: 'I believe that the mass of the nation feels about the war very much as you and I do, that is, they feel it to be a frightful failure of civilization that there should be a war at all between civilized western powers'.[34]

Shaw set out his views in his pamphlet *Common Sense about the War* and used his eminence to get away with much including exhorting soldiers on both sides to 'shoot their officers and go home'.[35] He perceived that the war would last a long time and take a terrible toll. Excoriated early on, his philosophy that 'one thing is to set to work immediately to draft the inevitable Treaty of Peace which we must all sign when we have had our bellyful of murder and destruction'[36] began to be accepted as the years went by. Shaw and the Elgars, like any of their fellow countrymen, would have been shocked by the unprecedented loss of life, firstly in the first few months of the war and then at Loos in the autumn of 1915. But the losses on the Somme exceeded these campaigns the following summer, and Shaw and his message no longer seemed anachronistic.

Once it was clear nothing could be done to halt the slaughter, Shaw changed his tune, and his energies began to be utilised more effectively. Shrewdly the authorities invited him to visit the front line, which inevitably made a deep impression upon him. Lytton Strachey gives us a memorable picture of Shaw at a public meeting, in full flight, dominating his audience as he dominated the stage.

> . . . and a large audience eager for a pacifist oration and all that's most advanced – and poor dear Mr Shaw talking about 'England' with trembling lips and gleaming eyes and declaring that his one wish was that we should first beat the Germans, and then fight them again and then beat them again and again, and again! He was more like a nice old-fashioned admiral on a quarter- deck than anything else.[37]

Nevertheless with all this concentrated energy and campaigning Shaw's time for writing was compromised, with the result that *Heartbreak House* was the only work of significance he wrote during the war.[38]

The challenge was great, if not impossible. W B Yeats (1865-1939) made his position clear at the time in his contribution to Edith Wharton's *The Book of the Homeless* published in 1916.[39]

A REASON FOR STAYING SILENT.

I think it better at times like these
We poets keep our mouths shut, for in truth
We have no gift to set a statesman right;
He's had enough of meddling who can please
A young girl in the indolence of her youth
Or an old man upon a winter's night.

It became apparent that only those who had seen and experienced the war would be able to 'tell'. Writers such as, Edmund Blunden, Ivor Gurney,[40] Wilfred Owen, Isaac Rosenberg, Siegfried Sassoon artists like Paul Nash and the composers Arthur Bliss and Ralph Vaughan Williams they 'knew' what Elgar could never know, but may have instinctively felt. Vaughan Williams, born in October 1872, was 42

LEFT: *Ralph Vaughan Williams by Sir William Rothenstein;* RIGHT: *Sir Hubert Parry*

years old when he joined the London Field Ambulance on New Year's Eve 1914, a decision with significant results.

> The change of style and musical language between, say, the pre-war *Songs of Travel* and the post-war cycle *Along the Field,* or *The Lark Ascending* (1914) compared to the *Violin Concerto* (1925) is so stark that the impact of his wartime experiences must be counted the major factor on his development as a composer.[41]

To speculate whether Vaughan Williams might have developed otherwise is futile; for it was inevitable he could not remain unaffected as an artist but also as a man. Sir Hubert Parry (1848-1918) perceived this when he wrote to the younger composer in January 1915, even if the peril to Vaughan Williams' life was largely in his mind.

> As to your enlisting, I can't express myself in any way that is likely to be serviceable. There are certain individuals who are capable of serving their country in certain exceptional and very valuable ways, and they are not on the same footing as ordinary folks, who if they are exterminated are just one individual gone and no more. You have already served your country in very notable and exceptional ways and are likely to do so again: and such folks should be shielded from risk rather than be exposed to it. We may admit the generosity of the impulse, and feel – I will not say what.[42]

This was the difference. Vaughan Williams, like Bliss, could and would tell of his experiences in his music afterwards. Remaining at home Elgar could tell of the *Fringes of the Fleet* but to portray the unimaginable slaughter of the Somme was impossible. Perhaps he came close in *For the Fallen.*[43] After the war those of Elgar's generation, those too old to fight, had to face the resentment of those that had fought, such as T E Lawrence.

> The old men came out again and took our victory to remake in the likeness of the former world they knew. Youth could win, but had not learned to keep: and was pitiably weak against age. We stammered that we had worked for a new heaven and a new earth, and they thanked us kindly and made their peace.[44]

Others, though, were more understanding and appreciative, even those of Lawrence's generation. In early 1917 Siegfried Sassoon wrote a poem on hearing Elgar's Violin Concerto for the first time. The programme also included the *Enigma Variations*, which he described as giving him 'as much pleasure as usual, which is a lot'.[45] That May Sassoon wrote to Binyon.

> I wish that those, who, like myself, have had their full share of the 'loathed business', could say that 'blessed are our eyes because they have seen' – But it is not so. For us it is mostly boredom & stark horror & fear.[46]

Frank Schuster wrote of the reaction of the young poet, Robert Nichols, invalided home and staying at The Hut. '... Sensible people like Yeats keep quiet, or express the feelings of non-combatants in the most touching & poignant forms imaginable as Elgar & Binyon. How often the sad last phrases of Elgar's 'For the Fallen' echo despondingly & yet somehow victoriously in my head!'[47]   Some, like Sir Edwin Lutyens (1869-1944), managed to bestride the pre- and post-war climates with success. That was achieved, to some extent by official patronage, as architect to the Imperial War Graves Commission for which he designed military cemeteries, the Stone of Remembrance found in all cemeteries and the cenotaph in Whitehall.[48] Lutyens also stayed in touch with the world that had nurtured his genius, and his feeling for the needs of a small community is demonstrated, for example, in the war memorial he designed for Mells in Somerset.[49]

Frank Schuster

As the war dragged on, Elgar's ill health increasingly ruled his life and it seemed he might only be cured by an operation. A benefit of this personal crisis was that few commitments then existed in the future. There were no conducting demands or commissions to fulfil, with the need to interpret what had become impossible and unimaginable. Perhaps it was inevitable that Elgar was restored to his true legacy and he began to write abstract music again. In good health, and at peace with himself the creative flame burned vigorously and exceptionally in an atmosphere uncluttered by other demands.

Paradoxically Elgar was now writing in a way that might have been attractive to post-war society. Unlike Lutyens his was not an official part of the post-war environment.[50] His fate was not that his music did not fit or was even out of date, but that he was seen as a part of that society which was partially responsible for the war. As such, Elgar's music came to be rejected by a generation that would soon want to hear Walton's *Façade* or Stravinsky's *Les Noces*.[51] Post war society did not want a concerto from those they saw had allowed the war to happen, but did not participate in the suffering or carnage. We can see that Elgar's unease during this time would have counted for nothing. Time alone would bridge the gap and turn the avant-garde of one generation into the establishment of the next. We have come to see the death of Alice Elgar in April 1920 as the temporary blanking out of Elgar's creative process, but that is only part of the story.

When it mattered, Elgar wrote some great and pertinent music. As the war changed so the demand for something profound changed too. In addition to the millions slaughtered, it became obvious the war had been a great disappointment, militarily. Sir Julian Corbett (joint author of the official *Naval Operations)* felt 'that the two really successful [British] operations in the whole war were the Falklands action and Allenby's campaign in Palestine'.[52] To these should be added the five months stand and counter attack of the British Army in 1918 which led to victory and an Armistice. The challenge then for any artist was how to express the emotion of the hour.

> The final campaign of 1918 – the last victorious 'Hundred Days' – is virtually an unknown story. The great catastrophes of the First World war have lingered in men's minds for six decades, *but* when the tide turned, the interest seemed to die away.[53]

Relief that the war had ended was then the dominant sentiment, and Elgar like many others, felt unable to write something for the peace. In anticipation of the Armistice, Laurence Binyon sent Elgar a draft of his *Peace* Ode, to which Elgar replied from Severn House on 5 November:

> . . . I think your poem beautiful exceedingly – but – I do not feel drawn to write peace music somehow – I thought long months ago that I could feel that way & if anything could draw me your poem would, but the whole atmosphere is too full of complexities for me to feel music to it: not the atmosphere of the poem but of the time I mean. The last two divisions VI & VII are splendid altho' I regret the appeal to the Heavenly Spirit which is cruelly obtuse to the individual sorrow & sacrifice – a cruelty I resent bitterly & disappointedly . . .[54]

Binyon, whose sure touch caught the mood and imagination of his country at the outbreak of war, seems to have found difficulty in finding the words for his *Peace*. His poem has neither the ecstatic reaction of Siegfried Sassoon's *Everyone Sang* nor the atmosphere that Masefield created in his *August 1914* of four years before. Relief, anxiety and anticipation are but three of the emotions that seem to be absent. The poem is set in seven numbered verses ('divisions'), and the following excerpts suggest how Binyon struggled to get to the heart of the issue and why Elgar found it difficult to embrace Binyon's words, as he had with 'For the Fallen' in 1915.[55]

I

Lovely word flying like a bird across the narrow seas,
When winter is over and songs are in the skies,
Peace, with the colour of the dawn upon the name of her,
A music to the ears, a wonder to the eyes;
Peace, bringing husband back to wife and son to mother soon,
And lover to his love, and friend to friend,

IV

Now let us praise the dead that are with us to-day
Who fought and fell before the morning shone,
Happy and brave, an innumerable company;
This day is theirs, the day their deeds have won
Glory to them, and from our hearts a thanksgiving
In humbleness and awe and joy and pride.

V

To sweeten and to cleanse our strifes and sins,
The furious thunderings die away and cease.
But what is won, unless the soul win peace?

VI

Not with folding of the hands,
Not with evening fallen wide
Over waste and weary lands,
Peace is come; but as a bride.
It is the trumpets of the dawn that ring;
It is the sunrise that is challenging.

VII

Peace, like the Spring, that makes the torrent dance afresh
And bursts the bough with sap of beauty pent,
Flower from our hearts into passionate recovery
Of all the mind lost in that banishment.
Come to us mighty as a young and glad deliverer
From wrong's old canker and out-dated lease,
Then will we sing thee in thy triumph and thy majesty,
Then from our throes shall be prepared our peace.

It is possible that Elgar may have reconsidered setting *Peace* or that Binyon misinterpreted his response, for he wrote to Elgar on 20 November.

> I have just got back from Birmingham. Where I have been lecturing & where I was so glad to hear that The Spirit of England had been finely performed to celebrate the armistice, & found your telegram & letter waiting for me. Of course I am only too glad if you take my poem & glorify it with music, & if anyone else should want to set it I shall say it is engaged. Indeed I hope very much that you will find the music coming.[56]

By not composing the equivalent of Haydn's *Nelson Mass* Elgar did not fail his public. It was not wanted. It is perhaps a relief that he did not attempt a celebration of victory, for we only have to remind ourselves of equivalent contributions to realise such pieces only have a short currency as their place in the repertoire quickly becomes anachronistic or even embarrassing.[57]

Few great or even good, long-lasting works of art emerge from war, but the First World War was an exception. It was a war that stimulated or compelled many of those who participated to express themselves in ways without precedent. Consequently we are aware of some fine poetry and paintings and subsequent literature from all sides in the conflict. But it is photographs and film, with their colourless skies that also remain vivid. America's civil conflict fifty years before had pointed the way and at last we can perceive, through photographs and for the first time film, the nature of war in death, in humour, in survival and occasionally in its grandeur. But this medium only served to bring the conflict into the home, revealing it to be bigger than any anticipated experience.

Elgar had to cope, like his contemporaries, with the difficulties of living during an unnatural time. A letter Elgar wrote to Sir Sidney Colvin on 17 April 1918 has often been quoted out of context: 'I cannot do any real work with this awful shadow over us ...'.[58] Elgar was then attempting to recover from his operation of the previous month. Above everything hung the ferocious attack and advance by the Germans, the *Kaiserschlacht* (Kaiser's Battle) which had begun on 21 March. It was this 'awful shadow' which then hung over Elgar and the country.

As we evaluate Elgar's work, we see that *The Starlight Express* and 'For the Fallen' can delight and move a new generation of listeners more than eighty years after the music was first heard. Charles Mott understood this when he wrote to Elgar on 12 May 1918, shortly before he died of wounds in France:

> There is one thing that 'puts the wind up me' very badly, and that is of my being wiped out and thus miss the dear harmonies of your wonderful works.[59]

Mott would have recognised the poignancy of the Binyon poem 'The Unreturning Spring', the last verse of which might have been the country's epitaph at the end of 1917:

> The year's pale spectre is crying
> For beauty invisibly shed,
> For the things that were never told
> And were killed in the minds of the dead.

We can never know precisely how Elgar responded to the war and its unprecedented length. We can observe the pressures he was under and guess that the slaughter and futility affected him as a sensitive artist. We can even suppose that he felt frustrated as he sought the inspiration to express the enormity of his feelings that would say something to his countrymen and which would lift them. He achieved this in *The Spirit of England* and partially in *Carillon*. However, even with this seemingly spontaneous work there were differences between Elgar and the Belgian poet, Emile Cammaerts (1878-1953). His daughter, Jeanne Lindley, who was also his biographer, recorded the writing of *Carillon* and the first performances of Elgar's setting.

> In October 1914, after the Battle of Antwerp, he [Cammaerts] wrote the poem which made his name a household word. He called it "Après Anvers", but when Sir Edward Elgar wrote his music for it, he renamed it "Carillon". The last stanza will give some idea of its popular ring and of the extraordinary restraint which characterises Kim's [Cammaerts] patriotism even at this moment of crisis:

> > Chantons Belges, chantons,
> > Même si il les belssures saignent et la voix se brise,
> > Plus haut que la tourmente, plus for que les canons,
> > Même si les bleeures saignent et si le Coeur se brise,
> > Chantons, l'expoir et le haine implacable,
> > Par ce beau soleil d'automne
> > Et la fierté de rester charitable
> > Quand la Vengeance nous serait si bonne!

> > (Sing, Belgians, sing,
> > Although our wounds may bleed
> > Although pour voices break
> > Louder than the storm, louder than the guns,
> > Although our wounds may bleed
> > Although our hearts may break,
> > Sing of hope and fiercest hate,
> > 'Neath this bright autumn sun,
> > Sing of the pride of charity,
> > When vengeance would be so sweet!)

> Many people recited those lines and their English translation which Tita [Brand] made. Dressed simply and quietly, Tita herself did so in the Albert Hall; Lalla Speyer [Vandervelde] repeated them wrapped in a Belgian flag; and Henry Ainley on an HMV recording; and always to the accompaniment of Elgar's rhythmic but slightly misleading music.

When Kim or Tita read, it was on a note of rising frenzy as the towns of the towns and suffering of their people were pictured. Before the last two lines of the poem, there was a break and the end came in a near whisper, almost as a prayer. Elgar's music with its crashing crescendo at the end does not really allow for such an interpretation.[60]

All the same, Cammaerts, in a letter to Elgar on 8 December 1914 the day after the premier of *Carillon* suggests that he was broadly happy.

> I cannot let this day pass without thanking you again for your glorious work. I have met a good many Belgians to-day and they all wonder how you managed to share so completely our pain and hopes. [61]

Binyon and Elgar, like other artists of their time, had to confront the unimaginable and the unprecedented. In some ways Binyon had the easier task. He reminded those of generations to come, as in his poem *Mid-Atlantic*, that they had a responsibility for their artistic heritage:

> Then sudden through the darkness came
> The vision of a child,
> A child with feet as light as flame
> Who ran across the bitter waves,
> Across the tumbling of the graves—
> With arms stretched out he smiled.
> I drank the wine of life again,
> I breathed among my brother men,
> I felt the human fire.
> I knew that I must serve the will
> Of beauty and love and wisdom still;
> Though all my hopes were overthrown,
> Though universes turned to stone,
> I have my being in this alone
> And die in that desire.

> On Board The 'Lusitania', December, 1914

By implication Elgar was required to produce music that was patriotic, inspiring, elegiac and funereal at the same time. When he did meet one or more of these demands, the response from his audience was one of enormous enthusiasm, contradicting the impression that the première of his Violin Concerto was the last time this happened. The first complete performance of *The Spirit of England* was met with the sort of response that fully justified its long gestation; and it is 'For the Fallen', as poetry and music, that stands the test of time and is relevant nearly a century later.

To meet the hour was largely impossible, but for much of the war Elgar did provide a mixture in his music which went some way to satisfying the demands of an equally uncertain and confused public. Frank Schuster realised this when he wrote to Elgar about the A flat Symphony, following the loss of a friend.

> As long as I have it I can bear my losses, although I thought when I went into the hall today that I couldn't. I felt then as I never have but as you, I fear, sometimes do – that life was not worth living & I would not be sorry to lose it. Then came your symphony – and in a moment I knew I was wrong. In it is *all love* – and love makes life possible. I wonder if you realise when you feel despondent & embittered what your music means to me – and therefore to countless others ... surely it must be *something* to you to know you are giving happiness & hope & consolation to your fellow creatures?[62]

NOTES and SOURCES

1. Wood, Henry: *My Life of Music* (Victor Gollancz, 2nd edition, 1946) p 288
2. All internees and prisoners of war, besides coping with the years of boredom and an increasingly poor diet as the British naval blockade became more and more effective, had to face the additional peril of the flu epidemic that swept across Europe at the end of 1918. The weakened Germans and many prisoners of war suffered, particularly, from its effect. See also the discussion of the Ruhleben prison camp, pp 99-100.
3. In 1844 the composer Francesco Cannetti begged Verdi to refrain from continuing the composition of *I due Foscari* he was also setting. Verdi, physically and mentally tough, had overcome the death of his first wife and their two children by the age of 30, and was not a character to be diverted from a determined, and contracted, course. (See Phillips-Matz, Mary Jane: *Verdi* (Oxford, 1993) p 169).
4. Letter of 5 July quoted in full in Hurd, Michael: *The Ordeal of Ivor Gurney* (Oxford, 1978) pp 75-76. (See also the letter from Hooey, Charles: *The Elgar Society Journal* vol XI, no 1)
5. Ricketts, Harry: *The Unforgiving Minute: A Life of Rudyard Kipling* (Pimlico, 2000) p 329. Mr Ricketts goes on to say: 'The story is usually told by Elgarians to Kipling's discredit; yet despite the songs' painful associations, he *did* give his permission, and there were regular performances over a period of six months.'
6. Rees, Brian: *A Musical Peacemaker: The Life and Work of Sir Edward German* (Bourne End, The Kensal Press, 1986) p 184
7. Wilson, Angus: *The Strange Ride of Rudyard Kipling* (Pimlico, 1977) p 305
8. Nicholson, Adam: *The Hated Wife: Carrie Kipling 1862 – 1939* (Short Books, 2001) p 89

9. Holt, Tonie and Valmai: *'My Boy Jack?': The Search for Kipling's Only Son* (Leo Cooper, 1998) p 133

10. Wood: *op cit*, p 289

11. Although see (later) the attitude to the more powerful figure of G B Shaw.

12. Foreman, Lewis: *From Parry to Britten: British Music in Letters 1900-1945* (Batsford, 1987) p 78

13. Moore, Jerrold Northrop: *Edward Elgar: A Creative Life* (Oxford, 1984) p 705

14. See p 16

15. Storr, Anthony: *The Dynamics of Creation* (Secker & Warburg, 1972) p 197

16. In August 1920, Elgar wrote to Sir Adrian Boult who was on a conducting tour of Austria and Germany asking him to 'give my warm greetings to Strauss ... you can assure him of my continued admiration &, if he will, friendship'. (From Moore, Jerrold Northrop: *Music & friends, Letters to Sir Adrian Boult* (Hamish Hamilton, 1979) p 45).

17. The reply of Marie Joshua to Elgar's letter to her recalled those earlier, happier, days: ' ... I remember his return from a visit to you, when you went over the Symphony, (dedicated to Richter as 'true artist, true friend') with him, which he was to introduce to us shortly. His enthusiasm was tremendous. "Oh!" he would exclaim, "it is so beautiful, so Elgarish ..." ' (Quoted in Moore, Jerrold Northrop: *Letters of a Lifetime* (Oxford, 1990) p 301). Richter died on 5 December 1916 - see p 91.

18. Ricketts: op cit, p 339

19. *Caractacus*: Cantata for soprano, tenor, baritone & bass soloists, chorus & orchestra, op. 35. First performed in Leeds, October 1898.

20. *The Spirit of England* was variously performed to celebrate victory. See letter of 20 November 1918 from Laurence Binyon to Elgar, p 226.

21. Binyon considered the 'glorious' opening night (12 March 1923) of *Arthur*, at The Old Vic, with Elgar in the pit, 'as one of the high points of his career'. It ran for 10 nights, but was not revived. Hatcher (*op cit*, p 224), comments on the elegiac mood and 'a language bleakly beyond emotion' even when Arthur confronts the adulterous Guinevere.

22. Hatcher: *op cit*, p 207

23. Hatcher: *op cit*, p 201

24. Hatcher, *op cit*, p 290. Professor Hatcher calls *The Burning of the Leaves* a far better poem than *For the Fallen*.

25. Gibbs, Philip: *The Battles of the Somme* (London, 1917)

26. Felix Aprahamian, (from a note of 1975) reproduced in the booklet accompanying the EMI recording of *Morning Heroes*, CDM 7 63906 2

27. W B Yeats, in his introduction to the 1936 edition of *The Oxford Book of Modern Verse* wrote that he was not including any poems by Owen because 'passive suffering is not a theme for poetry'. Quoted by Hynes, Samuel: *A War Imagined* (The Bodley Head, 1990) p 215

28. Kennedy, Michael: *Britten* (J M Dent & Sons Ltd, 1981) p 279

29. Moore: *Letters of a Lifetime* (Oxford, 1990) p 298

30. From the programme booklet for Clara Butt's 'Special Performances' of *The Dream of Gerontius* and parts 2 and 3 of *The Spirit of England*: 'To Women' and 'For the Fallen', in the Queen's Hall, London, 8-13 May 1916. See pp 247-8

31. Hynes: *op cit*, p 103
32. Lee, Hermione: *Virginia Woolf* (Chatto & Windus, 1996) p 349
33. This problem was not confined to Britain. Robert Chickering, in his *Imperial Germany and the Great War, 1914–1918* (Cambridge, 1998) p 138, makes the point that in Germany 'composers produced few remarkable pieces, with the exception perhaps of the *Variations for Orchestra* by Max Reger, Hanz Pfitzner's *Palestrina* and Strauss's *Die Frau ohne Schatten.*' Strauss spent much of the war in Garmisch working on *Die Frau*, substantially revising *Ariadne auf Naxos*. He also completed his *Alpensinfonie* in early 1915.
34. Holroyd, Michael: *Bernard Shaw,* vol II (Chatto & Windus, 1989) p 351
35. Holroyd: *op cit*, p 348
36. Holroyd: *op cit*, p 347
37. Holroyd, Michael: *Lytton Strachey* (Penguin, 1971) p 612
38. *Heartbreak House* is about the war but the war is never mentioned, although a Zeppelin raid occurs at the end. Shaw based the eccentric character of Captain Shotover on Commander Pocock the father of Lena Ashwell, the singer, actress and producer of *The Starlight Express.*
39. Wharton, Edith: *The Book of the Homeless* (New York , Charles Scribner, 1916) also contained poems by Binyon (*The Orphans of Flanders*) and Hardy (*Cry of the Homeless*).
40. Gurney, of course, also once set his own words, in *Severn Meadows.*
41. Connock, Stephen: 'The Death of Innocence', *Journal of the RVW Society*, no 16, (October 1999) p 12
42. Foreman: *op cit*, p 71
43. Kipling too recorded his memorial to the war in his poem *The Children* (*The Honours of War – A Diversity of Creatures*):

> Nor was their agony brief, or once only imposed on them.
> The wounded, the war-spent, the sick received no exemption:
> Being cured they returned and endured and achieved our redemption,
> Hopeless themselves of relief, till Death, marvelling, closed on them.

44. Lawrence, T E, from the suppressed introductory chapter for *Seven Pillars of Wisdom* (Quoted by Hynes, *op cit*)
45. Wilson, Jean Moorcroft: *Siegfried Sassoon: The Making of a War Poet (1886-1918)* (Duckworth, 1998) p 313
46. Hatcher: *op cit*, p 209
47. Moore: *Letters of Lifetime*, p 207
48. Kipling proposed the words for the Stone of Remembrance from Ecclesiasticus 44:14 'Their Name Liveth for Evermore' and those to be inscribed on every grave for an unidentified serviceman 'Known unto God'.
49. Elgar's reworking of 'For the Fallen' as *With Proud Thanksgiving* was specifically for the unveiling of Lutyens' cenotaph on 11 November 1920. It was not performed at the ceremony and had to wait until 7 May 1921 for its first performance. See pp 253 and 284.
50. With the exception of the commission of *With Proud Thanksgiving*.
51. *Façade* was first performed in 1922 and *Les Noces* in 1923.
52. Marder, Arthur J: *From the Dreadnought to Scapa Flow*, vol II (Oxford, 1965) p 124. Corbett, a friend of Sir Sidney & Frances Colvin got to know Elgar

whilst staying at Stopham Manor, near Brinkwells. Elgar wrote affectionately of Corbett to Sir Sidney Colvin on 26 September 1918. (See Moore: *Letters of a Lifetime*, p 319).

53. Terraine, John: *To Win a War: 1918 The Year of Victory* (Sedgwick & Jackson, 1978) p 13

54. Moore: *Letters of a Lifetime,* p 320

55. Hatcher: *op cit*, p 211. Professor Hatcher also says that 'Peace' falls far short of 'For the Fallen', lacking its tragic dimension [and] the elegiac lyricism Binyon shared with Elgar.

56. Letter of 20 November 1918 (from the collection of Raymond Monk)

57. The *Triumphlied*, op 55, composed by Brahms after the Franco-Prussian War in 1870 and *Song of Thanksgiving* of 1945 by Vaughan Williams are but two illustrations. We can certainly dismiss Khachaturian's *Stalin Cantata* that opens with the words 'Great leader for all eternity ... you bring happiness to the world'. Haydn could not have known about Nelson's victory at Aboukir Bay in 1798 when he completed his mass, but from the first performance it was known as the *Nelson Mass*.

58. Moore: *op cit*, p 717

59. Moore: *op cit*, p 719

60. Lindley, Jeanne: *Seeking and Finding, The Life of Emile Cammaerts* (SPCK, 1962) pp 102 – 103

61. Moore: *Letters of a Lifetime*, p 286

62. Kennedy, Michael: *Portrait of Elgar* (Oxford, 1968) p 228

Part Two

~ ~ ~

Elgar's Music in Wartime

CHAPTER 7

THE SPIRIT OF ELGAR
Crucible of Remembrance

John Norris

Perhaps it is because we are an island race that the British so tend to compartmentalise. Without the constant ebb and flow across ill-defined land frontiers, we think of ourselves as a homogenous nation identified by a clearly defined set of characteristics, breeding an insularity giving rise to a suspicion of anyone who does not fully share our ways and ideals. Of course, many within these isles do not match the entire stereotype and, while Elgar may not have come close to the norm to which he aspired, and certainly felt it, he was not alone. But caricature is a convenient shorthand, and so we have Elgar the provincial, born in Worcester, not London; Elgar the self-taught musician and therefore, to the musical establishment, an outsider; and Elgar the Catholic, a label rooted not so much in his Catholic upbringing as in his espousal of Newman's epic poem as the basis of his libretto for *Gerontius*, his first truly great choral masterpiece. Yet who can doubt[1] that Elgar found in Newman's words not so much an empathy with his own theology as a gripping storyline whose dramatic impact moved him to compose some of his greatest music.

And then there is Elgar the nationalist, the unswerving, jingoistic, blinkered patriot. This above all is the characteristic on which the wider public, and in particular his critics, focus, finding in a superficial examination of his music sentiments which attract some and repel others. Yet on what is it based? Not a great deal more, it seems, than Elgar's fondness of the *nobilmente* tempo and the words A C Benson provided to extend the appeal of, and royalties from, the trio tune of the first *Pomp and Circumstance* March.[2]

Bernard Porter explores the wider pointers to Elgar's nationalism in Chapter 4. Whether Elgar actively encouraged the nationalist tag or simply found it easier to go with the mood of the times is unclear. After years of struggle, he clearly relished the public acclaim that followed the *Enigma Variations* (but not yet from *Gerontius*) and he

FACING PAGE: *The Hampstead Special Constabulary, August 1914, with Elgar at the extreme left of the front row.*

knew that in the *Pomp and Circumstance* March he had a 'rattling good tune' that captured the public imagination. But the accompanying words did not arrive until the following year when, with encouragement from Clara Butt, Elgar included the tune as the finale of the *Coronation Ode*, written for the coronation of King Edward VII. Coronations are by definition nationalist, or at least monarchist, events and the words A C Benson produced for the occasion are wholly appropriate. But coronations are not everyday happenings.[3] Whether driven by financial considerations or simply a wish to ride on the tune's popular appeal, Elgar commissioned Benson to write a further set of words that would allow performance as a self-standing work. It is these words, now widely sung to accompany flag-waving performances of the march, that are familiar to all today. Written in the months following the British victory in the drawn-out Boer War, their stridency captured the unequivocal mood then prevalent in the country. But the product of a fervent nationalist? More a process of gradual evolution.

Elgar's subsequent use of the *nobilmente* marking simply sustained the pre-existing impression, as did his continuing friendship with royalty and the honours that flowed from it. The latter also helped ease a number of his senses of inferiority, the poor boy made good. In short, Elgar had no reason to dispel the notion that he was all for king and country, unswerving in his loyalty if perhaps insensitive to the plight of others. The image suited his purpose and he remained unchallenged by the deeper implications during the prosperous years of Edward VII. But the image remained more than the reality. Perhaps in *Falstaff*, composed as the signs of impending war grew ever stronger, we can first see outer signs of the inner conflict, the recognition at the moment of Falstaff's rejection by the newly promoted King Hal that royal and public patronage is fickle.

As other contributors to this book have noted, the war was, for the Elgars, a bitter personal blow: the way of life and society to which they had become accustomed could not survive and, even in distant England, the realities of war could not be escaped. The conflict between public persona and inner man became difficult to ignore. For many, the changes wrought in Elgar by the war first became apparent in the autumnal chamber works and the Cello Concerto (see Chapter 12), and it is true that Elgar did not provide many signposts to the transformation along the way. His sense of patriotic duty did not desert him and he threw himself into activities directed at helping the war effort: he joined the Hampstead Volunteer Reserve; he took on extensive conducting tours with the London Symphony Orchestra; and he wrote a number of shortish pieces intended to contribute more or less directly to wartime charities: *Polonia*, the three recitations and *The Sanguine Fan*. But in these he can be seen as a third party, donating his talents for the wider public benefit.

Of the major works Elgar wrote for his own satisfaction, one – *The Starlight Express* – is a light piece of escapist nonsense. Perhaps Elgar was attracted to it as a bulwark against the realities of the time. If so, the palliative effect was short-lived as Elgar fell out with the production and refused to conduct the première as had been planned. The decision seems extreme and one cannot but wonder whether differences with the producer camouflaged a deeper concern, perhaps over his involvement in so trivial a play at a time of national suffering, leading to the stubborn position he adopted. In contrast, the second work – *The Spirit of England* – addressed the war head-on, and the inner conflict could no longer be avoided.

It was Sir Sidney Colvin who first suggested to Elgar, in the early days of 1915, that he should write 'a requiem for the slain – something in the spirit of Binyon's *For the Fallen*'.[4] Colvin and his wife Frances were confidantes and supporters of many writers and other creative artists active during the early years of the century. They had known Elgar for at least ten years. Elgar corresponded regularly, with Frances Colvin in particular, and he shared with her husband a love of books and a fondness for unusual words and word-play. Their relationship never became particularly intimate in the manner of Elgar's friendship with Alice Stuart Wortley or Frank Schuster, but Elgar was nevertheless later to dedicate the Cello Concerto to them.

Colvin had been Keeper of Rare Prints and Drawings at the British Museum; Laurence Binyon was his assistant, becoming, on Colvin's retirement in 1912, his successor. Both had previously attempted to engage Elgar in operatic collaborations: in 1913, Colvin had acted as intermediary for the novelist Thomas Hardy in seeking to interest Elgar in composing an opera based on a Hardy novel, while Binyon had sought to entice Elgar on more than one occasion into a collaboration, with Binyon serving as Elgar's librettist. Elgar was to complain some years later that he had wanted to compose an opera that was 'heroic and noble' but he had only been offered 'blood and lust' plots.

The passage of time distorts. For many today, the perception engendered by the phrase 'war poet' is of the soldier fighting at the front who, as darkness falls, lays down rifle for pen to capture in verse the events of the day, the harshness of life in the trenches and the bitterness of war. The image is not too far removed from the reality of some well known names including Wilfred Owen, Ivor Gurney and Siegfried Sassoon. But the peak period for the writing of war poems was during the first months of the war, before the true nature of the developing struggle had become apparent. Newspapers, clamouring for readership through demonstrations of patriotism, published poems daily. Keith Robbins[5] estimates that no less than 1.5 million war poems were written in August 1914 alone.

Many of these were banal, insensitive efforts, full of 'bash the Hun' sentiment, from the pens of long-forgotten poets who never left the safety of Britain. A few, such as Rupert Brooke's collection of five sonnets published under the title *1914* and including 'The Soldier' ('If I should die, think only this of me . . .'), were of a higher calibre and attained a lasting public affection, despite their espousal of sentiments of righteous struggle and noble sacrifice that were soon to lose favour. Writing in the *New Statesman* on 26 September 1914, fellow poet J C Squire commented:

> What is wrong with most of these patriotic versifiers is that they start with a ready made set of conceptions, of phrases, of words and of rhymes, and turn out their works on a formula. Put England down as 'knightly', state her honour to be 'inviolate' and her spirit 'invulnerable', call her enemies 'perjured' and 'branded with the mark of Cain', refer to 'Trafalgar', . . . introduce a 'then' or two, and conclude with the assertion that God will defend the Right – and there's the formula for a poem.

Binyon does not fall conveniently into either category of poet. Born in 1869, he was too old to be called up to fight although he was eventually enlisted as a Red Cross orderly and, as such, reached the front in 1916. The poems for which he is now best known were all written in the latter half of 1914 and published in December of that year in a slim volume entitled *The Winnowing-Fan*. The populist sentiments of these months can be found, notably in *The Fourth of August*, which speaks of 'the hour of peril purified' and 'the grandeur of our fate', but also to a lesser extent in *For the Fallen*, in lines such as 'Fallen in the cause of the free' and 'Straight of limb, true of eye, steady and aglow'. And yet, for a poem which was first published – in *The Times* on 21 September 1914 – when the war was still less than two months old, *For the Fallen* shows remarkable prescience of the suffering to come. Ahead of its time, the poem was initially received without great enthusiasm and it was only as the public mood changed that the poem began to grow in popularity and critical acclaim.

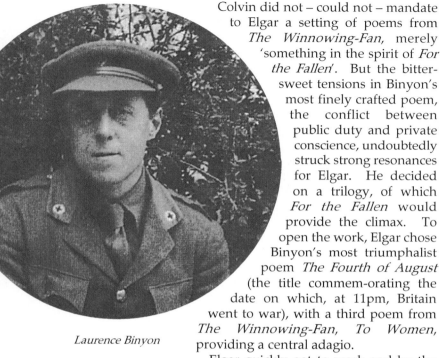

Laurence Binyon

Colvin did not – could not – mandate to Elgar a setting of poems from *The Winnowing-Fan*, merely 'something in the spirit of *For the Fallen*'. But the bitter-sweet tensions in Binyon's most finely crafted poem, the conflict between public duty and private conscience, undoubtedly struck strong resonances for Elgar. He decided on a trilogy, of which *For the Fallen* would provide the climax. To open the work, Elgar chose Binyon's most triumphalist poem *The Fourth of August* (the title commem-orating the date on which, at 11pm, Britain went to war), with a third poem from *The Winnowing-Fan*, *To Women*, providing a central adagio.

Elgar quickly got to work and by the spring of 1915 had completed sketching out the three settings. These sketches he played to his circle of friends, receiving their wide approval. They were, by general consent, considered deeply moving and Elgar was sufficiently encouraged to continue, expanding the sketches into full settings. But a chance meeting with a younger composer, Cyril Rootham, caused him to rethink his plans. Rootham confided to Elgar that he too was setting *For the Fallen* with provisional agreement from Novello to publish it.

Elgar was horrified at the implications of continuing with his own setting. Novello was the only significant publisher of large-scale choral works in Britain and, in Elgar's view, would be reluctant to publish two settings of the poem in close succession. Elgar assumed that Novello would choose his setting, thereby significantly reducing Rootham's chances of finding a publisher. Even if this analysis was wrong and Rootham was successful in having his work published, a setting by a composer of Elgar's stature would surely limit the opportunities for Rootham's work to be heard. To make matters worse, Rootham a pupil of Stanford, was now, like his teacher, installed at Cambridge. The unhealed rift between Elgar and Stanford was reflected in palpable anti-Elgar sentiments at the university which could only be exacerbated if Elgar were to proceed with his plans.

Elgar felt there was only one honourable course open to him. He confided in Rootham that he would not be continuing with *For the Fallen*; then, on 24 March, he wrote to tell Binyon the news:

> I cannot tell you how sad I am about your poems: I feel I cannot proceed with the set as first proposed & which I still desire to complete: but I saw Dr. Rootham, who merely wished to thank me for my 'generous attitude' etc. & said very nice things about my offer to withdraw – but his utter disappointment, not expressed but shewn unconsciously, has upset me & I must decide against completing 'For the Fallen' – I have battled with the feeling for nearly a week but the sight of the other man comes sadly between me & my music. I know you will be disappointed, but your disappointment is not so great as mine for I love your poem & love & honour you for having conceived it.
>
> I am going into the country & will see if I can make the other settings acceptable without the great climax.[6]

The last sentence alluded to the possibility considered by Elgar of continuing with just the first two poems. Had Elgar done so, he may of course have recast 'To Women' to provide a more climactic ending. But 'For the Fallen' was always intended to provide the dramatic finale to the work and anyone listening today to 'The Fourth of August' and 'To Women' in isolation can only be struck by the sense of incompleteness, of suspended desolation, in a work only half the length that *Spirit* eventually turned out to be. Some composers may have preferred it that way, but it wasn't Elgar.

Setting aside his own disappointment, Binyon replied to Elgar with an appeal to the composer's sense of patriotism and public duty:

> My dear Sir Edward,
>
> Your words about my poem touch me deeply. My disappointment matters nothing, keen as it is: but think of England, of the English-speaking people, in whom the common blood stirs now as it never did before; think of the awful casualty lists that are coming, & the losses in more & more homes; think of the thousands who will be craving to have their grief glorified & lifted up & transformed by an art like yours – and though I have little understanding of music, as you know, I understand that craving when words alone seem all too insufficient & inexpressive – think of what you are witholding [sic] from your countrymen & women. Surely it would be wrong to let them lose this help & consolation.[7]

Binyon even offered to write an extra verse, that beginning 'They fought, they were terrible . . .', for Elgar to set, but Elgar's mind was made up: he had given Rootham his word and there was no going back on it. And there the matter might have rested were it not for the persistence of Elgar's friends once word of his dilemma reached them.

First there was R A Streatfeild, a music scholar and writer who also worked with Binyon at the British Museum. He determined to visit Alfred Littleton, the long-serving chairman of Novello, and, with apparently little difficulty, persuaded him that Novello should publish both composers' settings. Sidney Colvin joined in, supported by his wife Frances, causing Alice Elgar to record in her diary for 11 April:

> Sidney overwhelming in his attack on E . . . E a little moved, I thought . . .

Rarely was Alice to respond so ambivalently to an attack on her beloved husband!

Elgar shifted his ground, claiming that there was no longer a market for his music. In the end, it was Colvin who, deploying his full range of persuasive powers, broke down the barriers of Elgar's resistance. In a letter alternately pleading and bullying in tone and appealing to Elgar's sense of logic and justice, he ended with a simple postscript:

> The above is not to be answered except by deeds.

Elgar took the hint. The following day, Alice's diary records:

> E turned to his beautiful music again, loved it himself. So there is hope.

Indeed there was. Within the year, Elgar had completed 'To Women' and 'For the Fallen', and an announcement to that effect appeared in *The Times* in March 1916.

Rootham, naturally, was disappointed. His was a simpler work, intended for performance by the smaller, local choral societies. We can empathise how, despite the fact that the work had now been published by Novello and despite (or perhaps because of) its appeal to a different, lesser audience, Rootham must have felt apprehensive that his own work would be overshadowed. But should Elgar have felt so constrained by Rootham's plans? It is difficult to see why. Such was the mood of the times and the appeal of the war poets to that mood, it seems inevitable that other composers would, both then and since, look to their poetry as promising source material for choral settings. Indeed, others did, as the list in the table below shows. A coincidence of interests, resulting in duplication of settings, appears inevitable.

Settings of Laurence Binyon's *For the Fallen*		
1915	C B Rootham	semi-chorus (or soprano, alto and bass soli), chorus, and orchestra or piano accompaniment
1916	Edward Elgar	soprano or tenor solo, chorus and orchestra
1929	Frederick Arthur Challinor	part song for male voices
1949	Arnold Walter	chorus and orchestra
1971	Douglas Guest	chorus and organ
1982	Mark Blatchly	for choir

But should that matter? Many composers have tackled subjects in the full knowledge that others have been there before. Elgar wasn't deterred from writing *Falstaff* by Verdi's opera, while the many scores based on the *Romeo and Juliet* plot appear only to have encouraged later composers to attempt their own encapsulation of the story. Elgar must have recognised that Rootham's setting of *For the Fallen* would ultimately stand or fall on its own merits and that, once published by Novello, Rootham was more likely to benefit from the interest in his own work from those wishing to compare it to Elgar's setting than to be suffocated by it. Elgar's comments to Binyon that 'Dr Rootham was in touch with Novello first – my proposal made his MS waste paper'[8] was not the 'bald statement of the case' Elgar claimed it to be.

But the surmounting of the obstacle erected by Rootham, allowing the completion of 'To Women' and 'For the Fallen' were not the end of Elgar's problems. There remained 'The Fourth of August' and its completion was to present Elgar with its own difficulties. Turning his preliminary sketch into a fully thought-through setting required a greater attention to Binyon's words. By and large, these presented no problem despite this being one of Binyon's more jingoistic offerings. But one verse caused Elgar significant discomfort, that beginning 'She fights the fraud that feeds desire on Lies . . .'

Elgar recognised the considerable debt he owed to the Germans individually and collectively. There was August Jaeger, Nimrod of the *Enigma Variations*, whose unstinting encouragement, criticism and selfless promotion of Elgar's music at Novello's had sustained the composer during his recurring moments of self doubt; Hans Richter, who had championed Elgar's music from the concert platform, conducting the premières of the *Enigma Variations, The Dream of Gerontius* and the First Symphony; Julius Buths, present at the poorly received Birmingham première of *Gerontius*, who, recognising the work's inherent greatness, arranged successful performances of the work in Düsseldorf in 1901 and 1902; the German audiences at those Düsseldorf performances who had responded in the manner Elgar wished but British audiences had up to that point failed to do; Richard Strauss who, on hearing the second Düsseldorf performance of *Gerontius*, proclaimed Elgar as 'the first English progressivist', thereby establishing a friendship that was to last into Elgar's years of loneliness following Alice's death; and Frank Schuster and the Speyers, father and son, whose friendship and magnanimity provided Elgar with the stability and some of the creature comforts which a successful composer might rightly expect but frequently lacked.

When, during the war, Thomas Beecham was asked where Elgar's friends had gone, he is reported to have replied 'They're all interned'. The cheap jibe was wide of the mark – Nimrod was by now six years dead, while Richter had retired to Germany on the outbreak of war, finding it expedient also to renounce his British honours – but it reflected the ambivalence of Elgar's position. How could a nation that had provided him with so much succour be one and the same as the 'Vampire of Europe's wasted will'? Even into the early months of 1916, Elgar's ambivalence was shared by a wider population among the thinking classes. The truly barbaric nature of the conflict was still not fully appreciated at home; to some, it remained a squabble between cousins and common sense would surely soon prevail. In such circumstances, voluble expressions of hatred toward the enemy could only inflame and, in so doing, indirectly extend the war. So Elgar put the incomplete first movement on one side and prepared for a first performance of 'To Women' and 'For the Fallen'.

Again, Clara Butt was instrumental in this. Believing the war had changed public attitudes toward death[†] with, in particular, an increased interest in the after-life, she organised a full week of consecutive performances of *Gerontius* at the Queen's Hall, London with herself and Gervase Elwes in the main solo rôles and the Leeds Choral Union in support. Profits were to go to the Red Cross. Concerns were expressed, however, over the viability of the project, despite the popularity *Gerontius* had by now attained. Hearing of Elgar's willingness to allow performances of his new work even

† - see page 103

though not yet complete, Butt seized on it as a means of broadening the appeal of the concerts.

The London performances were to begin on Monday 8 May 1916. By way of a dress-rehearsal for the choir, two preparatory concerts had been arranged for the preceding week, the first in the choir's home city of Leeds on 3 May thus providing the première for the two completed Binyon settings, with a second performance in nearby Bradford the following day. Despite suffering one of his frequent bouts of ill health, Elgar travelled north to conduct both performances, with John Booth singing 'To Women' and Agnes Nicholls as soloist in 'For the Fallen'.[9]   As with the London performances, *Gerontius* completed the programme, a tribute to the generosity of the promoters and the stamina of the audiences, for whom *Gerontius* is now usually considered sufficient in itself.

The concerts were an unambiguous success, both critically and financially. Despite the earlier concerns over viability, the London week sold out with many turned away, raising for the Red Cross in the process a figure variously reported as £2,700 [10] or £4,500.[11] Clara Butt commented that she 'had never heard more perfect singing' than in the performance given by Agnes Nicholls, and Alice's diary for 8 May also records:

> A. Nicholls' 'We will remember them' never to be forgotten.

Perhaps of greatest importance for Alice, King George V attended one of the London performances, accompanied by Queen Mary and Queen Alexandra. Alice noted in her diary:

> The King . . . was said to be much affected by 'For the Fallen', but *Gerontius* . . . was evidently too long for him.

More importantly for Elgar, the critics responded warmly to his new music. Even before the première, Ernest Newman had written:[12] 'Here in truth is the very voice of England . . .'; in an article[13] published during the week of the London concerts, he added 'The artist in [Elgar] gives him the power . . . of extracting from the crude human stuff of [his emotions] the basic durable substance that is art', while the music critic of *The Sheffield Daily*, reviewing the Leeds performance, recorded[14] that 'Never since *Gerontius* has Elgar given us music that carries so unmistakeable a ring of sincerity . . .' The crucial difference between the unthinking jingoism of *Land of Hope and Glory* and the emotional restraint of the new work had been grasped.

This page and overleaf :
Pages from the book of
words for Clara Butt's
season of The Dream of
Gerontius *in May 1916*

Under the immediate Patronage of
THEIR MAJESTIES THE KING AND QUEEN.
HER MAJESTY QUEEN ALEXANDRA.
HER MAJESTY QUEEN AMÉLIE OF PORTUGAL.
H.R.H. THE PRINCESS CHRISTIAN OF SCHLESWIG-HOLSTEIN.
H.R.H. THE PRINCESS HENRY OF BATTENBERG.
H.R.H. PRINCESS ALEXANDER OF TECK.
H.H. THE PRINCESS VICTORIA OF SCHLESWIG-HOLSTEIN.
H.H. THE PRINCESS MARIE LOUISE OF SCHLESWIG-HOLSTEIN.

IN AID OF THE
BRITISH RED CROSS SOCIETY
AND THE
ORDER OF ST. JOHN OF JERUSALEM IN ENGLAND.

MADAME

CLARA BUTT'S

Special Performances
OF THE

"Dream of Gerontius"
POEM BY   MUSIC BY
CARDINAL NEWMAN.   SIR EDWARD ELGAR.

AND THE FIRST PERFORMANCES IN LONDON OF

FROM

"To Women"   "The Spirit of England"
"For the Fallen"
POEMS BY   MUSIC BY
LAURENCE BINYON SIR EDWARD ELGAR

AT THE

QUEEN'S HALL,

MONDAY,	MAY 8TH, AT	2.30 P.M.
TUESDAY,	MAY 9TH, AT	7.45 P.M.
WEDNESDAY,	MAY 10TH, AT	2.30 P.M.
THURSDAY,	MAY 11TH, AT	7.45 P.M.
FRIDAY,	MAY 12TH, AT	7.45 P.M.
SATURDAY,	MAY 13TH, AT	2.30 P.M.

1916.

BOOK OF WORDS,
ONE SHILLING.

Under the direction of
MESSRS. IBBS & TILLETT,
19 HANOVER SQUARE, W.

Artists.

"To Women."
Solo   -   MR. JOHN BOOTH

"For the Fallen."
Solo   -   MISS AGNES NICHOLLS

"Dream of Gerontius."
Angel -	-	MADAME CLARA BUTT
Gerontius	-	MR. GERVASE ELWES
Angel of the Agony	-	MR. CHARLES MOTT
Priest	-	MR. HERBERT BROWN

CHOIR OF ANGELICALS.
MESDAMES

LILIAN DILLINGHAM	ETHEL MAUNDER	CLARA SIMONS
ETHEL DUNCAN	FLORENCE MELLORS	ISOBEL STUCKEY
EILEEN BOYD	NELLIE HATCH	LILIAN TOOLEY
MARY HILLIARD	ANNIE JOHNSON	BEATRICE WAYCOTT

CONDUCTED BY THE COMPOSER
SIR EDWARD ELGAR, O.M.

THE LEEDS CHORAL UNION

DIRECTOR OF THE CHORUS - DR. HENRY COWARD
ORGANIST - MR. JOHN GROVES, F.R.C.O.

THE LONDON SYMPHONY ORCHESTRA
LEADER - MR. W. H. REED.

COMMITTEES.

THE DUCHESS OF NORFOLK

THE DUCHESS OF SOMERSET

THE DUCHESS OF HAMILTON

THE DUCHESS OF RUTLAND

ADELINE, DUCHESS OF BEDFORD

MILLICENT, DUCHESS OF SUTHERLAND

THE MARCHIONESS OF LANSDOWNE

THE MARCHIONESS OF SALISBURY

CORA, COUNTESS OF STRAFFORD

THE VISCOUNTESS CURZON

THE LADY MAUD WARRENDER

THE LADY NORTHCOTE

THE LADY NORTHCLIFFE

LADY MILSOM REES

Mrs. AUSTEN CHAMBERLAIN

Miss MINNIE COCHRANE

Mrs. W. M. CAZALET

Mrs. WILLIE FOX

Mrs. WATERHOUSE

Mrs. WILBERFORCE

Rt. Rev. BISHOP BOYD CARPENTER

ARCHDEACON WILBERFORCE

The Hon. Sir CHARLES RUSSELL, Bart.

Rt. Hon. G. W. E. RUSSELL

FATHER BERNARD VAUGHAN

Rev. L. N. NIXON

Mr. W. P. MARA

———

LADY BRIDGE

LADY MACKENZIE

LADY STANFORD

LADY ELGAR

LADY COWEN

Mrs. F. H. CLIFFE

Mrs. LANDON RONALD

Mrs. W. H. SQUIRE

———

LADY ALEXANDER

LADY TREE

Miss ELLEN TERRY

Madame NAVARRO

Miss LILIAN BRAITHWAITE

Miss FAY DAVIS

Mrs. H. B. IRVING

Miss LILLAH McCARTHY

Miss OLGA NETHERSOLE

Miss MAY WHITTY

———

Madame ADA CROSSLEY

Miss ESTA D'ARGO

Miss MURIEL FOSTER

Miss ETHEL HOOK

Madame BLANCHE MARCHESI

Miss AGNES NICHOLLS

Miss SUSAN STRONG

Madame GLEESON-WHITE

Mr. BERTRAM BINYON

———

Mr. LEONARD BORWICK

Miss ESSIE FAULKNER

Miss MARIE HALL

Mr. MARK HAMBOURG

Miss MARJORIE HAYWARD

Mr. WILLIAM MURDOCH

Miss IRENE SCHARRER

Miss ELLEN TUCKFIELD

———

From this initial success, it was inevitable that other performances of one or both parts of the incomplete work would follow: Charles Hooey[15] notes in the first quarter of 1917 alone a series of regional concerts given by the Hallé Orchestra under Beecham; a performance in Walsall on 7 February 1917 in which the soloist for both parts was unusually a tenor, Frank Mullings;[16] and further performances of 'For the Fallen' by Agnes Nicholls in Manchester on 15 March and Bradford on 16 March as part of 'All-Wagner' (sic) concerts. Parallels between Elgar's music and that of Wagner had clearly been taken a little too literally!

But there remained that troublesome verse in 'The Fourth of August' that had stalled Elgar's earlier attempt to complete the work. As 1916 progressed, he hit upon a solution that allowed him to resume composition later in the year and take the setting of the first poem through to completion by April 1917. It is not recorded whether it was the pairing of the two completed settings with *Gerontius* in May 1916 that gave Elgar the inspiration he needed, but that in essence was his solution: as Binyon points his accusatory finger at German atrocity, Elgar underlines the message with a series of quotations from Gerontius's persecution at the hands of the Demons' Chorus. Three times the parallel is drawn but left unresolved: to suggest that Elgar had in mind a deeper, religious significance – a musical counterpoint to Peter's three denials of Christ, perhaps – is to enter the land of the more far-fetched solutions to the *Enigma*. But a more reasoned speculation is that, while the typical British attitude towards the German nation had by now collapsed into little but revulsion and hatred, Elgar still struggled with feelings of bewilderment and betrayal. We can only ponder the full significance these quotations from *Gerontius* conveyed for him.

The completion of 'The Fourth of August' opened the way for the first complete performance of the work and for many years this was accepted to have taken place under Elgar's baton at a Royal Choral Society concert at the Royal Albert Hall on 24 November 1917. Agnes Nicholls again appeared as the soprano soloist but with Gervase Elwes taking the solo lead in 'To Women'. The *Daily Telegraph* recorded that 'there was great enthusiasm at the end' of a programme that also contained works by Parry, Stanford and Sir Frederick Bridge, and the event received much generally favourable publicity.

But we are again indebted to Charles Hooey[17] for establishing that this was not in fact the first performance of the complete work. Three weeks earlier on 31 October, for example, there had been a concert approaching a rerun of the Leeds première the previous year when, at the same venue, Agnes Nicholls, Elgar and the Leeds Choral Union performed the complete work as a precursor to a performance of *Gerontius*. On this occasion, there was no tenor soloist in 'To Women', Gervase Elwes limiting himself to the rôle of *Gerontius* in the second half of the programme.

However, Mr Hooey has found an even earlier complete performance of *The Spirit of England*, given in Birmingham Town Hall on 4 October 1917 under the baton of Appleby Matthews; the soloist was the New

Appleby Matthews

Zealand soprano Rosina Buckman, and the programme also included *Carillon* and, 'by special request', *Weary Wind of the West, The Shower* and 'As Torrents in Summer' from *King Olaf*, as well as pieces by Mozart and Puccini. Matthews was an active local musician of some note, going on to help found in 1920 the orchestra that later developed into the City of Birmingham Symphony Orchestra, and then becoming the first conductor of the City of Birmingham Choir from 1921 to 1926.

The performance received an enthusiastic review in the *Birmingham Gazette* ('Mr Appleby Matthews . . . and his choir achieved a joint triumph in the three numbers . . . which filled the second half of the concert. A really magnificent performance from every point of view – precision, intensity, dramatism, and intelligence' – R J Buckley) while 'A.S.', reviewing in the *Birmingham Evening Dispatch*, gave a perceptive analysis of the now complete work:

Linked up in a completely successful performance with the second and third parts, the first part has a glory which is a new endowment for 'To Women' and 'For the Fallen'. The second part is shaded down by contrast to an even more beautiful truth and the third we find recapturing the glamour of the first. The grand rise at the end is not now simply an exultation; it is a return to the plane of the high beginning. With the three now public, the work is completely rounded, and it stands, definitely born of the war, worthy of the war, to survive the war.

There are pointers here to which we shall come back. Ernest Newman provided a review for the *Birmingham Post.*

Why, then, was a performance which was widely reviewed at the time subsequently overlooked for so many years, allowing its claim as a world première to be usurped by a later performance? Charles Hooey attributes it to 'war-weary reporters', 'carelessness, misunderstanding, or even indifference'.[18] Geoffrey Hodgkins, commenting on Mr Hooey's findings,[19] offers two more precise explanations. Firstly, the authoritative *Musical Times*, while recording elsewhere the inclusion of all three works in the Birmingham concert, quotes Ernest Newman's *Birmingham Post* review in such a way as to cloud the issue: the *Musical Times* reader could be misled into thinking that only 'For the Fallen' was performed at Birmingham, and presumably many were. But secondly, where was Elgar on the evening of the Birmingham première? Alice's diaries reveal that he was less than twenty miles away at The Elms, his sister Pollie's home at Stoke Prior near Bromsgrove. The concert receives no mention in the diaries or contemporary correspondence, nothing to suggest that Elgar even knew it was taking place.

Yet this seems barely credible, bearing in mind Elgar's long association with the venue which had already staged the premières of four of his major works.[20] Surely the promoters would have ensured that he received an invitation to a further première that extended that tradition. Perhaps through misunderstanding the invitation was never issued or was mislaid. But there was another tradition, that of Elgar as the conductor of premières of his own compositions. Did Elgar feel snubbed at being invited to Birmingham not to conduct but merely to listen? Was the Birmingham concert a late addition to the choir's season, organised after Elgar had already accepted the Royal Albert Hall commitment and so seen by him as a grab for glory? 'Première' is a somewhat arbitrary term since the designated performance is inevitably preceded by rehearsals, run-throughs and possibly a semi-private performance before an invited audience (*vide*

LEFT: *Agnes Nicholls;* RIGHT: *Caroline Hatchard*

the more recent première of the Elgar-Payne Third Symphony). Perhaps it was Elgar's wish that the Royal Albert Hall performance should continue to be recognized as the official première.

Following these three early performances, *The Spirit of England* quickly established a regular if none-too-frequent presence on the concert platform. But while Agnes Nicholls had all but monopolised the soprano rôle in performances of the incomplete work, her supremacy was soon to be challenged by a name new to the rôle – that of Caroline Hatchard, a popular British coloratura soprano during the first half of the twentieth century. Again it is Charles Hooey[21] who has traced Miss Hatchard's close association with the work. She first sang it at the Manchester première of the complete work on 15 December 1917, causing *The Musical Times* to describe her as:

> . . . a soloist who combined exquisite beauty and liquid purity of tone with a temperament so manifestly in sympathy with the spirit of the work . . . [Miss Hatchard] can be confidently expected to share with Miss Agnes Nicholls the task and privilege of revelation throughout Britain of the loftiest musical thought uttered in these fateful times.

Prophetic words, as *The Musical Times* subsequently plotted her progress through performances of *The Spirit of England* in Bristol on 23 February 1918 ('. . . with such competent principals as Caroline Hatchard, who took the solos in the first and third parts of the trilogy, and Mr Frank Mullings who contributed with rich expression the solo in the central section, a memorable reading of this notable war work was secured'); at the Halifax Choral Society's centenary performance on 14 March 1918 where she deputised for an ailing Agnes Nicholls ('. . . the soloist, Miss Caroline Hatchard, realizing fully the note of tender pathos that characterises the music'); with the Stockport Vocal Union on 24 March 1919 ('... an expressive performance that revealed much of the beauty and thoughtful appeal of the music') and the Croydon Philharmonic Society on 28 May 1919. A performance in Glasgow followed on 20 December 1919 and Hatchard continued to be associated with the work through the 1920s, including one performance of Wagnerian proportions at Hanley on 19 March 1925 in which, having taken the solo lead in *Spirit* in the first part of the programme, she continued after the interval in the soprano rôle in *The Apostles*. In later life, Hatchard became a professor at the Royal Academy of Music.

To commemorate the war dead, Sir Edwin Lutyens was commissioned to design the Cenotaph which stands in Whitehall, London. In January 1920, Novello asked Elgar if he would consider providing an arrangement of 'For the Fallen' suitable for performance at the unveiling ceremony, scheduled for 11 November 1920. Elgar rose to the challenge with an abridged version, reduced from eight verses to five, with a simplified accompaniment for military or brass band, organ or pianoforte, and no soloist. He called it *With Proud Thanksgiving* and dedicated it to the League of Arts, who had requested the arrangement from Novello. In the event, Elgar's arrangement was not used at the unveiling ceremony, nor in the music accompanying the burial of the Unknown Warrior at Westminster Abbey on the same day. Instead, Binyon's words are now read at the Cenotaph each November, reviving echoes of Oscar Schmitz's 'Land without Music' taunt [22].

With Proud Thanksgiving was instead premièred at the Royal Albert Hall the following May at a concert marking the jubilees of both the hall itself and the Royal Choral Society. The occasion, and other works on the programme demanded a full orchestra, however, and it was considered inappropriate to provide a military band for Elgar's new arrangement alone. The solution, one might have thought, would be to perform 'For the Fallen' in full but, possibly hoping to stimulate sales of the abridged version, Novello now asked Elgar to provide an orchestral accompaniment[23] to *With Proud Thanksgiving*. This he did, taking his orchestration for the full setting as his starting point rather than his arrangement for military band. This abridged orchestral version was used as the finale of the 'Pageant of Heroes', the penultimate section of the *Pageant of Empire* at Wembley in August 1924, and more recently revived in 1988 in a concert at Eton, given by the Broadheath Singers under Robert Tucker but, to the best of my knowledge, Elgar's arrangement for military band has never been performed.

The full *Spirit of England* continued to be performed regularly into the 1930s, however. A recording survives from that period of a BBC broadcast with Adrian Boult conducting the BBC Symphony Orchestra and Elsie Suddaby[24] as soprano soloist. But most will now know the work from two commercial recordings made and issued in the past 25 years. The first, from 1977 on the Chandos label, is of Sir Alexander Gibson conducting the Scottish National Orchestra and Chorus with the soprano Teresa Cahill as soloist. The second is a 1987 EMI recording under the baton of Richard Hickox, who ironically succeeded Gibson as Chandos' Elgar champion and embarked upon his set of recordings for the latter company of most of Elgar's major choral works; here he conducts the London Symphony Chorus and Northern Sinfonia, with Felicity Lott in the soprano lead. Both are commendable recordings. And if, for this author at least, the EMI recording has the edge, this must be balanced by the coupling of the Gibson recording with the *Coronation Ode*. The Hickox recording, in contrast, is supported by a rather mixed bag which includes Elgar's setting of *Land of Hope and Glory* as a separate song and a rather disappointing performance of his enchanting orchestral part-song *The Snow* that fails to match the captivating wistfulness of the recording, also on EMI, by Charles Groves and his forces at Liverpool.

So what of this piece that Elgar had struggled for so long to complete? Each poem has its own distinctive mood which Elgar captures in his setting, yet the three are inextricably linked with extensive cross-referencing and overlaid with a pervading air of resignation lapsing into sadness. This is not a celebration of war but a contemplation of its folly.

As has already been noted, 'The Fourth of August' is the most triumphalist of the three Binyon poems Elgar chose to set. Appropriately, after an eight-bar instrumental introduction built around an ascending single-bar sequence, which Gibson takes somewhat laboriously, the choir enters in full voice, confident and assertive in the major key, with a great upsweep on the opening words 'Now in thy splendour . . .'

The notes are the same as in the first occurrence of the sequence; the effect with choir is dramatically different. This is the spirit of England the audience no doubt expected, dominant, rampaging, victorious. The Nazi machine from the first movement of Shostakovich's *Leningrad Symphony* would be a fitting accompaniment at this point. The mood soon moderates somewhat, but remaining positive and courageous as the soloist returns at intervals to urge her troops on with shrill repetitions of the opening and other phrases.

Only as the troublesome verse is announced by three descending repetitions of the swirling four-note phrase that presages the 'Demons' Chorus' in *Gerontius*:

does the triumphal mood sour:

a defiant cry from the soloist which is taken up by the choir, and we are pitched into a turbulent maelstrom, punctuated by blasts of staccato fanfare (Example 4) which also mimic the Demons. The verse ends with a rhythmic throbbing from the basses (Example 5), reminiscent of the falling away of the 'Demons' Chorus' under the words 'Triumphant still' immediately before 39, and we are into calmer waters.

RIGHT: Ex 4

BELOW: Ex 5

The soloist emerges from this turbulence with a peaceful hymn of salvation, 'Endure, O Earth', that echoes 'To Women', and the choir, in hushed voices, twice intone the words 'O wronged, untamable, unshaken soul'. But the choir is only temporarily subdued. It is the words, not the music, that carry the message as the massed forces, unvanquished, regather strength and, under the marking *nobilmente e grandioso*, provide a forceful reaffirmation of England's superiority with a repetition of the opening verse 'Now in thy splendour go before us, Spirit of England, ardent-eyed . . .'.

'To Women' introduces a new Elgar. His favoured use of *nobilmente* earlier in this and other works conveys an air of grandeur touched at times with pomposity. Here, in 'To Women', he crafted a work as noble as any of his earlier utterances yet imbued through and through with a sense of humility, of desolation and of sadness. The tempo is an almost unbroken slow march emphasized by repeated arpeggios in the orchestral accompaniment, the plod of thousands of feet that conjures up images of newsreels showing defeated armies heading home. Binyon's words express the hopes, fears and pain of those left behind at home to await the return of their loved ones and the music mirrors these sentiments with moments of anguish and of peace.

The movement is dominated by the soloist, the choir's early contribution being limited to two verses ('Swift, swifter than those hawks of war . . . entered first a woman's breast'), the first rapidly delivered in a vaguely menacing chant, the second in more contemplative mood. But the marching feet return, heading inexorably, unremittingly towards the horizon. A central passage rises to a climax as the soloist sings 'From hearts that are as one high heart' and the choir answers 'Your hope, your dread, your throbbing pride'. And at the soloist's final words '. . . but not to fail', the main theme from the first movement reappears, *cantabile*; the choir's response is carried away on strains of the main theme from the soon-to-be-heard final movement.

'For the Fallen' was always seen by Elgar as the pivotal setting of the three and its length equals that of the first two together. It takes up where 'To Women' left off, the marching feet tempo supporting a quotation from 'To Women' which leads into a succession of quotations from elsewhere in the work, not least from 'For the Fallen' itself. The choir enters in tones of muted anticipation, the army now reformed and disciplined, distant but advancing. At the words 'Flesh of her flesh', the main theme, a soaring, wonderfully ethereal theme first heard at the end of 'To Women' and again in the orchestral introduction to the current movement, reappears.

As the army draws near, there are occasional demonstrations of force: a crescendo on the words 'Death august and royal' leads into a typically Elgarian second theme, a Mood of Dan[25] which he sketched in 1902:

and an *ff* marking for the lines 'There is music in the midst of desolation, And a glory that shines upon our tears', set to a more forceful rendition of the main theme. Suddenly, a brief fanfare interrupts the steady advance: the tempo changes to a quick, slightly playful march with meandering repetitions of a looping triplet figure:

capturing an unreal sense of joviality in an unreal war: 'They went with songs into battle . . . They sang their melodies of England, They fell open-eyed and unafraid'.   John Pickard[26] describes it as 'disembodied music', representing 'not real soldiers but ghosts'.

A change of time signature and a marked slackening of tempo bring us to arguably the best known verse of the war. Elgar altered Binyon's wording 'They shall grow not old . . .' to the more natural 'They shall not grow old . . .'; would he have dared to do so, one now wonders, if he had foreseen the popularity that Binyon's verse would attain. The orchestra introduces a new, longer meandering phrase.

Lacking rhythm and direction, it mocks the certainty of the first and, through a number of repetitions, creates a feeling of unease. 'At the going down of the sun' is sung to a lingering cadence:

a similar trick to that which Elgar employed in *The Kingdom* at the equivalent words 'The Sun Goeth Down . . .' Twice the choir sings 'We will remember them' over stark meanderings on woodwind and strings; twice the soloist answers, on the second occasion holding a fine *ppp* on the word 'remember', as if unwilling to let go. Further orchestral arpeggios lend a more resolute feel to a second verse given similar treatment, but it ends with the same dialogue between choir and soloist, emphasizing the point that this is a moment which no-one must be allowed to forget.

But time does not stand still: a short quasi-recitative dialogue between soloist and choir leads to the reappearance of the funereal tempo of the opening section, but the earlier sense of purpose and direction is now missing. In one of Elgar's bleakest passages, a constantly shifting key and gradual crescendo combine to create an empty, oppressive wilderness, the soloist reaching ever upward and outward in a desperate search for stability and truth. At last, at the words 'As the stars that shall be bright', doubts are resolved: a sustained key is reached and the Mood of Dan bursts forth, resolute and unrestrained, as the anguished past is put behind us.

This leads immediately to the climax of the movement, the soaring theme, no longer ethereal but triumphant, 'Moving in marches on the heavenly plain', marked *fff* and *Grandioso*. But there are no certainties in life and the moment soon passes: waves of emotion ebb away and we are left with an understated sense of hope and belief in the future as the movement ends in an air of contentment strongly reminiscent of the dying moments of the Second Symphony: *Spirit of England* meets spirit of delight.

Except that this is the spirit, not of England, but of Elgar, a musical encapsulation of his personal philosophy. The optimistic ending should not mislead us. This is archetypal Elgar, seen as long ago as *Caractacus* where intellectual somersaults allowed defeat to be projected as victory. But what *Spirit* portrays more vividly than any of Elgar's earlier music is the conflict, well recorded in the biographies, between the somewhat brittle confidence of Elgar's public persona and the insecurities of the inner man. That musical polymath David Owen Norris has likened Elgar's musical output to a striptease in which the shy Elgar gradually peels away the layers to reveal increasingly this inner persona. It can be glimpsed in the Second Symphony, a notably restless work in which conflicts are also finally resolved in the dying moments; it may be read into *Falstaff* if we accept that Elgar saw in his eponymous hero a measure of *alter ego*; but it is not until *The Spirit of England* that we finally see Elgar's true personality fully revealed.

It is not that Elgar used Binyon's words as a vehicle for an essentially autobiographical work, a second *Music Makers*. More that, in seeking to conjure up the musical imagery to enhance the emotions of Binyon's words, he was able to draw upon his own emotional experiences: the struggles against perceived injustices; the agonies of uncertainty; false optimism summoned to revive flagging hope; fond memories of better times now passed. From a work conceived and sketched at a time when all thoughts were of victory, not compassion, the British public were no doubt looking for the superficial sentiment of another *Pomp and Circumstance* to provide reassurance that national pride and determination would combine to defeat the German foe. Elgar refused, offering instead a much nobler sentiment, sincere and enduring, transcending earthly preoccupations, confident in the belief that when the fighting was over, enemies would be friends again. It was a vision to which Elgar's friends of whatever nationality could subscribe, a vision of a victory not over a human enemy but over human frailty. Ambiguous, uncertain, perhaps, the message may be, but it is above all a statement of Elgar's faith in the ability of the human spirit to overcome adversity, the spirit that enabled the provincial Catholic trader's son with no formal musical education to scale the pinnacles of the exclusive British musical establishment.

'. . . born of the war, worthy of the war, to survive the war' – how kind has history been to the *Birmingham Evening Dispatch* reviewer's assessment? The first element appears unchallengeable: without the war, there would not have been Binyon's poems for Elgar to set, and Elgar recorded his own wish for the work to be seen as a part of his contribution to the war effort through the dedication he added to the completed score:

> To the memory of our glorious men, with a special thought for the Worcesters

But the second and third elements are harder to assess. The worthiness of Elgar's settings, shunning bathos in favour of realism, is also beyond question but to link that to the worthiness of a transient if extended struggle is to invite too narrow a comparison, no more than a small part of the picture. Glorious men are not to be found only in uniform, preparing for battle. This is music that speaks to generations who have never known war.

Or does it? Despite an initial interest in the work that survived beyond 1918, the Second World War did not bring about a significant resuscitation of performances of the work. By now, Elgar's music had lost favour, and in the more recent regrowth of interest in Elgar, the work has remained firmly attached to its emotional origins. It is not a 'lost' work in the manner of *King Olaf*, where any performance is a noteworthy event: *Spirit* continues to be performed annually, but almost invariably on the anniversary of the ending of the conflict whose suffering Elgar sought to capture. For a work described by Michael Kennedy as 'the finest of all [Elgar's] laureate works',[27] coming 'close to *The Dream of Gerontius* as a manifestation of Elgar's 'insidest inside' '[28] and by Jerrold Northrop Moore as 'his finest music since the Second Symphony',[29] it deserves better.

NOTES and SOURCES

1. Doubters may wish to read *Providence and Art* (The Elgar Society), Geoffrey Hodgkins' thought provoking exploration of Elgar's religious beliefs.
2. The title 'Pomp and Circumstance' comes from Shakespeare (*Othello*, act 3, scene 3) who, despite a portfolio of historical plays presenting generally favourable portraits of the English monarchy, appears never to have struggled to cast off any non-artistic tags.
3. ... and appendicitis caused Edward VII's coronation to be postponed and Elgar to première his commissioned work at the following year's Sheffield Festival.
4. Letter from Colvin to Elgar dated 10 January 1915 (Worcestershire County Record Office 705:445:3453)
5. Robbins, Keith: *The First World War* (Oxford University Press, 1985)
6. Binyon family
7. Worcester County Record Office 705:445:6350
8. Binyon family
9. Hooey, Charles A: 'Spirit Insights', *Elgar Society Journal*, vol 9 no 6 (November 1996) p297
10. Moore, Jerrold Northrop: *Edward Elgar – A Creative Life* (Oxford University Press, 1984) p697
11. Ponder, Winifred: *Clara Butt, Her Life Story* (Harrap, 1928) pp167-8
12. *The Musical Times*, 1 May 1916
13. *The New Witness*, 11 May 1916
14. *The Sheffield Daily*, 4 May 1916
15. Hooey: *op cit*
16. Although Elgar had marked the score for soprano or tenor soloist, performances featuring a tenor, whether for the whole work or just one or two of the settings, are rare today. This was obviously far less so in the work's early years. In his *Elgar Society Journal* article,[9] Charles Hooey points to further performances featuring two soloists at Colston Hall, Bristol in February 1918 and in Croydon 1919.
17. Hooey: *op cit*, p298
18. Hooey: *op cit*, p296
19. *Elgar Society Journal*, vol 9 no 6 (November 1996), p302
20. *The Dream of Gerontius* in 1900, *The Apostles* in 1903, *The Kingdom* in 1906 and *The Music Makers* in 1912
21. Hooey: *op cit*, pp298-300
22. The German Oscar A H Schmitz wrote a book which he called *Das Lande Ohne Musik* (*The Land Without Music*). It was eventually translated into English, this edition being published in 1925. It does not discuss music.
23. The orchestral arrangement can be found in volume 10 of the *Elgar Complete Edition* (Novello, 1986), along with the full score of *The Spirit of England* and *The Music Makers*.
24. Hooey: *op cit*, p300
25. Dan was the bulldog of G R Sinclair, organist at Hereford Cathedral. The 'Moods of Dan' were musical sketches Elgar wrote in Sinclair's visitors book.
26. Pickard, Dr John: *Elgar's Marches* (lecture to the Elgar Society's London branch, 14 May 2001)
27. Kennedy, Michael: *Portrait of Elgar* (Oxford University Press, 3rd edition, 1987) p180
28. Kennedy, Michael: notes for EMI Records CDM 5 65586 2
29. Moore: *op cit*, p682

CARILLON

"CHANTONS, BELGES, CHANTONS!"

Poem by **Emile Cammaerts**

Music by **EDWARD ELGAR**

D. BRADDELL

NET CASH.
(with Piano Conductor) 6/-
with Piano Conductor) 3/6
.....each 6⁹
(Original with text may be hired

LONDON:
ELKIN & CO. LTD.
8 & 10. BEAK ST. REGENT ST. W.
NEW YORK: RICORDI
TORONTO: ANGLO-CANADIAN

NET
PIANO SOLO (Text ad lib) 2/-
PIANO SOLO (Simplified, no text)
ORGAN .....

CHAPTER 8

A VOICE IN THE DESERT
Elgar's War Music

Lewis Foreman

Melodrama – speech with music – developed as a distinctive genre in the mid-eighteenth century, and possibly originated with Rousseau's *Pygmalion* of 1762. Mozart in *Zaïde* of 1780 included two melodramas, while the dungeon scene in *Fidelio* provides perhaps the most celebrated example of the use of speech with music in opera, Beethoven also including such treatment in his incidental music for *The Ruins of Athens*, *King Stephen* and *Egmont*. Soon afterwards the wolf's glen scene in Weber's *Der Freischütz* provides another vivid early example that is still heard. Later Liszt wrote several melodramas, while in Berlioz's *Lélio* we have another score, occasionally heard today, in which melodrama finds a rôle. These examples, together with the first version of Humperdinck's *Königskinder* fuelled the turn of the century interest in melodrama which was later developed by Schoenberg and the Second Vienna School into notated *sprechtgesang*.

Before it was possible to amplify voices electrically, the rôle of speech reinforced by music on the stage had been a long-standing one. Music provided overtures and interludes in plays, and was used in the theatre both as entr'actes and to back speech, in a way that would later be adapted and developed by the cinema, and still later television. This use of music to excite an audience, or play upon their emotions, was particularly a feature of the theatre in the late nineteenth century. Sullivan made his reputation with his music for *The Tempest*, and British composers as varied as Stanford, Parry and Edward German contributed scores which were sufficiently memorable in their day to translate to the concert room, and indeed be arranged for popular ensembles from brass band to tea shop trios. The music written for the Greek plays at Cambridge, of which Vaughan Williams's music for *The Wasps*, of 1909, is probably the best known, a tuneful if a perhaps a somewhat rarified example of this tradition.

FACING PAGE: *The cover of the published piano score of* Carillon.

The orchestra as a means of giving continuity to the proceedings and keeping the audience excited was also a feature of the music hall, which by the early 1900s was becoming more formalised in grander buildings as syndicates built bigger and bigger 'variety theatres' [1] to attract larger and more popular audiences, the prime example in London being the Coliseum, which had opened in December 1904, and where Elgar appeared on many occasions between 1912 and 1917. The melodrama with orchestra, in the form of the sentimental or humorous monologue, was also a feature of the music hall and the dividing line between this popular medium and the aspirations of the concert repertoire can be somewhat hazy. It was against this background that Elgar would later contribute occasional works including his wartime recitations with music.

The melodrama as an art-form in its own right also had vigorous champions before the First World War. It is notable that the interest in the melodrama at the end of the nineteenth century, which in the concert hall we have largely forgotten a hundred years later, developed before there was any question of artificial amplification of the voice. Yet the reciter or orator in such a work frequently had to dominate the orchestra, doubtless taking a cue both from opera and from stage plays. It was for this reason that many composers expressed dissatisfaction with the form, Grieg for example, though the composer of an outstanding example in *Bergliot*, in the late 1880s warned his young friend Fritz (later Frederick) Delius of the impracticality of pitting a speaking voice against full orchestra, presumably from bitter experience.[2] When we encounter rare performances of such works today, the speaker is likely to be miked, the voice amplified. Yet hearing the first British performance of Delius's early melodrama *Paa Vidderne* at London's St John's Smith Square in 1984[3] was a vivid demonstration of the excitement that could be elicited by an orator having to strain to dominate a full symphony orchestra to deliver the text, and an insight into the effectiveness of such a work when it was first written, though *Paa Vidderne* was not heard in Delius's lifetime.

There was quite a school of such compositions in central Europe centred on the Czech composers Fibich and Ostrčil. Zdeněk Fibich was, after Smetana and Dvořák, the most prominent Czech composer of his day. Noted for operas and orchestral music, he wrote a succession of melodramas both for the stage – *Hippodamia* (a trilogy after Sophocles and Euripides) – and for the concert room. Six of the Fibich melodramas with three by Ostrčil were recorded on LP on

Supraphon 1112 2711-12G. A CD recording of *Hippodamia* is on Supraphon 543037-2.

This interest in melodrama possibly found its greatest success at the turn of the century in the work of the German conductor and composer Max von Schillings. Richard Strauss's three examples were written as vehicles for Ernst von Possart, the director of the Munich Court Theatre and a concert orator anxious to develop that aspect of his career professionally, and the two appeared in London in 1902 to great success, and most probably would have been heard by Elgar. It was for Possart that von Schillings wrote his large-scale melodramas *Kassandra* and *Das Eleisische Fest* in 1898 and *Jung Olaf* in 1911. Between them came *Das Hexenlied* ('The Witch's Song') first heard in 1902 with piano accompaniment and with orchestra the following year. It was toured by Possart and von Schillings and enjoyed a brief popularity.[4]

As well as providing an interesting precedent for Elgar's wartime use of the genre of spoken voice with orchestra, there is a more immediate link with Elgar, for the Gerontius at Düsseldorf in 1901 and 1902, and later in England at Westminster Cathedral and Liverpool was Ludwig Wüllner, about whose singing technique Elgar waxed lyrical.[5] As *Sprecher,* Wüllner became a celebrated exponent of von Schillings's *Das Hexenlied,* recording it in 1922[6] during the last phase of acoustic recording and again, with startling fidelity and immediacy, in 1933, a recording which has been reissued on CD[7] providing us a link not only to the architect of *Gerontius's* success but also to the power of the melodrama before Elgar. Elgar must have heard Wüllner in recitation, in which he was famous, both with musical accompaniment and without.

In the UK this interest in melodrama had focused on the Royal Academy of Music. It was Sir Alexander Mackenzie, Principal of the RAM for many years who asked for accompanied recitation in his choral work *The Dream of Jubal* (he called it 'a poem with music') in 1889. At the RAM Frederick Corder encouraged his pupils to write such works, and those who complied included Bantock, Corder's son Paul and Arnold Bax. The Society for British Composers, very much influenced by Corder, allocated a separate heading for 'Recitation Music' in its first two yearbooks,[8] including music by Hubert Bath, Herbert Bedford, Frederick Corder, Harry Farjeon, William Hurlstone, Emma Lomax and various other mainly young composers. Frederick Corder contributed to a very extensive book[9] on recitation, published at the turn of the century. This included many extracts for verse reading and recitation.   Probably the two best-known works for speaker and piano accompaniment are Grieg's *Bergliot,* first dating (in its piano version) from 1871, and Richard Strauss's *Enoch Arden* (also with piano) of 1897.   *Enoch Arden* is in two parts and in Gert Westphal's recording[10] with the pianist John Buttrick they run for a total of 64' 48", so is a substantial score. Strauss also made melodrama settings of Uhland's *The Castle by the Sea* and Salomé's dramatic monologue from Oscar Wilde's play, both of which have been recorded by Pamela Hunter.

The recent revival, by Pamela Hunter, of eight of the surprisingly effective melodramas of Stanley Hawley[11] well illustrate the genre. With piano accompaniment they include dramatic renditions of Edgar Allen Poe's *The Bells* and *The Raven*.   This treatment was found an apposite one for Poe's haunted imagery, later the Russian-American violinist and composer Arcady Dubensky producing a similar treatment of *The Raven,* with orchestral accompaniment, which was recorded by Leopold Stokowski in 1932, with Benjamin de Loache as narrator.[12]

A notable British advocate of the melodrama was Lena Ashwell, who during the war would become celebrated for her work with concert parties, generally known as 'Concerts at the Front' and for which she was appointed OBE.[13] It was in support of this Charity that Elgar contributed his music for the ballet *The Sanguine Fan* for a charity matinée.   Stanley Hawley's recitations were championed by Ashwell who had appeared in Grieg's *Bergliot* at an early Promenade Concert at Queen's Hall. But Hawley died suddenly in 1916 aged only 49 and at his memorial concert at the Wigmore Hall, Ashwell recited his melodramas with piano accompaniment by Sir Henry Wood. Ashwell first met Elgar over *Starlight Express* on 10 November 1915 she would be an important thread in his work during the next two years, and it seems very probable that she would have appeared in Elgar's *Carillon,* the most celebrated melodrama of its day.

Almost certainly the best known British examples of the spoken treatment of words with orchestra were the three wartime works that Elgar produced for emotional and nationalist occasions during the First World War.   They all set words by the now largely forgotten Belgian poet Emil Cammaerts, though in England during the Great War he was a big name.

In 1914 Elgar was no stranger to variety programmes and the music hall, his *Crown of India* – in its day one of his most popular works – being played in a mixed bill at the London Coliseum in March 1912. This was music intended to have a broad popular appeal – not only in tuneful music[†] and vivid and exotic stage settings, but also appealing to the popular political mood of the moment at the time of the Delhi Durbar when King George V was acclaimed by the states of India at a sumptuous ceremony. Elgar's more popular songs were also to be heard in the ballad slot in mixed music hall programmes.

Elgar's wartime recitations were conceived against this background, but his approach to his wartime patriotic works was not necessarily particularly patriotic *per se;* they were more works of protest at the war and its inhumanities. They first appeared in French, putting them out of the reach of the widest popular audience. But *Carillon* was soon issued in English, and in various arrangements, and was thus widely performed.

During the Autumn of 1914 *The Observer* published English translations of what became known as Emile Cammaerts' 'Patriotic Songs' ('Chants Patriotiques'). These included 'Après Anvers' and 'Le Drapeau Belge' both dated 'Londres, October 1914' and translated by his wife Tita Brand Cammaerts. Later Cammaerts' poem 'Une Voix dans le Désert', dated March 1915, appeared in *The Spectator*, though this time translated by Lord Curzon of Kedleston. They were collected in book form as *Belgian Poems* and published in the spring of 1915.[14]

Elgar's *Carillon* when it first appeared was a musical response to a deeply felt current event – one eliciting widely shared popular emotions. *Carillon* sets topical and emotional words responding to the 'rape' of Belgium, which generated an enormous following in its day. When Elgar attempted a sequel with the much shorter 'Marche militaire´ *Le Drapeau Belge*, he attracted a much smaller response. The moment had passed. Between these two, his second recitation, *Une Voix dans le Désert* was more reflective and for a modern audience can still be found touching. It included the poignant song

*nile
ammaerts
Vernon
ill*

† - the scena 'Hail Immemorial Ind' appears as track 14 on the accompanying CD

of the peasant girl whose home has been destroyed 'Quand nos bourgeons se rouvriront' ('When spring comes round again') beginning to touch wider sensibilities than its somewhat crude companions.   In all three recitations Elgar was articulating an emotional response to real events. Elgar's copy of Carillon was given him by the poet Cammaerts himself and was inscribed 'Après Anvers'. The fall of Antwerp (Anvers) was one of those key turning points in the breaking of inhibitions and was also the point at which the Allied depiction of the Huns as savages began. The peasant girl's song in *A Voice in the Desert* is littered with such names all of them once of great emotional significance in the fall of Belgium – Antwerp, Ypres, Nieuport, Dixmude, Ramscapelle – and an appreciation of them adds immeasurably to the emotional impact of the music.

The reviews pasted into the cuttings books covering the period of the war, now at the Elgar Birthplace Museum, are not always identified.   This is an extended extract from one of these to establish how Elgar's new work was received on 7 December 1914.

The principal feature of last night's concert of the London Symphony Orchestra at Queen's Hall was the first performance of Sir Edward Elgar's new incidental music to M. Emile Cammaerts' poem 'Carillion'. The poem is a lament over ruined Belgium, but also a glorification of the people which has preferred honour when shame would have been the easier way, and will prefer magnanimity when after victory when vengeance would be sweet. It is an inspiring subject for a musician, and it has nerved Elgar to one of his happiest and strongest achievements. The music moves irresistibly on a broad full stream of manly emotion to a series of noble climaxes. It is sonorous without clamour, and euphonious without weakness. It has stimulating rhythms, and the themes are strong.   From the technical point of view the way in which the whole moves over the insistent bell figure is a noteworthy tour de force. . . . The words were

lgar's "Carillon."

The musician's association with the word Carillon" is a war one. When the name is entioned there immediately leaps to his mind e thought of the inspired poem of Cammaerts ith its no less inspired musical setting by lgar.* Perhaps, if the musician has happened hear it as it was first performed in London, e will see again the crowded Queen's Hall, ill feel again the tense silence of an audience eply moved, will hear again the wonderful imax at the words, "A Berlin!" and then e still greater heights to which poem and music se, till the end comes on a note of triumph. et, though the bell theme is the very heart of e composition, and may be regarded as sym- olical of Belgium, it is not a Carillon theme that ngs out. Rather it is such a theme as we might ear on our English church bells. But to the nglishman it will never have this association. o him it is the true expression of a martyred ation—*Carillon* comes to him as the echo of elgium's cry for vengeance, and afterwards :—

Although our wounds may bleed, although our hearts may break,

'Neath this bright Autumn Sun,
Sing of the pride of charity
When vengeance would be so sweet

BELGIUM IN SONG.

Newcastle Visit of Sir Edward Elgar.

HARRISON CONCERT.

The cathedral bells of all Belgium seemed to ring out in triumphing tumult under the magic of Sir Edward Elgar's music in the Newcastle Town Hall last night. It was an unforgettable scene when M. Emile Cammaerts, the poet of Belgium, recited his thrilling verse to the accompaniment of Elgar's music. Something prophetic in the poet's ringing call, to which the orchestra gave mighty emphasis.

It was the last supreme item of a great programme. Sir Edward Elgar's orchestra- tion of the poetry is built upon the resound- ing chimes of cathedral bells, Belgium's resurrected bells. A moment later the whole vast audience uprose in our National Anthem. Belgium and Britain were one— the ravaged and the redeemer. "It made _____ ____ crying," blurted out a man

---

FACING PAGE:
Tita Brand and Marie Brema

THIS PAGE:
Selected press reports of early performances of Carillon

FOLLOWING PAGE :
The French actress Gabrielle Réjane, with a selection of cuttings showing press reaction to her appearance in Carillon

---

WORCESTERSHIRE ORCHESTRAL SOCIETY'S CONCERT.

ELGAR'S "CARILLON."

Saturday's concert of the Worcestershire Orchestral Society, given in the Malvern Assembly Rooms, was especially interesting from the fact that included in the programme was Elgar's "Carillon," which Birmingham, by the way, will have an opportunity of hearing at Mr. Percy Harrison's next concert. The music has had its origin in a poem by the Belgian Emile Cammaerts, which sings in profoundly moving tones the un- conquerable pride and hope of Belgium. As the poem, so is the music—simple but penetrating, high-spirited, woven out of the best that these ghastly times have bred in us. Both poet and composer have taken the line of the deeper and wiser humanism. Blackguard "hymns of hate" may be left to the literary blackguards who can write them and the deluded fools who can sing them: for those to whom the war, however it may end, means the shipwreck of almost everything they value in our civilisation, it is a poetry and a music grave and wise and noble that are needed— something that will help us to transcend the brutality and the disillusionment of the hour. Cammaerts's poem ___

REJANE DRAWS TEARS

SCENE OF EMOTION AT QUEEN'S HALL CONCERT.

MOVING BELGIAN POEM.

An unforgettable scene occurred yesterday afternoon at the Queen's Hall on the occasion of the first of a series of three orchestral concerts devoted to the works of British composers and organised by Mr. Isidore de Lara. The programme included Elgar's "Carillon," the wonderful setting of Emile Cam-

Daily Graphic, 20 April

A FEAST OF MUSIC.

REJANE'S TRIUMPH.

AN AMAZING SPECTACLE.

There remains, then, only to mention the soloists. Of these one was known here years ago in Opera. No one that saw Miss Mary Garden in "Manon" then will need to be reminded of how inevitable was the success of her operatic career even in the beginning. Yesterday, after singing "Dear River," from Goring Thomas's "Nadeshda," he added, by way of an extra, a trumpery little ballad that was completely out of place in a scheme in which so much interest and importance attached. At the last Madame Réjane's name is to be mentioned. In the course of its twenty-one years of existence Queen's Hall has witnessed many curious sights. But one takes leave to doubt if such a scene has ever before been enacted there as that which followed on Madame Réjane's marvellously indescribably beautiful recitation of Emile Cammaerts' noble words in the performance of Elgar's Carillon. That fine tribute to Belgium, as the public hardly need reminding, was contributed by Sir Edward Elgar to "King Albert's Book" on behalf of *The Daily Telegraph* Belgian Fund. The actual performance was unquestionabl

EMOTIONAL SCENE AT QUEEN'S HALL

There was a dramatic scene at the Queen's Hall yesterday during the rendering of Sir Edward Elgar's "Carillon," the wonderful setting of Emile Cammaert's poem, "Chantons Belges, Chantons," which the composer wrote for King Albert's Book.

Mme. Réjane, who recited the Belgian poem's lines, threw such intensity of feeling into them that many people in the crowded audience sobbed.

A great roar of cheers followed the last note of the music, and at a signal from Sir Henry Wood the orchestra broke into the "Marseillaise," and in the fiery strains of the French National Anthem the audience found vent for its emotion.

spoken with extraordinary emphasis (in French) by Mme Tita Brand.[15]

Clearly the success of the performance was to a considerable extent dependent on the histrionic delivery of the words by Cammaerts's wife:

> Perhaps one of the most impressive features of it all was the wonderful way in which Mme Tita Brand flung the splendid lines at the audience. The music, however, has caught the exact spirit of the poem, its pathos, and its proud, defiant feeling. The central theme is the simple one of a peal of bells, which is hardly evenr absent from the orchestral fabric . . . Always poetic and dramatic in feeling, it all has a fine sweep and rises to several impressive climaxes. Poem and music together produce a thrilling effect, and there were numerous recalls for poet, composer, and reciter. Sir Edward Elgar, by the way conducted his own music admirably.[16]

One or two journalists even wondered if Tita Brand had overdone it:

> The poem was recited in French by Mme Tita Brand. The wife of the poet, with astonishing and sometimes (it must be confessed) excessive vigour; but as she obviously felt very deeply one could forgive the excesses.[17]

The reception was so vigorous that it was programmed again on 17 December, when *The Daily Telegraph* noticed 'Yet, again, Elgar's Carillon aroused a storm of approval and appreciation on its second public performance'.[18] Performances quickly multiplied and in less than two weeks the music was published, in piano score, in *King Albert's Book*. As Stephen Lloyd recounts in his chapter on Bournemouth, it had its first provincial performance there in January 1915, the reciter being Mary Mackenzie, the daughter of the composer Sir Alexander Mackenzie who apparently went to the opposite extreme, giving a fairly flat undemonstrative rendition of the poem.

The work was widely performed, not least by the celebrated actor Henry Ainley, in 1914 aged 35 and then well-known as a romantic lead, who recorded a slightly abridged version with Elgar in January 1915 and then toured it with him. Possibly the most histrionic presentation came when the celebrated French actress Réjane appeared in it at Queen's Hall on 19 April 1915 in a concert conducted by Sir Henry Wood. Despite being on the point of retirement she:

> threw into the Belgian poet's lines such intense feeling and such dramatic force that the combined effect of words and music became almost unbearable . . . and long before she had finished the feelings of a crowded audience had been so played upon that many persons were sobbing. Then, after the last notes of the music, there came a great roar of cheering, not the ordinary applause of a concert audience, but an outburst of deep sentiment . . . Sir Henry Wood did the right thing. At a signal from him

CARILLON
EDWARD ELGAR

ARRANGED
for the
ORGAN
Price 2/-net cash

by
HUGH
BLAIR
may be performed in
public without fee
or license

ABOVE LEFT:
*The cover of
Hugh Blair's
organ version
of* Carillon

ABOVE RIGHT:
Henry Ainley

RIGHT:
*HMV's
advertisement
for the
recording
(March 1915)*

the orchestra broke into the 'Marseillaise' . . . but for ten minutes or so the atmosphere of Queen's Hall was more tense, probably, than it has ever been before.[19]

A variety of theatre people of the day became associated with *Carillon*, one notable actor being the Belgian Carlo Liten. This clearly did not go down well in all quarters, a newspaper review of a performance by Cammaerts himself in Liverpool noting:

> . . . the poem itself being declaimed with convincing earnestness by the author, M. Emile Cammaerts, and formed an agreable contrast to the stagey version offered by Mr Carlo Liten at the opening concert of the Philharmonic Society last year.[20]

Under the heading 'An Imperial Composer' another unidentified paper – possibly *The Daily Telegraph* writes:

> The wise man who put the songs of a nation before its laws was certainly not underrating the gift of song. 'To sing a sang for Scotia's sake' was for Burns the highest service he could do his country. Yet there is nothing that the minor poet or musician approaches with such easy assurance as the great mystery of song. Six weeks after the outbreak of war one London publisher had already received for approval three thousand patriotic songs. 'Tipperary' was the soldier's criticism of the efforts of his countrymen to find a voice for national feeling. Rather than sing the stuff that was offered him, the soldier sang a music-hall song without the remotest reference to the war. Perhaps it is a sign of the nations' good sense that the great stream of war songs has now become a mere trickle. The discovery that song writing and empty crowing are not the same thing is at least something. Even the most serious composer might hesitate before touching his harp to the tragedy of war.
>
> Only one British composer has so far sung of the war with any authority. Elgar may be regarded as the British musical laureate. . . No British composer has struck the Imperial note like Elgar, and no British composer combines so happily brilliance and the big manner. . . The music is clean and fresh, with a big emotional sweep, yet without any undue introspection – in a word British. His first and perhaps his best contribution to the music of the war was 'Carillon'. When it was written the cry of Belgium was fresh in British ears, and it appealed at once to the national heart and imagination. . . . Poem and music have the dignity of a noble grief, and all the exultation of heroic resolve.

Although Elgar wrote what was at the time the most celebrated wartime works in the concert hall, with *Carillon* and the widespread use of *Land of Hope and Glory*, the most long-lasting score written for a mass audience was Parry's *Jerusalem*. He had a lesser success with another similar setting, of John O'Gaunt's speech from Shakespeare's *Richard II*, called *England*. But his most potentially apposite short vocal work for the war, *A Hymn for Aviators*† which was sung by Clara Butt, finds him seemingly out of touch with the popular mood and it did not achieved the hoped-for circulation. On 13 May 1915, Parry attended the morning rehearsal for Butt's concert at the Royal Albert Hall and found it 'a perfect orgy of vulgarity'. Later, after the evening concert, he noted 'my Aviator's Song quite out of place'.[21] In fact Butt's recording, made late in 1918, was not issued until after the war in June 1919.

The early artistic focus of the war came with *King Albert's Book*,[22] published just before Christmas 1914.   This was very widely disseminated, and artistically stands at the stylistic crossroads between the old and the new. Just as the varied designs of war memorials at the end of the war would reflect contrasting artistic sensibilities so does this book. Assembled in a very short time by the popular novelist Hall Caine[23] and published in sumptuous style by *The Daily Telegraph* in conjunction with the *Daily Sketch* and the *Glasgow Herald* it consists of many messages from the great and the good, plus music and pictures and illustration representing a quite remarkable range of sensibilities.   In his introduction, Hall Caine wrote:

> The immediate object of this book is to offer, in the names and by the pens of a large group of the representatives men and women of the civilised countries, a tribute of admiration to Belgium, on the heroic and ever-memorable share she has taken in the war which now convulses Europe, and at the same time to invoke the world's sympathy, its help and its prayers for the gallant little nation in the vast sorrow of the present condition . . . Never, before, perhaps, have so many illustratious names been inscribed within the covers of a single volume . . . Out of the storm of battle a great new spirit of brotherhood has been born into the world, calling together the scattered and divided parts of it, uniting them in a single mind, a single sentiment, a single purpose, so that here, in love of justice and in hatred of oppression, speaking in many voices and many tongues but from only one soul, which enkindles the earth as with a holy fire, men and women of all civilised countries have drawn closer and clasped hands.

Altogether 26 paintings or drawing were reproduced in facsimile and a dozen pieces of music including Elgar's *Carillon*, were published in piano score, together with a photograph of King Albert of the Belgians as frontispiece. The music was:

> Mackenzie: *One Who Never Turned his Back* (Browning)
> Messager: *Pour la Patrie* (Hugo)
> Cowen: *Hail! Hymn to Belgium* (Galsworthy)

† -   Butt's recording appears as track 9 on the accompanying CD

Smyth: *The March of the Women* (extract)
Elgar: *Carillon*
Liza Lehmann: *By the Lake* (Song to be sung by Madame Clara Butt)
Edward German: Hymn [*Homage to Belgium, 1914*] (*Andante Religioso*)
Stanford: *But lo! There breaks a yet more glorious day* (Hymn tune)
Debussy: *Berceuse Héroïque*
Lange-Müller: *Lamentation*
Mascagni: *Sunt Lacrymæ Rerum!*
Johan Backer-Lunde: *She Comes Not* (Herbert Trench)

The Observer for 20 December 1914 surveyed the music in *King Albert's Book* and identified Elgar's *Carillon* and Debussy's *Berceuse Héroïque* as the two best numbers. One would not wish to disagree, and, indeed, considering the aspirations of the book, the quality of the music is remarkably limited.

Most of the senior British composers of the day wrote patriotic songs, choral music or marches in response to the war. Those that appeared in King Albert's Book, particularly by Mackenzie and Cowen are not among their composers' best, though Cowen enjoyed at least two popular patriotic 'hits' on record at this time with *Fall In* and *We Sweep the Seas.*[†] Indeed, Cowen's contribution to *King*

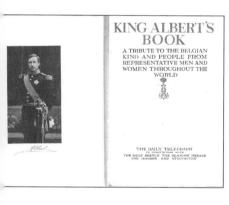

ABOVE: *The title page of*
King Albert's Book,
showing the portrait of
Albert, King of the Belgians

RIGHT: *Hall Caine*

† -   track 8 on the accompanying CD

By L. RAVEN-HILL.

"*You mark my word Jarge; that there Kayser 'll come to a bad end: I've 'ad my eye on un for many a day!*"

"*Plorans ploravit in nocte: et lacrymæ ejus in maxillis ejus ..... Manum suam misit ad omnia desiderabilia ejus.*" [*Lamentatio Jeremis Prophetæ. I.*]

By BERNARD PARTRIDGE

LA BELGIQUE: 1914.

Illustrations from King Albert's Book by L Raven-Hill, Bernard Partridge and Arthur Rackham

UNCONQUERABLE.

Albert's Book, the undistinguished *Hail! A Hymn to Belgium* sets even more undistinguished words by John Galsworthy beginning 'Men of Belgium! Honours own!/Ye who saved the Holy Grail' shows neither collaborator seeming to be comfortable with the limelight in which they have been placed by the request to contribute.

Viewed from a new century *King Albert's Book* is a useful *vade mecum* or touchstone of artistic sensibilities in 1914, most of them frankly backward-looking, and as far as many of the pictures are concerned it must have been the last occasion on which images of heroism could have been evoked by knights in shining armour (for example Frank Dicksee's 'Resurgam' and Briton Riviere's 'St George and the Dragon', RA's both). Another frankly Victorian image is A D McCormick's 'The Death of Admiral Blake'. The passing of the Cromwellian admiral is a subject also taken for an immediately pre-war choral work by the young Montague Phillips, setting words by Sir Henry Newbolt, which with its gorgeous central orchestral song remembering England 'Oh! To be there for an hour when the shade draws in beside the hedgerows' is almost a musical epitome of this idiom.[24]   There were also images of countries personified by statuesque women of which Arthur Rackham's 'Unconquerable' and the Punch cartoonist Bernard Partridge's 'La Belgique: 1914' must have had considerable power at the time. Perhaps the most effective and probably the most appealing to a wide British audience were the quietly humourous such as L Raven-Hill's cartoon of two old men, which by eschewing heroics and the past were the more effective.   It was in this ambience that Elgar's *Carillon* was published, perhaps being more in place than Debussy's *Berceuse Héroïque*.

Of Elgar's two later wartime recitations with orchestra *Une Voix Dans le Désert* and *Le Drapeau Belge*, neither achieved the impact or popular success of *Carillon*. *Une Voix Dans le Désert* first appeared in costume at the Shaftesbury Theatre, London on 29 January 1916, as a curtain raiser between 'Cav' and 'Pag' and enjoyed a short run. The reciter was Carlo Liten and the soprano Olga Lynn. Having two such now unknown names gives us little clue as to how it sounded, but the press reports clearly suggest seeing it in costume added to the impact:

> The scene is just a landscape showing everywhere the ravages of war, a shell-torn cottage with a fore ground of shattered bricks and mortar, and a background of red willows and the twinkling fires along the Yser.[25]

When *Fringes of the Fleet* became Elgar's latest work to catch the wider public's imagination, during 1917, that too was presented in costume, in this case four old tars seated round a pub bench. In a

The last page of Une Voix dans le Désert

mixed variety programme it could not fail and toured the country.

But it was *Carillon* which the public had taken to its heart, and throughout the summer of 1916 it had a run at the London Coliseum, with Carlo Littens as the reciter, which Elgar conducted himself. Later, in October a further run took place at the Coliseum, this time featuring Lalla Vandervelde, a Junoesque figure who, dramatically dressed in black appeared before a red drop-curtain. This too could not fail. In fact Vandervelde had first-hand knowledge of her subject as the daughter of Edward Speyer and the wife of Émile Vandervelde the socialist Belgian minister in charge of Belgian refugees in the UK.

The shortest of the three Elgar recitations is *Le Drapeau Belge* which was finished in the spring of 1916 but remained unperformed for nearly a year. The moment had passed for such things. It first appeared – with *Une Voix dans le Désert* – at Queen's Hall on 14 April 1917 recited by Carlo Liten in a birthday concert for King Albert of the Belgians. Elgar's heart seems to have been little in it but he appeared at Hamilton Harty's concert to conducted the first performance. It was soon forgotten.

Elgar's treatment of speaking voices with music may also be heard in *Starlight Express,* where he provides music in response to the standard theatre requirements of his day: this can be heard in the surviving tapes of the BBC's production broadcast in December 1965. The example overleaf, reproduced from Robert Walker's vocal score of the complete work, demonstrates how evocative such treatment could be, and how sensitive Elgar was to the requirements of the words.[26]

In 1919 Elgar seemed to have finished both with war and Empire, their valediction sung in the Cello Concerto. But there was to be an interesting postscript. In 1924 the Wembley Exhibition celebrated the Empire, and Elgar's music for the occasion consisted of a march and eight patriotic songs largely celebrating the Dominions and their ties to the 'old country'. One of them, 'Sailing Westward' has four optional additional texts to make it representative of those places, including India and South Africa, not otherwise covered – so if all were done there would be 12 songs in all, some for solo voice some for chorus, of which nine were sung during the pageant in August 1924.

With their words by Alfred Noyes this co-operation could not be less fashionable at the time of writing in 2001, and indeed they did not make much of an impact when they first appeared, but yet without the immediate wartime pressures to write another 'Land of Hope' they were in fact the no-nonsense patriotic songs he might have written before the war.

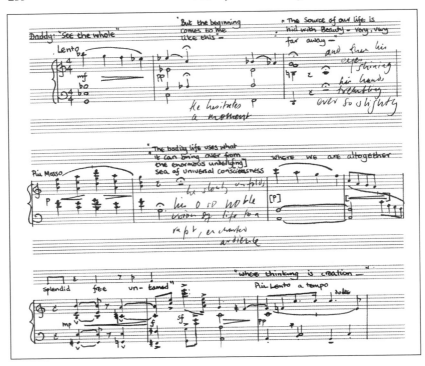

From 39 *in the vocal score of* Starlight Express, *showing Elgar's treatment of* speech over music

But, in the two key numbers 'The Immortal Legions' and 'A Song of Union' they had a more immediate rôle in 1924: remembrance. Here he was very much hymning the lost young men of the Somme, albeit in a language more suitable to the Boer War.

THE IMMORTAL LEGIONS (baritone and orchestra)[†]

Now, in silence, muster round her
   All the legions of her dead.
Grieving for the grief that crowned her,
   England bows her glorious head.
Round the ever-living Mother,
      Out of the forgetful grave,
Rise the legions that have saved her
      Though themselves they could not save.
Now the living Power remembers,
   Now the deeper trumpets roll –

† - track 15 on the accompanying CD

PAGEANT OF EMPIRE

NEW MUSIC SPECIALLY COMPOSED

Poems by
ALFRED NOYES

Music by
SIR EDWARD ELGAR

		Net. s. d.
The Empire March (1924) - - - - - - -		2 0
Shakespeare's Kingdom - - Song E flat (C to E flat), F, G -		2 0
The Islands (A Song of New Zealand) ,, F (C to E), A flat -		2 0
The Blue Mountains (A Song of Australia) ,, D flat (D flat to D flat), F -		2 0
The Heart of Canada - - ,, E flat (E flat to F) -		2 0
Sailing Westward - - - ,, F (C to E), A flat -		2 0
Merchant Adventurers - Song and Chorus E flat (B flat to E flat), F -		2 0

FOUR-VOICE ARRANGEMENTS

The Immortal Legions (S.A.T.B.) - - - - - -	0 6
Sailing Westward (S.A.T.B.) - - - - - -	0 6
With four alternative poems : Indian Dawn, The Islands, The Cape of Good Hope, Gloriana	
A Song of Union (S.A.T.B.) - - - - - - -	0 6

London
ENOCH & SONS L^D

Enoch House : 58, Great Marlborough Street, W.1

MELBOURNE :
ALLAN & CO.

NEW YORK :
ENOCH & SONS.

TORONTO :
THE ANGLO-CANADIAN MUSIC COMPANY.

PARIS :
ENOCH & CO.

Advertisement for the sheet music of Pageant of Empire, *showing the constituent numbers*

BRITISH - EMPIRE - EXHIBITION
THE
PAGEANT *of* EMPIRE
PROGRAMME—PART I.

THE WOODEN WALLS   *F. Brangwyn, R.A.*

Detail from the cover of the programme for Pageant of Empire, *21 July-30 August 1924*

> *Are there worlds beyond the darkness?*
> *Worlds of light beyond the darkness?*
> And a voice beyond the darkness
>   Whispers to her stricken soul:
> Mother of immortal legions,
>   Lift again thy glorious head.
> Glory, honour and thanksgiving,
>   Now, to our victorious dead.

The choral setting of 'A Song of Union'[†] draws together several threads, do you hear resonances in such verses as 'And peace was breathed on every sea' of *The Music Makers* and even *The Spirit of England*? Elgar underlines that the memorial mood is continuing with the funereal drums which underpin the opening stanzas of this number which, actually would be much more poetic without them. Despite the words hymning the 'love that linked our realm [ie the Empire] in one', lauding the Pax Britannica, here in his setting Elgar surely joins Parry in the closing bars of *Chivalry of the Sea* in contemplating the infinite, with an irreconcilable sadness.

† -   track 16 on the accompanying CD

WESTWARD HO !   15

MUSIC for PAGEANT, PART II and PART III.

MASTER OF MUSIC   ...   .   HENRY JAXON.

The greatest possible care has been taken in selecting the music, and British composers only are represented. Mr. Henry Jaxon has had the wide experience of Mr. I. A. de Orellana in assisting him in the selection and orchestration. The orchestra of 110 musicians has been specially selected from the London Symphony, Royal Albert Hall and Covent Garden Theatre (Opera) Orchestras.

The Choir (who have generously given their services) are members of the Alexandra Palace, Crystal Palace, Royal Choral, Ealing Choral, Harrow Choral, Northwood Choral Societies, and Wembley Choir, &c.

PART II.

THE DAYS OF QUEEN ELIZABETH.

EMPIRE MARCH (" 1924 ")	*Edward Elgar*
PRELUDE : IN THE MEADOWS (' Countryside ")	
	Eric Coates
THE OLD CRYES—CHERRY RIPE (Choir and Orchestra)	
	Anon
DANCES (" Henry VIII ") ...	*Edward German*
IN A COUNTRY LANE (" Summer Days ")	*Eric Coates*
SPIRIT OF PAGEANTRY (March) ...	*Percy Fletcher*
GLORIANA (Noyes)	*Edward Elgar*
LONG LIVE ELIZABETH (' Merrie England ")	
	Edward German
TE DEUM IN F	*Henry Smart*
IMPERIAL MARCH	*Edward Elgar*

THE ENGLISH FLEET IN THE MEDITERRANEAN—BLAKE AND THE BARBARY PIRATES.

" NERO " March	*Coleridge Taylor*
THE MARINERS OF ENGLAND (Choir and Orchestra)	
	John Pointer
PLYMOUTH HOE	*John Ansell*
AFRICAN DANCES	*Montague Ring*
BRITANNIA (Overture)	*A. C. Mackenzie*

THE PAGEANT OF SOUTH AFRICA.

THE CAPE OF GOOD HOPE (Noyes)	*Edward Elgar*
OLD " HOTTENTOT " MELODIES ...	—
PORTUGUESE MELODY	—
DUTCH BOAT SONG	—
OLD HUGUENOT DANCES ...	—
BOURRÉE	*Mouret*
AFRICAN SUITE	*E. D. Barcroft*
CAMP AND KAFFIR MELODIES ...	—
LIVINGSTONE EPISODE ...	*Hamish McCunn*
BAMBOULA	*Coleridge Taylor*
FROM WAR AND PEACE (Choir and Orchestra)	
	C. H. H. Parry
LAND OF HOPE AND GLORY (Choir and Orchestra)	
	Edward Elgar

THE EARLY DAYS OF INDIA.

INDIAN DAWN (Noyes)	*Edward Elgar*
INTRODUCTION (" Crown of India ")	*Edward Elgar*
MOGUL MARCH (" Crown of India ")	*Edward Elgar*
PERSIAN GARDEN (Scenes) ...	*Liza Lehmann*
INDIAN LOVE LYRICS ...	*A. Woodforde Finden*
OLD INDIAN DANCES	*Shankar*
MARCH (" Crown of India ") ...	*Edward Elgar*

PART III.

GEORGE III AND THE DEPARTURE OF CAPTAIN COOK.

EMPIRE MARCH (" 1924 ") ...	*Edward Elgar*
SYLVAN SCENES	*Percy Fletcher*
MINUET	*Dr. Philip Hayes*
MINUET AND PAGEANT MARCH ...	*Herman Finch*

A PAGEANT OF NEW ZEALAND.

THE ISLANDS (Noyes)	*Edward Elgar*
GOD DEFEND NEW ZEALAND ...	—
SEA CHANTIES ... Arranged by *Richard R. Terry*	
WHEN THE YELLOW KOWBAI BLOOMS	*W. G. James*
MERRYMAKERS (Overture)	*Eric Coates*
BENEDICTUS	*Granville Bantock*
WAITA-POI	*Alfred Hill*
TANGI	*Alfred Hill*
HARVEST DANCE	*Edward German*
EMPIRE MARCH (" 1924 ") ...	*Edward Elgar*

A PAGEANT OF AUSTRALIA.

THE BLUE MOUNTAINS (Noyes) ...	*Edward Elgar*
MARCH BLANC	*Herman Finch*
ADVANCE AUSTRALIA	—
THE LONG, LONG TRAIL ...	*Z. O. Eliot*
STOCK RIDERS' SONG	*W. G. James*
PLANTATION SONGS	*G. H. Clutsam*
SOLDIERS OF THE QUEEN ...	*Leslie Stuart*
IMPERIAL MARCH	*Arthur Sullivan*

A PAGEANT OF HEROES.

THE IMMORTAL LEGIONS (Noyes) ...	*Edward Elgar*
SOLEMN MARCH (Organ)	*E. H. Lemare*
NELSON PHRASES	—
WITH PROUD THANKSGIVING (Choir and Orchestra)	
	Edward Elgar

THE EMPIRE'S THANKSGIVING.

ANTHEM OF THE SISTER NATIONS (Binyon)	
	Nicholas Gatty
THE RECESSIONAL (Kipling) ...	*Herbert Bunning*

The Empire Pageant Council wish to thank the following music publishers for their kindness and courtesy in allowing their works to be performed : Messrs. NOVELLO & CO., BOOSEY & CO., ENOCH & SONS, CHAPPELL & CO., HAWKES & SONS, J. CURWEN & SONS, LTD., BOSWORTH & CO., RICORDI & CO., SCHOTT & CO., KEITH PROWSE & CO., ASCHERBERG, HOPWOOD & CREW, LTD., WEEKES & CO., WEST'S LTD., FRANCIS, DAY & HUNTER.

From the programme of Pageant of Empire, *21 July-30 August 1924*

A SONG OF UNION

The stars that wheel around the Sun
Proclaim the law that bound them.
Twas love that linked our realms in one
and Love in joy that crowned them!

> Then Freedom took her throne,
>   Freedom took her throne
> And peace was breathed on every sea
>   and music swelled around them;
> No more the dreams of war shall sound
>   When hearts and realms in
> Love are bound:
>   For Love binds all in one;
>   Love binds all our hearts in one.

In *The Pageant of Empire*, which took place in August 1924, Elgar recycled other music including three numbers from *Crown of India*, for the section 'The Early Days of India' which ended Part II. *The Pageant of Empire* ended with 'A Pageant of Heroes' followed by 'The Empire's Thanksgiving'. 'A Pageant of Heroes' which featured Elgar's 'The Immortal Legions' ended with *With Proud Thanksgiving*, his reduced version of 'For the Fallen'. We have no experience of the music written for the grand closing tableau, 'The Empire's Thanksgiving', which consisted of Nicholas Gatty's *Anthem of the Sister Nations* setting words by Binyon, and Herbert Bunning's setting of Kipling's 'Recessional'. Both these scores have vanished, and it is regrettable that Elgar was not tempted to stamp his personality on the proceedings by setting Kipling's most celebrated words.

It is salutary to discover that 'A Song of Union' is the one number which was not used during *The Pageant of Empire*. Elgar's wartime recitations were not heard again; they had served their purpose but they had been of their time. When, in 1942 a new version of *Carillon* was published, with new words by Binyon, its publisher was not to repeat his killing of the First World War, they found no takers and it disappeared without trace. Similarly Sir Edward Downes tells[27] of an attempt to produce *The Spirit of England* at a college of music on the outbreak of war in 1939, when the young choir refused to sing the words. Only now with the perspective of history can we experience Elgar's wartime music divorced from the very powerful emotions that engendered it: it stands such scrutiny remarkably well.

NOTES and SOURCES

1. For a summary history of the development of the music hall see Andrew Lamb's article 'Music hall' in *New Grove II*, vol 17 pp 483-6.
2. In his world première recording with the Royal Liverpool Philharmonic Orchestra conducted by Douglas Bostock, Peter Hall manages to strike a very persuasive balance between the heroic and the conversational (Classico CLASSCD 364).

3. On 7 February 1984. The speaker was Alan Hendrick with the Kensington Symphony Orchestra conducted by Leslie Head. A private recording of this performance survives.

4. For more on von Schillings and *Das Hexenlied* see Michael Beughold's extended booklet notes with the modern recording of the work on CPO LC 8492 (Martha Mödl, specherin; Kölner Rundfunkorchester conducted by Jan Stulen).

5. See Foreman, Lewis: 'Elgar and Gerontius: the early performances' in Hodgkins, Geoffrey (ed): *The Best of Me: a Gerontius centenary companion* (Rickmansworth, Elgar Editions, 1999) pp 162-235

6. Odeon Rxx80113/8; 0-8056/8

7. Grammophon 35000/2 reissued on Preiser Records 90294

8. *The Society of British Composers Year Book* 1906-7; 1907-08 (Pinner, Mddx, J B McEwen)

9. Corder, Frederick: 'Recitation with Music' in *Voice, Speech and Gesture: a practical handbook to the elocutionary art* by H Campbell, R F Brewer, H Neville, Clifford Harrison, F Corder, Stanley Hawley. Edited with notes and introduction by R D Blackman (first published 1895) New and enlarged edition, Charles William Deacon & Co., 1904

10. Jecklin - Disco JD 592-2

11. 'Romantic Melodrama' Pamela Hunter, reciter and Koen Kessels, piano (Discover DICD 920245)

12. Reissued on 'Philadelphia Rarities' Leopold Stokoski Society LSCD 20; further reissued on Cala CACD 0501

13. For Lena Ashwell's war work see her book *Modern Troubadours: a record of Concerts at the Front.* Gylendal, 1922.

14. Cammaerts, Emile: *Belgian Poems* (John Lane, The Bodley Head, 1915)

15. 'London Symphony Orchestra: New Work by Elgar' unidentified cutting 8 December 1914 in Elgar cuttings books at Broadheath

16. 'Carillon': London Symphony Orchestra Concert, *Daily Chronicle,* 8 December 1914

17. *The Daily News* 8 December 1914

18. Quoted in a press advertisement for Harrison's concert on 1 March 1915.

19. *Daily Graphic* 20 April 1915

20. Unidentified cutting, Elgar cuttings books, Broadheath

21. Parry's diary for 1915 at Shulbrede Priory

22. *King Albert's Book – A Tribute to the Belgian King and People from Representative Men and Women throughout the World* (The Daily Telegraph, December 1914)

23. Sir Thomas Henry Hall Caine (1853-1931), popular novelist and writer, made his reputation in the late 1880s and 1890s. He had been an associate of Rossetti's in his last days and was particularly associated with the Isle of Man.

24. When Montague Phillips' setting was revived in 1998 the Broadheath singers had to commission a new orchestration from William Llewellyn , the full score being lost.

25. 'Sir Edward Elgar's New Work: Simple Hymn-like Music Breathing Nobility and Devotion' *The Universe* February 1916

26. This number was, in fact, cut from the BBC's broadcast production.

27. In private conversation with the author.

CHAPTER 9

STARLIGHT AND FAN:
Escape and Reality in Wartime

Andrew Neill

Near where yonder evening star
  Makes a glory in the air,
Lies a land dream-found and far
  Where it is light alway.
There those lovely ghosts repair
Who in sleep's enchantment are,
In Cockayne dwell all things fair –
  (But it is far away).[1]

In his invaluable study, *Elgar and the Wonderful Stranger*, K E L Simmons throws light on the background to the production of *The Starlight Express* for which Elgar wrote the incidental music in late 1915, his opus 78.[2] Dr Simmons shows how the play was adapted for the theatre, throws light on the abandoned ideas for a first production in 1914, and the fraught circumstances leading to the first night. He also shows how the composer Clive Carey became involved with this first production and how this added to the musical controversies that dogged Elgar at this time. During 1914 Carey composed music 'of which three [songs] survive as his Opus 18: The Organ Grinder's Song ('Oh! Children'), the Dustman's Song ('The busy Dustman'), and the Gardener's Song ('Stars are seeding in the air').[3] After this proposed production was abandoned in October 1914, it would seem that Carey was the last to be informed.

Dr Simmons provides an analysis of Elgar's music with a clear breakdown of the fifty musical numbers in the Novello hire score. Space does not permit such musical analysis here, and readers are directed to this study as background to the following.

It seems that the problems a modern audience would have in accepting *The Starlight Express* existed in 1915. The play, which Algernon Blackwood and more particularly Violet Pearn adapted

FACING PAGE: *Lena Ashwell*

from Blackwood's novel, *A Prisoner in Fairyland*, was a substantially altered and simplified version of the novel. In many respects it was a new story, although its complexity and dramatic emphasis remained the same until the end, when Pearn imposed the Christian imagery of the Christmas Star upon the narrative, a decision that was, it has been suggested, 'grotesque and inappropriate'.[4]

It is unlikely that Blackwood's novel and *The Starlight Express* would have much currency today if it were not for Elgar's music, and indeed the whole idea of the play and its production has been called 'pretentious and naïve'.[5] Nevertheless, many listeners find it a magical example of Elgar's ability to write tuneful, poignant and memorable music conjuring up an atmosphere within a few bars. This description can apply equally to the *Wand of Youth* music, which also derived from an early Elgarian fantasy of escape from reality. However, Blackwood's conception is not about escape. It is about creating an environment for those involved in reality so that they can lead their lives more effectively. His five hundred-page novel is a large canvass on which to lay out his idea. *The Starlight Express*, although not ignoring this premise, subtly changes the emphasis of the story which, by the end, becomes an intrusive religious experience as the earth finds its star: the star of the nativity.

The 'Starlight Express' exists on two levels. Firstly as an invisible train of thought, and secondly as the old coach which the 'retired from business man' Henry Rogers' father had installed in the family garden at 'Crayfield' in Kent. It was here that Rogers imagined or even found the Sprites that provide the crew and make up the passengers of the Express both in his dreams and in the train of thought. It is the children of his cousin, John Campden, and Henry Rogers with their ability of getting 'out' of themselves whilst asleep that forms the dramatic momentum of the story. The play simplifies and shortens the story but leaves in a number of characters that do little for its momentum, such as the three Governesses and a Miss Waghorn. Introduced into the play is the children's Grandmother, but it discards figures like Rogers' secretary, Minks, and the Austrian Countess who becomes part love interest for Rogers and partly some sort of puppet master or deus ex machina.[6] Perhaps the most successful version of the story is that adapted by Raymond Raikes for BBC radio in 1965. Raikes further simplifies the plot, removing characters not essential to the drama and he tightens up the momentum of the story.[7]

A PRISONER IN FAIRYLAND

(THE BOOK THAT 'UNCLE PAUL' WROTE)

BY

ALGERNON BLACKWOOD

AUTHOR OF 'JIMBO,' 'JOHN SILENCE,'
'THE CENTAUR,' 'EDUCATION OF UNCLE PAUL,' ETC.

MACMILLAN AND CO., LIMITED
ST. MARTIN'S STREET, LONDON

1913

LEFT: *Title page of*
A Prisoner in Fairyland
incorporating the
illustration
'Per aspera ad astra'
by K W Diefenbach

RIGHT:
'The Organ Grinder's Songs'
incorporating the poster design
for the production.

THE ORGAN GRINDER'S SONGS * FROM
THE * STARLIGHT * EXPRESS
WORDS BY ALGERNON BLACKWOOD
* MUSIC BY EDWARD ELGAR *

1. TO THE CHILDREN.
2. THE BLUE-EYES FAIRY.
3. MY OLD TUNES.

PRICE EACH 2/- NET.

ELKIN & CO., LTD.
8 & 10, BEAK STREET, REGENT STREET, LONDON, W.
NEW YORK · G. RICORDI & CO · TORONTO · THE ANGLO-CANADIAN MUSIC PUBLISHING CO

If the play simplifies the characters it does not clarify the plot and it is left to Raikes to do so by restricting the 'unwumbling' through the writing of Daddy's book, Mother becoming a happy and efficient manager of a home, the restoration of Madame Jequier's finance and Jane Anne cleaning efficiently. From the beginning of the novel, Henry Rogers has had in mind a charitable gesture along the lines of 'disabled thingamajigs'. He suddenly abandons these plans in favour of 'unwumbling' Bourcelles. So we are left with a curious tale where miracles can be wrought through Star Dust collected in Star Caves where the 'interfering sun' puts off the great enterprise and where the 'wumbled' are eventually 'unwumbled'. It is neither very dramatic nor is it easy to become sympathetic to the characters, except for the children. The play also allows something of a transformation for Jane Anne who moves to a position of equality with her younger siblings, Monkey and Jimbo. She is a more shadowy figure in the novel. It is her seventeenth birthday as the play begins, but it is only towards the end of the novel that she comes into focus when she seems to attract Henry Rogers (his star Orion, hers The Pleiades). Any embarrassment this development might suggest is countered by the introduction of the Austrian Countess as the novel ends.

Blackwood's story is complicated and overlong. These points need examining further, particularly in an age obsessed with fantasy, as it might be that the novel's hour could now have arrived. Much has been made of the similarity between the novel and the youthful Elgarian fantasy behind *The Wand of Youth* music, where misunderstood children lured adults across a brook to be transfigured by a 'fairy feeling necessary for their well-being'. On examination this similarity appears to be slim. In Blackwood's play it is the children that lead the adults to self-awareness and the discovery of sympathy, but their Uncle Henry Rogers is already ahead of them. It was, however, during his childhood that Uncle Henry made the discovery that was to enrich the lives of the 'wumbled' inhabitants of Bourcelles. All are 'wumbled' in some way. That is to say the Campdens and their neighbours live out of sympathy in ways to produce muddle, discontent and ineffectiveness.

Dr Simmons, in his useful summary of Blackwood's career, makes it clear that Blackwood knew the country around Boudry and Neuchâtel well, and like the Campden family had spent time living there economically whilst writing 'more books'. So it is from experience and love of the area that Blackwood locates the Campden family in Switzerland. This serves the useful dramatic purpose of distance from Britain but causes difficulties in reconciling the very English sprites with the 'foreign' location the production requires. The explanation that the Campden's are living in Bourcelles for reasons of economy is further explained by the fact that Edward Campden, their eldest son, is studying for the Consular Service in Britain, which absorbs about a third of the family income.

In considering the attraction of *The Starlight Express* to Elgar, it is the play we have to examine. Clearly Elgar would have read the novel, but it is the play his music supports. Everything we know about November and December 1915 suggests he became absorbed and enchanted with the play. His notes to the typed script demonstrate his

Algernon Blackwood with Sir Edward Elgar (Raymond Monk collection)

involvement, almost page by page, including Pearn's symbolic ending with the introduction of 'The First Nowell'. Blackwood's story is not a religious one, although the transformation through sympathy (a rare commodity in wartime), which affects everyone in Bourcelles, can be likened to a conversion or even a transfiguration. The essence of Blackwood's conception would seem to be summarised by John Campden (Daddy), particularly in defining his fairyland, as Campden struggles to express the ideas for his novel to Henry Rogers.

Algernon Blackwood - cartoon by Venceslas Borowski

> You see, all light meets somewhere. It's all one I mean. And so with minds. They all have a common meeting-place. Sympathy is the name for that place – that state – they feel with each other, see flash-like from the same point of view for a moment. And children are the conduits. They do not think things out. They feel them, eh? For you see, along these little channels that the children – my children, as I think I mentioned – keep sweet and open, there might troop back into the village – Fairyland. Not merely a foolish fairyland of make-believe and dragons and princesses imprisoned in animals, but a fairyland the whole world needs – the sympathy of sweet endeavour, love, gentleness and sacrifice for others. The stars would bring it – starlight don't you see?[8]

§   §   §

> ...The Sun,
> Closing his benediction,
> Sinks, and the darkening air
> Thrills with a sense of the triumphing night –
> Night with her train of stars
> And her great gift of sleep.[9]

It is at night that Blackwood's tale comes alive. Despite the discursiveness of his novel, particularly his lengthy description of the 'scaffolding of the night' in chapter twenty-two, the anticipation for what can be achieved after dark, getting 'out' [of the body] is well conveyed. Unfortunately it takes a long time to get to the point, something the play inevitably reaches more quickly. This, though, obscures the ecstatic atmosphere, which we can see surrounds the children with the feeling that the world is about to be changed. In the one line 'Come, gentle night; come, loving, black-brow'd night', Shakespeare achieves all this, together with anticipation, desire and the feeling that night is a secure, wonderful thing. Blackwood's complicated world never reaches this level of simple clarity.

We are left with the need to answer two questions. The first is why Elgar was attracted to *The Starlight Express* and quickly committed himself completely to the project. The second is to attempt to establish why the production was a failure, despite the enthusiasm of certain members of a devoted audience and reviewers.[10]

In less than two months an enormous score was produced. It was only on 9 November 1915 that the critic Robin Legge who introduced him to the idea contacted Elgar. The next day Lena Ashwell brought the play to Severn House and laid it before Elgar. Taking all the factors relating to *The Starlight Express*, into account: the story, the production, quality of writing, characterisation and those involved in the production it is possible to guess that Elgar's enthusiasm derived from four factors:

1. His interest in the story and its surface comparison to *The Wand of Youth*. However, it is likely this comparison would have quickly dissipated.

2. Elgar's respect for Robin Legge and the friendships established with Lena Ashwell and Algernon Blackwood. This would have more than made up for the inadequate production and the possibility of the ill-disguised hostility of Violet Pearn, whose idea it was to adapt the play. She was not impressed 'by Elgar's music' and in a letter to Clive Carey on 26 December 1915 she wrote: 'He's [Elgar] done the songs before the curtain quite well. The rest of the music – and there is masses of it – bores me to tears'.[11]

3. The commitment, once made, had set his creative mind racing and there was, in fact, no going back. (Disappointment in the production and the atmosphere in the theatre was subsequently offset by the desire of HMV to make a substantial recording of some of the music.)

4. Elgar was happy to embrace something that would take his mind off the war and the fact that the Loos offensive was not going to conclude hostilities in 1915, after all. He would have also have been able to turn his back on his work in the Hampstead Volunteer Reserve.

If we ignore the problems of the production and the dissatisfaction of both Blackwood and Elgar with the designer's ideas, we can see that the seeds of failure were sown in the ideas that formed the basis of the novel. Even taking into account the quality of Elgar's music, this could not save the production. In wartime, audiences need something to take them out of themselves with tunes to sing and a mixture of pathos and joy. Even though they had their tunes it is difficult to see how members of an audience, in late 1915, could identify with the problems of the Campdens and the people of Bourcelles. These were hardly substantial and much less than for its audience, a people in a country at war.

J M Barrie's *Peter Pan* preceded *The Starlight Express* by ten years. Blackwood echoes one or two themes from the older model, but this perennial favourite is a more layered, complex tale, with good versus evil and the intellectually challenging prospect of eternal youth to consider. *Peter Pan* is also amusing and escapist. Lena Ashwell hinted at the problem when she wrote to Elgar: 'The play is half reality & half fairyland & it is your help in fairyland I want so much'. In *Peter Pan* it is clear what 'Neverland' is and who lives there. In Blackwood's book the distinction between reality and fairyland is blurred and, with the obvious exception of 'The Laugher' and 'Woman of the Haystack', the sprites were all largely part of the Edwardian world with which an audience would have been familiar.

The humour in *The Starlight Express* is, sadly, heavy-handed. *Peter Pan* has also stood the test of time, surviving competition from varied sources for nearly 100 years. Although Blackwood's novel is edited substantially for the play, the production still contained many unnecessary characters. It is difficult to sympathise with the disagreeable Grannie, the impecunious Governesses and the demented Miss Waghorn. These characters, particularly in Act I, are there presumably to provide amusement during the handing out of clothes from a box sent by relations in Edinburgh. Raikes, in his BBC adaptation, rightly discards this scene and therefore all of these personalities, leaving Madame Jequier as the only representative of the village. The result is a clearer, cleaner plot. There are fewer diversions through discordant characterisation and a clearer view of Blackwood's message, or rather the one distorted by Violet Pearn.

In seventy minutes, Raikes effectively distils the novel and its variation the play, into something acceptable that also includes most of Elgar's music. Even taking into consideration changes in cultural attitudes ('out' has developed a contemporary meaning far from

Blackwood's world), we need to ask basic questions such as, do we care sufficiently about this 'wumbled family', Daddy's big idea and the healing power of starlight? Also, do we believe in Henry Rogers, and his plans? After the enchanting idea for his childhood, and the magical evocation of his garden, the train and the sprites we are left to conclude that their mission is hardly adequate for creatures so attractive and inventive. As the sprites become more obvious in Act 3, hiding behind curtains and furniture, there is and probably was a risk of risibility. An audience has to care about all the issues in a play, the characters and the challenges that they face. In the final analysis perhaps that is where the play failed, for the audience – any audience, could not generate sufficient *sympathy* for the story, the characters and their 'unwumbling'.

ဢ ဢ ဢ

The following is a cast list and short synopsis of *The Starlight Express*.

The characters in *The Starlight Express* are:

> Daddy (John Henry Campden)
> Mother (Henrietta Campden)
> Grannie (The Irish mother of Henrietta)
> Jane Anne (eldest daughter of the above, aged 17, also known as Jinny)
> Monkey (younger sister of Jane Anne, aged 12)
> Jimbo (brother to the above, aged 10)
> Henry Rogers (Cousin of John Campden)
> Madame (Widow) Jequier
> The Tramp/Organ-Grinder
> Children ('Street Arabs' who accompany the Organ-Grinder before the curtain)
> Miss Waghorn
> Three retired Governesses
> Pleiades
> Sprites: (including the Tramp), Lamplighter, Gardener, Dustman, Sweep, Woman of the Haystack, Little Winds, and Laugher.[12]

From the novel we know that Mr and Mrs Campden have been married for over 20 years and are in their early forties. 'Daddy' is an author, struggling to find the key to his latest book, 'bigger than anything I have tried to say before'. The play gives 'Mother' an Irish accent, but we know little beyond the fact that she is not able to cope easily with being a housewife. Jane Anne is pretty and excited about 'putting up her hair' and embracing life. She is an enthusiast and subject to complicated and contrived sayings and malapropisms,

Charles Mott with the children on stage in The Starlight Express

because she is 'wumbled in her mind when she doesn't get her words right'. She is responsible for keeping the family apartment clean.

The two younger children occupy a more central rôle in the novel than in the play where they share more of the 'unwmumbling' with Jane Anne. Jimbo appoints himself 'seketary' to 'cousinenry'. It is they who have already learnt to get 'out' at night.

Prelude. Accompanied by the 'street arabs' the Organ-Grinder enters and sings 'To the Children'.

Act I. In The Den, a room in 'La Citadelle' in the village of Bourcelles, Daddy is seen struggling to write. Jane Anne enters, dusting, and they talk about his difficulties, the impending arrival of Cousin Henry Rogers (prompted by the sight of a lamplighter in the street). Monkey and Jimbo enter and we learn of their own secret 'star society'. They are excitedly anticipating the opening of the large box of clothes that has been sent to them by relations in Edinburgh.

They all converse about starlight, and ideas develop which Daddy notes, particularly the thought that starlight goes into Star Caves. There is one 'on the slopes of Boudry where the forest dips towards the precipices of the Areuse. You get all clothed and covered with it [starlight] and come out "soft-shiny" as it sticks to you, and so you "stick" to other people. That's sympathy'.

Mother enters. She is obviously concerned about their family problems and the various unpaid bills to which she wishes Daddy would attend.

Grannie then enters grumbling, followed by the ladies from the 'Pension Wistaria': Madame Jequier, Miss Waghorn and the three Governesses. The box is unpacked (a time for confusion as the clothes are tried on). No one is satisfied, except Jane Anne who finds some bleu gauze, spangled with gold that reminds her of her favourite stars, the Pleiades. She covers her head and dances about the room.

The Organ-Grinder knocks on the door and brings in Cousin Henry's luggage. 'He's a coming'. By now the Governesses have left and Cousin Henry steps into the room and is made welcome. From the window he admires the stars in the sky and this leads to conversation with Jane Anne. They realise they are 'star cousins', as his constellation is that of Orion. Monkey and Jimbo guess he is 'wumbled' too with his scheme for 'disabled – er – thingumajigs' and enrol Cousin Henry in their society. They tell him how they get 'out' and arrange for a meeting the following night on the slopes above the Areuse precipices. The children are sent off to bed, but not before Jane Anne tells her father she will try and get him 'out' and 'un-wumble' him. 'I'll come while you're dreaming'. The curtain falls.

Prelude to Act II. The Organ-Grinder sings 'The Blue-eyes Fairy'.

Act II, scene 1 (part 1). Cousin Henry, Monkey and Jimbo sit at the edge of the Pine Forest in front of a fire. In the background, amongst rocks, is the Star Cave but it is too narrow for them to enter. The Star Society meets and they fall asleep as the Scaffolding of the Night begins its formation. Sprites appear and the Organ-Grinder sings the curfew song. The sprites hide and the children awake.

Act II, scene 1 (part 2). The same scene, but it is now night. The children, now 'out' (as their bodies are at home asleep) stand in front of the Star Cave from which a shaft of light shines. A shooting star appears. It is Jane Anne gathering stardust, and to their surprise she is also 'out'. She emerges from the cave announcing that she is collecting stardust for Mother and Daddy. The Starlight Express arrives, from which the sprites emerge and enter the cave. At last Cousin Henry takes the children into the cave: 'Everybody's thin somewhere'. They follow the sprites, loaded with stardust, and Jane Anne urges them to help Daddy before the 'interfering sun' arrives.

Act II Scene 2. An interlude leads to a room in the Pension, the children and cousin Henry scatter stardust over the sleeping figures of Madame Jequier and Miss Waghorn.

Act II Scene 3. Jane Anne and the Sweep are trying to get Mother and Daddy 'out'. The others arrive with other sprites who help them with Daddy. The rising sun means they now have to wait until the following night, but then they will all be 'out'. The Dawn Song brings down the curtain.

Act III Scene 1. The Den now looks 'unwumbled'. Jane Anne is dusting and sprites are hiding about the room. Madam Jequier's debts have been paid and she comes over to thank Cousin Henry but also reveals that Miss Waghorn has died in her sleep. The three Governesses and Grannie are now much happier and Daddy is almost bursting with the ideas for his book and Mother is now much happier. The children plan to get Daddy 'out' that night and the curtain falls as sprites peer out from behind curtains and furniture.

Act III, Scene 2 The Waltz interlude leads to the Pine Forest again, by the Star Cave. It is now ablaze with starlight as the sprites load up with stardust. Cousin Henry and the three children enter with Madame Jequier. Mother follows. She is now 'out'. Miss Waghorn ('out for ever') passes across the back of the stage and at last Daddy arrives and thanks everyone for leading him to realise his inspiration. All now face the eastern sky and the Pleiades come down to earth and dance. The day star rises. It is the source of Daddy's light and inspiration and rose when a Child was born. It is the star of love, and all turn to face it as the curtain falls.

ꙅ   ꙅ   ꙅ

Lena Ashwell was the link to *The Sanguine Fan* ballet of 1917, Elgar's opus 86. Her 'Concerts at the Front', a high-profile charity, required continued nurturing. In Chelsea a committee had been formed to raise funds for causes, which would include that of Lena Ashwell. So it was that Ina Lowther was introduced to Elgar by Alice Stuart Wortley who was a member of the executive committee for the Chelsea Matinee. Mrs Lowther visited the Elgars at Severn House on 7 February to 'lay the Chelsea Ballet idea before E'. Her knowledge of dance meant that she had been commissioned to talk to Elgar about the ballet. This would be based on the design by Charles Conder, drawn in sanguine on a fan owned by another member of the committee Mrs John Lane the wife of the publisher.

Charles Conder (1868 – 1909) was born in Britain, but travelled to Australia in 1883 where he became a surveyor in the bush. He was eventually able to follow his true interests when he moved to drawing for newspapers. From this occupation he was able to study at the Royal Art Society in Sydney from where he moved to Victoria to work with the great painters Fred McCubbin, Tom Roberts and Arthur Streeton. Conder returned to Europe and worked in Paris and eventually London. At the end of his life he lived in Cheyne Walk, Chelsea. His sympathies lay in French art and he associated with Lautrec and Anquetin in Paris where he came to lead a more and more dissolute life, which contributed to his early death. His many paintings were widely admired by Oscar Wilde and his circle, who were 'much attracted by Conder's paintings on silk, especially the fans'.[13] When back in London he became part of the circle that included Laurence Binyon, William Butler Yeats and William

Charles Conder - a drawing by William Rothenstein

Rothenstein. In 1900 he became engaged to Binyon's first love, the Irish artist Elinor Monsell.

Rothenstein has left us a shrewd assessment of Conder. 'His art was based partly on his sense of style, of gesture, of artificial comedy, in a word, the comedy of Davenant, of Congreve, and of Watteau and Fragonard; and in large measure too, on his subtle observation of actual life. Each side of his nature helped the other. He had a great feeling for form, but because of an incomplete equipment, he was never able to attain the disciplined art of Watteau, of Gainsborough and of Fragonard. Yet Conder has a place in English art. He is one of the rare lyrical painters, singing now with the morning, innocence of the lark, now with the more sinister note of the nightjar.' [14]

Conder's Sanguine Fan leads the eye into the middle distance as a 'gentleman' in tri-corn hat, his hands clasped behind his back, talks to a lady seated on the ground. Trees, which fill the background to the right, open out to show a bright but clouded background that beckons the eye beyond the rising ground. To the right, another couple face the viewer. They are also dressed as in the mid 18th century. Stone cupids beckon to them. To the left Pan and Echo inhabit the same world, but their backs are turned to the human figures.

Part of the intention, for the one performance, was for well-known stage personalities rather than professional dancers, to perform the leading rôles. Consequently Gerald du Maurier took the part of Pan, Ina Lowther that of Echo, Fay Compton the First Girl and Ernest Thesiger the First Young Man. Ina Lowther's scenario took the following form:

SIR ADRIAN BOULT
London Philharmonic Orchestra
ELGAR
FALSTAFF-Symphonic Study

THE SANGUINE FAN-Ballet
Fantasia and Fugue in C minor
(transcription from J.S.Bach)

EMI

Sir Adrian Boult's LP recording of The Sanguine Fan, *the sleeve reproducing a fan designed by Conder*

Scene: – A glade. To the left there is an ancient shrine with a somewhat disfigured statue of Eros. To the right a little bridge spanning a dip in the glade. The ground rises slightly to the back of the scene.

Pan enters piping. He moves lazily across the scene, which seems redolent with his personality – he looks around in a sleepy way, and dropping his pipes, he curls himself up to sleep at the foot of a tree, against which he is hardly distinguishable.

Enter 1st Young Man, elaborately dressed in Louis XV costume. He walks quickly over to the shrine, evidently expecting to find someone waiting for him, but finding no one, he looks at his watch and seats himself at the foot of the statue, and takes out his snuff box.

At this moment two Ladies (also in Louis XV costume) enter hurriedly, talking and laughing together, and tripping gaily along. They almost reach the shrine before seeing the Young Man, who at their approach jumps up and goes forward to greet them. The Girls' manner immediately changes and they become prim and sedate, curtseying deeply to the Young Man, who bows in return. 1st Girl drops her fan in the excitement of the meeting, and the Young Man picks it up and returns it to her. This separates them a little from the 2nd Girl who is obviously de trop, and she wanders away where she meets 2nd and 3rd Young Men and 3rd Girl, who enter.

While they are greeting each other and talking, the 1st Young Man and 1st Girl have moved over to the bridge, the Young Man declaring his passion, which is reciprocated by the girl. As they reach the bridge, he takes her in his arms, kissing her tenderly. Their companions who have joined them unawares see this, and there is much laughter and chaffing until the culprits are forced to confess their love. Their companions insist on the happy couple complying with ancient the custom connected with the shrine of Eros, and blindfolding the 1st Young Man. They dance around him, drawing him to the shrine where, fate being against him, he chooses the wrong arrow (thunder) much to the consternation of his loved one, and a quarrel ensues as they wander from the glade, followed by their companions.

Echo now makes her appearance, dancing in gaily; she is very light-hearted and full of mischief. While dancing, she suddenly observes Pan asleep, and hastily picking up a handful of flowers, she runs across and throws them stingingly in his face, dancing away immediately with an innocent air.

Pan wakes angrily, and starting up he sees Echo, and at once falls madly in love with her. She leads him on, and they dance together until they finally fall exhausted and Pan, taking his pipes, plays to Echo and the glade vibrates with the passion of his song till at last he falls asleep.

Three Shepherdesses enter, bringing gifts for Pan, who they know haunts the grove. Every day they bring him offerings of fruit etc. They look to see if their carefully hidden gifts of yesterday have been received, and finding them gone, they place fresh fruits for the god. As they do so, they catch sight of Pan and Echo and creep silently away.

Re-enter 1st Girl, closely followed by 1st Young Man; she is evidently still angry with him, and he is entreating her for mercy. He laughs at her fears of disaster and tries to comfort her. But she will not listen to him, and in an outburst of temper he curses Eros, scattering the presents which lie at the god's feet.

As he does this, there is an ominous rumble of thunder which seems to vibrate the statue. The Young Man pauses abruptly, and Echo (who has been watching this scene) snatches up Pan's pipes, and creeping up to the Young Man, pipes to him temptingly of the world. The mortal girl, relenting a little, now makes advances to the Young Man. But the echo of the world has fired his imagination, and he will not listen to her but pursues Echo.

Meantime Echo has disguised herself as a mortal, and being now visible to the lovers, completely captivates the Young Man, who is enslaved by her attraction and is oblivious to all else.

As they dance, Pan rouses from his slumber, and recognizing Echo (who is in the Young Man's arms), becomes wracked with jealous wrath and utters one of his wild shouts, which strikes terror to the heart of the Young Man. Forsaking Echo, he runs to the shrine for protection. (The light grows dim, thunder rolls, and the glade becomes a whirling mass of shadowy forms, nymphs, satyrs, the winds etc). The Young Man, followed by Pan, reaches the statue. As he does so, Pan raises his arm as if to strike him. There is a vivid flash of lightning, apparently coming from the torch of Eros, and the Young Man falls senseless to the ground. The thunder rolls and dies gradually away.

Echo, having dropped her disguise, runs to Pan with her arms outstretched. The sun breaks through once more. Pan turns as if to strike her, but is again arrested by her beauty, and seizing her in a mad embrace, lifts her in his arms and runs off with her through the trees.

The mortal girl throws herself on her knees beside the prostrate figure of her lover. Pan pauses half way up the incline, looks back at them over his shoulder and laughs sardonically as the curtain falls.

Although this may have been escapism, hidden amongst the elegance and brittle decadence of 18th Century France, 'ingredients that might have attracted a Hofmannsthal and Richard Strauss',[15] there is a cynical aspect to the plot not out of keeping with the time. The composition of the score gave Elgar another month of concentrating on something other than the war, as well as pleasing the 'Windflower' (Alice Stuart Wortley). He scored the work more fully than the resources available for the revue (Flute for Echo on stage, single woodwind for Pan's answering clarinet, two horns, harp, percussion and strings), giving, in 'the wind solos throughout the work … a late Straussian poise and charm'.[16] Despite the proposed one performance, the quality of the music and those involved was matched by the contribution by the designer George Sheringham who was responsible for the costumes and scenery.

The story is a simple one with the gods controlling man and his destiny, unlike the real world outside which must have appeared

Ina Lowther dances in one of her productions, believed to be The Sanguine Fan

increasingly God-forsaken. This caprice was written and scored over a period of one month, an example of how naturally music flowed from Elgar's pen when the circumstances were sympathetic. As in *The Starlight Express*, he had produced something far more substantial and complex in a short time than might have been expected by the commissioners. This created an inevitable contrast to the other material in the review. The press at once recognised its difference to the rest of 'Chelsea on Tip-Toe', and the danger arising from that difference:

> If there was any chance of 'Chelsea on Tip-Toe' being revived, that various entertainment, presented at the Chelsea Palace last Tuesday in aid of 'Concerts at the Front', would deserve notice at length. But it is over and done with; and it must suffice to say that, on the whole, it was a very good joke at the expense of Chelsea and her great men, from the days of Rosetti to the day of John. The Conder ballet, with Sir Edward Elgar's music, was beautiful; the John heavy chorus was neither so beautiful nor so funny as it might have been. But the whole thing made a fairly original entertainment, not without appeal to lovers of wit and fun.
>
> Very graceful and charming, on the other hand, was the Conder ballet, written and produced by Mrs Christopher Lowther, with music by Sir Edward Elgar. Upon Mrs Christopher Lowther and Mr Gerald du Maurier fell the chief burden of the dancing and very pleasantly they acquitted themselves of the task.

For another writer cataloguing the items in the Matinee programme, the difference emerged thus:

> After this came something really beautiful—namely, the 'Conder Fan' ballet to music by Sir Edward Elgar . . . Here there was not only a 'pleasant fable of amorous Pan and fugitive Echo and passion-haunted eighteenth-century beaux and belles to lend the hint...' [17]

An attempt to save the ballet was made later on 22 May, when it was part of another variety show at a matinee performance put on at the Palace Theatre. Elgar added a Shepherd's Dance to the score for the shepherdesses who arrive at the half waypoint in the ballet. We have seen from Alice Elgar's diary that the Palace Theatre matinée was not a successful occasion, with the Ballet slotted into a programme of astonishing variety.

> May 22. E. & A. to Palace Theatre for Conder Ballet – Most things dull a <u>very</u> heavy dull audience – Why shd. Philanthropy make ladies so oppressively stupid? The Ballet a perfectly lovely gem – The music entrancing & <u>beautifully</u> played – Actors charming –lighting not quite right – The Italian Masque senselessly dull – lovely costumes.

The matinée was 'In aid of The War Emergency Fund of the Church of England Waifs & Strays Society under the gracious patronage of Her Majesty Queen Alexandra'. The programme began with an Overture by the Theatre Orchestra under the direction of Herman Finck and unfolded with the following:

Blanche Gaston-Murray singing a song and reciting a monologue, Daisy Kennedy, violin, then played works by Kreisler and Zimbalist. Gwendoline Brogden with the 'Palace Girls' in an excerpt followed this from Vanity Fair by Finck. Muriel Foster followed with Tosti's Farewell and Love went a-riding by Frank Bridge. Benno Moiseiwitsch then played Chopin's Impromptu in A flat, Etude in F and Chant Polonaise (arranged by Liszt). At last the bill announced:

'The Conder Ballet'
Written and produced by Mrs. Christopher Lowther
Music by Sir Edward Elgar OM, who will conduct the Orchestra

Pan	Mr Gerald du Maurier
1st Young Man	Mr Ernest Thesiger
1st Girl	Miss Fay Compton
2nd Girl	Miss Kathleen Blake
3rd Girl	Miss Doris Lytton
2nd Young Man	Mr C D Jeffries
3rd Young Man	Mr A Grayson
Echo	Mrs Christopher Lowther

Shepherds & Shepherdesses, Nymphs, Satyrs, Girls, Dryads, The Winds, Butterflies

The afternoon ended with Mr Finck and the Palace Orchestra taking centre stage again to be followed by Miss Dorothy Holmes-Gore will recite

'The Banquet'
An Italian Masque of the Renaissance
arranged by the Hon. Mrs. Harold Nicholson
The Dolmetsches perform in the 3rd Dance

The long afternoon finished with 'Mr. Nelson Keys auctioning by invitation', 'Miss' Ivy Shilling and Mr Fred Leslie in 'La Dame du Vaurien' from 'Three Cheers', an excerpt from 'Sir Walter Raleigh' and 'God Save the King'.

It was the infant Gramophone that rescued the music from complete obscurity as it did with *The Starlight Express*. On 24 February 1920, three years after the ballet had been forgotten, Elgar conducted a selection that would fit on one side of a disc. The opening minuet was linked to the Shepherd's Dance and that of Echo. Elgar worked on this arrangement a few days before the recording sessions that included music from *The Wand of Youth* and *Enigma Variations*; and that was the last heard of the music until EMI, Sir Adrian Boult and the London Philharmonic Orchestra rescued it over fifty years later.

NOTES and SOURCES

1. Duclaux, Agnes: *Cockayne Country*, quoted in Blackwood, Algernon: *A Prisoner in Fairyland*, chapter 8
2. 'Elgar and the Wonderful Stranger: Music for The Starlight Express' from Monk, Raymond (ed): *Elgar Studies* (Scolar Press, 1990)
3. *ibid*, pp 158-159
4. Harper Scott, Paul: The Starlight Express. A lecture given to The Elgar Society in University College, Worcester, 1 September 2001
5. Anderson, Robert: Elgar, J M Dent, 1993, p.268
6. Harper Scott calls the introduction of the Countess, in the last few pages of the novel, 'a disturbing twist'. It seems she had 'twisted every law of the physical universe just to bring him (Cousin Henry) to her. She had orchestrated all the wonders of his youth, set off the net of stars and thought alive the sprites. She had sought him all these years, [and her] introduction after the story appears to be over is, it must be said, something of a dirty trick on Blackwood's part and it changes utterly our reading of all that has gone before'.
7. Raikes was the son of Charles Raikes (1879-1945) who was considered as designer for the Starlight Express production. Charles Raikes was the son of a cousin of Alice Elgar.
8. Blackwood, Algernon: *A Prisoner in Fairyland* (Macmillan & Co, 2nd edition, 1928) pp 239-240
9. By W E Henley, quoted *ibid*, chapter 7)
10. See Simmons, *op cit*, p 183
11. Monk, *op cit*, p 181
12. In the BBC radio production of 1965 the Organ-Grinder (sung by Dennis Dowling) and Tramp were played separately. Grannie, Miss Waghorn, the Governesses, the Pleiades, the 'Children' and The Woman of the Haystack were not included.
13. Rothenstein,William: *Men & Memories 1872-1900* (Coward-McCann Inc, 1931) p 90
14. Rothenstein,William: *Men & Memories 1900-1922* (Coward-McCann Inc, 1931) pp 177-178
15. Anderson, Robert: *Elgar* (J M Dent, 1993) p 269
16. *ibid*, p 270
17. From a note by Jerold Northrop Moore accompanying the first recording of the ballet by Sir Adrian Boult, ASD 2970 (EMI 1974)

CHAPTER 10

AN ELGARIAN TRAGEDY
Remembering Charles Mott

Charles A Hooey

Elgarians and music lovers in general who visit the Somme area of northern France may find it rewarding to stop by the grave of a singer who was a special friend to Elgar, perhaps to say a prayer for this unfortunate free spirit who was cut down at thirty-seven years of age.

Charles James Mott was born about 1880, the son of Henry Isaac and Eliza Brockley Mott, who lived in the East Finchley/Highgate district in north central London, four or five miles from Covent Garden, his future stamping ground. It is unlikely proximity to the great hall of song influenced his development, but he did find music at an early age. As a boy chorister, he sang with St James's Church Choir at Muswell Hill in London. Upon reaching young adulthood, he fancied himself a banker but failed to consider its repetitive nature so, to ease the boredom, he would sing, softly, as he worked, thus giving rise to 'the legend of the singing bank clerk'. Such carefree behaviour in the 1890s did not go unnoticed, but happily his superiors were willing to help rather than chastise. They allowed him to stay as long as he confined his singing to after hours. This proved ideal and led Charles to study voice with Josiah Booth and later to work with Henry Stanley on finishing.

Good fortune continued to smile, as somehow his path crossed that of Baron Frédéric d'Erlanger, composer, financier and best of all, a force within the Royal Opera Syndicate. The Baron took to this brash young singer, bursting with grand ideas and pressed his case with his associates. As a result, young Charles was soon in Berlin studying with famous basso Paul Knüpfer. After a year of steady progress, Knüpfer was confident an audition with the Hofoper at Dessau would net Mott a two year posting as principal baritone. It did.

By 1906 he was back in London, pursuing his studies with Madame Novello Davies while eagerly awaiting chances to sing. An opportunity came on 26 October with Choughs, a prominent

FACING PAGE: *Charles Mott*

London-based society that offered concerts regularly in the Grand Hall of the Cannon Street Hotel, to sing in a variety show with Alex Webster, Fred Ranalow and a concertina player named Alex Price. It went so well he was welcomed back on 1 February, this time to share the stage with a promising newcomer, 'J F McCormack' along with Ernest Pike and Alfred Heather, Conway Dixon, Percy Frostick and Sydney Walter, G D Cunningham providing accompaniment.

Prior to the Spring Season of 1909, Charles approached The Royal Opera to see if he was still welcome. As a d'Erlanger prospect, he was greeted with open arms and signed as opening day on 26 April neared. But instead of singing a leading rôle or two,

Paul Knüpfer

he was fed a steady diet of small, support parts. In Meyerbeer's grandiose *Les Huguenots*, for instance, superb singing is needed – thus a performance is known as 'The Night of Seven Stars' – but when The Royal Opera gave its version in Italian on 9 June, Mott sang Méru, a Catholic noble, a player with only a few good lines. He could only watch the greats – Luisa Tetrazzini, Emmy Destinn, Giovanni Zenatello, Antonio Scotti, Marcel Journet, Alice O'Brien and Murray Davey – and dream of being one of those 'Seven Stars' someday.

Next we hear of him as a mainstay in a Wagner Festival staged in Buda-pesth, as it was known in 1912. The following February in Edinburgh, he sang with Carrie Tubb in music of Beethoven as part of an orchestral festival overseen in style by Michael Balling. They gave five concerts.

At this moment in time, Mott became involved with Raymond Roze, son of soprano Marie Roze, as he prepared to present six weeks of grand opera in English at Covent Garden. In fact, it seemed his main goal was to give his own *Joan of Arc* lots of exposure. A serious problem though was causing a delay; he lacked a top flight baritone. When Mott heard this news, he showed up asserting, 'I'm your man!' and settled in to prepare all the baritone tasks. Roze conducted his masterwork on 1 November 1913 with Mott as Philip, Duke of Burgundy. What is there to say of this dreary affair? Roze gave his all but *Joan of Arc* proved an unrelenting four hour bore, brightened only by the splash of colourful costumes. Roze remained optimistic, pushing it through no fewer than twenty performances! On 8 November, Mott could at last tear into a meatier rôle as Kurwenal in *Tristan Und Isolde* with John Coates and Marta Wittkowska, and then, on 4 December, accomplish the same as Telramund in *Lohengrin* with Coates and Lillian Granfelt. Finally, he donned toreador's breeches for *Carmen* with Violet Essex and Pauline Donalda.

Early in 1914, The Royal Opera began its own German Opera Festival at the Garden, retaining Mott for four of its five operas. First he took part in a most historic occasion. On 2 February, he sang the Second Knight of the Grail when Wagner's *Parsifal* was given, in German, for the first time in England. Heinrich Hensel was Parsifal, Eva von der Osten Kundry and his old mentor, Paul Knüpfer Gurnemanz. Artur Bodanzky conducted. One of the Flower Maidens was Rosina Buckman, a soprano from New Zealand, who would distinguish herself later as the first to sing Elgar's complete *Spirit of England*. *Parsifal* received fourteen performances.

The next night featured another 'first', Etiénne Méhul's *Joseph* with Johannes Sembach as the hero and Mott as Judah with Percy Pitt conducting. It was a Beecham initiative that a critic liked.

> Méhul's *Joseph* has hitherto been excluded from the English stage on account of its biblical libretto; and it is well that Mr. Beecham is the first to take advantage of the wider views which now prevail in such matters, to give us so beautiful a work.

It was repeated on 6, 9 and 17 of February.

Mott sang Melot when *Tristan und Isolde* was mounted on 11 February with Jacques Urlus and Eva von der Osten in the title rôles with Friedrich Plaschke as Kurwenal and Albert Coates conducting. In *Meistersinger* on 21 February, he sang the Nachtigal with Plaschke as Sachs, Claire Dux as Eva, Knüpfer as Pogner and August Kiess as

Kothner. Elgar came on 5 March, anticipating the final *Tristan und Isolde* but the curtain rose instead on *Die Meistersinger*, thus Elgar 'discovered' Charles Mott, now in Kiess's rôle. As a rule, Elgar disliked English singers but he warmed to Mott and decided to help him. On 16 March, he wrote to Percy Pitt:

> I wish you would cast Charles Mott for Kothner again – he is far and away the best I have ever seen – I have sent a note to Mr Higgins telling him this as he may not have been present on that chance evening.

Then to Mott himself he offered encouragement:

> I have seen more representations of the opera than I care to count, but have never seen this part done in so entirely satisfactory a manner.[1]

He also urged Ivor Atkins, coordinator of The Three Choirs Festival at Worcester, to have Mott sing in Gerontius, adding

> I wish you might (also) hear him as a possible Elijah – I think a little new blood wd do good. He sang some of it to me finely . . .[2]

For the next Garden season beginning on 28 April, Artur Nikisch conducted *Die Götterdämmerung* with an all-star array that included Gertrud Kappel, Peter Cornelius, Louise Kirkby Lunn, Paul Knüpfer and Charles Mott. His other activities that season, if any, remain unknown. On 28 July, the Company closed its doors as England prepared to wage war.

Elgar was still promoting Mott, writing to Atkins again on 1 June:

> I suppose Kirkby Lunn will do Gerontius; you did not tell me. What is Charles Mott doing? I hope you will like him. I heard him do (since Kothner) Gunther, & the Herald in *Lohengrin*, both good.

In fact, Atkins did hear Charles Mott, was duly impressed and engaged him to sing the Priest in *Gerontius* with Coates and Kirkby Lunn. Nothing came of *Elijah* nor of anything else as the festival was cancelled.[3]

With troops on the march, Mott turned his attention to a series of weekly concerts. In Bournemouth, he very likely sang Easthope Martin's *Speed the Plough* and the cycle *Songs of The Open Country*, music he much favoured.

Adelina Patti chose to bid her final 'farewell' at the Royal Albert Hall on Saturday afternoon, 24th of October 1914, determined to make her 'Great Patriotic Concert in Aid of the European War Fund' memorable. Patti herself sang with Mott, Carrie Tubb, Phyllis Lett, Plunket Greene, George Parker, the Royal Choral Society under regular leader, Sir

Frederick Bridge, the Queen's Hall Orchestra conducted by Sir Henry
Wood and the massed bands of H M Brigade of Guards led by Capt J
Mackenzie Rogan. The stage must have groaned.

Mott had his chance to sing *Elijah* in Nottingham on 4 November
with the Sacred Harmonic Society, Laura Evans-Williams, Frank
Webster and Helen Blain, Allen Gill presiding. Then, on 15 November,
came the sad news that Field Marshal Lord Roberts had died while
visiting troops in France. Atkins decided to hold a special service in his
memory on the 19th in the form of an organ recital with Mott to sing
'Proficiscere' from *Gerontius*. On the 21st Elgar wrote to Atkins:

> I am so very sorry I could not get down to Worcester on Thursday. What
> an excellent choice – proficiscere, & Mott, I hope, sang well.[4]

'Proficiscere, anima Christiana!', meaning 'Go forth upon thy
journey, Christian soul!', was music suiting the occasion, and with
Mott's skill and experience, surely it could not have been rendered
with more feeling; Elgar need not have worried.

§   §   §

The composer was now busy responding to a friend, actress Lena
Ashwell's need for incidental music for *The Starlight Express*, a play
she wished to produce at year's end in the Kingsway Theatre.
Authors Algernon Blackwood and Violet Pearn were drawing ideas
from Blackwood's own novel, *A Prisoner in Fairyland* while matters
of costume and scenery design were entrusted to Henry Wilson,
President of the Arts and Crafts Society. For the key rôle of the
Organ-Grinder, Elgar had designated Mott.

The play's theme was the significance of childhood vision in a world
sullied by the mistakes of grown-ups. Its timing was perfect for late in
the autumn of 1915 the Great War was crunching through its second
horrifying year, and if ever there was a monument raised to the
stupidity and wretchedness of the adult world, this was it. The authors
would discover to their dismay that trying to create a show with and for
children but with a powerful message for adults was not an easy task.

Blackwood wrote to Elgar on 15 December, acknowledging his
request that he see Mott in action.

> You want me to hear Charles Mott and I long to. I suppose you realise that
> your music is the most divine, unearthly thing ever written ..It makes me
> happy all day long, and I want to cry and sing. It will go all over the
> world, I know. I shall simply burst when I hear Mott sing it.

Blackwood wrote again on 21 December, now much concerned.

> Mr Wilson has designed the Sprite in the spirit of Greek
> fantasy..Lamplighter a quasi-Mercury, Gardener as Priapus, or someone
> else, and Sweep possibly as Pluto. It is a false and ghastly idea. There is
> nothing pagan in our little Childhood Play. It is an alien symbolism
> altogether. It robs our dear Sprites of all their significance as homely
> childhood Figures. Don't you think so too? If our Play means anything at
> all, it means God..not the gods. But Mr Wilson is obsessed with Greece..[5]

His concerns were aired far too late. On this rather ominous note *The
Starlight Express* opened at the Kingsway on 29 December 1915, on
schedule. To *The Musical Times* Mott was the key.

> A feature of the presentation is an organ-grinder, a kind of Pied Piper, who,
> with a group of children, makes his appearance before each Act. Some of
> the music allotted to this character is searchingly expressive – the first song
> particularly. Mr Charles Mott was a highly sympathetic exponent.

Rounding out the cast were V B Clarence who fussed as Daddy, the
frazzled author/dreamer, Ruth Maitland as a far more practical
Mother and Clytie Hine as The Laugher 'who sings trouble into joy.'...

> (The music) is certainly the main lure. It affords a glimpse of a quality of
> Elgar's genius that owing probably to lack of encouragement, has not yet
> been sufficiently explored. We had a foretaste of its potentialities in the
> *Wand of Youth* Suites, which resurrected some of Elgar's youthful fancies,
> and much of the music is deftly woven into *The Starlight Express*. The
> scoring is delightfully dainty ...dance-music especially is captivating, and
> many of the songs and other incidental music have conspicuous melody
> and rhythmic grace.[6]

After Mott's death was announced, Herman Klein wrote:

> His singing of the Organ-Grinder's songs acquires a double pathos, so full
> is it of tenderness, repose and sustained charm.

The music was superb, quite unlike anything previous from Elgar, the
singing actors as a whole were praised, but as expected, both story
and staging drew criticism. For such an auspicious time, Elgar was to
have conducted but four days earlier, Alice had suffered a severe
concussion when her automobile was struck by a taxi during a
wartime blackout. As well, Elgar had just lost a nephew to
tuberculosis; altogether, not a happy time. He chose to remain by his
wife's side as *The Starlight Express* took flight.

Wulstan Atkins, Ivor's eleven year old son, closely followed every
aspect, and of a meeting between his father and Elgar at the

beginning of January, wrote:

> Elgar told him that *The Starlight Express* was running at the Kingsway Theatre, and though he did not like the sets, he was pleased with the music and especially the songs.

Then after attending a performance:

> I expected to see Elgar conducting, but in fact the young Julius Harrison appeared on the rostrum. My disappointment soon disappeared, however, when Elgar's fascinating overture began and when the Organ-Grinder, Charles Mott, appeared on the apron of the stage to sing his first song, 'O children, open your arms to me'. Soon I was completely absorbed..[7]

Composer and critic Thomas Dunhill compared it with Elgar's other wartime works.

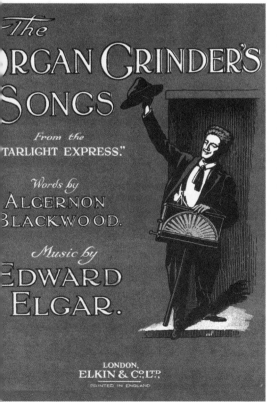

> Of slighter texture, but far more musical importance, were the delicate entr'actes and songs which Elgar wrote for Algernon Blackwood's fantastic children's play, *The Starlight Express* . . . the music which accompanied it does not deserve to be forgotten. It is of altogether finer quality than that of the ephemeral songs called *Fringes of the Fleet* .[8]

By avoiding the opening, Elgar escaped further upset while registering his displeasure. Why did the infernal staging have to differ so much from his childhood memories? As reports began to trickle in, his dark mood gradually lifted and he ended up attending regularly throughout January. His music was not enough however to stem the inevitable and the show closed after a single month.

Cover of 'The Organ Grinder's Songs' depicting Mott in the role.

Disappointed, Elgar's spirits were lifted nicely when executives from The Gramophone Company asked him to sign a new recording contract, offering to record four sides from *The Starlight Express* with Charles Mott in the bargain. Elgar held out for eight. They agreed and in 1916, what amounted to nothing less than a recording miracle, was achieved. Elgar saw it more as an opportunity to preserve forever his intense personal and private memories.

Mott revisited *Elijah* in Liverpool on 16 February 1916 with tenor Alfred Heather. Two days later, he was back at Hayes for the recording session as the Organ-Grinder; while Agnes Nicholls, another Elgar favourite, sang the Laugher's songs. All eight records were made on that one day. They were hurriedly produced and introduced two months later at a lavish press party in the Savoy Hotel. On 13 March, a set was thrust into Elgar's hands just as Blackwood arrived for an extended stay; it is easy to imagine these starry-eyed creators reliving their *Starlight* adventure thanks to the magic of the Gramophone. The Motts and child visited on the 26th to share tea and biscuits and presumably also had a chance to marvel at the recorded wonders.[9]

ഗ   ഗ   ഗ

That summer Mott must have meant to sing with Beecham's Opera Company in Manchester for his name appears on the roster in the programme for Stanford's *The Critic* on 10 May. No evidence was found to show he performed there at all.

Instead he became caught up in the frenzy attending Clara Butt's latest extravaganza on behalf of war relief. To give fellow Londoners a lift, something to ease wartime doldrums, Clara had devised a weeklong series of concerts with *The Dream of Gerontius* as the central element. Just the ticket, she felt, especially with the composer conducting, herself as the Angel, Gervase Elwes as Gerontius and Charles Mott as Angel of the Agony. On Mott she was adamant. He could not possibly refuse, or perhaps he felt he would benefit more, singing with Clara than being lost on a Manchester stage.

After pre-London airings in Leeds on 3rd May and the next day in Bradford, they moved to London to open a six-concert stand in Queen's Hall on 8 May. In his rôle, Mott 'sang with all the fervour of his strong temperament.' For an enormous audience on hand on 19 May when the King and Queen attended, Mott and Clara sang with Maurice d'Oisly as Gerontius, replacing an ailing Elwes. Beforehand,

The Fringes of the Fleet

LEFT:
*from HMV's
promotional
leaflet for*
Fringes of the
Fleet

Photo by Hana Studios, Ltd.

CHARLES MOTT

Assisted by Messrs. Frederick Henry, Frederick Stewart and
Harry Barratt, with orchestral accompaniment played by THE
SYMPHONY ORCHESTRA. Conducted by

SIR EDWARD ELGAR, O.M.

Words by Rudyard Kipling.

THE patriotic side of Elgar's genius has again found a remarkable expression in his latest song-cycle "The Fringes of the Fleet," which has delighted large audiences at the Coliseum for many weeks recently. England's glory and greatness have indeed always been a source of inspiration to our premier composer, whether it is of the past—as for example in "Caractacus"—or the present, as in "Land of Hope and Glory" and the "Pomp and Circumstance" Marches. Rudyard Kipling's fine lines on the heroes of England's matchless sea power, the men who do the "dirty work" on the ocean, have found a remarkable response in the composer, who has given us of his very best in this work.

The music of each of the four songs has the true atmosphere of the sea, and the breezy personality of these men who sweep the "mines reported in the fairway," who stalk the submarine in its lair, or take their chance with the deep as sportsmen. All of them have a rhythm and melody that haunts the memory with its sense of power and its splendid feeling.

12-inch Records 5/6

02734	"The Fringes of the Fleet"	... No. I.—The Lowestoft Boat.	*Kipling—Elgar.*
02735	"The Fringes of the Fleet"	... No. II.—Fate's Discourtesy.	*Kipling—Elgar.*
02736	"The Fringes of the Fleet"	... No. III.—Submarines.	*Kipling—Elgar.*
02737	"The Fringes of the Fleet"	... No. IV.—The Sweepers.	*Kipling—Elgar.*

The above songs are solos.   Published by Enoch & Sons.

BELOW:
*newspaper
cartoon from an
unattributed
cutting*

"FOUR ROUGH AND READY SAILORMEN YOU SEE UPON THE STAGE"

RIGHT:
A contemporary newspaper review of Fringes of the Fleet

BELOW :
The Fringes of the Fleet *at the Coliseum Theatre, June 1917:
from left to right,
Frederick Stewart,
Charles Mott,
Harry Barratt and
Frederick Henry*

the courage and daring of the men who make it their home and who spend their lives upon it. These songs conjured up in my mind images of fishing boats tacking their way through sunshine and storm, grey-coated men-of-war night and day defending the shores of old England from invasion ; mine-sweepers scouring the seas, alert patrol-ships darting alongside of vessels and demanding their destination and the name of their captain, brave old weather-beaten tramp-steamers from all parts of the world, and kindly light-ships tossing through the long dark night with their lights attached to their masts.

There was one glorious song whose delightful melody came wandering through my mind in particular. " The Lowestoft Boat " it was called, and Kipling's words and Sir Edward Elgar's music harmonise so completely that the song is a work of art. Indeed, all the breezy sea-songs which this great composer has so marvellously set to music in " The Fringes of the Fleet," sung by Charles Mott, form a song-cycle which is undoubtedly a masterpiece. Three more of these rhythmical songs of the sea I recalled as I sat there on the wet

was " Fate's Discourtesy," " The Sweepers," and " Submarines," and, gazing out with dreamy reminiscent eyes across the heaving grey-green water, it seemed to me that the American copy-writer had struck a big truth when he said that music was the universal language of the emotions, for if ever any composer expressed the emotions of the sea, Sir Edward Elgar did when he composed " The Fringes of the Fleet," and the Gramophone Co., Ltd., rendered humanity a service when they secured permission to record this great composition on their famous " His Master's Voice " Records. The song of the sea, and the story of the men who are in truth its children, has been caught and held, that all lovers of music and the out-of-doors may grow happy hearing it.

The rhetoric of the sea, with all its passion and restlessness, can only be adequately expressed through the medium of music. Music alone of all the arts can convey a sense of rapture, melancholy, joy or sorrow to the mind. It vibrates with the emotion of the composer ; it is redolent of wind on the hills and foam-sprayed cliffs, laughing waters, and the shining sunlit sea.

experts had scoffed at Butt's plan. 'A whole week based on oratorio will surely lose money,' they asserted, in words to that effect. In fact, many were turned away and a princely sum was raised for the Red Cross. Clearly Clara had judged the mood of the people better than anyone.

On 22 November, Mott faced Elgar's *Dream* again at a Hallé Concert in Birmingham, Elwes now filling in for Captain John Coates, who was called to military duty. The part of the Angel was sung by Dilys Jones. For a change of pace, he lined up with Agnes Nicholls and Alf Heather to sing in *Scenes of Hiawatha* in Liverpool on 6 March 1917. Sir Frederic Cowen conducted as Mott 'sang well' in perhaps his sole venture into the exotic music of Coleridge-Taylor.

In 1905 Elgar and his friend Frank Schuster had taken a fortnight-long cruise in the Mediterranean; the composer could relax, fanned by ocean breezes and be soothed by the dulcet tones of Lady Maud Warrender singing his own *Sea Pictures*. All were guests of Admiral Lord Charles Beresford. A dozen years later, he asked Elgar to set to music Rudyard Kipling's four poems, known as *Fringes of the Fleet*, reasoning that England's most brilliant duo could easily brew a tonic for sagging spirits. However, Kipling had just learned his son Jack was 'missing' at Loos, so he was in no mood to participate. Elgar chose to forge ahead and produced a cycle of four songs for four baritones, one to act as soloist, that singer again to be Charles Mott.

Dedicated to Beresford, the songs were arranged in order, gradually darkening in mood and then lifting gently at the end and were set in a 'broad saltwater style' as Elgar explained to Ernest Newman. They certainly captured the mood of the moment, not least because submarine warfare was much in the news. Beginning on 11 June with Elgar conducting, the songs were sung twice daily at London's Coliseum Theatre during a wartime entertainment. Curtain up, Mott, Harry Barratt, Frederick Henry and Frederick Stewart strode onstage as brawny and weatherworn mariners to begin singing before a rustic rural pub. They succeeded so well a provincial tour was organized to begin just as soon as the London run ended. On 4 July, the singers recorded the music.

Near the end of July, Elgar set to music a fifth song, Sir Gilbert Parker's poem 'Inside the Bar', in a part-song arrangement the singers recorded on 27 July before racing to the Coliseum for their final shows. Afterwards at a party on stage, levity was at a premium as everyone knew of Mott's imminent call-up. During a lull, Elgar presented a small silver ship wishing his friend 'clear sailing'.[10]

That summer and autumn, baritone George Parker filled in as *Fringes* was acclaimed in music halls throughout Britain, until the spirited adventure came to a thudding halt. In agony over his son's loss, Kipling had decided his poetry would no longer be used to glorify war. The troubadours limped back to the Coliseum on 1 December to end where they began.

Besides their musical allure, the songs hold special meaning for many, even today as Harry Howe in Kent explains:

> I have a soft spot for these discs as my father was a Regular in the Old Navy (1911-1946) and served in the Dover Patrol in both the First and Second Wars. The Dover Patrol was made up almost entirely of local Navy and Merchant Navy people, so a Dover Patrol ship sunk meant that a good many houses in Deal and Dover were bereaved. In Memoriam notices still appear in local newspapers for people lost in that fashion.

જી   જી   જી

Finally hearing his call, Mott enlisted at Paddington and was duly posted to the Artists' Rifles at Romford. During his training period, he tried all the while to keep his singing career afloat. In letters to Troyte Griffith, he proposed dates with the Malvern Concert Club but nothing materialized. He also spent much time tending to his wife who was taken seriously ill. Eventually he wrote to Griffith to make it clear a November 1917 date was impossible and the proposed recital would have to wait 'until after the war'.

With the Rifles, Mott encountered fellow singers Tom Kinneburgh and Roy Henderson. Roy, who lived to the grand age of 100, retained fond memories of his light-hearted fellow baritone. As he told it, 'The Artists' Rifles had in the battalion a Vicar from Essex (who chose) recruits needed to send suitable people for Officer Training and also to supply the 1st Battalion in France. One had to have an interview to get into the Artists' Rifles; it was selective. I was in the same hut (about thirty men) as Mott who was promoted Training Corporal. Mott was very popular and very kind to me personally but didn't conform to the spit and polish of the Battalion and was sent to France, where he became the life and soul of the Battalion there.'

Near the front, Mott scribbled a note to Elgar just four days prior to the battle. Reproduced here, his words, poignant and heart-rending, remain a critique of war as powerful today as then. Almost as it arrived came news of Mott's wounding and subsequent death.

Saturday 11th May 1918.

Dear Sir Edward,

This is a short note to let you know that all goes well up to the present. (You probably know by now that I have been 'out here' for about five weeks). I have enjoyed the experience immensely and look forward to heaps of 'fun' (admittedly of a rather grim nature) within the next few hours! I *know* you would feel the same. There is something grand & very fascinating about a battery of big guns & a shell that can make a hole in the ground big enough to put a motor-bus in – what a vast amount of pent up energy.

However, on passing over a shelled area I could not help deploring the waste of power, which if directed in another channel might preserve life instead of shatter it. There is something still very much wrong with a world that still sanctions war & something wrong with our practise of the various forms of religion too. One can only hope & pray that this war may wake the whole world up with a great tart and preachers & teachers rise up to the priceless occasion which this poor ravished bleeding world offers. It is groaning for the truth – so simple too.

If I were a preacher I would make 'Love, Unselfishness and Work' the burden of every text and the heads of every Govemment should do the same.

O, what a golden opportunity awaits everyone who cares to think at all. You, my dear Sir Edward realised this years before the war commenced. What consolation to recall your glorious Gerontius & that beloved work 'To the Fallen'. I shall be thinking a great deal of both works & have been of late.

There is one thing that 'puts the wind up me' very badly & that is of my being wiped out & thus miss the dear harmonies of your wonderful works [Mott here wrote hvo themes, one from the Violin Concerto, and one from The Starlight Express].

But I have a supreme confidence in my destiny & feel that I have some useful work to do in the world before I am called away.

Meanwhile the roar of the guns thrills me somehow, & I only dread my comrades coming to grief & seeing them wounded. I pray that they may all get through safely.

I will write you again with more details, if possible.

Hoping that you & Lady Elgar & Miss Elgar are all flourishing & with my heartiest good wishes & best regards.

Believe me

Yours sincerely

Chas. Mott[11]

In anticipation of the German spring assault, Lance Corporal Mott and his mates of The First Battalion London Regiment (Artists' Rifles), waited on 20 May in Aveluy Woods...then the dreadful business began. We can hardly imagine the scream of bursting shells, the chatter of machine guns, the hellish hail of metal...Charles fell, mortally wounded ..and two days later, he succumbed.   He was buried in Grave 2, Plot 11, Row C of Bagneux Military Cemetery, which is located south of Gezaincourt, two kilometres southwest of Doullens.

Should you wish to visit his grave, go first to Gezaincourt, turn at the Commonwealth War Graves sign and proceed south down a rustic trail that is often an adventure on rainy days, taking care as it suddenly veers to cross a rail line.   This once serviced a busy casualty clearing station..now there is just rusting rails, and the graves. Amidst a green and rolling countryside that could pass for southern England, Bagneux sits, well-tended but lonely, far from the beaten track.   Visitors rarely come. It is sad to see these white Portland stones now, row upon row, but in their quiet setting a feeling of respectfulness is ever present.

ﮒ   ﮒ   ﮒ

Roy Henderson spoke highly of Mott: 'He was a superb singer who would have been No 1 baritone in England had he lived. As a boy of 16, I heard him singing *Elijah* at Nottingham and was thrilled by his performance.' ... surely the occasion mentioned earlier. Apart from *The Starlight Express* and *Fringes of the Fleet,* he took part in a recording of Edward German's *Merrie England,* offering a robust and rollicking 'Yeomen of England'. However, the song that sticks in my memory is Frederick Clay's 'The Sands o' Dee', a tale of a young miss who, in gathering her sheep, decides to cross the sand while the tide is out...but fails to return in time. Her man laments ... there is a scream in the voice of this uncommon soldier as he expresses his grief and torment...and brings a lump to my throat every time.

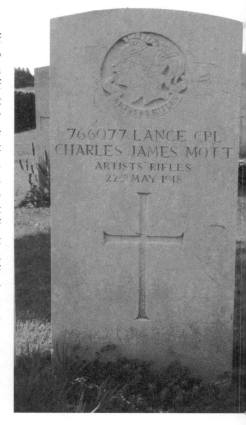

A MOTT DISCOGRAPHY
by Alan Kelly

Record-ing date	Artist(s) Matrix No	Title of Work	Catalogue Nos of 78s*
31-5-11	**Charles Mott**		
	13638e	Test - No title	
8-7-11	**Charles Mott**		
	ab13757e	Test - No title	
	ac5159f	"	
17-4-15	**Charles Mott (p)**		
	Ho769ac	Test - Wagner: Tannhauser: 'O Star of Eve'	
	Ho770ac	Test - Capel: Love could I only tell thee	
18-11-15	**Charles Mott (p)**		
	Ho1257ac	Hatton: Simon the cellarer	02615, D255
	Ho1258ac	" "	
	Ho1259ac	Clay: The Sands Of Dee	
	Ho2100ab	Tosti: For ever and for ever	4-2924, E71
24-11-15	**Charles Mott (organ Stanley Roper) (p)**		
	Ho1283ac	Mott: The Gift of Life	
18-2-16	**Agnes Nicholls, Charles Mott, Symphony Orchestra, Edward Elgar -** **Recordings from Starlight Express (Elgar)**		
	Ho1548 ac	Organ Grinder's Songs No 2 - 'The Blue-eyed Fairy' (Mott)	02640, D455
	Ho1549 ac	'The Laugher's Song' (Nicholls)	
	Ho1550 ac	" "	03473, D458
	Ho1551 ac	'Curfew Song', 'Orion' (Mott)	02642, D456
	Ho1552 ac	" "	
	Hol 553 ac	Organ Grinder`s Songs No 2 - 'The Blue-eyed Fairy' (Mott)	
	Ho1554 ac	'Hearts must be Soft' (Nicholls, Mott)	04151, D458
	Ho1555ac	" "	
	Ho1556ac	Organ Grinder`s Songs No 3 - 'My old Tunes' (Mott)	
	Ho1557ac	" "	02641
	Ho1558ac	a) 'Tears and Laughter'; b) 'The Sunrise Song' (Nicholls)	03472, D457
	Ho1559ac	Organ Grinder`s Songs No 1 - 'To the Children' (Mott)	
	Ho1560ac	" "	02639, D455
	Ho1561ac	a) 'The Woman of the Haystack'; b) 'Dance of the Little Winds' (Mott)	
	Ho1562ac	" "	02643, D457
	Ho1563ac	'Hearts must be Soft' (Nicholls, Mott)	

* - D and E prefixes denote double-sided records; all others were issued as single-sided records.

Record- ing date	Artist(s) Matrix No	Title of Work	Catalogue Nos of 78s
22-6-16	**Charles Mott (o Arthur Wood)**		
	Ho2884ae	Mott: Love's appeal	
	Ho2885ae	"	
	Ho2886ae	Mathesen: Royster Doyster	4-2764
	Ho2887ae	" "	
	Ho2888ae	Crichton: The Grey Watch	4-2795
23-6-16	**Charles Mott (o Arthur Wood)**		
	Ho1942af	Sullivan: Thou'rt Passing Hence	02676, D254
	Ho1943af	Reeve: The Friar of Orders Grey	02684, D255
	Ho1944af	Mackenzie: At the Sign of the Dragon: a) 'Mine Host'; b) 'The Pedlar's Pack', with piano	
13-12-16	**Charles Mott (o James Sale)**		
	Ho2406af	Roma: Can't You Hear Me calling, Caroline?	
	Ho2407af	" "	02706, D254
15-12-16	**Charles Mott (o James Sale)**		
	Ho3368ae	Sullivan: The Sorcerer: 'The Curate's Song'	4-2849, E71
	Ho3369ae	Squire: It's up to a Man	
	Ho3370ae	"	4-2898, E72
	Charles Mott (assisted by Frederick Henry, Frederick Stewart, Harry Barratt), **Symphony Orchestra, Edward Elgar -** **Recordings from Fringes of the Fleet (Elgar)**		
4-7-17	Ho2715af	3: 'Submarines'	
	Ho2716af	"	02736, D454
	Ho2717af	2: 'Fate's Discourtesy'	
	Ho2718af	"	02735, D453
	Ho2719af	1: 'The Lowestoft Boat'	02734, D453
	Ho2720af	"	
	Ho2721af	4: 'The Sweepers'	
	Ho2722af	"	02737, D454
27-7-17	**Charles Mott (p)**		
	Ho2764af	Clay: The Sands o' Dee	
	Ho2765af	"	02872, D464
	Ho3656ae	Mackenzie: At the Sign of the Dragon: 'The Pedlar's Pack'	
	Ho3657ae	" "	
	Ho3658ae	Mackenzie: At the Sign of the Dragon: 'Mine Host'	
28-2-18	**Gresham Singers**		
	Ho3106af	Caryll: O Honey, My Honey, Plantation Song (Not part of following set)	04256

Record- ing date	Artist(s) Matrix No	Title of Work	Catalogue Nos of 78s
27-2-18	**Bessie Jones, Edna Thornton, Charles Mott, Ernest Pike, Edward Halland,**		
	Joseph Reed, Violet Oppenshaw, Sarah Jones, Orchestra, Edward German -		
	Merrie England (German)		
	Ho3100af	'O Peaceful England' (Thornton, Chorus (all above) - set 11)	03616, D23
	Ho3101af	" "	
	Ho3102af	'The Yeomen of England' (Mott, Chorus (all above) - set 9)	02796, D22
	Ho3103af	" "	
	Ho3104af	a) 'In England' (Mott, Thornton, B Jones, Pike)	)
		b) 'The Sun in the Heavens '	) 04241, D26
		(Mott, Thornton, B Jones, Pike, Halland, Reed - set 17)	)
	Ho3105af	"	
1-3-18	**Merrie England (continued with same artists as 27-2-18)**		
	Ho3107af	a) 'When Cupid First the Old World Trod'	)
		(Song & Trio) (Mott, Thornton, B Jones, Pike)	) 04685, D28
		b) 'Robin Hood's Wedding'	)
		(Finale Act 2)(Full Company - set 22)	)
	Ho3108af	" "	
	Ho3109af	'Love is Sent to Make Us Glad' (Quintet)	
		(Thornton, B Jones, Pike, Mott, Halland - set 6)	04769, D20
	Ho3110af	" "	
	Ho3111af	'Two Merry Men A-Drinking'	
		(Mott, Pike, Chorus (all above) - set 20)	04243, D27
	Ho3112af	" "	
	Ho3113af	'The Month of May' (Opening Chorus Act 2)(Full Company)	
	Ho3114af	" " (set 16)	04684, D25
	Ho3115af	'Sing A-Down A-Down' (Opening Chorus Act 1)	
	Ho3116af	" " (set 2)	04678, D18
	H03117af	'O Who Shall Say That Love is Cruel' (B Jones)	

NOTES and SOURCES

1   Hodgkins, Geoffrey and Taylor, Ronald: 'Elgar and Percy Pitt', part II, in *Elgar Society Journal* vol 9, no 1 (March 1995) p 12
2   Atkins, E Wulstan: *The Elgar-Atkins Friendship* (David & Charles, 1984), p 256
3   *op cit*, p 261
4   *op cit*, p 267
5   Moore, *op cit*, p 294
6   *The Musical Times*, 1 February, 1916
7   Atkins, *op cit*, p 271
8   Dunhill, David: *Thomas Dunhill – Maker of Music* (Thames, 1997) p xxi
9   Neill, Andrew: The Great War: Elgar and the Creative Challenge, Elgar Society Journal Vol 11, no 1 (March 1999) p 23
10 see p 49
11 Moore, op cit., p 313

QUEEN'S HALL

Sole Lessees · Messrs. CHAPPELL & Co. LTD.

Polish Victims Relief Fund

"The Russians—to their Polish Brethren" · "In Brotherly Union of Strength"

Orchestral Concert

TUESDAY, JULY 6TH, 1915

AT 8.15 P.M.

CHAPTER 11

SOLIDARITY AND POLAND
Elgar's Opus 76

Joseph A Herter

The Great War (1914-18) did not inspire many Polish composers to write music 'for the cause.' If one recalls the political situation and borders of a non-existent Poland of that time, the explanation for this is simple. At the outbreak of the First World War, Poland had not existed as a sovereign nation for over a century. It had been partitioned by three of its neighbours and placed under their jurisdiction; these were the Austro-Hungarian, Prussian and Russian Empires. A public performance of a Polish patriotic composition in the partitioned lands would have been illegal and, for all practical purposes, impossible to organize. Turning the divided Polish nation into a battlefield also created a moral dilemma for the Poles who were forced to fight in the armies of their imperial rulers: that of having to go into battle and kill fellow Poles. At the war's outset, 725,000 Poles in the Russian, 571,000 in the Austrian, and 250,000 in the Prussian partitions were drafted into those countries' armies.[1] Even though each of the powers promised the Poles some form of autonomy after the 'victory' if they would fight for their side during the war,[2] writing music for *their* cause would have been promoting Polish fratricide as well. Moral support for the Polish cause through music would have to come from abroad.

A Pole who responded to the tragic situation into which Poland had been forced was the pianist and composer Zygmunt Stojowski (1870-1946). A student of Léo Delibes – and for shorter periods of time with Dubois, Massenet and Paderewski – Stojowski spent the last forty years of his life teaching and composing in New York. There in 1915, free from the retaliation of Poland's occupying powers, Stojowski took a political stance and wrote a cantata for solo voices, mixed chorus and orchestra, *A Prayer for Poland (Modlitwa za Polskę),* op 40. Stojowski's cantata, although long unperformed and forgotten, is one of the few works from the 'war to end all wars' which

FACING PAGE: *Cover of the programme for the first performance of* Polonia

was written on a spiritual base rather than on a totally patriotic one. The poem by Zygmunt Krasiński (1812-59) on which the cantata is based is addressed to the Blessed Virgin Mary. Using the appellation 'Queen of Poland' – a title which for centuries the Vatican has allowed Poles to use in the recitation of the Litany of Loreto – the poet calls upon Mary to 'End thou for bleeding Poland her deep anguish.' In writing about music as a voice of war in his book on twentieth century music, the noted American musicologist Glenn Watkins states:

> At various junctures throughout the twentieth century, man's search for spiritual values has surfaced in opera, symphony, and Mass; mystery play, ballet and cantata. Yet the period before the beginning of World War I to the conclusion of hostilities was not noticeable for a musical corpus with a pronounced spiritual base, and while the anxiety of a society on the eve of global conflict has frequently been seen as the root of the Expressionist movement, the number of musical statements that speak directly of the war of 1914-18 are few.[3]

Ignacy Paderewski (1860-1941) responded to the cause of Polish independence by writing his only choral work, *Hej, Orle biały (Hey, White Eagle),* for male chorus and piano or military band in 1917. This was the official hymn of the Polish Army in America, for whose creation Paderewski was largely responsible. The Polish Army in America consisted of over 20,000 enlisted Polish immigrants living in the United States, but who were not American citizens. This army trained in Niagara-on-the-Lake, Ontario, and later joined the Polish Army in France, which brought their number to over 35,000.[4] As the war came to an end, Feliks Nowowiejski (1877-1946) wrote an organ prelude entitled *Friede, schönstes Glück der Erde,* op 31, no 5 which was based on the Schubert *lied* of the same title. A former student of Bruch and Dvořák, and a well-known organist and composer throughout Europe, Nowowiejski was named an honorary member of the Organ Society of London in 1931.

It was with Edward Elgar's fantasia on Polish national airs, though, that the most outstanding, dramatic and nobly patriotic musical gesture for the Polish cause came into being during the First World War. Elgar, however, was not the first composer to have written a work entitled *Polonia*. The young Richard Wagner (1813-83), at one time sympathetic to Poland's fate, wrote an overture bearing the same title in 1836. In 1883, Franz Liszt (1811-86) also wrote a work entitled *Salve, Polonia*, an orchestral interlude from his uncompleted oratorio *The Legend of St Stanislaus*. All three compositions by Elgar, Wagner

ABOVE:
*Ignacy Paderewski
(1860-1941)*

RIGHT:
*Hej Orle Biały
(Hey, White Eagle),
his only choral work*

and Liszt make use of *The Dąbrowski Mazurka*, the hymn which was to become Poland's national anthem after it regained its independence. The title of Elgar's work, though, may not have come from the earlier works of Wagner and Liszt, but rather from compositions of the two Polish musicians most closely associated with the creation of Elgar's piece: Paderewski and Emil Młynarski.

Paderewski, to whom Elgar's Polish fantasia is dedicated, wrote his *Symphony in B minor,* op 24 and gave it the name *Polonia* as well. The symphony – Paderewski's only work in this genre – was inspired by the fortieth anniversary of the 1863-64 Polish Uprising and completed in 1909. The symphony was premièred in Boston on 12 January 1909, with the Boston Symphony Orchestra conducted by Max Fiedler. Paderewski uses the Polish National Anthem as well in this work. Unlike Elgar, however, who uses the hymn in its entirety, or Wagner and Liszt who write variations on the melody, Paderewski uses a motif from the hymn in the symphony's last movement *Vivace*. The motif is discreetly employed, one might even say – cleverly hidden – as a 'hope leitmotif' for the rebirth of Poland. Even listeners who are familiar with the opening phrase of the Polish hymn and its text *Jeszcze Polska nie zginęła, kiedy my żyjemy* ('Poland has not yet been lost so long as we still shall live') might easily let Paderewski's use of the motif pass without recognizing it.

Emil Młynarski (1870-1935), who was responsible for asking Elgar to make his noble statement in support of the Polish cause in April 1915, completed his *Symphony in F major,* op 14 in 1910. The composer did not give the title *Polonia* to his only symphony; rather it was a nickname given to the piece by other Polish musicians. The nickname is still often listed as part of the official title in catalogues of the composer's works. According to Tadeusz Sygietyński (1896-1955), a composer and the founder of the internationally renowned Polish Song and Dance Ensemble *Mazowsze,* Młynarski's symphony should bear this name because of its relationship in tragedy to Polish history as depicted in the cycle of paintings entitled *Polonia* by the nineteenth-century Polish artist Artur Grottger[5]. Młynarski, unlike any of the other composers whose works bear the same title, does not use *Jeszcze Polska nie zginęła* in his composition. Instead, he uses Polish dances – a mazurka in the third and a krakowiak in the fourth movements – and also employs the thirteenth-century hymn to the Blessed Virgin Mary *Bogurodzica* (Mother of God) which is still well known and sung by Poles today. This hymn, which has the

distinction of being the oldest recorded Polish melody and poetry in existence, was sung by Polish warriors as they went into battle against the Teutonic Knights.   The first seven notes of the medieval *Bogurodzica* are the exact same seven pitches of the opening theme of the *Kyrie* in Ralph Vaughan Williams' *Mass in G minor* of 1922. The première of Młynarski's *Polonia* took place on February 6, 1911, in Glasgow with the Scottish Symphony Orchestra performing and the composer at the orchestra's helm.

In addition to being a composer, Młynarski was also a famous

The opening phrases of the Polish medieval chant Bogurodzica and the Kyrie of Ralph Vaughan Williams' Mass in G minor. The latter is used by permission of Faber Music Ltd for the United Kingdom, Republic of Ireland, Canada, Australasia, South Africa, Jamaica, and Israel.

conductor and it is for his rôle in this profession that he is best remembered today. He was the first conductor of the Warsaw Philharmonic Orchestra (1901-05). In the first decade of the twentieth-century he guest conducted in Russia and in the British cities of London, Glasgow, Liverpool and Manchester. From 1910-15 he was the music director of the Scottish Symphony Orchestra in Glasgow. His association with Elgar also included collaborating with him and Thomas Beecham in presenting a three-day festival of British music in 1915.[6] It would also be Młynarski who would conduct the first Polish performance of *Polonia* at the Philharmonic Hall in Warsaw during the final days of the war on October 4, 1918.[7] Following the war, Młynarski's responsibilities included the directorship of both the Opera House (*Teatr Wielki*) and the Music Conservatory in Warsaw. After the war his guest conducting took him to the capitals of Europe and to major cities in America, where he joined the faculty of the Curtis School of Music in Philadelphia in 1929.

Elgar would not be the last famous composer to write a work entitled *Polonia*.[8] In fact, it was Elgar's composition which became a source of consolation and inspiration for one of Poland's greatest composers and conductors of the second half of the twentieth-century, Andrzej Panufnik (1914-1990). In search of political and artistic freedom, Panufnik escaped to the West and settled in England in 1954. As a conductor and Musical Director of the City of Birmingham Symphony Orchestra, he was responsible for a revival of Elgar's work during the 1957-58 season. Also showing Panufnik's affinity for *Polonia* is a 1997 BBC Radio Classics recording with Sir Andrzej conducting it in a 1978 performance with the BBC Northern Symphony Orchestra. As a composer, though, Panufnik gave credit to Elgar for his own 1959 orchestral work of the same title. In his autobiography Panufnik writes:

> It was not easy to start those spirited dances at a time of great loneliness... For a while I could not start. But then I started to think about Elgar's sombre and noble Polonia, a work most evocatively echoing the heroic and tragic elements of Polish history. I decided to use the same title but to adopt a completely different approach, so that the two works together might provide a full spectrum of the Polish spirit and colour. Elgar made use of Polish patriotic songs but also took some of Chopin's melodies, ending powerfully with the Polish National Anthem. In contrast I based my new-born Polonia on folk melodies and the vigorous, full-blooded rhythms of peasant dances.[9]

Elgar's compassion for the Poles' tragic suffering during the war served as an example for other English composers to make their own Polish musical statements in kind. Arnold Bax (1883-1953) saw a similar need to help the Poles during World War Two. Bax's response was *Five Fantasies on Polish Christmas Carols* which were dedicated 'To the Children of Poland' and scored for unison chorus and string orchestra. As Jan Sliwiński writes in the preface of the piano-vocal score of the Bax carols, the composer's arrangements were '. . . meant to turn the blood of war into the balm of love. British children were to have sung them in aid of their starving Polish brothers and sisters.' Another British composer, Benjamin Britten (1913-1976), also moved by the plight which Polish children experienced during WW II, took up the same theme in his choral work *The Children's Crusade,* op 82. Scored for children's voices, percussion, two pianos and electronic organ, this ballad is a setting in English of Bertolt Brecht's *Kinderkreuzzug.* It begins, 'In Poland, in 1939, there was the bloodiest fight.' The world première of Britten's work took place in 1969 on the fiftieth anniversary of Save the Children Fund, a British charity which was founded by Eglantyne Jebb to save starving Austrian children who were victims of a blockade imposed after the First World War.

Polonia was expressly written for the purpose of being performed at benefit concerts in aid of the Polish Victims Relief Fund, the raising of money for which was the primary activity of the Polish Victims Relief Committee. The Committee, which eventually established chapters in France, Great Britain, Switzerland, and the United States, was founded in Vevey, Switzerland in January 1915 by a group of eminent Poles who had planned the Committee's formation with Paderewski at his Swiss villa in Riond-Bosson. Jointly heading the Committee were Paderewski and Henryk Sienkiewicz (1846-1916), the author of *Quo Vadis?* and, in 1905, the first Polish laureate of the Nobel Prize for Literature. While calling upon others to assist hundreds of thousands of Poles, who were in desperate need of food, clothing and shelter, Paderewski himself donated more than $2 million from his own personal fortune to help his fellow countrymen.[10]

Paderewski sought the most influential people in each country to either organise, lead or join the four national chapters of the Committee. In the United States, it was former President William Howard Taft (1857-1930) who headed the American Committee. In France, Paderewski succeeded in obtaining the help of former French President Emile Loubet (1838-1929) to organise the Committee there. Great Britain was no exception. The British Committee consisted of a star-studded list of artists and high-ranking members of British society and government circles. Included with Elgar and his wife Alice were the famous English writers Thomas Hardy[11] and Rudyard Kipling. (Unfortunately, the Polish-born novelist Joseph Conrad refused to join Paderewski's efforts because of a disagreement about the way the French Committee had been organised). Other notable persons included the following: Arthur James Balfour; the Marquess of Crewe; the Duke and Duchess of Norfolk; the Duke and Duchess of Somerset; the Duchess of Bedford; the Marquis and Marchioness of Ripon; the Earl of Roseberry; former Prime Minister Lord Burnham; Prime Minister Asquith; future Prime Minister Lloyd George; Reginald McKenna; Winston Churchill; Austen Chamberlain; Lord Northcliffe; Lord Charles Beresford; and Viscount Edward Grey.[12] In the first several months of its existence, the British Committee's Polish Victims Relief Fund raised more than £50,000.[13]

The world première of Elgar's *Polonia* took place on 6 July 1915, with Sir Edward conducting the London Symphony Orchestra at Queen's Hall in London in a benefit concert for the Polish Victims Relief Fund. Other works in the concert included one movement from Młynarski's '*Polonia' Symphony* and Paderewski's *Polish Fantasy on Original Themes for Piano and Orchestra,* op 19.[14]

The thematic material for Elgar's composition is drawn from both traditional Polish tunes and from compositions by Frederic Chopin

Program

1. THE STEPPE: SYMPHONIC POEM . . . . Noskowski

2. POLISH FANTASY, for Piano and Orchestra . . . Paderewski

   Solo Piano, LEONARD BORWICK

3. PART II. OF SYMPHONY . . . . . Mlynarski

4. VIOLIN SOLOS . *(a)* " Légende " . . } Wieniawski
   (b) " Polonaise " . . .

   ALBERT SAMMONS

5. . . . . "POLONIA" . . . ELGAR

   (Specially composed by Sir EDWARD ELGAR for this Concert
   and dedicated to I. J. PADEREWSKI)

   Conducted by the COMPOSER

PART II

5a. SUITE . . 1. Thème Varié . . . . Stojowski
   2. Intermède Polonais
   3. Rêveuse et Cracovienne

6. SONGS . . . *(a)* " Nie płacz nademną " . . Karlowicz
   (b) " Idę ja Niemnem " . . . Paderewski
   (c) " Gdzie to jedziesz Jasiu ? ". . Polish Folk-Song

   J. CAMPBELL McINNES

   Accompanist . GEORGE REEDES

7. PIANO SOLOS . *(a)* Prelude in D minor, Op. 28, No. 4 . . Chopin
   (b) Mazurka, F sharp minor, Op. 6, No. 1
   (c) Etude in E minor, Op. 25, No. 5

   LEONARD BORWICK

8. DANCE OF POLISH MOUNTAINEERS . . . Moniuszko
   From the Opera " Halka "

   GOD SAVE THE KING

   Conductor . THOMAS BEECHAM

THIS AND FOLLOWING PAGES: *Three pages from the programme for
the first performance of* Polonia, *Queen's Hall, 6 July 1915*

SYMPHONIC PRELUDE . . . . . Sir Edward Elgar

"POLONIA"

DEDICATED TO PADEREWSKI

(First Performance)

THE composition of this symphonic prelude was prompted, in the first instance, by several (unmusical) motives which the composer has combined as happily, by writing the work, as he does his actual musical themes. These motives are best explained in Sir Edward Elgar's own words.

"It was suggested, two months ago, by M. Mlynarski that a 'Polish' piece should be written to help the Polish funds, as he told me so much had been done for Belgian charitable undertakings by the 'Carillon.' But the idea of writing an orchestral fantasy on Polish themes is not new to me, and curiously enough the suggestion, or rather influence, came in Herefordshire. The heir of the ancient family of Bodenham married, in 1850, a noble Polish lady, and from their descendant Count Lubienski-Bodenham, the squire of Bodenham while I lived in the adjoining parish, I heard much of Polish history, thought and feeling—supplementing the mere book knowledge. Very deeply regretted, this lovable gentleman died a few years ago.

"That some sort of symphonic prelude might be a practical and perhaps even a useful tribute to my friend Paderewski for the concert in aid of his countrymen, was the final inducement to weave into a concise orchestral movement some typical Polish themes."

The themes referred to are three in number, and were brought to Sir Edward Elgar's notice as suitable for a work to appeal to national feelings. They are all of them very popular in Poland.

Although the prelude is constructed around these themes, it is by no means a mere fantasia on the melodies. The music which the composer has woven out of them, and which he has adorned with many of his own characteristic themes, is as individual as any that he has ever written. One of the central ideas of the music, indeed, is a very striking heroic theme, which may be considered as an expression of the composer's personal admiration for Poland. It provides, as we shall see later on, the great emotional climax of the work, and is first heard, ringing out on the brass, after brief introductory phrases.

In the opening bars an appropriate atmosphere having been created by suggestions of the first of the Polish themes ("Z Dymem Pozarow"),

this is now played by 'celli, then repeated more fully. Soon the lower strings begin snatches of a martial air (the second Polish tune)

Ex. 3.

which is taken up by the full orchestra and very brilliantly discussed. The third tune—the national air "Jeszeze Polska nie zginela" ("Poland is not lost yet")—also now makes its appearance. It has a somewhat familiar ring to English ears.

Ex. 4.

The return of the noble heroic theme (Example 1) in stately manner, brings us to a remarkable episode, which has a very beautiful and poetic idea as its basis. The music fades away almost into nothingness, and from the silence there emerge, as it were, two great figures of Polish music—Chopin and Paderewski. Over a faint drum roll, and floating on harp chords, there comes a fragment of the former's familiar nocturne in G minor, tenderly and softly played by muted violas and 'cellos. Now follows a quotation from the opening of Paderewski's Polish Fantasy, and in a moment or two both the themes are heard simultaneously.

Before the vision vanishes the martial melody begins to mutter in the lower strings once again. Gathering in intensity it sweeps up to a great climax, where the "heroic" theme is thundered out by the brass, against an exciting *tremolo* in the violins. The emotional feeling of the climax is continued as the music plunges on into the stirring military theme, and then, still without a break, sweeps into the broad phrases of the hymn-like tune (Example 2), now treated in the characteristic harmonic style of the composer, with contrapuntal touches in horns and 'cellos.

For the brief remainder of the work, the themes are handled with new effect. Here, for instance, Examples 1 and 2 are combined thus :

Ex. 5.

and later on the composer brings back Example 4 in a very poetic version, to which a phrase on the violas gives special colour.

Ex. 6.

The music ends with a grandiose version of Example 4, the intention of the composer being to add a military band effect, and perhaps even voices, in the future.

and Paderewski.   The former include *Śmiało podniesmy sztandar nasz w górę (Bravely Let Us Lift up Our Flag)* also known as the *1905 Warszawianka* by Józef Pławiński; *Z dymem pozarów (With the Smoke of Fires)* also known as *Chorale* by Józef Nikorowicz (1827-1890) and *The Dąbrowski Mazurka* which has been the Poles' national hymn since the regaining of Polish independence.   The latter group includes the opening theme from Paderewski's *Polish Fantasy for Piano and Orchestra,* op 19   and   a   quotation   from   Chopin's *Nocturne no. 11 in G minor,* op 37 no 1.

In the introduction to the full score of *Polonia* Jerrold Northrop Moore states that it was Młynarski who proposed the Polish national melodies to be used, but that it was Elgar who selected the quotations from Chopin and Paderewski. These national melodies will surely be unfamiliar to the non-Polish listener. *The 1905 Warszawianka* is the first song used in the introduction of the fantasia. It is the two-measure dotted-rhythm melody which is first heard in the fourth bar as played by the bassoons and bass clarinet. Later, it is not only used as a transitional motif between sections of the fantasia, but the motif is also developed in two separate sections of the composition which give a unifying force to the work. Although the text of the song itself dates from the nineteenth-century and was written by Wacław Święcicki (1848-1900), it became popular when sung to a melody by Józef Pławiński and was used as an uprising song against the Russians in Warsaw in 1905.   This song became popular with workers' movements throughout Europe. It was translated into over a dozen languages and accompanied the revolutionary communist movement in many European countries.[15] The following hymn and the other Polish national hymns given below in English have been translated by the author.

> Bravely let us lift up our flag,
> Even though the storm of the unrestrained enemy rages,
> Even though their unbearable force treads us down,
> Even if it is uncertain to whom tomorrow belongs.
> Onward, Warsaw!
> Onward to the bloody fight, which is holy and just!
> March on, Warsaw, march on!

The second national tune *With the Smoke of Fires* or *Chorale* came into being following the Austrian Army's bloody suppression of the Cracow Uprising of 1846. As a national song, it best conveys the patriotic agony which the Polish nation experienced during the 123-

The 1905 Warszawianka
(By permission of Grupa Wydawnicza 'Słowo'.)

year-long period of partitions by the Russian, Prussian and Austro-Hungarian Empires.[16] Sung at both patriotic manifestations and at church services, the occupying powers soon forbade the public singing of this hymn. Punishment for performing the hymn was severest in the Prussian territories.

Elgar uses this melody twice in its entirety in his symphonic prelude. The first time is after Elgar's *nobilmente* original thematic material, which immediately follows the introduction, and the second time is just prior to the finale containing what is now known as the Polish National Anthem – *The Dąbrowski Mazurka*. Almost thirty years later, this hymn would be used once again to give the Poles courage when Radio London signalled the partisans in the nation's capital to begin the Warsaw Uprising of August 1944.[17] The *Chorale* written by Nikorowicz was sung to the tragic text of Kornel Ujejski (1823-1897).

> Our voices ring out to You, O Lord,
> With the smoke of fires and the dust of fraternal blood.
> The complaint is frightful; it is our last moan.
> From these prayers our hair turns gray.

Chorale (By permission of Grupa Wydawnicza 'Słowo')

By now the complaints have stopped
And the songs we know are none.
Forever a crown of thorns has grown into our forehead
As a monument to your anger.
To You we outstretch our imploring hands.

The last national tune used by Elgar is the Polish National Anthem which forms the basis of the fantasia's triumphant finale. The anthem's alternative title, *The Dąbrowski Mazurka,* refers to General Jan Henryk Dąbrowski, the leader of the Polish Legions who fought for Napoleon Bonaparte. The hymn dates from 1797 and was written in Reggio Emilia, Italy, by Józef Wybicki (1747-1822). The tune given to the hymn was a popular Polish folk melody. As it was sung by the legionnaires in their battles and journeys, the melody stayed with the Slavs in what is known as Yugoslavia and became the tune of their national hymn as well. The Serbs, however, sing it at a much slower tempo than the Poles do. For those familiar with the Polish national hymn today, it might sound as though Elgar ornamented the melody. Actually, this is the way the melody existed prior to 1918. Immediately following the establishment of the Republic of Poland, the Ministry of Education was given the task of making the melody easier for school children to sing. The passing notes heard in the last phrase of Elgar's setting of the hymn are noticeably missing in the post-war version. Although competitions were held after the war to search for a new national hymn, *The Dąbrowski Mazurka* became the official hymn on 26 February 1927. A translation of the hymn follows:

Poland has not yet been lost
So long as we still shall live.
That which foreign force has seized
We shall regain by the sword.
March, march Dabrowski!
From Italy to Poland!
Under your command
Let us rejoin the nation.

A listening guide for *Polonia* follows. The form of the piece is a free design. The work is scored for full symphonic orchestra and includes the following instrumentation: 2 flutes (2nd doubling on piccolo), 2 oboes, cor anglais, 2 clarinets, bass clarinet, 2 bassoons, contrabassoon, 4 horns, 3 trumpets, 3 trombones, tuba, percussion (6 players), 2 harps, organ and strings.

za two-im_____ prze - wo____ - dem,   zia -czym sie   zna - ro___-dem.

za two - im   prze - wo___ dem   zia -czym sie   zna - ro - dem.

The last phrase of the Polish National Anthem Jeszcze Polska nie zginęła. The first example shows how it was sung prior to 1927, while the second example illustrates how it is sung today.

Section	Bar nos.	Key	Comments
Introduction	1-20	A minor, C minor, A minor	Allegro molto : Original martial-like music by Elgar coupled with a two-bar motif based on bars 1 and 6 of The 1905 Warszawianka. Motif first appears at bar 4 when played by the bassoons and bass clarinet.
A	21-37	A minor	Nobilmente : A broad, heroic-sounding original melody by Elgar played by the full orchestra. The melody is chromatically altered during the second playing.
Transition	38-44	modulates	The rhythm of the Warszawianka is played by the percussion and violas while winds and remaining strings play a motif from Elgar's nobilmente.
B	45-92	E major	Poco meno mosso : The melody Z dymem pozarów (Chorale) is intoned by the cor anglais, which is later joined by the winds and strings, and finally with full orchestra joining on the last phrase. At a fortissimo dynamic level the lower brass play the penultimate four-bar phrase of the Chorale to a descending scale accompaniment by the rest of the orchestra. The music becomes softer and slower until piu lento at bar 85 where the violoncello is given the melody - slightly varied - as a solo.
Transition	93-100	E minor	Piu mosso, poco a poco : The Warszawianka motif is now extended into a four-bar phrase.
C	101-140	E minor	Allegro molto : The motif from Warszawianka is developed into an entire section using additional melodic material from other bars of the song as well.
A1	141-150	E minor	Elgar's nobilmente theme returns.
Transition	151-162	Modulates to G minor	Poco piu tranquillo : Change in mood, dynamics and colour. Tremolo strings lead to the modulation, after which the strings are muted.

D	163-210	G minor	In this section Elgar pays homage to Paderewski and Chopin. It begins with a quotation of the opening theme from Paderewski's Fantasia which in Polonia has been transposed a semitone lower from its original key. Played first by the violins, the phrase is echoed by the clarinet. This echo technique is then repeated between the clarinet and flute. At bar 186 the Chopin Nocturne is quoted by the solo violin. Expressive flexibility of tempo with markings of allargando, accelerando and a tempo are heard during Elgar's use of the Chopin.
Transition	211-229	Modulates	The Warszawianka motif and fragmented versions of the Chopin and Paderewski themes are heard simultaneously until the martial music of the Warszawianka completely dominates at bar 221, piu mosso, poco a poco.
C1	230-295	E minor	Once more the music of the Warszawianka is developed into a section of its own. Prominent is a motif based on bars 17 and 18 of the song where the text, Naprzód, Warszawo! (Onward, Warsaw!), appears. Dazzling chromatic runs accompany and, following the dramatic luftpause between bars 261 and 262, ascending chromatic scales are played con fuoco.
B1	296-311	A major	The Chorale returns accompanied by rising arpeggios in the harps and violins which add a sense of urgency in the pleading nature of this tragic song.
Transition	312-329	Modulates	The Warszwianka motif, the first four bars of the Polish national anthem and the first two bars of the penultimate phrase of Chorale are heard dovetailing each other, while at other times they are played simultaneously. The entire transition is played pianissimo.
Finale	330-379	F major	Moderato maestoso: A change from quadruple to triple time. The Polish national hymn dominates this section. The anthem is heard twice in its entirety. These complete settings are separated by short development of the mazurka at bar 349 animando. The final playing of the anthem at bar 360 Grandioso uses all the resources of the orchestra, including full organ, creating a glorious climax to the fantasia on Polish airs.
Coda	380-end	F major	Allargando al fine: Based on the dotted rhythm of the first bar of the mazurka.

BIBLIOGRAPHY

Bax, Arnold: *Five Fantasies on Polish Christmas Carols* (Chappell Music Limited, piano/vocal score, 1944)

Britten, Benjamin: *Children's Crusade*, op 82 (Faber Music Ltd, chorus part, 1969)

Chopin, Frederic: Nocturnes (Instytut Fryderyka Chopina & Polskie Wydawnictwo Muzyczne, 1951)

Davies, Norman: *God's Playground - A History of Poland*, volume II -1795 to the Present (Oxford, Clarendon Press, 1981)

Drozdowski, Marian Marek: *Ignacy Jan Paderewski - A Political Biography* (Warsaw, Interpress, 1981)

Dulęba, Władysław and Sokołowska, Zofia: *Paderewski* (Cracow, Polskie Wydawnictwo Muzyczne, 1976)

Elgar, Edward: *Polonia*, op 76. (Novello, full score in Elgar Complete Edition, vol 33, 1992)

Elgar, Edward: *Polonia*, op 76. Sir Adrian Boult & London Philharmonic Orchestra EMI, CFP 4527, 1975

Elgar, Edward: *Polonia*, op 76. Sir Andrzej Panufnik & BBC Northern Symphony Orchestra (BBC Radio Classics, 15656 91942, 1997)

Jasiński, Roman: *Na przełomie epok - Muzyka w Warszawie (1910-1927)* Warsaw, Państwowy Instytut, Wydawniczy, 1979

Jasiński, Roman: 'Pamięci Emila Młynarskiego' *Ruch Muzyczny*, no 7 (1960), pp 4-5

Kennedy, Michael: *Portrait of Elgar* (London, Oxford University Press, 1968)

McGinty, Brian: 'Paderewski' Paderewski Day Program, Warren, Michigan, Friends of Polish Art (1991) pp 27-33

Mechanisz, Janusz: *Emil Młynarski w setną rocznicę urodzin* (Warsaw, Teatr Wiielki, 1970)

Młynarski, Emil: Symphony in F major, op 14 'Polonia' (Ed Bote & G Bock, full score, 1912)

Moore, Jerrold Northrop: Preface to the Full Score of *Polonia* (London and Sevenoaks, Novello, Elgar Complete Edition, vol 33, 1992)

Mrowiec, Karol (chief ed): *Śpiewnik Kościelny Ks J Siedleckiego* (Cracow, Instytut Teologiczny Księży Misjonarzy, 39th ed, 1994)

Nowowiejski, Feliks: *Friede, schönstes Glück der Erde*, op 31 no 5 (Akademia Muzyczna im F Chopina, Utwory mniejsze na organy, 1994)

Paderewski, Ignacy Jan: *Polish Fantasy on Original Themes for Piano and Orchestra, op 19* (Ed Bote & G Bock, full score, 1895)

Paderewski, Ignacy Jan: *Symphony in B minor*, op 24 'Polonia' (Huegel & Cie, full score, 1911)

Panek, Waclaw: *Polski Śpiewnik Narodowy* (Poznań: Grupa Wydawnicza 'Słowa', 1996)

Panufnik, Andrzej: *Composing Myself* (London, Methuen, 1987)

Panufnik, Andrzej: *Polonia* (Boosey & Hawkes, full score, 1959)

Popis, Jan: *Notes for Paderewski Symphony Polonia*, CD recording (Polish Radio Studio S1 Music label, CD S1-001, Warsaw, 1991)

Reiss, Józef W Statkowski - Melcer - Młynarski - Stojowski Łódź: 'Wiedza Powszechna' *Wydawnictwo Popularno-Naukowe, muzyka i muzycy polscy*, no 18 (1949)

Stojowski, Sigismond (Zygmunt): *Prayer for Poland ('Modlitwa za Polskę')*, op 40 (Schirmer, piano/vocal score, 1915)
Vaughan Williams, Ralph: *Mass in G minor* (G Schirmer, Curwen Edition, choral score, 1922)
Wacholc, Maria (ed): *Śpiewnik polski* (Wydawnictwa Szkolne i Pedagognicze, 1991)
Wagner, Richard: *Polonia* (Breitkopf & Härtel, full score, 1908)
Walaux, Marguerite: *The National Music of Poland - Its Character and Sources* (London, George Allen & Unwin Ltd, 1916)
Waldorf, Jerzy: *Diabły I Anioły* (Polskie Wydawnictwo Muzyczne, 1988)
Watkins, Glenn: *Soundings - Music in the Twentieth Century* (New York, Schirmer Books, 1988)
Żmigrodzka, Zofia: *Notes for Ferenc Liszt Polonica* CD recording (Wifron Music label, WCD 028, Warsaw, 1994)

NOTES and SOURCES

1   Drozdowski, Marian Marek: *Ignacy Jan Paderewski - A Political Biography* (1981) p 68
2   Davies, Norman: *God's Playground - A History of Poland* vol II (1981), p 378
3   Watkins, Glenn: *Soundings* (1988), p 464
4   Drozdowski: *op cit*, pp 99-103
5   Jasiński, Roman, in *Ruch Muzyczny*, no 7 (1960), pp 4-5
6   Waldorf, Jerzy: *Diabły I Anioły* (1988), p 101
7   Jasiński: *Na przełomie epok - Muzyka w Warszawie (1910-1927)* (1979) p 282
8   Poles also use the Latin word for Poland, *Polonia*, in reference to its diaspora, ie the Polish community living outside of Poland.
9   Panufnik, Andrzej: *Composing Myself* (1987), pp 269-270
10 McGinty, Brian: *Paderewski* (1991), p 30
11 Moore, Jerrold Northrop: Preface to the full score of *Polonia* in the *Elgar Complete Edition* (1992), p xi
12 Drozdowski: *op cit*, pp 73-74
13 Dulęba, Władysław and Sokołowska, Zofia: *Paderewski* (1976) p 125
14 Moore: *op cit*, p xii
15 Panek, Wacław: *Polski Śpiewnik Narodowy* (1996) p 201
16 Walaux, Marguerite: *The National Music of Poland* (1916) p 13
17 Wacholc, Maria (ed): *Śpiewnik polski* (1991) p 57

Elgar at Brinkwells

CHAPTER 12

THE ROAD TO BRINKWELLS
The Late Chamber Music

Brian Trowell

War was foundering of sublimities,
Extinction of each happy art and faith
By which the world had still kept head in air.
(Robert Graves, 'Recalling War')

The meaning of 'the Brinkwells works'

Are we right to talk of 'the four Brinkwells works' as sharing some special qualities drawn from their birthplace? We don't usually talk of 'the Forlì works' or 'the Craeg Lea works' or even (a stronger analogy) 'the Birchwood works'. What did Brinkwells mean to Elgar? Was that cottage on the tree-girt hillside near Fittleworth, first glimpsed in May 1917, simply a 'country retreat', or did it represent, in a larger sense, a retreat from the great public conflict and from Elgar's own war-work into a private world of wood-music, sometimes mysteriously haunted? The Cello Concerto renounces grandiosity for ellipsis and concentration, but does it really enshrine the 'deep disillusion' of the war-poets as Basil Maine[1] suggested, and is it the case that, in Diana McVeagh's cautious phrase, 'It has come to seem as though [it was] his "war requiem"'?[2] Are we to hear in all four pieces, as Ivor Keys maintained, the ghostly after-life of a composer who had already sung his own artistic requiem as the 'singer who sings no more' at the end of *The Music Makers*?[3] The one thing that we can say for certain is that the works composed at Brinkwells present us in many respects with a new and different Elgar. It is not simply a question of a new medium and new techniques: if the Cello Concerto offers us, in the composer's phrase, 'A man's attitude to life', it is plainly not the attitude proclaimed in the Symphonies, still less that of the oratorios. The post-war Elgar seems to have abandoned E T A Hoffman's 'courage, confidence and faith', that optimistic belief in music's ability to celebrate 'the advent of the Divine' and make of humanity 'one universal church', which the composer had nailed to his masthead at the end of his inaugural lecture at Birmingham University in 1905.[4] What caused the change? What were the stresses that drove Elgar into a near-breakdown over the latter months of 1916 and early 1917 and for a time reduced his art almost to silence?

The Elgars on the home front: their general experience of war

When Great Britain so unexpectedly took up arms on 4 August 1914, Elgar at first threw himself with vigour into the national war effort, both as civilian and as musician, and so did his wife and daughter. For a truthful and connected impression of what life was like on the home front during the first two years of the war, seen through the eyes of a thoughtful upper-middle-class intellectual too old for military service, one cannot do better than read H. G. Wells' novel *Mr Britling Sees It Through* (1916). Much of the Elgar family's experience is mirrored in its pages: the horror at the attack on Belgium and the Bryce Report on atrocities; the rôle of the rather futile Special Constabulary and the Volunteer Reserve; good works with the Red Cross, with refugees, with the war-wounded; the fall in share prices and the shrinking of income from other sources; the issue of the non-involvement of the USA; the sense of unreality – or reality? – blotting out the long years of peace, and the questioning of the old life and its values; the recollection of happy Bavarian holidays and warm friendships with Germans, the admiration for German culture – with a corresponding inability to understand Lissauer's Hymn of Hate and the systemic nature of German state militarism; the destruction of towns and churches in Flanders and northern France; the killing of British civilians – the Zeppelins over London and the naval bombardment of east coast towns; the unprecedented horrors of trench warfare and the new weaponry that came with it – flame-jets and poison-gas as well as ever bigger guns; the submarines, the naval blockade and the shortages; the way the war obsessed every moment of one's thoughts; the unimaginable tolling of the daily casualty-lists in the newspapers and the loss or wounding of friends and relations; the Manichean sense of absolute evil. Mr. Britling loses his son; his thoughts turn towards a new social order and a league of nations, and he finds God.

Elgar appears to have lost no members of his family, though friends and associates died, such as Charles Mott, and close relatives of other friends were killed or wounded.[5] He may have moved leftwards in politics, if Lady Elgar's views are any guide: her diary records pleasure in the Russian Revolution, and in Lloyd George's landslide Liberal majority of May 1918. Elgar did not find God in the sense that Wells briefly did, but became more deeply entrenched in his view of the malignity of providence. When Laurence Binyon invited him at the end of the war to set his ode 'Peace' to music, he refused: 'the whole atmosphere is too full of complexities for me to feel music to it'. He seems to have sensed, like Robert Graves, that there could be no yearning for the old values suggested in Binyon's poem and in the work of Edmund Blunden and Siegfried Sassoon. He had no wish to hurt Binyon's feelings and praised his ode, especially the last two sections, but he could not stomach any reference to divine favour: 'I regret the appeal to the Heavenly Spirit which is cruelly obtuse to the individual sorrow & sacrifice—a cruelty I resent bitterly and disappointedly'.[6]

Elgar's war-music

As to his musical war effort, after three 'occasional' works, composition petered out in June 1917 with the completion of *The Spirit of England* and *The Fringes of the Fleet*. Writing to Ernest Newman about these last two, he seemed to draw a line under them with a certain relief: 'And this ends, as far as I can see, my contribution to war music'.[7] Yet, as Basil Maine observed, 'Elgar was the composer-laureate of the war no less than he had been of the Edwardian age. The public found in his music an expression of all the surging emotions of war-time and a solace for the fever of them.'[8] Solace there certainly was in *The Spirit of England* (1915-17), though Elgar had found it strangely difficult to complete the first movement of the trilogy where the words demanded angry music from him. He also offered comfort of a different kind, a brief escape from the grind of war, in *The Starlight Express* (December 1915) and *The Sanguine Fan* (March 1917). Or was this the beginning of his retreat?[9] Had he already begun to entertain misgivings about his rôle as a concert-hall militarist, composer of popular imperial marches and tub-thumping choruses such as we find (even before the Edwardian decade) in *The Banner of St George* and the finale of *Caractacus* and in many 'soldier's songs'?[10] *The Music Makers* also swells to the imperial theme; and in August 1915 he had, after all, gone so far as to add his signature to the 'Manifesto on National Service', published in *The Times,* which helped to pave the way for conscription seven months later.[11] But I suspect that by March 1916 he may already, like Mr.

Britling, have started to doubt the old certainties, and to wonder, reading every day the appalling lists of casualties, whether he had any responsibility for encouraging men to enlist. The poet W B Yeats, looking back on another contemporary conflict, more contained but no less bitter, wrote of his own contribution to Irish nationalism: 'Did that play of mine send out / Certain men the English shot?' [12]

Catholic outsiders, whose loyalty might still be suspected in some quarters, may have had to work harder than others to prove their patriotism. But Elgar had somehow succeeded in becoming in his own person a popular symbol of English jingoism, both in his carefully-cultivated military appearance and in the astonishing success he had achieved with *Land of Hope and Glory*.[13] Our 'second National Anthem' is an important image in Ford Madox Ford's splendidly heterodox trilogy of Great War novels depicting the experience and disillusionment of his hero Christopher Tietjens, a member of the Yorkshire squirearchy and, oddly enough, a Catholic and a Tory of the romantic eighteenth-century type like Elgar himself. 'God's England!' Tietjens exclaims in *Some Do Not* (1924), 'Land of Hope and Glory!' . . . 'Church! State! Army! HM Ministry: HM Opposition: HM City Man. . . . All the governing class! All rotten!' [14] In *No More Parades* (1925) Tietjens introduces the novel's title by describing how he came across a War Office official futilely 'devising the ceremonial for the disbanding of a Kitchener battalion', though the war was far from over. Elgar's tune is deconstituted like the troops: 'the band would play *Land of Hope and Glory*, and then the adjutant would say: *There will be no more parades*. . . . Don't you see how symbolical it was: the band playing *Land of Hope and Glory*, and then the adjutant saying *There will be no more parades?* . . . For there won't. There won't, there damn well won't. . . . No more Hope, no more Glory, no more parades for you and me any more. Nor for the country . . . Nor for the world, I dare say . . . None . . . Gone . . . Na poo, finny! No . . . more . . . parades!' [15] In *A Man Could Stand Up* (1926) Tietjens uses the song, in contrast, as a symbol of the continuity of military discipline and justice: when he is abused by an inspecting general out of personal enmity, he tells himself that as an officer he has the right to appeal to the Commander-in-Chief, and if necessary to the King in Council: 'It *is* a land of Hope and Glory!' [16] Elgar's song, and doubtless his persona, seem to have taken on a life of their own.

Something similar happened to Rudyard Kipling, another popular laureate and another non-military man whose early jingoistic poems, like Elgar's marches, show their author naively imagining that men marched into battle with joy and delight in their hearts. We are so used to Elgar's marches that we regard their nationalistic idiom as equivalent to that of Dvořák's *Slavonic Dances*, but they are not so innocent. If we put their glittering orchestral equipage and sheer catchiness to one side for the moment, we realize that they are really a kind of recruitment propaganda, showy street-processions like the example in *Cockaigne*,[17] but Time, which 'pardoned Kipling for his views', in W H Auden's words, has forgiven Elgar, 'pardons him for writing well'. (It is notable, though, that where a lesser composer might have responded to Binyon's 'They went with songs to the battle' in *For the Fallen* by regaling us with a quodlibet of army songs, Elgar's finer aesthetic sense chooses a more abstract, serious theme full of grim determination and purposeful striving.) Kipling, as is well known, changed his attitude after the loss in action of his only son: he bore a double burden of grief and guilt in that he had pulled strings to get the lad commissioned and sent to the front while still under age. His later war poetry concerns itself with problems of pain and fear, and of course a furious hatred of the Germans, and he turned to the devising of dignified memorials instead of recruitment-songs. Uneasy from the first at the very popular music-hall scene that Elgar made out of his pamphlet *The Fringes of the Fleet,* he eventually decided to ban further performances (thereby reducing the hard-pressed composer's income). Lady Elgar probably never forgave him for it, but I suspect that her husband came to understand.

Elgar's breakdown

What has all this to do with the Brinkwells music? If we are to gain some idea of his state of mind at the time, we need to look more carefully into the nature of the unrelenting physical and psychological breakdown that preceded its composition. Elgar himself well knew that his health problems were rooted in his emotional difficulties: as he wrote to Frank Schuster in November 1909 when his doctor puzzled over his persistent colds and sore throats, 'the poor man thinks it's nerves over composition – when it's only heartbreak for something or somebody else'.[18] His wartime ill-health eventually forced Elgar, after painful but unsuccessful electrical cauterizations of his throat, to undergo a tonsillectomy (no joke, in his sixtieth year) on 15 March 1917. Almost immediately afterwards, as he lay Tristan-like in a convalescent haze of pain, the 9/8 theme of the Cello Concerto drifted into his consciousness, to be followed very soon by ideas for the String Quartet; and it is clear from the sketches of the Brinkwells chamber compositions, and from the Elgar diaries, that they all rise from the same hidden aquifer of inspiration: work on any one of them was liable to be interrupted by the sudden advent of ideas for another. Ivor Keys thought that we might almost regard the sequence as a single sustained outpouring in thirteen movements. We need, I think, to speculate a little further on the origins of the spring that began to well up in March 1917.

There must be more to it than the discovery of the magical forested countryside around that Sussex cottage (where, however, the Elgars could still hear the distant firing of guns from across the Channel). Elgar's crisis was long in building. One index of it was his growing need for the company and consolation of Alice Stuart Wortley (his 'Windflower'). Even the circumspect Dr Moore writes that in November 1915 'His own Alice [Lady Elgar] could not fail to be aware of this affection turning toward obsession'.[19] What powered this need for special sympathy, understanding, perhaps confession, that she offered him when his own family could not? At that time, too, came Elgar's first escape from war-music, *The Starlight Express.* Another index, probably, was his growing need to get out of London and stay with his widowed sister Pollie Grafton and her family for a few days at Stoke Prior (where Alice Elgar never came), ten miles north-east of Worcester: two visits in 1914, no less than five in 1915; but his first visit of the following year (in April 1916) proved abortive, for he collapsed in the train and finished up in an Oxford nursing-home: this marks a sudden deterioration.[20] The crisis seems to have reached its most acute phase three months later, from 12 July 1916, when Alice Elgar's diary begins to note, but does not explain, her husband's increasing restlessness: 'E. out a good deal and wishing for the Country' [i.e. Stoke]. Two days later he decides not to go, but then leaves all the same on the 15th. He stays there for longer than the usual three or four days, and on the 20th Alice Elgar expresses some alarm: 'Seemed so long for E. to be away – A. missing him dreffully' [dreadfully]. But Elgar still did not come home. He arranged a meeting with the Windflower in Droitwich on the 24th (which his wife knew about) '& then drove round by the Elms [Pollie's home] & to the Common'. When the Windflower got back, Alice Elgar called round on the 28th to take tea with her, obviously to receive a report about her husband's condition and to confer on the best way of helping him. He, still restless, went on his own to Stratford (29th) and back to Stoke two days later. Then he decided, or more likely was persuaded, to go with his wife to the Lake District, where they were joined for a time by Lalla Vandervelde, another close friend who 'helped' with Edward. This impromptu escape lasted a full three weeks more until their return on 21 August, when 'E. hated coming back to town'.

His condition grew worse and worse, in spite of throat-paintings and cautery. On the 30th he set out for luncheon with Lalla and the Windflower, but had to return home, writing to the latter next day that 'I feel that everything has come to an end and am very unhappy'.[21] What was it that had come to an end? Neither letters nor diaries afford any clue. He went for a few days to Edward Speyer's house at Ridgehurst, but on 6 September reported to the Windflower, home again, that 'I am better but not happy: . . . this is a dreary matter-of-fact world I am in now—& not worth living in'.[22] Why 'now'? What had changed in his life? No-one has looked into this. On the 15th—again at Stoke—he wrote to her that he had enjoyed some relief at the Berkeleys' home, Spetchley Park, 'But I am very sad—& cannot *rest* even here [i.e. at Stoke], so after *one* night I restlessly go home'.[23] In London he continued intermittently ill, though capable of some visits, theatre excursions and professional activity. On 20 December he wrote to congratulate the Windflower on the peerage awarded to her husband; but he himself remained deeply depressed:[24]

> Everything pleasant & promising in my life is dead – I have the happiness of my friends to console me as I had fifty [*sc.* 'thirty'] years ago. I feel that life has gone back so far when I was alone & there was no one to stand between me & disaster – health or finance – now that has come back & I am more alone & the prey of circumstances than ever before.

So far as we can tell from Elgar's own utterances, this was the very nadir of his despair. It is odd that, in publishing this letter, both Dr Moore and Michael Kennedy pass over without comment the phrase 'fifty years ago', which does not make sense. Elgar cannot have been referring to his condition in 1866, when he was nine years old, and 1876 seems almost as unlikely. He must surely have meant 'thirty years ago', 1886, or more precisely the year between October 1885, when his former fiancée, the violinist Helen Jessie Weaver, emigrated to New Zealand, and October 1886, when he gave Alice Roberts her first violin lesson. Why should this sudden access of war-time despair have transported him backwards to that period of his life?

Old wounds reopened

Elgar was then in his late twenties and indeed miserable, a provincial violin-teacher whose career as a composer seemed to be going nowhere. His bad times had begun a year before that, in the spring and early summer of 1884. On 21 April of that year he wrote to his friend Dr Charles Buck that 'My prospects are about as hopeless as ever. I am not wanting in energy I think; so, sometimes, I conclude that 'tis want of ability & get into a mouldy desponding state which is really terrible.' On 20 July he declined Buck's invitation to attend his wedding: 'I will not worry you with particulars but must tell you that things have not prospered with me this year at all, my prospects are worse than ever & to crown my miseries my engagement is broken off & I am lonely . . . I have not the heart to speak to anyone.' [25] He told very few people about his first engagement, not even, apparently, his daughter Carice. (He revealed it to Ivor Atkins only in 1932-3, after more than forty years of close friendship, and evidently in terms which led Atkins to conclude that 'this had profoundly affected much of Elgar's music',[26] in particular the Violin Concerto and the 'Enigma' Variations, the thirteenth of which Atkins arranged to be played at Elgar's memorial service in Worcester Cathedral, along with the Theme, 'C. A. E.' and 'Nimrod'.) In August 1895, no doubt on learning that Helen, who had apparently had smallpox and now had tuberculosis, was to seek a healthier life in New Zealand, Elgar enshrined his love for her in a touching song with these words by John Hay (but the composer's emotionality destroys the literary form of the poem by repeating and even altering certain phrases):

> Through the long days and years
> What will my lov'd one be,
>   Parted from me?
>
> Always as then she was
> Loveliest, brightest, best,
>   Blessing and blest.
>
> Never on earth again
> Shall I before her stand,
>   Touch lip or hand.
>
> But, while my darling lives,
> Peaceful I journey on,
>   Not quite alone.

On 7 October 1885 Elgar wrote to Buck, after visiting him in Settle, 'Miss W. is going to New Zealand this month – her lungs are affected I hear & there has been a miserable time for me since I came home.' [27]

Helen Weaver's children, real and imaginary

That is the last overt mention of Helen Weaver in the Elgar documents, though I have suggested, agreeing with Wulstan Atkins and his father, that it was she who took ship in the thirteenth of the Enigma Variations and was the original mother, as Alice Stuart Wortley was the 'stepmother',[28] of the Violin Concerto.[29] I have also speculated about Elgar's *Dream Children* (1902), his first and most mysterious revisiting of the music of his youth (for Helen and he were childhood friends): I think that the wistful little pieces depict the imaginary children that they might have had together, had they married, just as Charles Lamb's essay, quoted in the work's epigraph, depicts his 'dream children' by 'fair Alice W-n', whose love he also had had to renounce. (Elgar claimed disingenuously that he could not remember why he had composed it.) With the discovery that Helen Weaver, by then Mrs John Munro, had *two* children, a boy and a girl, I became fully persuaded that my hypothesis was correct.[30]

That information came largely from the researches of Dr K E L Simmons and from *The Thirteenth Enigma?* (London, 1988), by Cora Weaver, a relation of the Weaver family by marriage who was able to supplement her privileged local knowledge with useful investigative skills. Helen Munro's children were Kenneth, born 7 July 1891, and Joyce, born 16 February 1893: they would have been eleven and nine years old in 1902. How could Elgar have known about them? Their uncle, and Helen's brother, was Frank William Weaver (b 1855), five years older than her and also a decent violinist, and a good friend of Elgar, who collaborated with him over many years in various local musical activities. Elgar kept in touch with him and his family after Helen had left: Cora Weaver says that his sons Francis Schubert (b 1891) and Bernard John (b 1895) studied the violin with Elgar – perhaps rather unlikely in the case of the younger, but Elgar was still teaching as late as 1898. The boys and their mother Fannie became Catholics in 1900-01, and in 1902, according to Cora Weaver, 'Frank and Fannie's youngest child, Maria Theresa, was born on September 2 and was baptised at St George's five days later, with Edward Elgar as her godfather.' Noticing from Alice Elgar's diary that Edward went to Spetchley on 7 September 1902 and that she attended mass at St George's on her own, I concluded that Elgar must have become godfather by proxy. A check on the baptismal register, however, and Dr Simmons' work, revealed that the godfather was one 'Sylvi O'Brien' and that Elizabeth O'Brien stood in as proxy godmother for Lucy Pipe

- who was Elgar's sister.[31] Family tradition was not quite accurate, then, but even if Elgar was not present, his wife was, and his sister stood sponsor. Elgar was evidently in contact with the Weavers long after Helen had left, and would surely have heard news of her.

Lieutenant Kenneth Munro

It is not known whether Helen Munro revisited England, but her son came over – though not for pleasure. Four months after the outbreak of war, as Cora Weaver tells us, Kenneth Munro, aged twenty-three, joined the Wellington Infantry Regiment as a second lieutenant on 31 December 1914. Promoted first lieutenant in February 1915, he embarked for the Dardanelles as a member of the ANZAC force, reaching the staging-post of Suez on May 26. The Gallipoli landings were of course a wasteful and bloody exercise, and he was one of the many wounded. I have no date for this, and do not know the nature of his injuries, but on 31 August 1915 Kenneth Munro arrived in London for care and recovery at The Royal Free Hospital, Hampstead, where he seems to have stayed until 24 January 1916, when he 'was moved to Grey Towers', a depot for New Zealand troops, in Hornchurch, Essex. While in or based at the Hampstead hospital, he apparently spent five months within short walking distance of the Elgars' home in Netherhall Gardens, Hampstead.

It is hardly credible, since Kenneth still had relatives in Worcester and Elgar twice visited Stoke during this period, that they should not have known of each other's existence and whereabouts. Did they make some kind of contact? Alice Elgar's diary contains no hint of such a thing, but it is very unlikely that she would have referred in its pages to this revenant from her husband's past. As Carice Elgar Blake was later to tell Dora Powell, 'no mention was ever made in a diary of anything disagreeable or vexing'.[32] Alice noted on 5 November 1916, when Edward was alone at 'The Hut' in Maidenhead with his host Frank Schuster, that he was 'Seeing many soldiers from the Hospital' and enjoyed 'Much interesting talk with Soldiers Frank entertained from Hospital'. This was no doubt a near-by one, but it is perhaps worth remarking that around this time Schuster took under his wing Leslie ('Anzy', from ANZAC) Wylde, 'a handsome young New Zealand officer who had lost a leg at Gallipoli—and awoke in hospital to find Frank Schuster bending over him'.[33] Was Elgar talking to New Zealanders?

Kenneth was still at Grey Towers on 22 March 1916, so Cora Weaver says, when the New Zealand soprano Rosina Buckman sang in a concert there. By then he was once more fit for active service, and had been or was to be honoured with three awards, the 1914-15 Star and the British War Medal and Victory Medal. In April 1916, after a short recuperative stay in Egypt, the New Zealand Division landed in France and took up positions near Hazebrouk, where Kenneth rejoined them. Presumably he left England for France and eventually the Somme in late March or early April. If Elgar knew that Kenneth, already wounded in action, had returned to the front line, it would have made him very anxious; and the first really serious symptom of his declining health was, as I have said, his complete collapse in the train to Stoke on April 8 . . .

The second stage of Elgar's crisis began, as I have shown, on July 12 1916. When he opened his *Daily Telegraph*[34] that morning and scanned the 'Roll of Honour' of casualties on the Somme, he would have been horrified to see, amongst the names of the dead (p 5, col 1), 'Munro, Lieut. K., New Zealand Infantry'. Kenneth had been killed in action with fifty other New Zealanders on July 3. London and Hampstead seem immediately have become intolerable for Elgar, who, as we have noted, launched out on his unusually protracted flight to Stoke and thence to the Lake District, his mind beginning to whirl in the maelstrom of misery which we have illustrated above from his subsequent letters to the Windflower. It can only have been Kenneth Munro's death, I suggest, which made him feel that 'Everything has come to an end' and delivered him back into that earlier period of loss and loneliness thirty years before in 1885-6.

The Spirit of England: its 'fourth part' and first performance

A peculiarly agonizing aspect of his grief would have been the knowledge that Helen Munro's suffering must have exceeded even his, and that he was unable to comfort her. One's mind turns back to the second part of *The Spirit of England,* a setting of Binyon's 'To Women', which ends with a picture of the wives' and mothers' bravery and suffering, their hearts 'Burningly offered up, to bleed, / To bear, to break, but not to fail!' Elgar did not need to look far for examples of the womenfolk's anxiety: his own sister Pollie Grafton's boys were in the forces. But one wonders when exactly he may first have learned that Kenneth Munro had enlisted: did he know about it early on, when the young lieutenant was facing the dangers of the Dardanelles? On July 20 1915 Alice's diary records that Elgar played some music, obviously including *The Spirit of England,* to G R Sinclair and was 'raser [rather] worried wanting to alter some chords in his England music afterwards & rather tired'; on the next day she again noted: 'E. raser worried over his music & wanting change'.

While this may refer to Part 1, it is perhaps more likely that he was meditating on the revision that he is known to have made in the ending of 'To Women', at figure 10 . The extraordinary final phrase of the soprano solo, as emended, links with the return in the orchestra of the 'Spirit of England' theme from Part 1 to reveal its origin in the slow movement of the *Serenade* for strings, Op 20 (see Example 1: (a) is the 1st Violin theme from the *Serenade* at 9 bars after letter L , where it returns to form the movement's climax, and (b) the revised end of the soprano solo with part of the theme in Violin I at figure 10 of 'To Women'). On the autograph manuscript of the *Serenade* he had written, in 1892, 'Braut helped a great deal to make these little tunes'; Alice was by then his 'Braut' (bride or fiancée), but so also had Helen Weaver been . . .

There are two further mysteries connected with *The Spirit of England*. Part 1, 'The Fourth of August', was incomplete when Kenneth Munro died.[35] But when Henry Embleton visited Elgar on 23 January 1917, as Alice reported in her diary, he 'urged E. to have 3rd part of Apostles ready for him for March ['next' omitted?] year & 4th part of Spirit of England for this March—Wish he might.' A fourth part? That does not look like a mistake, and indeed Elgar seems to have considered the idea of adding an extra movement to *The Spirit of England* around this time, perhaps prompted by Kenneth Munro's death. In the previous month, on 10 December 1916, Alice reports that Laurence Binyon came to tea, 'Talking about a new poem': had he been

summoned with this in mind? On the 16th he tried to call on the
Elgars again, '& arrived at Hampstd. Tube but cd. not venture to find
way in fog.' There is a letter from him in the Elgar Birthplace Museum
Library which bears this out, preserved in a folder (Item 490) headed
'Poems. / Set to Music' [pencilled:] 'or suggested', no. 52. The letter,
headed 'Sunday', begins: 'I think this is better. But if you don't like it,
I will try again', and goes on to regret the fog and the abandoned visit.
With it is a draft entitled 'Before the Dawn', eventually published as
the penultimate poem in *The Cause: Poems of the War* (London,
[1918]), p. 114, but not included in Binyon's *Collected Poems* of 1931.
The draft, which Binyon appears to have left with Elgar on the 10th,
or posted to him before the 16th, runs:

> Blacker the night grows ere the dawn be risen,
> Keener the cost, and fiercer yet the fight.
> But hark! above the thunder and the terror
> A trumpet blowing splendid through the night.
>
> It is the challenge of our dead undying
> Calling, <u>Remember! We have died for you.</u>
> It is the cry of perilled earth's hereafter—
> Sons of our sons—<u>Be glorious, be true!</u>
>
> Now is the hour when either world is witness;
> Never or now shall [<be>, *del.*] we be proven great,
> Rise to the height of all our strain & story,
> Ay, and beyond; for we ourselves are Fate.

The first stanza is cancelled, with a line drawn through it. With his
letter Binyon must have included a suggested revision, which Elgar
has re-copied below the poet's signature:

> Heavy the hour before [the stars be risen] ?
> Keener the cost, more terrible the fight
> Hearken, above the thunder and the terror
> Sound of a trumpet blowing thru' the night

Elgar was evidently not satisfied with this as a memorial, and must have
asked for another poem, which is the next item in the file, no 53, in
Binyon's hand. It is a draft of the final poem in *The Cause* (p 115), there
entitled 'To the End', and was also omitted from the *Collected Poems*:

> Because the time has stript us bare
> Of all things but the thing we are,
> Because our faith requires us whole
> And we are seen to the very soul,
> Rejoice! from now all meaner fear is fled.

Because we have no prize to win
Auguster than the truth within,
And by consuming of the dross
Magnificently lose our loss,
Rejoice! We have not vainly borne & bled.

Because we chose beyond recall,
And for dear honour hazard all,
And summoned to the last attack
Refuse to falter or look back,
Rejoice! We die, the Cause is never dead.

But this too seems to have been too general or too magniloquent for Elgar's purposes, and he did not in the end add a fourth part to *The Spirit of England.* It would of course have been difficult to contrive a further depiction of mourning which would contrast sufficiently with the pre-existing three.   Or was he still too close to his grief to transmute it into music?

The remaining mystery relates to the first performance of the completed trilogy. This, as Charles A Hooey pointed out in 1996,[36] was not, as had been thought, in Leeds on 31 October 1917, with Embleton's Choral Union and Elgar's then favourite soprano, Agnes Nicholls; nor was it the London performance with the Royal Choral Society at the Royal Albert Hall on 24 November, again with Nicholls but with Gervase Elwes taking the solo in Part 2. No, the première was entrusted to the little-known Appleby Matthews and his Birmingham choir, with The New Orchestra and a single soloist, Rosina Buckman.   It took place on 4 October, and was clearly advertised as the first performance in *The Musical Times* for October 1917 (no 896, p 460). Now an Elgar première, and particularly of such a work, cannot have happened by accident. Composer and publisher must have arranged it. Elgar himself could have attended, since he went to Stoke that day, which was less than fifteen miles away. If so, however, he was there incognito and took no bow, since the newspaper reviews do not mention his presence. Perhaps he felt that the first performance of a work whose music he had dedicated 'to the memory of our glorious men, with a special thought to the Worcesters' ought to take place, if not in Worcestershire, which in wartime lacked the resources to mount it, then at least in reachable distance of the Worcestershire kith and kin who might wish to attend. Perhaps he was thinking more particularly of Kenneth Munro, a Worcester man at one remove, and his Weaver relatives. The choice of a leading New Zealand soprano, Rosina Buckman, who had sung in a concert at Kenneth's camp, may also have been no accident. According to Ernest Newman, she 'was seemingly moved rather too deeply to have complete command of her voice, but she made a noble centre figure for the music.'[37]

Another New Zealander; and an unknown dead war-poet

Yet another New Zealander crops up rather mysteriously in Alice Elgar's diary less than three months after Kenneth Munro's death. On 24 September 1916, 'A[rthur] Alexander, a N. Zealander (Musician)' came to tea, and Edward was '<u>vesy</u> [very] kind to him'. Why this special kindness? The young man, a pianist and composer, had only recently returned from New Zealand.[38] Had he known Kenneth? Did he bring news of Helen Munro and her family's reaction to their loss? Alexander was invited back a month later on the evening of 29 October to join a distinguished gathering to whom Clara Butt 'sang some of the 1st No. of the Spirit of England', then incomplete, and 'It sounded gorgeous'.

I end this section with one more enigma. It is a poem sent to Elgar from a soldier living under bombardment in the front line in France, typed or copied in violet, and undated.[39] Its blank verse, with echoes of Milton, Wordsworth and Browning, is clearly the work of an amateur poet, though not without a certain power:

WITH THE GUNS

Last night I dreamed the universe was mad,
And that the sun its Cyclopean eye
Rolled glaring like a maniac's in the heavens;
And moons and comets, linked together, screamed
Like bands of witches at their carnivals,
And streamed like wandering hell across the sky:
And that the awful stars, through the red light,
Glinted at one another wickedly,
Throbbing and chilling with intensest hate,
While through the whole a nameless horror ran;
And worlds dropped from their places i' the shuddering.
Great spheres cracked in the midst, and belched out flame,
And sputtering fires went crackling over heaven,
And space yawned blazing stars: and Time shrieked out
That hungry fire was eating everything !
The scorched fiends, down in the nether hell,
Cried out, "The universe is mad—is mad!"
And every giant limb o' the universe
Dilated and collapsed, till it grew wan,
And I could see its naked ribs gleam out,
Beating like panting fire—and I awoke.

Underneath the poem the presumed author has added, and underlined, ' <u>'Twas not all a dream; – such is the world to me.</u>' Then came his initials, and ' – In France'. But Elgar, presumably (who else?), has deleted the initials, scratching them completely away with a knife, and substituted a cross, bounded by full stops and quotation marks, thus: – '. + .' – to show that the writer has died. Who was this literate young officer (for only an officer would have had access to a typewriter or typist)? And why did Elgar wish to keep his poem, yet obliterate the evidence of the poet's identity? He kept one of Charles Mott's pencilled letters safe enough;[40] Mott's style of writing, plain and direct, makes no pretension to literary skill, and he wrote that 'the roar of the guns thrills me somehow', so he is an unlikely candidate. The poets at the front whom Elgar knew (Robert Nichols[41] and Laurence Binyon, who served as a Red Cross orderly for a time in 1916) survived the war, and in any case, as I have said, the poem does not seem to be the work of a professional writer. I do not know whether Kenneth Munro had any literary skill or aspirations, but he had enjoyed a decent education at Nelson College, an exclusive boarding-school in South Island. If he were the author, one might readily understand why Elgar treated his poem so strangely.

Return to 1917; return to composition

We need not look much further into Elgar's condition during 1917. The Windflower knew that his only real hope of relief lay in composition, and persuaded him in February to take on the commission for *The Sanguine Fan,* two centuries away from thoughts of the war. One wonders whether she and the Beresfords combined to press Elgar to complete the songs from Kipling's *The Fringes of the Fleet,* a project first mooted a year earlier, in January 1916; the performances kept him occupied and brought him income as a conductor too, in spite of ill-health and air-raids. He would have needed no prompting to finish *The Spirit of England.* All this activity may have helped to dull his anguish, but it taxed his strength, and his physical condition grew worse and worse until a surgical operation became necessary. And then, in its aftermath, the Brinkwells works slowly began to well up into his mind.

The first idea to take shape, in March 1918 as I have said, was the 9/8 theme for what became the first movement of the Cello Concerto.[42] The first surviving sketch and an early copy of it afford no hint that a concerto was intended. The former bears the indications 'II' [Violin

II], 'Va', 'Cello' and again 'II' at respectively bars 9, 11, 13 and 15 of the movement (numbered as it now stands, with the Introduction). That is not quite how Elgar eventually disposed the music; but whether he meant it for orchestral strings or solo string quartet cannot be determined. Most of his time in 1918 was taken up with the chamber works, but on 19 July, when he briefly worked on his sketch again, he talks of it as orchestral, for he noted in his diary 'Began orchestrating 9/8'. And this is the only work that Alice Elgar can have meant when on 27 August she noted in hers that the conductor Landon Ronald, who was visiting them, 'loved the mysterious Orch. piece and wants it dreadfully'. Why 'mysterious'? Had Elgar not disclosed his intentions even to her, or, if he had, did he ask her not to reveal them? We do not know at what point it became a Cello Concerto, but it was before December 1918. In *Elgar as I Knew Him*, W H Reed tells how, when he played over the original sketch with Elgar at Brinkwells 'after the signing of the Armistice', the composer 'said [it] was to be a 'cello concerto'. This would have been during Reed's visit of 3 December 1918, then (he had also stayed there for a few days earlier in the year, from 29 August). His later book *Elgar* repeats the story and confirms the date, since he places the visit later than the Elgars' burglary at Severn House; he there describes the sketch more precisely as 'the first movement of a cello Concerto (first section)'.[43] When Elgar played some of it to Ronald again on 2 June 1919, it was definitely as a cello concerto, and thereafter he worked hard to finish it. The score was posted off to Novello on 8 August. The first Brinkwells work to be conceived had become the last to be completed, and Elgar, preparing to leave for Hampstead, seemed to know that he would compose no more major works there (or perhaps anywhere). The comments he made in a letter to the Windflower on 22 September 1919—unless we are to believe that he has destroyed a major work of whose nature and existence the archives contain no hint—can only refer, surely, to his most recent composition, the Concerto: '. . . I want to get away—strange: but the Studio is sad sad & I feel I have destroyed the best thing I ever wrote & that it had to be so.'[44] He has evidently 'destroyed' a piece of music by putting it to some other use in such a way as to disguise its original nature and purpose.

It now seems possible that the 'mysterious Orch. piece' may have started life as an elegy for the loss of Kenneth Munro, a tribute of the kind that Elgar had paid to several of his friends, but which was hardly capable, in this case, of public exhibition. (He could of course, thanks to the generalizing power of music, have turned it into a universal elegy for the war dead.) The descending contour of the 9/8 theme, a three-limbed sequence which is then three times repeated at the same pitch, is curiously reminiscent of the rather similar procedure at the beginning of another well-known elegy—for solo cello—the *Élégie,* Op 24 (1883), by Gabriel Fauré, whose chamber music Elgar much admired.[45]   Both melodies may suggest grief bowing before the inevitable, Elgar's at first a quiet, accustomed, long-meditated sorrow, Fauré's a strong, immediate outburst with a single repetition, pianissimo; and there may be the suggestion of a body slowly lowered into a grave.   Elgar's theme is longer and more complex, and he introduces subtle alterations into the repeats, not shown here (see Ex 2: (a) is Fauré's opening, (b) Elgar's Concerto, at figure ⌐1⌐):

The bareness of Elgar's unaccompanied theme also recalls the disconsolate unaccompanied octaves for cellos and basses which open Schubert's 'Unfinished' Symphony (another composer who meant much to him), particularly where at figure ⌐3⌐ Elgar's solo cello turns the last bar upwards to a *b*—and to B minor!; even more where this is doubled by the orchestral bassi at 6-7 bars after ⌐6⌐ (see Ex 3: (a) is Schubert's opening, (b) the Concerto, leading into figure ⌐3⌐):

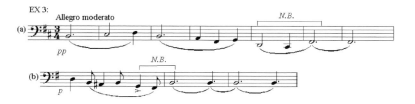

At the first harmonization (figure 2), the chord chosen and the shape of the initial three notes call to mind the opening song of *Die Winterreise*, 'Gute Nacht' ('Goodnight'): the desolate chord—over a tonic pedal, like Elgar's—with which Schubert emphasizes 'eingezogen' ('came hither', in 'A stranger I came hither') later becomes a tolling ritornello figure and accompanies 'nun ist die Welt so trübe' ('now is the world so dreary'). (See Ex 4: (a) gives bars 8-10 of the Schubert, (b) his bars 24-8, (c) Elgar's Concerto at figure 3):

Before moving on to more general considerations, it is worth noting that the opening theme of the second movement of Elgar's String Quartet—generally believed to be a nature portrait with 'captured sunlight', in Lady Elgar's phrase—begins with a rhythm and a profile which hint that he may have been musing on the second of the *Dream Children* pieces: both bear the direction 'piacevole'

(charming, amusing, pleasant). Is the later movement a picture of children at play in the sun? The mature Quartet theme is of course much more complex and artful (see Ex 5: (a) is the Quartet tune, omitting the quaver octave *c* on the first beat which completes the rhythm, (b) is the opening of *Dream Children* No 2):

Programmatic ideas in the Brinkwells music: the context

To Basil Maine, and to the audiences who first heard the Brinkwells music, Elgar seems to have given not the slightest hint that the works enshrined any hidden meanings. Maine therefore asserted that they marked a return to 'abstract' composition – a quality particularly characteristic of chamber music – after several years of involvement with the setting of poetic texts and with theatre music. (His views on the Cello Concerto are put forward as his own.) That would appear to square with various hints and rejected ideas in the composer's letters and his wife's diaries, indicating the kind of music that he did *not* wish to compose.   He ignored William McNaught's naïf suggestion on 9 October 1916 that he should 'write a Bugle call symphony very appealing to all the army'. Two years later, on 27 September 1918, we find Alice Elgar apparently regretting that he had not expressed his feelings about the war in a symphony: she heard in a passage from the slow movement of the Piano Quintet (bars 44-85?) 'another lament wh. shd. be in a War Symphony'. When Sir Gilbert Parker, recently recruited to provide an extra item for *The Fringes of the Fleet*, called in on 30 November 1917 and 'Hoped to do some scene to collaborate with E.' – doubtless on a martial theme – nothing came of it. Elgar did not set the poem by A H Clough – which can only have been 'Say not the struggle naught availeth' – pressed on him by Alice and the Colvins and specially copied out for him by Alice on 13 June 1918. We have seen above how he resisted setting Binyon's 'Peace' ode: this was also urged on him by Sidney Colvin, to whom he replied firmly that '*Peace* music is off'.[46] He had plainly had enough of public war-music and disliked the expectations aroused by his status as composer-laureate. If he still had feelings to express about his wartime experience – and he surely had – he would encode them privately in 'abstract' forms.

There were other motives, probably, which impelled him towards chamber music at this time. One may have sprung from the way in which, as we have seen, he had been plunged back into the 1880s by his emotional crisis of 1916. As Robert Anderson and Jerrold Northrop Moore make clear in their admirable Foreword to Vol 38, *Chamber Music*, of the *Elgar Complete Edition*, to this period belong many unsuccessful attempts to compose chamber music. Like the octogenarian Verdi redeeming his early failure in comic opera, *Un giorno di regno,* by re-creating the genre in *Falstaff,* he may have wished to prove himself by returning in mature triumph to the field of chamber music (and he must have played over some of his early attempts, surely, with the expert violinist Helen Weaver). His remarks on Fauré's chamber works show not only sincere admiration, but also a resentment that the German hegemony in London concerts, symbolized in the figure of Joachim, had deprived Fauré's very different works of a fair hearing.[47] This feeling would have been sharpened by the war. It is curious that Claude Debussy, a musician hardly to be considered as in the same camp as Elgar, also planned a cycle of six chamber works at this time; he proudly signed himself 'musicien français', much as Elgar, in the programme for Clara Butt's grand patriotic concert of 10 October 1914, advertized his appearance as 'By permission of Chief Inspector King, of the Hampstead Special Constables'. (Of course, the wartime decline in concert life and the difficulty of assembling large forces may also have led these composers, like Stravinsky, to write for smaller ensembles.) The movement to establish a native British tradition of chamber music, headed by W W Cobbett, in fact antedates the war: Elgar had been approached by the Worshipful Company of Musicians in those years with a commission for a string quartet, but at the time had let the matter lapse. Only after his Quartet had been published did Cobbett remind him about it and eventually persuade him to accept the fifty guineas.[48] This forgotten commission, nationalist in intention, may consciously or unconsciously have prompted him to provide a corpus of works to head an English tradition of non-Teutonic chamber music.

Programmatic associations in the Elgar literature

We may now approach the question of meaning in these 'abstract' works with a better sense of motivation and context. Over all of them, to a greater or lesser extent, an aura of 'wood-music' has descended. Elgar loved trees, certainly, and recuperated his spirits by making himself into a competent woodman. But the point of working with his hands, surely, was to free his mind to work elsewhere. The accretion of mysterious 'wood-lore' around this music has been well studied, especially in relation to the Piano Quintet, by Michael Pope, in his Foreword to the Eulenberg miniature score of that work (1971). None of it appears to come directly from Elgar himself, but from W H Reed's two books on Elgar and his earlier article on the chamber works in W W Cobbett's *Cyclopedic Survey of Chamber Music*, 2 vols (Oxford, OUP, 1929), where he speaks of a group of dead trees on a high plateau near Brinkwells 'with gnarled and twisted branches . . . a ghastly sight . . . beckoning and holding up gaunt arms in derision', whose sinister influence makes itself felt in all three chamber works; he also points to the Spanish or Moorish or Oriental quality in the first movement of the Quintet. Reed knew Elgar well, of course, and had played through his sketches with him on frequent visits to Brinkwells. Lady Elgar's diary also records scattered comments on the group of dead trees, endorsing the legend that they are 'sad' and 'dispossessed' beings in a dance of 'unstilled regret' for their accursed fate. In Basil Maine's biography of 1933 a footnote on p 268 of the *Works* volume fills this out with what he says is a local legend, that the trees were a group of sinful Spanish monks struck dead by divine retribution for their 'impious rites'; he connects them particularly with the Quintet's first movement at five bars after figure ⃞4 , to which Reed had alluded: 'The Spanish character of this theme suggests that the composer had this legend in mind'. There is indeed a just possibly Spanish, or more accurately gypsy element in the Phrygian semitones that colour bars 78ff of the first movement of the Piano Quintet; and the 'Romance' of the Violin Sonata hints remotely at a kind of triple-time *bolero*. But there were never any Spanish monks in England, let alone Sussex, and no monastic establishment is recorded closer to Brinkwells than three miles to the south, not near the trees. The local legend, if it ever existed, is untraceable today. Alice is more helpful, I think, when she associates with the Brinkwells works Elgar's remarkable words and music for the partsong 'Owls', a sinister picture of nature's nihilism and indifference to death and decay. No doubt Alice discussed all of her ideas with Reed: but did Elgar? Reed does not say so. Maine, too, does not say that his information came from Elgar. One's belief that Lady Elgar may have been fantasizing is increased when she later associates Bulwer Lytton's *A Strange Story* with the Quintet, a novel which is concerned with the occult, but not with dead trees and thunder-blasted Spanish monks. Pope is right to suspect that another visitor to Brinkwells, Algernon Blackwood, an expert spinner of uncanny tales, may have played an inventive part in all this. A further insight into Alice's tendency to fantasize in a proprietorial manner about her husband's music may be seen in her post-hoc reinterpretation of his First Symphony after a performance on 6 January 1916: 'The great tune so majestic & beautiful. Then the wild underspirits & vain things conquered by it—Then the pagan tune absolutely a picture of the Huns & the great struggle ending in absolute triumphant Victory of the great rights of humanity—so wonderful & uplifting.' The eight-year-old pre-war Symphony has become prophetic indeed.

Other possibilities

Elgar himself, as is well known, mistrusted the literalism and onomatopoeia to which programme music could easily descend, presumably because it might limit, rather than stimulate, both the composer's imagination and the listener's response. His public pronouncements on the meaning of his works are always rather general and imprecise, though he liked to hint at enigmas; even his private observations to friends are almost as vague, mysterious and tantalizing, never concrete, and often phrased as questions. He evidently wondered at the blasted trees near (it seems) Bedham; but his artistic response would have been poetic and generalizing. In 1917, would they not have reminded him, not of the misdemeanours of Spanish ecclesiastics (such as the Capuchin Ambrosio and the nuns in Matthew Lewis' notorious Gothic horror-novel *The Monk* (1796), source of many an opera-plot), but rather of the shattered trees in the war-torn landscapes of Paul Nash, first exhibited in London in June of that year?[49] Several of his pictures show 'the shell-chopped trees that fang the plain', as Edmund Blunden described them in his poem 'The Zonnebeke Road'. Others, and much war art and photography besides his, depict demolished buildings and churches, and as early as 21 September 1914 the Elgars 'Heard of the destruction of Reims [sic] Cathedral—Much upset'. If Elgar propped up a fragment of plainsong, lintel-like, in the piano octaves at the opening of his Quintet four years later (a possible allusion to the first four notes of the *Salve Regina,* but then why only four?), and if he commented on it with horror in the shuddering revulsion of the accompanying string figures, what was more likely to have been in his mind, Spanish monks misbehaving, or the desecration of the smashed churches in Belgium and northern France? (Those 'bare ruin'd choirs' would also have reminded Elgar, a Catholic, of the destruction of English monasteries at the time of the Reformation: either memory might have led him to describe the Quintet's first movement to Ernest Newman as 'ghostly stuff'.[50]) The sorrow and regret at figure 1 then become a much more understandable sequel, and the angry 6/8 at figure 2 an entirely justified call to arms. After the return of the regret at figure 4, may not the broken, irregularly limping phrases from bar 79 onwards be heard as a helpless wringing of the hands, the sense of beauty (major) oppressed by grief (minor)? A 'Spanish' interpretation (and why should the pizzicato chords at figure 5 represent a guitar, since they suggest neither a *rasgueado* nor a dance-rhythm?) would tend to set this apart as a quite new section, whereas the music develops logically and audibly from the first three notes of the opening piano octaves (here repeated in the bass *a,g,a*) and also in the tune above, whose rhythm, moreover, extends that of the 'shuddering' figure. At figure 6 this is re-cast as more confident, joyful music, as of a people reaching up against the oppressor in communal purpose. At figure 8 the opening music returns, to be reworked into four-bar phrases at 9 and into a tight, regular fugato at 10: is not this a nation pulling itself together and organising for war? Bernard Shaw disliked the fugato, which Elgar defended:

> it was meant to be square at that point and goes wild again—as man does . . .[51]

These must be soldiers, then, running wild in the heat and frenzy of battle. The wildness is achieved with a rising semiquaver figure, derived from bar 79, and tremendous antiphonal conflict between piano and strings; at the climax of the warfare (14) – a varied recapitulation – a triplet form of the semiquaver figure links it with the variant of the strings' music at 2, first heard in bars 49-51. The wheel has come full circle, for this in turn derives from the opening three notes of the 'plainsong'. So one might continue. The point is not, however, that my interpretation of the movement is necessarily right, but that thoughts of 'Spanish monks' distract one from the free play of the listener's imagination and experience of life which Elgar felt that his music should evoke. But it may be that, having refused to write any more self-proclaimed 'war music', he welcomed his wife's diversionary imaginings as a kind of smoke-screen.

Elgar's comment proved to be of some use here. What else did he himself say about the Brinkwells works? A remark to the Windflower after a performance of the Piano Quintet on his seventieth birthday in 1927 suggests that she was in some way present in it, or knew what it was 'about': 'the Quintet is not of this world; but you know more of this than I do'.[52] The slow movement delivers a message of peace, but also an aching regret, and it may be that Canon W H T Gairdner was right to hear in the finale (which revisits memories of the first movement) 'a second chance of a blessed, healthy, sane life in a restored world';[53] to some writers, however, its thematic invention has seemed to fall below Elgar's best. He was aware that his Brinkwells music would appear in some ways old-fashioned, and in writing to offer the dedication of the Violin Sonata to Marie Joshua on 6 September 1918 he said

> I fear it does not carry us any further but it is full of golden sounds and I like it[:] but you must not expect anything violently chromatic or cubist.[54]

This was still to be three-dimensional music, then, using the perspective of tonality. Though 'abstract', it would not be analytical or synthetic but would depend on the traditional language of feeling.[55] Whose music would he have considered cubist? Probably that of Picasso's friend Stravinsky: he knew *The Firebird* and *Petrushka* and, if Alice Elgar's comments are to be trusted, did not like them. Later on, after his wife's death, his sense of isolation and his unhappiness over recent developments in music are evident in some remarks to Ernest Newman:

> music I loathe--I did get out some paper—but it's all dead. . . . The old life is over and everything seems blotted out. . . . I see little in the musical world which wd. be pleasing to you—it all seems "gone ugly".[56]

To Alice Stuart Wortley he described the first movement of the Sonata as 'bold & vigorous', and so it is, save for the strange static interlude beginning at figure ⑤; he defined the Romance as

> fantastic, curious . . . with a very expressive middle section: a melody for the Violin—they [Landon Ronald and W H Reed] say it's as good as or better than anything I have done in the expressive way: this I wrote just

after your telegram about the accident came [a very painful broken leg] &
I send you the pencil notes as first made at that sad moment . . . The last
movement is very broad & *soothing* like the last movemt of the IInd
Symphy[.][57] I have been sketching other things which are full of old times

– like the Sonata itself, presumably. In other words, it was full of his
feelings for the Windflower, which never found finer or more original
expression than in the astonishing outpouring of endless and
cadenceless melody in the Romance, from figures 28 to 34, of which
he enclosed a sketch. This is a single span no less than 58 bars long,
and in its first version the violin's line was not interrupted by the rests
that he later introduced into it three bars after figure 30 and five bars
before 34.[58] It is exactly the same kind of purely Elgarian melody that
he later enshrined, in more contained fashion, in the third movement
of the Cello Concerto – another totally original creation.

During the finale of the Sonata there are hints at the 'Bliss' motive
from Wagner's *Ring* in the theme beginning at figure 43, and
perhaps at a phrase from Isolde's *Liebestod* in the eighth bar after 41
and later. It is very surprising to discover that the return of twenty
bars of the tune from the slow movement at figure 53 of the finale
was not part of Elgar's original plan, since such a backward reference
at such a point is characteristic of him. The change was apparently
motivated by news of Marie Joshua's death, but it is the Windflower's
melody, and it provides a perfect counterpoise to the rather restless
striving of the finale's other thematic material. The music is
transposed so as to begin in E major and put into 3/2 time instead of
3/4: the sketch makes it clear that a slower tempo is intended by the
direction 'L'istesso tempo' (omitted in the published version) and the
note, 'Keep in this tempo: *not* as in the Andante'. A more surprising
alteration is the intrusion into the piano part, in the two bars before
figure 54, of the third phrase of the theme of the 'Enigma' Variations
(and at 54 Elgar has changed the violin's *e* to an *a*, noting on the
sketch 'more final here, so A'). This third phrase of the 'Enigma', so I
have suggested, was conceived to the words 'Nulla chieggio' from the
Tasso pseudo-quotation copied at the end of the score of the
Variations: 'I ask for nothing'. A tribute to Marie Joshua, then,
encloses a tribute to the Windflower, which refers to a tribute (as I
maintain) to Helen Weaver. This is indeed to 'draw three souls out of
one weaver', as Elgar once wrote to A J Jaeger.[59]

Of the String Quartet he spoke rather less, and it keeps more of its
mystery. He advised Harriet Cohen in 1932 not to lead off with it in a

concert of his chamber works, because it 'starts in rather a phantom-like way',[60] and certainly it is easy to hear the hoarse whisper of some gaunt visitant in the depressed, modal harmony[61] and strangely-spaced homophony of its opening bars. But whose ghost is it? I think I must agree with Ivor Keys that it is Elgar himself, awakening hollow-eyed after long and disturbed sleep—with a start of surprise in the curious rhythm of the second bar, since he finds himself in 1918 and not the 1880s. He tries to speak, but at first can only whimper, and sends for music-paper to set his thoughts down . . . (I recall my own recovery from a tonsillectomy in my forties. Fanciful? I admit it, but do not repent.) The thoughts come crowding fast and cause him to elaborate the texture with a profusion of detail springing from his mastery of counterpoint and expert knowledge of stringed instruments. It is the kind of detail that some find restless, overloaded, even neurasthenic in the large orchestra of the Second Symphony: in the string quartet it has found its ideal medium, but players would be well advised not to take the music too fast. Another reason is the constant incidental modulation of key:[62] though the general tonal framework is clear enough, Elgar makes frequent play in this work and elsewhere in the Brinkwells music (eg the first and second movements of the Violin Sonata, the second movement of the Cello Concerto, the harmonization of the opening melody of the second movement of the Piano Quintet) with the ambiguity between a tonic and its relative minor, or sometimes its mediant. (It is curious to find Stravinsky doing something very similar when he re-interpreted the harmonic language of classical tonality in such works as the *Symphony in C* of 1938-40.)

I suspect that Elgar was referring to this technical feature, nowhere carried to greater lengths than in the second movement of the Quartet, when he told Troyte Griffith years later that there 'there is something in it that has never been done before'.[63] In this I disagree with Professor Brian Newbould, though admiring his sensitive analysis of the movement's form. Look at the harmonization of the first 23 bars (see Ex 6). In this pure three-part writing, which here recalls Handel's (and over two-fifths of the movement is composed essentially in three parts), C major is the only key which holds the harmonies together; yet, after the initial octave *c*, there is no firm chord of C major except on the first beats of bars 15 and 17, where it is so approached that it feels like the submediant of E minor; there is only one half-cadence, an unusual one, on to the dominant (bar 6); in bar 23, however, the ear eventually accepts the *g* sharps quite naturally as *a* flats ushering in the return of the theme in C. (There is a pencilled note in the sketch, in which Elgar tells himself to repeat bars 7-8 with a new continuation, 'Bis 2nd to A ped C ♮' – so as to lead to A minor (bars 15ff) over a pedal *c.*)

EX 6

Moving on, the fleeting arrivals on to an E minor chord (bar 36) and its dominant (bar 41) are made to feel like interruptions of G major. An extraordinary play of three-part permutations then leads to the first firm C major cadence for a foreshortened repeat of the opening five bars. The MS note runs 'to Bar 5 to E dom[inan]t then 2nd theme'. But again the new tonic of A minor is destabilized with C major, G minor, F sharp minor, D major, though returning in bars 71 and 97 as the only tonic (with its cognate A major) which holds all these together. At bar 107, long pedal *g*s set in, which feel like like preparation for the return of C, but the harmony refuses to settle, and fourteen bars of ambiguous permutations supervene before the expected rearrival and recapitulation. At bar 183 the brief return of the opening is again truncated to five bars, to land on the dominant of D minor. At bar 228 the *g* pedal of bar 107 becomes, in one sense rather unexpectedly, a pedal on *c*, the hoped-for tonic; but the harmonic play, and the return of the permutations at bar 245, now also placed over the same pedal, keep the music in the air and allow a gradual relaxation to the final muted repeat of the opening at bar 261. It is again reduced to five bars, though Elgar had originally written six and altered it at the last moment by excising the fourth bar and ingeniously joining up the seam (which Newbould thinks had 'never been done before'). This seems to me pretty clearly designed to match the earlier foreshortenings in phrase-length and to throw a stronger rhythmic emphasis on to the surprising unaccompanied *d* of the viola in bar 265. Repeated, this gives rise to further hesitation and excision. Finally, the pedal theme of bar 15 is approached from what can now only be C major, and varied, still over a *c* pedal, with the ambiguous *g*sharps acting firmly as *a* flats. This is one of Elgar's most perfect movements;[64] from a technical point of view it evinces a complete Brahmsian understanding of classical tonality and a subtle skill in exploiting the gravitational relativity of key-areas in a new and unexpected way. I have expressed the view that the movement represents the bustling activity of charming children gravely enjoying themselves in intensely serious play—perhaps Elgar's *Dream Children*. It seems unnecessary to go along with Lady Elgar's imagery for the last movement, with her 'galloping squadrons': this is another of Elgar's shoulder-squaring finales, facing the future with confidence and unexpectedly renewed vigour, with only a momentary misgiving in the four bars before figure 49 .

The Cello Concerto had a much longer gestation than the other Brinkwells pieces, and the initial early inspiration of the 9/8 theme seems to have become transmuted, so I have suggested, into a work differing in some important way from Elgar's original intention. Knowledge of its first kernel or template, however, allows us to recognize in many of its themes Elgar's astonishing ability to derive new material of distinct character from a single generic outline. If we consider the 9/8 theme itself and look at the first two-bar unit (which is twice repeated in sequence, a sixth lower, to form the remainder of it), the initial five notes seem to have generated the last five by inversion and reversal of values (see Ex 7 (a)). The opening of the initial cello solo, whose first four notes also usher in the second movement and which returns complete at figure 79 near the end of the last movement, is derived from the outline of the 9/8 theme (Ex 2 (b) above) in its first four notes (marked with a cross in Exx 7 (a) and (b)) and also in the way in which it is extended by means of three descents in slightly varied rhythmic sequence to a bottom *e*. The rising fourth of the opening is answered – denied? – by the falling fifth at the end. The effect is to convert the 9/8 idea into a Zeus-defying gesture (the opening fourth), which is however compelled to acknowledge defeat and to bow down to the decree of malevolent providence – surely a musical translation of the 'cruelty I resent bitterly & disappointedly' of Elgar's letter to Binyon of 5 November 1918 (see above): Elgar has arrived at the nihilism of King Lear. After a pathetic repeat four bars before figure 1, he introduces a gently questioning, upward-looking phrase – 'Must it be?' – which melts away into the 9/8 theme as if in a cinematic dream-dissolve.

If we turn to the slow movement, where the tune proper begins (up-beat to bar 9), the same four-note opening gesture, now decorated with a dip to the lower octave, is transformed so as to become the tender sympathy, shared anguish, and counsel of acceptance that this extraordinary music conveys—it seems to me that this must originally have been addressed to Kenneth's mother, or to all bereaved mothers (see Ex 7 (c)).[65] In the 'quasi Recitative' that marks the return to E minor at the beginning of the last movement (figure 42), the template returns yet again. The rising fourth is now depressed into a minor third (which was of course present in the 9/8 theme), and once more its first phrase is extended through the familiar descent in triple sequence (see Ex 7 (d)); this is repeated in varied form, and is to become the main subject of the last movement proper, linking that too, therefore, with the 9/8 theme. First, however, the rising phrase, which had been pathetic at four bars before figure 1, is turned in the cadenza before 44 into a repeated speech of protest, each attempt muted by a *diminuendo,* but culminating, with its upward arpeggio, in a terrifying shout of accusation.

EX 7

All this thematic integration has made itself felt mostly in the rhetorical introductions prefacing the first, second and fourth movements. It is mainly by this means, I think, that Elgar has succeeded in making a convincing four-movement concerto out of what was probably intended as a single-movement Elegy. (All his other memorial pieces are in one movement.) Why does he need four movements, when his Violin Concerto, like most concertos, has only three? The slow third movement seems an entirely appropriate pendant – 'For Women'? – to the elegiac first. He probably composed it second, since Alice's diary originally described the present second movement ('diddle, diddle') as the third; that might possibly explain why she made a curious and uncharacteristic mistake in laying out the instrumentation of the Adagio for full orchestra—did she still think at that point that the present second movement was to be the third? Having conceived two slow movements, Elgar would naturally have needed to design a fast movement showing off the traditional virtuosity of a concerto to separate them. The fantastic will-o'-the-wisp scherzo that he produced stands in place of the weightier concerto-style Allegro that we might have expected. The movement has nothing elegiac about it (nor does the main body of the finale): this is doubtless why Elgar told the Windflower that he had 'destroyed' his original idea. He linked his Allegro Molto to the Elegy by means of a strange prefatory 'RECIT.' (figures 18 - 20) which is much more portentous than the ensuing musiic. What does it mean? Elgar sets off with a quiet *pizzicato* repeat of the concerto's opening, which becomes menacingly louder and faster with each chord until the full orchestra interrupts it with a sudden and unexpected hammer-blow. Some will call me naïf, but I venture to suggest that this and what follows depicts the shock of dreadful news: Elgar reading the announcement of the death of Kenneth Munro. The fragment of scherzo theme feels like spiders down the spine. The stricken mind is at first numb, uncomprehending (bars 3-6): can it be? Then, with a move from E minor to the more tender G or C major (bars 18-19), he thinks of the mother. An accelerating crescendo of horror leads to an outbreak of protest in the 'Lento', breaking down into chromatic grief. The three bars before figure 20 repeat the harmonic process more containedly and lead with greater composure into the 'scherzo', but it seems a hollow joke.

The other virtuoso Allegro, the finale, also avoids elegy for most of its course, and is also a kind of bitter joke. After its own introduction, it sets off as a grim, grotesque and obsessive dance, whose God-defying gesticulations are doomed to failure. The brief attempts at lyrical tenderness at figure 47 end in ridiculous prat-falls, after which the theme's aspirations frenziedly resume but are forced down to earth. At figure 59 the principal idea returns, marked with the familiar Elgarian 'nobilmente'; but this is satirical, for the line is doubled by the lower strings of the orchestra, so that the new phrasing merely makes the theme appear heavy, Falstaffian and clumsy. At figure 66 , however, we reach a throbbing pause on the dominant of F sharp minor, and heartbreak and anguish supervene: this extraordinary but tightly-organised lament, the most dense and chromatic music that Elgar ever wrote, seems to enshrine Wilfred Owen's 'Futility': 'Was it for this the clay grew tall?' A brief reference to the consolatory opening of the slow movement melody leads to a resumption at figure 72 of the opening statement from the first movement, now marked, as though the intervening music had explained its significance, 'QUASI RECIT.' After that, a terse seventeen bars of the demonic dance conclude what was to be Elgar's last major work. In some respects, I think that Elgar might have chosen for it another epigraph from Owen: 'My subject is War, and the pity of War'. Maine was right. This is all quite unprovable, of course; but I do not see how the concerto can be adequately performed without bringing some such intense life-experience into it.

He never completed another major work. That much-talked-of Piano Concerto remained a sketch. Convinced of the cruelty of God, he was never going to compose the third part of the *Apostles* trilogy. For several years, oppressed further still by the death of his wife on 7 April 1920, he felt that he had 'reached the end . . . my whole past is wiped out & I am quite alone': not even the Windflower could comfort him.[66] Paying tribute to Alice Elgar in a letter to Ivor Atkins of 30 December 1922, he implied—surely overstating the case—that his pessimism was constitutional and had always dogged him, tracing it back to the time of *The Black Knight* (1889-92): he is only partly jesting when he speaks of 'the malevolence of the Creator of all things' and 'the horrors piled on by the aforesaid beneficent fiend', concluding that he 'should have . . . joined Job's wife in the congenial task of cursing God.'[67] It would not have softened his nihilism if he had learned that Helen Munro's other child, her daughter Joyce, had died of inherited consumption on 6 October 1921. Helen's husband was to die on 14 September 1925, and she herself, of intestinal cancer, on 23 December 1927. Elgar again revisited music from the time of his association with her in the *Severn Suite* (1930) and *Nursery Suite* (1931). He formed new relationships and recovered his spirits sufficiently to attempt, but not complete, a third symphony and an opera. But he was never to regain the zest, the belief in the meliorative power of music, that sense of 'sublimities', that 'happy art and faith', in Robert Graves' words (see my epigraph) which the war had knocked out of him. We are lucky that Brinkwells at least enabled him to recuperate his health and artistic abilities for long enough to transmute that sense of loss, and the pity of it, into enduring music.

NOTES and SOURCES

1. *Elgar: His Life and Works* (London, 1933) vol i, *The Life*, p 206
2. 'Elgar', *The New Grove,* 2nd ed (London, 2001) p 121, col a
3. '"Ghostly Stuff": The Brinkwells Music', in Monk, R (ed): *Edward Elgar: Music and Literature* (Aldershot, 1993) pp 108-120
4. Elgar, Edward (ed Young, P M): *A Future for English Music* (London, 1968) p 61
5. Killed: Isabel Fitton's brother Hugh, Lady Barttelot's first husband, Carice

Elgar's first beau, Mansfield Evans. Wounded: Hubert Leicester's son Philip. Some writers have found it strange that Elgar at one point expressed himself as more shocked at the slaughter of horses than at the death of soldiers, but this was very early in the war, and the men, unlike the horses, were volunteers (see Moore, J N: *Edward Elgar: Letters of a Lifetime* (Oxford, 1990) p 277). It is hard today to imagine what a horse-drawn cavalry war must have been like. The following lines, though poor verse, give some idea (from Graves, Arnold F: *The Turn of the Tide* (London, 1916) p 9):

> There, where our troopers charged that day,
> A thousand dying horses lay.
> 'Twas terrible to hear them neigh.
> Yet there was no one by to lend
> A hand their agony to end.

6. See Moore: *Letters of a Lifetime*, p 320. By the time Binyon came to publish his ode in *The Four Years: War Poems* (London, 1919, pp 165-9) he had removed all trace of any 'appeal to the Heavenly Spirit', perhaps in an attempt to persuade Elgar to change his mind and set the poem to music: according to Michael Kennedy he almost succeeded (*Portrait of Elgar*, 3rd ed (Oxford, 1987) p 277). In the end he had to content himself with Nicholas Gatty's setting of 'An Anthem of the Sister Nations' (Binyon, *op cit*, pp 163f and note on [170]).
7. Moore, *op cit*, p 307. The children's song *Big Steamers* (June 1918) hardly counts.
8. Maine, *op cit*, p 205
9. But Elgar would have known that escapist music was important to fighting-men: see the soldier's letter of November 1917 in Moore, J N: *Edward Elgar: A Creative Life* (Oxford, 1987) pp 694f. Siegfried Sassoon uses the memory of great music to make a similar point in his poem 'Secret Music'; but in 'Dead Musicians' he says that great music cannot revive for him the 'memory of my friends who died': it is only 'fox-trot tunes' that can summon their ghosts (*Collected Poems* (London, 1947) pp 32f, 92f). Elgar made another attempt to escape in summer 1917 (and perhaps August 1918) by sketching further male-voice part-songs on poems from the Greek Anthology . There are enough drafts, all save one incomplete, for two further sets. Many of these sketches, of course, must belong to 1902, but Alice Elgar refers in her diary for 12 July 1917 to 'E thinking of beautiful Scene from Greek Anthology [;] beautiful idea': this must refer to the remarkable fugal treatment of Plato's 'Peace, wooded crags', translated by Richard Garnett (British Library Add MS 63153, f 27r).
10. Whatever his feelings in 1917, he composed two more marches after the war, and both words and music for the marching-song *Zut! zut! zut! zut!* The earlier 'soldier's songs' include, we ought not to forget, an unpublished anti-German marching-song of 23 March 1909, also to his own words, which are lost save for the final exhortation 'Wake!' (originally 'Rise': see BL Add MS 63160, f 55v, and Young, P M: *Elgar, OM: A Study of a Musician* (2nd ed, London, 1973) p 140); and the lost *Song for Soldiers,* or *The Roll Call,* with words by Harold Begbie, withdrawn and apparently destroyed after its performance at Clara Butt's patriotic concert in the Royal Albert Hall on 10 October 1914 (it is not listed in

the programme, which the R A H Archive Dept kindly copied for me, but Alice Elgar's diary confirms that it was sung); the text was not published in any volume of Begbie's verses, but was probably taken from a newspaper. Elgar was apparently ashamed of these two, but not of his song for Sir Francis Younghusband's Fight for Right movement, intended to give a spiritual dimension to the war; it was sung by Gervase Elwes at the same R A H concert as Parry's *Jerusalem* on 28 March 1916, and sets six fine lines from Book II of William Morris' *The Story of Sigurd the Volsung and the Fall of the Niblungs,* beginning 'When thou hearest the fool rejoicing'. I am also now able to identify two further incomplete sketches for settings of patriotic verse by Kipling: one is from *The Fringes of the Fleet,* 'Farewell and adieu to you, Greenwich ladies' (BL Add MS 69835, ff 6v-7r); the other a setting of Kipling's 'The Choice' (presumably April or May 1917), celebrating the entry of the USA into the war, identified from the heading 'Kipling', the metre and the three words 'Who bade us' (v6): this would have been a large setting for chorus and orchestra (BL Add MS 63155, ff 43v-5r and 51r).

11. See Moore, J N: *A Creative Life,* p 687
12. 'The Man and the Echo', *The Collected Poems of W B Yeats* (London, 1952) p 393
13. At the outbreak of war, he and A C Benson tried to remove the exhortation to imperial aggrandizement of the refrain 'Wider still and wider . . . make thee mightier yet' by substituting:

> Gird thee well for battle, bid thy hosts increase,
> Stand for faith and honour, smite for truth and peace,

but the revised version never caught on (though its militarism is no less fierce). See Moore, J N: *Letters of a Lifetime,* pp 277-83.
14. I have omitted some musical commentary which seems incomprehensible, though Ford, son of the music-critic Francis Hueffer, once thought of studying at the Royal College of Music: 'Land of Hope and Glory! – F natural descending to tonic C major: chord of 6-4, suspension over dominant seventh to common chord of C major. . . . All absolutely correct! Double basses, cellos, all violins: all woodwind: all brass. Full grand organ: all stops: special *vox humana* and key-bugle effect. . . .' (Penguin Books edition, 1948, pp 116f).
15. Penguin Books edition, 1948, p 19
16. Penguin Books edition, 1948, p 172
17. The marching soldiers on the illustrated cover to *Cockaigne* are wearing pith helmets, so this is a recollection of the Diamond Jubilee procession and unmistakably imperialistic (cf the reproduction in McVeagh, *op cit,* p 119).
18. Moore: *Letters of a Lifetime,* p 213
19. Moore, J N: *The Windflower Letters* (Oxford, 1989) p 156
20. Moore: *A Creative Life,* pp 671, 685f, 695
21. Moore: *The Windflower Letters,* p 169
22. *Ibid,* p 169
23. *Ibid,* p 170
24. *Ibid,* p 172
25. Moore: *Letters of a Lifetime,* pp 10f
26. Atkins, Wulstan: *The Elgar-Atkins Friendship* (Newton Abbot, London & North Pomfret, Ve, David & Charles, 1984) p 477

27. Moore: *op cit*, p 112

28. Moore: *The Windflower Letters*, p 50, letter to Schuster of late May 1910

29. Trowell, Brian: 'Elgar's use of Literature', in Monk, R (ed): *Edward Elgar: Music and Literature* (Aldershot, Scholar Press, 1993) pp 182-326

30. *Ibid*, pp 241ff, 284. Elgar omits from his epigraph Lamb's phrase 'The children of Alice call Bartrum father', which reveals that she now had children, but by another man: this completes the analogy with his own situation.

31. I am grateful to Tony O'Hanlon, Parish Administrator of St George's Catholic Church, Worcester, for his kindness in sending me a facsimile of the relevant entry.

32. Powell, Mrs Richard: *Edward Elgar: Memories of a Variation*, 4th edn, rev & ed by Powell C (Aldershot & Brookfield, Ve, 1994) p 84. The earlier diaries, nevertheless, contain from time to time the cryptic abbreviation 'A.w.b.', 'a.w.b.', once 'A.w.braut', which I interpret as 'angry with Braut'.

33. Moore: *The Windflower Letters*, p 245

34. The Elgars would surely have taken the *Telegraph;* on 22 July 1918, Edward noted in his diary 'DT did not come.'

35. Elgar had difficulty setting Binyon's lines at figure $\boxed{10}$:

> She [England] fights the fraud that feeds desire on
> Lies, in a lust to enslave or kill',

eventually using themes from the Demons' chorus in *The Dream of Gerontius*. He may have thought the verse poor at this point ('desire on' rhymes with 'iron') and hoped that the ever-obliging Binyon would improve it. He did, later on, but not much! – to:

> She fights the force that feeds desire on
> Dreams of a prey to seize and kill

(*Collected Poems of Laurence Binyon: Lyrical Poems* (London, 1931) p 206). Apropos Elgar's stopping work on *For the Fallen* because of the Cambridge composer Cyril Rootham's prior rights in the poem, I may as well record here what my music-teacher the Rev W C M Cochrane – who passed on to me his love for Elgar's music – told me at Christ's Hospital in *c*1948. He had read Music at Cambridge in the early 1930s, and recalled that Rootham, who was vain about his compositions, was known there as 'van Roothoven'. Cochrane attended a lecture by Rootham in February 1934 on the morning when Elgar's death was announced. Rootham began with the remark, 'Well, gentlemen, I see that a would-be English country gentleman has died', whereupon the whole class got up and left.

36. Hooey, Charles A: 'Spirit Insights', *The Elgar Society Journal,* vol 9, no 6 (November 1996), pp 296-301, with useful additional note by the Editor on p 302

37. Newman's review, from *The Birmingham Daily Post,* was more accessibly reprinted in *The Musical Times* for November 1917, vol 58, no 897, p 506.

38. Alexander, who had been a pupil of Matthay at the RAM, had returned to New Zealand (via Australia) on a concert tour before the outbreak of the war (see p 95). I am grateful to the editor for identifying him: see Foreman, Lewis:

From Parry to Britten: British Music in Letters 1900-1945 (Batsford, 1987) pp 66, 91 and pl 15.

39. It is in the folder 'Poems Set to Music or suggested', item 490 in the Birthplace Library, already adduced, no 34.
40. Moore: *Letters of a Lifetime*, p 313
41. The poem that Nichols read to the Elgars on 16 January 1921, whose title is missing from Carice's diary, though she says it was dedicated to her father, must have been 'Plaint of a humble servant', item 7 in his *Aurelia* (London, 1920), pp 59-61, 'For EDWARD ELGAR'; it is about the humble jackass whom Christ rode on the first Palm Sunday, and resembles Chesterton's better-known 'The Donkey'. Item 15, 'Swansong', is dedicated to Philip Heseltine [Peter Warlock].
42. Most of the information in this paragraph is taken from the excellent Foreword and source-descriptions in Anderson, Robert and Moore, Jerrold Northrop (eds) *The Concertos (Elgar Complete Edition*, vol 32 (London, 1988)). See also Anderson, R: 'Toward a Flawless Work', in *Affetti musicologici* (Festschrift Z M Szweykowski), ed P Poźniak (Krakow, Musica Iagellonica, 1999), pp 433-9.
43. Reed, W H: *Elgar as I knew him* (London, 1936, reissued 1973) p 64; *and* Reed, W H: *Elgar* (London, 1939, reprint with additions of 1949) p 123
44. Moore: *The Windflower Letters*, p 230
45. Moore: *Letters of a Lifetime*, pp 388, 390f; Alice Elgar's diary, 30 November 1919: 'E liked the Fauré Quartet vesy muss' [very much]—a piano quartet, but which of the two?
46. McVeagh, Diana M: *Edward Elgar: His Life and Music* (London, 1955) p 66; Kennedy, M: *op cit*, p 277
47. See footnote 44 above
48. McVeagh: *op cit*, p 67, relates the little-known story, which explains why Elgar also resurrected a youthful piano trio at this time, feeling he should do more to earn the fee (but did not complete it).
49. I cannot prove that Elgar knew Nash's highly-acclaimed work, but Alice attended the Belgian Exhibition 'Art at the Front' on 15 February 1917; she 'saw pixtures [pictures] etc', which might have been Nash's at Gimpel Fils, on 22 June 1917; and on 6 March 1918 saw 'wonderful War pictures at Grafton galleries'.
50. Letter of 5 January 1919, in Moore: *Letters of a Lifetime*, p 321
51. Moore: *op cit*, pp 323f
52. Moore: *The Windflower Letters*, p 313
53. For Gairdner's personal view of the whole Quintet, see Appendix 2 of my 'Elgar's Use of Literature', *op cit*, p 288.
54. Moore: *Letters of a Lifetime*, p 316. Marie Joshua was half-German, so a dedication to her would have been a kind of statement at that time. She refused the honour, but after her death her daughter allowed it, putting only her initials, however, on the title-page. Mrs Joshua had been a sterling friend, sending many gifts, culminating in a cheque when Elgar was ill (which was returned). Her letters (at the Worcestershire County Record Office) reveal a boundless admiration, placing Elgar even above Brahms. Alice's diary calls her his 'prophet' and reveals that she so worshipped the Master that at first she felt it would be a sort of *lèse-majesté* to take tea in his presence.
55. He would not have welcomed the splintered imagery of the modernists, T S

Eliot's use of past glories in *The Waste Land* (1922) as 'fragments I have shored against my ruins' (any more than he would have enjoyed the same poet's satirical up-dating of a Roman victory procession in the statistics of his 'Triumphal March', which implicitly criticizes his own military marches); nor, I think, would he have agreed with Ezra Pound that the war was being fought:

> For a botched civilization, . . .
> For two gross of broken statues,
> For a few thousand battered books.

(*Hugh Selwyn Mauberley* (1915), end of section V). A poem on the war that he did greatly admire was Masefield's magnificent 'August, 1914' (*The Collected Poems of John Masefield*, London, 1923, new and enlarged edn of 1938, pp 372-4) – a countryman's view. See Atkins: *op cit*, p 265.

56. Letter of 7 April 1920, in Moore: *Letters of a Lifetime*, p 244
57. The connection with the Second Symphony is endorsed by a later letter to the Windflower of 19 October 1924, after a performance of the Violin Sonata by Thibaud and Cortot, where he quotes a Shelleyan phrase that he had once applied to the Symphony: 'I *do* like the Sonata "written in dejection" [because she was not there for him to play it to?]—but what tunes!' (Moore: *The Windflower Letters*, p 296).
58. See MS 28 at The Elgar Birthplace Museum Library. Late in his life, in December 1932, he played this movement over with Vera Hockman: 'He was delirious with joy over the Romance: "Oh, this is a *lovely* passage – I nearly always cry when I hear it, but I am not lonely today – we are together –I am so happy."' (Quoted from her typescript memoir in Moore: *A Creative Life*, p 795.) So the music sprang from loneliness, not consummation. It is worth recording here that the 'piece of the Sonata sketches' that Elgar gave to his Brinkwells neighbour Lady [Gladys] Barttelot on 17 August 1919, as Alice's diary records, is no longer traceable: I am grateful to Sir Brian Barttelot, Bart, and to Lieutenant Commander W N N Diggle, RN, for kindly searching their archives in answer to my enquiry; it was probably the violin part for the unrevised finale.
59. From Shakespeare's *Twelfth Night* (Young, P M (ed): *Letters to Nimrod* (London, 1965) p 22)
60. Moore: *Letters of a Lifetime*, p 457
61. As Ivor Keys points out, the modality is a fleeting inflection inside an essentially classical use of tonality. We are not in the world of Vaughan Williams, but of Fauré, with minor-mode dominant chords and triads on the flat seventh.
62. But against this we must set an opposite and balancing quality found elsewhere in the Brinkwells works, which may conflict oddly with sonata style: a tendency towards harmonic stasis within a section, towards statement and repetition rather than development. See, for example, the first movements of the Cello Concerto and Piano Quintet. This is also to be found in Haydn's late quartets, and in Schubert.
63. Quoted from Griffith's MS reminiscences in Moore: *A Creative Life*, p 731. Brian Newbould's discussion of the movement is in '"Never done before": Elgar's Other Enigma', in *Music & Letters*, vol 77, No 2 (May 1996), pp 228-41.

64. Elgar knew it was a winner: it is a pity that his suggestion to Henry Wood that it might be transferred to string orchestra was not, apparently, taken up (see Moore: *Letters of a Lifetime, op cit,* p 338).

65. One is tempted to find a funerary significance in the very beautiful phrase and progression first heard 6 bars before figure 37, in that it recalls bars 21-2 of the opening movement of Verdi's *Requiem* at the words 'et lux perpetua [luceat eis]'; that may be just, but it has come into the concerto via *The Music Makers,* eg at 2 bars after figure 39. Something quite like it may also be found in the Romance of Elgar's Violin Sonata at figure 32.

66. Moore: *The Windflower Letters,* p 246

67. Moore: *Letters of a Lifetime,* p 212

Part Three

~ ~ ~

Reference Section

AN ELGARIAN WARTIME CHRONOLOGY

compiled by Martin Bird

This narrative of Elgar's life for the period from July 1914 to November 1918 is given as far as is possible in the words of the participants, with their original punctuation and errors retained. It is taken from a longer, unpublished compilation by the author, covering the whole of Elgar's life and is intended to complement the chronology given elsewhere in this book, notably in the first chapter. It should be read in conjunction with that chapter as duplication has been reduced as far as is practical. A list of sources appears at the end.

July 1914

Elgar … had now committed himself to Embleton to write Part 3 of The Apostles, and had already collected around him all the books, drafts, etc., which he had used in the original composition. He had decided not to go abroad this year, but to take a long holiday in Scotland before starting serious composition. He expected to be fully occupied on the work in September and therefore only to come to Worcester for the first part of the Festival.
Wulstan Atkins

08 I am leaving for Worcester via all sorts of places today & shall be at the Mayor's *[Hubert Leicester]* tonight.
Elgar-Ivor Atkins

After dinner, it being a warm evening & very light, he suggested a walk & so he & I lit pipes & started off up Barbourne. He knew every house & street. When near Thorneloe he said he would like to call on his sister Mrs Pipe in Barbourne Terrace … Then we strolled back to the Whitstones … About 10 o'clock Father came in & E. seemed very glad to see him. Then the fun began, & for an hour or more E. rattled out funny tales of the old days in Worcester ... his eyes rapidly opening & shutting & his pleasure in his memories was evidently intense.
Philip Leicester

09 E. at the Leicesters – Had a car & took his sister Lucy for a drive – So sweet & dood – Then rehearsal of Gerontius – Then motored to Stoke –
Alice diary

10 E. returned, he liked seeing the country & all well D.G.
Alice diary

I arrived home at 4.15 all safe but very hot.
Elgar-Alice Stuart Wortley

11 The chorus sounded fine to me & better than ever. I am going away for six weeks – as at present arranged – & I hope you will get a good holiday.
Elgar-Ivor Atkins

18 Very busy settling up everything for house & wages &c &c &c
Alice diary

19 Unsuspectingly on July 19th, we left London travelling by night to Glasgow, and then on by easy stages to Inverness. Our objective was Lairg, but on arrival we took an instantaneous dislike to the place and to the hotel in particular. We had booked for two weeks but somehow we managed to extricate ourselves and went on to Gairloch. This entailed a railway journey to Achnasheen and then a thirty mile drive to the Gairloch hotel. The taxi driver was slightly drunk and Father and I in the back of the car with our hearts in our mouths sang nonsense songs of which we had built up a

good repertoire over the years; this at least distracted us and prevented our staring at the edges of deep precipices or watching with great uneasiness the edge of Loch Maree which came right up to the side of the road with no fence … We luckily arrived safely and found the hotel delightful. It had lovely grounds, sands quite near and lovely walks. Time passed all too quickly. But the news of the assassination of the Archduke was very disturbing and it was very difficult to get any news. Eventually we sent a telegram to Novello's to try and learn something of the situation.   Carice Elgar

24   At Lairg – Gale & pouring rain – Depressed with the place – After lunch telegraphed to Gairloch & heard cd. have rooms & cd. be met. Decided to go. Much gayer after decision.
                                                                                            Alice diary
26   Finer – Began to like it very much. Walked about –   Alice diary
29   E. & C. fished all the morning. A. joined them in aftn. Really, dearly, A. found it rather monotonous   Alice diary

This is the most wonderfully beautiful place we have ever been in except Bavaria. We look straight across to Skye, an ever varying object, sometimes shimmering grey, sometimes magically blue, & the mountain views are gorgeous. I wish you were here to walk & talk & sketch.   Alice-Troyte Griffith

August 1914

02   How truly awful all the news is – I cannot think of anything else – yes there's one other thing – we get very little news & I have been wiring to London as trains are hours late – posts very vague and newspapers scarce & old: thanks for those you sent – we shall remain here until the 9th & longer if we can so please write as often as you can & tell me news, not only of the war, for which I hunger   Elgar-Alice Stuart Wortley

03   Heard from Muriel Germans marching through Luxembourg. More reassured as to our position –   Alice diary

04   My cold possesses me. *[Added by Rudyard Kipling]* … incidentally Armageddon begins.
                                                                                   Caroline Kipling diary

Readers should refuse service from a German or Austrian waiter.   Daily Mail

I do not think there were anywhere two persons more distressed at the catastrophe than the German Ambassador Prince Lichnowsky and his wife Mechtilde. Only a few weeks before I had given a private concert in the Embassy with my orchestra, and the couple were devoted to music, being constantly seen at the Opera and Ballet. Of an amiable South-German stock, they were both of them heartbroken at the breach between their own country and one to which they had become attached, and felt that in some way they had made a pitiable failure of their diplomatic mission. Strictly speaking, this was true …   Thomas Beecham

05   Frightfully anxious for news. Had a telegram saying Germany had declared war against us. The Govt. proclamation dates war from 11 P.M. on Augt.4. May God preserve us. Our conscience is clear that we tried all means for peace & waited at our own disadvantage in patience & forbearance. So we can go on with a brave heart. Glorious spirit seems to pervade all. Saw the Territorials start on the old Char-a-Banc. Splendid spirits. All flocked out to see them shaking hands & waving. Very thrilling –
                                                                                            Alice diary

Those who saw the London crowds, during the nights leading up to the Declaration of War saw a whole population, hitherto peaceable and humane, precipitated in a few days down the steep slope to primitive barbarism, letting loose, in a moment, the instincts of hatred and blood lust against which the whole fabric of society has been raised.

Bertrand Russell (The Nation, 15/08/14)

I am quite ill with the awful business – but that is nothing – the confusion is terrible & reduces me to a sort of comic despair – when you find that five pound notes are of no use, where are you? there is no change here! We were to return by steamer to Lochalsh – today we are told the steamers have no crews & are stopped – we shall see. The weather is too awful: I want to be assured that you are quite well

Elgar-Alice Stuart Wortley

07 I fear this awful war is trying you more than a great many people with your festival coming on: I hope you are well & prepared for any anxieties which may occur – I suppose there is no thought of abandoning the festival. You will let me hear any news you can.

Elgar-Ivor Atkins

08 *It was decided to postpone the Worcester Festival.*

09 The public vehicles were all commandeered to carry the territorials & were so occupied for two days – gradually all the guests left & we are now the only people left except an elderly gentleman & his wife. We decided to leave by the steamer – but this was also commandeered to pick up reservists &c. from the islands – since that voyage it has ceased to run. In the meantime both the hotel motors are hopelessly broken down & the necessary parts must come from Glasgow & now only the road is usable so the repairs may not be completed for a month. The last charabanc informed me on Friday that he wd. not return – So we felt that all was over but to our delight he arrived here last night & we hope & trust that tomorrow (Monday) will see us on our way south. We have great difficulty over money as English 5£ notes will not be accepted anywhere.

I purposely refrained from any rush or excitement but I am returning to London as soon as possible to offer myself for any service that may be possible – I wish I could go to the front but they may find some menial occupation for a worthless person.

Elgar-Alice Stuart Wortley

10 War was declared, of course, on August 4th but we were unable to leave until the 10th as every available vehicle was commandeered to fetch the Territorials and the Lovat scouts from the entire district, and the little steamer was collecting men from the islands. It was very moving to watch these men going off every day and all the way to London we were aware of the vast movement of men.

Carice Elgar

11 Arrived about 6 at Edinburgh – Many soldiers dining &c –

Alice diary

12 Did not care for Hotel. A. thinks real disgrace to Edinburgh to keep such slums & have children so miserable & neglected looking & sickening to see women, one quite old, bent under heavy sacks coming up hill – never saw such a sight any where else. E. found he did not want to stay so to leave next day –

Alice diary

13 Started about 9.30 – E. left us at Carlisle to go to Leeds to see Mr. Embleton. A. & C. reached home about 6.30.. Thankful to find all well. House looked lovely – So strange & dull wisout E –

Alice diary

14 Very busy unpacking &c &c. E. returned in early aftn. Did not see Mr. Embleton. Our thoughts all in the war –
                                                                                      Alice diary

We are all here safely & trying to be calm & be prepared for anything.
                                                                      Elgar-Alice Stuart Wortley

The Elgars, never given to over-optimism, were in the depths of despair when I called at Severn House on Friday.   **Rosa Burley**

15 *First performance of Sospiri, conducted by Henry Wood, at the first Promenade Concert of the season.*

I fear I have never read my morning paper with the diligence of the average Englishman; and when war was declared, so far as I was concerned, it came as a bolt from the blue … We opened our first concert with the national anthem and La Marseillaise to a crowded house in whose demeanour one could trace no signs of war or thoughts of war.   **Henry Wood**

16 On the following Sunday when I spent the day with them, things were no better.
                                                                                      Rosa Burley

17 Once home, Father did not lose a minute in offering his services for the war … He went to Hampstead Police Station and was sworn in as a Special Constable … My Mother, full of indignation, embarrassed us by going into the local shops and asking how many recruits they had.   **Carice Elgar**

He was very excited about it, and donned armlet, belt, and hat; he also had a truncheon, which he handled rather gingerly, I thought.   **W H Reed**

C. to work for Navy League & first aid –   **Alice diary**

c20 *Elgar wrote to Arthur Benson asking for new words to Land of Hope and Glory.*

24 Financially Alice & I and Carice are absolutely ruined – we can see daylight for a year & are quite happy – I envy the lazy fat Beasts opposite – whose property I have to guard!
                                                                      Elgar-Alice Stuart Wortley

All thanks for sending so quickly. Alas! the words will not do … Forgive this bald & businesslike note, but I am in great haste & you know I wd. write blandly if the occasion admitted – I do not know how to thank you for what you have done. It may save time if I enclose a skeleton which you may clothe with ardent & palpitating flesh & blood.
                                                                      Elgar-Arthur Benson

25 I'll turn to again, today or tomorrow & see if I can do anything – but I'm not strong in the Vengeance line, & indeed I don't see what there is to revenge as yet – we have hemmed in Germany tight all round for years, in the Good-natured unsympathetic way in which we Anglo-Saxons do treat the world, & the cork has flown out! I haven't the faintest doubt that the patriots in Germany are saying 'How long, O God, how long?' with precisely the same fervour & spontaneity.   **Arthur Benson-Elgar**

Here we are busy and doing what we can to help. Carice Red Crossing from morning till night – Alice generally sympathetic … We reduce our staff, finding them good places – no panic, please, only stern law & order & goodwill all round.
                                                                      Elgar-Frances Colvin

26 How will this do? Please make any comments & criticisms.   **Arthur Benson-Elgar**

27 A million thanks – excellent. But the 2nd & 4th lines must be of six syllables. I hope you can carve it down.   Elgar-Arthur Benson

28 Here is a new draft – You will see some alterations … I am sorry to have given you so much trouble over all this, & you have been very kind & patient.   Arthur Benson-Elgar

30 I am very busy with things that are in themselves slight, but the assumption is that I am releasing a better man, which is pleasing.   Elgar-Rosa Burley

September 1914

05 Should have gone to Madresfield as planned for Festival – E. busy – & may have to go out in the night. any night –   Alice diary

06 E. suddenly wrote the Song for Soldiers Begbie's words.   Alice diary

08 It wd. have been 'Gerontius' tonight at Worcester Fest – but for Hun Kaiser. Mr. Reed came. Felt he must thinking of the Festival.   Alice diary

12 *'Householder's Return' for a Parliamentary Recruiting Committee:*
There is no person in this house qualified to enlist: I will do so if permitted.   Elgar

13 Sir, I have to acknowledge the receipt of your letter of the 9th inst, in which you ask that a special constable shall be detailed to visit The Hut for an indefinite period. I must point out that it is necessary to receive fuller particulars than those contained in your letter … On receiving your reply the matter shall be proceeded with at once.
                                                                          Elgar-Frank Schuster

16 I have been asked to make some suggestions for the (sort of) certificate we would like for our S. Constabulary … Can you suggest anything for a border connecting the 'views' (pictures) of Hampstead etc.   Elgar-Troyte Griffith

21 Heard of destruction of Reims Cathedral – Much upset. Felt must go & see Westminster Abbey was there so E. & A. went – Saw the Bath Chapel & Banners & Crests – Nice gosing out togesser –   Alice diary

22 *Elgar went to stay with his sister Pollie and her family at Stoke Prior, the first of many such wartime visits.*

23 A. to Dentist & did not like Dr. Budden   Alice diary

24 It is too lovely in the country but it is lonely also – so I come back – I want news, news.
                                                                    Elgar-Alice Stuart Wortley

26 This is only to say thanks for your suggestions for the certificate – they will give the donor some sort of a guide.   Elgar-Troyte Griffith

October 1914

01 Sydney *[Loeb, Richter's son-in-law]* can visit him *[Elgar]* and tell him that neither bad politics nor the smoke of gunpowder will come between us.   Hans Richter-Mathilde Loeb

09 E. to rehearsal Albert Hall. Fearing Antwerp must fall.   Alice diary

10 *First performance of The Roll Call in the Royal Albert Hall in a patriotic concert organized by Clara Butt in aid of 'H. M. the Queen's Work for Women Fund'.*

11 Called on … Elgar. He sent his love to Richter & said he much regretted he had not waited until he was better informed (re Drs degree).   **Sydney Loeb diary**

[Richter had resigned his honorary doctorates from Oxford and Manchester]

15 How are you & how are things in general? I have not written since the postponement notice – it all seemed too sad & what could one say? Your disappointment must have been greater than ours – although you know the festival is the one thing I look forward to with real joy.   **Elgar-Ivor Atkins**

E. to Manchester 8 A.M. train. Comfortable start. Lovely day – Rehearsal in aftn. & Concert in evening –   **Alice diary**

Elgar conducted the Halle Orchestra in their first wartime concert – Enigma Variations, 'It comes from the misty ages' from The Banner of St. George, Tchaikovsky Symphony No. 4 and Lalo Symphonie Espagnole with the Halle leader, Arthur Catterall.

Elgar was one of the conductors who came to us during the war. He had been an amateur bassoon player and always came to have a chat with me. Being interested in the instrument he would discuss it potential and difficulties, and it was rarely that his compositions did not have what he called 'twiddly bits' for the bassoon. One such 'bit' is in 'Dorabella' (from the Enigma Variations), where the bassoon goes off like a rip-rap for no reason at all.   **Archie Camden**

16 E. returned all well D.G. & had had most successful concert & good audience – & cheered altogether.   **Alice diary**

19 E. at The Hut but motored home late after dinner A.S.W. brought him.   **Alice diary**

20 E. busy – A. to Chelsea but found no pupils – not well enough from inoculation.
                                                                      Alice diary

21 A. to Chelsea but heard C.O. ordered classes to be discontinued – Her pupils quite dismayed & sorry.   **Alice diary**

24 … touched by your kind letter and we appreciate this friendly greeting and mark of confidence at a time when sense of fairness and proportion and logic seems to have forsaken a section of the people.   **Edgar Speyer-Elgar**

November 1914

01 *Sir Ralph Hall Caine was preparing "King Albert's Book", an anthology to be published by the Daily Telegraph in aid of the Belgian Fund. Elgar initially declined to contribute.*

07 I do hope your decision is not absolutely final. I can hardly imagine the book without you. At the same time I realise your position. You would naturally want to do something worthy of your great distinction to appear in a book of such importance, containing the contributions of the most illustrious of your living confreres … If it had been possible for you to write any new piece of music on this immense theme I am sure you would have done it already.   **G Ralph Hall Caine-Elgar**

10 E. thinking of his wonderful Carillon Music & talked on telephone to Made. Cammaerts.
                                                                      Alice diary

Almost overcome by the reading of this poem, Elgar, with tears in his eyes, rushed to his desk and wrote music to fit in with the words in such a way that it could be recited up and down the country, so that all should know through the poet's burning words what sufferings were being endured, and with what spirit, by our little ally, Belgium.

W H Reed

Like the rest of us, he had been deeply moved by the German invasion of Belgium and when he read Emile Cammaerts's stirring poem Carillon he at once decided to make a setting for it. But Edward's attempts at fitting words to music had never been very happy and had not grown happier with the passing of the years ... When, therefore, he told me of the project I ventured to suggest that he should not try to tie himself to the metre of the words ... but that he should provide an illustrative prelude and entractes as background music for a recitation of the poem. This he did with immense success.

Rosa Burley

11   E. to Stoke –   **Alice diary**

12   Elgar ... came over to Worcester and spent much time in the cathedral with my father, who played to him many of his favourite works on the organ ... He had told Atkins that he had almost finished a patriotic composition for orchestra, Carillon.

Wulstan Atkins

I went to Worcester & had the joy of sitting in the old Library in the Cathedral amongst the M.S.S.   **Elgar-Alice Stuart Wortley (13/11/14)**

16   *Elgar back to Severn House, with his niece Madge Grafton.*

18   *Elgar finished Carillon and sent it to the publishers, Elkin.*

Alice Wortley heard it in its complete form & was good & kind enough to give approval.   **Elgar-Frank Schuster**

December 1914

07   The first performance of the Carillon was given at Queen's Hall ... and has remained in my memory for more reasons than one. Cammaerts's wife was the actress Tita Brand, whose mother Marie Brema had first sung the part of the Angel in Gerontius at Birmingham fourteen years earlier, and it seemed fitting that she should declaim her husband's poem. But unfortunately Mme Brand-Cammaerts was enceinte and in order to conceal this fact an enormous bank of roses was built on the platform over which her head and shoulders appeared rather in the manner of a Punch and Judy show. Mme Brand put such energy into the performance that both Edward, who was conducting the orchestra, and I, who was sitting in the audience, trembled for the effect on her, but patriotic fervour won the day and the Carillon was performed without mishap.   **Rosa Burley**

11   Concert for Belgians – M. v Defaux, M. Jongen, – Beuland, LaPrade, Made. Delacre & an American performed most beautifully also a delightful choix. Large audience – really a great success. Fine aftn & house looked lovely. Sarah a splendid help. Many Belgian guests, result £36.10-0- for artists & Belgians –   **Alice diary**

I am sorry I saw so little of you today at our music but I was torn in many pieces: I hope you liked some of it. I rushed out & had a very refreshing walk after it all as I

wanted air & refreshment – both of which I had & am now better for the rest from
crowds & police work.   **Elgar-Alice Stuart Wortley**

12   Finishing restoring things in house – E. very pleased & satisfied at result of Concert.
                                                         Alice diary

23   A. to Sir Maurice for ear deaf from cold – Then to do some shopping for presents for
     Christmas & various things.   **Alice diary**

25   The Christmas of 1914 I … spent with them at Severn House and it was good to find
     that our old friendship, which had tended to cool during the long periods of
     separation, was becoming closer and warmer than it had been at any time since the
     old days at Malvern.   **Rosa Burley**

30   The war has altered many attitudes, closed some vistas, opened others & has shifted
     many narrow points of view, but it has tightened friendships & I hold yours fast.
                                                         Elgar-Anthony de Navarro

January 1915

01   The Year opens laden with anxieties. May God keep England & may a glorious peace
     crown the year & our splendid Army & Navy.   **Alice diary**

03   E. to rehearsal at Albert Hall – Carillon & lunched at Cheyne Walk – A. & C. to "Bert"
     were given a box – Carillon <u>very</u> beautiful but acoustics so trying as usual – C. Collier
     very good.   **Alice diary**

10   Why don't you do a wonderful Requiem for the slain-something in the Spirit of
     Binyon's For the Fallen?   **Sidney Colvin-Elgar**

17   *The Elgars went to the Royal Albert Hall for a 'Grand British Concert' conducted by*
     Landon Ronald. Sammons played the Elgar Concerto. The concert opened with
     Ronald's A Birthday Overture, and Edward German conducted Spring and Autumn
     from his Suite – The Seasons.

21   We went on to U.S.A. Consulate General – Ill mannered priggish people except one
     decent man who showed us to the right room but there we might have sat for
     unlimited time till A. walked up to the <u>Man</u> & began. He was tolerable then – but
     U.S.A. had to learn elementary manners.   **Alice diary**

24   I had given over this morning to the dentist but he was so expeditious that I found I
     had some time on my hands & went to the British Museum. I saw Binyon.
                                                         Elgar-Sidney Colvin

29   E. to Hayes & A with him. Adlington car … E. had good record then Mr. Ainley came
     & all seemed pleased.   **Alice diary**

     Who can forget the thrill of his Carillon with the dramatic Henry Ainley declaiming to
     the music?   **Fred Gaisberg**

31   Not out – Very cold – Mr. S. Wortley & Alice to tea – saw E.'s old M.S. books &c.
                                                         Alice diary

February 1915

03 A. & C. to Percy Anderson beginning to paint his (C's) picture – **Alice diary**

07 Nice afternoon Laurence Binyon Jebb Scotts H. Brooke & Mrs. Miss Broome – Much pleasant talk & gramophone playing. **Alice diary**

09 *Elgar started his setting of Binyon Poems "Spirit of England".*

E. put off going to Tree's Dejeuné & composed violently. Went later & conducted the Carillon. **Alice diary**

14 I got home safely & had a very good time; nice people large house & dogs; the latter quieter than all else altho' all else is quiet: I think the dogs are bored; a burglar broke in sometime ago & the dogs welcomed him & sat up pleased to see visitors: so I am assured by the host ... Your mother purrs, the logs hiss, the rain pours, the urn bubbles, I smoke, all is on the surface peaceful joy & yet – I say many things which are not in the mass! **Elgar-Carice**

16 E. to Cl. Butt to go through 'Gerontius' – Very cold & frosty – Meeting at Mansion House for Music in War time – **Alice diary**

18 *Elgar travelled to Bradford, returning on the 20ʰ.*

19 *E conducted the Berlioz Te Deum with the Hallé in Bradford* ... which was not lacking in a certain splendour and gravity. **Review**

21 E. & A. to "Bert" for E. to hear Dvorak Symphony *[the "New World", which he was to conduct on an LSO tour].* **Alice diary**

22 *Elgar resigned as a Special Constable.*

My relief was very great. **W H Reed**

26 E. said A. might try & get Cousins to come with him on the Tour – to A.'s relief & delight the telegraphic answer soon came Yes – A. so thankful – **Alice diary**

[Cousins had been his valet from 1905 until the beginning of the war.]

March 1915

01 ... went on tour all over England and Scotland with Percy Harrison of Birmingham, an impresario who organised these provincial tours each year. The London Symphony Orchestra, with the Belgian pianist, Arthur de Greef, and Constance Collier, who recited Carillon in French, formed the concert-party. **W H Reed**

Elgar conducted the first concert of the tour in Birmingham.

02 *Elgar conducted LSO concert in Liverpool.*

03 I have bought this odd little paper at a corner odd little shop on purpose for you: the young lady said 'What initial will you have?' – I had not thought of an initial – & of course was going to say 'W.' – It seemed to be the rule to have an initial – so here it is & means Edward.

I loved my letter this morng. All well & no cold. **Elgar-Alice Stuart Wortley**

The tour continued to Manchester, with a concert that evening.

04 *Elgar conducted LSO concert in Sheffield.*

It is quite warm & fine & I have wandered about these depressing streets trying to find something to look at – it is early closing day which adds to the dullness.

Elgar-Alice Stuart Wortley

05 *Elgar conducted LSO concert in Glasgow.*

06 *Elgar conducted LSO concert in Edinburgh.*

07 When we were in Edinburgh one Sunday, Sir Edward and I took a taxi-cab and drove out to Queensferry on the shores of the Firth of Forth. We could see across to Rosyth, where several cruisers which had been engaged at the Dogger Bank were being overhauled and having their wounds attended to. We were very thrilled about the submarine nets which we were told stretched right across under the Forth Bridge – and then we drove back and thought how awful it all was, and how much we hoped that it would all be over quickly.

W H Reed

08 *Elgar conducted LSO concert in Newcastle.*

09 *Elgar conducted LSO concert in Leeds.*

16 A. in bed all day – Truly dreadful cold – E. to see old books – A.S.W. to tea – Dr. Blair to dine with E. So he was not by his souse –

Alice diary

17 E. to Rehearsal. A. joining him there with fur coat –

Alice diary

18 *Elgar conducted Symphony No. 2 and Carillon (Ainley) in a Royal Philharmonic Society concert at Queen's Hall. Percy Pitt conducted Vaughan Williams "Wasps" Overture and Stanford's Songs of the Sea with The Stock Exchange Male Voice Choir and Harry Dearth. Parry conducted the first London performance of his Tone Poem 'From Death to Life'.*

The Philharmonic Society's all-British concert, held in Queen's Hall last night, contained more interest for the student of musical evolution in this country than for the music-lover pure and simple. A concert which represents Elgar side by side with composers born a decade earlier demonstrates forcibly the way in which he has epitomised the musical aspirations of more than one generation.

Philip Heseltine (Peter Warlock), Daily Mail (19/03/15)

20 E. angelically good to At. G. & Gertie & Cousin Lesley who came to tea

Alice diary

25 E. at Stoke. Went to Worcester & saw old places –

Alice diary

26 We could not however get away from the conviction that if two settings of the verses in question were published about the same time, one of them would certainly prove a failure, & with you in the field we naturally feared that Dr. Rootham's work would be the one to suffer. In such cases the disappointed composer invariably blames the Publisher.

Henry Clayton-Elgar

April 1915

01 E. returned – such joy to have him back – He & A. into town –

03 *Elgar, encouraged by Charles Stuart Wortley, added his name to the Committee of Paderewski's Polish Relief Fund.*

13 It was suggested … by Mr. Młynarski, that a Polish piece should be written to help Polish funds, as he told me so much had been done for Belgian charitable undertakings by the Carillon. But the idea of writing an orchestral fantasy on Polish themes was not new to me, and curiously enough the suggestion, or rather the influence, came from Herefordshire. The heir of the ancient family of Bodenham married, in 1850, a noble Polish lady, and from their descendant, Count Lubienski-Bodenham – the Squire of Bodenham while I lived in the adjoining parish – I heard much of Polish history, thought and feeling that supplemented mere book knowledge. Very deeply regretted, this lovable gentleman died a few years ago. That some sort of a Symphonic Prelude might be a practical, and perhaps a useful tribute to my friend Paderewski, for the concert in aid of his countrymen was the final inducement to weave into a concise orchestral movement some typical Polish themes.
Elgar

I heard with great distress last night that my wife's utmost petition to you on behalf of us all seemed to be in vain and that you persist, now that the original occasion for such a misfortune has passed away, in abandoning the scheme on which we had built such hopes. Well, it is cruelly hard on that fine poet & fine fellow, my friend Binyon, to whom the association with you would have brought just the lift in fame & status which was lacking to him and which, since the war began, he has so splendidly deserved.

Do the work you had promised & begun – do it for those who love you – do it for the thousands for whom it will express what is deepest & most sacred in their souls, do it for your country & the future & to honour and justify the gift that has been given you. I cannot bring myself to believe – nor to crush the hopes of the poet by having to tell him – that in the end you will not consent. –
Sidney Colvin-Elgar

15 E. to lunch with L. Ronald & Edward German.

17 E. to drill on College ground in aftn. Rather too cold for him.

21 Młynarski came rather upset as E. did not approve programme & altered it. Delighted that E. contemplated a Polish Musick, & much excited at the beginning. Alice diary

22 C. heard she had the post in the Government Censorship – Very pleased. Alice diary

23 My hand is shaky: I have just been doing rifle exercise Elgar-Alice Stuart Wortley

24 E. to Rehearsal at the Albert Hall at 11 – To Concert in afternoon – Fine performance of the 'Carillon' but a dull audience – Did not even rise in 'Land of Hope & Glory' – wh. Kirkby Lunn sang magnificently – Alice diary

To College at 10.15 and then to Albert Hall for the rehearsal of the afternoon's concert … I never heard such a tremendous volume of sound as that produced by the Recruiting Bands and the Coldstreams together in the empty Hall … Back to the College for lunch with professors … Concert at 3 … Had to attend to receive the King and Queen Mary and Queen Alexandra. My chorus from St. Cecilia went with spirit and the whole programme, especially a March for drums and fifes, was very effective and arousing.   **Parry diary**

26 *The Elgars travelled to Stratford-on-Avon for F. R. Benson's Shakespeare Festival, and saw The Merchant of Venice in the evening.*

27 *Merry Wives of Windsor.*

28 *Romeo and Juliet.*

Mary de Navarro motored over – Very dear & nice – Embraced E. at front door! Took E. & A. for lovely motor drive to Wilmcote to Shakespeare's Mother's house – 2 attached cottages not kept up at all.   **Alice diary**

29 *Twelfth Night in the afternoon, and Richard III in the evening.*

30 *Coriolanus.*

May 1915

01 E. & A. left Stratford. Said farewell to nice Bensons who were grateful to E. & keen about schemes for next year.   **Alice diary**

08 Our dear dear Wedding day.   **Alice diary**

10 Our principle is that the merchant traffic must look after itself, subject to the general arrangements that are made.   **Winston Churchill**

13 *Elgar conducted the Violin Concerto with Albert Sammons at Queen's Hall.*

14 … the occasion of the most astounding exhibition of violin playing that has been heard in London from any artist for many a long day. This is a big statement, but it was fully justified by Mr Albert Sammons' superb performance … The mingled strength and tenderness of his tone, coupled with brilliance of execution and flawless intonation, made of his performance a miracle of beauty.   **Philip Heseltine, Daily Mail**

18 Concert here … Music in War time Society. Really a great success – nice attentive audience only wishing to be pleased E. very kind & good – Result £26 – Miss Paget delighted –   **Alice diary**

24 Empire Day. E. put up the Flag – <u>Lovely</u> day.   **Alice diary**

27 I have worked hard at the Polish piece & to-day do not like it. I want help.
                                                        Elgar-Alice Stuart Wortley

June 1915

01 E. finishing little touches to 'Polonia – Very fine.   **Alice diary**

02 E.'s beloved Birfday – Think he will end by liking his presents vesy muss! – Went to Mr. Elkin with his Polonia – It is brilliant & beautiful –   **Alice diary**

03 *From June 3rd – 5th Elgar was with Frank Schuster at The Hut. Pausing only to lunch at Severn House, he left for Stoke Prior, where he stayed until the 10th.*

05 In 1915, when she was fifteen, *[Ellen Faulkes]* worked for Mrs Polly [*sic*] Grafton at the Elms Farm, Stoke Prior … During the twelve months that Ellen was there Sir Edward came to stay three or four times … He always came alone. Ellen wondered at this, and at the fact that though Pollie, Edward and the Grafton children talked together so often on many subjects neither Lady Elgar nor Carice were ever mentioned. One day Ellen asked Mrs Grafton why Sir Edward's wife never came with him. Mrs Grafton hesitated, frowned, and said, 'She does not care for travel.' And those were the first and last words that Ellen ever heard on the subject.

Sir Edward was always a very welcome guest, his visits eagerly looked forward to. He slept in the boys' room, walked the dogs on the common, enjoyed a glass of beer, and drove to Mass at the little church at the bottom of Rock in the trap with Pollie each Sunday morning. Though he had a keen sense of humour and was a great joker at times, Ellen remembers him as a quiet and reserved man with a gentle voice which he never raised. He still spoke with more than a hint of the rounded accents of his native Worcester and the faint double vowel sounds that mark a midland man.

Letter from Nicholas Hale to Alan Webb

08 I had a lovely day yesterday in my own land & today had an and & lonely time in Birmingham: the prints of Worcestershire which I went to examine are worthless almost & I had a wasted journey: **Elgar-Alice Stuart Wortley**

11 *From June 11ʰ – 15ʰ Elgar was busy checking and correcting the score and parts of Polonia, and working on For the Fallen. From June 16ʰ – 19ʰ, he was again with Pollie.*

16 E. working at the Binyon music all the morning A. wis him to Euston – The train nearly left wisout him as he was telling A. what Orch. to set – A. raser mis as she got on omnibus going wrong way, (pease not beat) & hates those crowded streets. Took a taxi to Baker St. **Alice diary**

18 Your dear letter came this morning at Stoke & I have travelled here since. Here I remain until tomorrow – Saturday – afternoon & I get back to Severn House in the evening. It is lovely here – flowers sun & everything except good news, alas! **Elgar-Alice Stuart Wortley**

Elgar and Hubert Leicester looked in briefly. E told Atkins that he was checking the parts of a new orchestral work, Polonia, which he had written in aid of the Polish Relief Fund, and dedicated to Paderewski. He also said that he had recently joined the Hampstead Volunteer Reserve and was enjoying his rifle practices at which he was now becoming quite an expert. **Wulstan Atkins**

19 Expecting E. home A. began setting Orch. for E. for L. Binyon Music. E. home quite safes – D.G. pleasant little visit to the Leicesters – Drove to Sherridge, Kempsey, saw almost all old friends – Hydes, Munns, Norburys &c – & poor nice Will in a farm house – Mary Clifford returned as parlour maid – **Alice diary**

22 *The Elgars joined the Stuart Wortleys in their box at the Royal Albert Hall to hear Landon Ronald's performance of Enigma.*

26 *Elgar's concert was in the afternoon, after which he returned home to Severn House.*

Most wonderful, however, is Bournemouth's splendid detachment from war panic, when it is remembered how many of the great provincial festivals have been cancelled and how few independent recitals and concerts have been given in London.

Bournemouth has quietly and without fuss provided its own quota of eligible fighting men in the nation's crisis. But that epic motto 'Business as usual' means to Bournemouth also music as usual, and the work done in that direction since the war began is unparalleled in the United Kingdom.   **Daily Telegraph**

July 1915

02 We send you very many thanks for your kind present, we are very proud & delighted to have your poems from you. They give us so much real pleasure ... (I am proud of my association with two of them)   **Elgar-Emile Cammaerts**

Landon Ronald conducted Enigma and Carillon with his Guildhall School of Music students' orchestra.

E. to Rehearsal ... returned very cheerful saying the Orch. was so good & Variations so well played ... E. A. & C. to Concert – Quite a delightful evening. Miss Burley, her pupil & Miss Hawkshaw with A.'s tickets, there – & vesy joy E. sat most of the time by A. all thro' the Variations. Beautifully played. Landon is great, Carillon splendid & E's new Trumpet effect thrilling. Most emotional meeting in Artists' Room, the Landons, M. Mossel, Liten &c – E. had a tremendous reception, the real roar I like to hear for him. Lovely warm night, drove back thro' Park in open taxi E. vesy serene & likes it all. D.G. for such a happy interlude in our anxious days –   **Alice diary**

04 To tea Sidney Colvin & Mr. Streatfeild then Mr. & Made. Dern & M. Carveye who brought Cello & no accompanyist. Found Kol Nidrei & E. played for him before anyone came & again later ... Rather exhausting as the foreign gentlemens cd. not talk English – & A. had so many to talk to at once.   **Alice diary**

05 *Elgar rehearsed Polonia in preparation for its first performance next day. Beecham conducted the rest of the programme, given in aid of the Polish Victims Relief Fund.*

... it is not to be wondered at that the composer received a tremendous ovation after its first performance. It will always remain an inspired work of art, a gorgeous treat for those who desire richness combined with musical spirit and scholarliness of the highest order.   **John F Porte**

07 A line to congratulate you heartily on the success of Polonia last night. It was a pity the audience was so small, but they certainly amply made up for their lack of numbers. While it was very pleasant to hear the appreciation of the music, it was (as I think I mentioned to Lady Elgar) almost more so to notice the really warm & almost affectionate note one could distinguish in the reception given to you personally.   **William Elkin-Elgar**

08 E. not so vesy well – Went into town –   **Alice diary**

09 E. out & in, better, but not quite recovered – A. to lunch with Mrs. Joshua ... Going thro' Park heard P. & Circumstance No.1 & stopped & listened – Band played it very well – E. came down on chance of meeting A. on omnibus & came exactly at the right moment. A. vesy peased.   **Alice diary**

12 Now that this battalion is on the eve of departure for France, it does not strike me as absolutely out of place to write and express my real gratitude to you for the many hours of pleasure you have given me through your music. So many similar effusions have possibly reached you that they have become unbearably boring, but you will not think me impertinent, I know, when I state that 2 Ibs. out of the modest 35 that I am allowed to take out with me as necessary kit are taken up by the scores of your variations and second symphony.   Arthur Bliss-Elgar

15 *The Elgars went to a dinner at the Royal Automobile Club.*

We are a little early for our dinner party so I stepped in here *[Athenaeum]* to wait
    Elgar-Alice Stuart Wortley

16 *Elgar working on his Carillon 'follow-up' – Une Voix dans le Désert.*

It was angelically good of you to help me with my bourgeois tune; here it is sans accpt. I shall be so grateful if you will verify it; I have put it exactly as you left it with me – or me with it – yesterday except the small matters mentioned below: Elgar-Percy Pitt

20 E. to dentist. A. with him into town & then on to Waterloo & Liphook – Mrs. Caulfield's car met her with Miss Burley – <u>Lovely</u> drive & <u>lovely</u> paradise of a place – delicious house &c – Mrs. C. very nice & Cicely quite delightful – Walked about & into wood, just like Birchwood woods, scent & all   Lovely views – Through Hawkshaw grounds, over green drive to Station – & so back.   Alice diary

When the war prevented my visit to Russia I had gone to live for a time with Admiral and Mrs Caulfeild at their beautiful old house, Hookland, in West Sussex. Rosa Burley

Dr. Sinclair to dinner, E. so dood & played to him – Dr. S. much impressed. He seemed so pleased to be here & so devoted – E. raser worried wanting to alter some chords in his England music afterwards & rather tired –   Alice diary

21 E. raser worried over his music & wanting change – Started for Stoke about 2 – Decided to take Hookland for possible dates in Augt. A. so delighted. Felt we <u>must</u> go there –
    Alice diary

23 *Lady Elgar went to The Hut, where she was joined later from Elgar, who had come from Stoke Prior.*

24 I have been down to my sister in remote Worcestershire & found your valued advice here. I am busily amending my M.S. & once more express my gratitude to you for your fraternal help.   Elgar-Percy Pitt

26 E. left the Hut early for rehearsal at Coliseum – A. back to lunch with E.   Alice diary

29 E. turning to the Binyon Poems again –   Alice diary

Many thanks for the photos of Shiff *[the resident dog at Hookland]*. Greet him for me & thank the dear child for the pictures of my friend & confidant! He knows a lot & when he finds communicable speech, in the next world, he will astonish, to insulting point many winged angels!   Elgar-Rosa Burley

He was not a man who could be said to be fond of children but the beauty and charming manners of the young Caulfeilds, who greatly admired his music and whom he first met early in 1915, won his friendship and affection from the start. Rosa Burley

30 Sunday is impossible as many people are coming & Mr. Reed comes at 3 o'c to play thro' the 'Voix dans le désert' – so you will please come here then – it will be amusing to hear it with the Violin – later Litens etc   Elgar-Alice Stuart Wortley

August 1915

01 Very nice afternoon – Mr. Reed came to play string parts of 'Voix dans le Desert' & Mrs. R. with him. Then Liten & M. Viseur came, such an interesting man in the new Khaki Belgian uniform – a poet too – E. played the Voix &c & some Binyon – Liten recited. *Alice diary*

02 *From August 2ⁿᵈ – 14ᵗʰ, Elgar conducted Carillon throughout its summer run at the Coliseum with the Belgian actor Carlo Liten: two performances each day.*

E. to Coliseum in aftn. A.S.W. there & took E. for drive – E. to Coliseum in evening. Very good reception – *Alice diary*

05 *Lady Elgar's September 1914 poem 'England, August 4. 1914' was published on the front page of 'The Bookman'.*

Lady Elgar, several of whose songs have been set to music by her husband, the famous composer, sends us the following lines, commemorative of England's entry into the World War. *Editor of 'The Bookman'*

E. to see Clara Butt about conducting Gerontius. E. went out & brought in a Bookman for A. & gave it her with tight clasped tisses & wrote her name on it E. vesy peased – *Alice diary*

06 E. to Coliseum in aftn, driving with Maud & Mrs. R. Brooke Very good performance, A. drove down with him in evening & sat in the car – great success – Maud & Mrs. R. Brooke to lunch – Very nice time. E. played. the Voix to Maud who loved it & then amused her with 'Ruth' wh. she sang all the way in the car. *Alice diary*

Means of locomotion during the War did not include private motors; owing to the rationing of petrol for official purposes only. Even taxis were difficult to get, and when I was dining out within a possible radius of Great Cumberland Place I used to proceed in a Bath chair, to the great amusements of my hosts – a very comfortable process, as it enabled me to be wheeled inside the front door in bad weather. *Maud Warrender*

08 *Elgar spent the day at The Hut.*

10 *Rudyard Kipling met his son John in London for the last time, prior to John's posting to France. Two days later Kipling himself went to France to write an account of the war.*

12 Then we left the pier with a quick stealthy turn and two destroyers came out of the warm grey sea ... and fell in alongside us on either side, sort of lounging along to keep pace with our modest 22 knots. The Channel was full-packed with traffic – and there were certain arrangements for the discomfort of roving submarines, which were very nice to watch. *Rudyard Kipling*

14 E. finished the fortnight at the Coliseum – <u>Most</u> successful A. drove down & waited for him in car – *Alice diary*

15 John leaves at noon for Warley. He looks very straight and smart and young, as he turned at the top of the stairs to say: "Send my love to Dad-o". *Caroline Kipling diary*

16 *The Times published a 'Manifesto on National Service' signed, amongst others, by Elgar, Charles Beresford and Neville Chamberlain.*

... an organised effort to carry on the war ... every fit man must be made available ... for the fighting line, or ... for National Service at home.   **The Times**

In the summer of 1915 ... the Caulfeilds offered Hookland to the Elgars for a few weeks. They accepted and the change did Edward good.   **Rosa Burley**

Started for Hookland – tiresome slow train – Lovely day. E. tired of journey & wanted to go home in the middle of it – A. vesy anxious he shd. like it. Difficult to get all luggage on to Taxi but it was done & E.A. & driver well wedged in. Cd. not get out to open Gate. Chauffeur sd. "perhaps some one will be coming by!" but at last managed it. E. thought it beautiful. All the house left so nice & ready & all welcomy & pleasant.   **Alice diary**

19 C. came down for the day ... long walk with E. & Shiff – Enjoyed her day. West's Victoria to return – A. drove with her.   **Alice diary**

Rooads do be bad, doan't it?   **Albert West**

20 I have a large dog friend 'Schiff' who has adopted me & takes me for walks in the wildest places he knows them all & I tell him everything!   **Elgar-Alice Stuart Wortley**

29 ... in the middle section I have brought in remote & I trust with poetic effect a theme of Chopin & with it a them of your own from the Polish fantasia linking the two greatest names in Polish music – Chopin & Paderewski.   **Elgar-Paderewski**

30 Left Hookland – Very sorry to leave ... Found all well at Severn House –   **Alice diary**

31 E. restless & wanting to go away again –   **Alice diary**

September 1915

02 *The Elgars decided to join the Stuart Wortleys for their Lake District holiday at 'Walls', a house lent by Charles Stuart Wortley's cousin Lord Muncaster. Elgar left on September 6th, leaving Alice to sort out Severn House.*

07 A. & C. watched & watched raid. E. said we were to go down in basement but could not leave this extraordinary sight ... Sad tragedies in some of the streets from the fiendish thing.   **Alice diary**

"Why have the Zeppelins come so often to London, though the Allied aircraft never reach Berlin" the terror-stricken populace complained. In the shops, on the 'buses and by the roadside the rumour spread that London had no protecting aircraft until September 8th 1915, when, after a raid more terrible than its predecessors, some fighting planes were withdrawn from France. When Parliament reassembled, six days later, Members asked why the defence of London had not yet been considered.   **Sylvia Pankhurst**

10 I am just leaving & meeting Alice at Foxfield & we pay a visit & ramble a little after, & so home ... It is too heavenly here & at Ullswater – weather exceptionally lovely –
                          Elgar-Troyte Griffith

15 E. mowed nettles & we all worked & made bonfire –   **Alice diary**

The bonfire was a source of great delight to Sir Edward and Mr Wortley, who enjoyed themselves like boys over it, being nevertheless very scientific as to the lighting and management of it! Clare helped, under their instructions. Mrs Wortley and Lady Elgar viewed it from afar, beseeching them not to set themselves on fire!   **Clare Stuart Wortley**

406   *Oh, My Horses! - Elgar and the Great War*

19 Lovely day – Bonfire still going on – After lunch most of the party to meet Beresfords. All arrived. –   **Alice diary**

20 E. & A. left Walls – Alice. C.S.W. & Claire all at the station with us – Very early & saw miniature Ry. & stroked the infant engine. They nearly wept to part with us. Then along looping "curly" journey on Furness Ry. At last arrived at Lakehead & got onto steamer. lovely all up Windermere, great broad calm lake – At Ambleside drove on coach into the town. had tea & had <u>lovely</u> walk to Grasmere past Fox Hove – E. rather tired & slept after arrival – such a welcome at Hotel –   **Alice diary**

22 Lovely day, quite hot – Disappointed at first that no coach went to Ullswater to take luggage so had to give up our intended walk over the pass there – but had a delightful walk to the Garmisch-like part below Basedale Tarn –   **Alice diary**

23 *Elgar went from Grasmere to stay with Sinclair at Hereford. Lady Elgar returned to Severn House.*

We left the Lakes yesterday mg. Alice went home & I left her at Crewe & came here.   **Elgar-Alice Stuart Wortley (24/09/15)**

25 *Elgar went to Stoke Prior to stay with Pollie and family, returning to Severn House on June 27ᵗʰ.*

27 *John Kipling missing in action.*

Your son behaved with great gallantry and coolness and handled his men splendidly. I trust that your great anxiety may be allayed by definite news of his safety soon. Please accept my most heartfelt sympathy. I had a great affection for him.   **John Bird (Company Commander)**

October 1915

02 *Elgar rehearsed* Polonia *at Queen's Hall in the morning, and then conducted* Carillon *which was starting another run at the Coliseum, with Lalla Vandervelde, nee Speyer, reciting.*

[I preferred to stand] outside the drop curtain, which was bright red. As I should be dressed in black the contrast would be striking, and I could use the curtain to lean against, or to clutch – for "business".   **Lalla Vandervelde**

05 *Elgar somehow fitted in a performance of Polonia at Queen's Hall in between his two Coliseum performances.*

E. to Queen's Hall to rehearse Polonia. A. wis him. Gorgeous to hear. E. to Colosseum in aftn. Then after dinner to Queen's Hall A. & C. wis him Glorious performance, most exhilarating & lovely. A. was swept away with enjoyment. E. had a great reception when he appeared & a <u>great</u> ovation afterwards. Then to Coliseum. Made. V. rather trying. No amusement to E. as it was with Liten – A. & C. waited in car –   **Alice diary**

08 A wrote very burningly 'Pay, pay, pay' – *[a poem condemning the "Yankee men" for staying neutral.]*   **Alice diary**

16 E. & C. to Stratford – C's plans for her holiday with Rosamund having fallen through. A. all by her souse – Percy called & had pleasant talk –   **Alice diary**

19 We went into Leamington & I sent you the very soiled & bedraggled print of Calder – burn it – it is of no value but I wrote a word on its very smoky back – We leave for Stoke at Midday & I look for letters there –   Elgar-Alice Stuart Wortley

22 I was so sorry to hear via Carice, that you have been attempting influenza & that you do not really like it now you have it; it is extremely careless of you & I hope most sincerely that you are much better. C. will have told you or will tell you of our sudden flight to the Midlands on account of the sudden change of plan by her friend. I rushed home yesterday (leaving the child at Stoke) as I go on to Bournemouth tonight to be in time for a rehearsal tomorrow – also I have a detestable cold which I am sure is worse than yours –   Elgar-Rosa Burley

23 *Elgar's concert in Bournemouth included the Violin Concerto with Albert Sammons, Carillon, and the second Wand of Youth Suite.*

25 *E conducted Carillon with Madame Réjane at a LSO concert at Queen's Hall. Beecham conducted Berlioz's Roman Carnival, Mozart's Eine Kleine Nachtmusik, Delius's In a summer garden and Rimsky-Korsakov's Scheherazade.*

… the great French actress, Réjane, whose consummate artistry and white-heat of enthusiasm swept the audience off its feet, and created a sensation in the concert-hall the like of which London can never have witnessed either before or since.   Thomas Dunhill

28 E. turning to his great Music for Binyon Poems again –   Alice diary

November 1915

03 *Elgar went to The Hut, staying until November 7th.*

08 *Elgar went to Leeds for a rehearsal, and a concert the next day.*

09 I rang you this morning about an important matter with Lena Ashwell.   Robin Legge-Elgar

Robin Legge has encouraged me to ask you if you would consider writing music for a play I hope to do at Christmas by Algernon Blackwood. The play is half reality and half fairyland & it is your help in fairyland I want so much. There is a great mystic quality in the play which I am sure will help people to bear the sorrows of the war, & the end is really wonderful in its beauty. Would you ring me up tonight & say if I may come to see you about it.   Lena Ashwell-Elgar

11 E. into town for lunch. Met A. at Kingsway Theatre & L. Ashwell gave a box. Alice S. W. with us. Enjoyed 'Iris intervenes' extremely. Lena wonderfully clever in it. Much thought as well as amusement in it. The only play or novel in which a woman has the sense to say 'Nothing wd. make me believe it' (tale about her Husband) Even if it were absolutely proved I'd not believe it' A. clapped & was joined by someone – Tea with Lena A. afterwards very nice & interesting.   Alice diary

15 I had a 'meeting' author producer & composer this a m & decided to do the music – consider the amount of help I shall want & the responsibility! Tomorrow we go to Leeds – home on Thursday …   Elgar-Alice Stuart Wortley

I am no playwright; I possess none of the necessary talents. I have never started a play on my own initiative. In 1915 when A Prisoner in Fairyland was at its high peak of circulation a Miss Violet Pearn obtained my permission to adapt it as a play for children. Music only emerged as quite an afterthought. Elgar's name cropped up. I had never met him and knew next to nothing of his music. However, various people, myself amongst them, were bold enough to approach the great man. He at once fell in with the proposal.   **Algernon Blackwood**

I was so delighted to see you were to be Mayor & Mayoress again; it is most patriotic of you to give up so much time, money, labour & everything for the good of the dear old city: I feel so proud to know you both &, although thanks are not of much use, I send you mine for so splendidly upholding the honour of our town.   **Elgar-Hubert & Agnes Leicester**

17 *Elgar conducted Caractacus with the Leeds Choral Union.*

Immense audience & gave E. great reception. He asked if Dr. Coward might conduct Nat. Anthem joy for Dr. C. just what E. wd. think of. Great Concert, best Caractacus ever done E. thinks. A really <u>great</u> Concert –   **Alice diary**

In the trenches, very cold, do not feel very fit. P accidentally shoots himself cleaning rifle, a sad loss – letter from Lady Elgar.   **Arthur Bliss diary**

19 *Elgar started work on The Starlight Express.*

Occupying practically the whole of the time he could spare from his duties in the Hampstead Volunteer Reserve during the months of November and December, the fantasy was produced for the Christmas holidays on 28th December.   **W H Reed**

20 *The Elgars saw L'Enfant Prodigue at Duke of York's Theatre. Landon Ronald played the piano on the first night. John Barbirolli was a 'cellist in the pit band, with long trousers* "which hurt under the armpits".

24 … we heard a lot about the Starlight Express. It is so disgusting that it is not to have your music … They have got Elgar to do the music … and apparently Lena Ashwell and Algernon Blackwood go about saying in perfect seriousness that the play is being produced by God. I think you are well out of it, as I imagine God would be as tiresome to collaborate with as Stanford.   **Edward Dent-Clive Carey**

27 Is 'Sir Elgar' already writing an opera? From him something great will be expected!
                                                        Hans Richter-Sydney Loeb

December 1915

04 *Elgar conducted Carillon at a Royal Choral Society concert, the main item being Haydn's Creation, conducted by Sir Frederick Bridge, with Agnes Nicholls, John Coates and Bertram Mills.*

07 Mr. Ronald is carrying on the business negotiations between Sir Edward Elgar and Miss Lena Ashwell for a new Play shortly to be produced. Mr. Chas. Mott is one of the artists. Mr. Ronald thought that he could arrange the matter should we wish records to be made.
                                                        Gramophone Company Minute

08 Ballet Mistress came. E. much absorbed in his work –   **Alice diary**

10 I have been so sumptuously busy over the play – slow copyists – inferior & rejected singers etc etc that all the nicest things in the world, & you the best of all, have had to be neglected, but not forgotten.   **Elgar-Clare Stuart Wortley**

12 J. Harrison *[conductor of 'The Starlight Express]* to go through the music with E. & stayed to lunch.

Alice diary

I am glad you smell the Severn in my music.

Elgar-Julius Harrison

c13 I hear that Mr Wilson, the artist, has designed the Sprites in the spirit of Greek fantasy – Lamplighter a quasi-Mercury, Gardener as Priapus, or someone else, and Sweep possibly as Pluto. It is a false and ghastly idea. There is nothing pagan in our little Childhood Play.

Algernon Blackwood-Elgar

Another difficulty that 'might have arisen' is the scenery and dresses. Because when anything hasn't been dramatised before (Mr. Blackwood's Sprites, for instance) it is a matter not only of giving 'airy nothing a local habitation and a name', but clothes as well – a much more complicated proposition. But Mr Wilson, the president of the Arts and Crafts Society, knew exactly what Mr Blackwood's Sprites looked like and did. In fact, he seemed to know just as much about it as the authors, Mr Blackwood and Miss Pearn. So that difficulty did not arise!

Lena Ashwell, The Referee (26/12/15)

15 *Elgar completed the score of The Starlight Express.*

20 … it has been a real joy to have something so pure & simple to do & Blackwood is an unusual man – & sympathetic to me.

Elgar-Sidney Colvin

21 *Elgar's nephew William Henry Elgar died from TB at the age of 25.*

23 *Funeral of Elgar's nephew. The Elgars did not attend*

24 *Elgar and Blackwood attended a dress rehearsal.*

25 I know what you're feeling. Probably you can guess what I'm feeling. Can we do anything? I am so inexperienced in these things … This murder of my simple little Play (qua words) I can stand, for the fate of my books has accustomed me to it; but this suburban, Arts & Crafts pretentious rubbish stitched on to your music is really too painful for me to bear.

Algernon Blackwood-Elgar

26 It is a very happy play, which will, I hope, cheer everyone up. The extraordinary intuitive grasp which Miss Ashwell has shown has been a very keen delight to me. Her enthusiasm and her zeal are beyond anything I could have expected.

Algernon Blackwood, The Observer

27 *Lady Elgar suffered concussion when her taxi was involved in an accident.*

28 Your friend *[Harry Griffiths, the set designer]* has entirely ruined any chance the play had of success – he's an ignorant silly crank with no knowledge of the stage at all & has overloaded the place with a lot of unsuitable rubbish & has apparently never read the play! He ought to be put in a Home!

Elgar-Troyte Griffith

29 Poor dear Alice is quite laid up with a taxi accident – better now, but in bed & will be there for a long time I fear. She mercifully remembers nothing about the collision – a perfect blank.

Elgar-Ivor Atkins

The play was, unhappily, not very successful, but the music which accompanied it does not deserve to be forgotten.

Thomas Dunhill

It was a terrible production … It was financed by a man in loving memory of his wife and there were bits put in because the dear departed would have liked them.

Violet Pearn-Val Gielgud (date unknown)

January 1916

01 *[Message to cast]* Best wishes to all good Cockaigners! May they all be un-Wumbled &
have plenty of star-dust.
Elgar

May this year bring hope & Victory – & blessed Peace. A. in bed – Starlight Express
every day. E. there very often –
Alice diary

04 In case I do not see you – I cd. not leave today but go tomorrow ... to Stoke for a few
– very few – days
Elgar-Alice Stuart Wortley

[Later] I tried to get to the theatre to-day but could not; I heard a good solid report of
a cannon about four o'clock & the people called out Zeppelins. I shall be at Stoke I
think until Monday
Elgar-Alice Stuart Wortley

19 *Elgar signed a contract with Elkin to publish the voice and piano arrangement of Une
Voix dans le Désert, and commissioning a third 'Belgian' piece, Le Drapeau Belge.*

25 Mr. Muir wished to know whether any of Kipling's poems, set to music by Sir Edward
Elgar, were ready. Mr. Ronald stated that Sir Edward had refused to continue the
writing of these musical accompaniments and that therefore the matter had been
dropped.
Gramophone Co. Minutes

29 This piece was performed nightly for a week after its production. The work met with
considerable success at first and is well written and interesting. There is a charm in
"The Starlight Express" music ... that is free from artificiality or affectation. It is the
work of a musician of good-nature, and it might well be revived, at any rate at
Christmas time. Elgar among the realm of the children is as natural as the same man
who, in large symphonic work, expresses the triumph of simple faith.
John F Porte

February 1916

05 A. out by her souse into town for 1st time. Real effort to go – First to Sir Maurice & then
to a Shop – E. not out – much –
Alice diary

06 I received by the same post as your very welcome letter, one from Lady Elgar who has
now recovered from her motor accident.
Arthur Bliss-Francis Bliss *[his father]*

14 It was reported that all arrangement had been made for recording 'The Starlight
Express' under the conductorship of Sir Edward Elgar, on Friday next, and that Agnes
Nicholls had been engaged to do the soprano solos and duet for a fee of £30.
Gramophone Co. Minutes

18 I ... took records of his music for a play, a fairy-tale of Algernon Blackwood's called
The Starlight Express, with that fine soprano, Agnes Nicholls, and a great baritone,
Charles Mott.
Fred Gaisberg

He had a great fancy to have me do this ... He was very excited about these records, and
if I may say so, very pleased with the way I did it.
Agnes Nicholls-Jerrold Northrop Moore

26 *Elgar completed the full score of To Women.*

27 *Elgar rehearsed with the LSO at Queen's Hall for another tour.*

28 Elgar then went on another Harrison tour with the London Symphony Orchestra,

Arthur de Greef touring with them as solo pianist. Elgar conducted a piece by de Greef for piano and orchestra called Melodies flamandes and the third Brahms Symphony among other items … he became very sure of himself as the tour progressed, and he conducted the same works night after night in each town. I remember specially a most impressive performance of Brahms's Third Symphony, which he adored.   W H Reed

Elgar conducted the first concert of the tour in the Mansion House, Birmingham.

29 *Elgar conducted LSO concert in Manchester.*

March 1916

01 *Elgar conducted LSO concert in Liverpool.*

I am 'on the wing' as Byard said – touring with the L.S.O.   **Elgar-Rosa Burley**

02 *Elgar conducted LSO concert in Newcastle.*

03 *Elgar conducted LSO concert in Glasgow.*

04 *Elgar conducted LSO concert in Edinburgh.*

05 E. home all safe & well. D. G.   **Alice diary**

07 The tour was interesting: the varieties of lighting *and drinking* restrictions are puzzling but I suppose are devised with knowledge & to a good end.
     You will have seen that, owing to the N. countrymen's enterprise the Gerontius performances at Queen's Hall are to be, & that Binyon's poem will be done:
     Elgar-Frances Colvin

14 Mr. Gaisberg … to lunch. Very interesting talk   **Alice diary**

As a guest at Severn Lodge … I never felt otherwise than at perfect ease. The spirit of wholesome goodness emanating from Lady Elgar permeated their home. In no other house have I, as a guest, felt so free from restraint.   **Fred Gaisberg**

15 You must have realised then, as now, that the weight of your name as a composer against mine would spoil my chances, not in the matter of publication only. So that your generous action (which I made as public as I could) is completely negatived by what you have since done. I fail to reconcile your first letter to me with the action which (without giving me a hint of what you have done) you have since taken.
     Cyril Rootham-Elgar

21 *The Elgars attended a preliminary meeting at the Royal Automobile Club about the Clara Butt Red Cross Concerts planned for May.*

E. & A. to meeting about Gerontius music for the week – E. did not speak. Looked <u>too</u> unhappy … Mr. Blkwd there. Mr. Embleton to lunch – seemed more devoted & nicer than ever –   **Alice diary**

Isn't it time … that art in England should try to express a new attitude of the English mind towards life after death? … We are a nation in mourning … I want people to come … and to realise some spiritual truths, and to give them a week of beautiful thoughts.   **Clara Butt (Daily Telegraph)**

23 E. busy arranging Song for Muriel Foster.   **Alice diary**

26 Muriel came & was delighted with Handel song E. arranged for her. A. not out – E. & A. Blackwood to lunch at Cheyne Walk, our guest looking mis at having to go out! – In aftn Mrs. Caulfeild & Miss Hawkshaw Anthony Bernard & Mr. Rogers – M. Cammaerts – Mr. & Mrs. Mott & child, Mr. Streatfeild – seemed very successful –
Alice diary

28 I fully understand that I am taking what you may well consider an unwarrantable liberty in venturing to interfere in a private matter, but I cannot refrain from doing so in the hope of removing a misunderstanding which seems to have arisen between you and Sir Edward Elgar regarding your respective settings of Laurence Binyon's 'For the Fallen'.   **Richard Streatfeild-Cyril Rootham**

28 Our dear guest *[Algernon Blackwood]* left – said he had never had such a visit in his life – Frightful Storm snow, wind &c – very devastating all over the country – Quite frightening here –
Alice diary

29 E. intended going into country but suddenly developed bad cold – & trains all delayed by storm & all snow & horribly cold.
Alice diary

30 A. to arrange about a typewriter for E. It came up & E spent hours practising & writing wild flights
Alice diary

31 My dear Mrs. Stuart-Wortley (!!!!)
How is that for a beginning? This machine is beyond praise & knows exactly what to say and how and when to say it! How frightful it looks printed like this; it is not to be borne.
My dear Windflower, — this is much smaller type and more befitting, — you said I must never use type in writing to you, but I m u s t practise this new machine which gives all the foreign accents and is a great amusement ...   **Elgar-Alice Stuart Wortley**

April 1916

02 E. not very well but resolved to go to Coliseum Had to wait a long time, went into Nat. Gallery & went to sleep – Not at all well. A. in bed
Alice diary

06 *HMV gave a luncheon at the Savoy to launch the Starlight Express records.*

It is ... magnificent to relate that the Gramophone Company has recorded the whole play, allowing us to be quite independent of theatres. The vocal parts were taken by competent artists and the whole fantasy sounds, we think, just as Elgar would have conceived it. It is another case in which we have to be thankful for the composer's insight into the gramophone possibilities.   **John F Porte**

11 I have just found your Stoke letter here – Alas! I was taken ill in the train & removed from it to a Nursing Home at Oxford – so strange so instead of Stoke I have been taken by some unknown good person to the Acland Home where I have been lying till today when Carice escorted me home. I am of course better but not well – I went out too soon after Influenza & collapsed in the train   **Elgar-Alice Stuart Wortley**

14 I visited the Elgars when they were at Severn House. I remember very well going up the hill there, entering this large house, and Lady Elgar being very kind, and hearing Elgar upstairs playing some phrase over and over again on the piano.   (Afterwards I discovered that this phrase came from an 'occasional piece', Le drapeau Belge). He soon stopped and came down, and there he was – the first time I met him – aloof, shy, speaking to me in his soft Worcestershire voice, and taking me in with his rather curious blinking eyes.

Arthur Bliss

… slim young man in uniform.

Carice Elgar

15   The complete work is entitled 'The Spirit of England' Consists of settings for Tenor, or Soprano solo, chorus & orchestra of three poems by Laurence Binyon, – published in The Times & now included in the volume of poems inspired by the great war 'The Winnowing Fan.' Music sketched and nearly completed twelve months ago. The whole work bears the inscription 'My portion of this work I humbly dedicate to the memory of our glorious men, with a special thought for the Worcesters. 'Edward Elgar. 1915.

Elgar-Ernest Newman

27   Sir Edward … set Binyon's For the Fallen … I, being enlisted under the Derby Scheme and doing war-work, was luckily not sent away, so was able, though there was not much time for music in those terror-ridden days, to get together a few string players and take them up to Severn House to try over the string parts for Binyon's poem. This we did also with Le Drapeau Belge and The Spirit of England, Sir Edward filling in the wind parts on the piano.

W H Reed

Our music – which was meant for you – went beautifully & the men played like angels

Elgar-Alice Stuart Wortley

May 1916

02   *Elgar conducted a rehearsal in Leeds of To Women and For the Fallen.*

Here in truth is the very voice of England … moved to the centre of her being in this War as she has probably never been moved before in all her history.

Ernest Newman (Musical Times, 05/16)

03   *Elgar conducted the first performance of 'To Women' and 'For the Fallen' with Agnes Nicholls, the Leeds Choral Union and the Halle Orchestra. Gerontius, with Clara Butt, came after the interval.*

… had never heard more perfect singing.

Clara Butt *[of Agnes Nicholls]*

04   *Elgar conducted a second performance, in Bradford.*

Elgar has made the orchestra his chief speaker. The words, whether sung by the soloist … or the choir, are chanted as an accompaniment to the orchestral music. They stand in the background, inspiring the feeling of each musical thought … Until the climax of "For the Fallen" The reticence in the vocal music is a thing which seems to show Elgar's sense of responsibility. A larger chorus singing such words as those of the final part of "To Women" might become blatant.

The Times (06/05/16)

05   At the Behrens – Very kind. entirely obsessed by Bradford – even said <u>have</u> you good Drs. in London!

Alice diary

06   So nice to be in London again after Bradford's very local atmosphere –

Alice diary

08   *Elgar conducted a sold-out week of performance of To Women, For the Fallen and Gerontius organised by Clara Butt at Queen's Hall for the Red Cross. The soloists were Agnes Nicholls, Clara Butt, Gervase Elwes and Charles Mott.*

Charles Mott … gave a striking rendering of that marvellous cry of the Angel of the Agony; and Clara Butt … surpassed anything she had ever done, revealing in herself the great nobility and the artistry called forth by this inspired work. Maud Warrender

A memorable feature of the musical season was an Elgar Festival at Queen's Hall on behalf of the British Red Cross Society. As the results of six performances of his "Dream of Gerontius," which the composer conducted, a large sum was handed over to that organisation. Hazell's Annual

The record success of the series smashed the hoary fiction that oratorio is exhausted with one performance. The audiences were astounding in quality and quantity. King George, Queen Mary, and Queen Alexandra attended, and the Royal box was always a picture. Henry Coward *[conductor of the Leeds Choral Union]*

These performances attracted great attention; as the Angel, Dame Clara, dressed in white lace, took a position high up behind the orchestra in Queen's Hall, level with the organ. Ivor Newton

How can I ever tell you dear Edward what we felt today or how deeply moved we both were – it is all quite wonderful &just what one wants at this time – & at all times – it will live always – 'For the Fallen' especially will always be the one great inspiration of the War. My heart is full of warm gratitude to you – but my eyes are sore with tears & I can't write – but we both send you our heartfelt love & congratulations – Bless you. Frances Colvin-Elgar

09 The enormous audience continued on Tuesday evg. & everything was even more perfect – Alice diary

11 This was a specially beautiful evening. Alice diary

12 Another superb performance. Feeling thankful E. had kept well enough so far – Alice diary

15 I am so glad you like the new things … Thanks for pointing out the grammatical errors … I now see there are fifths – what ARE we to do? Elgar-Ivor Atkins

16 The more I think of your work on Saturday the more I glory in it … the whole work is so noble, so poetically patriotic and splendid that I have no words to tell you what I feel about it. And there it is, a living thing in my soul and mind, – and I just want to thank you. Mary de Navarro-Elgar

18 *From May 18th to 23rd the Elgars took a holiday in Eastbourne.*

26 I sent, instead of carrying, the K. John relics to the Dean – I wonder what you think? I rescued them on the chance of their being genuine & Canon Wilson & the Dean accept them Elgar-Ivor Atkins

June 1916

02 *The Elgars travelled to Worcester together, then Elgar went on to Stoke Prior to stay with Pollie, while Lady Elgar went to the de Navarros at Broadway.*

03 I am here & much better – so far: it is lovely and – lonely. I rest & play with the dog & cut down thistles. Your telegram came – love & thanks Elgar-Alice Stuart Wortley

Very lovely at the Court Farm. Cuckoos & flowers &c – Many walks with M. de N. & good news of E.
Alice diary

06 Elgar … visited my parents and spent some time in the cathedral seeing the King John relics, and in the new Music Library.
Wulstan Atkins

08 Raser worried about E. & telegraphed.
Alice diary

15 E. met A. In Worcester. A. rather agitated leaving Broadway as car seemed late. Went to see the China King John Tomb – & E. to see his brother. E. raser better but so sorry to leave country. So A. raser mis – C. & all well at home. D.G.
Alice diary

24 *From June 24ᵗʰ – 26ᵗʰ the Elgars stayed with Edward Speyer at Ridgehurst.*

29 *Percy Scholes went to Severn House to interview Elgar for an article in the October 1916 issue of 'The Music Student'.*

Once at the summit, and admitted into the house, the interviewer is happy. He sinks back into an arm chair, Sir Edward sits up to his library table ready for business and the questioning begins.
Percy Scholes

July 1916

01 *Start of the Battle of the Somme.*

06 *[Enclosing miniature score of Cockaigne]* Good luck.
Elgar-Arthur Bliss

One of my most treasured possessions is a miniature score of Cockaigne which he sent me, and which … retains the mud marks of the trenches.
Arthur Bliss

08 *The Elgars spent the weekend at The Hut, returning on July 10ᵗʰ.*

11 We got back from the Hut yesterday afternoon: I spent my time like Old Mortality renovating old inscriptions. It was lovely to see (between the rain-storms) but not restful with four soldiers in the house & only A. & myself as other guests … I may go to my sister any day but all is vague, uncertain & unprofitable.
Elgar-Alice Stuart Wortley

12 E. out a good deal & wishing for Country –
Alice diary

15 *Elgar went to Stoke Prior to stay with Pollie.*

19 I went out to Bridgnorth yesterday such a lovely place so curiously placed on a hill with my beloved windflowerish Severn winding round it: but I am not well today, alas! … The weather is lovely now but it has brought out millions of FLIES!
Elgar-Alice Stuart Wortley

20 In the middle of July Elgar was again staying with the Graftons. He came over to Worcester on the 20th. He told the Atkins that he and Alice were going up to the Lakes for a few weeks.
Wulstan Atkins

24 E. lunched with A.S.W. at Droitwich & then drove round by the Elms *[Pollie's house]* & to the Common –
Alice diary

August 1916

01 A. started to Bridgnorth   So excited to know <u>when</u> wd. meet E. Looked for him at Worcester, then at Droitwich & <u>then,</u> at Arley with head out of window saw him. Both had such real excited joy in meeting   He had a garland of clematis & threw it over A.'s head – He had been at Bridgnorth to see room &c & came back to Arley to meet A. Looked better & very keen about the holiday. <u>Intensely hot.</u>   Alice diary

02 E. & A. at Bridgnorth. Wonderful place, more like a foreign rock village. Walked all around. A. rather disappointing! as she did not mind the heights suspension bridge as E. thought she wd. <u>Very</u> hot. Had a taxi after tea & drove by Quatford &c. Very nice country. Saw such a lovely old, red brick empty house   Decided to go to Ullswater next day   Alice diary

03 *From August 3ʳᵈ – 21ˢᵗ the Elgars holidayed in the Lake District.*

11 *Lalla Vandervelde joined the Elgars at Ullswater. She left on August 16ᵗʰ.*

16 We leave on Friday for P. of Wales Hotel Grasmere … We have rain storms but lovely times in between … Alice is much rested & this has done her any amount of good – she thinks it is good for me but I stay on for her sake. I do not know when we shall arrive in town:- next week I think   **Elgar-Alice Stuart Wortley**

22 Sir Maurice came to see E. & gave him tonic &c – promised improvement – Alice diary

26 I do not improve much. We are just back from the Lakes & I have had a little throat examination & it seems that some small trouble there affects me: this trouble is being 'eliminated' – by nauseous means – & in a few days I shall be all right: it is said so, but I await in impatience … I am glad my uncle *[Henry]* keeps fairly well. he was 87 this week!   **Elgar-Ivor Atkins**

31 I was so sorry about yesterday – I started out but had to return – not well – today – the same feeling … I feel that everything has come to an end & am very unhappy –
                                                   Elgar-Alice Stuart Wortley

September 1916

02 *Elgar went to Ridgehurst for the weekend.*

He came to me one day and said that a dear old friend of his, Mr. Edward Speyer, who lived at Shenley, wanted him to go there for a week-end and take me with him … He had been a personal friend of Brahms, Goldmark, and many other famous musicians of his time; and music was his one subject. Knowing this, I took my violin, expecting that there would be music on the Sunday.

Unfortunately for our host's plans, Sir Edward had just learnt a new game at the billiard-table, a kind of pool with coloured balls … as soon as tea was over we had to go at once to the billiard-table and learn the new game. This went on until it was time to dress for dinner. Then Suggia arrived. During dinner the new game was explained to her, with the result that, after coffee, Suggia, Mrs. Speyer, and myself had to begin a fresh game with him. In vain poor Mr. Speyer produced some sheets of music to discuss with Sir Edward. They were glanced at hurriedly and put down again because it was his turn to play. The game went on until bedtime.   **W H Reed**

03 The same thing happened next day … nothing could interest him for long except that new game, which we all played again until bedtime. **W H Reed**

04 Next morning, full of sincere thanks to our host and hostess for a most enjoyable week-end … we left Elstree without having played a single note. Mr. Speyer might as well have entertained Lord Lonsdale. **W H Reed**

E. returned early, & had had a pleasant time & looked all the better for change –
Alice diary

06 I am better but not happy … I am not sure if I am going to Stoke but, as the weather is quite bright this morning, I may go at any moment … **Elgar-Alice Stuart Wortley**

08 The Elgars *[came]* down to stay with the Berkeleys at Spetchley Park for about a fortnight, and Elgar was proposing to wander about the park and fish for the first week, after which he intended coming on to Worcester. **Wulstan Atkins**

12 Happening to be in Worcester one summer day I met Mr. Robert Berkeley on his way to a council meeting; he told me that Elgar was staying at the Hall and suggested that I should run down there … As I was nearing the Hall I was hailed by someone from the lake. It was Elgar. He brought the punt to the bank and conveyed me to the middle of the lake, where I passed with him one of the golden summer afternoons of my life, talking about this and that. He had felt, he told me, an irresistible urge to be alone, and had excused himself on the plausible ground that he wanted to do some composing.
Ernest Newman

14 A. & E. left Spetchley after early lunch – with much regret & most affectionate farewells & wishes for us to come again … E. wrote lovely words in their copy of Gerontius & found a poultry poem for Betty. **Alice diary**

The Gerontius copy was inscribed: 'In Spetchley Park, 1869'. *Elgar went on to visit his sister Pollie while Lady Elgar returned to London.*

15 I am just passing on my way home from Spetchley. Alice & I paid a week end visit to the Berkeleys- a visit which was prolonged day by day – lovely place where I played as a child, 3½ miles from Worcester – Deerpark, fishponds etc etc – I caught 70 good fish! But l am very sad – & cannot rest even here, so after one night I restlessly go home
Elgar-Alice Stuart Wortley

16 E. left Stoke & went to Holmbury S. Mary to stay with Lalla & other friends
Alice diary

18 E. returned from Holmbury S. Mary – quite safes & looking well – He did not care about the place for a 'prolonged stay', but had had a pleasant time. **Alice diary**

October 1916

01 Zepp raid late at night. A. heard shouting. but guns were too far away. Joy at another brute being brought down at Potter's Bar. Crew taken prisoners by a single Special – It fell near a cottage but did not touch it - Marvellous for the 4th to come down without damaging anyone as it fell **Alice diary**

03 I have been hoping to hear from you. I did not go away & see no chance of going for a long time … I feel you are all safer on that coast than here but it is good to know that we can capture the Zeppelins sometimes. **Elgar-Alice Stuart Wortley**

08 The other afternoon a friend of mine saw three or four urchins in the Finchley Road playing with a toad – to the toad's evident discomfort. Sir Edward Elgar appeared on the scene, and for the sum of two pence rescued the reptile and bore it off in triumph. The appearance of a Symphonic Poem on this occurrence will be awaited with some interest, if not anxiety.

Daily Mirror (10/10/16)

20 *The Elgars went to see Mary Anderson (de Navarro) at His Majesty's Theatre in W S Gilbert's Pygmalion and Galatea.*

21 How wonderful & how beautiful! Thank you again & again for this view of your art: I was so happy during the performance – I do not go to see or hear my friends as I suffer such acute agonies of nervousness for their sakes, but yesterday was a thing of joy. Bless you!

Elgar-Mary de Navarro

22 I was so pleased to see you in the theatre, that I did what I never do: I bowed specially to you – and at once they sent me word I must bow to the Queen – whose presence I forgot.

Mary de Navarro-Elgar

26 A.S.W. came to tea & played the lovely phrase of Piano Concerto.

Alice diary

November 1916

01 *Winifred Norbury stayed with the Elgars from November 1ˢᵗ – 3ʳᵈ.*

04 C. did splendid work in greenhouse – rescuing & repotting plants massacred by casual gardener –

Alice diary

12 E. not very well, down to luncheon – Very nice afternoon. Lady Horridge, Lalla, Lady Petre, Eleanor Berkeley – & Mansfd. Evans (mufti) unexpectedly came & was announced as Percy Anderson! Much gramophone – Lalla stayed to dinner, great Indian pool game – *A*. won –

Alice diary

The whole place was full of interesting people. Eleanor Berkeley quickly mixed with the guests, leaving me to sit down to a good talk with Carice on a sofa. As I came to know her, I found her rather miserable at this time, asking 'Who am I amid all this throng?' Once she said: 'Kitty, I'm sick of eminent men!'

Lady Petre

13 E. better – D.G. Busy arranging Violin Concerto for Gramophone.

Alice diary

15 Give my love to my friends & all the artists who worked with me, when you meet them. They are with me in my waking hours & in my dreams, & my thoughts of them are always good & pleasurable. With thankfulness I think of the hours I spent with them. They were the happiest of my artistic life.

Hans Richter-Mathilde Loeb

20 E. A. & C. (Lansdown Car) to Albert Hall in evening. Very beautiful rehearsal of 'For the Fallen' – A. Nichols' voice & rendering wonderful in that great space – Then on to Queen's Hall to hear the Violin Concerto – Salmons played most wonderfully but Safonoff conducted so badly, boisterous heavy & no real reading of the wonderful work –

Alice diary

22 *Elgar went to Manchester to rehearse the chorus for a performance of Gerontius which he conducted next day with Gervase Elwes, Muriel Foster and Charles Mott.*

24 E. left Manchester at 7.30 – & arrived at the Albert Hall at noon in time for his Rehearsal of 'For the Fallen' –

Alice diary

27 *Elgar conducted the second Symphony at a [Royal] Philharmonic Society concert, deputising for Landon Ronald, who was ill. Beecham conducted rest of the programme: Wagner, Mozart, Tchaikovsky and Bantock. Elgar had had three rehearsals for the Symphony.*

E. sat with A. for 1st part rather boring & then conducted the Symphony <u>most</u> splendidly, a wonderful beautiful performance. **Alice diary**

Poor Elgar – The orchestra positively scrambled through the symphony as if they had never before seen it. If it had been a work of mine I should have gone home & vowed 'never again without three <u>long</u> rehearsals'. In fact, as I had never heard the work before I felt quite sick about it. Performances of this kind do far more harm than good.
Frank Bridge-Edward Speyer (30/11/16)

December 1916

01 E. to see Lalla in her new flat – painted most garish colours under Mr. R. Fry's direction – then on to see Lan, who was better. **Alice diary**

04 Cabinet crisis settlement not announced yet. We are longing for Asquith to go –
Alice diary

05 *Hans Richter died; Asquith resigned, replaced by Lloyd George.*

James White had acted as general business adviser to my father over his London interests … It was during the late autumn that he one day startled me by saying: "Your friend Mr. Asquith won't be long where he is." I sought out … a close friend of the Prime Minister *[and]* told him in detail of the existence of an intrigue to oust his leader in favour of Mr. Lloyd George. **Thomas Beecham**

11 I am very unwell indeed and do not know what to make of it – I suppose it is the old thing but I can make no plans at all. I have to go to the Gramophone Coy on Saturday but I am waiting for further information as to time & mode of conveyance
Elgar-Alice Stuart Wortley

16 No lunch till just 2.45 – E. vesy tired & headache – L. Binyon tried to come & arrived at Hampstd. Tube but cd. not venture to find way in fog. **Alice diary**

The Concerto has achieved world-wide popularity, but it is fortunate that the interpretations of two historic combinations have been recorded for the gramophone. These two are Albert Sammons and the Queen's Hall Orchestra under Sir Henry J. Wood, and Marie Hall and the Symphony Orchestra under Sir Edward Elgar himself. Albert Sammons and Marie Hall have given refined and impressive renderings.
John F Porte

Mr. Gaisberg reported that Sir Edward was delighted with his Violin Concerto records. He had at his home the records of the Competition of this same Concerto, and Sir Edward and Mr. Gaisberg carefully compared these sets of records, and in Sir Edward's opinion our recording was superior. **Gramophone Co. Minutes (23/01/17)**

17 E. vesy unwell. headache &c. down to lunch – Moved blue sofa to fireplace wh. was comfy for him. **Alice diary**

18 Saw Charles S. Wortley was to be made a Peer – Telegraphed congratulns. **Alice diary**
23 Alice S. W. came in afternoon – Brought E. his Lavender Water present & A. dear

pottery bowl of White hyacinths – & C. a nice umbrella – E. & A. walked with her to Finchley Rd. omnibus –   Alice diary

28 Lalla to lunch & stayed for tea – Mrs. Hunter & 2 children came – (formerly Jaeger) Gave them little presents.   Alice diary

Elgar lying on a sofa and Lalla Vandervelde "adoring him"   Mary Jaeger/Hunter

January 1917

01 May the N. Year bring hopes for some prosperity & health to E. & C.   Alice diary

02 All good wishes to you both for the New Year – I should have written days ago but the inevitable fog killed all good intentions for four days – I have been in bed.
                                                                               Elgar-Frances Colvin

04 E. not very well. Meant to take Miss Burley out to lunch & have tea with Colvins but gave it up. Colder but bright & sunny. Thrushes singing in the morning now –
                                                                               Alice diary

09 Sir Edward is still indisposed, and he is not able to see friends or visitors. Mr. Gaisberg stated that he had received a letter from Lady Elgar saying that as soon as Sir Edward was fit she would acquaint Mr. Gaisberg with the fact so that he could pay Sir Edward a visit.   Gramophone Co. Minutes

11 I wonder how you are: I went to the doctor yesterday & am no better today; I am trying the dentist this afternoon but I do not see beyond to-day! … Troyte is 'coming' for a day or two   Elgar-Alice Stuart Wortley

12 E. seemed better D.G. Troyte came.   Alice diary

16 To A's relief coke arrived!   Alice diary

28 Ever since Elgar had sent the proofs of For the Fallen to Atkins in May 1916, the latter had been considering how he could arrange a performance in Worcester Cathedral. Towards the end of January 1917, plans were sufficiently advanced to enable Atkins to write to Elgar, putting forward his ideas and asking him to come down to conduct For the Fallen.   Wulstan Atkins

Your letter is thrilling!! I must say at once that on March 7th I am in Leeds, so that makes the 8th in Worcester impossible. How about the 15th? The only difficulty ahead (& which, wretchlike you don't suggest) is the SOPRANO SOLOIST What is to be done? All else, – you (supreme) at the organ, chorus, (all old &) new friends, my (very own) Cathedral – all beside the Woman, seems perfect.   Elgar-Ivor Atkins

February 1917

02 (As I write a dense yellow fog envelops the house). I really do not know of any singers – no doubt some are to be had – other than Agnes or Carrie Tubb. Stick to March 15th, please – it will suit me far better than the 1st – it would be Ide-le (!!) – better perhaps 'Ide-al', classic allusion – for me to give reasons for this. (No, I did not wilfully lead up to this colossal pun).   Elgar-Ivor Atkins

It was decided that For the Fallen should form the centrepiece of the largest memorial service yet held in the cathedral. Subscribers to the Worcester Festival Choral Society announced that they would provide all the expenses in connection with the service. This solved the difficulty regarding the soloist ... and Carrie Tubb was engaged to sing the soprano part.   **Wulstan Atkins**

03 E. busy with arrangements for Gramophone – out to lunch   **Alice diary**

05 I want to tell you about a wonderful viola player who played at my recital last Thursday. I never heard anyone to approach him. His name is Lionel Tertis. It would be splendid if you could write something for him to play – it would be a great chance.
                                                              George Sinclair-Elgar

06 I have a most terrible cold & do not know when I shall be out.   I must go to the gramophone on Friday.   **Elgar-Alice Stuart Wortley**

07 *Ina Lowther, wife of Christopher Lowther, visited Severn House with a proposal for a ballet based on Conder's Fan.*

E. in bed & his room all day but raser better – just came down in fur coat to see l. Lowther. So glad Gramophone day at Hayes postponed.   **Alice diary**

George Robertson Sinclair died at 53 from heart attack. He was staying the night in Birmingham after a rehearsal of the Choral Society.

I found him a fussy, typical bachelor, who soon disillusioned me about passing my LRAM in one term – a year at least would be needed, even if I worked my hardest. He was a sound teacher and would brook no slackness, but looking back on that brief period I cannot say that I enjoyed working with him. Dan had been succeeded by Ben, who snuffled, snorted and slobbered, and in fact the whole house smelt of a mixture of dog and general stuffiness.   **Lady Percy Hull**

08 My father was stopped by a friend just opposite the window of the Worcester Herald offices near the Cross. While they talked I looked in the window, and after looking at some photographs I saw an item headed 'Well-known Cathedral Organist Dies'. It was a short announcement that George Robertson Sinclair had died the previous night in a hotel bedroom in Birmingham. He was a special friend of ours, having brought my father with him as assistant when he came from Truro to Hereford in 1889. He had been with my parents on many holidays abroad, and I had known and loved him ever since I could remember.   **Wulstan Atkins**

09 I have just opened the paper & seen the sad, sad, sad news of Sinclair.   I am overwhelmed & sorrowful and quite unable to see things as they are, & alas! are to be! I have no news beyond the Telegraph, & am confined to my room with a severe cold, so I am in the greatest state of tension ... Poor dear old fellow – he was here & dined with us only last week or just before & was full of projects & good will. I grieve!!
                                                              Elgar-Ivor Atkins

11 E. at home rather a cold – Maud rang up & asked to come to lunch – Miss Burley here too. E. played new music to Maud & also some gramophone wh. touched her deeply – Ina Lowther about Ballet Music, then for tea, late, K. Petre & Eleanor & a Valentine Fleming, a nice Eng. country girl. then Lalla to tea –   **Alice diary**

12 We do not sufficiently realise how much the Church owes to its Cathedral organists and its chapel-masters …. amid many difficulties, over-burdened with the toil of teaching, and with little encouragement from the ecclesiastical authorities, those men have worked with enthusiastic zeal in the service of their Church and of their art.

Canon A Bannister [Sermon at Sinclair's funeral]

13 E. going on happily with his new music – C. Stuart of Wortley took his seat in House of Lords.   Alice diary

16 A. to stores about Electric tray &c – E. writing <u>lovely</u> Fan music –   Alice diary

18 Ina Lowther came to go through music of Fan – Sidney Colvin to tea – E. talked with marvellous fund of information of 18th century, pleasant long visit. Percy Anderson to dinner, charmed with E.'s Fan music. Nice evening, he seemed to enjoy it very much.

Alice diary

19 Darkest fog in the morning seen at all this winter. Cleared later It nice & mild – E. orchestrating Fan music – Copyist came & took some away. Did not like it gosing out of the house –   Alice diary

21 E. very intent orchestrating his booful Fan music. Much warmer, quite mild, bulbs showing –   Alice diary

24 E. heard his Uncle Henry Elgar was dangerously ill. Gray sunless day, not cold. E. not vesy well did not go to Dentist. After lunch E. & A. to Kilburn by train & walked some way. A. not liking it <u>at all</u>.   Alice diary

25 E. had a telegram to say his Uncle had passed away the previous evening.

Alice diary

28 *Elgar recorded the first Bavarian Dance, Cockaigne, the Prelude to Gerontius, and some of the Wand of Youth*

March 1917

02 E. busy with R. Kipling Songs –   Alice diary

Some time before, Admiral Charles Beresford had asked Elgar for a setting of some of Kipling's poems. Elgar took some of the 'Barrack Room Ballads'.

03 Busy preparing for journey to Leeds – E. busy with R. Kipling songs –   Alice diary

04 I have been unwell & frightfully busy. We go to Leeds tomorrow for Mr Embleton. Send a line to me at Queen's Hotel.   Elgar-Ivor Atkins

05 My dear Windflower:
    Oh! this weather! & I was dreaming yesterday of woods & fields &, perhaps, a little drive round Harrogate – or a little play journey to Fountains or some lovely remembrance of long ago idylls, & now deep snow. Well, I have put it all in my music & also much more that has never happened.
    A. & I are just starting but I must send a line to say how glad I was you came yesterday.
    I kiss your hands, Love, EE

Elgar-Alice Stuart Wortley

Mr. Broadhurst came re R. Kipling Songs – Much telephoning Mr. Elkin had score of Fan. Started for Leeds from King's Cross – Full train but quite good journey. A's telegram never reached Mr. Embleton so not there to meet us – Desolate! Tried round the station, so cold & dreary, & found cab & then Mr. E. waiting for us in Hotel. Dined with him & nice Norley & Whitehead & Dr. Coward, & then E. to Choral Rehearsal – not A. Very good. E. changed & had supper with Mr. E. & Committee – Dear Mr. E. pleased.   Alice diary

06 I think of the old days here – how happy we were before the war! The service here is beyond belief – e.g. I ordered breakfast at 8.40 sole & porridge – at 9 o'c the young lady came back to say they had no sole: I sd. What have you? She didn't know: then she went away for ½ an hour to find out … Chorus excellent & best soloists – I fear the orchestra may be poor tomorrow but who cares?   Elgar-Alice Stuart Wortley

07 Very very cold – Mr. E.& Dr. Coward lunched with E. & A. – Mr. E. to tea with us – E. & A. to Concert in car – <u>bitterly</u> cold & snowy. <u>Immense</u> audience standing &c – & many turned away. Seemed most <u>wrapt</u>. Beautiful performance. E. conducted masterfully & splendidly. Everybody impressed & delighted.   Alice diary

08 I am just home & found your p.c. dated the 2nd just arrd. What times we live in …. Great performance last night. At your leisure send me a schedule of times of rehearsal etc. I fear my time will be very hurried as I must clear up my poor dear old uncle's affairs. He left no will.   Elgar-Ivor Atkins

09 E. busy with his Fan music. made a lovely Variant in the 18th Cen. theme – Most disarming & lovely – After lunch had car & took his music to Wyndham's Theatre Saw Gerald De Maurier who said E. wd. become absorbed in his music & keep him standing on one leg while he dwelt on a note.   Alice diary

12 Your letter just recd & I note the times. But, alas! I am in bed!! I got an awful chill in the unwarmed train *[coming back from Leeds]* & have been nursing ever since: the doctor is just coming and I am straining every nerve to get a decent report. I am coming to Worcester if I can stand. I hope it will be all right but you must prepare a substitute.   Elgar-Ivor Atkins

13 The doctor came & will let me out! But I am a dessicated worm: we arrive at 4.40 & go straight to the Star. I will be ready for your rehearsal. On Thursday I shall want some time for business (my uncle's affairs) & I float away early on Friday to be in time for rehearsals here. *[Sanguine Fan]*   Elgar-Ivor Atkins

14 That evening the Elgars dined with my parents and I spent some time with them. I recall Alice as short and affable, but disconcerting to a boy because she would come very close when she talked to you, a habit to which I was not accustomed. Elgar talked quickly, often moving about, often with a twinkle in his eye which put me at once at ease.   Wulstan Atkins

15 E. to Cathedral with Ivor. to his Uncle's rooms to settle affairs – A. to Cathedral & Ivor showed her his <u>lovely</u> library, sweet old place, where he is collecting E.'s works – Then E. rehearsed with Ivor & A. went off to call on Lucy. She seemed pleased – then to the Leicesters & saw Agnes. Then E. & A. lunched at the Deanery – Lovely old house – Very friendly & impressed by E. Lady I. Magneson there & others & Ivor. Then E. & A. fled out to Spetchley in rattley old car – lovely there & such a welcome. Miss

Willmott there (not desired). Then A. to Hydes, found them sitting by fire like Philemon & Baucis. So pleased to see A. E. rested. Evening in Cathedral <u>most</u> impressive & beautiful. Enormous audience. For the Fallen deeply touching. Ivor played Prelude <u>wonderfully</u>. Two devotees walked 8 miles home, 2 girls by themselves, after it. Wonderful evening.   Alice diary

After the opening prayers the music began with the cathedral choir singing unaccompanied Psalm 23, 'The Lord is my Shepherd'. Elgar stepped on to the rostrum and, after a silence, he lifted his baton and my father on the organ played the Solemn Prelude which opens For the Fallen and leads into the chorus, 'With proud thanksgiving, a mother for her children. England mourns for her dead across the sea.' The second stanza begins 'Solemn the Drums thrill', and I can still hear the roll of the King's School drums and feel again the shivers which went down my spine. It is impossible to convey the emotions which raced through my mind as that intensely moving performance proceeded, or to describe how avidly I followed Elgar's beat, but anyone who has been privileged to take part in a performance under Elgar's baton, when he himself was completely and absolutely carried away by his music, will know how he played upon his singers and how they gave him results which they had no idea they were capable of.

For the Fallen ends with the chorus singing very quietly 'To the end they remain', and the final chord dying away into space. Absorbed in this music I was completely unprepared for, and shattered by, after a short silence, the first notes of the 'Last Post', which came from the darkness of the distant Lady Chapel. Even now I cannot hear the 'Last Post' without recapturing some of the terror I felt at that utterly unnerving sound.   **Wulstan Atkins**

16 E. & A. left at 9 train. Hubert Leicester came to see us at station – He looked so ascetic & fine Acting Mayor the evening before – nice ceremonial & impressive great sword up behind his raised seat – Startling news on opening paper at station Revolution in Russia & Czar deposed – May it have all success!   Alice diary

A sort of springtide of joy has broken out all over Europe.   **J Ramsay MacDonald**

20 *Elgar conducted the first performance of The Sanguine Fan, as part of 'Chelsea on Tip-Toe', a 'Review of Modern Chelsea', at the Chelsea Palace Theatre.*

Ina Lowther designed her own costume. It was typical of her not to have a finished headdress, but she had wild grass and buttercups (showing the wildness of love, Pan, etc.) and a Pipes of Pan to mime playing upon. She circled round and round the young man with her pipes, eyeing him seductively. At the end Du Maurier (Pan) looked superb, utterly sardonic and unyielding as he half carried Echo off, his arm around her shoulder, looking back on the dead young man and desolate girl.

Winifred Lawford *[one of the dancers]*

22 A week ago today! I am so sorry I have been unable to write before this but every second has been taken up – the worry of the amateur entertainer is endless. Now, how different from the well-devised & perfectly working ceremony at Worcester under your management. The Fan Ballet was lovely & you must see it – some of the entertainment was a disgrace – low & vulgarly uneducated.   **Elgar-Ivor Atkins**

April 1917

07 Windsor Castle. Six degrees of frost in the night. The United States declared war against Germany yesterday by a large majority in the Congress: 373 to 50.

King George V diary

11 A. lunched with Mrs. Joshua – & took her the large photograph of Richter. Much overcome with emotion but glad to have it. Drove A. to Baker St. with lovely chocolates! Very kind –

Alice diary

12 I sent The Fourth of August to the publishers today so that our work, complete in three divisions, will appear some day. Thank you for allowing me to set your splendid poems. I fear I have been a very long time, but the difficulty over the one poem last year put me off somewhat & it has taken me all this time to overtake the first careful rapture.

Elgar-Laurence Binyon

13 E. & A. to Queen's Hall for E.'s rehearsal – De Greef seemed to go on with his Concerto indefinitely so the invaluable Elkin had to stop him – Orchestra lovely & E.'s works beautiful – The 'Voix' 'so wonderfully remote & poetic. Very wet & gray –   Alice diary

The Drapeau Beige makes a fine noise. I am tired because I finished the remaining Binyon thing & The Spirit of England is at the printer's – it went yesterday. Tea with Frances yesterday & much talk, interesting all round. My plans are vague, depending mostly on weather as it is still too cold for Stoke, alas!   **Elgar-Alice Stuart Wortley**

14 If you are seeing the Dean please tell him that 'Red House Hill' is Rainbow Hill. The Red House still exists & is now called Marlbank. S. T. Dutton lived there; it is an old house (200 years) & now much built in … If the old Red House (which has oak floors etc) had been more free from surrounding new buildings I wd have ended my days in it – it is for sale.   **Elgar-Ivor Atkins**

In the afternoon E conducted part of a Concert to celebrate the birthday of King Albert of Belgium: Une Voix dans le Désert and the orchestral première of Le Drapeau Belge, both with Carlo Liten. The remainder of the concert was conducted by Hamilton Harty.

Very stupid management of Belgian Concert, hardly any notices in papers – & few people heard of it & might have had a much larger audience –   Alice diary

23 Alas! My dear W – we packed & got to Paddn. & then I was not well enough to go – so we drove home & here I am with a splitting head & a broken feeling of disappointment.   **Elgar-Alice Stuart Wortley**

25 Proofs of the beautiful Spirit of England came so E. put off starting till 1.40 train – Muss better D.G. A. to Paddn. with him & perhaps wd. have gone to Oxford or Worcester but E. felt muss better & had good journey   Alice diary

26 My dear W.
        Here are a few of your prototypes – I am quite well & arrived in good order; a cuckoo yesterday & a swallow to-day! Juno has not forgotten me & the meeting was more exciting than ever.   **Elgar-Alice Stuart Wortley**

May 1917

02   ... he visited the Atkins and spent some hours playing over the proofs of The Spirit of England which he had brought with him. The first section, 'The Fourth of August', was new to Atkins ... He also told Atkins that they felt they must find a cottage in the country near London where he could retreat when he wanted to compose.   **Wulstan Atkins**

... the 'studio', a large timber shed near the cottage, erected by the previous owner who was an artist.   **Wulstan Atkins**

05   A. to Norwood after lunch. Tried new omnibus to Herne Hill – Rather chilly wind. So peased to see them all. At. Vee looked wonderful – Willie still not very well but so kind & all of them so welcoming – A. much flattered & spoilt. At. G. & Gertie there, At. G. looking pulled down by her illness – A. not back till 8-15 or so – came by Gypsy Hill –   **Alice diary**

09   E. to Novello – Found his 4 Augt. Spirit of England had stirred the House – It was thought so wonderful. E. to see Mr. Stoll who liked the idea of the Kipling Songs at Coliseum – Then to Enoch to consult them about it – Lunched at Athenaeum – Home quite pleased with day – May it have all good results.   **Alice diary**

24   I am so glad you saw the ballet – there were many shortcomings. We are just starting & this is a temporary farewell. We shall be back in ten days or so.   **Elgar-Alice Stuart Wortley**

Lovely day, quite hot – E. & A. left Severn House for 10.20 train – Comfortable journey. but E. went fast asleep, A. thought there was another station first & they narrowly missed Pullborough altogether: A cart came for luggage & E. & A. walked. A. missed turn & but a kind farmers daughter showed them a short cut. Very late for lunch & very starved – E. badsley headache in aftn. but thought it "too lovely for words" & satisfied with house much to A.'s relief. A. very busy making it look a little nice –   **Alice diary**

26   I am delighted to tell you that Edward's first exclamation was 'It is too lovely for words' & he was quite pleased with the house & has loved every minute since we came – So you may think how relieved & pleased I felt. I am in the garden & before my eyes lies a wonderful deep wood & low hills beyond & then the Downs, larks are singing as there are some fields as well, & a nightingale is heard sometimes, & in the evening the nightjars go whirring around on the fringe of the wood – It is a most extraordinarily lovely spot. Endless walks & paths in the woods – There is also a Carpenter's bench & tools &c & E. has already made me 2 rustic footstools – Today Carice is to arrive & I am going in to meet her,-   **Lady Elgar-Alice Stuart Wortley**

27   E. feeling sleepy – but gardening violently with Carice helping –   **Alice diary**

30   E. wd. not walk so A. & C. went to Stopham. The most exquisite spot. a wide green, the old Church, great clump of gorgeous rhododendrons in Rectory Garden & great shrubbery presumably the Barktolls' place. We asked for key of Church at Rectory, the Rector took us in seemed very shy and disliked us! but became humanized later, showed us 4 wonderful brass monuments.   **Alice diary**

The village of Stopham is on a miniature scale and it all seems in a sense closely woven in with the story of the old house; for it is but a step from the garden along a grass-grown path to the small church, dedicated to St. Mary. Here the dark, rather stern-looking, grey tower with its small rounded Norman windows shelters that melodious bell upon which are depicted the royal arms and the sentence, Fox Augustina Sonat in Aure Dei. It calls the few who constitute the village community to prayer … The lover of ancient brasses can surreptitiously raise the carpet and discover some that have been here for centuries, portraying again the figures, from 1498 onwards, of successive Barttelots who were interested in Stopham. **Viscountess Wolseley**

June 1917

07 I was sorry to miss the Hut, or rather you, last week: we went to Sussex & it is divine: simple thatched cottage & a (soiled) studio with wonderful view: large garden unweeded, a task for 40 men. The 'Navy' turn will come off at the Coliseum next Monday – I shd. have told you earlier but there have been troubles as Mott is called up. However I hope all will be well. The Admiralty are taking great interest in it & on Monday NIGHT We hope to have a great shew of Admirals & gold lace in the front row. I need not tell you that Lady Maud has done everything to help. I went to Harwich yesterday to get the correct Kits for the men. **Elgar-Frank Schuster**

The Fringes of the Fleet come off at the Coliseum next Monday for three weeks & I shall stew here. If anything shd. happen – you may have a 'furlough' or something – you must come to the cottage. I walk about in shirt & pants all day. **Elgar-Troyte Griffith**

09 Rehearsal (orchestra) at Coliseum – Very good. **Alice diary**

10 Mott, Stuart, Henry, Barett, & Mary Crawshay & Mrs. Arkwright to lunch – (Had Harrod waiter) Delightful time, they seemed to enjoy all immensely – Went thro' songs after lunch **Alice diary**

11 To-night at nine o'clock the turn comes off – of course this afternoon also but I am not sure of the time. We did want you yesterday as I had the quartet – luncheon here. I wanted you but we had Mary Crawshay & Mrs. Arkwright to balance things.
Elgar-Alice Stuart Wortley

Elgar conducted the first performance of Fringes of the Fleet at the matinee at 2.30, and again at 8. 'Fringes' was part of a long review produced by Oswald Stoll which included George Graves in 'What a Lady', Charles Cochran's production of 'Hello! Morton', Florence Smithson, etc. etc.

A man is generally made to look his best on the stage, but it is not so with Sir Edward Elgar at a matinee. You feel that with his morning coat and brown boots he is going to crown himself with a silk hat! He is a handsome man with a good colour, but the limelight makes him pallid of hue and patriarchal of appearance. In the conductor's chair he is a prince … **Daily Chronicle (30/06/17)**

The Fringes of the Fleet are by far the most important of Elgar's works without Opus number. They comprise some of the most popular music of the day, but nevertheless, are worthy to be ranked with the composer's other fine works. There is no mistaking the breezy atmosphere of the whole, while the sentiments are always stirring and savour of the national spirit of English seamen. Altogether we consider them, both as regards words and music, a noble tribute to those noble men, the merchant seamen of the European War period. **John F Porte**

Elgar seems to have enjoyed experiences of this kind, and to have been gratified by the friendly greetings which he received from the music-hall audiences. **Thomas Dunhill**

The success of 'Fringes' meant that the Coliseum run was extended, and Elgar continued to conduct two performances a day until the end of July.

13 ... the Songs go well but I have a continual fear that the drilling will kill Mott! Do let me know when you can come: **Elgar-Alice Stuart Wortley**

Raid in morning. heard guns but cd. see nothing. Sad sad list of casualties – **Alice diary**

The raid, by 15 German aircraft, killed 97, including 42 women and children, and injured 439. A school in the East End was hit.

Considering that the "Fort of London" had been drenched with the "ghastly dew" of aerial navies barely three hours before Parliament met on June 13, Members showed themselves in uncommon calm.   **Punch (17/06/17)**

14 A. to Nat. Gallery, after ½ hour or so there, all were herded into basement, raid said to be on way. A. cd. not bear not being with E. if raid came so an official let her out at some back door & she "sprinted" up to Coliseum. Much enjoyed Songs & went again in evg. with E.   **Alice diary**

15 *Elgar treated the band plus Arthur Croxton, Manager of the Coliseum, to lunch at Gatti's.*

16 I hope you are home safely. I am sitting here *[Athenaeum]* with the storm crashing round wildly. How lovely it was this afternoon – Like old times & I hope you were amused.   **Elgar-Alice Stuart Wortley**

17 McNaught tells me, to my great satisfaction, that you will write something about the new Binyon thing: it is the simplest of all, as I felt the subject shd. be treated so.

Do not dwell upon the Demons part:- two years ago I held over that section hoping that some trace of manly spirit would shew itself in the direction of German affairs: that hope is gone forever & the Hun is branded as less than a beast for very many generations: so I wd. not invent anything low & bestial enough to illustrate the one stanza; the Cardinal invented (invented as far as I know) the particular hell in Gerontius where the great intellects gibber & snarl knowing they have fallen: This is exactly the case with the Germans now:- the music was to hand & I have sparingly used it.

And this ends, as far as I can see, my contribution to war music.
                                    Elgar-Ernest Newman

23 Enormous audience & great enthusiasm – E. had bought some extra properties herring &c. in the morning.   **Alice diary**

25 *Elgar wrote an extra song, the unaccompanied 'Inside the Bar', with words by Gilbert Parker. It was dedicated to 'The 4 Singers'.*

26 The Recording Dept. reported that they had arranged to record The Fringes of the Fleet, which is now being performed at the Coliseum, with Charles Mott and the Chorus of three voices which is being used at such performances – Sir Edward Elgar to conduct.   **Gramophone Co. Minutes**

July 1917

01 I have had a very pleasant letter from Clayton & the firm will send to your Library the f.s. of the 'Light of Life', orig M.S. at my request they will send it direct to you, so no inscription will be thereon & something suitable to their generosity & my good feeling can be added when I come down. As to 'Froissart': their memd. records that the M. S. was sent to me in 1901 but I cannot find it! If it does turn up it shall fly to you at once.

I wish you cd hear & see the songs at the Coliseum, it is a huge piece of honest jovial heroism & a great success.   Elgar-Ivor Atkins

02 E. stayed in morning. After lunch he & A. started togesser he went on to Coliseum & A. to find a dress, which she did, very nice but expensive   Alice diary

04 *A recording session for 'Fringes':* E. & A. started just before 9 for Hayes, car sent for us. Very nice drive there front window open pleasant cool air – Very fast driver. All so kind & nice at Gramophone, & much work done for the rekkards. They shd. be good. Very heavy rain – Lunch there with nice kind little goblin man & nice Mr. Darby, Mott who motored with us to Coliseum. A. home by tube – E. had a very great ovation again.   Alice diary

11 E. & A. dined at the Cavour & A. went in to Coliseum for the Songs – Quite wonderfully given now – & enormous audience.   Alice diary

13 This is a sad note to say our party on Sunday is 'off' We shall have the records some other day. Frank rang up very pathetically (he is really ill I believe) begging me to go, so I shall go to luncheon on Sunday   Elgar-Alice Stuart Wortley

14 E. sd. it was an uproarious evening, & all tickets taken for 3 days! & Mr. Croxton wants The Fringes to go on for weeks – at Coliseum – E. raser tired – Tried the new Fringes' records – Quite <u>wonderful</u> Sweepers so splendid –   Elgar-Alice Stuart Wortley

15 *Elgar went to The Hut and stayed the night.*

The Hut was somewhat sad: Claude, Lionel Holland Mad: V, myself & Frank: much rain & consequent shutting up in small rooms: I … came home on Monday very tired as I had not slept much – Holland's valet in the next, communicating, room to mine seemed to sneeze or cough all night. Frank was very dear & kind, but he has really aged a good deal during the last three months or so.   Elgar-Alice Stuart Wortley (17/07/17)

19 On 19 July my father was in London and he went to the Coliseum to hear The Fringes of the Fleet. He found Elgar there and shared his box. He told me that he enjoyed the evening immensely. The songs were clearly very popular with the large audience which contained many members of the armed forces on leave. Towards the end of 1917 HMV issued the records which they had made earlier in July of the five songs from The Fringes of the Fleet. These records were probably the first Elgar records I ever heard. They were played to me by a young officer friend, then on leave, on a portable Decca gramophone, which he was taking back to the trenches with him.
                                                                      Wulstan Atkins

22 To me the great hope of Edward Elgar standing out as a master-mind in musical composition after the war is shown by his wonderful setting of Rudyard Kipling's songs of Sea Warfare. In these songs you get the real right magic of British seafaring spirit, of the open air, of the sea. The music smells of salt-water, and you feel that here at last is work which to its hearers gives added confidence that from the Great War Edward Elgar will obtain impressions to which his musical genius will give magnificent utterance.   **Arthur Croxton (Manager of the Coliseum) Sunday Evening Telegram**

25   E. to Coliseum – A. to Maples & Heals to see if dining room Carpets were hurrying to come to Severn House – they were not –   **Alice diary**

27   I was present at a very pleasant little function on the stage of the Coliseum yesterday evening. It consisted of the presentation of a silver inkstand to Sir Edward Elgar, who for the last month or so has been conducting the performances of his musical setting of "The Fringes of the Fleet". Lady Elgar was present, as was Lady Shaftesbury. So, too, was Mr. Charles Mott, who, I understand, is about to leave for the front. It was a picturesque little scene. Tiny tables were placed all over the stage, at these was an abundance of tea, cakes and speech-making.   **Daily Mirror (28/07/17)**

30   E. feeling raser throaty &c to see Sir Maurice at 2.30 A. met him there. Sir M. gave a very good account of E. D. G. – E.& A. to Coliseum, A. heard Parker, very good – then bofe home.   **Alice diary**

George Parker replaced Mott for the forthcoming provincial tour.

Yes, Mott has gone with the rest of the heroes, while those who can afford to pay are let off. Why does not someone, not a musician, interfere? The Songs go to Manchester on the 13th, Leicester on the 20th, but I do not think I shall go with them.   **Elgar-Alice Stuart Wortley**

31   Mr. Clayton handed to us last week the mss. of your setting of Sir Gilbert Parker's 'Sailor's Song'. We have since heard the Song sung at the Coliseum under ideal conditions, but we think that so much depends on the conditions that, when deprived of them, the Song is not likely to prove successful amongst those choirs who favour the more ordinary form of Glee or Partsong, & that its circulation is on that account likely to be restricted. Under these circumstances we are returning the mss. with many thanks to you for giving us the opportunity of considering them.   **C J May (Novello & Co.)-Elgar**

E. to see oculist about glasses &c – then to Coliseum. A. in car wis him to Coliseum waited in dressing room – Very fine performances much enthusiasm –   **Alice diary**

August 1917

06? *Elgar went to stay with Pollie and her family at Stoke Prior.*

08   I have no news: everything just as usual: the country silent no birds sing: but it has been lovely; to-day heavy rain: I am looking out trains to Manchester but they are vague & the posts here worse – days seem to go by & no post in or out. I will let you hear further plans   **Elgar-Alice Stuart Wortley**

11   I travel on Sunday: a week (as you know) at M. then a week at Leicester & after that quite uncertain. Alice is going to Hereford & may go on to Gloucestershire: but our proceedings after Leicester are uncertain but I think it very doubtful if I return to London until Sep: 8th for the Chiswick week: we shall see.   **Elgar-Alice Stuart Wortley**

A. to Hereford – lovely journey after agitating morning. Housemaid (Wallet) wishing to leave at once & A. not liking Lloyd to be alone. Great rest in train & lovely to see

"our own country" again. Nice dear Miss Thomas extricated A. from crowd & she & A. walked up to Castle St. Such a warm welcome – nice to see it all again – No view of new factories from arrival side –
Alice diary

12 E. to Manchester from Stoke – wrote to A. from Birmingham where he rested at Hotel – arr. all safe D.G. ... walked up past Plas Gwyn – Looking from road it seemed like gazing over a Welsh mining village & strong smell of chemicals was blowing up –
Alice diary

13 1st day at Manchester. Had a rehearsal & 3 performances –
Alice diary

14 Before the tea party Catherine drove A. to see Dr. Sinclair's grave in such a lovely place with the high heaven overhead so quiet & peaceful
Alice diary

16 I have been so occupied even in this ancient city, I take the first moment to write to you. First I am thankful to tell you I have had excellent accounts from Edward, confirmed by a nice letter from Mr. Henry & E. tells me all goes well – You may think how strange it seems to be here without him & I have been longing for him to be here & see some of the lovely places ... I have seen such numbers of old friends & it has been so touching to have such warm welcomes – Today I am to go on to Hasfield Court Gloucester till probably Wednesday, & tomorrow I am to be taken over to Redmarley & it is most thrilling to think of seeing my old home which I love so much.
Lady Elgar-Alice Stuart Wortley

I am glad to report that in spite of depressing weather here, Sir Edward still keeps bright and cheery and when in our dressing room gives us vast entertainment with his flow of wit and anecdote.
Frederick Henry-Lady Elgar

I am glad you 'feel' Stoke – that is a place where I see & hear (yes!) you. A. has not been there since 1888 & does not care to go & no one of my friends has ever been but you. No one has seen my fields & my 'common' or my trees – only the Windflower and I found her namesakes growing there – aborigines I'm sure – real pure sweet forest folk.
Elgar-Alice Stuart Wortley

17 I hope you are both well & that the rain has been less with you than with me here.
Elgar-Sidney Colvin

Thought so much of E. & when he was at Hazeldine & our walks there – Willie Baker motored me over to Hazeldine – Rather gray & rainy but not much rain – Lovely & thrilling to see it again. The great oak gone & the beloved ash tree perished – other trees immensely grown, the cedar & pine on bank, altering the prospect. The house charming, so much what we shd. like to have done & never could. West windows &c Want the upper room (old spare room) for E.'s study. Lovely furniture & old Raikes portrait & engravings &c – Miss Newberry very nice. Shady walk lovely & glade amidst the beeches – Thro' wood rather wilder than we had it – Garden lovely –
Alice diary

18 E's last day at Manchester. All had gone well & he had been well D.G.
Alice diary

19 *Elgar and the 'Fringes team' travelled to Leicester.*

20 Thinking of E. his first day in Leicester (afterwards Mr. Henry told me there were great audiences & enthusiasm)
Alice diary

22 Heard we cd. have cottage for fortnight & took it –
Alice diary

I wish you were here, it's such a nice town. I leave on Saturday night or Sunday It wd do you good to have a clear day here: send a wire if you can come & you shall be met but I fear your holidays may be over   **Elgar-Rosa Burley**

24 The appearance of Sir Edward Elgar conducting his own music is a great draw.
                                                                          Leicester Pioneer

25 E. finishing at Leicester ... All went well with 'The Fringes' A, returned. Sybil Baker stayed with her till train started, preventing her being submerged by crowd.   **Alice diary**

26 E. safes home to lunch – D. G. Looked a little tired – It seems atrocious but mean spirited R. Kipling wants to stop 'The Fringes' continuing.   **Alice diary**

28 Intended starting for Brinkwells – but a great gale blew torrents of rain so put off going. Terrible weather all day   **Alice diary**

31 Lovely day at last. Gray morning but sun came out. We did enjoy it. A. going to P. O. again but met Sidney Colvin & returned with him.   **Alice diary**

September 1917

03 E. & A. in Mr. Aylwyn's pony carriage to Petworth. Walked around & then lunched at The Swan – Found town very uninteresting. Then into Park, also very uninteresting & E. slept under a tree –   **Alice diary**

05 It is lovely here but I am tired of lovely vistas which end in nothing. We return on Saturday night as I must have Sunday to prepare for Chiswick Empire. We went over to see the Colvins on Monday & I found them well & rejoicing in the weather, which has become good at last. They are in a highly civilised (residential I shd. think) village, quite lovely for them but I shd. die of it – here we are quite wild & free.
                                                                    Elgar-Alice Stuart Wortley

After tea E. & A. walked to Stopham Bridge. <u>Very</u> massive & fine – 14th century. The house damp & cheerless looking. Church beautiful & the old farm & houses – Thunderstorm & torrents of rain –   **Alice diary**

Although the old house that guards the passage over the river has been much altered by successive owners ... the bridge remains practically untouched, and the embrasures, or sharp angles forming recesses in the roadway of the bridge that project over a portion of the river show clearly where the archers were supposed to stand to take aim in the event of an attack from the river-side. Motors pass with some difficulty across the narrow roadway, which is steep in ascent if they come from Pulborough, necessitating a change of gear very naturally not considered by the ancient builders of the bridge. The foot-passengers are, however, safe, and are grateful to the archers of Edward ll's time for the angles in the masonry that enable them hurriedly to seek refuge from the oncoming traffic.   **Viscountess Wolseley**

08 A. busy packing & settling everything. E. & Lalla through lovely wood ways – Started after tea, A. persuaded E. to drive as he wd. get hot & then chilled. A. & Lalla walked to Church where E. had sent back carriage. Nice old Mr. Aylwin made touching speech about "Missy" (Carice) whom he '<u>respects</u>'. Good journey back.   **Alice diary**

10 *From September 10ᵗʰ – 15ᵗʰ Elgar conducted 'Fringes' twice each evening in Chiswick.*

E. & A. to Chiswick & E. investigated Theatre & rehearsed. A. returned. E. & A. in car in evening A. waited till "2nd house" & then went in. Hated E. Retford Songs. Then 'The Fringes' were splendid as ever. E. & A. home togesser –   Alice diary

15 I have been very unwell all the week & sadly worried about everything. I 'got thro' the Chiswick week but had to be taken down & brought back every evening – I mean convoyed as I was so giddy. This morning I feel better for the first time – Next week Chatham. I fear the Songs are doomed by R.K. he is perfectly stupid in his attitude ... I will tell you, too long to write – about our wild expedition – the crew & Alice & me – from Chiswick on Saturday night to the Coliseum – Mrs Pat Campbell suddenly ill & they begged me to go & give the songs   Elgar-Alice Stuart Wortley (18/09/17)

24 *From September 24th – 29h the Elgars were in Chatham for yet another week of 'Fringes' performances. In the event, most performances were cancelled because of air raids.*

25 Alice & I are here – no performance last night – terrible gun firing – raid etc etc they expect one every night. I am not well as the place is so noisy & I do not sleep – the guns are the quietest things here. I long for the country & Stoke.   Elgar-Alice Stuart Wortley

E. sd. the room was not to be borne – A. explored & E. & she settled on a back room, very unattractive & moved into it – Roamed around & down to Rochester – fine old Castle, but not attracted by any of it –   Alice diary

26 E. & A. desperate at Chatham – To Canterbury ... Lovely day – & Canterbury so beautiful.   Alice diary

27 We are not enjoying Chatham, what a place! Last evening however, 'The Fringes' were actually performed & recd. with wild enthusiasm, more than ever, but you may think it has been rather like a nightmare to be here since early Monday & a raid each evening so no performance cd take place – utter darkness prevailing.
     Lady Elgar-Alice Stuart Wortley

29 ... no car at Charing Cross on account of Raid Came by Tube but home safely at last very late.   Alice diary

A member of Oriana Choir, singing in a Prom at Queen's Hall: ... Carmen Hill was singing, when we heard the ominous sounds outside, but we all sat tight. The next item was a bassoon solo. In the middle of it there was a crash, and then a cracking sound, and a shower of plaster began to fall from the roof of the Promenade, which was packed. Even Sir Henry Wood himself glanced rather anxiously up at the roof, though still wielding his baton. The bassoonist, however, kept merrily on; and we realized it could only be shrapnel which had dislodged the plaster. The soloist got a rousing encore and treated us to 'We Won't Go Home Till Morning', amidst cheers and laughter. After the concert no one was allowed to leave the Hall. We prowled round the passages and had some coffee, until one of the orchestra nobly returned to the platform and struck up a waltz. We were soon dancing over the floor and really enjoying the experience. We were not released until about 1 a.m.   Mrs. M. Currie

30 So thankful to wake up at home, after trying Chatham –   Alice diary

October 1917

01 *Elgar was due to go to Stoke Prior, but was too exhausted. An air raid prevented him travelling next day, and he eventually left on October 3ʳᵈ.*

02 Mansfield Evans came to stay the night … Capt. M. <u>extremely</u> nice. E. seemed to enjoy the evening & pweaked & told stories & we laughed very muss – Quiet evg the first for some time
Alice diary

Captain Mansfield Evans, a boyfriend of Carice – was later killed in war. They had … a knight-and-lady relationship. The Elgars were not at all easy as regarded young men. Carice … was like Georgina Podsnap in Dickens. I have actually heard her say under her breath at the approach of someone, 'Oh, go away! go away!' And when Mansfield Evans asked if she had missed him Carice, ever anxious to escape from the centre of the picture, nervously jerked out: 'Oh, not in the least, thank you'.
Winifred Davidson

Winifred Davidson, a close friend of Carice, was Mrs. Joshua's grand-daughter.

04 *Appleby Matthews, organist of Birmingham Cathedral, conducted the first performance of complete Spirit of England in Birmingham Town Hall, with New Zealand soprano Rosina Buckman, New Birmingham Orchestra and his own choir. Despite his relative proximity at Stoke Prior, Elgar did not attend the performance.*

Mr Appleby Matthews is in close affinity with the Elgar mood, and he and his choir achieved a joint triumph in the three numbers … which filled the second part of the concert. A really magnificent performance from every point of view – precision, intensity, dramatism, and intelligence.
Robert Buckley, Birmingham Gazette

The Spirit of England trilogy made Elgar our national minstrel in a finer way that the Land of Hope and Glory song did.
A J Sheldon

I am safely here in pouring rain which I don't mind: I had a good rest in the train & wonderful! began smoking a pipe again which is a mercy: so soothing to the nerves. I do hope you are safe & well, I hope this weather will stop the raids. I have just 'signed on' for the Coliseum next week so I hope to return on Sunday night & find you well & gay next week. Juno is quite well & gave me the warmest welcome.
Elgar-Alice Stuart Wortley

05 Though unknown to you, I feel I must write to you tonight. We possess a fairly good Gramophone in our Mess, and I have bought your record Starlight Express: 'Hearts must be star-shiny dressed'. It is being played for the twelfth time over. The Gramophone was Anathema to me before this War because it was abused so much. But all this is changed now, and it is the only means of bringing back to us the days that are gone, and helping one through the Ivory gate that leads to fairyland, or Heaven, whatever one likes to call it. And it is a curious thing, even those who only go for Rag-time revues, all care for your music. Our lives are spent in drunken orgies and parachute descents to escape shelling or Bosch aeroplanes. In fact, the whole thing is unreal, and music is all that we have to help us carry on.
Captain J Lawrence Fry-Elgar

On the same day 'Windflower' sent a box of clothes to The Elms for the family.

06 Oh! how cd. you send so much: the merest trifles wd. have given these dear children pleasure & now they are distracted with joy. The opening of the box reminded me of the 1ˢᵗ Sc. in the Starlight: such joy & wonder – you would have loved to have seen it all.
Elgar-Alice Stuart Wortley

07 Very excited expecting E. who arrived in very fair time 9.42 train –   Alice diary

08 *From October 8ᵗʰ – 13ᵗʰ Elgar again conducted 'Fringes' at the Coliseum.*

10 E. into town – A. met Alice & Claude Williams at Coliseum nice seats & they enjoyed
'The Fringes' & wd. not stay for anythg. afterwards then tea at the Lyons & then as
they were starting met E. who pweaked to them. Then E. & A. returned to Coliseum
to see the Swing Ladies – Very good – E. stayed for evg. & A. returned & came in car
& fessed him home.   Alice diary

17 *Elgar went to the Hut, where he was joined on October 20ᵗʰ by Lady Elgar. They
returned home of October 22ⁿᵈ.*

21 Lovely day. Tints beautiful Thought river & Hut never looked so lovely. Lady Wemyss
& sister came over in morning. Played crazy croquet in aftn & Spelka in evening.
Alice diary

29 Domestic crisis in the morning! so pleasant. E. & A. left 1.30 train for Leeds … Mr.
Embleton met us & the usual drive in old shawridan to Queen's Hotel. Dear Mr. E. doing
<u>all</u> he cd., fires &c – rooms rather altered & improved – Then E. & A. & Mr. Embleton to
Choral rehearsal. Very good. Lovely to hear 4th Aug. for 1st time.   Alice diary

30 Fine morning. E. & A. started for York. Wandered round, the sun shone on the
Minster & the beautiful decoration looked like lace – Lunched at Station Hotel & then
walked about round old streets &c & then to Minster again & back to Leeds – Mr.
Embleton had E. & Committee to dinner. E. seemed quite amused & the Committee
spoke seriously to him that he must go on & they want the 3rd part Apostles.
Alice diary

31 *Elgar conducted the complete Spirit of England and Gerontius with the Leeds Choral
Union. Agnes Nicholls and Gervase Elwes were among the soloists.*

November 1917

01 *Elgar was due to go to Stoke Prior, but was too exhausted. An air raid*

We live in a nightmare in this hotel – nothing ever comes! meals arrive anyhow – at
anytime except the hour for which they are ordered. A very fine chorus & fine orch. –
& then! – dear Elwes cd. not sing – suddenly failed – no time to find a substitute – so
after all – he just came on to the platform & whispered a few phrases & spoke it: just
like praying –   Elgar-Alice Stuart Wortley

02 *The Elgars moved on to Huddersfield, for Spirit of England and Gerontius with the
Huddersfield Choral Society next day.*

Rehearsal in aftn A girl substituted to save Gervase Elwes – <u>Very</u> poor singer. A. much
perturbed – Orch. wild but better than expected.   Alice diary

07 E. not feeling vesy well. A. raser agitated – Went with E. to Euston. 9.20 train. E. muss
better & started. Said often "I wish you was coming." A. found telegram when came
in saying all safes at Birmingham, where he met May – D.G.   Alice diary

Queens Hotel, Birmingham. Passing through
My dear W.
  I am really on my way to Stoke   Elgar-Alice Stuart Wortley

14 Elgar … came over to Worcester. He told Atkins that they had now found a cottage ('Brinkwells'), which he thought would prove ideal, and that in its peace he would he able to write real music. **Wulstan Atkins**

16 I shall he home very soon now as I have a silly chorus rehearsal on Monday evening – alas! **Elgar-Alice Stuart Wortley**

17 E. at Stoke – A. mis at not hearing & telegraphed, nice answer to come tomorrow. **Alice diary**

19 *Elgar did not conduct the chorus rehearsal of Spirit of England as he was again feeling giddy. He was able to conduct the final orchestral rehearsal at the Royal Albert Hall on November 23rd.*

24 *Elgar conducted the first London performance of Spirit of England, soloists Agnes Nicholls and Gervase Elwes. The concert also included Parry's Naval Ode – 'The Chivalry of the Sea', and Stanford's 'Songs of the Fleet and A Carol of Bells.*

[Spirit of England] Very poor stuff for the most part. Justified choral writing. Like a sentimental part-song. The Choir sang Chivalry splendidly, but I don't think the audience liked it. **Parry diary**

This was an almost harrowing experience and I remember that Gervase Elwes, who had taken part, told me that he hardly knew how they had all got through it. The war casualties at that time were heartrending and almost every member of the choir must have lost a close relative or a friend. **Rosa Burley**

The solo part in The Fourth of August, as also in For The Fallen, was quite beautifully sung, as it deserved to be, by Miss Agnes Nicholls, and the composer (who conducted) was also well served by Mr. Gervase Elwes, the soloist in the middle section of the completed work. There was great enthusiasm at the end. **Daily Telegraph**

26 *From November 26th – December 1st Elgar conducted the final run of Fringes of the Fleet at the Coliseum.*

27 Are you coming to the Fringes – the funeral this week. so sad. Perhaps you will have tea – I have such a nice sitting room at the Colis: **Elgar-Alice Stuart Wortley**

December 1917

01 *Elgar was due to go to Stoke Prior, but was too exhausted. An air raid*

Most of what I do is not worth much from a financial point of view, and if I do happen to write something that 'goes' with the public and by which I look like benefiting financially, some perverse fate always intervenes and stops it immediately. **Elgar**

03 E. vesy porsley. Sir Maurice came & gave him admirable medicines – not out at all – **Alice diary**

07 E. still very unwell. Sir Maurice came & ordered bed for 2 or 3 days & new remedies, very kindly sent them. **Alice diary**

15 *Elgar cancelled his Hallé/Manchester date (only the second time he had ever had to pull out of a concert engagement.) R H Wilson conducted Spirit of England in his place, and Beecham conducted Mozart's Magic Flute Overture, Beethoven's 5th Piano Concerto and Rimsky-Korsakov's Scheherazade (which replaced Falstaff).*

23 It was a dreadful evening for you to be out – the damage appears to have been unworthy of the means as usual – I found a heavy piece of shell case & two smaller pieces in our garden, either one enough to end a passenger. I am just the same alas! But I have stopped all medicine & take long walks, lonely. Elgar-Alice Stuart Wortley

27 Sir Maurice came & decided to bring a tummy specialist Dr. Hale White evidently very disappointed & puzzled over E – Alice diary

Dr. Hale White was a Senior Physician at Guy's Hospital.

29 How dear & kind of you to send those splendid looking pheasants, arrived today – They are so appreciated & will make such a nice change for E – It was dear &,sweet of you to send them Also the Shortbread which is a great feature at aftn. tea … The Dr. promises improvement. E. is down again this aftn. & I trust will be feeling better very soon – Lady Elgar-Alice Stuart Wortley

January 1918

01 What will this year bring forth – A momentous time. We pray & trust for complete victory – the triumph of right & humanity over fiendish barbarity. E.. much the same – I pray he may soon be well – these weeks are so sad & anxious to see him still ill – E. with A. in car to see Sir Maurice who tried testing mouf, nose, &c. found all very well – D.G. Alice diary

06 A. to Albert Hall, met C. in Mrs. Lan's box – Maud W. & Alice S. of W. there too – A. met Maud waiting for omnibus at Hyde Park Corner & both struggled in & out – Most <u>wonderful</u> performance of the 1st Symphony – Mrs. Lan said Lan went off like a child with delight to rehearsal, loving it so much. The great tune so majestic & beautiful. Then the wild underspirits & vain things conquered by it – Then the pagan tune absolutely a picture of the Huns & the great struggle ending in absolute triumphant Victory for the great rights of humanity – so wonderful & uplifting. Alice diary

The interpretations by Landon Ronald of Elgar are remarkable for their insight and wealth of expression, and are generally accepted to be the most authoritative. The full extent of the famous conductor's work to make the British public understand the genius in their midst, we are expressly forbidden to mention, but should the facts ever come to light, the world will see yet another example of the self-love of true genius for fellow genius. Perhaps the most wonderful part of Mr. Ronald's work is the attention and applause he obtained for both symphonies at Albert Hall Sunday afternoon concerts. John F Porte

09 We are nearly snowed up but I have struggled out on to the heath very cold. I am not so well internally & suffer much. Elgar-Rosa Burley

Father still seems to have been unwell early in the year and his Dr, Sir Maurice Abbott-Anderson, gave him tests of his nose and throat, and the test was satisfactory. In spite of this, he decided a few days later to have an X ray test; also negative and the whole condition was ascribed to a 'dropped stomach' for which electric treatment, and later a special belt, were recommended. It was a great relief to know that there was nothing radically or organically wrong. Carice Elgar

28 E. vesy badsley – E. & A. to Sir Maurice – who promised he shd. be better soon – Alice diary

February 1918

10 I have been laid up for so long that I seem to have lost touch with my oldest friends and you are now one of the oldest, although it seems but a little time since we first met at Miss Smart's and you talked of Jokai and 'Eyes like the Sea'. Good book that, – – someone has stolen my copy, which I resent but which I cannot blame ... Well, I wish you were here: I have had a long and dreary time and should like a sight and a word, but these wry-necked times make it almost impossible to move. I have been a worm and shut up, more or less, for three months. I am ashamed to tell you the amount I have read during this inevitable leisure: leisure most undesired by me. But I have come across scarcely any thing new worthy of note ... I am hoping to be about again shortly but am not capable of much work. You must not mind the wearisome length of this and don't think I expect a long reply as you are so busy.   **Elgar-Troyte Griffith**

For the next few weeks he seems to have been very much up and down, after which he began to go for long walks; to the Cemetery at Highgate for instance, I happened to be free and to go with him, and we were completely staggered by its immensity and its astounding monuments. He went too to a lot of sale rooms and bookshops. Lady Stuart of Wortley, Algernon Blackwood, Sidney Colvin, Lalla van der Velde were frequent visitors, as also were the John Fortescues, who had just bought a lovely old house in Hampstead. This seems too to have been the beginning of friendship with the Bernard Shaws, as Lalla took Father to lunch with them.   **Carice Elgar**

17 ... he took me carefully through the entire score of In the South, which I was including in some concerts in the Queen's Hall in 1918. I can still see him sitting at the piano with the score in front of him, giving me his comments as he turned over the pages.
                                                                          Adrian Boult

18 *Boult conducted the LSO in the second of a series of four concerts promoted by him. The programme included In the South and Vaughan Williams' 'London' Symphony. Vaughan Williams and Holst were in the audience. The orchestra was led by W H Reed, and contained only 28 strings players.*

When the Reserve Centre office broke up in 1916, I was offered a job in the War Office, concerned with the German Press. Hardly had I begun, when I ran into Fred Marquis (later Lord Woolton) ... Marquis insisted on my transferring to the War Office branch in Tothill Street where he was gradually assuming control of the country's leather resources. Work as his personal assistant took me almost to the end of the war, and also, with Marquis' permission, enabled me to organize four concerts with the London Symphony Orchestra in the spring of 1918. When I got possession of the score *[of the Symphony]*, I was just beginning a tour of the West Country to boost Marquis' most ingenious scheme for a war-time standard boot to suit all pockets.   **Adrian Boult**

Arrangements have been made for a range of samples of War Time Boots to be placed upon the Market by Manufacturers under the general supervision of the War Office. MR. A. C. BOULT, an Officer of the Department, will he Present between the hours of 2-30 and 4 p.m. on Friday, 18th January, when retailers (in Shrewsbury and the surrounding Districts) are particularly requested to attend with the view of discussing any difficulties, and the representatives of the local press are invited to meet Mr. Boult at 2-30 p.m. on Friday, 18th January.   **Poster**

At the end of the concert orchestra and audience (about equal numbers) collected in the basement bar at Queen's Hall until the "All clear" had sounded.

Adrian Boult, The Star (04/04/35)

In all the hurry of Monday I never had the opportunity of thanking you (1) for doing my symph (2) for giving such a fine performance – it really was splendid you had got the score right into you & through you into your orch:

Ralph Vaughan Williams-Adrian Boult (25/02/18)

Sir Edward seemed in better health but is not yet quite well.   William Gaisberg

26 E. with A. to Dentist, Mr. Phillips. Sir Maurice met E. there – Took off crown to tooth – E. seemed better that afternoon.   Alice diary

March 1918

06 Father, though apparently better, was not really well and Sir Maurice, after consultation with Mr. Tilley, the throat surgeon of the day, strongly urged the removal of his tonsils and Father agreed. It worried Mother considerably that he should have such an operation at his age, 61.   Carice Elgar

10 *Despite Elgar's continuing illness, Sunday afternoons continued to be a hive of activity at Severn House. On March 10th W. H. Reed's string quartet entertained a large party.*

They played beautifully & sd. it was such a pleasure to come & to play in this room – Everyone loved it – the rooms looked beautiful … All really great success.   Alice diary

12 I am going on Thursday, I can't say where.   Elgar-Alice Stuart Wortley

14 He went into a nursing home in Dorset Square … and had the operation next day. All went well and the operation was fully justified as the tonsils proved more poisonous even than they had suspected.   Carice Elgar

15 A long day of suspense as the opn was not till 3 P.M. E. was very calm, & bore the long suspense wonderfully. Then the nurse came & injected something in his arm to <u>dry</u> up saliva &c. Then Sir Maurice fetched him & he went downstairs so simply & cheerfully – A. went down to waiting room & as she entered just caught a glimpse of E. in his blue dressing gown, entering the Theatre – A. spent an anxious horrible 40 mins. then Sir Maurice & Tilley came & told her all was well. Sir M. showed her the worst tonsil all over abscess matter & a black stone, pea size, in it. A. not let go up so went home, returned at 7. found E. in great pain not knowing how to bear it, agonising to A. They gave him an injections & in 10 mins he was sleeping peacefully. A. had to leave him –   Alice diary

Nursing Home Operation on Throat Tilley surgeon   Elgar diary

16 Drs. satisfied – Dreadful pain & misery for E – Very dood & patient. A. wis him all day. & home late – Drefful to see him suffer –   Alice diary

Loveliest weather Nursing Home   Elgar diary

On his return Elgar wrote the opening theme of Cello Concerto.

At Severn House the night I returned. Very full, sweet and sonorous.

Elgar – note on sketch

The sketch is interesting because it is covered with his comments as usual, but they are inscribed with a typewriter instead of in his own handwriting. This was a new toy, and had to be used. The instrument did not lend itself to variations except in its black and red ribbon. The original jumps from one colour to the other in the most erratic manner.   **W H Reed**

25 I have had some trouble with my throat and did not dally with fate but went straight off to an operation and the resulting getting well, – which is worse than the disease! I am at home again and creep about as becomes one who has lost much both in flesh and fine weather.   **Elgar-William McNaught**

April 1918

01 E. (with A.) to Mr. Tilley Very pleased with throat & <u>promising</u> recovery – Lunched at Cavour but E. says not again.   **Alice diary**

03 Writing E minor stuff   **Elgar diary**

The weather has been cold and ungenial but A. and I have been experimenting in luncheons in town to try to acclimatise me: it is weary work but I think I am better on the whole. We lunched at Canuto's (Saturday) at Cavour's (Monday) and at Scott's (Tuesday) and I have borne it moderately well.   **Elgar-Alice Stuart Wortley**

05 I have had a bad winter, one illness after another and the entertainment culminated in a throat operation (vilely painful) and a spell in a nursing home, which was not cheering. I have been home for more than a week now and things are settling down but I am not yet strong by a long way. It is hoped that we shall get away to the cottage soon …   **Elgar-Ivor Atkins**

08 The cottage is in Sussex – I'll send you the proper address when we arrive; it is a divine woodland place and remote from the spoor of man.   Perhaps you might come!
                                                                                  Elgar-Ivor Atkins

We are hoping to get to the cottage and I yearn for a pig so keep me awake to your proceedings – and the pig's. If yr PIG is born on AP: 26th, as is hoped, what shall you call him? … Defoe was buried on that day and D. is a fine and wholesome name for a pig … I shall hope to see him one day before the sausage stage.   **Elgar-Troyte Griffith**

10 A. to Sir Maurice, who promises E. shd. be better & supports driving him to Hut, if car is permitted – A. is to find out – E. better.   **Alice diary**

11 Today I am not so well & tomorrow, Friday, Alice & I go to Frank's; A. for the week-end & I, if well enough, stay on.   **Elgar-Alice Stuart Wortley**

15 Set lines for eels – no luck. A. left by 3.40 train Had new watch Frank bot. in India 12/6 A telegram (about nine) Safe arrival etc.   **Elgar diary**

16 Snow & rain all day. dreadful weather not out & very unwell Long letter from Colvin Saw in paper announcement of Ffrangcon Davies' death   **Elgar diary**

23 Walk in a.m. F. & E. to tea in Maidenhead Muriel & Mr. Boult arrd. at 5.54. – cards.
                                                                                  Elgar diary

25 Left Hut. Lovely day Mr. Wylde motored me home Left at 1.30 arr'd Severn House

3.10 Mrs. Joshua sent cheque to Alice. On return Home found an empty house in Fitzjohn's Av. taken over by Air Force much drilling in roads every day   Elgar diary

27 At home all day – packing for Brinkwells & clearing up. Did not go out.   Elgar diary

Mother was meanwhile very busy arranging for the move to Brinkwells for recuperation. She had to think what would be wanted in the country as there was a scarcity of furniture and comforts there and also the business of shutting up Severn House safely. Father's only contribution to all this was choosing tools which he would need for the woodwork he did and the repairs and small improvements he made.   Carice Elgar

30 E. vesy unwell – A. very very busy.   Alice diary

Fine day – called on Inc. Tax surveyor Very dull person   Elgar diary

May 1918

02 <u>Arrived Brinkwells</u>   Alice diary

The great removal day was May 2nd, and they went by train and were met by Mr. Aylwin with his pony cart and luggage cart and a warm welcome. I had joined them at Victoria, and Father and I walked up. We had a warm welcome too from Mrs. Hewitt, who 'did' for us.   Carice Elgar

03 Forgive this machine but we have no INK! the goods have come from Petworth & the ink is omitted so I feverishly dash off this for Carice to post in London as under the latest regulations this is a two-day post; please remember this. We arrived all safely & I walked up to this really divine country place; I am not well and feel desperate about getting better but we must hope: it was so sweet of you to see me through that luncheon and afterwards: it made our departure a human thing. I will write properly soon. It is dreary for Carice to return to town but she sticks to duty; we had a walk in the heavenly woods and I killed one of your friends, length 2 ft 2 in.!!   Elgar-Alice Stuart Wortley

06 E. very busy clearing workshop &c. A. with new curtains &c &c. Rambled around. Woods so wonderfully lovely, with great gardens & borders of flowers.   Alice diary

Finer. Mark killed a large adder in wood. E. brought the corpse to house for identification – an ugly brute – planted Mustard & Cress on Sacking   Elgar diary

Mark *[Holden]* was a character. He went with the house, like the tool-shed or the chestnut wood. I don't think he had ever been more than five or six miles from Fittleworth in his life. He looked after Sir Edward's comforts and helped about the house and garden. He was a man of few words, very unimpressionable. Mark was a character after Sir Edward's own heart. His monosyllabic replies were quoted again and again.   W H Reed

10 … lunch (good) at Swan bought lamp etc coffee & milk jugs. walked thro' village & home (by fields to Stopham) … put up bedstead in Studio etc. etc. not too tired A walked well Mark shot a pigeon 6d & rabbit 1/-   Elgar diary

11 This is just a short note to let you know that all goes well up to the present … I have enjoyed the experience immensely and look forward to heaps of 'fun' (admittedly of a rather grim nature) within the next few hours! I know you would feel the same.

There is something grand & very fascinating about a battery of big guns & a shell that can make a hole in the ground big enough to put a motor-bus in – what a vast amount of pent up energy. There is one thing that 'puts the wind up me' very badly & that is of my being wiped out & thus miss the dear harmonies of your wonderful works. But I have a supreme confidence in my destiny & feel that I have some useful work to do in the world before I am called away. **Charles Mott-Elgar**

12 We are settling down & seem to have been away years, when I think of you, but when I look round here it seems as though we have only lived in it a moment. The woods are full of flowers, wonderful – some anemones still left but just leaving us for a year, bluebells & primroses etc … it really is lovely here – food good & plentiful – much beer! – but do not mention it. **Elgar-Alice Stuart Wortley**

13 I miss you very much but I work very hard & have been smoking – (I am now) – again to my great contentment, I eat & sleep marvellously but I have the taste still, which is vexing. I have done heaps of things: we sorted out & dusted all the oddments in the workshop, I've set up the sundial which is a great joy when there's any sun. I put on the oilskins (Fringes) & tramp the woods in the heaviest rain & it is great enjoyment … Today it's raining cats but is warmer. Everything is getting tidied up except (as you will well guess) this writing table, which is a scandal. **Elgar-Carice**

15 Lovely day. A. & E. walked to Petworth bought tobacco & tools. lunched Swan & then on to Tillington to the Colvins – tea lovely afternoon Trap (lady driver) back to Well Diggers Arms & then walk home **Elgar diary**

17 *Lalla Vandervelde came to stay at Brinkwells.*

20 *Charles Mott wounded during the Second Battle of The Marne.*

Bank Holiday E. not so vesy well – but busy in Workshop & Lalla helping to clear – A. & Lalla to Mrs. Elliott's cottage in aftn. Lovely view from Spring Farm, sat on Bank & wondered at it. **Alice diary**

21 Very hot. Saw to Veg. Marrows Saw man making hurdles (Oak) Saw hawk entangled in wire fence by Hen house – large Snake by Barn: found Tits nest in oak by wood yard. L.V. left for London 8.21. Clock weight fell in the night 3.20!. **Elgar diary**

Charles Mott died of his wounds.

His singing of the Organ Grinder's songs acquires a double pathos, so full is it of tenderness, repose and sustained charm. **Herman Klein (Mott obituary)**

24 Very cold early, feared it might be miserably cold for Alice S. of W – Day improved & grew sunny & warm. E. with Mr. Aylwin to station & met Alice S. of W. A. started to meet them but they turned thro' wood – E. & A. mis at missing & E. trying to find her – Alice delighted with everythg. enjoying herself like a baby child – **Alice diary**

25 Heard Mott was wounded **Elgar diary**

26 Much frightened at lunch, eating gooseberry tart. E. got something in his throat, cd. Not see anythg. After much coughing &c. E. got it up, a sharp, cruel twisted piece of wire, **Alice diary**

28 Up early. Worked at fowl run put up vice on bench A.S.W. left 3 o'c train. weather changing – cooler **Elgar diary**

June 1918

02 Very hot cloudless day: 8 Tomtits in wall. Put strong stay to east end workshop Cider
put in cellar   **Elgar diary**

I cannot tell you how overjoyed we were to receive your letter from Holland and to
know that you are so far safely on the way home, for you cannot be held up much
longer it seems certain. You have had a dreadful time with those appalling Yahoos the
Prussians and it is a mercy you have been allowed to leave their unsavoury clutches.

I have had a bad winter and the evil days culminated in a severe operation on my
throat; we are in this lovely cottage in the woods, high above the world in peace,
plenty and quietness and I am trying to get well and strong to do something useful
again.

We shall welcome you home with enthusiasm and I trust the post of organist in
your own cathedral will be yours. I was only too glad to do what I could to further your
claims ...   **Elgar-Percy Hull [who had been interned at Ruhleben, near Berlin, and released to Holland]**

Sunday Joon the Tooth
Darling:
When you go to Hampstead will you seize the TROMBONE, which shd be
hanging on the wall in the workshop & give it over to the household (I do not know
who is now in charge) and ask them to clean it thoroughly. Be careful how you handle
it as it may slip apart and bruise; if you hold it at first by the lower part you will jolly
soon see what slips about, ... but it may be stuck from accumulated verdigris. When
cleaned I will instruct 'em what to do next. I am giving it to the Y.M.C.A. It's vilely
dirty, I fear.

The country wits your coming and so do I, – also a cask of cider which arrd
yestere'en and the tapping thereof will be a sollum serremony between you & me!
Perhaps!   **Elgar-Carice**

03 Mrs. Joshua sent box of wonderful good things for E.'s birfday.   **Alice diary**

Worked at Fowl run etc. turned much cooler A. & E. in eveng walked to Little Bognor
past old mills to Lady Maxse (out) Large parcel (Fortnum) from Mrs. Joshua.   **Elgar diary**

05 It is difficult to believe that dear Charles Mott is dead; dead of wounds in France. I am
overwhelmed: a simple, honest GOOD soul.   **Elgar-Anthony Bernard**

06 Cloudy – but no rain worked at wood paths – etc. A. in pony cart to Petworth & the
Colvins About now Ministry of food wrote asking me to set Kipling's child's Food song
for the good of the cause to be pubd. in special No. of "The Teacher's World"   **Elgar diary**

The birthday 'went off' very quietly with the assistance of your good asparagus: it was
wrong of you to send a valuable present but it was enjoyed. It is, of course, lovely here
& requires much weeding: however, the gardener has been furiously attacking the
weeds & the place looks much more civilised than last year despite your frantic efforts
with Carice If you know anyone requiring 'Willow-bark' (I think that's right) I can
supply it by the ton. I hope you are well: I am rested but do not get well at all & never
shall. But I am strong & eat & sleep & work work work.   **Elgar-Rosa Burley**

07 Carice arrived. A & E met her on road. Brought Lobsters & plaice from Windflower
Saw Nightjars in wood   **Elgar diary**

`08 Carice arrived all safely, but, dear Alice, you really are too good sending such lovely things, thank you very much but you really should not have thought of so much. The jam is hailed with real joy! & will be most valuable, & the delicious dates & Chocolate, & supply of tea & biscts. but those you really are too spoiling to send. E. so enjoyed some of that gigantic Lobster – says it is the best he ever tasted.   **Lady Elgar-Alice Stuart Wortley**

Now that the Food Controller has got into his stride, the nation has begun to realise the huge debt it owes to his firmness and organising ability, and is proportionately concerned to hear of his breakdown from overwork. The queues have disappeared, supplies are adequate, and there are no complaints of class-favouritism.   **Punch (07/18)**

11   Headache – colossal A. to F.worth post in p.m. E. met her – worked at garden seat Recd. permit to fish.   **Elgar diary**

12   Lovely day – A. & E. walked to auction sale at Swan F'worth – home (thro woods both ways) to lunch Grace (p. maid.) came Sidney Colvin drove over to tea walk in wood Clover carried   **Elgar diary**

14   Proofs of little children's Food song came: rushed to station with them L.V. arrived walked up & in evening round Bedham   **Elgar diary**

The occasion seemed to call for something exceptionally simple and direct, and I have endeavoured to bring the little piece within the comprehension of very small people indeed.   **Elgar**

17   Warmer – pleasant day. E. & Lalla to Fishing pond. E. did not catch anything. back to lunch & Lalla to station, Mr. Aylwin. He went down again for Muriel Foster, E. & A. met her & she walked this end of the way with E. <u>Enchanted</u> with the place –   **Alice diary**

24   E. to Fishing Pond – A. grew a little anxious & went to meet him, found him happily fishing. Returned togesser, & met Carice a very little way in wood – Just between us, A. in front, an adder crossed the path. E. killed it. C. all safe & well, good journey …
                                                                                    Alice diary

26   Carice left at 6.20 a.m. (Aylwin) for Pulboro' Early tea: then A. & E. to River (Arun) by Brick works caught several very small things – brought none home   **Elgar diary**

27   Sidney Colvin to tea. E. & A. to Bognor Pond. stayed late & warmed dinner our souses –
                                                                                    Alice diary

July 1918

01   A. & I walked to Petworth and back on Saturday & none the worse for it – No not Petworth – Tillington a mile further I mean – we had tea (& talk) with the Colvins: he is rather a weakling alas! You must get over to them when you come next week (?)
                                                              Elgar-Alice Stuart Wortley

I am better but not fit for the world & don't seem to want it – I get a few fish & read & smoke (praise be!) but there are about six people I want to see & you are one – number one I mean the rest follow. Dear Frank how are you? sacrificing your whole life for others you forget to tell us and we have to take it for granted that you are well.
                                                                  Elgar-Frank Schuster

08   Lalla arrived about 1 – in Governmt. car. Looked very ill –   **Alice diary**

11 (Stormy) L.V. here still Very high wind & storms of rain Sidney C. to tea & much talk of his translation of 'Demeter' walk in eveng Bedham School A to Fittleworth between lunch & tea
Elgar diary

13 E. & Lalla to river. Most lovely morning. No fish – but lovely out. took lunch – Lalla left in Car at 4.30 – A. with her to P. O. walked back. – Mrs. Hewitt left for 2 days – E. & A. had to do dinner.
Alice diary

14 Mad: Vandervelde has been here to rest: she has been very ill indeed & a week at the Hut made her worse if anything. So Alice thought a real rest wd. do her good: it did but she was lying about here all day and rather (!) incommoded us; but A. & I have been feeling that it is selfish of us to have this lovely place all to ourselves & want to be useful in repairing broken nerves.
Elgar-Alice Stuart Wortley

Very wet & misty – most unpleasant day – Mrs. Hewitt away. E. & A. did breakfast. Mrs. Haggis came for lunch, E. & A. did dinner. Very trying here with the hateful back premises – quite different if at home –
Alice diary

16 This envp has been directed two months & I never used it hoping you were coming here & that we should talk. I am better but not up to much pen work. I spare you the typewriter tho' with ill effect as you see.
Elgar-Troyte Griffith

… (blepharitis, blessed word!), which has made wreading and riting all as wrong as I have spelt 'em.
Elgar-Sidney Colvin

18 Finer morning. Starlight telegraphed coming by 10... train. E. walked to meet him but missed the telegram lady but asked at post & heard Starlight cd. not get into train coming by next. So disappointing. A. tried in vain for pony cart, so walked to station & met him. So nice to see him – Much struck with scenery & loved it all. After tea E. & he to sinister trees …
Alice diary

We played another record, and before I could turn it over Elgar rather dreamily talked about visits that Algernon Blackwood had paid them at 'Brinkwells', and what an ideal guest he was to have at a country cottage, a fine walker and talker, a keen athlete and a rare expert at pole-jumping. He told how he had cut a long pole for him, and how he had demonstrated his art by leaping on to the top of a tall, barred gate, jumping over a hedge, and by long horizontal jumps.
Wulstan Atkins

25 E. began Garden house, opening out vistas – worked so hard.- Promised to be perfectly lovely –
Alice diary

26 Stormy. worked at wild garden in a.m. in afternoon heaviest rain for hours ever known. Road washed cruelly. Carice came. A. started to meet her driven back by rain. E walked down road & met her near Targrove Then heavy thunder & rain in torrents
Elgar diary

28 Finer – A. & C. saw lovely butterflies in the wood – E. & C. for walk in aftn. C. had to return. Mr. Aylwin took her to Pullborough –
Alice diary

31 A. poorly badly but better D.G. White (colour) washed Garden House & made steps – Very hot Began to use reading lamp after dinner
Elgar diary

August 1918

03 Finer & some sun earlier Aylwin to meet Alice Wortley at 3.55. She had (wisely) arrd. by early train & rested at the Swan (lunch)   Elgar diary

05 Very wet & stormy. E. & A. of W. to river later –   Alice diary

06 Stormy & wonderful cloud effects. A. S. of W. left for 3-train – Mr. Aylwin drove her. She told us afterwards good journey to Horsham. there thought she wd. not get into train at all. at last got into a 3rd as the 10th passenger.   Alice diary

15 E. heard from Ramsden that Piano was "on rail" Began to make floor for garden room. Mark found 'slabs' sawn off pines.   Alice diary

This was the Steinway upright given to him by Professor Sanford in Plas Gwyn days, and long in storage.

17 Rainy – placed floor in garden room before Bkfast: worked at it all the morning. S. Colvin & E. V. Lucas to tea – A. & E. to Fittleworth for letters – A. had a lift in carr. Delightful visit (Mark said "NO")   Elgar diary

19 A day of great excitements: first the Blind has arrived & is the greatest success; you are so clever knowing the exactly right thing in every case – it is, of course, too good (refined & delicate) like the plane & all of you, for everyday use, but it makes the garden house yours more than ever. And the piano arrived in the same waggon & is now in the Studio & I have been playing away: it is the old one we had in Hereford & is quite good still. I am hard at work at music I hope. Then, when the blind & the piano were arriving the postman brought the lovely brass nails; they are lovely & I wish I could add a circle of them to your tray. A. is overjoyed with the sight of the blind – & of me with music paper again.   Elgar-Alice Stuart Wortley

20 Dull morning but afterwards hot fine. Wrote some music.   Elgar diary

The start of the Violin Sonata.

21 It is so wonderfully beautiful just now, I must say it over again! & the Garden house quite delightful with its lovely blind – a 1000 thanks it is so complete & perfect, lovely green shade, & pretty acorns &c – & now I expect E. told you the Piano is in the Studio, I call it the music room now, as E. seems delighted to have it, & has been playing lovely tunes – Such a joy to hear again – & to see him reconciled somewhat to thinking of them!   Lady Elgar-Alice Stuart Wortley

22 Carice & Sarah Allen arrd in afternoon – Very fine & hot   Elgar diary

Sarah Allen was a devoted maid who began her service as a very young girl at Hazeldine House & who nursed Lady Roberts in her last illness & remained with my Mother until she married. Later on she came back to us & was the greatest comfort. We all felt as long as she was there everything would be perfectly all right. She remained with us after my Mother's death but became a victim of a most painful form of neuritis & died in 1923.   Carice Elgar

24 Lovely day – sunny & hot. Mr. Aylwin's Clover field finished – lovely scent.
                                                                                Alice diary

Second movement of Violin Sonata.

26 A. very busy preparing change of rooms &c ready for Lan. E. busy & happy over his music – Much shocked to hear Alice S. of W. had had an accident & broken her leg – so sorry – such misery suffering for her. **Alice diary**

27 Rather stormy & gray. E. very busy with booful new music – A. drove down to meet Lan. & drove & walked back – So delighted Lan was really here – He heard the new music after lunch & loved the mysterious Orch. pieces wants it dreadfully, & much liked the <u>Sonata</u>. He had a walk with E. they talked <u>music,</u> & Lan was very amusing too – **Alice diary**

28 L. Ronald left after Bkfast weather improved Gleaning wheat by Mr. Aylwin's permission – **Elgar diary**

29 Mr. Reed came by 3 – train in time for tea – Very nice evening in Studio **Alice diary**

When I arrived, Mr. Aylwin, a neighbouring farmer, met me at the station with a pony and trap, it being rather a long way to Brinkwells and difficult to find unless one was acquainted with the district; also I had a bag and a fiddle-case. We jogged along through some wonderfully wooded country, along a road which twisted and turned continually, until at last we came to about half a mile of straight road rising up a fairly steep hill, with chestnut plantations on either side. At the top of the hill, looming on the sky-line, was what at first sight I took to be a statue; but as we drew nearer I saw it was a tall woodman leaning a little forward upon an axe with a very long handle. The picture was perfect and the pose magnificent. It was Sir Edward himself, who had come to the top of the hill to meet me, and placed himself there leaning on his axe and fitting in exactly with the surroundings. He did these things without knowing it, by pure instinct.

He set me at once to cut down some chestnut-poles. Happily, before I had time to cut myself down, Lady Elgar wanted a tub for some domestic purpose or other; and, as there was a big barrel up at the house doing nothing, he produced a long two-handled saw with which we sawed the barrel in halves successfully and presented Lady Elgar with two tubs. A sudden relapse into experimental chemistry was precipitated by a plague of wasps in the garden, the greengage-tree being the attraction. Cyanide of potassium was clearly indicated; so he obtained some from the local chemist., and arranged that we were to go out about an hour before sunset, to intercept the wasps on their return to their nest.

I was not surprised when, after tea, Lady Elgar took me on one side and said, "I am so glad you have come: it is lovely for him to have someone to play with". **W H Reed**

30 Mr. Reed very happy here. E. & he to Bognor pond back to lunch – no fish. Played about in wood &c getting special sticks. Played Sonata again in evening, then cribbage – **Alice diary**

fiddled, fished & fooled walked to river no fish cut sticks etc lovely day **Elgar diary**

I woke up about half-past four in the morning to find Sir Edward standing by my bedside fully dressed, with a pair of Wellington boots which he wanted me to put on. He had on a similar pair of boots himself. When we went out, the extraordinary coldness of the dew-drenched grass convinced me of their necessity He was perturbed because he had been seized with an uneasy feeling about those wasps which lay in heaps on the road. It suddenly occurred to him that children going early to school would see them and might be led up to the hole, where they would find the wool with the deadly cyanide on it. He could sleep no more, so came to fetch me. **W H Reed**

31 E. & Mr. Reed played through Sonata again. The 1st Movement now seems as beautiful as the beautiful 2nd. Sarah sat below Studio <u>entranced</u>. A. busy packing for E. never understood the chance of getting to Ridgehurst & cd. Not think why E. talked of it! – E. drove down for 3.13 train & C. walked with Mr. Reed. – A. with E. to top of lane – E. seemed in such good spirits over his music &c – & so cheered with good news.

Alice diary

Sonata with Reed Cut sticks. E. to London with Reed to 34 Kens Sq. *[Lalla Vandervelde's flat]*

Elgar diary

At my first visit the Violin Sonata was well advanced. All the first movement was written, half the second – he finished this, actually, while I was there – and the opening section of the Finale. We used to play up to the blank page and then he would say, "And then what?" – and we would go out to explore the wood or to fish in the River Arun.

W H Reed

September 1918

02 E. & Lalla to Ridgehurst, Mr. Speyer & E. long talk – E. so glad to go there – Lovely day.
Alice diary

03 Shopping lunch Soho left Vic at 3.45 to Petworth A. & C. met me walked up. Lytton's Novels came
Elgar diary

04 Writing Sonata Sheep came to graze
Elgar diary

06 Misty morning. C. left at 6.20 – E. saw her into pony cart So sorry for her holiday to be over – Most lovely day, warm & all looking exquisite. More good news – D.G. for such happiness & to be in such a lovely place –
Alice diary

I fear your last delightful present was not ever acknowledged, we are so very sorry but between the three of us – for Carice has been here – the letter was never written: please forgive truly repentant chocolate eaters. I have been writing music again & have nearly finished a Sonata for Violin & Pianoforte – so nearly finished that I can almost consider it out of my hands but, as you know, the last stage is the critical time & it may require much trimming – I hope (& think) not. However I am so anxious & selfish that I write before the thing is printable to know if you will allow me the honour to dedicate it to you: it will give me the greatest gratification if you will allow this …
Elgar-Mrs. Joshua

I have been writing much music & I had Mr. Reed with his violin here for a clear day. I had asked him for a week but W.O. duties called him. I had made such a nice (for me nice) plan to bring him over to you & play thro' the new stuff (which implicates a violin) to Frances & you before anyone else. I am so very sorry this idea could not become a real thing.
Elgar-Sidney Colvin

It was good of you to write – we hope the dear patient is progressing well & without pain; I know she is always interested in my music & I have been writing a lot; if you think she is well enough I would write & tell her about it but I hesitate to do so as she may be better without letters even about music.
Elgar-Charles Stuart Wortley

07 Whiskey & wine came Sonata Misty morning & again hot & fine Tried Cribbage with A
Elgar diary

08 I am sending you a line at Mother's wish, as she has caught a chill, I am sorry to say. But she is anxious not to postpone her heartfelt thanks for your letter – She hopes to be able to write herself to-morrow and to explain why, although she is quite overwhelmed by the great honour that you suggest, she feels it would not be right for her to accept it. **May Davidson-Elgar** *[Mrs Joshua's daughter]*

Wrote proposing to buy underwood. **Elgar diary**

10 Sunny & then storms Thunderstorm in aftn. A. to Fittleworth P. O. after tea. E. met her. E. writing his booful Sonata – Marie Joshua died suddenly, did not hear of it till following Saturday 14th great shock to us. **Alice diary**

11 All goes on as usual as regards the scene & surroundings. Our local cook, whom you saw, has gone to her returned soldier husband & we have Alice's former maid Sarah whose rheumatism is better & her niece is coming as cook etc. I suddenly took to writing music! & have nearly 'done' a sonata for Violin & piano in E minor. Ronald & Reed both like it – what I played to them, a little to Ronald & more to Reed, for whose use I copied out a violin part & we played & thought you ought to be here to help generally: a sad little chair with a pencil is beside the piano now. The first movement is bold & vigorous; then a fantastic, curious movemt with a very expressive middle section: a melody for the Violin – they say it's as good as or better than anything I have done in the expressive way: this I wrote just after your telegram about the accident came & I send you the pencil notes as first made at that sad moment. You will make nothing of it from this but a better copy shall come as soon as you can play again – I hope this will be very soon. The last movement is very broad & soothing like the last movemt of the IInd Symphy. I have been sketching other things which are full of old times. **Elgar-Alice Stuart Wortley**

12 Heard from Stopham Agent that the **Wood reeve** wd call regarding the underwood Rose came. **Elgar diary**

13 E. writing Sonata – Not out far – Mr. Newbury *[vicar]* called went on parishing & then back to tea – Seemed to enjoy himself – E. most genial **Alice diary**

14 Writing. Heard saddest news of Mrs. Joshua's death: roofing felt came **Elgar diary**

15 You will now have heard that my beloved Mother passed away suddenly on Tuesday morning – and it is my sacred duty to write to you about her thoughts and feelings (as far as I can interpret them) which she would have expressed in her intended answer to your letter –

I must first tell you that your thought of dedicating your new work to her, filled her with radiant and exalted joy – and I shall carry with me always and always a feeling of gratitude to you, such as I can never express, for giving her this crowning happiness and greatest honour of her life and for thus making her last days on earth, days of purest bliss and thankfulness –

She spoke to me of … her reasons for feeling that she could not accept this honour – She said that in her mind, there was one great chain binding the immortal works of Bach-Beethoven-Brahms-Elgar – and that no ordinary human being was worthy of being linked to these master-pieces, that your first Great Symphony bore the dedication 'Hans Richter-true artist-true friend' and that the wonderful Violin Concerto 'contains the Soul of –' and that she was not fitted to be included in this Spiritual Cycle –

To the, last, her thoughts were centred on the letter she was going to write to you and her mind was dwelling on all the great and beautiful things that meant so much to her – Art – Your Art – and the Suggested Dedication – Dear Sir Edward – her life would not have had this wonderful fulfilment, but for your last letter – I am eternally grateful.   May Davidson-Elgar

Violin Sonata dedicated to 'M.J. – 1918'

I was so very touched and overwhelmed by Sir Edward's beautiful thought – I could not say how much – but wanted to tell you and him – I feel sure that my dear Mother would be happy with this silent dedication – She always spoke of the sacredness of Sir Edward's work – and she would not think that this took away from it – I am convinced –
                                                              May Davidson-Lady Elgar (?24/09/18)

A favourite short walk from the house up through the woods brought one clean out of the everyday world to a region prosaically called Flexham Park, which might have been the Wolf's Glen in Der Freischutz. The strangeness of the place was created by a group of dead trees which, apparently struck by lightning, had very gnarled and twisted branches stretching out in an eerie manner as if beckoning one to come nearer. To walk up there in the, evening when it was just getting dark was to get "the creeps."
                                                                                      W H Reed

16 The <u>Reeve</u> came. I bought the near underwood for £3. & proceeded to cut a. boundary warm & rainy. Maids' tea party A. & E. to Stopham Manor to tea (Corbetts) very nice walk home posted Lavender to Windflower   Elgar diary

Sir Julian Corbett was Director of the Historical Section of the Committee of Imperial Defence.

The fruit trees blossoming within the orchard near by beckon to us to explore more of the beauties of Stopham Manor, that subsidiary dwelling of those who owned the large house near the Bridge, that home compact in shape, mellow and well-toned in soft shades of reds and yellows … The first thing we notice is that for an ancient house it is remarkably well placed, standing upon the summit of a small hill that overlooks the Arun valley. A rough trackway leads across the meadow-grass and, as we approach, we gain a side view of the northern and perhaps the oldest side, which is said to have been rebuilt in 1485 and is consequently medieval and sombre-looking in character. It is small wonder that such a homely old house should win the hearts of those who live in it …   Viscountess Wolseley

18 Reed came per Aylwin 4 o'c played Sonata & sketch Vtett. also wooded in wood (wet night)   Elgar diary

The Sonata … was finished first, and he wrote out whole sections of the Quartet and the Quintet for violin, so that when the author came to Brinkwells he could play them, Elgar condensing the rest from his sketchy score, playing it on the piano and getting a better idea of it with the aid of the violin than he would have done by just playing what he had written over on the piano.   W H Reed

19 Reed here. much fiddling at Sonata. he left at 5.0 revised <u>"edn"</u> – Played thro'
                                                                                      Elgar diary

23 After the operation on my throat we came to this cottage & have been here ever since, & are likely to remain: it is divine, & I have bought 1½ acres of wood to cut down &

want an axeman badly! ... I have also made a table & have written a Sonata for Vn & Pf on it, & the latter (that is the piano part) requires much consideration & advice from Firapeel.   Reed, dear man, has run down from London twice, & we have 'done' the Sonata & by'r lakin I think you will like it – it's the best of me.   **Elgar-Ivor Atkins**

26 E. very happy over his music & woods wd. not come out. C. gave up coming owing to wicked railway strike.   **Alice diary**

28 Dr. Spear for Sarah. Electricity E. not vesy well & very disappointed at not feeling so – His eye wh. was struck with a chips using chopper in wood, not quite well. Dr. Spear here for Sarah looked at it & said it <u>was</u> all well – D.G. A. to P. O. & found splendid War news on all the fronts – so thankful. Fire in dining room in Evg. 1st time.   **Alice diary**

30 E poorly all this week Wrote a little & worked in wood   **Elgar diary**

October 1918

01 I am supposed to be going to Frank on the 14th so as to be near for the Palace (Fringes) Charity affair (C. Beresford) & a recording at the Gramophone & a 'comic' concert that L. Ronald is getting up – but I have had – at the thought of town life – a recurrence of the old feelings & have been just as limp as before the nursing home episode.
        Elgar-Alice Stuart Wortley

Sent Sonata to Novello   **Elgar diary**

03 *Germany and Austria request armistice.*

05 Much music being written but E. not at all well – A. concerned about him – Excursions to wood. Splendid news on all sides – D.G.   **Alice diary**

07 Rather finer – E. very hard at work A. to P. O. – E. met her – E. muss better. He lay on the sofa before dinner & A. read poetry things to him. Suddenly at dinner he said "I feel all right again" – & seemed so – D.G.   **Alice diary**

Finer. Germans suing for peace E. better   **Elgar diary**

Hubert Parry died.

Yes, we have had an irreparable loss, you and I and all of us. He was the foundation of our musical life, and no-one can express what we all owe to him, not only for his work but for keeping our world clean & good & great ...
        Harry Plunket Greene-Herbert Howells (13/10/18)

You have asked me in very touching words to write an article on our late Director as a Composer ... Frankly it would be impossible for anybody to carry out a task in a few weeks which would require years for adequate treatment, and you will forgive me if I do not rush in where angels ought to fear to tread ... Schumann once wrote of the impossibility of appreciating the height of peaks when the spectator was too close to the mountain ranges. It requires, above all things, time. Time to go to a sufficient distance, and time to explore the peaks themselves. This is true of Parry as of any other great writer. It is not for a contemporary but for the next and succeeding generations to write upon. Therefore you will forgive me if I content myself with these few words. I can guess what the verdict of coming centuries will be, but I will not charge a jury which is not yet in the box. If my words are few, my heart is full; and you will understand.   **Charles Villiers Stanford, RCM Magazine**

08 E. possessed with his wonderful music, 2nd Movement of 4tet – Varied by excursions to wood – Much excited over news. Germans ask for terms. Trust & hope that nothing short of dictation will be thought of … read of Hubert Parry's death previous day – Last day of birthday year full of serious thoughts & thankfulness for year with beloved –
Alice diary

09 Gale & rain again – E. repeats "Storms are sweeping sea & land" – E. possessed with his lovely new music – the 4tet – Writing the 2nd movement, so gracious & lovable – A. birfday – & Sarah's –
Alice diary

10 Packing up for short trip to London.
Elgar diary

11 A. & E. to London stayed Langham Promenade Concert
Elgar diary

12 Severn House
Elgar diary

14 The Sonata was first played privately, with W H Reed as violinist and Elgar at the Piano in Elgar's home. Among the guests were Schuster and Ronald, who was so impressed that he begged Elgar to allow him to give the first public performance of the work with Reed.
Wulstan Atkins

16 *The Elgars attended Parry's funeral service in St. Paul's. The service was taken by the Archbishop of Canterbury. The organists included Walter Parratt, Walford Davies and Ivor Atkins, and Hugh Allen conducted the Cathedral, Temple, RCM and Oxford Bach Choirs.*

…the crowd was so great that, in my capacity of steward, I had considerable difficulty in finding places for him and for Lady Elgar
Thomas Dunhill

[The music] reached its noblest moment in Sir Hubert's own Motet 'There is an old Belief', wherein the unison passage at the words 'That creed I fain would keep, and hope I'll ne'er forgo' gave us the most vivid moment, the most vital memory of a beloved man, the greatest uplifting in that inspired service.
Herbert Howells

Some felt God's presence, I felt his presence the great noble soul pervading everything the wonderful inspiring influence which will dwell on and on after we are all dead.
Sir Arthur Ponsonby diary

We came up hurriedly on Saty and – as the printers were clamorous for the M.S. – we had an impromptu 'party' & Reed & I played the Sonata twice – before tea & after. Frank came & the Colvins & the Fortescues, Lan. Ronald Muriel F & one or two others: we missed you dreadfully & were saying it did not seem right to do it without you. It was liked … I am going to the Hut today & come up for C. Beresford's affair (Naval charity) at the Palace Theatre next week. We go back to Brinkwells in a fortnight's time & I am wondering if you will be home before then & if you wd. be equal to hearing the Sonata if Mr. Reed wd. come with me & play it to you? … The air does not agree with me & I long to get back to my quiet woods.
Elgar-Alice Stuart Wortley

17 at Hut A to Sir M. about 'Wen' A. cold operation postponed
Elgar diary

20 I have just tramped over to rank Schuster's at Bray and back, where I had a very pleasant lunch. La Grosse Lalla was there … also old Edward Elgar, who seemed an amusing old bird, and Adrian Boult. It was a pleasure to be with comparatively human intelligent beings again, even tho' it entailed a walk of eleven miles thro' the rain.
Aldous Huxley

21 E. from Hut for rehearsal of 'Fringes' (C. Beresford's Matinee) Fog retd to Hut
Elgar diary

We are only here for a few days: we have been at the cottage in Sussex all the summer & have spoken of you again & again wondering if you wd. ever come there for an entirely solitary (lovely) quiet time in the hills & woods. Do think of it: we go back till Christmas in 10 days time & if the autumn is fine we shd. welcome you with the greatest joy. There is just the simple cottage – a large garden – a wood – & a big studio right away down the garden. I wish with all my heart you cd. come.

I've written a lot of music including a String quartet & a V. & P Sonata & an incipient Quintet – I only mention this because I should like to dedicate the last named to you if it is ever finished.

P.S. We have been very sad over Parry's death & now, dear old McNaught it is too terrible   **Elgar-Ernest Newman**

22 E. to London – rehearsal Matinee Fringes. <u>Palace Theatre</u> Slept at Severn House
                                                          Elgar diary

It was reported that Sir Edward is going to record his Variations for us. The only difficulty is in arranging in cuts. Mr. Ronald thought this was excellent.
                                              Gramophone Co. Minutes

23 *Elgar went to the Hut, where he was joined two days later by Lady Elgar.*

28 E. & A left Hut. No taxi at Paddn E. rehearsal of 'Toy Sym.' concert in afternn played cymbals (L. Ronald's)   **Elgar diary**

I must explain that Irene Scharrer, Myra Hess and Muriel Foster had each to have a mug of water in which to blow their toy instrument 'The Nightingale' so that the desired result might be obtained. At rehearsal this must have been a somewhat wet proceeding for Sir Alexander, who was sitting just in front of them, although at the time no word of complaint escaped his lips. At the performance, however, no sooner did the warble of the nightingales commence, than Sir Alexander quietly put down his violin and producing a large umbrella from somewhere, opened it, rested it on his shoulder and then immediately resumed his playing. It was all done so quietly and unostentatiously that it was a good minute or two before either the audience or the orchestra realised what had taken place. Then a roar of laughter ensued and as I have said it was only a miracle that prevented the whole orchestra stopping.   **Landon Ronald**

29 Sir Maurice, Barrow & anr doctor – A's 'Wen' removed E then sick many times
                                                          Elgar diary

I should have written before but at Brinkwells I managed to (adroitly) send a chip into my sound eye & we had to scrimmage up here, where we have been torn in pieces & hope to be able to get back to the cottage in a day or two. Alice has just had a little operation: removal of a 'wen' sort of thing. She is going on quite well & shd. be about again soon.   **Elgar-Rosa Burley**

31 to Cheyne Walk with Reed to play to Alice Wortley Claude there Reed – dinner
                                                          Elgar diary

November 1918

02 E. to Ridgehurst trains at Finchley Road! 'Nip round with yr bag'   **Elgar diary**

03 E. at Ridgehurst Made them very happy, & in aft. played all kinds of old romantic music to them, Mr. Speyer sang & shouted & seemed quite young again.   **Alice diary**

04 E. back from Ridgehurst early Alice diary

05 Very busy with music Lunch at home Elgar diary

Yes. I recd your letter from France & awaited your return which I am glad is safely accomplished. I think your poem beautiful exceedingly – but – I do not feel drawn to write peace music somehow – I thought long months ago that I could feel that way & if anything could draw me your poem would, but the whole atmosphere is too full of complexities for me to feel music to it: Elgar-Laurence Binyon

07 Alice's operation was much more of an event than we anticipated & than she knows even now – there is a large wound. The doctors refused to let us go *[back to Brinkwells]* & all plans had to be altered by telegraph etc etc & endless confusion of course ... My writing new stuff has been held up by the confusion & I am in despair at ever overtaking it – our coming away – which was necessary – has been a tragedy for my music, alas! Elgar-Alice Stuart Wortley

08 Sir Maurice & Mr. Barrow came at 8.30 – & took off A's bandage & put on plaster. Such a relief to have bandage off. Said we might leave on Monday – Alice diary

09 I have a lot of new stuff to show you & should send on proof if I cd get them but ... times are difficult: however you shall see everything as soon as possible: a Sonata for V. & Pf ought to find a responsive thrill in you – I hope it will, because if it does I know it's all right. Elgar-Ivor Atkins

10 E.& C. to Colvins in aftn & then to Lalla's tea party. The Belgian Ambassador Monsieur de Moncheur thanked E. for all he had done for Belgium. A. busy preparing. Alice diary

11 Armistice – ran up Flag. Car to Victoria. A.& E. to Fittleworth 1.36. Flags ... Lalla at Victoria Threshing barley at Brinkwells Elgar diary

Arriving in exile at Count Bentinck's castle in Holland:
"If it is possible I should like above all a cup of hot English tea." Kaiser Wilhelm II

Riotous joy and triumph and flags and motor-lorries of drunken Dominion soldiers and crowds and crowds ... Jelka Delius

The joy which overtook the whole nation at the conclusion of all hostilities would have been almost too great to bear had it not been tempered by the thought in every one's mind of the terrible cost at which this great and victorious end had been achieved and the irretrievable loss of human life it had demanded. Elgar himself was much affected in this way. He felt no hilarity, only a deep thankfulness that the horror and strain was over, especially for those who had endured the worst of it. W H Reed

November 11th, at 11 a.m. – an unforgettable date (11-11-11, 1918) – the sound of the maroons announced the end of hostilities. I flew out of my house in Great Cumberland Place and went straight to Buckingham Palace to write my name, and there I remained the whole morning within the gates, from where one could see the amazing crowds whose first thought had been, like mine, to go to the Palace as a tribute to the King. Lord Farquhar, then Lord Steward, took me up to his room to look at the thousands of people reaching as far as the Admiralty Arch. It was a magnificent, spontaneous outburst of loyalty. Queen Victoria's Memorial was covered with those who had climbed all over it. The Guards Band played "Tipperary" and other soldier songs. And several times in answer to the cries of "We want King George! We want

King George!" H. M. came out with the Queen on to the balcony and finally made a simple, effective speech.   **Maud Warrender**

13 Very bright & cold – E. very busy. A. walked to P.O – Papers very exciting & interesting –   **Alice diary**

14 We arrived all safely & found everything ready. It is cold but vividly bright weather & the woods divine: there are still leaves & the colours ravishing. Music does not go on yet: my poor dear A. has a cold & keeps her room – I doubt if she will be able to stay here but we shall see.   **Elgar-Alice Stuart Wortley**

19 Not so cold – All as usual –   **Alice diary**

Sort of neuralgia from cold winds   **Elgar diary**

SOURCES

Books

Allen, Kevin: *August Jaeger - Portrait of Nimrod* (Ashgate, 2000)

Atkins, E Wulstan: *The Elgar-Atkins Friendship* (David and Charles, 1984)

Beecham, Sir Thomas: *A Mingled Chime: Leaves from an Autobiography* (Hutchinson, 1944)

Birkenhead, Lord: *Rudyard Kipling* (Weidenfeld & Nicolson, 1978)

Bliss, Sir Arthur: *As I remember* (Faber and Faber, 1970)

Boult, Sir Adrian: *My Own Trumpet* (Hamish Hamilton, 1973)

Burley, Rosa & Carruthers, Frank: *Edward Elgar: The Record of a Friendship* (Barrie & Jenkins, 1972)

Camden, Archie: *Blow by Blow* (Thames Publishing, 1982)

Colls, R & Dodd, P (eds),: *Englishness Politics and Culture 1880-1920*, (Croom Helm, 1986)

Coward, Henry: *Reminiscences* (Curwen, 1919)

Dibble, Jeremy: *C. Hubert H. Parry: his life and music* (OUP, 1992)

Dunhill, Thomas: *Sir Edward Elgar* (Blackie, 1938)

Fifield, Christopher: *True Artist and True Friend* (Clarendon Press, 1993)

Foreman, Lewis: *Music in England 1885-1920 as recounted in Hazell's Annual* (Thames Publishing, 1994)

Foreman, Lewis: *From Parry to Britten: British Music in Letters 1900-1945* (Batsford, 1987)

Gaisberg, Fred: *Music on Record* (Robert Hale, 1936)

Godfrey, Sir Dan: *Memories and Music* (Hutchinson, 1924)

Graves, Charles: *Hubert Parry* (Macmillan, 1926)

Greene, Harry Plunket: *Charles Villiers Stanford* (Arnold, 1935)

Jacobs, Arthur: *Henry J Wood, Maker of the Proms* (Methuen, 1994)

Kennedy, Michael: *Barbirolli: Conductor Laureate* (MacGibbon & Kee, 1971)

Kennedy, Michael: *Portrait of Elgar* (OUP, 1968)

King Albert's Book (The Daily Telegraph, 1914)

Maine, Basil: *Elgar: his Life and Works* (Bell, 1933)

McVeagh, Diana: *Elgar: His Life and Works* (Dent, 1955)

Monk, R (ed): *Elgar Studies* (Scolar, 1990)

Moore, Jerrold Northrop: *Elgar on Record* (OUP, 1974)

Moore, Jerrold Northrop: *Edward Elgar - A Creative Life* (OUP, 1984)

Moore, Jerrold Northrop: *Elgar and his Publishers* (OUP, 1987)
Moore, Jerrold Northrop: *Letters of a Lifetime* (Clarendon Press, 1990)
Moore, Jerrold Northrop: *Music and Friends Letters to Adrian Boult* (Hamish Hamilton, 1979)
Moore, Jerrold Northrop: *Spirit of England: Edward Elgar in his World* (Heinemann, 1984)
Moore, Jerrold Northrop: *The Windflower Letters* (Clarendon Press, 1989)
Mr Punch's History of the Great War (Cassell, 1919)
Newton, Ivor: *At the Piano* (Hamish Hamilton, 1966)
Palmer, Christopher: *Herbert Howells a Centenary Celebration* (Novello, 1978)
Pankhurst, Sylvia: *The Home Front* (Hutchinson, 1931)
Porte, John: *Elgar and his Music: An Appreciative Study* (Pitman, 1933)
Porte, John: *Sir Edward Elgar* (Kegan Paul, 1921)
Redwood, Christopher (ed): *An Elgar Companion* (Sequoia, 1982)
Reed, W H: *Elgar as I knew him* (Gollancz, 1936)
Reed, W H: *Elgar* (Dent, 1939)
Ronald, Sir Landon: *Variations on a Personal Theme* (Hodder & Stoughton, 1922)
Roscow, Gregory: *Bliss on Music* (OUP, 1991)
Vandervelde, Lalla: *Monarchs and Millionaires* (Thornton Butterworth, 1925)
Vansittart, Peter: *Voices from the Great War* (Jonathan Cape, 1981)
Warrender, Lady Maud: *My First Sixty Years* (Cassell, 1933)
Wolseley, Viscountess: *Some of the smaller manor houses of Sussex* (The Medici Society, 1925)
Wood, Sir Henry: *My Life of Music* (Gollancz, 1938)
Young,Percy: *Alice Elgar: Enigma of a Victorian Lady* (Dobson, 1978)
Young, Percy: *Elgar, O. M.* (Collins, 1955)
Young, Percy: *Letters of Edward Elgar, and other Writings* (Bles, 1956)

Newspapers & Journals
Allen, Kevin: 'Elgar's letters to Rosa Burley', *Elgar Society Journal* vol 9, nos 4 (March 1996) & 5 (July 1996)
Boult, Sir Adrian, *The Star* (4 April 1935)
Buckley, Robert: *Birmingham Gazette* (4 October 1917)
Daily Mirror (10 October 1916 & 28 July 1917)
Daily Telegraph, The (25 November 1918)
Hodgkins, Geoffrey & Taylor, Ronald: 'Elgar & Percy Pitt' part II, *Elgar Society Journal* vol 9, no 1 (March 1995)
Hull, Lady Percy: 'A memoir of Elgar', *Elgar Society Journal* vol 7, no 1 (January 1991)
Smith, Barry: 'Elgar & Warlock', *Elgar Society Journal* vol 12 no 1 (March 2001)
Times, The (6 May 1916)

Unpublished
Alice Elgar: diary
Edward Elgar: diary
Elgar, Edward: letter to Anthony Bernard
Hale, Nicholas: letter to Alan Webb, Curator, Elgar Birthplace Museum

BIBLIOGRAPHY

In the following bibliography place of publication is assumed to be London and is only stated if otherwise.

Elgar Cuttings Books (39 vols) at the Elgar Birthplace Museum. Here reference has largely been made to Vol 12 1914-1919.

Binyon, Laurence: *The Winnowing-Fan: poems on the Great War* (Elkin Matthews, 1914)
Binyon, Laurence: *Collected Poems* 2 vols (Macmillan, 1931)

Elgar Society Journal
The Musical Times
The Music Student

Grove's Dictionary of Music and Musicians :
   3rd edition (ed Colles, M A) 5 vols (Macmillan & Co, 1928)
   5th edition (ed Blom, Eric) 9 vols (Macmillan & Co, 1954) Supp Vol (1961)
   New Grove 1st edition (ed Sadie, Stanley) 20 vols (Macmillan Publishers Ltd, 1980)
   New Grove 2nd edition (edSadie, Stanley; executive editor John Tyrrell) 29 vols (Macmillan/Grove's Dictionaries, 2001)

(a) Elgar

Allen, Kevin: *August Jaeger - Portrait of Nimrod. A Life in Letters and Other Writings* (Aldershot, Ashgate, 2000)
Anderson, Robert: *Elgar in Manuscript* (The British Library, 1990)
Anderson, Robert: *Elgar* (The Dent Master Musicians) (J M Dent, 1993)
Atkins, E Wulstan: *The Elgar-Atkins Friendship* (Newton Abbott, David & Charles, 1984)
Blackwood, Algernon: *A Prisoner in Fairyland* (Macmillan, 1913)
Burley, Rosa and Frank Carruthers: *Edward Elgar, the record of a friendship* (Barrie & Jenkins, 1972)
Bury, David: *Elgar and the Two Mezzos* (Thames Publishing, 1984)
Culshaw, John: 'Was Elgar a Nationalist Composer?' *The Mercury* No 4 (July 1949) pp 6-8
Gardiner, John: 'The Reception of Sir Edward Elgar (1918-c1934): a reassessment' *Twentieth Century British History* Vol 9 (1998) p 3
Harrison, H Wells: 'Edward Elgar's Settings of Cammaerts' Poems' *The Music Student* (July 1916) pp 313-4
Hodgkins, Geoffrey: *Elgar: a bibliography* Offprint from *The Music Review* vol 54 No 1 (1993) pp 24-62
Hodgkins, Geoffrey: *Providence and Art - A study in Elgar's religious beliefs* (Rickmansworth, The Elgar Society, 1979)
Hodgkins, Geoffrey, ed: *The Best of Me: a Gerontius centenary companion* (Rickmansworth, Elgar Editions,1999)
Hodgkins, Geoffrey and Ronald Taylor: Elgar and Percy Pitt *Elgar Society Journal*

vol 9 no 1 (March 1995) p 12

Hooey, Charles A: 'Spirit Insights' *Elgar Society Journal* vol 9 no 6 (November 1996) p 297

Keeton, A E: 'Elgar's Music for "The Starlight Express"' *Music & Letters* (January 1945) pp 43-6

Kennedy, Michael: *Portrait of Elgar* (Oxford University Press, 1968; rev and enlarged edn 1982)

Kent, Christopher: *Edward Elgar a guide to research* (New York, Garland Publishing, 1993)

Knowles, John: *Elgar's Interpreters on Record - an Elgar discography* (Thames Publishing, 1985)

Lace, Ian: 'Elgar & Empire' *Elgar Society Journal* vol 10 no 3 (November 1997)

McVeagh, Diana M: *Edward Elgar His Life and Music* (J M Dent, 1955)

Maine, Basil: *Elgar his life and works* (2 vols, 1933, reprinted as one, Bath, Cedric Chivers Ltd, 1973)

Monk, Raymond, ed: *Elgar Studies* (Aldershot, Scolar Press, 1990)

Monk, Raymond, ed: *Edward Elgar Music and Literature* (Aldershot, Scolar Press, 1993)

Moore, Jerrold Northrop: *Elgar A Life in Photographs* (OUP, 1972)

Moore, Jerrold Northrop: *Letters of a Lifetime* (Oxford, Clarendon Press, 1990)

Moore, Jerrold Northrop: *Elgar on Record: The Composer and the Gramophone* (Oxford, OUP, 1974)

Moore, Jerrold Northrop: *Edward Elgar: A Creative Life* (Oxford, OUP, 1984)

Moore, Jerrold Northrop*: Elgar and his Publishers, Letters of a Creative Life* (2 vols, Oxford, Clarendon Press, 1987)

Moore, Jerrold Northrop: *An Elgar Discography* (British Institute of RecordedSound,1963) (Reprint with corrections from *Recorded Sound* vol 2 no 9 (January 1963))

Moore, Jerrold Northrop: *Edward Elgar The Windflower Letters Correspondence with Alice Stuart Wortley and her Family* (Oxford, Clarendon Press, 1989)

Moore, Jerrold Northrop: *Spirit of England - Edward Elgar in his World* (Heinemann, 1984)

Pirie, Peter J: 'World's End: a study of Elgar' *Music Review* (May 1957) pp 89-100

Powell, Mrs Richard: *Edward Elgar - memories of a Variation* 4th ed, rev and edited by C Powell (Aldershot, Ashgate, 1994)

Redwood, Christopher, ed: *An Elgar Companion* (Ashbourne, Derbyshire, Sequoia Publishing in association with Moorland Publishing Co Ltd, 1982)

Reed, William H: *Elgar As I Knew Him* (Victor Gollancz, 1936)

Sheldon, A J: *Edward Elgar* (Office of The Musical Opinion, 1932)

Sotheby's: [Sale Catalogue] 9 February 1976. Lots 73-77 comprise letters to the Kilburn family from Carice Elgar, Lady Elgar and Edward Elgar, with extensive quotations from the letters pp18-21

Sotheby's: *The Novello Collection* [auction catalogue] London 15 May 1996

Taylor, Ronald: *A Chronological List of Live Broadcasts of Elgar's Music by the BBC November 1922 to February 1934* (New Barnet, Privately printed, 1996)

Weaver, Cora: *The Thirteenth Enigma? The story of Edward Elgar's early love* (Thames Publishing, 1988)

Young, Percy M: *Alice Elgar - Enigma of a Victorian lady* (Dobson, 1978)

Young, Percy M: *Elgar O M* A Study of a Musician (Collins, 1955. Extensively revised, White Lion Publishers, 1973)

Young, Percy M ed: *A Future for English Music and other lectures* (Dennis Dobson, 1968)

Young, Percy M, ed: *Letters to Nimrod. Edward Elgar to August Jaeger 1897-1908* (Dennis Dobson, 1965)

Young, Percy M, ed: *Letters of Edward Elgar and other writings* (Geoffrey Bles, 1956)

(b) General: music

Ashwell, Lena: *Modern Troubadours: a record of Concerts at the Front* (Gylendal, 1922)

Bainton, Edgar L: 'Musical Personalities at Ruhleben' *Musical Opinion* (February 1919) pp 279-80

Bashford, Christina and Leanne Langley eds: *Music and British Culture 1785-1914* (Oxford, 2000)

Bax, Sir Arnold: *Farewell, My Youth and other writings by Arnold Bax*, edited by Lewis Foreman (Aldershot, Scolar Press, 1992)

Beughold, Michael: Von Schillings and *Das Hexenlied (*extended booklet notes with the CPO recording) CPO LC 8492 (Martha Mödl, specherin; Kölner Rundfunkorchester conducted by Jan Stulen)

Bliss, [Sir] Arthur: *As I Remember* (Faber & Faber, 1970)

Boult, Adrian Cedric: *My Own Trumpet* (Hamish Hamilton, 1973)

Brian, Havergal: *Havergal Brian on Music. Selections from his Journalism* edited by Malcolm MacDonald Volume One *British Music* (Toccata Press, 1986)

Brown, Malcolm: 'Music fit for heroes' *Radio Times* Vol 237 No 3234 9-15 (Nov 1985) p 3

Carley, Lionel: *Delius A Life in Letters* 2 vols (Aldershot, Scolar Press, 1983, 1988)

Colles, H C: *Walford Davies - A Biography* (OUP, 1942)

Connock, Stephen and others: 'VW and the First World War' issue of *Journal of the RVW Society* No 16 October 1999 Includes: 'The Edge of Beyond' and 'The Death of Innocence' by Stephen Connock; 'Vaughan Williams as an Officer' by Alan Aldous; 'Where Shelled Roads Part - RVW, Britten and the Great War' by Roger Juneau; 'Henry Steggles on VW in the Great War' (from *RCM Magazine* Easter Term 1959, vol LV no 1) pp 21-24

Corder, Frederick: 'Recitation with Music' in *Voice, Speech and Gesture: a practical handbook to the elocutionary art* by H Campbell...R F Brewer...H Neville...Clifford Harrison...F Corder...Stanley Hawley... Edited with notes and introduction by R D Blackman (first published 1895. New and enlarged edition, Charles William Deacon & Co, 1904)

Cross, Mark, ed: *Armistice Festival: complete programme guide* (London and Oxford, Armistice Festival Ltd, 1988) (Reviewed: *Financial Times* 8 November 1988) p 23

Dannatt, George: *Heroes of the Somme* [Programme for] Concert by NELP Chorus, Hatfield Philharmonic Chorus and Harlow Chorus Royal Festival Hall, 20 Nov 1985(Includes Dannatt's article 'War and the Creative Impulse' and his notes for *Banks of Geen Willow* (Butterworth), *The Spirit of England* (Elgar) and *Morning Heroes* (Bliss))

Dunhill, David: *Thomas Dunhill - maker of Music* (Thames Publishing, 1997)

Ehrlich, Cyril: *First Philharmonic. A History of the Royal Philharmonic Society* (Oxford, Clarendon Press, 1995)

Ehrlich, Cyril: *The Music Profession in Britain Since the Eighteenth Century. A Social History* (Oxford, Clarendon Press, 1985)

Ferguson, John: *The Arts in Britain in World War I* (Stainer & Bell, 1980)

Fifield, Christopher: *True Artist and True Friend. A biography of Hans Richter* (Oxford, Clarendon Press, 1993)

Foreman, Lewis: *From Parry to Britten - British Music in Letters 1900-1945* (B T Batsford, 1987)

Foreman, Lewis: *Music in England 1885-1920 as recounted in Hazell's Annual* (Thames Publishing, 1994)

Foreman, Lewis, ed: *Ralph Vaughan Williams In Perspective - studies of an English composer* (Albion Press for The Vaughan Williams Society, 1998)

Forsyth, C: *Music and Nationalism* (London, 1911)

Godfrey, Sir Dan: *Memories and Music - Thirty-Five Years of Conducting* (Hutchinson, 1924)

Graves, Charles L: *Hubert Parry His Life and Works* 2 vols (Macmillan, 1926)

Gray, Cecil: *A Survey of Contemporary Music* (OUP, 1924)

Gurney, Ivor: *Ivor Gurney War Letters* a selection edited by R K R Thornton (Manchester, Carcanet New Press, 1983)

Howes, Frank: *The English Musical Renaissance* (Secker & Warburg, 1966)

Hurd, Michael: *The Ordeal of Ivor Gurney* (Oxford, OUP, 1978)

Jacobs, Arthur: *Henry J Wood - Maker of the Proms* (Methuen, 1994)

Kennedy, Michael: *Adrian Boult* (Hamish Hamilton, 1987)

Kenyon, Nicholas: 'Memory of war' *The Listener* (7 November 1985) p 38

Lamb Andrew Lamb's article 'Music hall' in *New Grove II*, vol 17 pp 483-6

Lloyd, Stephen: *Dan Godfrey Champion of British Composers* (Thames Publishing, 1995)

Mackerness, E D: *A Social History of English Music* (Routledge & Kegan Paul, 1964)

Martland, Peter: *Since Records Began - EMI The first 100 years* (B T Batsford, 1997)

Moore, Charles Willard: *The Solo Vocal Works of Ivor Gurney* Thesis Mus D, (Indiana University, 1967)

Palmer, Christopher: *Herbert Howells - a centenary celebration* (Thames Publishing, 1992)

Parry, C H H: *College Addresses delivered to pupils of the Royal College of Music* (1920)

Pirie, Peter J: 'World's End' *Music Review* (1957) p 89

Pirie, Peter J: *The English Musical Renaissance* (Victor Gollancz, 1979)

Ponder, Winifred: *Clara Butt - Her Life Story* (Harrap, 1928)

Rees, Brian: *A Musical Peacemaker - the Life and work of Sir Edward German* (Bourne End, The Kensall Press, 1986)

Roscow, Gregory, ed: *Bliss on Music: Selected Writings of Arthur Bliss 1920-1975* (Oxford, OUP, 1991)

Rust, Brian: *London Musical Shows on Record 1897-1976* (Harrow, General Gramophone Publications, 1977)

Rust, Brian: *Gramophone Records of the First World War: an HMV catalogue 1914-18* (Newton Abbot, David & Charles, nd [1974])

Scholes, Percy A: *The Mirror of Music 1844-1944* 2 Vols (Novello & Co Ltd and OUP, 1947) (especially: 'The First "Great War" (1914-18)' vol 2 pp 887-892)

Scott, W H: *Edward German an intimate biography* (Cecil Palmer, Chappell, 1932)

Shaw, Martin: *Up to Now* (Oxford, 1929)

The Society of British Composers Year Book 1906-7; 1907-08; 1912 (Pinner, Mddx, J B McEwen 1906-12)

Stanford, [Sir] Charles V: 'Music and the War' *Quarterly Review* (1915) reprinted in *Interludes: Records and Reflections* (John Murray, 1922) pp 102-124

Stradling, Robert and Meirion Hughes: *The English Musical Renaissance 1860-1940 Construction and deconstruction* Routledge, 1993

Trend, Michael: *The Music Makers - Heirs and rebels of the English Music Renaissance Edward Elgar to Benjamin Britten* (Weidenfeld & Nicolson, 1985)

Wood, Henry J: *My Life of Music* (Victor Gollancz, 1938; revised edition 1946)

(c) General: non-musical sources

[Begbie] 'Poetry' [some notes about Harold Begbie] *Stand To!* [The Journal of the Western Front Association] No 62 (September 2001) p 31

Bentley, Gilbert: *The Evolution of National Insurance in Great Britain; the origins of the Welfare State* (Aldershot, Gregg Revivals, 1966)

Binyon, Laurence: *The Winnowing-Fan* (Elkin Matthews, 1914)

Bourke, Joanna: *An Intimate History of Killing* (Granta, 1999)

Cammaerts, Emil: *Belgian Poems* . . (John Lane, The Bodley Head, 1915)

Cannon, John, ed: *the Oxford Companion to British History* (OUP, 1997)

Chickering, Robert: *Imperial Germany and the Great War, 1914 – 1918* (Cambridge, CUP, 1998)

Colls, Robert and Philip Dodd: *Englishness Politics and Culture 1880-1920* (Croom Helm, 1986) (includes Jeremy Crump:' The Identity of English Music: The Reception of Elgar 1898-1935' pp 164-190)

Dawson, Graham: *Soldier heroes - British adventure, Empire and the imagining of masculinity* (Routledge, 1994)

Dibble, Jeremy: *C Hubert H Parry His Life and Music* (Oxford, Clarendon Press, 1992)

Eagleton, Terry, Frederic Jameson and Edward Said: *Nationalism, Colonialism and Literature* (Minneapolis, University of Minnesota, 1990)

Ehrlich, Cyril: *the Piano - a history* (Dent, 1976)

Foreman, Susan: *From Palace to Power: an illustrated history of Whitehall* Brighton, (The Alpha Press in association with Sussex Academic Press, 1995)

Gibbs, Philip: *The Battles of the Somme* (London, 1917)

Hatcher, John: *Laurence Binyon Poet, Scholar of East and West* (Oxford, Clarendon Press, 1995)

Hobson, J A: *Imperialism: a study* (London)

Holt, Tonie and Valmai: *'My Boy Jack' - the Search for Kipling's Only Son* (Leo Cooper, 1998)

Horne, John and Alan Kramer: *German Atrocities in 1914 - a history of denial* (New Haven, Ct, Yale University Press, 2001)

Keegan, John: *The Face of Battle* (Barrie & Jenkins, 2nd edn, 1988)

Keegan, John: *The First World War* (Hutchinson, 1998)

King, Alex: *Memorials of the Great War in Britain: The Symbolism and Politics of Remembrance* (July 1998)

Ketchum, J Davidson: *Ruhleben - A Prison Camp Society* (Toronto, University of Toronto Press, 1965)

Kipling, Rudyard: *The Irish Guards in the Great War* vol I (Staplehurst Spellmount Ltd, 1997)

Krebs, Paula M: *Gender, Race and the writing of Empire* (Cambridge, CUP, 1999)

Lee, Hermione: *Virginia Woolf* (Chatto & Windus, 1996)

Lindley, Jeanne: *Seeking & Finding. The Life of Emile Cammaerts* (SPCK, 1962)

Mackenzie, John: *Propaganda and Empire. The manipulation of British Opinion 1880-1960* (Manchester, 1984, Manchester UP, 1997)

Massie, Robert: *Dreadnought Britain, Germany, and the coming of the Great War* (Random House, 1991 (Canadian Edition))

Morris, James: *Pax Britannica the climax of an Empire*   Faber, 1968 (Harmondsworth, Penguin, 1979)

Mrinalinj, Sinha: *Colonial Muscularity* (Manchester, Manchester University Press, 1995)

Nicholson, Adam: *The Hated Wife - Carrie Kipling 1862-1939* (Short Books, 2001)

Panayi, Panikos: *German Immigrants in Britain During the 19th Century, 1815-1914* (Oxford & Herndon VA, Berg, 1995)

Porter, Andrew: *The Nineteenth Century: The Oxford History of the British Empire V3* (Oxford, OUP, 1999)

Porter, Bernard: "Monstrous Vandalism: Capitalism and Philistinism in the works of Samuel Laing (1780-1868) *Albion* Vol 23 (1991) p 2

Pulbrook, Ernest C: *The English Countryside* (B T Batsford Ltd, 1915)

Read, Donald: *Edwardian England* (Croom Helm, 1982)

Ricketts, Harry: *The Unforgiving Minute - a life of Rudyard Kipling* (Pimlico, 2000)

Robbins, Keith: *The First World War* (OUP, 1985)

Rothenstein, William: *Men and Memories 1872-1900* (Coward-McCann, 1931)

Rothenstein, William: *Men and Memories 1900-1922* (Coward-McCann, 1931)

Rutherford, John: *Forever England - reflections on race, masculinity and empire* (Lawrence & Wishart , 1997)

Said, Edward: *Orientalism* (New York, Vintage Books, 1979)

Salmon, Edward and Major A Longden: *The Literature of the Empire The Art of the Empire* (London, 1924) (The British Empire - A Survey, vol II, Collins (1924)

Shaw, G B: *Fabianism and the Empire* (Grant Richards, 1900)

Storr, Anthony: *The Dynamics of Creation* (Secker & Warburg, 1972)

Tuchman, Barbara: *August 1914 (The Guns of August)*, (Constable & Co, 1962; Papermac edition, 1991)

Wharton, Edith: *The Book of the Homeless* (New York, Charles Scribner, 1916)

Wilson, Jean Morcroft: *Siegfried Sasson - the Making of a War Poet (1886-1918)* (Duckworth, 1998)

Yeats, W B: *The Collected Poems of W B Yeats* (Macmillan, 1952)

DISCOGRAPHY

This discography lists selected commercially issued recordings of the main works discussed, plus Elgar's music recorded during 1914-18 by the composer and others. Many works of the period, for example F S Kelly's *Elegy in Memory of Rupert Brooke*, Parry's *The Chivalry of the Sea*; John Foulds' *A World Requiem*, Lilian Elkington's *Out of the Mist* and Elgar's *In Proud Thanksgiving* have never been recorded. For a selection of popular and patriotic First World War recordings see *'Oh! It's a Lovely War' Songs and sketches of the Great War 1914-1918* Vol 1 on the CD41 label (001). This includes McCormack's recording of *Tipperary*, Helen Clarke's version of *Your King and Country Want You* and Ernest Pike's once best-selling recording of Haydn Wood's *Roses of Picardy*.

Two notable recordings promoted by the conductor Barry Collett are issued by Pearl (and are particularly discussed by Bernard Porter in Chapter 4):

Elgar: War Music (Pearl SHE CD 9602)
(*Carillon*; *Le Drapeau Belge*; *Fringes of the Fleet*, *Inside the Bar*, *Une Voix dans le Désert*; *Polonia*, with Teresa Cahill (sop), Richard Pasco (Narrator); soloists; Rutland Sinfonia conducted by Barry Collett

The Unknown Elgar (Pearl SHE CD 9635)
(21 vocal pieces including *A War Song*; *Fight for Right*; *Follow the Colours*; The King's Way; *The Birthright*; *Big Steamers*; *Chariots of the Lord*; *Sailing Westward*; *The Immortal Legions*) all with piano (or organ) accompaniment, except *The Birthright* which has trumpets and side drum.

For Dan Godfrey and Bournemouth see the discography in Stephen Lloyd's book *Dan Godfrey: Champion of British composers*. For Mott see Alan Kelly's discography *supra* pp 323-5.

RECORDINGS BY AND OF ELGAR 1914-1918

Elgar's recording sessions were discussed in considerable detail by Jerrold Northrop Moore in *Elgar on Record* and before that in his *An Elgar Discography*, first published as an issue of *Recorded Sound* (Vol 2 No 9 January 1963). For a comprehensive Elgar discography see John Knowles' *Elgar's Interpreters on Record*. Elgar's complete acoustic recordings were reissued on LP and subsequently on CD in five volumes by Pearl (GEMM 9951-5). The wartime recordings are on the first two CDs of this set, the songs from *Starlight Express* with Mott and Agnes Nicholls on GEMM 9951. A variety of other early Elgar recordings have been reissued for the Elgar Society by Dutton on four historical CDs. These are cited individually where appropriate below.

SELECT LIST OF CD RECORDINGS OF ELGAR'S MUSIC DISCUSSED

Big Steamers
>Tudor Choir/Barry Collett Pearl SHE CD 9635

The Birthright
>Tudor Choir/Richard Allen; Chris Holleworth; Paul Dovey (trumpets); Colin Goldsmith (side drum); Ken Burley (pf)/Barry Collett Pearl SHE CD 9635

Carillon (All recordings in English**)**
>Richard Pasco (Narrator); Rutland Sinfonia/Barry Collett Pearl SHE CD 9602

Cello Concerto
>Beatrice Harrison (vlc)/Symphony Orch/Elgar Pearl GEMMCD 9953
>Squire (vlc)/Hallé Orchestra/Harty Pearl GEMM 0050
>Du Pré (vlc)/LSO/Barbirolli   EMI CDCS 56219-2
>Navara (vlc)/Halle Orchestra/Barbirolli Testament SBT 1204

Chariots of the Lord
>Stephen Holloway (bass); Barry Collett (pf) Pearl SHE CD 9635

Coronation Ode
>T Cahill (s); A Collins (con); A Rolfe Johnson (t); G Howell (b)/Scottish Orch Choir/Scottish Orchestra/Gibson Chandos CHAN 6574
>F Lott (s); A Hodgson (con); R Morton (t); S Roberts (b)/CUMS, Kings College Ch/New Philharmonia O/Philip Ledger EMI CMS 7 64209-2

Crown of India: March
>Munich Symphony Orchestra/Bostock Classico CLASSCD 334

Le Drapeau Belge (Recorded in English**)**
>Richard Pasco (Narrator); Rutland Sinfonia/Barry Collett Pearl SHE CD 9602

Falstaff, symphonic study op 68
>New SO/ElgarHallé Orch/Baribirolli EMI CDM 5 66322-2
>LSO/Elgar EMI CDS 7 54560-2 [Elgar Edition Vol 1] or CDM 5 67296-2
>LSO/Collins Beulah 1PD15
>LPO/Handley Classics foir Pleasure CFP 573 722-2

Fight for Right
>Stephen Holloway (b), Barry Collett (pf) Pearl SHE CD 9635

Fringes of the Fleet
>Paul Kenyon; Stephen Godward; Simon Theobald; Russell Watson (baritones); RutlandSinfonia/Barry Collett Pearl SHE CD 9602

[Fates Discourtesy and Sweepers]
>Keith Falkner (bar) w piano ELGAR SOCIETY Vol 2 CDAX 8020

The King's Way
>Teresa Cahill (sop)/Barry Collett (pf) Pearl SHE CD 9635

Land of Hope and Glory
>Margaret Balfour (con)/Philharmonic Choir/LSO/Elgar [The Elgar Edition Vol 2) EMI CDS 7 54564 2

Pageant of Empire (Sailing Westward; The Immortal Legions) Chorus and piano
>Tudor Choir/Ken Burley (pf)/Barry Collett

Piano Quintet in A minor
Harriet Cohen (pf) Stratton Quartet (rec 1933) Dutton CDLX 7004
Peter Donohoe (pf) Maggini Quintet Naxos 8.553737

Polonia
(abridged) Symphony Orch/Elgar Pearl GEMMCD
LPO/Boult   EMI CDM5 65584-2
Munich SO/Bostock   Classico CLASSCD 334

Rosemary
New SO/Elgar   EMI CDS 7 54568-2 [Elgar Edition Vol 3]
Northern Sinfonia/Richard Hickox HMVC HMV5 72830-2
Northen Sinfonia/Marriner EMI CDM 5 65593-2

The Sanguine Fan
LPO/Thomson   Chandos   CHAN 7038
English Northern Philh/D Lloyd-Jones Naxos 8.553879

The Spirit of England
T Cahill (s); A Collins (con); A Rolfe Johnson (t); G Howell (b)/Scottish Orch
Choir/Scottish Orchestra/Gibson Chandos CHAN 6574

The Starlight Express
(8 sides) Agnes Nicholls (sop)/Charles Mott (bar)/Symphony Orch/Elgar Pearl
GEMM CD 9951
(4 sides) Alice Moxon/ Stuart Robertson and orch on Elgar Society Vol 1 CDAX
8019
V Masterson (s), D Hammond-Stroud, LPO/Handley EMI CD-EMX 2267

String Quartet
Stratton Quartet (rec 1933) Dutton CDLX 7004
Magini Quartet Naxos 8.553737

Violin Sonata
Y and H Menuhin EMI CDM5 66122-2
H Bean (vln), D Parkhouse (pf) Classics for Please CD-CFP 4632

Une Voice dans le Désert (Recorded in English)
Richard Pasco (Narrator); Rutland Sinfonia/Barry Collett Pearl SHE CD 9602

A War Song
Stephen Holloway (b), Barry Collett (pf) Pearl SHE CD 9635

The Wind at dawn - song
Mette Christina Østergaard (ms)/Munich SO/Bostock Classico CLASSCD 334

OTHER MUSIC DISCUSSED

Hyperion's song recital 'War's Embers' (CDA 66261/2 - two CDs) includes songs by
the principal British musical casualties of the war including Butterworth,
Denis Browne, Farrar, Kelly and Gurney.

Melodramas by Stanley Hawley and Strauss, performed by Pamela Hunter and
Koen Kessels (piano) are on Discover International DICD 920245

Bax, Sir Arnold: Five Fantasies on Polish Christmas Carols
>   St Angela's Singers/Divertimenti/Peter Broadbent   Ensemble (cassette only)
>   ENS 112; ENS 136
>   Bel Canto Voices/Plymouth Festival Orchestra/Philip Brunelle   Pro Arte LP
>   PAD 192

Bliss, Sir Arthur: Morning heroes
>   Brian Blessed (orator), East London Choir/Harlow Choir/E Herts Chor/LPO/M
>   Kibblewhite Cala CACD 1010
>   Richard Baker (orator)/BBC Symphony Chorus/BBCSO/Groves Carlton BBC
>   Radio Classics 15656 9199-2
>   John Westbrook (orator)/Liverpool Philharmonic Choir/RLPO/Groves   EMI
>   CDM 7 63906 2

Bliss, Sir Arthur: The Storm (Music for The Tempest)
>   Nash Ensemble/Brabbins Hyperion CDA67188/9

Bridge, Frank: Lament - for strings
>   English String O/William Boughton Nimbus NI 5366
>   RLPO/Groves EMI CDM 5 66855-2

Britten, Benjamin: Children's Crusade
>   Wandsworth School Boys' Choir/Chamber Ens/Britten London 436 393-2LM

Butterworth, George: Banks of Green Willow
>   **LPO/Boult Belart 461 354-2**

Butterworth, George: A Shropshire Lad - Rhapsody
>   **LPO/Boult Belart 461 354-2**

Cowen, Sir Frederic H
>   Cowen's 78s were reissued on LP by Rare Recorded Editions (RRE 190). This
>   includes *Fall In* sung by Stanley Kirkby from Winner 2713 .

Delius, Frederick: Paa Vidderne - melodrama
>   Peter Hall (narrator)/RLPO/Bostock Classico CLASS CD 364

Delius, Frederick: Requiem
>   R Evans (sop)/P Coleman-Wright (bar)/Waynflete Singers/Bournemouth
>   Symphony Chorus & Orchestra/Richard Hickox Chandos CHAN 9515

Dupré, Marcel: 3 Preludes and Fugues, Op 7
>   John Scott (org) Hyperion CDA 66205
>   J Fishell (org) Naxos 8 553919

Farrar, Ernest: Heroic Elegy; Rhapsody No1, The Open Road; Variations for Piano and Orchestra; The Forsaken Merman; English Pastoral Impressions
>   Howard Shelley/Philharmonia Orchestra/Alasdair Mitchell Chandos CHAN
>   9586

German, Sir Edward: Have You News of My Boy Jack?
>   Clara Butt (con)/Beecham Symphony Orchestra/Beecham EMI 8 CD set SH
>   1001

Greig, Edvard: Bergliot, op 42
>   Lise Fjeldstad (narrator)/Trondheim SO/Ole Kristian Ruud Virgin Classics
>   VC5 45051 2

Howells, Herbert: Piano Concerto No 1 in C minor Op 4 (compl. Rutter)
>   Howard Shelley (pf) BBCSO/Richard Hickox Chandos

Młynarski, Emil: Symphony in F major, Op 14 'Polonia'
National Philharmonic Orchestra/Kazimierz Korda MUZA PNCD 074

Nowowiejski, Feliks: Christmas in Poland - organ Op 31/4
R Innig (organ) MDG MDG 317 0973-2

Nowowiejski, Feliks: Polish Fantasy, 'Christmas Eve at Wavel Cathedral in Cracow
R Innig (organ) MDG MDG 317 0973-2

Paderewski, Ignaz: Polish Fantasy - piano and orchestra Op 19
T Tirino (pf) Polish National RSO/M Bartos

Paderewski, Ignaz: Symphony in B minor 'Polonia', Op 24
BBC Scottish SO/Maksymiuk Hyperion CDA 67056

Parry, Sir C H H: From Death to Life
English Symphony Orchestra/William Boughton Nimbus NI 5296
LPO/Matthias Bamert Chandos CHAN 8955

Parry, Sir C H H: England
London Philharmonic Chorus and Orchestra/Boult (Sir Adrian Boult 80th Birthday Concert) AS Disc AS 534

Schillings, Max von: Das Hexenlied
Martha Mödl (specherin)/Kölner Rundfunkorchester/Jan Stuken CPO 999 233-2

Stanford, Sir Charles Villiers: Organ Sonata No 2
J Payne (org) Marco Polo 8 223754
D Hunter (Org) Priory PRCD 445

Stanford, Sir Charles Villiers: Songs of the Fleet (1. Sailing at Dawn; 2 The Song of the Sou'Wester; 3 The Middle Watch; 4 The Little Admiral; 5 Farewell)
see the CD with this book for a recording of 'Farewell'
Harold Williams (bar)/LSO/Stanford Pearl LP GEM 123
B Luxon Bournemouth Symphony Chorus/BSO/N del Mar EMI CDM 5 65113-2

Stanford, Sir Charles Villiers: Songs of the Sea
B Luxon Bournemouth Symphony Chorus/BSO/N del Mar EMI CDM 5 65113-2

Smyth, Dame Ethel: The Boatswaine's Mate (Mrs Waters' recit and aria 'If only I were young again')
Tommie Crowell Anderson (sop)/Opera Viva Orchestra/Leslie Head Opera Viva 2LP set OV101/2
Eiddwen Harrhy (sop)/The Plymouth Music Series/Philip Brunelle Virgin Classics VC 7 91188-2

Smyth, Dame Ethel: The March of the Women
The Plymouth Music Series/Philip Brunelle Virgin Classics VC 7 91188-2

Strauss, Richard: Enoch Arden
Gert Westphal (spkr)/John Buttrick (pf) Jecklin-Disco JD 592-2
Claude Rains (spkr)/Glenn Gould Sony Classical SM2K 52657

Vaughan Williams, Ralph: A London Symphony (original 1914 version)
LSO/Richard Hickox Chandos CHAN 9902

Vaughan Williams, Ralph: Mass in G minor
Corydon Singers/Matthew Best Hyperion CDA 66076

CONTRIBUTORS

MARTIN BIRD
Martin Bird discovered Elgar in the days when the composer *always* featured in the list of A-level Music set works. Early retirement from the computer department of a major airline a few years ago has allowed Martin to concentrate on his musical interests. A double bassist with the Bushey Symphony Orchestra and a number of other ensembles, he has compiled a massive but as yet unpublished chronology of Elgar's life, of which a truncated version of the relevant years appears in this book.

JEREMY DIBBLE
Jeremy Dibble is Reader in Music at Durham University. Author of *Sir C Hubert H Parry: His Life and Music* (1992), he has written widely on British and Irish music of the late nineteenth and early twentieth centuries including articles, essays, and contributions for *New Grove 2*, the *New Dictionary of National Biography*, the *Revised Oxford Companion to Music*, *Musik in Geschichte und Gegenwart*, and *Thoemmes Dictionary of Nineteenth-Century British Philosophers*. He has just completed a companion volume on Stanford for Oxford University Press and an edition of Parry's Violin Sonatas for *Musica Britannica*.

LEWIS FOREMAN
Lewis Foreman took early retirement from the Foreign & Commonwealth Office in 1997 and now concentrates on a range of musical activities including repertoire research and advice for a number of record companies. He is the Music Trustee of the Sir Arnold Bax Trust and the Administrator of the Sir George Dyson Trust. A contributor to *New Grove*, his many books include *British Music Now* (1975), *Bax: a composer and his times* (2nd ed 1987), *From Parry to Britten: British music in letters 1900-1945* (1987) and *Vaughan Williams in Perspective* (1998).

JOSEPH A HERTER
Joseph Herter was born in America of Polish descent and studied music at the University of Michigan, and later conducting with such as Robert Shaw, Seiji Ozawa and Kurt Mazur. Since 1974 he has been resident in Poland and regularly conducts orchestras throughout the country, and has become well-known for introducing major works by Western composers. He has been a guest conductor at the Warsaw Opera, and is the founder and conductor of several ensembles, including the mixed chorus Schola Cantorum, and the cathedral boys choir Cantores Minores.

CHARLES HOOEY
Charles Hooey lives in Canada and is a member of the Elgar Society. He has a passionate interest in singers of the early part of the 20th century, and it was research into one of them, Caroline Hatchard, which led him to discover that the first complete performance of *The Spirit of England* was given in Birmingham on 4 October 1917, described in an article in the Journal of the Elgar Society.

STEPHEN LLOYD

Stephen Lloyd was for 17 years Editor of *The Delius Society Journal*, and his first book was a biography of Delius's great friend, H Balfour Gardiner (CUP 1984). His other books have included a history of Sir Dan Godfrey and the Bournemouth Municipal Orchestra (Thames 1995), a comprehensive collection of Eric Fenby's writings on Delius which he edited to mark Fenby's 90th birthday (Thames 1996), and more recently *William Walton: Muse of Fire* (Boydell & Brewer 2001) in anticipation of the centenary of Walton's birth. He has also contributed to books on Elgar and Grainger as well as chapters on Delius, Walton and Bliss in Ashgate's 'Music and Literature' series.

ANDREW NEILL

Born in Bath, Andrew Neill joined the Elgar Society in 1967, becoming its Secretary in 1978 and Chairman in 1992, a position he still holds. As Secretary, Andrew arranged the 1984 Royal Festival Hall concert to commemorate the fiftieth anniversary of Elgar's death, which led to his involvement in a number of recording projects including that of *Scenes from the Saga of King Olaf* which EMI made in 1985. Since then he has been closely associated with the issue of a number of Elgar's recordings. During 2000 and 2001 he was closely involved with the establishment of The Elgar Society Edition, a charity formed to complete the publication of a scholarly edited edition of Elgar's music. Since 1984, he has also been a trustee of The Elgar Birthplace.

JOHN NORRIS

An Elgar Society member since the mid-1980s, John Norris set up the Society's website in 1995. A chance meeting in the Cabinet Office the same year with Lewis Foreman led indirectly to the formation of Elgar Enterprises in 1999,which John has since run. But the need to remain in full time employment and the consequent daily journey into Central London provides the opportunity to write the occasional article about Elgar, including two chapters for the first volume in this series (*The Best of Me*) and the current chapter.

BERNARD PORTER

Bernard Porter comes from Essex, was educated at Cambridge, has taught there and at Hull and Yale universities, and is currently Professor of Modern History at the University of Newcastle. His books include *The Lion's Share: A Short History of British Imperialism 1850-1995* (3rd ed Longman, 1996). He is presently writing a book on the domestic impact of the empire on Britain.

BRIAN TROWELL

Brian Trowell lives in Oxford, where he was Heather Professor of Music from 1988 to 1996. Before that he spent 18 years at King's College, London, latterly as King Edward Professor of Music. His research interests lie in late mediæval English music ands in the life and music of Handel and Elgar. He has also worked as an opera coach, conductor and stage director, and was for three years head of opera for BBC Radio 3. He has translated many operas, among them several of Handel's which he staged for the first time in modern revivals.

A Note on the Compact Disc

The compact disc which accompanies this book consists of historical recordings from commercial 78s and a number of recordings from a concert given in 1975 which explored the repertoire discussed in the text. We have tried to present the historical recordings in the highest possible quality from nearly mint originals. Here we provide Elgar's celebrated wartime recordings of *Carillon* and *Fringes of the Fleet*, the latter with Charles Mott, who was killed so soon after making this recording. These are set in context by other topical recordings of the period featuring music by German, Cowen, Parry and Paul Rubens. The recording of Clara Butt has been carefully checked to find the most accurate pitch for making our copy, sometimes a problem with Butt's recordings. Also included in this section is 'Farewell' from Stanford's *Songs of the Fleet*, which was sung widely during the war, here in a recording from 1934 made by the popular baritone Peter Dawson.

Secondly, through the good offices of the conductor Leslie Head, we are able to present more modern recordings taken from Mr Head's London concert on 30 October 1975, from a private recording never intended for wider circulation. This concert featured the legendary BBC announcer Alvar Lidell, who came out of retirement specially to perform the three Elgar melodramas, of interest to all interested in the period for the fact that they were performed without microphone, the recording giving a remarkably good idea of Lidell's impact in the hall. Unfortunately the technical quality of *Le Drapeau Belge* has proved not to be good enough for it to be used, but we are grateful to the Estate of Alvar Lidell for approving the use of the two recordings included here.

Leslie Head's concert included the scena 'Hail! Immemorial Ind' from *Crown of India* and two movements from *Pageant of Empire*, all with orchestral accompaniment. We feel that Mr Head, his soloists, chorus and orchestra well demonstrate the power of Elgar's orchestration to project even the most occasional works.

The commercial recording of 'Spring Offensive' was made by Basil Maine, himself a distinguished Elgarian, in the early 1930s. As the creator of the rôle of the orator in Bliss's *Morning Heroes* it provides a useful footnote (discussed in chapters 3 and 6) to any study of music and the First World War.

The editor and publisher would like to thank Michael J Dutton and Dutton Laboratories who managed the technical processing of all recordings for their issue here. The compilation and remastering is ℗ and © Elgar Editions, 2001.

Contents of the Accompanying Compact Disc

This book is published with a compact disc of historical recordings located in an envelope on the inside back board. The following is a detailed list of tracks. For timings, see disc insert.

1   Elgar: *Carillon*   HMV 20522; 20523
    Henry Ainley (speaker)/Symphony Orchestra/Elgar   recorded 29 January 1915

    Elgar: *Fringes of the Fleet* (wds: Kipling)
2   *The Lowestoft Boat*   HMV 02734   4   *Submarines*   HMV 02736
3   *Fate's Discourtesy*   HMV 02735   5   *The Sweepers*   HMV 02737
    Charles Mott/Frederick Henry/Frederick Stewart/Harry Barratt (bars)/
    Symphony Orchestra/Elgar   recorded 4 July 1917

6   Sir Charles Villiers Stanford: *Farewell (Songs of the Fleet - 5)* (wds: Newbolt)   HMV C 2694
    Peter Dawson (bar)/chorus and orchestra   first issued November 1934

7   Sir Edward German: *Have You News of My Boy Jack?* (wds: Kipling)   HMV 03572
    Louise Kirkby Lunn (con)/Orch/German   recorded 19 July 1917
    (with 'chorus' in final verse: Bessie Jones/Edna Bennie/Elsie Williams/Nellie Walker)

8   Sir Frederick H Cowen: *We Sweep the Seas* (wds: M Corelli)   HMV 02557
    Harry Dearth (bar)/Symphony Orchestra/Cowen   recorded January 1915

9   Sir C Hubert H Parry: *A Hymn for Aviators* (wds: Mary Hamilton)   Columbia 7174
    Clara Butt (con), Harold Craton (pf)   recorded 1918 issued June 1919

10 Paul A Rubens: *Your King and Country Want You* (wds: P A Rubens)   Columbia 2467
    Maggie Teyte with orchestra   recorded 1914 or 1915

11 Elgar: *Carillon*   public concert
    Alvar Lidell (orator)/Kensington Symphony Orchestra/Leslie Head   October 1975

12 Elgar: *Voice in the Desert*   - 13 Song: 'When Spring Comes Round Again'   public concert
    Alvar Lidell (orator)/Valerie Hill (sop)Kensington Symphony Orch/Leslie Head   October 1975

14 Elgar: *Crown of India*: 'Hail! Immemorial Ind' (wds: Henry Hamilton)   public concert
    Carol Leatherby (con)/Kensington Symphony Orchestra/Leslie Head   October 1975

15 Elgar: *Pageant of Empire*: 'The Immortal Legions' (wds: Henry Hamilton)   public concert
    Anthony Ransome (bar)/Kensington Choir & Symphony Orch/Leslie Head   October 1975

16 Elgar: *Pageant of Empire*: 'A Song of Union' (wds: Henry Hamilton)   public concert
    Kensington Choir/Kensington Symphony Orchestra/Leslie Head   October 1975

17 Sir Arthur Bliss: *Morning Heroes*: 'Spring Offensive'(wds: Wilfred Owen)   Decca F 5219
    Basil Maine (orator) with drums   recorded c 1934

INDEX
compiled by Susan Foreman

References to photographs are given in *italics*. Musical works are listed under the name of their composer except for Elgar, where they are listed as main entries. Except for London, urban geographical entries appear under the name of the town or city in which they are located.

The Elgar Society was formed in 1951 with the objective of promoting interest in the composer and his music. With a number of significant achievements to its credit, the Society is now the largest UK-based composer appreciation society with ten regional branches in Britain and about 10% of its membership resident outside the UK. In 1997 the Society launched its own Internet website (http://www.elgar.org) with the aim of spreading knowledge of Elgar around the world and, in the process, attracting a greater international membership. This was followed in 1999 by Elgar Enterprises, the trading arm of the Society, whose purpose is to raise funds for the Society's charitable projects through the sale of books, CDs, CD-ROMs and other material about the composer and his music, and in October 2001 by the launch of the Elgar Society Edition, a scheme to publish a uniform edition of all the composer's music.

All enquiries about membership should be addressed to :

David Morris, 2 Marriotts Close, Haddenham, Aylesbury,
Bucks, England HP17 8BT
telephone : +44 1844 299239; fax : +44 870 734 6772
e-mail : membership@elgar.org

On-line and postal membership application forms
can be found on the website at:

'http://www.elgar.org/5memform.htm'

ᔍ   ᔍ   ᔍ

The Elgar Foundation was established in 1973. Its objectives include supporting the Elgar Birthplace, the cottage in which Elgar was born in Lower Broadheath, some three miles west of the city of Worcester. The Birthplace and the adjacent Elgar Centre now house a collection of memorabilia associated with the composer. They are open to the public daily throughout most of the year.

To check opening times or for further information:
telephone +44 1905 333224; fax +44 1905 333426;
e-mail: birthplace@elgar.org